MW01268543

Persistence of Memories of Slavery and Emancipation in Historical Andover

Persistence of Memories of Slavery and Emancipation in Historical Andover

The Massachusetts Woman Enumerated as
a "Slave" in the 1830 U.S. Census
and the Family of Rosanna Coburn from
Enslavement to Contingent Freedom

26 october 2021

Edward L. Bell

S

Shawsheen Press
Boston

Designed and composed by James T. Connolly

Indexed by Diane Brenner and the author

Printed and bound by Bridgeport National Bindery, Inc.

Shawsheen Press logo by Jesse M. Kahn

Oak branch ornament from Vectorian Free Vector Pack (http://www.vectorian.net)
licensed under Creative Commons Attribution 3.0 Unported

Library of Congress Control Number: 2020901423

ISBN: 978-0-578-65395-2

First edition

Contents

List of Figures

Preface

Historical Andover—which includes North Andover and Lawrence in Essex County, Massachusetts—became famous as a hot center of pre-Civil War antislavery activism. Why then was a 100-year-old Andover woman then-residing at the Andover almshouse officially counted as a "slave" in the 1830 federal census? The "slave" officially counted in the fifth United States Census for Massachusetts has been a long-standing historical enigma. Never before or since has a slave appeared in a federal census for the nominally "free" state that had judicially abolished slavery. The designation of a free person as a "slave" was a singular departure from practice that nevertheless was accepted by Congress in 1832. It remains an official statistic that has mystified historians interested in slavery and emancipation in Massachusetts.

The identity of the unnamed centenarian woman enumerated as a slave in June 1830 is unknown. Federal correspondence files for the 1830 census that likely included letters to and from the census takers to clarify that matter were destroyed, and no other contemporaneous records or reports have been found that named the elderly woman counted as a "slave." But there was another women living in historical Andover through the first two decades of the nineteenth century, also one hundred years old and older, who had been born in Africa and endured slavery. Whoever the other woman was at the almshouse in June 1830, it was not the African-born Phillis, a free woman who had self-emancipated herself and her children by September 1790 and who died before January 5, 1829 when she was 101 years old. As with the unidentified woman at the almshouse, and so also with Phillis' extended family, government officials persisted in considering their former enslaved status long after their emancipation. Phillis' family's experiences with local and state poor relief practices in postemancipation Andover answers the question as to why that other free woman was officially designated a "slave" in the 1830 federal census.

Phillis' extended family was comprised of her spouse Booso (she was born in Africa, he in the West Indies, and both were enslaved in Andover); their

children born enslaved in Andover including their daughter Rosanna Coburn; Rosanna's husband Titus Coburn (enslaved in the adjoining towns
of Reading and Wilmington, then manumitted before he moved to Andover); Titus' daughter Jennie (also called Jane/June, freeborn in Wilmington, who stayed with the family in Andover); and, Rosanna's daughter
Colley Hooper who was freeborn in Andover. All received poor relief from
the town, intermittently over many years. The state partly reimbursed Andover for the town's costs of providing them poor relief. The town considered Phillis' family to be nonresident "state paupers" because of the family's
history in enslavement. Massachusetts towns sought and received state reimbursement for poor relief provided to emancipated slaves and their children. The "slave" designation of the centenarian woman at the almshouse in
the 1830 census was intended to document that woman's former condition
in slavery and thereby to deny the town's financial responsibility for her
support. When the federal census takers arrived to enumerate the inhabitants of the Andover almshouse, the almshouse superintendent identified
that woman as a "slave" to bolster the town's position that some other entity
should bear the cost of that formerly enslaved woman's institutional care.
The evolving and complicated state law regarding paupers and residency,
which determined whether a town or the state was responsible for the costs
of supporting impoverished former slaves and their children, challenged local and state officials in their decision-making.

The presence and movements of formerly enslaved individuals and their
born-enslaved or born-free children, when residing in one town or another,
became matters of dispute when any of them required economic support.
Town poor relief officials sought reimbursement from other towns or the
state for the costs of supporting them. Disputes about economic responsibility for poor relief provided to former slaves and their children reached
the state's highest court in the late eighteenth and nineteenth centuries. In
deciding poor relief cases involving former slaves and their children, the judiciary examined and reinterpreted the murky history of judicial abolition
in Massachusetts, only to establish that the impoverished people were legally free and thus not the economic responsibility of the private citizens who
had formerly enslaved them. Embedded in those judicial narratives of poor
relief cases were "legal fictions" of instant and statewide judicial abolition
by the state constitution or by previous case decisions ("common law"). Regardless of the records of previous court decisions that did not plainly and
unambiguously emancipate the state—and despite evidence of enslavement
in Massachusetts that persisted after the adoption of the state constitution
in 1780 and subsequent to those previous court decisions that were only

thought to have emancipated the state—jurists writing about the history of judicial emancipation established the myth of sudden statewide freedom merely for legal utility to decide the cases that were then before them in postslavery Massachusetts. That legal fiction was applied in poor relief cases involving former slaves and their children retrospectively to establish their present legal emancipated status, so that jurists could decide which town, if not the state, was financially responsible for supporting them.

The tenacious historical myth of immediate statewide emancipation by the 1780 state constitution, or by the once obscure and now famous 1781 and 1783 freedom suits of Brom and Mum Bett and of Quock Walker, influenced judicial decisions of poor relief cases, as those decisions then came to be relied upon in the significant 1836 decision of Commonwealth v. Aves. To decide that an enslaved girl called Med brought from Louisiana to Massachusetts was free, Supreme Judicial Court Chief Justice Lemuel Shaw declared in *Aves* that slavery had been abolished in this state from the adoption of the 1780 state constitution going forward in time. The 1836 *Aves* decision was the first instance of that notion that appeared in a judicial decision of record, with instant, statewide applicability and with the power of reliable precedential authority.

Significant moments in the biographies of Phillis' family, from their enslavement to their contingent freedom, were considered by town and state officials when the family required poor relief. The established legal decisions about circumstantial financial responsibilities of towns, or the state, for poor relief provided to formerly enslaved people and their children had implications for Phillis' family. The town of Andover, where they lived, considered them to be the responsibility of the state because of their family history in enslavement.

A state-appointed commission of two state representatives investigated to clarify legal residency of paupers throughout Massachusetts, including some formerly enslaved, and published their report in 1847. For Andover, the commissioners considered the genealogies of Rosanna Coburn and her daughter Colley Hooper, and the biography of Lucy Foster (a woman well known to African diaspora historians and archaeologists worldwide) to ascertain whether they were town residents or were state paupers. The commissioners applied established law (which was generally obscure to local officials who were not usually legal professionals) to conclude that former slaves born in those towns were legal town residents: if indigent, they were the financial responsibility of those municipalities and not the state. Andover overseers of the poor immediately contested the state's determination that Andover-born Rosanna Coburn and her daughter Colley

Hooper were town paupers. The town's attorney, who was also one of the overseers of the poor, argued case law and precedent of practice to support Andover's contention that formerly enslaved inhabitants were state paupers. Ultimately, however, state reimbursement to Andover for supporting Rosanna and Colley was disclaimed by the state commissioners. The town of Andover continued to provide support to Rosanna and Colley until at least 1856.

The commissioners accepted that Lucy Foster—practically a lifelong Andover resident—was a state pauper, but only because she was born elsewhere. Former slaves born elsewhere were deemed to be nonresident state paupers, even if they had been enslaved when children and remained as practically lifelong inhabitants of towns. The state commissioners interpreted an 1844 statute to require that state paupers be full-time almshouse residents to receive state support. The commissioners discovered that overseers of the poor in many towns were unaware of the 1844 law, but if the town overseers had read it, they could have understood the law differently. The requirement that state paupers be supported "actually and entirely [...] the whole number of days" did not specify almshouse residency. The state commissioners' expansive interpretation of the 1844 law allowed them to deny reimbursement to towns for state paupers when poor individuals still managed to live on their own or with others. For the formerly enslaved Lucy Foster—deemed a state pauper only because she had been born-enslaved in Boston—the state reduced Andover's reimbursement for the cost of Foster's full year of support to cover only two weeks when she was at the almshouse before she died.

Rosanna Coburn obtained a Revolutionary War veteran widow's pension in 1854 on account of her late husband Titus Coburn's military service. Curiously, the awarding of the pension to Rosanna was celebrated in local and abolitionist newspapers as a significant achievement of equal treatment by the federal government, although many people of color were granted veteran pensions. Historically, Rosanna became an emblematic counterpoint to the former practice of generational slavery in Andover. Rosanna Coburn's town and state death records prepared in 1860 by the Andover town clerk denoted her former condition perplexingly: the notation of her place of birth in Andover in the official death records was annotated with "a slave". Official vital records for several people in Andover included similar notations about their former enslaved status. Antislavery sentiments were encoded in Rosanna Coburn's "memorial narratives" of her obituary and gravestone. Local history projects remembered her long after her death in 1859 as the "last" slave born in Andover. This book considers the evolution of historical representations and memories of Rosanna Coburn and of her contemporaries who became "known far and wide".

My microhistorical focus on people of color in a Massachusetts town revealed specific, factual information about a family's transition from enslavement to a contingent freedom. Biographical sketches drawn of Phillis, Booso, Colley Hooper (Elizabeth Coburn), Titus Coburn, and Rosanna Coburn foregrounded their documented moments in time, and investigated historical lacunae, ambiguities, assumptions, and misapprehensions about them and others known to them. Their biographical stories, and the experiences of people of color in adjoining Essex and Middlesex county places who had Andover connections, expand understandings about historical Massachusetts and the New England region. More broadly, from the perspectives of modern scholars of slavery, emancipation, and the persistent period called *postslavery* and *postemancipation*, these experiences are appropriately considered in view of the history of the Atlantic World and beyond.

Persistence of Memories of Slavery and Emancipation in Historical Andover brings forward research discoveries about fascinating people of many ancestries and heritages, connected together and integral to New England histories, artifacts, cultural traditions, and historic places. Their ordinary and extraordinary lives in historical Andover and surrounding localities are remembered today, some even internationally. The enduring and pervasive historical memories of many familiar Andover people of color are remarkable to consider. The detailed and precise documentation provided by this research effort is indispensable to guide further investigation of historical sources that await the attentions of interested fellow researchers. This study's essential findings, informative endnotes, and a bibliography of incisive sources deepen views of the persistent echoes of enslavement, emancipation, and postemancipation in Atlantic World and global perspectives.

Editorial Conventions and Notes about Sources

Historical Andover

When referring generally to "Andover" I mean the historically larger town, and I often prefix "historical" to emphasize that. The city of Lawrence was formed in 1847 from a part of Andover, and the town of North Andover was set off in 1855. The history of historical Andover is shared in common with Andover, North Andover, and Lawrence.

"Race" and people of color

Following modern practice, I put "race" in quotation marks to emphasize that the ambiguous idea is unscientific and contemptuous. Bounded notions of "race" are complicated ideological constructs that varied in place and time, subjective position, and perceptions. Developmental psychologies of modern populations show how familial, social, and cultural biases of "race" are inculcated and expressed even neurologically: from an early age, socialized modern humans learn advantageous and disadvantageous perceptions about self-identity, group affiliation, degrees of esteem and impartiality, and degrees of prejudice and disdain. Modern socialization processes implicating "race" are not transglobal culturally. Ancestry (genetics) and heritage (identity) differ from "race."

While "race" is unreal, racism is discernible and many racialized terms were invented and used. When it came to calling people names, there were a slew of words available. Familiar racialized terms are ubiquitous in the records and writings about people of color in historical Andover and the region generally. Rendered with variable spellings, I quoted racialized terms from documents as data to be pondered. As detailed in this work, meaningful racialized terms purposefully applied to some individuals changed during and again after their lives. A linguistic study of the practice and evolution of racialized terms is possible with this area's rich documentary heritage. Cultural historian Angela Michele Leonard undertook one such study using nineteenth-century newspaper texts published in Haverhill,

Massachusetts, and her findings were important to my interpretations. Leonard's penetrating analytic methods could be applied to more types of narrative texts, more localities, regionally, and for even longer time spans. From Leonard's investigation, it is notable that in this area in the early nineteenth century the range of racialized terms attenuated: terms used for colors (e.g., "black" and "white") became more frequently employed (imprecisely and synonymously) to convey perceptions of "race" as an artificially rigid and mutually exclusive binary. In the later twentieth century, "Black" was typically capitalized and perceptively became the preferred alternative to "Negro." Racialized terms employed in places and moments are a linguistic form of "marking" (i.e., "markedness"). Axiomatically in linguistic theory, marking consciously and unconsciously conveys subjects of heightened interest and concern to writers and speakers. Ironically, the evident effort to especially designate people of color in historical writings proves useful for researchers to identify people of color and to further investigate moments of their biographies. Literary and cultural historian Lois Brown appreciated the double-edge of problem and advantage of racial designations in historical texts: "Sometimes I cursed that anything about Negroes was relegated to the back of a book at best. Sometimes I thanked heaven that anything about Negroes was relegated to a back of a book and thus had a discrete section of its own."[1]

Demarcating people deemed to be people of color with racialized terms (but not to do so for people deemed not to be people of color) peculiarly and incongruously discloses that notions of "race" were only attached to people of color. The practice reveals obvious positioning of domination and subordination, evident even today when meaningfully coded but actually inaccurate terms such as "minorities," "ethnic," and "urban populations" are employed casually. Categorizing people of multiple ancestries and heritages (people whose parentage was simultaneously from both dominating/not of color and subordinated/of color people) was a problematic that required specialized terms and pseudoscientific typological assignments. In some times and places, people of multiple ancestries and heritages were calculated to have fractionalized "blood quanta" and the related "one-drop rule" deemed a person with an ancestor of color was a person of color. These old ideas are extremely dangerous and bring to mind political inventions of "racial purity" that physical anthropology, population genetics, the archaeology of human movements, and genealogy prove to be absurd.

Although the phrase is hundreds of years old, my gloss of "people of color" is deliberately used in a modern way in an intentionally respectful manner, realizing there is no escaping alterity, privilege, and contradiction when such distinctions are made. I can only offer resolution of the dilemma by appealing to my conscious intentions in practice and application as a documentalist. In another sense of the word, it is indeed a personal privilege to apply my skills as a researcher to this documentary endeavor. My twenty-first-century project is respectfully intended to honor people in history by searching, bringing forward, and highlighting biographical information about historical people, people with diverse ancestries, heritages, and relations, as the lot of us modern people have.

Names

Variations of names of historical individuals posed research, interpretive, and editorial challenges. Several factors entered into my decisions as to which form to use when referring to historical persons. I favored using the seeming preference of an individual based on their writings, sometimes the name they have come to be known by in history, and the fullest rendering of a name. I was attentive to name changes during a person's lifetime. Names were sometimes ascribed to persons by writers intending to regularize names or to identify individuals, but they themselves and others who knew them may never have used that form. Chiefly while enslaved and for a time thereafter, individuals were known by a single first name and my phrasing reflected that period of their lives. For familiar people, such as Rosanna (also called Rose) Coburn and her daughter Colley Hooper (also more rarely called Elizabeth Coburn, but seemingly only by others), I often referred to them familiarly by first name as a stylistic choice in composing sentences.

I quoted name variations that I noticed in historical documents, suspecting that phonetic spellings may have captured pronunciation or what was misheard by the writer. While Titus Coburn has become known by that name historically, spelling variations of, e.g., "Cober" and "Colburn" may approximate his own regionally distinctive pronunciation. Similarly, "Sibson" was used for Dinah and Caesar Simpson, and may reflect their pronunciation, but I favored the fuller rendering. Spelling variations that may preserve speech patterns are interesting linguistically, but in citations and references to works that are strictly arranged and indexed under particular spellings, specific spelling was necessarily indicated (e.g., alphabetized and indexed names in *Massachusetts Soldiers and Sailors of the Revolutionary War*, the published *Vital Records* series, deeds, probate, etc.). Some indexes, such as grantor and grantee indexes to deeds, helpfully provided a concordance of spelling variations: all index entries were gathered under one heading, and other spellings were cross-referenced to the main entry. To identify individuals, and to differentiate same-named individuals such as father and son, I sometimes added a suffix in brackets ("[Sr.]") and used titles (e.g., "Hon."; "Col."; "Esq.", etc.).

Quotations and scholarly transcriptions

Except when indicated in each instance, quotations are literal and verbatim. I preserved spelling, capitalization (sometimes difficult to be certain in manuscript sources), superscript abbreviation (but not the accompanying superscript dot, single, or double lines), abbreviation symbols (& and +), punctuation, italics, underlining, etc. Connecting or terminal punctuation was not silently added to quoted material, but placed outside closing quotation marks. My consistent practice to accurately convey quoted material without alteration of added connecting and terminal punctuation differs from more common editorial practice that favors appearance over substance. Within quotations I used brackets for emendations and bracketed ellipses for deletions. Brackets that appeared in the original material quoted were noted. Line breaks, hyphenated word divisions at line endings, and other related textual features were generally not preserved in quotations, except when specifically indicated (e.g., by a bracketed slash [/] to indicate a line break) and as otherwise explicated in an endnote indicating a formatted transcription.

Interlineated matter—typically words written above a line of text, with a caret or some other symbol that indicated where the writer intended the material to be inserted—was brought into the line of quoted text and framed with bracketed carets [^]. When I quoted material that had used double quotation marks (indicating it was quoting from another source), I changed the double quotation marks to single quotation marks to differentiate them from mine. The obsolete long or descending *s* (ſ) was transcribed as *s*. As indicated in each instance, I substituted *u* for *v* in quotations from printed sources that had transcribed differently those interchangeable letter forms in seventeenth-century handwriting. Among other authentic orthographic matters in historical sources that differ from modern, ever-evolving writing and editorial practices, creative and phonetic spelling was not unusual and there was no need to call attention to those. Explanatory emendations were supplied when it seemed that misapprehension or mystery might otherwise occur to an attentive reader. Use of *sic* ("thus" from *sic erat scriptum*, "thus it had been written") was limited to indicate noticed error or to emphasize that an unexpected form in a quotation was indeed as it appeared in the source. I have strived for accuracy and precision and beg indulgence for any unintentional error.

Abbreviations and bibliographic data in scholarly apparatus

Abbreviations in endnotes for frequently cited works appear at the beginning of the notes. Abbreviations in the scholarly apparatus include n.d. (no date), n.p. (not paginated), s.l. (*sine loco*, no place of publication specified), and s.n. (*sine nomine*, no publisher named).

In the references cited, authorship and minor details of capitalization and punctuation within titles may be rendered differently on title pages of original works. Those matters also may be recorded differently in the catalog records of libraries and archives prepared in adherence to technical cataloging rules, and in the records of metadata in digitized collections prepared with different rules. Consequently, it can be difficult to correlate original items, library and archive catalog records, and metadata. When I noticed obvious errors and related problems in catalogs or databases, I notified the data managers.

Authorship of some anonymous works was identified or may be attributed, as explained in the notes and in some references, and those works are listed in the references cited under those authors' names. When authorship of anonymous works was identified with certainty or attributed by consensus in scholarly tradition, then brackets were placed around author names in the references cited. If information was noticed in sources that suggested alternatives but authorship of an anonymous work could not be reliably concluded, then the reference to the anonymous work was placed in the "Anonymous" section in the references cited, which section is organized alphabetically by full title including any articles (a, an, the). Suggestions of possible authorship for those cases were explained in notes.

In references to works by the same author that were published with slight variation of the author's name, the fullest regular rendering was used and bracketed information was supplied to render names consistently so that works by the same author are grouped together in the references cited. For the reader's ease, the brackets that enclose information in references to reliably attributed authors of anonymous works, or to authors' consistently rendered names, were dispensed with in endnotes (e.g., "[Poor(e)]" in references is "Poore" in endnotes).

"Corporate authors" that are governments (cited in endnotes as, e.g., Town of Andover; or, Commonwealth of Massachusetts) are alphabetized in the references cited by placename (Andover, Town of; Massachusetts, Commonwealth of). Government files on individuals (cited in endnotes as, e.g., Rosanna Coburn, Death record) are alphabetized in references by surname (Coburn, Rosanna, Death Record). Otherwise, as expected, references to works by corporate authors that are organizations (e.g., The Trustees of Reservations) are alphabetized by the organization name including the leading article that is part of the full organizational name.

I preferred to render titles as they appeared exactly on the title page of the original work, especially for historical printed and manuscript works. Within some titles, explanatory emendations were supplied in brackets. In referenced titles, capitalization was sometimes regularized and punctuation may have been silently provided when only implied on title pages, such as commas supplied to separate parts of a title, or a full colon supplied to separate subtitles. Published authors will understand that graphic designers, editors, and typographers employ punctuation or not, and use other graphic conventions merely for design considerations when preparing title pages. Those artistic choices may not comport with authorial intention and such creative variation may be noticed differently by readers, by catalogers in libraries and archives, and by other scholarly bibliographers. Rather than always impose an artificial and modern uniformity, the complicated and irregular bibliographic features of many historical works were expressed intentionally so that researchers could confidently identify referenced sources. For some long-running and continuing serial works, such as the Massachusetts *Acts and Resolves* or the Andover *Annual Town Reports*, the titles and other publication data expressed on the title pages of each volume varied from year to year, but the generic names of the series were used in citations and references. Only for particular referenced acts and resolves of the Massachusetts legislature (e.g., Massachusetts Chapter 1 of the Acts of 1703), did I supply the particular bibliographic data from the variant title page of the volume in which it appeared. For legal documentation, I employed legal style citations and references (as further explained below) rather than humanities style because the legal style system is used by judicial archives, law libraries, and online legal databases. For the same reason, I followed the specialized bibliographic style used for United States congressional publications and statutes.

Microforms and digital formats

I frequently used microfilm and digital images of manuscript and printed material. If reformatted versions required an exceptional system to readily locate and identify images of bibliographically problematic items (e.g., unpaginated manuscript record books lacking consistent volume titles, appearing in sequence on microfilm with its own bibliographic complications and inconsistencies, sometimes later digitized and indexed by image number), then I added the exceptional information about the reformatted edition to citations and references to assist researchers to rapidly find the particular item.

With some historical documents, there may be multiple reformatted versions of the same original material, such as created by separate and duplicative microfilming projects; or paper reproductions made from microfilm images; or digitized microfilm, etc. The reformatted editions might bear variant titles making it difficult initially to realize that the contents of the reformatted editions overlap to some degree. Details about multiple reformatted editions of particular historical materials are provided in notes and references. Otherwise, such as with digitized printed books, newspapers, and other historical material readily found online, I may not specify that I used reliable reformatted versions rather than the original. Historical information provided in the notes but not included in the references cited was indicated in each instance. That information was accessed online (such as by colleagues and me and shared in email communications, which they were interested to pursue and document further, or were tangential sources). Email communications with me were indicated in notes but also were not listed in the references. Regarding citations and references to online sources that include URLs, when the URL no longer functions then the Internet Archive's collection of sampled websites can be searched using its Wayback Machine to see the appearance of the cached webpage near the date that I accessed it.

Microform reproductions of this region's town, parish, and ecclesiastical manuscript records are increasingly difficult to locate. Master negatives may not be preserved for some series to make fresh user-copies to replace scratched and worn microfilm at libraries. The preservation condition of remaining copies of microfilm is concerning. Microfilm made on cellulose acetate-based film stock ("safety film") is rapidly deteriorating, alarmingly. Reformatting projects of historical Andover municipal and ecclesiastical records differ in scope, coverage, and image quality. Consequently, digital images created from the monochromatic microfilm carry along those uneven aspects. While some reformatting projects overlapped in imaging the same materials, identification of original materials was problematic, and indexing systems vary among them to describe what items appear in which order.

The reformatting projects include the following: circa 1960 by North Andover Historical Society with Andover Historical Society (NAHS/AHS) on 26 reels of microfilm with a typed index, printed reproductions made from microfilm of one or more volumes, and provisional typed transcriptions of some town records; in 1971 by the Genealogical Society of

Salt Lake City, Utah (GSU), on microfilm, and in the 2000s by FamilySearch as digitized images of that microfilm much of which presently is only viewable at Family History Centers and FamilySearch affiliate libraries; circa 1972 by the North Andover town clerk on six reels of microfilm, and beginning in 2004 by the town clerk and historical commission as digitized images of at least parts of the NAHS/AHS and town clerk microfilm, with additional digital imaging of historical records; and, in 1998 by Jay Mack Holbrook of Archive Publishing/Holbrook Research Institute on 246 microfiche (ISBN 0-87623-397-3).

My bibliographic data include GSU Microfilm Reel numbers—called *GS numbers* by FamilySearch—because those reel numbers are used to find the FamilySearch catalog record for particular microfilm reels and to access their digital images on familysearch.org. The original GS numbers are provided in FamilySearch catalog records, and that GS number appears as the first digital image of the digitized microfilm. As microfilm reels were digitized, FamilySearch assigned an additional DGS number (abbreviating *Digital Genealogical Society*). There were two earlier microfilm numbering systems used by the GSU, but not applicable to the 1970s series of GSU microfilm that I used which were given third-system GS numbers. Yet another microfilm numbering practice (an alphanumeric system) was once used by GSU, but seemingly only temporarily for production and tracking of commercially supplied (user) copies of reels of GSU microfilm. I mention that other temporary numbering practice only because library catalog records (and possibly scholarly bibliographic citations) have noted the temporary production numbers. That temporary alphanumeric (e.g., "2174C/2175A" for GSU Microfilm Reel 878787) appeared at the very beginning of the microfilm reel, before the microfilm frame with the actual GSU Microfilm Reel number, and that temporary alphanumeric was also printed on the original microfilm box label as-supplied by GSU. That temporary alphanumeric is not used by FamilySearch, the microfilm frame in which it appeared was (sensibly) not digitized, and so the alphanumeric is not useful for locating the reel or its digital version.

Middlesex County municipal and ecclesiastical manuscript records dating through 1830, including those of the adjoining town of Wilmington that I used, were microfilmed by Early Massachusetts Records, Inc., in the early to mid-1970s, following the GSU filming of selected municipal records statewide. I used the Early Massachusetts Records, Inc. microfilm series and the printed guide at the Boston Public Library's Central Library. The Massachusetts Historical Society also has the Early Massachusetts Records, Inc. microfilm (additional to the Middlesex

County records in that series are Gloucester, Essex County, records), the printed guide, and that organization's project records. The Congregational Library continues with a long-term project to create digital images of congregational church manuscript records, which I used for Essex and Middlesex County places. Public libraries in Andover and in several of the surrounding towns have digitally reformatted portions of their local history collections, but it is chiefly printed material. Andover's Memorial Hall Library hosts digital images of published annual Andover town reports, two volumes of 1960s typed provisional transcriptions of Andover town meeting records (1656–1776), along with other items in their local history collection. The State Library digitally imaged Andover annual town reports in its collection.

Judicial sources

Judicial sources cited to and referenced in this monograph are a distinctive type of historical documentation that requires more extended explanation. Understanding how and why judicial documentation was created, organized, transformed, and preserved or not, and apprehending conventional practices in citation and referencing systems for legal documents, are important for locating and interpreting historical information. Familiarity with historical legal processes, rules, and terminology opens up the contents and meaning of historical legal documents. Legal documents employ seemingly familiar words that are actually specialized and technical vocabulary with specific legal meaning and implication. Judicial documents have abbreviations and annotations that are not explicit but which embody specialist understandings and rules of legal practice and process. A few helpful introductory guides and more specialist works on historical legal practice are listed in the references cited. I used many other general reference sources, legal dictionaries, and digitized historical legal works to assist my studies.

To provide summary background to understand and utilize historical legal sources, the remaining part of these notes touch on the following topics: technical "legal fictions"; unpublished judicial documentation; court case titles called *captions*; the changed name of the same Common Pleas court; judicial orders called *executions of judgment*; three archival collections of legal papers; court clerk record-making practices; probate court materials; Revolutionary War veteran pension application files kept by the county Common Pleas court and separately by the federal government; published judicial decisions; and, historical legal documents preserved in places other than official government archives.

Legal fictions

Using legal documents for historical research requires background knowledge to perceive significant data and to avoid misunderstanding and unfounded assumption. Peculiarly, writs that commenced civil actions were commonly peppered with fictitious assertions that only appear to be specific facts but which were not literally true. The formalistic *legal fictions* required in these writs for civil actions were legal. No one objected to or challenged fictions because they were required for technical legal reasons: to adhere to traditional, centuries-old legal form and rules. Law professor and historian David Thomas Konig explained, comfortingly, that "legal fictions [...] made no innate sense outside the artificial reason of the law".[2] Legal fictions were employed to make substantive issues fit within the frame of accepted form and rules so that a civil action could proceed. To emphasize, a modern reader of these writs must discern and separate factual clues from fictitious formalism, which is challenging because the latter ordinarily specified dates, places, and events that can seem to be literal statements. Legal fictions were also used in a parallel, abstract manner in case decisions when jurists made legal findings that required them for the sake of conformance with the internal logic of their decisions. Legal findings that were actually legal fictions were abstractions and distillations of an ideal stated as truth. Legal findings were purposeful and intentional: they allowed substantive issues to be decided that depended on the findings being held as true. In that regard, fictive legal findings may not have been historically true, but they were legally true.

Referencing and archival arrangements of unpublished judicial documentation

Citations and references to unpublished, manuscript judicial documentation of the records of case decisions (called *records*), to the court *dockets* (the list, prepared by the clerk, of cases intended to be heard during a term of court with an abbreviated record of the actions taken for each case), and to the case *file papers* (documents for a case filed with the court) include, by convention, the *term of court* which is rendered as a month and year. In actuality, the term of court began in that month and year, but the term usually did not conclude within that month and year. The court clerk recorded the date that the court term commenced and usually recorded the date that the term adjourned. When a specific date was indicated for a judicial action, then that date was noted in the citations and the corresponding reference in the references cited (e.g., records of hearings held by the Essex County Court of General Sessions of the Peace specified the actual date of the hearing).

Court clerks used the term of court to organize their dockets, the records of case decisions made each term, and their files of case papers. Dockets for each term appeared consecutively in docket books, which in earlier times were called *minute books*. Records of case decisions and other matters decided and ordered by the court were likewise recorded sequentially for each term in record books. The record books were usually paginated, and although the pagination system might vary, by convention a matter appearing as a court record of decision is cited only to the first page number of the decision (unless quoting from or referring to another page). When a leaf-type page numbering system was employed, the page number was given to the sheet of paper or leaf, and both sides of that leaf are considered to have the same page number. I referred to the leaf number (called a *folio*) without distinguishing it was a folio rather than a page number, and I did not specify front (recto) or back (verso) of the leaf. Clerks prepared rough indexes that appear at the beginning or end of whole volumes of record books, but their arrangement and precision differ from modern indexing practices. File papers for each case were gathered together, labeled with the *case caption*, and each separate case file was placed alongside other case files from the same term of court in which all those cases were concluded.

Clerk practices varied and developed over hundreds of years, and the results of their record-making and record-keeping systems could be later rearranged as pages from their books might be disbound, rebound, separately filed, renumbered, repaginated, reindexed, etc. and file papers might be reorganized as well. In instances when original documentation has been rearranged and new numbers were assigned to items using a consistent identification system (such as with the Suffolk Files Collection, described below), then the conventions of that system were followed in citations and references.

Case titles and captioning practices

Full bibliographic references to unpublished judicial documentation and to published reports of cases are alphabetized in the references cited under the name of the first party of the case caption, or by the name of the subject of the judicial file (e.g., Andover v. Canton; Bishop, John v. John Hathorne and Edward Richards (In re Mall Indian); Coburn, Titus, Revolutionary War Pension Application File; Francisco, In re; Frye, Sarah, Probate file papers; Quimby, Robert, Presentment of).

Sometimes, in abbreviation or by inadvertence, court clerks rendered case captions variously. When more than one person appeared as plaintiff/appellant or defendant/appellee, the clerk might abbreviate the case caption as, e.g., Smith et al. v. Jones et ux. (ux. for *uxor*, "wife"). Names might be spelled differently among documents, apparently to no consequence other than to passing notice of researchers. In the references, I indicated captioning vagaries that I noticed. When cases were heard on appeal, sometimes the order of the names of the parties might be reversed. Or, the names might not be reversed even though the losing defendant was the appellant who might ordinarily be listed first when the case was appealed. So that all the related judicial documentation for each cited case, even if appealed, appears together in the references cited, I maintained the original case caption as the leading reference to the documentation even if the caption changed upon appeal.

In the seventeenth-century court records and files of the Essex County Quarterly Courts and the Court of Assistants, and in the eighteenth-century records of the Essex County Court of General Sessions of the Peace, in the documentation that I used, cases were not captioned by the clerks in the now-familiar manner of plaintiff/appellant v. defendant/appellee. Only for ease and consistency in citations and references, I editorially created captions for historically uncaptioned court cases, explaining when I did so because my editorially created captions do not appear in the judicial documents.

By convention, while full case names are not italicized, shorthand mentions of a case are (such as *Aves* referring to Commonwealth v. Aves). In text and notes when referring generally to the now-famous freedom suit cases of "Mum Bett" and of "Quock Walker," I placed the familiar generic names for their cases in quotation marks because they were captioned differently historically and the "Quock Walker" cases were multiple. Full references to their judicial documentation are listed under their proper case captions: "Mum Bett" refers to Brom and Bett v. Ashley (first heard at Berkshire County Court of Common Pleas and then appealed to the Supreme Judicial Court [SJC] in 1781). "Quock Walker" refers to Walker v. Jennison; to Jennison v. Caldwell and Caldwell (the first two cases were heard at Worcester County Court of Common Pleas, then both were appealed to the SJC in 1781); and, finally, Commonwealth v. Jennison (a serious criminal matter so heard as a case of original jurisdiction at the SJC in 1783). The decisions of the "Mum Bett" and "Quock Walker" cases were unpublished. Several published transcriptions of the records and file papers of the cases are at variance with the manuscript judicial documents.

The Inferior and Circuit Court of Common Pleas

In citations and references to matters at the properly full-named Inferior Court of Common Pleas, I dispensed with "Inferior" following the trend of modern historiographic practice. "Inferior" was dropped from the name

in 1782, and in the first decade of the nineteenth century the court was renamed the Circuit Court of Common Pleas. Historical consensus appears
to be that the changes were in name only. In my precise citations and references to judicial archives, I used the full proper name of the Essex County
Circuit Court of Common Pleas for the Middle Circuit to specify records
of decisions and files of that court, including that court's nineteenth-century case documentation and its files of original Revolutionary War veteran
pension applications, to distinguish those from the records, dockets, and
case files created by its eighteenth-century predecessor.

Executions of judgment

Separate orders, called executions of judgment, commanded the sheriff to
implement (execute) a court's decision (judgment). Executions directed
the sheriff to seize and sell property to obtain the money owed to a winning party that, despite the court decision, had not been paid by the losing
party. In records, dockets, and in case files, executions of judgment were frequently indicated, sometimes by short abbreviation with the date that the
execution was issued. The obvious potential confusion of an execution of
judgment with a warrant to carry out a sentence of death is the reason that
the proper term for an execution may be rendered differently in non-judicial contexts, such as "Notices to seize property" in an archival finding aid.
Ironically, alternative renderings of the proper term may be confusing to
those who understand the difference.

Suffolk Files Collection

The Suffolk Files Collection includes file papers for court cases heard
1629–1799 by the SJC and its predecessor courts (among which were the
seventeenth-century Court of Assistants that heard appeals from the early county courts, and the immediate precursor of the SJC called the Superior Court of Judicature or SCJ). Regardless of the name, the Suffolk
Files Collection includes file papers from cases heard in all the counties
by the SJC and its predecessor courts. The justices of the SCJ and then
the SJC once rode circuit among all the counties and held court at each of
the county venues. The papers from the case files for legal actions that had
been heard in all the counties—as well as the case files of the lower courts
in Suffolk County that were also brought into the collection—were largely
once stored at the old Suffolk County Courthouse, and hence the name of
the artificially created collection.

During a late nineteenth- to early twentieth-century archival reorgani-
zation and indexing project, the file papers were chronologically sorted,

grouped generally by case into separate files, and then assigned unique *file numbers.* The vast, artificially created collection has 1,289 large-format volumes, with at least 175,581 uniquely numbered files containing more than 250,000 papers. However, while effort was made during sorting and organization to group file papers from the same case in the same file, papers from different cases are found in a single file, and papers related to a single case are scattered among different files. The collection has multiple types of indexes that are mutually exclusive (e.g., entries in the "county" indexes may not also appear in other indexes), so locating pertinent documents ordinarily requires using several indexes.

The Suffolk Files Collection preserved at the Supreme Judicial Court Archives (Judicial Archives) at the Massachusetts Archives in Boston, has been microfilmed, and the microfilm has been digitized by FamilySearch although in their catalog the collection is confusingly called "Suffolk County (Mass.) court files, 1629–1797." Confusion also ensues from bibliographic citations used by some researchers to refer to the assigned file numbers of those created assemblages of file papers. Some misnamed the file number as "case number" or "docket number," which the file numbers are neither. Again to emphasize, the file numbers were assigned in the late nineteenth and early twentieth century, and thus the file numbers in the Suffolk Files Collection do not appear in the dockets and records of case decisions created long before that time.

Middlesex Folio Collection

The Middlesex Folio Collection of Middlesex County court file papers (and other documents found in courthouse storage) is also an artificially created assemblage preserved at the Judicial Archives. According to the FamilySearch catalog entries for their microfilm of the indexes and folios, the file papers in the collection span from 1636 to 1798, but different year spans are indicated in their own catalog records and in other sources. The separate FamilySearch catalog records that include links to their digitized microfilm of the Middlesex Folio Collection and card indexes are titled "Colonial county court papers, 1648–1798"; "Folio index cards, 1650–1800"; and, "Card index to births, deaths, wills, and miscellaneous court records, 1600–1799." The court papers appear to have been sorted and arranged only generally chronologically and placed within numbered packets called *folios.* The folios have summary listings of contents with names, dates, and subjects, but the listings are not always complete and accurate. The numbering system for the folios and the individual items within the folio envelopes is unwieldy and complicated. Genealogist Melinde Lutz Sanborn (now Byrne) indicated that the collection was created in the 1930s, and that the file card indexes were hastily prepared, faulty, and incomplete.[3] The unsatisfactory arrangement, numbering, and indexing of the collection—combined with multiple, partial, overlapping, and poorly executed reformatting episodes in photostat and microfilm that are insufficiently documented—make using the collection extremely challenging and time-consuming. Sanborn advised using the rough chronological arrangement to search the contents of each folio. Thus, if the term or a date of a court decision is known from the court records of decisions, related file papers might be found in that manner.

Massachusetts Archives Collection

Administratively separate from the Judicial Archives is the well-known compiled collection of original documents in the Massachusetts Archives Collection (MAC, also called the Felt Collection), assembled in the 1830s by Rev. Joseph Felt with additional volumes created by others in the late nineteenth century. Like with the Suffolk Files Collection, original documents were placed scrapbook-fashion on pages within large-format volumes. Eight topical volumes (Volumes 38B, 39–44, 282) titled "Judicial" contain chiefly file papers regarding civil, criminal, and probate cases, but also judicial appointments, orders, rules, and case decisions, from the General Court, Court of Assistants, and SCJ dating 1640 to 1799. Judicial documents, mostly file papers, were also placed in other topical volumes of the series (e.g., there are court clerk-captioned case file papers in other volumes, and part of Volume 273 has wills and inventories but probate file papers were also placed in other topically titled volumes). There is no single index for the entire MAC that consists of 328 numbered volumes, sixteen of which volume numbers are suffixed with either letter *A* or letter *B* for a total of 336 once separately bound volumes (some volumes were subsequently disbound to better preserve original documents). The contents of the MAC volumes can be searched, variously, by a card catalog, or for some volumes only by tables of contents and name indexes within volumes, or for 24 volumes only also by an online database. Some volumes in the series have no finding aids. The MAC and the card catalog are at the Massachusetts Archives Division of the Secretary of the Commonwealth, Boston, within the same building as the Judicial Archives. FamilySearch's microfilm of the MAC has been digitized under two FamilySearch library catalog records, "Massachusetts State Archives collection, colonial period, 1622–1788" and "Massachusetts State Archives collection, colonial and post colonial period, 1626–1806." FamilySearch microfilmed only a portion of the card catalog and presently (2020) has not digitized all the reels that are listed under the library catalog record as "Card index to the Massachusetts Archives."

Clerk numbering practices

Regarding numbering of documents as practiced historically, in the dockets that they prepared for each term of court, court clerks regularly numbered cases in the order they appeared in the docket, and sometimes wrote that number on the associated file papers for each of those cases. When cases were continued to a following term, in the docket prepared for that next term of court, the clerk listed all the cases to be heard—first the continued cases from the previous term and then the new cases. The clerk freshly numbered all the cases listed in the docket that were intended to be heard during that term, and then sometimes updated the related new docket number on the file papers for each of the continued cases. In the books of the records of case decisions, court clerks sometimes sequentially numbered cases in the order that they were recorded, and sometimes that case number might also be written in the docket or on file papers. Unlike with modern case numbering systems, earlier clerk practices could be inventive and idiosyncratic. While such artifacts of bureaucratic record-making practices that appear on documents should be properly explained in scholarly transcriptions and quotations, the various numbering systems used by court clerks to temporarily track and designate entries and related documents may be of little interest to modern researchers, and not directly helpful to locate, differentiate, and interrelate associated archival records. I specified numbering and pagination, and explained any vagaries, when that information would seem to best assist a researcher to rapidly locate and identify a particular archival document.

Probate documentation

The Judicial Archives has vast collections with many archival series containing documents of interest to historians. Best known are the series created by the probate courts. Their components and the searching avenues required to locate related information in them vary by period and court, but usually consist of four main groups: *indexes* of names; *dockets* that summarize actions of the probate process; *records*, which are copies of information transcribed from the file papers; and, the *file papers* that are the original documents filed with the court (original wills, inventories, accounts of estate administration, guardianship papers, orders issued by the probate judge, etc.). Digitized microfilm images of probate indexes, dockets, and records are available through FamilySearch. For my purposes, the file papers were most revealing. The original probate file papers from the Essex County and Middlesex County registries of probate have been scanned, digitized, and indexed in a joint effort by the Judicial Archives and New England Historic Genealogical Society. (Digitization and indexing of probate file papers from other Massachusetts counties that I did not use for this research are also completed or in progress.)

Revolutionary War veteran pension application files

Federal pension applications for Essex County veterans of the Revolutionary War were first made through the Essex County Circuit Court of Common Pleas for the Middle Circuit. Essex County court clerks made copies from their original application files and sent those copies to Washington, D.C. Differences among the original documents in the county court files and the copies in the federal files were merely scrivener's errors, and explain incongruities evident in the copies. Later applications by widows and children of veterans were made directly to a federal office. Some of those later application files also include certified copies of records created by clerks, such as a certified copy of a marriage record made by a town clerk for the purpose of proving that the pension applicant was married to the veteran. Federal pension application files may thus contain copies of documents, as well as unique original material. Digital images of the federal pension application files are freely available through the National Archives online catalog.

Referencing published SJC decisions and "extended" official records

Published reports of court case decisions of the SJC appear in the series known as *Massachusetts Reports* that began to be published in 1805. Only somewhat similar to my citations and references to unpublished judicial records of decisions (and the associated docket entries and file papers, all of which require more information to quickly locate and identify that material), citations and references to published reports of case decisions are rendered in more straightforward legal style. The volume number precedes the name of the published series, while the page number of the first page of the decision follows the name of the series: "18 Pick. (35 Mass. Reports) 193, at 208" means that a report of the decision was published in *Massachusetts Reports*, Volume 35—retrospectively numbered after Volume 18 of Pickering's published series of reported case decisions, which series and other series were subsumed into the *Massachusetts Reports*—that page 193 is the first page of the reported decision in that volume, and that the particular matter I noticed or quoted appears at page 208. By convention, the name of the

xxxii   *Editorial Conventions and Notes about Sources*

published *Massachusetts Reports* series (and its encompassed predecessor series reported by Williams, Tyng, Pickering, Metcalf, Cushing, Gray, and by Allen) is abbreviated and is not italicized in citations or references. The year or term of court was added to citations of published decisions when that information was significant to my point, such as to trace chronology; the term of court in which a decision was made was included in the references to published reports of decisions. While I have not used them, the Judicial Archives of course has the court's own official, original records of SJC case decisions that had been reported and published by others. Especially for the earlier published reports of case decisions, the official records of SJC decisions in the Judicial Archives may differ from the published reported versions: archivist Elizabeth Bouvier beguilingly referred to the official records of decisions as "extended" records.

Judicial documents elsewhere

Documentation for all Massachusetts judicial matters is not all preserved, and not all is at the Judicial Archives or the administratively separate Massachusetts Archives Division of the Secretary of the Commonwealth which agencies cooperatively occupy spaces and share resources in the Massachusetts Archives building. File papers and other judicial documents that are public records landed in other repositories or have found their way to private hands. Genealogical and historical research guides to court documents and citations of referenced manuscripts in scholarly works assist to ascertain locations of public legal records. Some historical Essex County judicial documents that are public records were long ago placed on deposit at Phillips Library (formerly part of the Essex Institute and now Peabody Essex Museum, and once located in Salem, then Danvers, and now in Rowley). At the time, Phillips Library afforded better preservation, access, and security for the fragile records than the old Salem courthouse. The Boston Public Library's Rare Books and Manuscript Department has a large number of judicial file papers from the Court of Assistants (and other Massachusetts courts) that heard matters involving Essex County subjects. In future, public judicial records may be transferred to the modern facilities of the Judicial Archives that are curated at regional Trial Court Record Centers and at the Massachusetts Archives building. Researchers should ascertain the present location of original archival materials prior to scheduling a visit to see them.

Private legal records

Additional to official judicial public records, there are many other kinds of documents relating to legal matters: professional notes, files, diaries, financial records, etc. created and kept privately by judges and attorneys, and legal documents kept by families that had occasion to interact with the judiciary such as during probate proceedings. Those records may be preserved by their descendants or at private or public archival repositories. Private legal records encode significant information that does not appear in or which better explain matters only allusively summarized in official judicial archives. I used many private records created by legal professionals in this study. Drawing out and linking legal events which occurred and then were done with, to fuller biographies of the many people involved with those legal matters is accomplished with non-judicial documentary sources that have their own complexities and complications. Careful attention to my bibliographic data will allow researchers to rapidly relocate the particular documents that I referred to, and to seek other pertinent and related information in meaningfully organized archival collections and their subseries.

Introduction

In the historical town of Andover, which includes the now-separate municipalities of North Andover and the south part of Lawrence, preserving memories about people of color connected to the historical area has long figured in its documented, remembered, and represented historical traditions. Biographical sketches and historical representations of Andover's historical people of color are integral to the town's cultural traditions and historical cultural geography. Andover's narrative cultural heritage includes oral histories of memories, stories, and anecdotes. It includes writings that relied on information from oral traditions, from a vast documentary heritage of original records, from previous history writings, from artifacts preserved as heirlooms associated with individuals and their families, and from knowledge of historical places and structures linked with them. Historical Andover's archivists and curators of collections, librarians, public historians, genealogists, educators, and preservationists, as well as historical researchers, archaeologists, and writers drawn to the famous town's cultural resources, continue to seek, bring together, and purposefully convey meaningful information about people of indigenous Native and African ancestry and heritage associated with this area. They have been neither forgotten nor ignored. Memories persist of people of color in historical Andover, and knowledge about them connects them to places, objects, documents, and to other people, including ourselves.

Biographies of several Andover people of color, people who were in ways ordinary and extraordinary in their time and after, are also remembered today nationally and even internationally. Andover's Lucy Foster (1767–1845) is featured in a multitude of internationally disseminated scholarly articles, books, bibliographies, textbooks, and encyclopedias on the history and archaeology of the African diaspora and about American historical archaeology generally. Salem Poor (1744–1802) became a nationally significant figure representatively for his valor and gallantry at the Battle of Bunker Hill. His first wife, Nancy Parker (fl. 1752–1825), became mentioned with him, typically and imprecisely styled as Salem Poor's "Indian" wife. During their lifetimes, at their deaths, and after, Pompey and Rose Lovejoy (1724–1826 and 1727–1826), Rosanna Coburn (1762 to 1767–1859), and Cato Freeman (1768–1853) were featured in newspaper articles that circulated statewide and nationally. Locally, all those more generally known individuals, along with Andover residents Barzillai Lew Jr. (1777–1861), Allen Hinton (1835, 1837, 1844, or 1847–1912), and Alice Hinton (1870–1951) among several others, are remembered because their names appear again and again in historical projects through the efforts of public historians in Andover, North Andover, and Lawrence.

It is surprising that persistent memories of several people of color associated with historical Andover are so broadly known. History projects, in a manner familiar to most everyone, so often focus on momentous people and events of national, regional, or thematic import. Regularly, history projects feature inspiring great leaders and achievers in politics, business, military service, science, medicine, mathematics, literature, music, arts, and other areas of the humanities. People of color have been conspicuous among them throughout history. So rarely do we hear, read, and see information about the lives of more ordinary people of color who were born, lived, and died in the places we reside and visit. In Andover there were individuals who, during their lifetimes, were among the most ordinary, laboring people. Others gained sufficiently to be property owners, farmers, and businesspeople. Some had been held in captivity as slaves, others freeborn. Some men, while enslaved or free, bravely joined with other Andover men on military excursions. Some women and men prospered economically, others maintained themselves and their loved ones, others experienced abject impoverishment, and sometimes these same people went through reversals of fortune, for better or for worse. Among them were particularly gifted and notable individuals who gained admiration and respect for their talents, courage, wisdom, and generosities. Others were remembered for different reasons. Whatever experiences and eventualities came to them, during their lifetimes they were familiar to other townspeople, and at their deaths people made effort to honor and commemorate the lives of many people of color connected to historical Andover. They are named and remembered to this day.

This scholarly monograph explores two main topics in the history of people of color in historical Andover. First is the longstanding mystery of the 100+ year-old woman of color counted as a "slave" at the Andover almshouse in the 1830 federal census.[1] That was the only instance when a slave was counted and officially accepted by Congress in any federal census for Massachusetts, a state that had legally abolished slavery by over 170 years of individual judicial actions made by people of color and their allies. The singular appearance of a person denominated a slave in the nominally "free" state of Massachusetts was controversial at the time and has perplexed historians ever since.

Second, this study explores the biographies of members of Rosanna Coburn's extended family. Rosanna Coburn, a locally well-known woman of color, was meaningfully designated at her death in 1859 as the last person to have been born in the town as a slave. Her mother Phillis was born in Africa and her father Booso was from the West Indies. Both were taken captive, taken away from their people and their homelands, and were brought to Andover as slaves. All their other children, Rosanna's siblings, were also born in Andover as slaves. In 1778 Booso prevailed when he legally challenged his enslavement. By 1790, Phillis and all the children and another enslaved man named Cato, there at the late Sarah Frye's farm and felt hat manufacturing workshop, had self-emancipated on their own terms as a group: they had "taken their Freedom".[2] Just as perplexing as the official designation of a "slave" in the 1830 federal census, the former status of Rosanna Coburn and that of several other formerly enslaved, contingently free people in Andover was considered by local and state officials during their lives. Rosanna Coburn's former status as a slave was specially denominated in her official local and state death records, as was done for the death and marriage records of several other Andover residents.

The designations employed in official records were purposeful and deliberate. During their lives, when formerly enslaved people such as Rosanna Coburn (and her freeborn daughter Colley Hooper who lived in her mother's household throughout her life) required economic assistance from the town, their former status figured in determining whether the town or the state was responsible for the cost. The designation of the centenarian woman at the almshouse in 1830 as a "slave" was intended to establish her former condition and to bolster the town's position that some other town or the state should bear the cost of that formerly enslaved woman's institutional care. Legal standards decided whether a formerly enslaved person or their descendants who needed poor relief was the financial responsibility of the town where they lived presently, of another town where they were born or formerly lived, or of the state. Those decisions were made based on individual biographical details of birth place, of residence of their former slave owner, and other considerations that evolved in legal decisions about poor relief made by the state Supreme Judicial Court. The state's murky history of judicial abolition was considered by jurists in making decisions about poor relief for formerly enslaved people and their descendants.

The later appearance of notations about former enslavement in official town and state death records for Rosanna Coburn had a different meaning in a different context. In January 1860 when the Andover town clerk prepared Rosanna Coburn's official death records for the town and separately for the state, under the column for Rosanna's place of birth, he wrote "Andover. a slave". For the state vital records that he prepared, he or another hand underscored "a slave". Andover town clerks made several similar notations in marriage and death records of formerly enslaved people.[3]

When Rosanna Coburn died in 1859, it was at the zenith of local attention to national issues of slavery and its abolition. Andover was a nexus of antislavery, abolitionist, and antisegregation activism. The civil violence then raging in Bleeding Kansas about that issue was another facet of the national conflict that occupied the attention of Andover townspeople. Some Andover residents materially supported antislavery settlers connected to Andover who had moved to Kansas in hope of making it a "free" state.

The presence of formerly enslaved people in town was known to many: some had escaped from distant slave states and settled in Andover, others came to Andover as visitors or settlers from other New England towns, and there were inhabitants such as Rosanna Coburn who had been born and enslaved there. To local activists opposed to slavery, the living survivors of enslavement reminded them of the town's own disconcerting history of generational slavery. Their emancipated presence among the townspeople embodied their present ideal to end slavery nationally. Rosanna Coburn's death was a moment to reflect that the last living reminder of the town's past practice of slavery had truly passed into history, while looking forward to when the nation too might achieve what Andover had accomplished by ending the practice of slavery in their town. Rosanna Coburn's elaborated gravestone epitaph prepared in or before 1861 memorialized that she was "born a slave in Andover and the last survivor of all born here in that condition". To underscore the finality, her epitaph indicated that she had left no descendants.[4]

The surprising initial report of four slaves in Massachusetts counted in the fifth federal census of 1830—corrected to one slave before the final census tally was accepted by Congress—was not evidence of persistent slavery in an ostensibly "free" state (Figures 1–2). Rather, the designation as a slave of the centenarian woman living at the almshouse in the Essex County town of Andover in 1830, revealed the practice of Massachusetts town overseers of the poor to officially designate formerly enslaved people as nonresidents. By doing so, towns sought and received state pauper reimbursements for supporting formerly enslaved people, some of whom were in fact legal residents of Massachusetts towns and thus not "state paupers." Towns received state funds to support formerly enslaved town residents as late as 1846 when a state commission rejected the practice for former slaves who were legal town residents.

The identity of the sole person ever counted as a slave in a federal census for Massachusetts likely will never be known. The 1830 census population schedules named only the "head of household"—in this instance, the almshouse superintendent. Statistics about occupants of a residence were provided after the name of the head of household. Federal correspondence files for the 1830 census that probably included letters to and from the census takers to clarify that matter were destroyed. No other contemporaneous records or reports have been found that named the elderly woman deemed a "slave."

Nevertheless, the initial, preliminary report that four slaves had been counted in the nominally "free" state of Massachusetts became a matter of immediate public controversy, skepticism, and speculation. The initial count of slaves in Massachusetts and other "free" states prompted a Congressional inquiry that led to the eventual adjustment of the Massachusetts count to one slave. The official Congressional acceptance of the census statistic of one slave in the state, which has ever since been included in editions of the authoritative *Historical Statistics of the United States*, has been a long-standing and perplexing mystery.[5] The next part of this monograph examines that matter.

Realizing that presumably the Andover almshouse superintendent characterized the almshouse resident as a slave, that she herself was not asked, leads to consideration about how and why town and state officials persisted to specially denote other formerly enslaved Massachusetts residents.[6] That practice was for discerning legal responsibility to provide either municipal or state poor relief funds to former slaves and their progeny. A state commission, which examined state pauper claims submitted by towns for the fiscal year 1845, investigated the genealogy of Phillis' daughter Rosanna (Rose) Coburn and her granddaughter Colley Hooper (Elizabeth Coburn). The state officials considered the Andover family's history to determine whether Rosanna and Colley were "town paupers" or "state paupers." Phillis and Rosanna's former enslavement in Andover, and particularly Rosanna's birth in Andover as a slave, established Rosanna and Colley's legal settlement in Andover.[7] Phillis herself had been consulted by Andover overseers of the poor for reliable genealogical information, not recorded in official vital records, to establish accountability for private, municipal, or state funding to care for destitute people.[8]

The "laws of settlement" as they were called had evolved over centuries in Massachusetts statutory and common law (case law, legal principles established as precedent in case decisions). By the early nineteenth century, common law determined that residency ("settlement") for a former slave was in the town of their former owner. Later the law nuanced that former slaves were "state paupers" if they were born long ago in a different town than where they were living presently. In crafting their decisions in which the common law was made about settlement of former slaves and their descendants, jurists employed technical "legal fictions" that differently remembered the timing and effects of previous judicial decisions, unpublished decisions that had occurred decades prior and which were preserved only in obscure manuscript court records. In deciding settlement law cases decades after judicial abolition had been achieved, jurists fictively proposed that slavery had been abolished even earlier by the adoption of the 1780 state constitution with its guarantees of freedom, liberty, and equality. Their technical legal findings, while historically fictive—as jurists themselves realized that the subjects of the disputes and many others actually remained enslaved after 1780—were legally effective, for they allowed the jurists to proceed in their rational decisions to decide which town or the state was responsible for economic support required by the poor.

This study considers finer details of the tenebrous legal history of judicial abolition in Massachusetts for several purposes. Legal abolition was eventually consequential at moments in the lives of Phillis and Booso's extended family and others in Andover and surrounding towns who enter into this study. To eventually leave enslavement they relied upon the effects of that protracted and uneven process of judicial abolition, what historian Margot Minardi appreciated as having only provided a vague "sense that slavery was defunct in Massachusetts".[9]

The technical details, timing, and results of Massachusetts freedom suits are not well-known and understood. Historical investigators have not always been so curious and applied to seek, examine, carefully transcribe, and fully document original archival records about these unusual and consequential legal actions for freedom. A more sophisticated and accurate story about Massachusetts judicial abolition is revealed when the archival documents are studied with specialist understandings of technical legal vocabulary, rules, and processes, rather than with undue assumption and mere speculation. My closer examination of notable legal cases, some long-famous, others obscure, appear in expansive narrative endnotes to enthuse further serious research into Massachusetts freedom suits. While so many lawsuits for liberty have figured importantly in historical projects about

Massachusetts judicial abolition, embodying the collective achievement by enslaved people and their allies, the full corpus of archival documentation relating to Massachusetts freedom suits remains undiscovered in the vast judicial archives.

A longstanding myth still prevails that emancipation arrived in Massachusetts suddenly by one final court decision or another, which was not the case. The myth of instant, statewide emancipation was founded in misunderstanding the merely technical, idealistic, and purposeful employment of retrospective legal fictions by jurists to bolster their decisional rationales. Misunderstood legal fictions matched proudly righteous historical traditions of the nominally "free" state. How Massachusetts came to abolish slavery in the state, to outlaw slavery and the slave trade here, has engaged and befuddled historians since the late eighteenth century. Decades of efforts by legal historians have conveyed that important historical conclusion about the state's history of enslavement and judicial emancipation: enslavement did not end instantly and statewide, but continued here long after. The historical facts of the persistence of actual slavery and related situations along a continuum of "unfreedom" helps to understand how other people of color discussed in this study remained in those confining and dependent, servile situations long after the long-supposed and mythical sudden ending of slavery and the slave trade statewide. A large part of the expansive endnotes comprises documented examples of people remaining enslaved or in slave-like or ambiguous laboring circumstances in Essex County after the once-believed moment of judicial abolition. What may be gleaned of their individual biographical moments, their circumstances, movements, and fates, is sketched in the narrative endnotes to encourage other researchers to further pursue that topic statewide.

While "slave trade" is ordinarily thought to refer to material support and implementation of schemes to initially kidnap and sell groups of people, wholesale as it were, by the Middle Passage, passed between ships at sea, smuggled through hidden coastal places, docked at ports, in the despicable trade—and I also chiefly use the phrase in that more common sense—any buying, selling, or exchange of persons was part and parcel of the slave trade, whether cash or barter was involved or not. Thus, participation in the slave trade included end consumer retail exchange of slaves, including persons obtained by gift or disposed for free as many infants were in Massachusetts. While many will disagree that testamentary bequests, inheritance, and gifts of enslaved persons was "participation in the slave trade," and I do not go so far here as to characterize that as such, to my mind that practice too was a part of the same globally scaled traffic in people as property.

At Rosanna Coburn's death in 1859, her official town and state death records prepared by the Andover town clerk explicitly and curiously denoted
her birth status as "a slave" and literally underscored that last word in the
state version of the vital records he prepared. The extra notations were not
required and had no legal operative effect, but followed a practice by town
clerks when creating vital records for several other formerly enslaved Andover residents. The town clerks' notations reflected their efforts to historically encode that representationally significant biographical detail.[10]

Rosanna Coburn became legendary in Andover, and came to be
remembered as the "last" slave born in Andover. During her lifetime, a
detail of Rosanna Coburn's biography—that she received a Revolutionary
War veteran widow's pension from the federal government—was proudly
announced first in the town newspaper, then in national abolitionist
newspapers as a significant achievement by a woman of color for equitable
treatment.[11] After the Dred Scott decision was released in 1857, among
other African American soldiers, Titus Coburn's Revolutionary War service and his pension were lionized to criticize Chief Justice Taney's opinion.[12] The granting of the pension to Mrs. Coburn for Titus Coburn's
service was even mentioned in private correspondence from the Unitarian
minister Theodore Parker (a leading figure in the abolition movement) to
the national historian George Bancroft who was seeking information in
1858 about the roles of "Africans" during the Revolutionary War.[13]

Rosanna Coburn's obituary mentioned the pension, but also included
a detailed historical summary of her extended family's history in slavery
and freedom, reaching back to her mother Phillis born in Africa and her
father Booso born in the West Indies.[14] Her original gravestone conveyed
publically that Rosanna was "born a slave in Andover and the last survivor
of all born here in that condition". Her long epitaph featured also that she
was granted the pension "as a widow of a soldier of the Revolution." The
present gravestone that replaced the original marker in 2002 added additional biographical information: it named her husband Titus Coburn, her
mother Phillis, her father "Benjamin"; it identified her parents' geographic origins in Africa and the West Indies; and, it named her former owner
Joshua Frye, using the common New England euphemism of "servant"[15]
(Figures 21–23).

Distinct from the reasons for the official bureaucratic practice that specially denoted formerly enslaved Massachusetts residents in obscure government records seen by very few, Rosanna Coburn's public "memorial
narratives"[16]—her obituary published in 1859 and her gravestone epitaph
prepared in or before 1861—encoded didactic historical and political

messages about antislavery, abolition, and antisegregation sentiments in Andover before and around the time of the outbreak of the Civil War.[17] This monograph biographically traces Rosanna Coburn's extended family, beginning with her African-born mother Phillis. The public familiarity of Rosanna Coburn, her husband Titus Coburn, and other Andover people of color during their lives; the detailed knowledge of their survivance and re-silience locally and now known far more broadly; and, the persistent mem-ories of them long after their then-ordinary lives are remarkable to consider.

Rosanna Coburn became "known far and wide"[18] to many "early change agents and culture workers"[19] interested in the history of American enslave-ment and emancipation. Their projects championed political efforts for ob-taining civil rights and more equitable treatment of people. The literary and cultural historian Barbara McCaskill recognized the "desire to recover the lost voices of those who were enslaved and those who bought, sold, and owned them. It invites us to think about the polyvocal nature of African American [...] history" because "we still struggle to come to terms with this past and to liberate ourselves and our communities from its unwelcome descendants—racial bigotry, social intolerance, fear of and resistance to change—that have attached to us and not let go."[20]

This narrative considers other people in Andover and elsewhere that in-teracted with Phillis' family, and also people who figured in their historical representations by generations of writers and public historians. My research and writing project "performs the cultural work of memorializing those other unrecorded, unrecognized souls, and it points to a process of inquiry as tantalizing and tangled as their story."[21] There are several such "tanta-lizing and tangled" complicated narratives in the archive about the cente-narian woman counted as a slave in the 1830 census and about Phillis and her extended family of Booso, Colley Hooper, Titus Coburn, and Rosanna Coburn. In each of their biographical summaries, information and events common to them recur among the summaries because family members ap-peared together in the same sources. Their singular and mutual experiences connected them, just as the stories told about them become familiar to us.

Some readers are less drawn to recondite details in meticulously document-ed historical sources, to tracing previous and relevant scholarship, to discur-sive and nuanced treatments about finer and technical points of intellectual and legal history, and to particular biographical and historical information about related people and topics. In this monograph I chose to place that ma-terial in expansive, narrative endnotes, in the style of legal history writing but unusual in most other historical texts. Several endnotes are presented unconventionally and indulgently as short, digressive articles that follow research avenues and sketch out genealogies of scholarship. As with mutually presented biographical information that recurs, intellectual and historical topics are iterant to emphasize important matters or to consider information from another perspective. I delve into those related topics separately from the main narrative to encourage deeper awareness of intellectual and historical contexts about experiences of people in historical Andover and Massachusetts generally, and to persuade interested researchers to pursue further consideration of people and subjects through the references cited.

I engage with vast and ornate archives and bring forth their components that can be readily identified and located using the bibliographic apparatus. Detailed and particular historical data and the profusion of citations to documentation are intended for fellow researchers to locate, evaluate, and interpret productive sources in many research avenues. In consideration of time and effort required for that task, I mention promising archival record series that I have not fully explored, and occasionally when I had searched records but found no pertinent information. For the convenience of researchers and archival collections reference staff, I made particular effort to explicitly identify unique artifacts such as documents and objects, and to indicate where the original items are preserved. I frequently noted the availability of primary sources reformatted as photocopies, microfilm, or digital files that broaden access to and ease searching of the encoded information. Throughout this project I especially relied on digital sources to access information from unique documents and compiled databases, and to read scarce editions of published works that are scattered among the world's libraries and archives. In considering evidentiary potential and evidentiary limitations in sources, I commented on their degrees of organization, disorganization, and differential preservation, on their archival arrangement, cataloging, and indexing, and on their interpretations by others. I considered ambiguities and lacunae in the sources and attempted to detangle evident confusion, misapprehension, error, and the repetition of accepted speculations and errors that then became factoids, to better guide researchers to locate and understand authentic and reliable historical materials.

My choice to supply minute and particular points in veritably and frequently literally genealogical detail has more fundamental intentions. First, the preserved original source material demonstrates the factual and incontrovertible evidence of the presence, experiences, relationships, and remembrances of people of color and their contemporaries in historical Andover. The mass and complexity of primary and secondary historical sources relating to the people, topics, connections, and contexts of historical Andover comprise the authentic foundation of its historical and cultural traditions.

I am particularly interested in how information representatively appeared and was transmitted in fixed forms of local historical traditions, erudition, and scholarship. Historical practices and historical products are, of course, forms of ongoing cultural traditions that convey what knowledge was considered to be specifically meaningful.

Second, my application of a microhistorical approach contrasts with historical writing traditions that create sweeping narrative from a selected few illustrative examples of primary sources suggested to be representational. In that popular narrative style, with enviably elegant source citations, anecdotes drawn from historical sources are woven seamlessly in narratives that metaphorically extend the selected information to convey a regularity or to impose a normativity that may have not existed in all places, at all times, and among all people. An incident that occurred momentarily at some place in historical Andover was not precisely experienced or remembered monolithically and generally. Its recounting does not necessarily demonstrate the way all similar occurrences played out throughout the town or county or river drainage that metaphorically represents "Massachusetts," that conceptually encompasses "New England" or "The North," or that functions as a synecdoche for "The Nation" or "North America." When removed from particularly meaningful temporal, geographic, historiographic, intellectual, and cultural contexts, historical material treated as merely illustrative can seem to be paradoxically ahistorical.

In writing, I kept close to documentary texts. I related particular information about people (such as dates and amounts of poor relief) in an effort to show the sorts of proofs of their existence at historical moments encoded in bureaucratic notations made about them and in records that they themselves participated in creating. I expect that each of them would be surprised to learn that details of such transitory events were preserved and rediscovered. They might have balked that such small events as receiving a load of firewood had no import in the meaningful arc of their lives. For this documentalist project, any notation naming a person of interest was important, and oftentimes tiny details proved to figure significantly when considered in relation to other information or when put in broader context.

During their lives, Rosanna Coburn and Colley Hooper allied to values of privacy, modesty, and public respectability. Yet, their names appeared in published town and state reports as having received poor relief. The mother and daughter were known to many public and private persons as having received intermittent public assistance in food, supplies, cash, housing, and medical care. If, when, or to what degree having to rely on public assistance and charity was stigmatizing or embarrassing to them is unknown. They were well-known in town and in places near and far. Their names appeared on antisegregation petitions sent to the state legislature; Rosanna was interviewed and related her extended family's history that was recounted in a local history column published in the town newspaper; Rosanna's Revolutionary War veteran widow's pension was reported in local and national newspapers; and, by those articles her pension was known to abolitionist-era historians. Rosanna Coburn was remembered as vivacious, personable, intelligent, and highly regarded. One, some, or all of the historical people featured and figured on these pages might have thought it an arrogation to use their biographies as opportunities for propaedeutic considerations of broader historical developments and interpretive themes. I expect there would be contestation about suppositions and meanings entailed in that mode of biographical narrative-making that has intellectual goals beyond the autonomy and authenticity of their particular lived experiences. Perhaps one or some might have appreciated my intentions in creating this renewed attention to their biographies as a genuine effort to learn more about them to honor their astonishing lives.

I intend in this monograph, through its main text, illustrative figures, discursive endnotes, and attendant bibliographic apparatus, to invite multivocal, polysemous considerations and reconsiderations of historical experiences of people of color and their contemporaries in historical Andover and its connected places. My treatments of this information acknowledge interpretive limits of sources, are grounded in factual evidence, are contextualized in time and culturally relevant geography, and favor alternative, plausible explanations rather than assumption and speculation which more ordinarily reflect presentism, subjectivism, and essentialism entailed with objectivism. Postmodern historical narratives favor explicit, reflexive consideration of "position" and "authorial location" to convey, e.g., humility, gratitude, dependence, capacity, privilege, authority, intentions, methods, subjective perspectives, and other allied postcolonial meta-considerations such as contemplating the historical sociological context of historical collections of papers and objects in archives and museums. As a person of my time, these ideas influence my writing and channel my attentions to what I find interesting. This monograph was conceived and structured to convey information about people and subjects in history that assuredly others will find interesting, challenging, perplexing, and ultimately mysterious. By vicariously joining with me as I explore and comment on these discoveries and rediscoveries, we can each take our place in ongoing historical traditions that form and reform our views about cultural heritage that we find meaningful to us.

Slaves in the 1830 Census Returns for Massachusetts

Four enslaved women, all over 55 years old, were reported in the provisional returns of the fifth federal census of Massachusetts[1] (Figure 1). The enumeration of slaves in a "free" state led to confusion and consternation. Among several writers who jumped to the same conclusion, Thomas Price in *Slavery in America* (1837) asserted that the women were "sojourners from slave states" traveling with their owners. Charles Bowen in *The American Annual Register* (1832) believed there was an "Error in return. There are no slaves in Massachusetts," as was the count of five slaves in New Hampshire and six slaves in Maine, but that the 14 slaves in Rhode Island and 25 slaves in Connecticut were accurate. To resolve the contradiction about the presence of enslaved persons in "free" states that had outlawed slavery legislatively, judicially, and constitutionally, nineteenth-century compilers presumed that the four Massachusetts women were travelers.[2]

William Lloyd Garrison and Isaac Knapp, Massachusetts abolitionist newspaper publishers, resolved the inconvenient 1830 census data by rationalizing that slavery in Massachusetts was illegal, *ergo* the four women counted as "slaves" did not exist! In the premiere issue of *The Abolitionist* (1833), the presence of the four slaves in the 1830 census for Massachusetts, as well as the slaves counted in the "free" states of New Hampshire, Maine, Ohio, and New York, was acknowledged but reported in the tabulated state data in the column for "Slaves" as zero. The numbers of the counted "Slaves" were not then added to the column for "Free Blacks". A note explained that because the previous 1820 census had reported no slaves, "and it is admitted on all hands that slavery cannot legally exist [...], we have thought it would be a misrepresentation to report any slaves as existing. [...] Therefore there can be no slave[s] there now."[3]

The confusion about the slaves initially counted in Massachusetts, Maine, and Ohio in 1830 prompted Massachusetts Congressman John Davis to propose a House resolution for the United States Secretary of State (under whose office the census was conducted) to investigate and report on that matter in 1832.[4] Secretary of State Edward Livingston reported to the

House of Representatives that two of the Massachusetts women were in fact free persons of color, explaining that numbers had been inadvertently placed in an incorrect column of the population schedules. The other two Massachusetts women, Livingston averred incorrectly, had been properly characterized as slaves. Secretary Livingston indicated that both slaves were women 100 years old or more. Astonishingly, Livingston asserted that one of the women counted as a slave lived with Prince Walker's family in the town of Barre, Worcester County, Massachusetts. Prince Walker, a former slave of Nathaniel Jennison, was the brother or son of Quock Walker who brought the now-celebrated 1781 freedom suit and was the subject of the 1783 related court actions involving Jennison.[5] However, Livingston was mistaken: the miscount of a slave in Barre was due to another clerical error[6] (Figure 3).

The remaining one slave woman had been counted at the Andover almshouse. She was tallied under the entry for almshouse Superintendent Joseph Cummings, among the 54 almshouse residents, 11 of whom (including the "slave") were people of color (Figures 4A, 4B, 5). Superintendent Cummings characterized the elderly woman at the almshouse as a slave. She herself was not asked her status by the census official. Only a "free person, more than 16 years of age, whether heads of families or not," was asked: "What number of Female Slaves were there, on that day [June 1, 1830], in this family, including any who might have been occasionally absent?"[7] By reporting her status as a slave, the town hoped to recoup its expenses for her support from her owner, another town, or the state.[8]

Only heads of households were named in the 1830 census, so the woman's identity and biography are not known. Research of town and state records did not identify the woman.[9] She would have been formerly enslaved in Andover, or in another Massachusetts town, or was an escaped or abandoned slave from another state.[10] John Hannigan, a history doctoral student and reference staff at Massachusetts Archives, tentatively suggested Rosanna Coburn's mother Phillis as a potential candidate for the woman counted as a slave in 1830. However, as a result of my further research, Phillis was excluded as a candidate because she had died long before the Census Day of June 1, 1830.[11] Phillis—born in Africa and formerly enslaved by the Frye family in Andover—was said to be 90 years old in 1820, and she was later said to have died at the age of 101.[12] Phillis was named in town records among individuals who received town poor relief prior to 1830, but she cannot be the woman counted as a slave at the almshouse in 1830 because she died prior to January 5, 1829. On that day, the Andover treasurer made payment "for a coffin for Phillis Wid[ow] of Boos".[13] Phillis may have gone to the almshouse for a brief time before her death, or more likely she passed away at home. Her death was not recorded by the town clerk or in church records, and so no entry appeared in the published *Vital Records of Andover*. But Phillis and her extended family depended on public support periodically. The 1830 census schedules for Andover listed the household headed by her daughter Rosanna Coburn, the 62- to 68-year-old widow of Revolutionary War veteran Titus Coburn. Rosanna lived with her daughter—Phillis' 44-year-old granddaughter—Elizabeth (Colley Hooper), the stepdaughter of Titus Coburn.[14] The enslavement of Phillis, her daughter Rosanna, and other members of Phillis' extended family figured throughout their lives and after in official determinations of eligibility for town and state poor relief. Their formerly enslaved condition was also remembered in local history traditions to the present day.

Although others cannot be excluded, thus far documentary records do not suggest any identifiable candidate for the woman counted as a slave in 1830 that meets the criteria of age, former enslavement, who received town or state support, and not obviously present in a household separate from the almshouse in 1830. Whoever the centenarian woman was at the almshouse who was counted as a slave, she would not be remembered as "the last slave" born in Andover. It was Phillis' daughter Rosanna who was encumbered with that appellation. After her death in 1859, Rosanna became an historical representation of the town's "last" slave, although several formerly enslaved people—born elsewhere—lived in Andover after Rosanna's death. The historical idea of Rosanna Coburn as the town's representative "last slave" symbolically conveyed the finality of the former *practice* of slavery in Andover that contrasted with and extolled the town's social and political evolution as a significant locus of antislavery, abolitionist, and antisegregation activism.

Federal census officials and the federal marshals or their assistants in Massachusetts likely exchanged letters about the "slaves" counted, seeking information and providing clarification to answer the 1832 Congressional inquiry. The name of the woman called a "slave" might have been revealed in that correspondence. Regrettably it appears certain that the letter books were destroyed circa 1908, and thus far no persuasive documentary clue has been found in other local, state, or federal records to identify that woman.[15]

In the corrected federal report of the aggregated population statistics for 1830, the official version used for Congressional reapportionment, the supposed enslaved woman living with Prince Walker in Barre was discounted, as indicated in an errata sheet that accompanied the corrected report. The official count of one enslaved woman in Massachusetts in 1830, the woman residing at the Andover almshouse, was accepted by Congress in 1832 and thus remains an official historical statistic[16] (Figure 2). While the woman's identity continues to be an enduring mystery, the motivation of the almshouse superintendent to assert her status as a "slave" was chiefly fiscal. That town official considered that her former enslavement absolved the town of responsibility for the cost of her care.

"She was a colored woman . . . known far and wide":

The Persistence of "Slave" Denotations in Historical Andover

Massachusetts towns charged the state for support of formerly enslaved inhabitants, as if they had established no residency in any town. The nineteenth-century practice was among the ways that Massachusetts towns disregarded or were unaware of fine points in the evolved state laws of settlement that established the scope and responsibility for town and state pauper relief. Providing for poor people in need was tempered with controlling expenditures from the public fisc. Towns expended considerable funds to support their own town poor, the poor from other towns, and state paupers who had established no town residency. State reimbursements were never sufficient to meet town outlays for state paupers. Yet, the practice to officially designate a free person of color as a "slave," to continue to denote and to emphasize the former enslaved condition of free persons in official records, was not a fine point in a state that had judicially abolished slavery by evolving the common law and interpreting state constitutional law.

Slave owners had been economically responsible for their slaves and their slaves' children. Some elderly slaves with no other home, no family of their own, and little strength left for wage labor chose to remain enslaved, advantaging the only realistic prospect available for shelter, heat, food, clothing, and health care. Financial records, probate file papers, and other related documentation could determine in each instance if the dependant arrangements continued as before with no wages; if the servant was treated as property, being leased for a term, being hired out for day labor, or transferred in probate; and, as to whether the servant was free to leave without being characterized as an escapee subject to detention, return, and punishment. There were other facets of slavery per se, there were ambiguous, slavery-like situations, there were gradations along a continuum of "unfreedom," and positional viewpoints mattered.[1]

The 1703 state law that required owners to post a bond with towns for support of manumitted slaves who might become paupers had fallen into desuetude. The adjoining town of Wilmington voted in March 1777 to support any of the town's manumitted slaves as they did other town poor, who were freed within a month of the vote. With that impediment removed, manumissions ensued for at least two enslaved women. In the manumission he prepared for his slave Dinah, the Rev. Isaac Morrill restated the particularity of the town vote, that it applied to "Such Negroes as were within one month freed by their masters". The town offered residents who owned slaves only 30 days to free them to be assured that the town would support their former servants in need. On the day of the vote, Cadwallader Ford, Jr. (the son-in-law of Rev. Morrill, and also the town clerk) and his father (who had been elected meeting moderator) recorded their opposition to the vote and the proceeding of the town on that matter. Cadwallader Ford, Esq. and Jr., wrote that they had provided the town with "The Reason &c." for their objection, but they did not record their reasoning. It is impossible to know if their opposition was because the 30-day sunset clause was too limiting; or alternatively, whether they were disinclined to manumission generally; or whether they did not wish to share the costs of supporting other families' former slaves; or what procedural flaw they surmised in the meeting and the vote. They specified the "Vote, and proceeding of [...the] Town" on that matter. Perhaps the town clerk considered the burdensome bureaucratic record-keeping required to provide certainty as to which manumitted slave was eligible for town support. As it turned out, only two Wilmington slave owners came forward within the 30-day period to manumit two enslaved women.[2]

By the early nineteenth century, common law had evolved that established residency ("settlement") for a former slave in the town of their ex-owner. It was later established that if a former slave had been born in a town different than where they were living, then they were "state paupers." Evolving state settlement law made it difficult for former slaves to establish legal residency in other towns and it constrained mobility.[3]

In Andover, some free persons of color established residency, some bought or inherited property, some settled in enclaves. Others like Nancy Parker and her son Jonas lived on their own, occupying land.[4] Other people of color, freed after having been enslaved by townspeople for decades, were not accepted as residents by the selectmen of Andover. Some former slaves remained in town anyway. There were also visitors who came and went. There were movements, and there were connections and relations with people from adjoining towns and more distant places (Figure 6).

In early to mid-nineteenth-century Andover, all the free people of color whose employment can be discerned were skilled and semiskilled laborers and farmers. Surely some went into maritime trades. Among the men were several veteran soldiers. Some individuals such as Pomp and Rose Lovejoy gained income through cooperative spousal labor, by making and selling home-baked cakes and root beer, or beer, or ale during the town's Election Day festivities, and for other gatherings, including funerals.[5] Others worked doing spinning, cleaning, laundry, and other skilled tasks for local families, and by taking in boarders. Angela Davis (the scholar, cultural commentator, political activist and organizer) dialectically proposed that even unpaid gendered household labor—how women "cooked, sewed, washed, cleaned house, raised the children"—should be considered "meaningful" labor. Nancy Parker was paid to spin wool or flax and to do laundry for other families: she was remembered historically as "the champion spinner of the region". Parker's reputation as the area's most accomplished spinner could have been a point of personal pride, and would have benefitted her business dealings. Dinah Simpson and Lucy Foster also processed wool and flax for cash and barter in exchange for goods and supplies. Rosanna Coburn with her daughter Colley had a home garden, gathered wild berries that they traded for flour, and brokered for a local farmer selling his eggs to an Andover household. Paid and unpaid labor for themselves and their families created a sense of autonomy, identity, control, and belonging. It was "essential to the *survival*" of them, their families, and their "community." Part of their survival strategy required intermittent poor relief.[6]

Claiming freedom did not entail equality. Emancipation brought a measure of autonomy and personal responsibilities, and more abstractly the benefits and obligations of being an inhabitant of Massachusetts. Historian Gary B. Nash summarized that "[l]egal emancipation did not confer full political rights, equal economic opportunity, or social recognition."[7] "Freedom" was contingent and cabined socially, politically, legally, and economically. Participatory politics was engaged in by petitioning, and degrees of economic security were achieved by a few. At times, Phillis and her extended family partly depended on municipal support for their survival. Rosanna finally achieved financial sufficiency for the last five years of her life, thanks to her Revolutionary War widow's pension.

Intersecting perceptions about "race," age, gender, marital status, social station, religious persuasion, health, and so forth circumscribed personal experiences as they offered creative opportunity for action.[8] The degrees of the "rights" obtained with emancipation were constrained by personal, cultural, social, and legal ideologies (historically situated and experienced "realities") entailed by gender, religion, age, physical capability, health, marital status, economic position, and mercurial perceptions of "race." An audaciously achieved freedom was attenuated but could be advantaged. Many challenges and opportunities came with created, experienced, and perceived identity: how one perceived one's complex *self*, and how others viewed and treated their *selfhoods* as a male or female; as a person of a certain age; as a person of color; as a single, attached, married, deserted, divorced, or widowed person; as a wife or husband; as a mother, father, or other kin relation; as a neighbor, friend, a Christian and a parishioner or not; as a laborer or broker or as a customer or client; as a pauper, dependent, or benefactor; as a resident, stranger, or "foreigner"; as sick or healthy, and so on. The lineage connections sought in creating a family, perhaps in contacts sought and reestablished between people separated by enslavement, and the social and economic networks fostered or ignored with neighbors, townspeople, customers, merchants, and religious and political authorities figured in people's senses of identity and how others identified them. The range and content of these interactions and movements, however, are mostly elusive for lack of documentary evidence.[9]

As the eighteenth century turned into the nineteenth century, a prevailing intersectional discrimination posed obstacles to labor, habitation, interactions, and mobility. Persistent slavery designations and pervasive racial labeling maintained and reproduced separateness in a manner familiar to us still.[10] People of color, leader-types among them, transmitters of legal and other strategic information, rallied resources and allies. People of color succeeded to obtain liberty, as well as the economic and logistical support required to confront the intersections of gender, "race," and economy, among other perceived axes of oppression and opportunity.

Andover bore economic costs providing for many people who could not fully provide for themselves, people without family or friends able or willing to support them adequately. A growing population among the town poor was previously enslaved and had been the economic responsibility of their former owners. Enslavement had created a fundamental economic disadvantage. Formerly enslaved adults, children, and other dependents arrived to only a contingent freedom with few tangible resources and little or no cash. When a crisis occurred, an already tenuous situation could quickly become desperate. Intermittent financial assistance that was provided by towns through provisions, supplies, and medical care, was part of broader survival strategies developed by formerly enslaved people and their descendants.

Manumitted or self-emancipated people of color, children and adults in circumstances dire or ordinarily needful, were among the town poor who suffered homelessness, hunger, illness, injury, disability, or decrepitude that precluded laboring for sufficient wages. Several Massachusetts towns sought state assistance for formerly enslaved people who town officials considered had not achieved resident status—despite that generations of their families in slavery and contingent freedom had lived among and with them.[11]

In 1846, a two-person gubernatorial commission was organized to examine and in 1847 reported on pauper accounts submitted in 1845 by towns for reimbursement by the state. The commissioners found that the overseers of the poor of Andover (and two other towns) persisted in characterizing settled residents as slaves, and on that basis sought state pauper funds to reimburse itemized town expenditures for their support.[12] The history of the evolution of the common law and statutory law about paupers supported by Massachusetts towns and the state, particularly paupers who were former slaves, was understood by legal professionals in reference to the murky history of judicial abolition of slavery in Massachusetts. The prevailing professional legal view, the commissioners discerned, was not inculcated uniformly among town overseers of the poor:

> [T]he law was not only imperfectly understood and incorrectly applied, but often grossly neglected.
>
> That [...] is not [a] matter of surprise. Few of the men composing the different boards of overseers belong to the legal profession, and many retain the office but for a single year, and perhaps have never had a case arise which necessarily directed their attention to the law of settlements, and feeling, as most men on those boards do, the duties of the office to be a burden, for which they receive no adequate compensation, they are content rather to follow in the footsteps of their predecessors, than to burden themselves with the necessary investigation, to ascertain what their duties, under the existing laws of the Commonwealth, are.
>
> But the opinions which some persons entertain of the law and of their duty under it, and the practice which prevails in many towns, consequent upon these opinions, are matter[s] of astonishment.[13]

The commissioners' specific findings about the charges submitted to the state by Andover for ten individuals indicated only that the town overseers of the poor had misconstrued as "state paupers" two individuals—Rosanna and Colley—who were legally town residents, and that the town had charged the state for support of three others during times when they were not living at the town almshouse, which the state commissioners disallowed. Of the entire amount of reimbursement provided by the state to

Andover in 1845 that totaled $170.78, the commissioners determined that the town "overcharged" the state $93.07.[14]

When the Andover overseers of the poor were informed of the results of the commissioners' visit to Andover in 1846, they immediately contested the commissioners' findings. On November 18, 1846, Andover attorney Nathan W. Hazen, who was also an overseer of the poor, prepared a letter on the town's behalf that cited case law to support the overseers' view that Rosanna Coburn and her daughter were state paupers, with no legal residency in any town, because Rosanna had been born a slave.

<u>1846</u>   Andover Nov. 18, 1846
No. 3.   John Sargent, Esq.
                Sir,
      We write in conformity
with the desire of the Commission to hear
further from us in relation to the case of
Rosanna Coburn a State Pauper. —
      Upon enquiry we do not find
any material variance in [^] the [^] facts relative
to her origin from than stated to you by
herself.
      From her statement it appears very
clear that she was born in this Commonwealth and was the child of slaves;
in which case according to the decision
in the case of Littleton v. Tuttle 4 Mass. Rep.
123 [i.e., 128 n], She was born free, and being the
progeny of slaves merely, tho born in this
town, stands in the same predicament
with her daughter Elizabeth whose want
of settlement is admitted.
      It seems to us that the case of Andover
v. Canton 13. Mass. Reports 547 and of
Lanesboro v. Westfield 16 Mass Rep. 74
are ~~entirely~~ [^] quite [^] decisive that Rosanna
Coburn [^] upon the facts stated [^] has no settlement in this town.
      If you are not satisfied with
this view of the case [^] & will notify us [^] we will give it
a further examination
                Yours very Respectfully
                N.W. Hazen
[_ _]&on behalf & c[15]

No correspondence from the state commissioners was preserved in the overseers' letter book, but attorney Hazen did not persuade them.[16]

In their report issued on February 1, 1847, the commissioners' findings of "overcharges" for Andover indicated that the town overseers were not cognizant of the changed common law of settlement made by court decisions, which determined whether a pauper was the financial responsibility of a town or the state. Moreover, the commissioners concluded that overseers from many towns were "not aware" of an 1844 resolve passed by the state legislature requiring that reimbursement for support of state paupers would be provided only for the particular days when they were "actually and entirely supported [...] the whole number of days", which the commissioners interpreted as requiring residency in municipal almshouses. The commissioners' findings of the "overcharges" for Andover, pivoting on obscure and complicated legal rules, were repeated throughout their report for all the Massachusetts municipalities that also continued to follow the same practices they had for decades, and which theretofore had been accepted by the state.

In the *Annual Town Report* for 1847, in their statement dated February 25th, the Andover overseers of the poor William Johnson, Jr., Joseph Shattuck, Jr., and Nathan W. Hazen advised the town of the commissioners' February 1st decision. The Andover overseers' view was that the town was not legally required to return the partial state reimbursement for the town funds expended on individuals that they considered were state paupers, and who had been supported, in part, outside the almshouse. "Commissioners appointed by the Legislature have reported at the present session that 122 towns have overcharged for the support of State paupers. The alleged overcharges of this town [...include partial state reimbursement for support of "Rose and Elizabeth Coburn," Lucy Foster, and two other women.] The objection to the charge for the support of these persons arises mainly from a Resolve of the Legislature passed in 1844; but it is apprehended that the law has not been repealed by the Resolution referred to [i.e., the resolve], and that the town is entitled to retain the money it has received."[17]

The state commissioners' interpretation not only denied the town reimbursement of funds they already expended for state paupers, it also posed practical problems for towns that partially supported "worthy poor" adults outside the almshouse setting who had no present need for institutionalization. Poor inhabitants, predominantly elderly women, who could still manage to live on their own or with others avoided the indignity, regimented supervision, lack of privacy, vulnerability, and contagion of almshouses. Requiring that all the state paupers instantly move to town almshouses would overcrowd the facilities, straining institutional staffing and resources.[18] The 1844 resolve provided no exception for children who were customarily indentured with local families. Except for those with profound disabilities, almshouses were not ordinarily considered to be appropriate, long-term settings for children of tender years and above, but the *Annual Town Reports* enumerated children living at the Andover almshouse. In 1845, the auditors that prepared that town report related that "The number of children in the Workhouse, and other circumstances, well known to the Town, have induced the Overseers [of the Poor] to employ a female teacher to take charge of the children there."

The printed town annual report for 1846 expressed ongoing concerns about the town's financial expenditures for providing support outside the almshouse: "It is believed that the amount paid on their account the present year [March 1845–February 1846], is somewhat less than the average of the sum paid for some years past. It is much to be doubted if too much has not been paid in this manner. It may be very difficult to deny the partial relief that may be asked, and not easy to lay down any general rule upon the subject; but we have concluded to advise that the town instruct the [O]verseers of the Poor, that as general rules, 1. that relief should be afforded only in sudden or extreme cases, and 2. that so far as may be avoided, no person should be allowed to expect partial relief as a certain resource."[19]

Andover had characterized, as state paupers, the formerly enslaved Lucy Foster, and the formerly enslaved Rosanna Coburn with her daughter Elizabeth (Colley Hooper). All three women were longtime, practically lifelong Andover residents. But Andover sought and received state reimbursement for their support on the basis of Lucy having been born in Boston and enslaved in Andover; and, that while Rosanna and Colley were born in Andover, Rosanna had been enslaved and Colley was the daughter of a slave. The state pauper accounts for Andover printed in the Massachusetts *Acts and Resolves* series include state reimbursements to Andover for Lucy Foster, for Rosanna Coburn from 1831 to 1843, and for her daughter Colley ("Elizabeth C. Coburn") from 1839 to 1843. Because they were named in the 1847 state commissioners' report that concerned claims for state paupers reimbursed in the fiscal year 1845, the town had submitted claims for them that fiscal year as well. Presumably, claims were submitted to the state for other years, but the names of state paupers were not specified in the published state pauper accounts for those years. The printed town annual reports did not consistently list names of those that the town considered to be state paupers, but both Rosanna and Colley were indicated to be state paupers in 1832, 1843, and 1845–1847. In the 1851 town report, Colley

("Elizabeth Coburn") was listed among state paupers but her mother was not.[20]

Lucy Foster was brought from Boston to Andover when she was four and enslaved by Job and Hannah Foster. Lucy was baptized at South Parish church in 1771. In 1791, Lucy was "warned out," a bureaucratic declaration to deny financial responsibility for her support. She stayed in town, became a member of the South Parish church in 1793 where her son Peter was baptized that year, and in 1812 she inherited a small lot where she had a cottage. She remained in Andover, and she died at the almshouse in 1845 within two weeks after being brought there. Seemingly because Lucy was born in Boston—despite her having been enslaved by Andover residents from the time she was four years old, and having resided in Andover for 74 years—the state commissioners agreed with the town that Lucy had not established legal residence. The requirements of the settlement laws were complex and evolved during Lucy's long life, but she had not been formally accepted by town meeting or able to obtain sufficient property to establish residency. The state commissioners allowed the town's charge for only 14 days of Lucy Foster's care (set at 7 cents per day) while she was at the almshouse, because of their position that state funds were only allowed for "entire" support, not the partial support she was provided when Lucy lived outside the almshouse.[21]

"Black Lucy" Foster became well known internationally among students of the African diaspora because her homesite was the subject of a 1943 archaeological investigation by Adelaide Kendall Bullen joined by her husband Ripley, both of them affiliated with the Robert S. Peabody Foundation for Archaeology at Phillips Academy in Andover. That project has been retrospectively appreciated as pathbreaking in the then-incipient field of American historical archaeology for its focus on a residence of a contingently free, formerly enslaved woman of African ancestry. Lucy's biography and the meanings of the site have been scrutinized and continue to offer promising insights. Lucy Foster is among several enslaved and freed people of color in Andover, people who were, in their time, among the most ordinary and not even middling sort, who continue to be named and remembered hundreds of years after their passing.[22]

Rosanna (Rose) Coburn was the daughter of Phillis and Booso. Phillis was a slave in the Frye family in Andover, so when Rosanna was born she became a slave.[23] The family history of Rosanna and her parents in slavery was key to both the town and the state's consideration of Rosanna and her daughter's eligibility for state poor relief. The 1847 state commissioners' report summarized what they ascertained of the two women's circumstances:

Rosanna Coburn and Elizabeth Coburn, mother and daughter, were colored persons, living and keeping house together, and the town furnished each with the amount of the State allowance; and beyond that they were dependent upon their own labor and casual charity.

Rosanna Coburn states that her father was the slave of Samuel Chickering, of Andover, and that her mother was the slave of Joshua Frye, of Andover; that she supposes she is 76 years old, (she is returned as 78 years of age;) in either case she was born before her parents were liberated by the adoption of the constitution in 1780, and, if born a slave, would take the settlement of her master. One of the overseers testified, that he presumed the mother of Rosanna Coburn was a slave at the time of Rosanna's birth, but was not positive as to the fact.[24]

In the state commissioners' view, the Andover residency of Rosanna's parents' former owners, and her birth in Andover, established that Rosanna and her daughter Elizabeth (Colley Hooper) were legal residents of Andover, and so were not the responsibility of the state. The state disallowed reimbursement for Rosanna and Colley's support in 1845.[25]

Regarding the commissioners' reference to the Massachusetts Constitution, neither that in 1780 nor the "Mum Bett" and "Quock Walker" cases in 1781 and 1783 actually, instantly, or effectively ended slavery at the time in Massachusetts. They affected nothing, actually, for Phillis' family listed as chattel in their owner's estate inventory in 1781. They affected nothing for Cato Phillips (later Cato Freeman) who remained enslaved in Andover by the Phillips family until 1789. They affected nothing for numerous other enslaved people in Essex County and elsewhere in Massachusetts who continued to be treated as legal property in probate court filings, a practice accepted and approved by county probate judges.

What the commissioners were indicating, for the purposes of their legal findings about Rosanna and Colley, was the generic legal status of Rosanna's parents from 1780 forward, as considered *retrospectively* from their perspective of the common law as it stood in 1847. The state commissioners correctly applied the law as it was in 1847 to conclude that Rosanna and Colley were not state paupers. The commissioners' legally correct view and their proper application of the common law was entirely consistent with the 1836 judgment in Commonwealth v. Aves. In 1836, Chief Justice Lemuel Shaw novelly declared in *Aves* that "it is sufficient for the purposes of the case before us, that by the constitution adopted in 1780, slavery was abolished in Massachusetts, upon the ground that it is contrary to natural right and the plain principles of justice." In *Aves*, Shaw stated what legal minds and the public understood, that Massachusetts had judicially abolished slavery long before. To authoritatively articulate the common and constitutional law as it was understood in 1836, Shaw employed a legal fiction that in Massachusetts legal history there was "an unbroken series of judicial decisions" that abolished slavery in reliance on the 1780 state constitution.

Despite Shaw's fictive assertion, there actually was no "unbroken series of judicial decisions" on that point that could be relied upon to have established binding precedent. The *Aves* case decision was the earliest certain and explicit judicial finding that slavery was (retrospectively) illegal per se in Massachusetts, from the adoption of the state constitution in 1780, going *forward* in time. That legal finding was despite the historical fact that people were actually still enslaved in Massachusetts after 1780, including Rosanna and her mother. It did not matter for the purposes of the state commissioners' generic legal finding in 1847—that Rosanna was born a slave and thus became a resident of the town of her owner—but the commissioners did not know that Rosanna's father Booso had sued and won his freedom in 1778, and that Rosanna and her mother Phillis along with all the other Frye slaves had "taken their Freedom" before September 1790.

Popular notions that all slaves were instantly freed upon the adoption of the state constitution in 1780, or by the decisions of the "Mum Bett" (1781) and "Quock Walker" (1781, 1783) cases, or more vaguely during the Revolutionary War, persist mythically despite contrary historical evidence but more to this point, *legal* evidence. The difference is conceptually challenging between historical facts of persistent slavery, on the one hand, and on the other the evolution of the common law made by court decisions of record that incorporated fictive statements (legal fictions: fictive, retrospective assertions made only for the purposes of discerning and applying current law to current matters). Legal historian David Thomas Konig explained that "legal fictions [...] made no innate sense outside the artificial reason of the law". Historically and factually, people literally remained (illegally) enslaved in Massachusetts possibly into the early nineteenth century. Legal historian William E. Nelson concluded that "there is no way of knowing how many blacks remained enslaved [...] because they lacked either the means or inclination to bring suit for their freedom. Thus, as has often been the case with race relations in American history, compliance with the law did not occur nearly as rapidly as the law itself changed." Phillis and the other Frye family slaves did not sue for their freedom. Instead, they became aware of the changed common law, and by September 7, 1790, all six of the Frye slaves had "taken their Freedom" on their own volition, as a group. Sarah Frye's estate administrator, James Ingalls, did not dispute their self-emancipation, and the probate court judge Benjamin Greenleaf "accepted and allow'd" it.[26]

The history of Phillis' extended family in slavery, then in contingent freedom, assists to understand how and why Rosanna was encumbered by persistent official "slave" denotations throughout her life, and even at her death. Rosanna's former enslavement was not only noted in obscure bureaucratic records: it was declared overtly on her gravestone that pronounced she was the "last" slave born in Andover. Rosanna achieved notoriety during and then after her lifetime in newspaper articles and history writings, ensuring that the condition of her former enslavement remained in the public consciousness. Forgotten stories about her and her family have been rediscovered. Rosanna Coburn and her family have become known and remembered by many more, in farther places, and in more ways than any of them might have imagined.

The archive for Phillis' family is diverse. As with all historical "texts," primary documentary sources and secondary historical writings about them are fragmentary and ambiguous in their disclosures and concealments, and all are multivalent. All such texts are artifacts, filtered through and transformed by participants involved with their creation, observation and interpretation, reproduction, preservation, or destruction: such is the nature of fixed or fugitive cultural things.

The absence of information for Phillis and most of her extended family in official vital records for births, marriages, and deaths is unexceptional in historical Massachusetts. The inclusive, detailed, systematized, and coetaneous recording of vital statistics, as a municipal and state civil registration process, did not *begin* in Massachusetts until the early to mid-nineteenth century. Lack of gravestones (or for that matter, records of burial locations) is also not uncommon, eliminating those alternative sources for biographical data. Charlotte Lyons, historian at South Church in Andover, conveyed that of approximately 1,500 Andover people whose deaths before 1800 are recorded in any sources, and who were likely to have been interred at the South Parish Cemetery, only 113 gravestones naming them are preserved there. The simple statistic that roughly 93% of known pre-1800 decedents are now in unmarked graves at that cemetery, and realizing further that many people's deaths went unrecorded, conveys that monumenting graves with enduring stone markers was likely never commonly practiced for most people in historical Andover.[27]

The general absence in ecclesiastical archives of baptism, marriage, or death records for most of Phillis' extended family also suggests that their momentous life affairs occurred mostly separate from the churches and without ministers. Perhaps they were conscious of and disaffected by the institutional discrimination and segregation that was common in New England Congregational churches. If so, whether they attended Sabbath Day services anyway or refused to participate eventually or altogether is not ascertained. After a time, enforcement of mandatory church attendance waned.[28]

Phillis' and Booso's African and West Indian heritage supposes that rituals and ceremonies that surely accompanied their family's births, marriages, and deaths involved traditions different than Colonial British American Christian ways. Booso's earlier name was reported to be Jubea or Jubah. The ten-year-old child called Juba in Sarah Frye's 1781 inventory was probably Phillis and Booso's son, later called Jack. There are diverse African and African-derived cultural and geographic sources and meanings for the name Jubea or Jubah. Following African-derived traditions, two of Booso's children, Hepzabeth Boose (1774–1814) and Jack Booz (Juba, 1771–?), used their father's single "given" name as their surname.[29] The story recorded about a man named Boise or Bowser, who may have been the same man as Booso, has action that resembles African and Caribbean magic or ritual traditions that have their own historical depths and complexities: "He would grow wild when recounting the history of his capture by slavers; and, drawing a huge knife, would make furious attacks upon the trees, thus taking revenge upon an imaginary foe." Also in line of traditions known among many people of recognizing revered individuals as community historians, Phillis preserved genealogical information in her memory.[30]

Because women were economically disadvantaged, women of color even more so, and more likely than men to require public assistance, their biographical moments were more usually noted by government record makers tracking poor relief expenses in Andover. Moments in their lives were captured in bureaucratic notations by the Andover overseers of the poor, the town treasurer, the town clerk, state legislative staff, and other county, state, and federal officials. Detailed and complex genealogical and historical data appeared in a voluminous Revolutionary War veteran and widow federal pension application file for Titus and Rosanna Coburn. Biographies about Rosanna Coburn and her family members were conveyed during and after her life in newspaper articles, stories told and written about them, historical exhibitions of a ring she owned, even in her gravestone epitaph. Public interest in Rosanna Coburn was how the history of Phillis' extended family came to be recounted.

The next sections of this monograph are structured as biographical summaries of Phillis, Booso, Colley Hooper, Titus Coburn, and Rosanna Coburn. Facts and assertions in each biographical summary recur in other summaries because family members appeared together in the sources. Their experiences singularly and together joined them and make them familiar to us. The matrifocal structure of the presented history of members of Phillis' extended family is partly a function of the nature and content of the archival record. With Phillis having been a community historian who preserved genealogical information in her memory, it is particularly fortunate to be able to follow her family line.

Phillis (fl. 1727?–1828) and the ending of legal slavery in Massachusetts

Phillis was born in Africa. Her daughter Rosanna's 1859 obituary—in part reciting an earlier interview published in 1853—related that Phillis was ten years old when she landed in Charlestown, Massachusetts, sometime between 1737 and 1745.[1] Her arrival at the dock on Boston Harbor was nearly the final stop on a terrifying journey that began with capture and separation from her parents, relatives, playmates, neighbors, and the leaders of her homeplace. She may have been born in a free or enslaved family. Phillis was taken from them and shipped from the West African slave markets to the West Indies in a dark, foul, crowded hull. If Phillis were then soon transshipped to Boston, she would have arrived with an African child's cultural knowledge, but with no fluency in English speech or ways. If she had been taken from Africa as a very young child and remained in the West Indies for a while, she may have begun to learn English and maybe other languages there.[2] A Charlestown merchant may have bought her from the ship's captain, and Joshua Frye (1701–1768) of Andover probably purchased Phillis there. Frye would have brought her to Andover on horseback or by cart or coach. The 25-mile trip took about three hours to at most six hours.[3]

If Frye purchased her soon after she landed in 1737–1745, and if she was at that time still unfamiliar with the new culture, then Phillis would have entered his household understanding little English beyond a few words she began to glean. A ten-year-old girl, a stranger to the country, with no facility in its language, rules, foodways, dress, and tools, inept in laboring tasks wanted of her, was not immediately serviceable to Joshua's second wife Sarah Frye (1712–1781). As a child, Phillis would have been sold for less than a young adult. If Phillis was purchased when Joshua was a legislator from 1755 to 1756 (she would then have been about 28 or 29 years old), then she would have been accustomed to English speech, ways, and things, and been an immediately useful servant to the Fryes.

From 1737 to 1756, Sarah Frye had two to three children at home. In 1737, Mary, the daughter of Joshua's first wife Mary Dane Frye (1695–1729) and named after her, was 11 years old. Phillis may have been put with Mary to learn what was expected of her and how to go about it. Around 1737 Sarah was pregnant with a son, born 1738 and who died in 1747. Her next son (the third among three sons named Joshua) was born in 1748. Phillis could have helped Sarah and Mary tend to the boys. Sarah and Joshua had lost four children within a month in 1738: scarlet fever, diphtheria, smallpox, and measles took many in the region at that time.[4]

Joshua Frye's probate file papers have no inventory of personal property that would have listed all his slaves. A year before he died, the 1767 tax valuation indicated only one slave in Frye's possession. Perhaps Phillis was not in the Frye household until after 1767 when she was 40 years old. However, the 1767 valuation for Andover has discrepancies, compared to earlier counts of slaves.[5] Of his slaves, Mr. Frye's 1764 will mentioned only one: "my Negro Servant Boy named Cato". He was 5 years old in 1764, if his age of 22 was correct in his mistress' 1781 inventory. In his will, Frye named the enslaved boy Cato in a contingent legacy arrangement. Cato was first to be his widow Sarah's slave. Mr. Frye's next plans for Cato were ambiguously written in the will. Frye's intentions were either that when his eldest son Joshua (1748–1819) became 21 years old, Cato would then belong to him, or after Sarah Frye's death, Cato would serve either or both of his sons, Joshua and John (1750–?).[6]

Sarah Frye was the main beneficiary of her husband's estate, and she inherited the family's slaves. Sarah's 1776 will indicated that she continued the family hat manufacturing operation as well as managed her farm with its expansive real estate. The slaves must have worked in her agricultural and manufacturing interests, and inside the house. After her death, the inventory of Sarah Frye's possessions itemized objects of adornment, personal care, labor, diversion, hospitality, and rest for herself, her guests, her slaves, and others who came and went to her house, her lands, and her shop.

The 1781 inventory of Sarah Frye's property appears to have been organized not generally by location, but rather by groups of like objects, beginning with clothing, then gold and silver objects, then beds, and so forth. "The Negroes Bed" appeared as the fifth and last bed in the list of beds: the best bed (£10), the next best bed (£4 2s.), another next best bed "in the North Chamber" (£3 6s.), another bed "in the little Room" (£3 10s.), then the "Negroes Bed" (12s.), then sheets, pillow cases, a table cloth, and napkins. There were 20 tin-glazed earthenware ("Delph") plates, six bowls of the same, three porcelain ("China") cups and saucers, and 3 cream-colored earthenware cups and saucers, but only two wine glasses and two glass beakers (probably for serving wine). There were many pewter plates and other pewter vessels. The "Great Wheel" (£3), "Foot Wheel" (£8), a reel (£4), and a "Hand Wheel" (£1 6s., listed near the end of the inventory with "a Spit" and "old Curtains") were for spinning wool yarn (and possibly also flax into linen yarn or thread) that Sarah Frye's female slaves, hired females, or she herself might do from time to time. No other required tools and machines for processing wool or flax to prepare it for spinning, and no weaving loom were indicated, so perhaps the material arrived processed and the yarn or thread sent out. There were many other household, agricultural, and husbandry objects not summarized here but of fascinating interest to material culture historians.

Sarah Frye's gentility was suggested by her elaborated household furnishings. Furniture included several tables and chairs, and there was specialized kitchen equipage for cooking, food processing, serving, and storage. Household members, visitors, and dinner guests were amply accommodated. The cooking, serving, and eating objects, the tables and chairs, and other private and public household goods and spaces evoked expression of the Frye's elite class. Her late husband Joshua had been a town selectman (1752–1753), state representative (1755–1756), and town treasurer (1762–1764). A measure of wealth and gentility was expressed to the Frye's guests and neighbors by the presence of many servants. Of course only the prominent and wealthy were able to possess multiple slaves. Slave labor supported Joshua and Sarah's public and private endeavors and aspirations. The six slaves Sarah owned were the last of her possessions to be listed in her estate inventory. An undated draft of the inventory did not include the slaves, so at some point prior to May 1, 1781 the committee of three Andover men assigned by the Probate Court to undertake the inventory—John Farnham, Moody Bridges, and Nathaniel Lovejoy—decided to add them. The inventory listing the six slaves was presented to the Probate Court by the estate executors James Ingalls and Asa Forster and it was accepted by Probate Judge Benjamin Greenleaf on June 5, 1781.[7] In Massachusetts, slave labor was integrated with merchant capitalism at several economic levels, in household, local, and regional economies, in the broader Atlantic world, and farther.[8]

The oppressive nature of New England slavery is critical to conceive because it was mischaracterized in historical narratives that retrospectively minimized the atrocious realities of Northern slavery. "Every modern historian who has studied the institution of slavery agrees that slavery in the Americas was inherently brutal, violent, oppressive, and dehumanizing. Its

evil and immorality are neither magnified nor diminished by individual instances of exceptional brutality or kindness."[9]

Revisionist histories created following the Revolutionary War, then
during the rise of antislavery and abolitionism, and then again following
the Civil War attempted to favorably compare slavery in households, farms,
trades, and industries in Massachusetts, New England, and sweepingly "the
North," to plantation slavery in Southern states and the Caribbean. Revisionist narratives of New England regional exceptionalism typically included one or more of the same themes: the comparatively fewer slaves here,
fallacious notions that slaves were unimportant to the region's economy, assertions of fictive kinship of slaves as family members, the sharing of meals
at the same table, examples of paternalistic or benevolent treatment, and
the euphemism of "servant."

Defensive Southern anti-Reconstruction writers delighted to expose the
hypocrisy by recounting anecdotes of brutality and oppression committed
by Northern slave owners. Counternarratives that aggressively challenged
revisionist tracts of Massachusetts exceptionalism appeared in the mid- to
late nineteenth century: most famous was *Notes on the History of Slavery in Massachusetts* (1866) by the New-York Historical Society librarian
George H. Moore. Less well-known is that Moore's 1869 publication of a
transcription of an Andover manuscript brought Massachusetts historical
revisionism and its critique to a national reading audience. The manuscript
was "A Form for a Negroe-Marriage" written by South Parish Church Rev.
Samuel Phillips. The conditional marriage vows, written for his own slaves
who married in 1760, expressed that the duties of slaves to their master and
mistress took precedence to their duties to each other as a married couple.[10]

Many, now-historical narratives about African Americans in Massachusetts are infected with patronizing treacle and racist anecdotes, accompanied with stereotypical parodies of distinctive pronunciation, expression,
and vocabulary (speech patterns or patois), gesture, dress, and appearance,
that a perceptive modern reader should approach with skepticism. Even in
these racist portrayals, a discerning reader can appreciate evidence preserved
in these texts of intelligent and knowing agency, resistance, and defiance by
enslaved and free people of color in their crafty linguistic code-switching,
concealment, inversion, and other kinds of sociological signification. In
historical New England, diverse and creative cultural practices and identities evolved chronologically and varied geographically. Ways, ideas, and
material objects derived from many heritage traditions.[11]

At times, enslaved people ate with their owners and their guests at the one
and only meal table in those households.[12] At times, enslaved individuals

may have been thought of affectionately and conceived to be part of their owner's family while actually more often treated, if serviceable, as "vendible property" (as historian Peter Benes put it so aptly). In New England, slaves were typically referred to with the seemingly gentler-sounding euphemism of "servant" that masked hardworking lives marked by surveillance, lack of control, segregation, confinement, objectification, base brutality, and familial isolation.

Historian and anthropologist Robert K. Fitts discerned that slaves housed in their master's domestic spaces were under an intense degree of oppressive control and oversight of their actions, space, and movements and had less time to themselves than enslaved people who were housed in separate quarters. Historian Jared Ross Hardesty appreciated degrees of patriarchy and paternalism "structured by ties of deference and dependence", that were reinforced, negotiated and resisted. Historian Kerima M. Lewis recognized that cohabitation of slave and owner families allowed enslaved persons to monitor the movements of household occupants, and used their intimate knowledge of space and objects also to their advantage. In historical Andover, cohabitation of enslaved people and other dependent servants was common. By the last decade of the eighteenth century, when enslaved or formerly enslaved people remained with the families that they had long-served, and as they aged and became less serviceable, sometimes the families arranged for separate housing for their servants. Rural Essex County towns, with few people of color, meant that social opportunities with people of their own stations and heritages were relatively constrained in comparison to urban places with more people of color.[13]

Social gatherings of extended families of owners, guests, and their accompanying servants were occasions for people of color to notice each other, to be noticed, and to be introduced. Other occasions for meeting occurred when slaves or free laborers from one family were lent to another in reciprocal laboring arrangements. Phillis and the West Indian man named Booso who became her spouse may have met in that manner. He was enslaved by the intermarried Andover Osgood-Chickering families. Slaves could also earn cash doing extra labor for another family after their chores for their owners were done. Physical segregation of enslaved and free persons in houses, churches, and at mealtimes, where other people of color were present, diversions during errands or travels, and their own social gatherings provided opportunities for enslaved and free persons of color to be together and to communicate with each other beyond the immediate surveillance of masters and mistresses. It was during those occasions, when people were away and together, that news and information was exchanged. Enslaved and free people of color learned about and considered various opportunities and alternatives, such as for laboring and residency arrangements, and legal developments about cases sued in courts where enslavements were being challenged and freedom obtained. Booso learned about freedom suits and that was how he gained his liberty in 1778. Enslaved and free people of color attained legal consciousness of a variety of practical subjects.

Phillis and Rosanna appear among the other named slaves in Sarah Frye's probate file papers (1776 will, 1781 estate inventory, and 1790 accounting and distribution). The 1781 inventory of Sarah's estate itemized six "Negroes young & old": Cato 22 years old, Juba 10, Titus (uncertain numeral, 8?), Tory 6 months, Phillis 42, and Rose 12 (Figure 7). The ages specified, if by them, may have been a concealment by them, or the ages may have been misstated by the inventory takers to increase market value (older adults and very young children were less monetarily valuable as slaves).

Rose, Juba, Titus, and Tory were probably all Phillis' children. Cato was unrelated, a lone enslaved boy present in the household before Phillis arrived, and had come of age with her in the household. Phillis had borne 14 children, according to an 1853 interview with her daughter. No records have been located for the ten other children. Booso was the father of at least several if not all of Phillis' children. That interviewer also mentioned Rosanna's late brother Jack Booz who worked as a waiter. Jack was "represented by our old people as having been one of the most polite men ever known. He became so popular as a waiter at parties, that the elite of his day invariably secured his services on such occasions." Jack was probably the child called Juba in the 1781 inventory, named after his father's earlier name Jubah or Jubea (later Booso, rendered variously). Jack Booz used his father's later first name as his surname, following African-derived traditions.[14]

Sarah Frye's 1776 will ordered that her slaves be sold "as soon after my Decease as Such Persons can be found to purchase Them as will Treat Them with that Justice & Humanity which is due to Such Servants" with the proceeds divided between her sons Joshua, Jr. and John. Sarah's plan was that the money earned selling Rosanna and Juba would go to John Frye, and the proceeds of selling Phillis and Cato would be divided between John and Joshua. At the time she wrote her will, however, she indicated that John had left America and she doubted he would ever return. The stipulations in Sarah's will that proposed to separate Phillis from her children, to divide siblings from each other, to sell off all of them, interjected insecurity and danger. Sarah's directives that Phillis and her family would be parted and sold made obvious the limits of the "Justice & Humanity [...] due to Such Servants".[15]

To modern sensibilities, Sarah Frye's debasing order to separate a family and to sell them as vendible chattel while invoking the phrase "Justice & Humanity" is transparently hypocritical. Frye's expression nevertheless reflected a perceptual change about slaves-for-life. Historian David Brion Davis understood that "by the eve of the American Revolution there was a remarkable convergence of cultural and intellectual developments which at once undercut traditional rationalizations for slavery and offered new modes of sensibility for identifying with its victims. [...T]his growth of antislavery opinion signified a profound cultural change [....] [S]lave emancipation required, as a *precondition*, a basic shift in moral perception."[16] Historian Emily Blanck echoed that there was "a deep change in the social order" and a "tremendous shift in thinking about race." The shift in thinking about "slaves" as mere property, to recognizing the humanity of "enslaved persons" with natural rights to liberty, allowed efforts toward general emancipation in Massachusetts.[17]

In considering "the force of public opinion and the last years of slavery in Revolutionary Massachusetts," the historian T.H. Breen pointed to the Stamp Act riots of 1765 when "ordinary people developed a heightened consciousness of freedom and equality in their lives." Breen recognized legislative petitioning by free people of color, pamphleteers and newspapers, and also "contradictory opinions" and "competing views" that defended unfree labor. Bridging the two dominant explanations of "publick opinion" and "heroic legal narrative" that led to the "collapse" of the system of enslavement in Massachusetts were the jurymen in freedom suits who became "unwilling to defend social and economic categories of unfreedom." In freedom suits (examined further in the next chapter about Booso), "the traditional defense of human property had lost most of its persuasive force in this society."[18] Historian Margot Minardi recognized that early Massachusetts historian Jeremy Belknap retrospectively outlined the "complex interplay between public opinion, ordinary people's activism, and legal reform". Incremental victories of each and every successful action instigated by enslaved people and their allies against those trespasses worked to evolve the law and influenced public opinion. Those cultural changes are the very intellectual roots of a foundational period in the nation's long, interrupted, and still-imperfect history of seeking liberty, equality, and equal treatment by recalcitrant government, institutions, society-at-large, and individuals.[19]

Beyond local and regional events that fostered "political literacy"—in historian Manisha Sinha's phrase—transatlantic "political rumor and information networks" spread news of slave rebellions and ideas about liberty long simmering in eighteenth-century antislavery and abolition movements. Foregrounding the earlier strategic actions of resistance and revolt, with the intellectual influences of people of color who shaped emancipative political expectations, conceptually and geographically enlarge the roots and shoots of later antislavery, abolitionist, and colonizationist movements apparent in historical Andover. What, if any, participatory roles, and what intellectual and sentimental influences did local people of color have in local abolitionist, antislavery, and colonizationist groups in early to mid-nineteenth-century historical Andover? There were daily interactions with formerly enslaved local people and their descendants who labored at the same tasks they did in previous conditions of servitude. To what if any degree did local individuals with their known histories and genealogies connected with local generational slavery—some with histories of having sued for freedom, others having claimed their own freedom on their own accord, others by self-purchase, others manumitted—impress themselves and others to become involved with local, state, and national anti-segregation and antislavery efforts? Direct and indirect influences for political strategies and ideologies were most discernible in Andover's famous nineteen-century residents, visitors, and correspondents: Frederick Douglass, The Hutchinson Family Singers, George W. Latimer, Wendell Phillips, Calvin and Harriet Beecher Stowe, George Thompson, Sojourner Truth, and William Lloyd Garrison.[20]

Historian Joanne Pope Melish considered that the gradual and protracted process of ending slavery in northern states, combined with the historical amnesia of generational slavery, involvement with the slave trade, and the economic entanglements of northern industry with plantation slavery, were powerful factors in rising discrimination and hardening racist thoughts in New England: "The erasure of a local history of slavery had devastating consequences for people of color. Without a history of enslavement to account for the disproportionate poverty and illiteracy of free people of color, whites could explain these circumstances and justify discrimination against black people as 'natural' consequences of [the racist idea of] blacks' own innate inferiority", rather than deriving from disadvantages and inequities inherent to enslavement and its attendant ideologies. Historian Rhett S. Jones traced out that "gradual coalescence of racist thought," a dehumanizing ideology that undergirded and perpetuated legal discrimination long beyond the Revolutionary era.[21] The "gradual coalescence" that Jones inferred socially and culturally was detected in subtle and unsubtle linguistic structures and processes that historian Angela Michele Leonard teased out of early nineteenth-century newspaper articles published in Haverhill, Massachusetts.

In her article, "The Instability and Invention of Racial Categories in the *Haverhill Gazette* (MA), 1824–1827," and in her book *Political Poetry as Discourse*, Angela Michele Leonard undertook a fine-scaled linguistic analysis focused on news stories about "blacks" (what she called "black referent newstexts") published in the nearby Essex County town from 1824 to 1827. Leonard's discourse analysis of the contents and semiotics of the news articles detected conceptual inheritances and further developments in common use and understanding of specific racialized vocabulary "to disclose the construction of race as it is ideologically imbricated". Leonard's penetrating study revealed a transition from multiple racial terms used for several "subgroups" of people of color toward a binary conception of "blacks" and "whites". *Words* that had been used for the "multiple yet distinct black subgroups"—the familiar "recurrent racial signifiers" of "free," "slave," "negro," "colored," "African," "mulatto," and "black"—*literally create[d] racial subgroups*" in thought and deed. The semantic "units [...the "recurrent racial signifiers"] coalesce[d] into a distinctly descriptive and derisive single, congregated, constructed black identity". Leonard concluded significantly that emancipative judicial decisions and ameliorative legislation "did not nor could it mandate against prejudicial behavior and the rejection of the 'negro' as a free man subject to all the rights and privileges of American citizenship in Northern white society. Racially motivated legislation effectively sustained the white hegemony and blocked blacks from access to most social institutions [....W]hites were especially prejudicial towards the aspiring, trained, educated, and accomplished free blacks." Leonard's analytic findings are particularly important to understand "a gradually spreading antislavery sentiment" and its fiery node in Andover, and at the same time the rise of "colonizationist rhetoric" (overtly expressed in the *Haverhill Gazette*) that proposed to expatriate African Americans to Africa.[22]

The African colonization movement was particularly pernicious as it embraced a stigmatizing ideology that was "derogatory and negative" and viewed "blacks as Society's undesirables." Colonizationist schemes found common cause among some African American Nationalists (as separatists, transnationalists, etc.), American racists (anti-"white" and anti-"black"), pro-segregationists of the latter ilk, abolitionists, missionaries, enthusiastic émigrés to Liberia, among others. These ordinarily incompatible ideologies were not oxymoronic with colonizationism when liberty, equality, due process, and "full citizenship" were not simultaneously advocated.

Shifting the gaze to another perspective, utopian visionaries intent to establish an autonomous sovereignty outside the United Sites did not consider established and then-ongoing African traditions of enslavement,

panyarring (pawnship), other social practices of unfreedom, African participation in the slave trade, and, according to historian Paul E. Lovejoy, the
apparent absence of any broad antislavery or abolition movement in the
African continent until sometime in the nineteenth century. Historian and
sociologist Mimi Sheller conveyed that a few contemporary postcolonial
theorists once alighted on a now-rejected idea that "'Western' concepts of
freedom, equality, and citizenship [were themselves...] tainted ideologies
that [...] supported imperialism and colonial rule". Yet, other scholars of
postemancipation and postslavery in African and Caribbean regions (here
I am quoting Giulia Bonacci and Alexander Meckelburg) insisted that
"existing notions of abolition being a 'Western' endeavor" were initially
reactionary and thus extremist, with no historical depth or identifiable cultural source other than from the minds and reinforcing readings of a few
modern intellectual theorists. Progressive liberalism was and remains appealing in times and at places, suggesting that while notions of liberty and
its counterpoise may vary, freedom from enslavement and other forms of
captivity is desired normatively and cross-culturally among detained people. That is an entirely different matter than the unreflective construction of
grander historical narratives about enslavement, emancipation, and degrees
of cabined "freedom" of postemancipation in historical America: the sort
of history writings that historian Walter Johnson deemed to merely "take
the temperature of a historical process with a foreordained outcome" and
thereby reproduce "a single story of progress: the metanarrative of racial liberalism—the story of black freedom and racial acculturation, of how black
slaves became American citizens."

Although long-established and ongoing African traditions of enslavement, etc. and slave trading were not in the purview of colonizationist advocates, to prospective émigrés from the United States to Africa, remaining
in this country was not ideal if prospectively they might foresee ceaseless
struggle against segregation, rising hostility, and violence predicated in
thickening ideologies of "race" and status characteristic of postemancipation in postslavery societies. Further research is needed to explore the
popularity of colonizationist promotion in historical Andover, but in the
1830s individuals associated with the Andover Theological Seminary and
Phillips Academy initially supported colonization before directing their efforts toward abolition in this country.[23]

Along with ideological and political changes about slavery and "race,"
practical calculations were also afoot. Historian Jared Ross Hardesty saw
an increase in manumissions during the economic recession that followed
the French and Indian War. He sensibly considered that the apparent in-

crease in manumissions has to be counted in view of growing numbers of enslaved people. Historian Gloria McCahon Whiting's recent, comprehensive analysis of probate records from cases dating 1760 to 1790 in historical Suffolk County (then including what is now most of Norfolk County) showed a precipitous decline in slave owning beginning in 1775, while manumissions by will rather than bequeathing slaves to devisees increased five-fold from 1775 to 1790. Whiting also realized that the decrease in the total number of manumissions during that period was due to the declining number of people held in bondage. Whiting's preeminently significant research findings suggest in part an economic aspect of the waning of slavery in that locale, and by extension likely in other Massachusetts places, as a consequence of the economic disruptions of the Revolutionary War.[24]

There were also ideas at work based in political socioeconomics: within the emerging class-consciousness of wage laborers, resentment arose to the competition of unpaid slave labor, with violence directed to both the enslaved and to their owners. I am uncertain precisely when, where, and among whom those matters were formative to emancipative ideas in Massachusetts: in 1795 John Adams said that they were, yet those troubles also coalesced earlier and later in different places. Then and here too, antipathy was matched with heightening racist treatment of contingently free and enslaved people of color, especially toward individuals who had achieved economically, socially, and literarily. Great thinkers such as W.E.B. Du Bois recognized that such resentments and violence were internecine and misdirected as both enslaved and contingently free laborers of whatever heritage were oppressed and exploited by the same individuals, emphasizing always that the enslaved suffered far worse.[25]

This rangy and ragged, indeed revolutionary transformation in the cultural, intellectual, economic, political, and legal landscape was an historically essential period for people of color in Massachusetts. Following several freedom suits won by enslaved Andover people, in 1778 Booso strategically left his enslavement by an uncontested lawsuit, examined in the next chapter. The change was consequential for Booso, Phillis, their children, and for Cato too, because it permitted them to reach a most significant decision and take action. Cato, Phillis, and all her children emancipated themselves as a group without having to bring a lawsuit. By 1790, when Sarah Frye's estate was finally distributed and accounted, the administrator reported that the "6 Negroes appraised at £24 [...] have since taken their Freedom" (Figure 7).

Nevertheless, as directed by Sarah's will—"one half of my wearing apparrel [*sic*...] I give to my Female Negro Servants"—the administrator delivered to Phillis and Rosanna their share of Sarah's clothes valued at £4 9s. 4¼p. Significantly, their self-emancipation was recognized and accepted by the legally appointed administrator of Sarah Frye's estate and by the Probate Court too, which reflected understanding and acceptance of the revolutionary change that had occurred. Yet, the racial appellation "Negro's" used when naming Phillis and Rosanna in the distribution of Sarah Frye's clothes showed that even though they had detached themselves from slavery, racial terms continued to be attached to them. Their former condition of enslavement continued to be invoked throughout their lives. The practice of appending racial terms in speech and writing connoted, as it created, otherness.[26]

The indifferent practice of making civil registration entries of vital statistics of births, marriages, and deaths posed practical challenges to individuals who needed that information on occasion, such as to prove parentage to establish freeborn status in freedom suits, or to establish spousal or parental relationship of widows or children seeking federal veteran pension benefits. Individuals instead relied on sworn affidavits (and depositions in court for freedom suits) prepared by witnesses and others with pertinent knowledge. Birthplace, parentage, status as enslaved-at-birth or freeborn, and place(s) of residency, was also considered in determining whether the cost of support that Andover provided for poor individuals was the responsibility of other towns or of the state. Town officials relied on Phillis' memory for details of community genealogies not recorded in vital records to make decisions about claimants for poor relief. Rosanna Coburn's obituary related that her mother "Phillis was often consulted in the latter part of her life by the overseers of the poor, with regard to the pedigree of persons applying for help, and her memory was so remarkably retentive that the information was reliable."[27] Rosanna's enduring cognitive abilities were remarked upon too. Her epitaph said she had "intelligence" and "retained all her faculties in a singular degree to the last".[28] Phillis' remembrance of community lineages provided important information to the overseers of the poor: it helped to establish responsibility for paying poor relief, whether it lay with solvent relations, the town, other towns, or the state. Phillis was well known to the town officials because she and her extended family themselves received poor relief intermittently.

In 1800, Phillis was living in Andover with her spouse Booso. The 1800 federal census enumerated five people of color in Booso's house, the membership of which is uncertain. Presumably the household included Phillis, and it may have included three of their adult children, Juba (Jack), Titus, and Tory (perhaps about 30, 27, and 20 years old, respectively), or the others may have been boarders. (That year, Phillis' daughter Rosanna and granddaughter Colley were presumably living with Titus Coburn in the adjoining town of Wilmington).[29] Booso had probably died before 1810. Entries in the third federal census suggest that Phillis was living in Andover with her daughter, granddaughter, and her son-in-law Titus Coburn, who bought land with a building there in 1809 that he sold in 1811.[30]

As a reconfigured family household, Phillis, Titus, Rosanna, and Colley took care of each other as needs arose, as they could or did, in their own ways and capabilities. Beginning in March 1816, the Andover overseers of the poor began roughly quarterly payments to Titus Coburn for "supporting" (or "for support of") Phillis. Payments were usually $6.50, but $4.50 in February 1818 and $9.00 in July 1818 could be accounted for by costs calculated over shorter or longer periods. In two instances the term used was "boarding" (August 1819, January 1820) but the amount paid is identical and the terms seem to have been synonymous, conveying inclusive support to sustain her while she lived with him. The town's payments to Titus for supporting Phillis continued to April 1821 (Titus died May 5, 1821), when the town began paying Rosanna in July 1821 to help with the cost of caring for her elderly mother.[31]

The fourth federal census in 1820 did not enumerate heads of households of people of color in Andover, so household membership cannot be ascertained from that census.[32] However, an 1820 document in her son-in-law's pension application indicated that Phillis, then 90 years old, was supported by Titus Coburn, presumably in the same house with Rosanna and Colley. Due to an injury, by then Titus was unable to labor to support his household: "His family [...] are all incapable of taking care and supporting themselves, and they have had assistance from the town for many years past". Titus died in May 1821, further jeopardizing Phillis' situation.[33]

The Andover overseers of the poor began to reimburse Rosanna in July 1821 for "supporting" Phillis (sometimes phrased in terms of "boarding" or "supplying" but the amount is identical and the terms seem to have been synonymous). Payments were usually the same $6.50 that Titus Coburn had received. Exceptional amounts paid to Rosanna were $8.67 in March 1823; $13.00 in August 1825, January 1826, October 1826, and February 1827; $6.00 in July 1826; and, $8.50 in July 1827. The variable amounts could be for cost of support calculated over shorter or longer periods, or for exceptional outlays. The overseers continued to reimburse Rosanna for supporting Phillis until their final payment to her in late February 1828. The town made two reimbursement payments (itemized by treasurer payment number) on behalf of Phillis on March 10, 1828: the first to her physician,

Dr. Nathaniel Swift (No. 3, $4.95), and the second payment to William Jenkins who delivered wood to Rosanna Coburn's house (No. 7, $13.81). In September 1828, a man was reimbursed for $15.28 worth of unspecified items for "Phillis Boos" that were delivered to Rosanna's house. In February 1829 two other Andover men were paid for wood deliveries to the house (February 2, 1829, No. 40, for "Phillis" $2.50; February 16, 1829, No. 49 to "Rose Coburn" $2.00). These payments came to the men during their busy winter season. A billing for a wood delivery that was paid in June 1829 (No. 24, $2.00) may be a delayed reimbursement of a winter delivery, or was fuel needed in the late spring. The interval between delivery of goods and services and reimbursement is unknown.[34]

Phillis was visited by local doctors, it seems at her home, but it is possible she was seen at their office-residences. The town contracted with doctors to provide medical care for the poor at the almshouse, and for poor residing outside the almshouse. When a doctor was paid for those services by the Andover treasurer—routinely described as "for medicine and attendance"—the payment record separately listed (1) the aggregate amount for all the patients the doctor saw at the almshouse who were not named individually, in contrast to (2) the names of patients that he attended to, who lived apart from the almshouse. Those entries convey that an individually named patient was not an almshouse resident. Sometimes "state pauper" would be indicated for those individually named who had been seen by doctors. That special notation, and rarely "foreigner," was infrequently indicated in treasurer's entries, but its purpose was for seeking state reimbursement; likely it also indicated that they were being supported with a local resident rather than at the almshouse. None of Phillis' extended family had "state pauper" indicated in the manuscript treasurer records, even though for a time they were deemed state paupers by the town. Entries for other individuals whose support was reimbursed by the state—such as treasurer's notations for Lucy Foster—also lacked "state pauper" designation, so the notating practice was not consistent. In the printed town annual report, Rosanna and her daughter were characterized as "State Pauper" in 1832, 1843, and from 1845 to 1847, while Colley alone was so-designated in 1851 but her mother was not.

In the portion of the manuscript town records that I searched, entries for Phillis' medical care show she was seen nearly annually, 1817–1819, 1821–1824 (amounts for her routine visits ranged from $0.50 to $1.09) and then she was not seen again until 1827 when Phillis was possibly about 100 years old (fees increased, $2.17 then $2.75). That year and continuing until 1828, Phillis was seen by her physician more frequently. One reimbursement (August 20, 1827, No. 12) was for $6.75—about two-and-a-half times the previous charge ($2.75). The next bill was for $3.57 (February 4, 1828, No. 46). The final town reimbursement to Dr. Swift for his medical care of "Phillise Boose" was made on March 10, 1828 (No. 3, $4.95). The much higher August 1827 billing of $6.75 must indicate that Phillis had a health crisis around that time. Understandably at her advanced age, Phillis required more care, including more medical attention, reflected in the upward trend of the billings.[35] At the time when Phillis was residing with them, Colley also may have been experiencing issues that required Rosanna's attention.[36] Caring for Phillis at their home may have eventually become untenable for Rosanna and Colley. Phillis may have entered the almshouse for a brief time, although there is no documentary evidence such as seen in treasurer's payments to men who had moved people to the almshouse, or in entries in the *Vital Records of Andover* noting deaths at the almshouse.

Phillis died before January 5, 1829. On that date the town treasurer made the following entry: "An order to Stephice Holt for a coffin for Phillis Wid[ow] of Boos".[37] Rosanna Coburn's 1853 interview reported that her mother died at 101 years old.[38] If Phillis had died at the almshouse, she would have been buried at the almshouse cemetery. More likely, Phillis passed away at home and was buried at another Andover cemetery.[39]

Booso (fl. 1755–1800), freedom suits, and the establishment of home and family in community after slavery

Rosanna's father Booso was born in the West Indies. He was married there and had four children when he was taken away from them. According to his daughter Rosanna's interview and obituary, he was first known as Jubah or Jubea, and may once have been called Benjamin.[1] While it could as well be another individual, a person named Juba appeared among a list of men and women in a Boston merchant's account book, under entries for "Negro's Receiv'd from Barbados in the Year 1729".[2]

In Andover, Booso was a slave of Deacon John Osgood (1683–1765). Booso then became a slave of Samuel Chickering (1704–1788?) who had married Deacon Osgood's daughter Hannah (1710–1761) in 1728, and perhaps he was later a slave to their son Samuel Chickering (1732–1814). The year of Booso's birth, when he arrived in Andover, and his death are not yet ascertained. Booso, Boso, Booss, Booz, etc. had many variant spellings. The Dutch origin of the name suggests Booso lived on one of the Dutch Caribbean islands or in Suriname, and that in turn makes it likely he was multilingual.[3] Rosanna Coburn's interview and obituary asserted that her father was called Booz Chickering, but neither that expression of his name nor "Benjamin" has been found in any other sources. Booso may be the same or a different man known as Boise or Bowser. Booso as Boassee (Bussen) must be the same man: he and Moriah, each indicated as a "servant" of Samuel Chickering, were married at the North Parish church in February 1755. Hepzabeth Boose (1774–1814) may have been his and Moriah's daughter. As with Rosanna's brother Jack Booz, Hepzabeth followed an African-derived custom to use her father's name as a surname. The ten-year-old child named Juba listed in the 1781 inventory of Sarah Frye's estate could be a diminutive form of Booso's former name rendered as "Jubah" or "Jubea".[4]

Booso won a freedom suit against Samuel Chickering (a "Currier" or leather worker) in 1778. Chickering did not appear at court, and an order was issued that "Booso recover [...] his Liberty & [...] be no longer held in Servitude".[5]

Decades of successful lawsuits for freedom advanced the common law of personal liberty in favor of enslaved persons in Essex County. These Essex County lawsuits for liberty were tried as civil actions chiefly in the Court of Common Pleas. Essex County Common Pleas freedom suits are known, so far, from 1766 to 1782. So far, only one freedom suit (1722) has been found in the records of the Essex County Court of General Sessions of the Peace. The General Sessions court more usually addressed criminal matters, referrals and appeals from local magistrates, and county administrative business. Civil complaints were properly brought to the Court of Common Pleas.[6]

The earliest freedom suits in Massachusetts were initiated by and on behalf of Native women, men, and children. There are two early freedom suit cases known from what is now Essex County. One that involved an Indian girl named Mall was heard in 1660 in the Essex County Quarterly Court (the precursor to the Common Pleas and General Sessions courts). The other brought by an Indian man named James may have been first heard by a town magistrate, but it was heard by an Old Norfolk County Quarterly Court of which no record was preserved. That case was appealed to the Court of Assistants in Boston prior to March 1672, and a paper filed by the appellee in response to that appeal is the only discovered record of that significant legal action. Legal strategies in freedom suits focused on the particular circumstances of the laboring arrangement, challenged claims based on established law of contract, indenture, and servitude, and invoked humanistic and religious principles. The late seventeenth- and early eighteenth-century cases brought by people of Native ancestry developed Massachusetts law and practice, and established expectations in legal and public minds for the slew of Essex County freedom suits brought in the mid- to late eighteenth century. Their cases were particularly important to evolve the common law principle that descendants of Indian women could not be legally enslaved for life. Juries and judges regularly freed people of maternal Native ancestry on the principle that they were born free.[7]

Slave owners eventually realized the futility of defending civil actions brought by enslaved persons as case after case (usually) granted them freedom, court costs, and money damages. When cases went to trial, juries nearly always freed the enslaved plaintiff. Attorneys representing plaintiffs and defendants in freedom suits sometimes negotiated settlements or agreed to binding arbitration that precluded costly appellate actions. That strategy reduced expenses, travel, time, and aggravation for both parties. When slaves challenged their captivity and possession as property in court, their owners typically capitulated, realizing the futility of defending enslavement in the changed legal landscape of late eighteenth-century Essex County. Frequently slave owners did not bother to appear at court to answer to their slave's lawsuits, and thus many enslaved persons won their liberty by default.[8]

Launching a freedom suit was among many modes of resistance and refusal by several Andover slaves over many decades. Perhaps to characterize freedom suits as "revolutionary actions" per se, begs only a precisely denotative question as to whether those lawsuits were truly acts of revolt. Historian Douglas R. Egerton heuristically circumscribed revolutionary acts as those that "consciously challenge the established class structure of slave societies." Obviously, using the judicial system to bring freedom suits, adhering to its formalistic rules and hierarchical authorities, was acceding to rather than rebelling against that social institution. The judiciary undergirded hegemony of the established class structure, and thereby reinforced the social norms of "hierarchy, deference, and dependence" that historian Jared Ross Hardesty emphasized. Legal historian David Thomas Konig acknowledged that freedom suits "might arguably be seen, to be sure, as allowing the law to provide legitimacy for slavery by making a relatively insignificant concession to a statistically small number of successful petitioners". Yet, the formalism and rules of the Massachusetts judicial system provided the very process that permitted ordinary people, even enslaved individuals, to come into court and bring actions against powerful individuals.

Egerton refused to accept too-limited conceptual boundaries to demarcate revolt from resistance. Egerton stressed that "the distinction between resistance and rebellion itself is a misleading one, and not merely because the varieties of rebelliousness were so varied." Historian Sylvia Frey estimated that "the shape and degree of slave resistance was roughly proportional to the possibilities inherent in their situations." Even the mode of escape "was a major form of resistance inasmuch as it destroyed property and thereby undermined the wealth and power of the master." Most interestingly, Frey saw in "prerevolutionary resistance" "ideology, strategy, and meaning in African patterns of resistance and warfare." Force and violence was central to abolitionist political rhetoric and used strategically and tactically.[9]

While my research that compiled summaries of the protracted history of Massachusetts freedom suits brought from 1660–1784 demonstrates that the legal tool for emancipation had a long and complicated evolution, several historians have recognized an apparent upsurge in freedom suits

that coincided temporally with what is generally considered to be the commencement of the revolutionary era in Massachusetts with the 1765 Stamp
Act protests. Taken together, the so far identified nine successful suits for
liberty dating 1769–1779 that involved people in Andover, could be connoted as "revolutionary" in that other sense of having brought a fundamental change to the enslaved and their owners.

Surely obtaining liberty, whether by judicial declaration or otherwise,
was a consequential moment for individuals, their families, friends, and
allies. It was consequential to their former owners too. All the courtroom
drama and formalities, the performative aspects of legal speech and comportment, one's name being called out by court officers and spoken by attorneys, judges, and witnesses, being asked to sign one's name, seeing papers
where one's name appeared, were focused moments for and about them.[10]
Modern sensibilities need to be measured to fairly consider the place and
import that these transitory legal actions had in the full biography of the
people involved and affected. To modern eyes, the excitement of reading
preserved, information-laden judicial records naming these people, the
nuggets of biographical information they contain (albeit many matters
merely fictive legal formalism[11]), and the historical evidence of efforts to
gain freedom from enslavement are very appealing to our enduring ideals
of liberty and equality. These legal actions, which could sometimes extend
over a long while, nevertheless concluded. For many, their time in court and
the result might have been the most significant event in their lives. But surely for others there were other, even more personally important moments in
their lives before and after their court cases.[12]

Booso's enslavement in a household separate from Phillis and his children
confronted and complicated his patriarchal role as husband and father and
her matriarchal role as wife and mother, in whatever ways and to whatever
degrees gendered roles and domesticity figured in their self-identities and
aspirations. Separation, not cohabitation, posed another complication to
Phillis and Booso in parenting their children. Historian Kendra Field deftly
summarized that one major "emblem of slavery was the denial and destruction of family bonds, and the vision of an emancipated future rested upon
the security of family and kinship." The absence of vital records makes it
impossible to determine the role and relationship of Booso's wife Moriah,
and his daughter Hepzabeth whose mother is not known, with Phillis and
her children. Moriah may have separated from Booso, she may have died
before Booso and Phillis became spouses, or they all may have created an
extended familial configuration for a time. Recall that Booso had a wife and
children in the West Indies; and, while Booso and Moriah's marriage was

solemnized in Andover, there is no marriage record discovered for Booso and Phillis.[13]

When he became a contingently free man in 1778, Booso regrouped his family that had remained with Joshua Frye, then Sarah Frye, then their son Joshua between 1781 and 1790 when Phillis, Rosanna, Cato, Juba (Jack), Titus, and Tory had all "taken their Freedom".[14] The 1790 federal census population schedule for Andover listed two separate households, at some distance apart, both headed by women named Sarah Frye. The first Sarah Frye household had only one "white" female. But the second Sarah Frye household perplexingly counted only three "all other [non-"white"] free persons" with no "white" person in that household. I guess that second household was the property of the late Sarah Frye (died 1781) where her former slaves continued to live and work. Perhaps they were Cato, Rosanna, and her then approximately three-year-old daughter Colley, or perhaps not. The 1790 Andover census for the household of "Rose Chickering" had only four non-"white" persons: perhaps she was the woman later known as Rose Coburn, and if so, gave or was called by the name of the family that had enslaved her father Booso.[15]

The 1800 federal census enumerated the Andover household of "Booss" with five people of color, the membership of which is uncertain but was himself, probably Phillis, and three of their children, Juba (Jack), Titus, and Tory.[16] So between 1790 and 1800, Booso had established his own household in Andover. At some time, "Booz and Phillis had a house on the Salem Turnpike, a short distance north of the house of William Peters." Perhaps they occupied that property like other formerly enslaved, free people of color did elsewhere in Andover.[17]

In the Andover treasurer/overseers of the poor records are numerous dated entries (itemized by payment number) for Booso, whose name was variously expressed. Among them, for example, are "An order to pay Boso a free Negro for Boarding his daughter Rose" (March 15, 1790, No. 10), an order to "pay Booso in part for supporting a Negro Child thirty weeks", with another order "to pay Booso in full", and with a third order that same day "to pay James Barnard for his finding provision for Boso + Family" (June 21, 1790, Nos. 46, 47, and 50).[18]

The overseers of the poor in Andover placed needful children and adults of color with families of color and with other families to provide care for them on behalf of the town. Booso, Pompey Lovejoy, Cato Freeman, Caesar Freeman, Dudley Dole, among others were reimbursed by the town for providing support services to several people in need. The male heads of those households were reimbursed by the town for services that were largely the responsibility of wives and daughters: feeding, bathing, nursing, and laundry. Booso's household boarded, probably meaning fed and housed, the woman known as Member (Remember Sawyer), as did several other Andover families. Remember was a former slave of either or both Dr. Thomas Kittredge (1746–1818) and his son Dr. Joseph Kittredge (1783–1847). Remember Sawyer died at the latter's house in 1825. Town records frequently did not specify which Dr. Kittredge was meant. Member stayed with Booso's family from January through March of 1793. Perhaps Member gave birth to her daughter Phillis Russell when she stayed with Booso's family. "Member" and "Members child" were moved from household to household in Andover over many years, and sometimes separated. Additional entries of payments to others for caring for (e.g., "boarding") Member and her child continued until at least 1804, and included Cato Freeman, Elisha Phelps, Benjamin Parker, Isaac Russell, Widow Phoebe Parker, Joseph Bradley, and Peter Johnson. Most interestingly, there were at least two payments for "Schooling" Member's child in 1799 and 1800. There may be more entries of payments to Booso for Member or her child, for caring for other people, and for payments to others for intermittent provision of food, supplies, and services to Booso and to his extended family. During the time when Member lived with Booso's family, he himself required a doctor's visit, and medicine was prescribed.[19]

The absence of Booso, Phillis, or other members of their family from three overseers of the poor expense lists dating 1801–1803 only suggests that the family might not have received any support during that period and were getting by without town assistance. However, the last of the three lists that compiled expenses for that period is inconsistent, not listing one person's name ("Cesar Sibson") who appeared on the second of the three lists. Additional research in the town manuscript treasurer and overseers of the poor records is needed to compile more data for Phillis and Booso's extended family.[20] Booso's absence in the 1810 federal census, and his daughter's husband Titus Coburn heading a household in Andover that year, approximates Booso's death before.

Colley Hooper (Elizabeth Coburn) (1786?–1857) and Andover antisegregation petitioning

Rosanna's daughter Colley Hooper (Elizabeth Coburn) had multiple heritages, with her African and West Indian maternal grandparents and her father unknown.[1] She was called "colored" in the town and state death records and in a notation about her death made in the North Parish church "Minister's Book." While the racial term might have been meant only generically, perhaps—or not—it indicated a father of European ancestry. Speculation that Rosanna's pregnancy was a result of coercion or violence has no evidentiary foundation, but is among several possibilities. Rosanna and Colley's choices to use and retain the surname Hooper is intriguing, but no explanation has emerged other than the supposition that Hooper was the father's name. Colley was named, in honor or memory, after a person of color with that same forename who lived in Sarah Frye's household before Colley Hooper was born. On October 8, 1770, an Andover doctor visited and dispensed medicine to the "Negro Garl Colle" and then billed the costs to Sarah Frye. The cognomen could have belonged to one of Phillis' children, such as Rosanna, before Colley Hooper was given that name.[2]

Colley was born in Andover and seems to have lived with her mother her entire life. Colley chose the familiarity and security of staying with her mother. Conceivably, Colley may have had somatic or psychological developmental issues that required her mother's lifelong attention and support. Colley's signed statement for her mother's 1854 pension application (albeit written by another) was lucid and indicated that she had access to her early childhood memories. Colley "distinctly recol[l]ects when she was six years of age, of being present at the marriage of her mother [...] to [...] Titus Coburn". Yet, her mother appointed her executor John Parnell to be Colley's trustee to manage Colley's finances. The trustee arrangement might suggest that Rosanna did not consider Colley fully capable of managing her own finances. The prospective idea might, rather, have originated with Andover attorney Nathan W. Hazen who created the will. Rosanna may have simply acceded to the trustee arrangement, and deferred to Hazen's experience in the complicated moment of finalizing her last will. As it would turn out, the arrangement was not needed because Colley predeceased her mother. Colley developed "consumption" (possibly pulmonary tuberculosis or any other sort of wasting disease) that would have incapacitated her when the effects were pronounced, and the disease eventually killed her.[3]

Colley and her mother—according to Colley her mother was then known as Rosanna Hooper—moved from Andover to the adjoining town of Wilmington. Her mother married Titus Coburn there in 1792.[4] Titus, Rosanna, and Colley returned to Andover, likely near or soon after Booso's death between 1800 and 1810, conceivably to be near Colley's grandmother Phillis, then about 70 to 80 years old. Phillis could have assisted Rosanna and Colley and cared for Titus who was painfully injured and could no longer labor by 1820. He died the next year. If she were able, Colley could have helped Rosanna care for Titus, and for his daughter Jennie (Jane/June) who had stayed with them in 1816, and for Phillis who persisted to 101 years of age. Her grandmother passed away before early January 1829, but whether at home or at the almshouse is not known. Rosanna and Colley's two-person household was enumerated in the 1830 federal census.[5]

Whether Colley attended school, or for very long, is not known. She signed her name by mark, as did her mother and stepfather[6] (Figures 8–17). Colley and Rosanna's written names appear on two antisegregation petitions sent to the state legislature in 1842. On both petitions, their names are written by the same hand and Colley's name is the last signature. On the petition to repeal the racialized marriage laws, the names were written as "Rosanna Coban" and "Colly Coban".[7] On the petition against discrimination based on color in Massachusetts railroad cars, the name "Colly Coban" was written.[8] The writing of others' names on petitions during this incipient era of women's door-to-door canvassing and at gatherings for antisegregation, antislavery, and abolition was an ordinary practice, done on behalf of petitioners who were illiterate in writing, and should not be considered forgery. That practice ensured that individuals who could not write their names but could only sign by mark were still able to courageously, publically profess their concurrence with the petition's prayer through an amanuensis. The presence of Colley and Rosanna's names on the petitions indicate that they were known within a local network of committed women activists who mobilized in one of the few direct political routes available to females.[9]

Colley predeceased her mother by two years, dying from "consumption" in 1857. She was interred at the South Parish Cemetery, initially in an unmarked grave, at or near where her mother's grave would be later marked with a stone that indicated their co-burial. Her death record said her age was 70. Throughout their lives when officials demanded their ages, Colley and her mother gave varying answers.[10] The intrusive encounters may have reminded them of being counted and asked their ages for Sarah Frye's estate inventory that in historian Daina Ramey Berry's estimation, assigned them "external values" in contrast to their perceived "self worth".[11] "Dissemblance," as configured in historian Darlene Clark Hine's term of art, "created the appearance of openness and disclosure but actually shielded the truth of their inner lives and selves." Clark's "dissemblance" was one of many "forms of resistance" that advanced the deliberate function of emotional concealment to game oppressive and confrontational situations.[12] Privacy, modesty, and public respectability were gendered virtues in ideologies of womanhood. Rosanna and Colley's knowing practice may have been personally and mutually satisfying. Privacy preserved, in scholar Lois Brown's phrase, a "fragile but resilient interiority."[13] To whatever degree and in what circumstances Rosanna and Colley were self-conscious of their moments of fragility or strength, when they were asked their ages they were in control of personal information and manipulated those situations.[14]

Titus Coburn (1740 or 1756–1821) from enslaved soldier to manumitted yeoman landowner

Titus Coburn likely was born a slave and may have hailed from Dracut where Coburn families, including people of color with that surname, were prodigious. Dracut adjoins Andover to the northwest across the Merrimack River, and Titus Coburn had connections with people from that town during his lifetime. The earliest certain records of him indicate that he was baptized in 1767 at the Second Church of Christ in Reading and that he arrived in Wilmington in the spring of 1774. Titus was brought to Wilmington from the adjoining town of Reading by his owner, Capt. Edward Hircom (fl. 1720–1781)[1] (Figure 6).

During his military service during the Revolutionary War, Titus Coburn was not a legally free man. Massachusetts offered no direct mechanism for enslaved men to be manumitted by their service as patriot soldiers. Coburn served a turn at the Crown Point Expedition in 1776 as a substitute for Capt. Hircom.[2] Titus Coburn later enlisted as a soldier for the town of Wilmington, serving nine months with the Massachusetts line as a private. Around 1779 he was described as 22 years old, 5' 6" tall, "complexion, negro". The specific dates of his service vary in documents included in his veteran's pension application and in the published summaries of his service records, the years spanning 1778 to 1780. He said that he spent most of his military service at West Point, N.Y.[3] Titus Coburn signed by mark a request for nine months military pay in 1787, seven years after his service.[4]

Titus was named as "my Negro man Titus Cobur" in Capt. Edward Hircom's 1781 will. Hircom's will also named "my Mulatto Woman Peggy". Hircom's will included a stipulation that manumitted Titus and Peggy upon Hircom's death: "My Will is + I further order that the said Titus + Peggy have their Liberty and that each of them be Free Persons im[m]ediately after my Decease". Hircom bequeathed all his clothes to Titus "excepting my best coat", and half of what Hircom called his outdoor movables and husbandry tools. Peggy and Titus together shared an inheritance of half of Hircom's buildings (including the easterly part of the house, the barn, and the outbuildings), half the 200¼ acres of land including a garden (the will devised *half* his land to be shared by Titus and Peggy, but on the same day Hircom deeded *all* his land to them), and all of Hircom's livestock—a horse, "half a large pair of oxen", six cows, five young cattle, a steer, five sheep, and four pigs. Peggy alone inherited all the furniture, money, notes, and bonds (except for half of one bond), and any remaining personal property.[5]

Hircom named as his executor Nathaniel Russell, "who lives with me in the house". Russell was likely a relative through Edward Hircom's previous marriage to Priscilla Russell. While Hircom was a widower, Nathaniel Russell's wife Sarah and their four children were also present in the household. Nathaniel Russell was bequeathed the easterly and best parts of the house, half of the barn and outbuildings, half the land, half the tools and outdoor moveables, and half of a £93 6s. 8p. bond. Hircom's "best coat" was not otherwise specifically devised in the will (so by default to Peggy), which may have been an oversight. Hircom may have intended that his gentleman's coat was more appropriate to Nathaniel than to Titus, or perhaps Hircom anticipated to be buried in it.[6]

On the same day that Hircom wrote his will (July 14, 1781), he executed a deed to "Titus Cobur Negro" and "Peggy Hircum Mulatto" for the parts of the buildings just as he had specified in his will. But, unlike in the will that devised half of his 200¼ acres of land to Nathaniel Russell and the other half of his land to be shared by Titus and Peggy, in the deed Edward Hircom conveyed all his land to Titus and Peggy. Edward did not also execute a deed for Nathaniel Russell, indicating that Edward's special effort for Titus and Peggy was made to ensure that they received his property as he intended.[7]

Edward Hircom's deliberative and willful acts embodied his vision that the emancipated Titus and Peggy, with Nathaniel and Sarah and their children, all living together in separate parts of one domestic structure, would be fully provided to continue operation of his farm. Edward Hircom's intentional vision by his will and deed was above and beyond his contemporaries. He implemented a plan to ensure that Titus and Peggy were not merely manumitted, and not merely bequeathed token amounts of cash or secondhand items less interesting to other devisees. Prospective manumission by will and small bequests of money to slaves appear in probate documents, sometimes with appreciative words for their longevity of loyal service. In many historical texts of this region, "loyalty" and "faithfulness" were frequently invoked for people in servitude. The terms carried connotations of obedience that concealed negotiations, contestations, and resistance to subservience. More typically of course unfree people—whether slaves-for-life or constrained by some other type of involuntary, dependent, or compelled laboring arrangement—were devised in wills as objectified chattel. Foreknowledge of such bequests of freedom and money that would arrive upon a master's or mistress' death, or of plans to separate and sell enslaved families, was information that might be guarded by slave owners. Desperate circumstances, motives and means, could converge and prove to be prematurely fatal. Such mechanistic arrangements established by will, implemented by estate administrators and affirmed by probate court judges, perpetuated slavery and slave-like practices long past the supposed moment when legal enslavement and related shades of unfree laboring practices had receded in Massachusetts.

Nathaniel, Titus, and Peggy inherited considerably valuable personal property and the expansive, working farm of 200¼ acres. The inventory that was completed October 5, 1781 included the land and buildings appraised for £600, and movable goods, livestock, and agricultural produce that together was valued at £187 15s. 8p. The "5664 old Continental Dollars" were so depreciated as to be practically worthless, so their value was not indicated by the appraisers. Additionally, there were many notes and bonds from individuals, but also a "Continental Note" from 1777 ($200), two "State Note[s]" from 1777 (£32 17s.), and four "Wilmington Treasur[er]s Notes" (£309 8s.) from 1777 and 1778. Probate of the estate was completed in four years, from September 1781 to September 1785. It was during that period of probate that the 1781 deed from Edward Hircom to Titus and Peggy was recorded, specifically on June 5, 1782.[8]

As a newly propertied free man, Titus Coburn was involved in several real estate transactions in Wilmington, selling land in 1785, 1786, and 1792, and buying it in 1785 and 1792. These transactions included parts of the land and buildings on the Hircom farm, and probably adjoining or nearby parcels. (As a newly positioned woman, Peggy Hircom purchased real estate between 1782 and 1789 and sold it between 1782 and 1793, although for this project her transactions were not all traced. Nathaniel Russell disposed of his part of the farm and the dwelling house in July 1788.) The nature, content, and timing of the deeds for these land transactions by Titus Coburn reveal information about important moments in Titus Coburn's life in Wilmington.[9]

Titus' first real estate purchase was in September 1782: he bought nine acres of Wilmington upland and swamp for £27 12s. A month and a half later he sold the same parcel for £24, losing £3 12s. Both transactions were not recorded until May 1785. That apparently unsuccessful real estate speculation may instead have been a way to raise cash, or perhaps an effort to obtain additional land for farming and husbandry that Titus Coburn soon decided was not necessary.[10]

"Titus Cober" married "Vilot Noble" in August 1785.[11] In November 1785, Titus sold to Peggy all the land parts of the farm that Capt. Hircom had granted him, including his shared right in "the Mill House" and the barn, but Titus did not sell her his shared portions of the dwelling house. Titus and his wife Violet resided at the farm: in that sale to Peggy, Titus reserved "a good Priviledge in the [...Barn] to keep a Cow & to lay Fodder for said Cow so long as I shall dwell in my House here in this place" and "Vilot Wife of the said Titus" assented to the sale by releasing her dower rights.[12] Nathaniel Russell and his wife Sarah probably left the property in July 1788, when he sold his part to Samuel Eames, Esq. (1755–1834).[13] "Squire Eames" who had witnessed Capt. Hircom's will in 1781, would later also purchase Titus' portion of the former Hircom farm in 1791, Peggy's portion in 1793, and he officiated the marriage of Titus Coburn and Rosanna in 1792. In April 1789 Peggy sold to Titus two parcels of land totaling seven acres, one of which was four acres of woodland on the farm. That deed was not witnessed until January 9, 1792; it was recorded nine days later.[14]

Titus and Violet had a daughter Jennie born in May 1789. Seemingly Jennie was the same person called Jane or June in 1816. At the time of Jennie's birth, her parents were indicated by the nineteenth-century compiler of the Wilmington vital records to be "Servants of Ebenezer Jones."[15] Such notations were made in town or church records to indicate present enslavement (which implicated ownership of children born to a slave, sponsorship of slave baptisms, and sometimes the assent granted or denied by an owner for marriage of their slave); to indicate free status of persons of color (when used with the term "late" to mean a former slave); to indicate indenture that might require consent of a master or mistress; or, intended to identify single-named persons. If the note in the published nineteenth-century vital records is correct (and I suspect it is not), when Jennie was born, Titus and Violet were laboring for Ebenezer Jones (circa 1724–1791), presumably for remuneration as both Titus and Violet were free persons. If the couple and their daughter temporarily lived with Jones in 1789, they did not stay long because Titus had his own household the following year.

In 1790, "Titus Cobur" had three other people in his household, presumably Violet, Jennie, and Peggy, at the former Hircom farm.[16] On December 25, 1791, Titus—"with Vilot my now married Wife consenting"—sold whatever he retained of the former Hircom farm to Samuel Eames. That sale included the two parcels of land (seven acres total) that he purchased from Peggy in 1789, and his portions of the dwelling house.[17] Peggy Hircom sold her remaining share of the former Hircom farm to Samuel Eames in March 1793. By June 1794, Peggy Hircom was living in Andover, where she married Samuel George.[18]

Titus and Rosanna met in Wilmington, and they were married on September 6, 1792 by Samuel Eames.[19] In Wilmington in 1800, the census population schedule shows seven people of color in Titus Coburn's household, presumably including Rosanna and Colley.[20] Lack of vital records makes it impossible to determine if Violet was still living, and if so, how long she stayed and when she separated herself and her daughter from Titus. But for a time Titus created a household configuration that included Titus' new wife Rosanna and her daughter Colley, Peggy, and three other people. Violet and Jennie may have been among them, or the three other persons could have been farm tenant laborers.[21]

In 1809, Titus Coburn purchased just over an acre of orchard and mowing land with a building in Andover for $230. Nearly three years later, he sold the same property for the identical sum to Sarah Stevens, a widow in 1811.[22] If the Coburns lived in the undescribed building, or whether after the sale they moved into Phillis' house "on the Salem Turnpike, a short distance north of the house of William Peters", is not known.[23] Perhaps Widow Stevens allowed the family to stay as her tenants. The 1810 federal census population schedule for Titus Coburn's Andover household counted four persons of color, himself, and presumably Rosanna, Colley, and his mother-in-law Phillis.[24]

For a brief period in 1816, Titus Coburn's daughter Jennie (then called Jane or June) joined them in Andover during a time when she required medical care. She was about 27 years old. The Andover treasurer paid Titus "for supporting his daughter in part" on June 8, 1816. The next payment entry that day was to Dr. Nathaniel Swift for (generically) "medicine and attendance" for "June Coburn" ($6.54), and four months later Dr. Swift was reimbursed for his treatment of "Jane Coburn" on October 7, 1816 ($2.08). Dr. Swift's charges are several times more than he charged for routine visits. The "black man at Titus Coburns" around that time may be related to the appearance of the daughter, and he may have accompanied Jennie (Jane/June) to the Coburns. The unusual entry only indicated that this "black man at Titus Coburns" had been given 50 cents.[25]

The year 1816 was called "Poverty Year." It was awfully cold throughout the year, an exceptional and consequential event remembered by many chroniclers in New England. Andover's first history book, Abiel Abbot's *History of Andover* (1829), concisely noted that both 1816 and 1817 were

"Remarkably cold seasons, frosts early, most of the corn destroyed by frost." A Dracut historian conveyed that there were "frosts every month and snow every month, except July and August" that devastated crops. "In September the corn froze to the center of the cob and apples froze on the trees." The effects on the food supply caused "great hardship and suffering for the families". A Wilmington farmer commented on the "scarcity of pigs, as few farmers kept a hog over winter. That year, pigs were killed that would not be allowed to live and that were not fit to die." By August, "there was a great cry for pigs." A writer in Franklin County, Massachusetts, said "Breadstuffs were scarce and prices high and the poorer class of people were often in straits for want of food [...] and people were obliged to rely upon their own resources or upon others in their immediate locality."[26] The cold weather of 1816 may be in part why Coburn's daughter and the "black man" came to stay at Titus and Rosanna Coburn's house during that year, why the overseers provided extra support to Titus for his daughter and the half-dollar given the "black man", and may be also reflected in Andover's poor relief costs that year and the next. Recall that in March 1816, the town overseers of the poor had commenced to reimburse Titus for supporting his mother-in-law Phillis. All the women in the household likely cared and labored for each other and the men, and friends and neighbors may have helped too.

Titus Coburn learned that he was eligible for a Revolutionary War veteran's pension, and applied April 8, 1818. He was sent his pension certificate in September 1818, providing him $8 per month; his first payment included a semiannual allowance and retroactive amounts totaling $87.20. Regular payments were made on March 4th and September 4th of each year to the Boston branch of the United States Bank, where presumably Titus went twice a year to receive his money[27] (Figure 8).

Titus Coburn was a defendant in a March 1819 debt case for which he did not appear at court to answer, so he lost by default. He had made a promissory note in 1818 for $35.72 to Moses Wood (1779–1867), a clerk at the Andover general store called Shipman's (Figure 9). Moses Wood endorsed Coburn's promissory note over to Wood's Boston wholesalers, a firm called Gurney and Packard, who sued Titus. After the Boston men won and Coburn did not pay the court judgment of $40.93 that included his outstanding debt, interest, and court costs, the court issued an order to the sheriff (called an *execution*) to carry out the court's judgment.[28]

Titus' case was among fifteen related debt cases brought by Gurney and Packard against Andover men between 1818 and 1820. All the lawsuits were won by the plaintiffs when none of the Andover men appeared in court and all defaulted. The court records of decisions note that (for all but one case) executions were issued by the court ordering the sheriff to take action to satisfy the Boston creditors. (One case record ends abruptly with the conclusion of the decision not written out by the clerk, the part that would have noted the issuance of an execution of the court's judgment.) In three cases, executions had to be issued twice.

All but three of the fifteen Gurney and Packard lawsuits involved promissory notes that had been endorsed over or made directly to the Boston business by Moses Wood. Of those twelve cases, eleven involved Andover men who bought (or whose families had purchased) goods from Shipman's store. The eleven promissory notes ranged from $19.97 to $67.19, with the simple average of $37.09. The men gave Moses Wood their notes for their purchases, which Wood then signed over to Gurney and Packard. The twelfth case was brought by Gurney and Packard against Moses Wood himself who owed by far the largest amount of money to his wholesalers by his own notes to them: $3,015.02. The other three of the fifteen Gurney and Packard lawsuits were against another merchant, a shoemaker, and a farmer who had written promissory notes to the Boston firm. Those three Andover men did business directly with the Boston wholesaler.[29]

The Andover debt cases occurred during the national economic collapse known as the Panic of 1819. Economic historian Daniel S. Dupre vividly summarized the progression of economic effects at international, national, regional, local, and individual scales:

> Merchants [...] scrambled to liquidate their assets to cover debts owed to foreign creditors, and [...] in turn pressed smaller merchants and shopkeepers [...] for payment on merchandise sold on credit. Those small-scale merchants [...] scrambled to stave off bankruptcy by pressuring their customers, usually farmers, to pay off their debts. But falling crop prices and the scarcity of specie or reputable bank notes made that difficult, forcing both merchants and farmers to face foreclosure and the sale of property.[30]

The file papers for the Gurney and Packard case against Titus Coburn include the $35.72 note from Coburn to Wood written July 18, 1818, and endorsed the same day by Wood to Gurney and Packard. Coburn made a payment of $10 on October 11, 1818, but no further payments were recorded on the back of the note. On December 1, 1818 the clerk of the Essex County Court of Common Pleas issued a writ against Titus Coburn. The writ stated the creditor's claim (using the full amount of the original note of $35.72 but not mentioning the $10 payment or the $0.52 interest) and asserted damages to them of $60. The writ ordered the sheriff to "attach" (i.e., to seize, to make legal claim to) Coburn's property and to summons Titus to appear in court to answer to the lawsuit at the December 1818 term. The attorney for the Boston grocers, Amos Spaulding, signed the writ to guarantee for the plaintiffs in the event they lost. To ensure the obligation of the sheriff to execute a levy on real estate, Spaulding wrote "Mr Officer attach sufficient estate by order of Creditors". The deputy sheriff served the writ on Coburn on December 5, 1818, and "attached about Two acres of Land within [*sic*] the building thereon on which said Coburn now lives & improves & lying on the road from Wid[ow] Phebe Abbot to Ezekiel Wardwell's in South parish Andover, as the property of the within named Coburn". At the time, however, Titus Coburn owned no real estate. He had sold his acre with a building in 1811. The property attached by the sheriff may have been Phillis' occupied house and land where Titus lived with Phillis, Rosanna, and Colley, but there is no record that Phillis or her late husband Booso owned that real estate. Nevertheless, even rented property not owned by the defendant could be attached by the sheriff. The case must have been continued from the December 1818 term to March 1819, when Titus lost by default for not appearing. The court awarded the plaintiffs only the outstanding debt of $26.89 and their costs of $14.04.

On July 21, 1819, the court issued an order to the sheriff to execute the court judgment against Titus Coburn for $40.93 plus additional costs for the execution process. The resolution of the case cannot be determined because the records of the execution were not located in the Supreme Judicial Court Archives. Because Titus Coburn was a pauper with no real estate, the sheriff had other options, including gathering and selling produce from his improved fields, seizing any rents he might have paid the landowner, or putting him in jail. Even so, the creditors may never have collected.[31]

When federal pension eligibility requirements changed, Coburn reapplied in July 1820 and his Revolutionary War pension was continued; he was paid to March 4, 1821. An inventory of Titus Coburn's possessions in 1820 was required for his reapplication. The inventory listed no real estate, and only agricultural tools and household goods: shovel, hoe, axe, tongs, chest, six chairs, six cups and saucers, mirror, scythe blade with its handle, and a pitchfork, the value of which totaled $6.15. The enumerated items could have included possessions inherited from Edward Hircom between 1781 and 1785. The tools hint that the family had a home garden. They probably kept poultry and maybe a cow. The 1820 pension application indicated that "he owes a number of debts" and that he was unable to perform any labor due to an injury. Differently from the 1820 federal pension application file in federal archives, the 1820 Essex County Circuit Court of

Common Pleas version of the application appears to have original marks of Titus Coburn[32] (Figure 10). The 1820 federal census population schedules for Andover did not enumerate households headed by persons of color, instead provided aggregate statistics for the 61 people of color in the town. Titus Coburn's family members do not appear on a list of supplies delivered to the town poor from 1820 to 1821, but the household received intermittent town support during that period. Further research is needed into the town treasurer and overseers of the poor financial records to compile all the entries for the extended family.[33]

Titus Coburn's will included two religious sentiments, opening with "In the name of GOD amen", and for his "sound mind and memory" he expressed "blessed be almighty GOD". Besides being written the day he died when ethereal thoughts would be expected, the formulaic phrases are common to wills. Titus was illiterate in writing and signed by mark: because only copies of the will were preserved, the identity of his amanuensis cannot be determined by the original handwriting.[34] If Titus was a church-going man later in his life, no record has been found. He was baptized in 1767, likely at 11 years old. His marriage to Violet in 1785 was performed by the Rev. Isaac Morrill at the First Church of Christ in Wilmington when he was likely 29 years old.[35] His marriage to Rosanna in 1792 was officiated by Samuel Eames, Esq., apparently not a minister, so it was probably a civil ceremony.[36]

Titus Coburn passed away on May 5, 1821, probably at his house. He was most likely 64 years old, not 81 as indicated apparently erroneously in town records. He could have been buried in any of the Andover cemeteries open at that time. Long after his death, his estate was probated in August 1854, coincident to Rosanna Coburn's application for her Revolutionary War veteran widow's pension. While probate process for the estate of that impoverished man, with few personal possessions and probably little if any savings, was not accomplished thirty-three years previously, Rosanna's attorney Israel Perkins evidently thought it was necessary to do so for her federal pension application that he was preparing. Somehow, someone, most likely his widow, had kept Titus Coburn's original 1821 will, and it was brought in to Probate Court, the session for which was conveniently held at Andover.

Joining Rosanna and her attorney for the probate proceedings were two surviving relatives of the (by then deceased) witnesses to Titus Coburn's 1821 will. The son of one witness, and the son and nephew of the two other witnesses, affirmed the authenticity of the original signatures of the three Andover men who had witnessed the will. Also accompanying Rosanna that August day was Barzillai Lew [Jr.] (1777–1861, an Andover man of color, the same-named son of the Revolutionary War veteran, 1743–1822, who lived in Dracut). Lew deposed that he was "well acquainted" with the late Titus Coburn and with Rosanna, and "well remember them as man and wife", that he *read* Rosanna Coburn's petition to the Probate Court, he affirmed the facts of it, and then he signed his name. It may have been the literate Lew who informed Rosanna that she was eligible to apply for the widow's pension and connected her to Israel Perkins. That Danvers attorney simultaneously prepared a pension application for Lew and his two sisters based on their father's Revolutionary War service, and Perkins also assisted them with their mother's estate.

Regrettably for historians, the original 1821 will was not retained by the court clerk (the original document may have been fragile and worn), and only a copy of Titus Coburn's will was made for the probate court file papers. That copy of the will was then used to make another copy for Rosanna Coburn's widow's pension application to further demonstrate the fact of her spousal relationship and other facts that were not otherwise sufficiently documented in official government records.[37]

Rosanna (Rose) Coburn (1762 to 1767–1859) among the last survivors in historical Andover born in slavery and a representative icon to its past

Rosanna Coburn, the daughter of Phillis and Booso, was born a slave to Joshua Frye. Rosanna's birth in Andover at the Frye's can be inferred. Because of the different ages she gave or was said to be during her lifetime and at her death, it is impossible to know what year Rosanna was born. It can be estimated that Rosanna was born sometime between 1762 and 1767, but no entry for the event appears in town or church records. Likewise with the uncertainty of her mother's birth year: if Phillis were born in 1727, then she would have been between 35 and 40 years old when Rosanna was born. Rosanna told two stories independently (rendered in writing by others and published in 1847 and in 1853) that her mother was Joshua Frye's slave. The chronology is also disorderly, but Rosanna's story published in 1853 indicated either that Phillis became Frye's slave when Phillis was a young girl (about ten years old in 1737–1745) or otherwise when Phillis was a young woman (about 28 or 29 years old in 1755 –1756). Considering together Rosanna's two separately told stories that her mother was enslaved by Joshua Frye; that Phillis, Rosanna, and Juba are devised in Sarah Frye's 1776 will; and, their listings in Sarah Frye's 1781 inventory with the child Titus and the infant Tory, indicates that those four children were all born in slavery at the Frye's in Andover. The state commissioners presumed that Rosanna Coburn was born in Andover because her mother and father were slaves of Andover residents. The Andover official interviewed by the commissioners in 1846 expressed his uncertainty about Rosanna's biography: "One of the overseers testified, that he presumed the mother of Rosanna Coburn was a slave at the time of Rosanna's birth, but was not positive as to the fact."[1]

At Joshua Frye's death in 1768, she and her mother became slaves to his widow Sarah Frye. The widow's death in 1781 threatened the cohesion and security of Phillis' family, because Sarah's 1776 will had ordered their sale. When the men appeared in May 1781 to take inventory of Sarah Frye's property, they counted, named, provided ages, and set a value for the lot of them. Anxieties about their separation and future circumstances with new owners would have been dreadful. By September 1790, she and her mother with all the other Frye slaves (Rosanna's siblings and Cato) had "taken their Freedom".[2]

Rosanna's father Booso had already gained his freedom in 1778 by suing his owner for his liberty. Booso's legal action presupposes he obtained "legal consciousness" and he may have knowledgably encouraged Phillis, the children, and Cato that they could assert their freedom without having to go to court. Knowledge of decades of favorable common law decisions that granted freedom to enslaved people in Andover encouraged Phillis and the other Frye slaves to claim their own liberty.[3]

Around 1785 Rosanna became pregnant—by whom is not known, but she was between 17 and 23 years old.[4] Her daughter Colley Hooper was born in Andover about 1786. She and Colley moved to the adjoining town of Wilmington. Her daughter claimed that her mother used the name Rosanna Hooper when there. Rosanna met Titus Coburn in Wilmington. He had been married previously to Violet Noble in 1785, and also had a daughter born in 1789 called Jennie (later, in 1816, seemingly the same person called Jane or June). Rosanna and Titus married in 1792 when Colley was six years old, and they lived together in Wilmington through August of 1800 in a house that had four other people.[5]

After her father Booso died between 1800 and 1810, Titus, Rosanna, and Colley returned to Andover, presumably to be near her widowed mother Phillis, then maybe 73 to 83 years old. Titus, Rosanna, and Colley may have moved to Phillis' house located "on the Salem Turnpike, a short distance north of the house of William Peters." The site of Phillis and Booso's house became a landmark: "After the building was demolished, the oven remained standing fifteen years."[6] Alternatively, Phillis may have joined them at the property Titus Coburn purchased in 1809 that was described as orchard and mowing land with a building. When he sold that property in 1811, if the building was their home, they may have stayed on as farmer-tenants to the new owner, a widow named Sarah Stevens. Decades later, beginning by at least 1843, Rosanna and Colley lived in a rented house. It had a garden that provided them some food, and they may have traded or sold some of the yield to others. That rented house may be the same place where Rosanna and Colley were residing by at least 1852, located on Missionary Lane (now Woodland Road, east of Phillips Academy)[7] (Figure 18).

From spring to autumn 1816, Titus Coburn's daughter Jennie (then called Jane or June, about 27 years old) had reappeared and stayed with the Coburns during a time when she required medical care. If whatever was affecting her required home nursing, Rosanna, Colley, and Phillis (if she were able) would have done that work. The appearance of a "black man at Titus Coburns" around that time may be related to the daughter's visit, and he may have accompanied Jennie (Jane/June) to the Coburn's house. The Andover overseers of the poor made a single reimbursement of $5.00 to Titus "for supporting his daughter in part" while she stayed with the Coburns. The modifier "in part" indicated either that the amount was for only part of the time, or part of the costs for his household's support of the daughter, or that costs for another matter was included.[8]

Rosanna's husband Titus applied for a Revolutionary War veteran's pension in 1818, and the initial first payment of $87.20 included retroactively owed amounts and a semiannual allowance. Thereafter, Titus received $96 a year, paid biannually in Boston until March 1821. Economic circumstances became increasingly tenuous for the household. Titus was sued for a debt in 1819. A sheriff appeared at their home twice: first to order him to court, which he ignored, and then to enforce payment of the court judgment against him. By exerting himself in heavy labor, Rosanna's husband injured himself severely and painfully. His laboring days were over before 1820. Rosanna and Colley must have provided most of the nursing care that Jennie (Jane/June) required in 1816, that Phillis required in her advanced years, and that Titus required by his aggravated injury. He died on May 5, 1821. Phillis could have cared for people in the household as she was able.

The Andover overseers of the poor reimbursed Rosanna for supporting Phillis while she lived with Rosanna and Colley. Payments were made about each quarter, usually the same $6.50 that Titus Coburn had received. Exceptional amounts paid to Rosanna for supporting her mother at home were $8.67 in March 1823; $13.00 in August 1825, January 1826, October 1826, and February 1827; $6.00 in July 1826; and, $8.50 in July 1827. The variable amounts could be for cost of support calculated over shorter or longer periods, or for exceptional outlays.[9]

Phillis had a health crisis around August 1827, inferred from an exceptionally high medical bill that the Andover overseers of the poor had paid that month. She was perhaps 100 years old.[10] Rosanna was between 63 and 68 years old that year, and Colley also required Rosanna's attention. At the time when Phillis was residing with them, Colley's long-term health issues from "consumption" (pulmonary tuberculosis or any other wasting disease) may have become palpable. Colley Hooper lived with her mother her entire life. Only conceivably, Colley may have had other issues, such as somatic developmental disabilities or a psychological disorder, although the statement she made in 1854 for her mother's pension application was lucid and showed that her childhood memories were intact. Yet, four months later, when Rosanna prepared her will, Rosanna did not consider that Colley was capable of managing her own financial affairs and appointed the executor to act as Colley's trustee. Caring for Phillis at their home might have become impossible for Rosanna and Colley to manage. If so, Phillis could have gone to the almshouse, or maybe neighbors helped instead. Phillis likely died at home, probably in late 1828.[11]

The federal census for 1830 showed two people in Rosanna's household, two females aged 35 to under 55, and 55 to under 100. Rosanna and Colley remained together as a two-person household, appearing in federal and state census records for 1840, 1850, and 1855, their reported ages varying considerably. Throughout their lives, when officials demanded that they state their ages, Rosanna and Colley's answers were knowingly modest and they remain enigmatic.[12]

Rosanna, probably together with Colley, gathered wild blueberries that Rosanna exchanged for flour, and brokered for a local farmer selling his eggs to an Andover household. It may have been Rosanna or another "Mrs. Coburn" who was paid in January 1853 by North Andover farmer John Foster for two weeks of work "taking care" of his wife after the birth of their daughter in late December 1852.[13] When Rosanna Coburn was interviewed by a newspaper reporter in 1853, she called her own daughter "her 'one chicken.'" The reporter said that Rosanna and Colley "have been provided with a comfortable house, by the kindness of benevolent friends, and the little assistance they receive from the town, with the charities of the community, sustain them."[14]

Rosanna Coburn received small annual payments from the Samuel Phillips and Samuel Abbot Funds for the Relief of Indigent Persons in the South Parish in 1824 ($1.75), 1836–1845 ($2.00), and 1846–1854 ($3.00).[15] She appeared on a list of the town poor that was prepared for the state in January 1834. Wood fuel was supplied to Rosanna Coburn's household in March and December 1839.[16] A notebook kept by an Andover overseer of the poor from 1843–1845 has a list of food provisions and other items provided to Rosanna Coburn around 1843.[17] The *Annual Town Reports* listed Rosanna or both she and Colley among people named as receiving support outside the almshouse for 1832, 1835–1839, 1845–1848, and 1850–1856. In the town reports, Rosanna Coburn was named but Colley was not, even when Rosanna shared a home with her daughter in 1832, 1835–1839, 1848, and from 1852 to 1856. In those years, the support provided for a named person was as the head of a household. Furthermore, in the published town reports, both Rosanna and Colley were specially designated as "State Pauper" in 1832, 1843, and from 1845 to 1847, while Colley alone was indicated to be a state pauper in 1851 but her mother was not. In the 1850–1851 town reports, Rosanna was indicated to have received "medical attendance".[18]

In her 1854 will, Rosanna bequeathed all her possessions to her daughter Elizabeth ("commonly called Colly", i.e., Colley Hooper). Simultaneously, Rosanna established Andover tailor John Parnell (1796–1867) to be her executor and a life trustee for Colley, suggesting she might not have expected that her daughter was fully capable of managing her own affairs independently. Rosanna may, however, have simply acceded to her attorney's recommendation to name a trustee for Colley. In either case, the trustee arrangement was not required because Colley predeceased her mother.[19] At some point Colley became ill, a wasting sickness called at the time of her death "consumption," perhaps pulmonary tuberculosis, but it could have been another dissipating disease. The town clerk recorded Colley's age at her death as 70 years in 1857. Rosanna would have been between 89 and 95 years old when her daughter succumbed. Two years after Colley's death, the writer of Rosanna's obituary complimented her agreeable public countenance that concealed her sadder personal experiences: "Rose was strictly honest, always in good spirits, and would enjoy a laugh as well as any young person."[20]

Rosanna Coburn became known during her life for having been a granted a Revolutionary War widow's pension for her husband Titus Coburn's military service. Her application stated that "the reason why, she has never presented her Claim, for pension before this time, is, that she was poor and destitute and no person offered to aid her."[21] But many people became involved in testifying and preparing prodigious documentation on behalf of her application. Her legal advocate was attorney Israel Perkins of Danvers. Perkins was also the attorney who assembled Barzillai Lew [Jr.]'s pension application on behalf of Lew and his two sisters, which commenced the same day as Rosanna Coburn's application. Perkins was executor of Lew's mother's estate. It may have been through Andover resident Barzillai Lew [Jr.] (the son of the nationally known African American Revolutionary War veteran), that Rosanna learned that she was eligible to apply for the widow's pension. Lew was among the many people who made affidavits and witnessed documents for Rosanna Coburn's pension application, as well as for her 1854 probate petition for her late husband's estate that provided supportive documentation for her pension application. The lack of official vital records for Titus and Rosanna Coburn's family required a formida-

ble and expensive effort to locate deponents, prepare their sworn affidavits, have the statements witnessed and attested before appointed officials,
whose appointments were validated by certificates prepared by the office of
the Massachusetts Secretary of the Commonwealth. The lengthy pension
application with its highly detailed, formalized documentation that established facts, identities, and legal relationships was estimable.[22]

The granting of Rosanna's pension by the federal government was celebrated in newspapers as a triumph of equitable treatment. That singular
news is interesting because so many other people of color who were Revolutionary War veterans, their spouses, and their children also received
pensions. Historian Margot Minardi appreciated that people of color especially faced significant legal, documentary, and bureaucratic impediments
in their veteran pension applications: "securing a military pension was not
only a way for veterans [and their survivors] to make ends meet. African
American[s] [...] also saw pensions as a means to assert their claims to equal
citizenship in the young republic."[23] Perhaps it was intentional and strategic
that no racial terms appeared in the Coburns' pension applications, except
for the one instance of "Negro" stated in the copy of Titus Coburn's death
record included as supporting documentation.[24]

After news arrived that Rosanna's pension was approved by the War Department in 1854, the local *Andover Advertiser* newspaper published an
article in late September under the headline, "A Windfall." The Andover
story was picked up in mid-October by William Lloyd Garrison's abolitionist newspaper *The Liberator* published in Boston. Garrison's note was
then reprinted in *Frederick Douglass' Paper* published in Rochester, N.Y.:
"Rose Coburn, a colored woman of South Andover, 88 years of age, has obtained from Government the sum of three hundred dollars besides expenses. She is also, hereafter, to receive $95 annually as a pension. The Andover
Advertiser facetiously remarked that 'It is understood that a future marriage
would cut her off from the annuity.'" The Ohio abolitionist newspaper
The Anti-Slavery Bugle reprinted *The Liberator* article in early November
1854.[25] The Unitarian minister and abolitionist Theodore Parker alluded
to Rosanna Coburn in an 1858 letter to national historian George Bancroft, writing that Titus Coburn's "widow now lives in Andover, (Mass.),
and draws a pension."[26]

The anonymous 1853 interview with Rosanna Coburn, in the *Andover
Advertiser* series of interviews with elderly residents about local history,
"Sketches of Octogenarians," began as the column characteristically did
with a Biblical passage. For Rosanna, it was Song of Solomon 1:5–6: "I am
black, but comely, O ye daughters of Jerusalem, as the tent of Kedar, as the

curtains of Solomon."[27] For the conclusion of her 1859 obituary, the same writer again conveyed Rosanna's racial alterity or "otherness" by allusion and elegy: "Although possessed of 'a skin not colored like our own,' but few were more highly regarded, and only few leave a better record behind them. Peace to her ashes."[28] Variants of the oft-quoted phrase "guilty of a skin not colored like our own"—tailored from lines by English poet William Cowper—were used ironically and moralistically in many antislavery and abolitionist texts.[29]

Scholar Lois Brown's analysis of "memorial narratives" frames the "Sketches" and the obituary writer's "pronounced religiosity" and moralizing. The as-published form of the information presented has been, of course, mediated during the ethnographic moment of the interview, the writer's compositional practices, and even by the unseen hands of the newspaper editor and typesetter. Personally significant genealogical and biographical information remembered and related by Rosanna during the interview was processually "transform[ed from] cultural values and memory into multicultural morals and history." The writer of the interview and obituary valued Rosanna Coburn's information to document Andover's history and the genealogy of its people, and was moved to signal a position about broader political issues of the day.[30]

In January 1860, Andover town clerk Edward Taylor recorded the circumstances of Rosanna Coburn's death that had occurred on March 19, 1859. He entered the information in the official vital records that she was 97 years old, a widow, and died of old age. Under the column for Rosanna's place of birth he wrote "Andover. a slave". In the state vital records that he prepared, he or another hand underscored "a slave"[31] (Figures 19–20). Taylor's additional, nonconforming entry is intriguing. Whatever his purpose to note her former condition in the permanent town and state records, it was another instance where her enslavement was officially attached to her identity.[32] The town and state vital records, although public records, were hardly seen in contrast to her published obituary and her gravestone.

The historical, genealogical, and biographical sketch about Rosanna and her family created in 1853 was repeated with slight change by the same writer for Rosanna Coburn's 1859 obituary. Both were sources of fixing the family's history, Rosanna's biography particularly, in local oral and written historical traditions. The obituary was the source of some details used by the writer[33] of the original gravestone epitaph (of which there are five varying transcriptions from circa 1863 to 1864, 1880, 1896, 1975, and 2002). The age provided in the obituary and on the gravestone is 92. The obituary described Rosanna as "strictly honest, always in good spirits, and would enjoy a laugh as well as any young person." The earliest transcription of the gravestone epitaph said, "She was a person of great honesty vivacity and intelligence". Both indicated that she received a pension for her late husband's Revolutionary War service, subtly linking idealization of the patriotic war for "liberty" with citizenship.[34]

Rosanna Coburn's gravestone itself prompted memories. A short, untitled news note in 1896, about resetting grave markers at the South Parish Cemetery recalled that "stories told by the old folks of Rose Coburn are quite interesting. She was a colored woman who was known far and wide".[35]

Andover and North Andover historian Sarah Loring Bailey may have drawn information from the "Sketches" and obituary when she wrote that "In the Old South Burying Ground is the grave of the last slave born in Andover, Rose Coburn, wife of Titus Coburn. She was daughter of Benjamin, a slave brought from the West Indies, and Phillis, brought from Africa at the age of ten years, a servant of Mr. Joshua Frye." Bailey then quoted Rosanna Coburn's epitaph, the details of which vary among other texts with transcriptions of the original stone, including mistaking "vivacity" on the gravestone for "veracity" (Figures 21–23).

> Here lies buried the body of
> Rose Coburn
> Who died Mar. 19 1859 aet 92 years
> *She was born a slave in Andover and was the last survivor of all born here in that condition.*
> *A pension was paid to her as the widow of a soldier of the Revolution.*
> *She was a person of great honesty, veracity and intelligence and retained all her faculties in a singular degree until the last.*
> *Also her daughter Colley Hooper died aged 58, who died first, neither of them leaving any descendants.*[36]

Bailey's book, in turn, became a standard source for Rosanna's most remembered biographical detail, recollected to this day.[37] Her legendary notoriety as "the last slave" attenuated her biography. Whether or not precisely correct, certainly the memory of Rosanna Coburn as the town's "last survivor" of slavery resonated with Andover's nineteenth-century antislavery and abolitionist constituency.[38] She became an emblematic representation of the finality of local slavery, and her grave marker was an historical object lesson as a counterpoint to Andover's antislavery and abolitionist activism. Whereas the wording of Rosanna Coburn's gravestone epitaph seemed to arrest her in her former condition, the words on Pompey Lovejoy's adjoining gravestone signaled his biographical transformation: "Born in Boston, a slave: died in Andover a freeman [...] Much respected, as a sensible amiable and upright man."[39] As with Coburn's gravestone epitaph, so too did Pompey Lovejoy's epitaph represent the town's history of emancipation. The proximity of their two distinctively worded grave markers and their similar histories as formerly enslaved people encouraged historical writers to consider Coburn's and Lovejoy's biographies together when composing narratives about generational slavery and its abolition in Andover.

Perhaps the earliest detailed portrayal of Pompey Lovejoy was an historical writing published in 1858 that concluded by quoting his complete gravestone inscription. Published in the *Andover Advertiser* just 32 years after Lovejoy's death, the anonymous article "Pomp and Pomp's Pond" was linguistically marked with past temporal referents throughout. In the opening sentence alone, the writer used *old, old, old, time-marked,* and *older.* Reminiscent of Romantic period travel literature describing Old World antiquities, the article invoked the historicalness of the place where Pompey and his wife Rose Lovejoy had their cabin and garden, where their nieces Flora Chandler and Dinah Chadwick worked and stayed for a time with the elderly couple. In suitably ornamented style and sentimental tone, the Romantic writer described the archaeological ruin of "the now demolished domicil" being overtaken by nature.

> Here may be seen the outlines of the little cellar where Flora kept her ale; and scattered around are the fragments of the old kitchen-place, where she brewed it, and where she baked her '*lection cake.*' [...]
>
> Around these ruins is the old garden plat, once teeming with vegetables and garden herbs [...] where *Pomp*, in his declining days, might often be seen, supported by two sticks [....] *Pomp* was a genuine undiluted son of Africa, as his baudy [i.e., bandy] legs, ebony complexion and facial developments testified. [...] With his amiable wife, *Rose*, and his sable companions, *Flora* and *Dinah*, he spent his time in quiet preparation for his exit". [...] He died as he had lived, peacefully, and in charity with all mankind; and if his sphere in life was humble—his abilities and acquirements limited, and his race degraded, there are those still living who remember his virtues, and others who would do well to imitate him.

As with Rosanna Coburn's original gravestone that said she left no living posterity, the article conveyed that "no descendant survives" Pompey and Rose Lovejoy, before concluding with a transcription of Pompey Lovejoy's entire gravestone inscription.[40]

Especially following the Civil War, characterization of the nature of slavery in Massachusetts was utterly transformed and historicized.[41] Objects associated with formerly enslaved people of color in Andover became venerated heirlooms displayed at commemorative events that were occasions of remembrance and history-making. A ring once belonging to Rosanna Coburn was lent in 1896 and 1897 for historical exhibitions in Andover and Boston. The exhibitions were produced under the leadership of Andover pillar Salome Jane Abbott Marland (1850–1920), the wife of Maj. William Marland (1839–1905), with other women on the town's 250th anniversary committee from the Andover chapter of the Daughters of the Revolution. Exhibition catalogs were prepared for these "loan collections" that described the item and lender. The Andover catalog for the May 1896 exhibition, arranged as part of Andover's 250th anniversary celebration, described it as "Gold ring, worn by the last slave in Andover." The lender, indicated as Mrs. Benjamin Brown, was Susan F. Burr Brown.[42] The Boston exhibition catalog prepared in 1897 by the Daughters of the Revolution of the Commonwealth of Massachusetts, *Catalogue of a Loan Collection of Ancient and Historic Articles*, indicated that the keepsake was lent by Mrs. Eliza R. Doe Flanders, who was Susan Brown's half sister: "The ring bears what is thought to be the word, 'Assurance.' It is supposed to have been presented to her at the time she was freed." More likely it was a gift when she was granted her widow's pension, or perhaps it was her wedding ring.[43] Andover historian and genealogist Charlotte Helen Abbott wrote in 1896 that Rosanna Coburn's gold ring was then "in possession of a friend whose mother knew the old slave well." Rosanna Coburn's ring came into Susan Brown and Eliza Flanders' possession, probably through their mother Eliza Davis Burr Doe who must be the woman to whom Abbott referred.[44] Like her gravestone, Coburn's ring became imbued with a meaningful story about her enslavement and emancipation.

The *Boston Globe* connected Rosanna Coburn's ring and her gravestone in its 1896 report of the loan collection assembled for Andover's 250th anniversary program, and realized the general educational purpose of the effort that resounded beyond Andover:

> Many of the features to be brought out at the celebration are not only of local interest, but have lessons to teach to all. [...]
>
> A loan collection, in charge of Mrs. William Marland, is to be an educator of all who give time to the study of the varied departments. [...]
>
> The bridal ring of the last negro slave of the town will prompt many to step out a little distance from the loan hall and there study a

memorial of that institution that once flourished so extensively in the colonies of New England.

"Here lies buried the body of Rose Coburn, who died March 19, 1859, aet 92. She was born a slave in Andover, and as the last survivor of all born here in that condition a pension was paid to her as a widow of a soldier of the revolution. She was a person of great honesty, vivacity and intelligence, and retained all her faculties in a singular degree to the last."[45]

Appreciating the goals and purposes of the didactic messages conveyed by exhibition of Rosanna Coburn's ring and by reciting Rosanna Coburn's epitaph, the *Boston Globe* article broadened Rosanna Coburn's historical representativeness to acknowledge New England slavery and its abolishment.

Conclusions

The only "slave" ever counted in a federal census for Massachusetts was denominated by the Andover almshouse superintendent to deny her legal residency in town and to avail reimbursement for her care. Whoever the woman was that was designated a "slave," her biography, the biographies of the other ten people of color at the Andover almshouse in 1830, and more inclusively the history of people of color in historical Andover and surrounding localities are stories that I encourage others to pursue further. I have sketched out many research avenues for those and interrelated subjects in the discursive endnotes, and provided leads to informative sources.

Generations of Phillis' extended family became entangled in the practices of Andover officials that characterized, as nonresidents, formerly enslaved, free people of color who were long-time town inhabitants. Town officials purposefully and persistently asserted former slave status of individuals to seek state reimbursement for their support until the state rejected the practice. Entries about members of Phillis' family and other formerly enslaved, free people in Andover were engrossed in official government records and in historical productions that continued to explicitly reference their former enslaved status. Even Rosanna Coburn's town and state death records created in 1860 officially denoted that she was born "a slave." Official vital records created in Andover for other formerly enslaved people included similar notations.

Phillis' daughter Rosanna Coburn was remembered, her gravestone epitaph conveyed, as having been "born a slave in Andover and the last survivor of all born here in that condition."[1] Rosanna Coburn became historicized as the last living representative of the practice of slavery in Andover. A gold ring she once owned engraved "Assurance" became meaningfully imbued with a story about her gaining freedom and being the "last slave in Andover" and was integrated with commemorative exhibitions of historical objects in late nineteenth-century Andover and Boston.

The part of Rosanna Coburn's uncommonly long epitaph about her en-slavement was seemingly included as a tribute to her life passage from its beginning in adversity. The pensive melancholy of the final line that Rosan-na and Colley left no descendants was a definite terminus for the last liv-ing person to be born a slave in Andover, as it represented that slavery in Andover had passed, in cultural historian Blanche Linden-Ward's bucol-ic phrase, "putting the past under grass." Linden-Ward, in *Silent City on a Hill: Landscapes of Memory and Boston's Mount Auburn Cemetery*, con-veyed that didactic, patriotic, and sentimental memorials—the Bunker Hill Monument, Plymouth Rock, even graves of renowned Puritans such as the ancient Mather tomb at Copp's Hill in Boston that was ornamentally fenced in the nineteenth century—were created out of a "historical or com-memorative consciousness". Those efforts were the result of "community ac-tion to finance [civic and] funerary monuments to exemplary individuals in hopes of cultivating shared civic values and producing a virtuous citizenry through moral philosophy". As "history and death" were equated, the mon-uments themselves were "historical agents" in "landscapes of memory".[2]

On a far smaller scale but sourced in that same didactic ideal, Rosanna Coburn's modest gravestone, through its atypically elaborated epitaph, me-morialized "the last survivor" of local slavery while encoding the moral cer-titude of antislavery shared by many in Andover. The prominent location of the gravestone and its unusually long epitaph reinforced the virtuousness of antislavery ideals that had been fostered by decades of ardent moral per-suasion and political actions near and far. Local knowledge of Rosanna Co-burn's enslavement in Andover was a nuanced complication during a period of intensifying local agitation about slavery nationally. Between 1854 and 1861, Andover antislavery activists centered at the Free Christian Church invested in the New England Emigrant Aid Company (formerly Society) that funded settlers in the Kansas Territory with designs to make it a "free" state. Andover residents collected supplies and money for Kansas settlers from their town. Distressing letters from Andover émigrés in "Bleeding Kansas" were published as newspaper dispatches in the *Andover Advertis-er*. Rosanna Coburn's gravestone and her gold ring were small and modest monuments to an ordinary person who became emblematic of greater is-sues that would soon after her death bring the nation to war. By the time Rosanna Coburn's headstone was engraved and the probate process was completed in June 1861, the Civil War had already started.[3]

Andover South Church historian Charlotte Lyons considered that Rosanna Coburn's gravestone epitaph "affirmed long-term generational slavery in Andover."[4] To memorialize Rosanna as the last person born in slavery in Andover was to affirm the cessation of the town's historical practice of enslavement and publically adumbrate changed attitudes opposed to slavery. The portrayed remembrance of Rosanna Coburn as the last slave was not equally and universally shared, nor were the intended messages stable in resonance or meaning. But for allies of antislavery and abolitionism, particularly following the Civil War, Rosanna Coburn's historical transformation to an icon of the ending of local slavery distinguished her. As the town's symbolic last slave, she represented historical distance from the practice of slavery in Andover, while it confirmed certainty in modernist ideals of moral reformation in the practice of antislavery and abolitionist activism by Andover residents.

The public remembrance of Phillis' extended family, repeating biographical details about them and other people of color in the town's history-making traditions, drawing meanings from historical documents, artifacts, and places associated with them, provide glimpses into their true biographies in view of the long process of emancipation and the consequences of conditionally liberated survivance in historical Massachusetts. History-making projects about the family and other formerly enslaved people connected with the town reflected the sentiments of Andover's antislavery, abolitionist, and legal equality activists.

Modern memories of experiences of people of color in slavery and emancipation in historical Andover and the surrounding localities persist because of the devotion of archivists and curators of historical collections, librarians, public historians, genealogists, educators, preservationists, historical researchers, archaeologists, writers, and artists drawn to the famous area's cultural resources. Local history information is conveyed in books, photography, news articles, historical pageantry and drama, social media postings, exhibitions, websites, and in specialized databases and guides to archival and object collections. Preserved historical documents, objects, narratives, and historic places prompt recollections and make connections by, with, and about people of color. The preserved and cherished material culture of the records and artifacts, the historiography and informed oral history traditions, and the revered places connected with historical Andover comprise its actual and authentic cultural heritage. Its vastness, complexities, and mysteries are awesome. Local knowledge about people of color in historical Andover is astonishingly particular, detailed, and interrelated geographically, temporally, and thematically. Popular and scholarly knowledge of people of color connected to historical Andover, their experiences in enslavement and their survivance in contingent freedom, is astounding in its national and even international reach.

During my research forays and during the writing and editing of this monograph, I met and corresponded with so many encouraging people in the present municipalities of Andover, North Andover, and Lawrence who evince an abiding enthusiasm and interest about the history of people of color in and connected to their communities. A cadre of local history professionals, volunteers, and avocationalists were generous with their time and efforts to convey information and to guide me to sources and places. Within and beyond the historical area, I was encouraged in my project because it supported parallel projects in public service scholarship that seek to diversify, deepen, and reframe historical portrayals of people of color in local places that are most meaningful to our everyday experiences.

Historical interpretations recognize and celebrate contributions of historically significant personalities. People of color, leaders among them, learned, taught, and leveraged legal processes in their own everyday lives, with their kin, friends, and allies, and within consciously assembled communities. People of color and their allies through multiple practices of resistance and opposition shifted ideologies, and through freedom suits they changed the common law to judicially abolish slavery in Massachusetts. Andover townspeople's engagements in civic participation, education, religious life, business, the military, science, medicine, mathematics, arts, music, literature, and scholarship enrich, affirm, and inspire. Public history projects proudly remember that the historical town was a major nexus of abolitionist activism with civil disobedience that threatened considerable danger to those who participated as escapees, shelterers, and conveyers on the Underground Railroad. Local history projects recount focused and nationally minded activities of people within and connected to the historical town that financially and materially supported the Kansas settlement effort that brought the territory into the Union as a "free" state after appalling violence and mayhem. The contributions and sacrifices of Andover people in the military and at the homefront during wartime, and national and international missionary, educational, social, and political work are commemorated and interpreted.

Pain is palpable in the difficult knowledge that there never will be melioration about generational enslavement and analogous oppressive situations of family disconnection, servitude, and dependence; about participation in the slave trade and its economic tentacles; about slavery's attendant racialized categorizations and ideologies; and about the quotidian experiences of oppressions, hostility, and violence that characteristically persist in post-slavery societies. Historical and ongoing negotiations of intersecting disparate treatments of people of many ancestries, many heritages, and each and all of our ascribed and experienced identities are common cause because intersectional processes, their effects, and their opposition are common to all. Concerted and genuine efforts in the municipalities that encompass historical Andover persevere to acknowledge and tenderly educate about complicated and agonizing parts of local, regional, national, and global history. Particular attention is drawn to historical treatments of people of color and its obstinate echoes in contemporary experiences in modern society to educate young minds, to instill empathy and civility, and to advance social justice and equity interests that are vital to everyone in a civil society.

There are encouraging group efforts in Merrimack Valley places to identify and improve social, economic, educational, and health disparities and to address issues of inclusion, equity, dignity, and justice among many vulnerable and disproportionately affected populations. These organizations have proposed and created projects that reference historical persons and events connected with the area in reflection and for inspiration. Historical understandings about the causes, effects, and treatments of systemic disparities, and about the political and logistical solutions developed and applied historically by strategic social reform advocate-activists and their allies to confront corresponding issues, can inform and map strategic routes to be implemented that address our continuing and parallel concerns.

The unprecedented accessibility in the first quarter of the twenty-first century of historical information from print, manuscript, graphic, and artifact sources benefits interested residents, visitors, and researchers to learn about the places and roles of people of color in the historical area. All these ongoing cultural activities of cherishing, remembering, transforming, and transmitting historical information are how meaningful memories of people of color in historical Andover persist to our times.

Figures

[Doc. No. 263.] 5

STATE OF MASSACHUSETTS.

COUNTY.	AGGREGATE.	SLAVES.	FREE.	FEDERAL OR REPRESENTATIVE.
Suffolk - -	62,163	-	62,163	62,163
Nantucket - -	7,202	-	7,202	7,202
Plymouth - -	43,044	-	43,044	43,044
Hampshire - -	30,254	2	30,252	30,252
Bristol - -	49,592	-	49,592	49,592
Middlesex - -	77,961	-	77,961	77 961
Norfolk - -	41,972	-	41,972	41,972
Barnstable - -	28,514	-	28,514	28,514
Worcester - -	84,355	1	84,354	84,354
Hampden - -	31,639	-	31,639	31,639
Franklin - -	29,501	-	29,501	29,501
Dukes - -	3,517	-	3,517	3,517
Berkshire - -	37,835	-	37,835	37,835
Essex - -	82,859	1	82,858	82,858
Total Massachusetts -	610,408	4	610,404	610,406

Total population of Massachusetts - - - -			610,408
Of which are—			
Free.—White males - - -	294,685		
White females - - -	308,674		
Total whites - - -		603,359	
Colored males - - -	3,360		
Colored females - - -	3,685		
Total free colored - - -		7,045	
Total free - - - -		610,404	
Slaves.—Females - - - -		4	
			610,408

FIGURE 1. The initial 1830 census abstract for Massachusetts, with four slaves. United States House of Representatives, *Abstract of the Returns of the Fifth Census*, 22d Cong., 1st sess., Doc. 263, 1832, 5, courtesy United States Census Bureau.

5

MASSACHUSETTS.

NAMES OF COUNTIES.	Total population.	Slaves included in the foregoing.	Representative numbers.
Suffolk, { City of Boston, 61,392 / Residue of county,771 }	62,163	- -	62,163
Nantucket, - - -	7,202	- -	7,202
Plymouth, - -	43,044	- -	43,044
Hampshire, - - -	30,254	- -	30,254
Bristol, - - -	49,592	- -	49,592
Middlesex, - - -	77,961	- -	77,961
Norfolk, - -	41,972	- -	41,972
Barnstable, - - -	28,514	- -	28,514
Worcester, - -	84,355	- -	84,355
Hampden, - - -	31,639	- -	31,639
Franklin, - -	29,501	- -	29,501
Dukes, - - -	3,517	- -	3,517
Berkshire, - -	37,835	- -	37,835
Essex, - - -	82,859	1	82,859
Total aggregate of Massachusetts, - - -	610,408	1	
Representative number for the State, ...	....	....	610,408
The representative ratio, 47,700, multiplied by 12, the number of representatives, gives.....	....	....	572,400
This, deducted from the whole representative number of the State, leaves the residual fraction........................	....	....	38,008

FIGURE 2. The corrected 1830 census abstract for Massachusetts, with one slave in Essex County. United States Department of State, *Abstract of the Fifth Census of the United States, 1830*. Washington, D.C.: F.P. Blair, 1832, 5, courtesy Google Books.

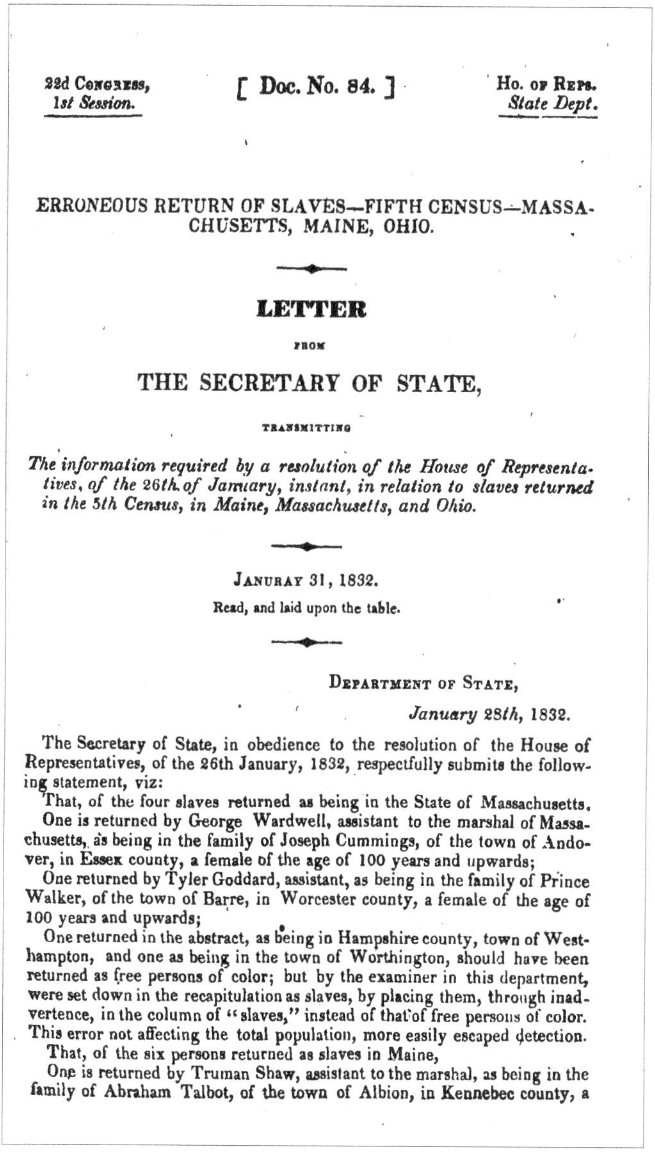

22d CONGRESS, 1st Session. [Doc. No. 84.] Ho. of Reps. State Dept.

ERRONEOUS RETURN OF SLAVES—FIFTH CENSUS—MASSACHUSETTS, MAINE, OHIO.

LETTER

FROM

THE SECRETARY OF STATE,

TRANSMITTING

The information required by a resolution of the House of Representatives, of the 26th of January, instant, in relation to slaves returned in the 5th Census, in Maine, Massachusetts, and Ohio.

JANURAY 31, 1832.

Read, and laid upon the table.

DEPARTMENT OF STATE,
January 28th, 1832.

The Secretary of State, in obedience to the resolution of the House of Representatives, of the 26th January, 1832, respectfully submits the following statement, viz:

That, of the four slaves returned as being in the State of Massachusetts,

One is returned by George Wardwell, assistant to the marshal of Massachusetts, as being in the family of Joseph Cummings, of the town of Andover, in Essex county, a female of the age of 100 years and upwards;

One returned by Tyler Goddard, assistant, as being in the family of Prince Walker, of the town of Barre, in Worcester county, a female of the age of 100 years and upwards;

One returned in the abstract, as being in Hampshire county, town of Westhampton, and one as being in the town of Worthington, should have been returned as free persons of color; but by the examiner in this department, were set down in the recapitulation as slaves, by placing them, through inadvertence, in the column of "slaves," instead of that of free persons of color. This error not affecting the total population, more easily escaped detection.

That, of the six persons returned as slaves in Maine,

One is returned by Truman Shaw, assistant to the marshal, as being in the family of Abraham Talbot, of the town of Albion, in Kennebec county, a

FIGURE 3. Portion of United States Secretary of State Livingston's report to the House regarding his initial findings about the four slaves counted in Massachusetts. Joseph Cummings was superintendent of the Andover almshouse. The secretary erred when he asserted that a slave resided in Prince Walker's household in Barre. Edward Livingston, "Erroneous Return of Slaves–Fifth Census–Massachusetts, Maine, Ohio," January 28, 1832. United States House of Representatives, 22nd Cong., 1st sess., Doc. 84, January 31, 1832, 1, courtesy Library of Congress.

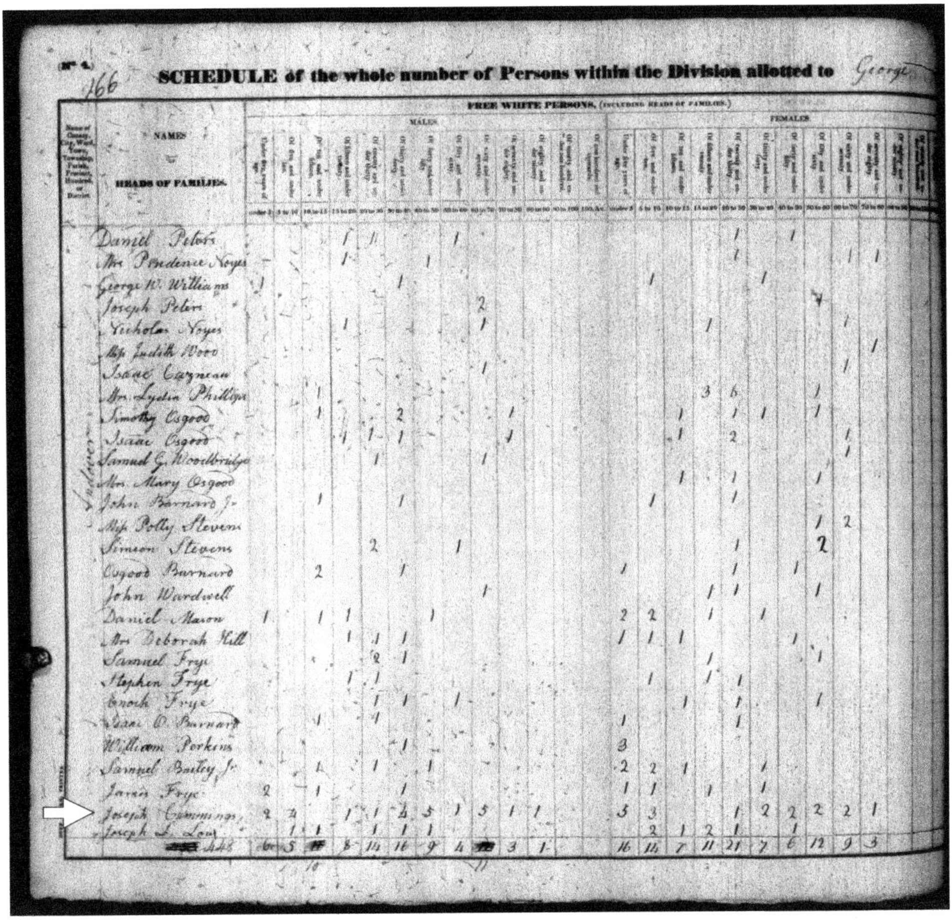

No. 4. 166 SCHEDULE of the whole number of Persons within the Division allotted to George

NAMES OF HEADS OF FAMILIES.

FREE WHITE PERSONS, (INCLUDING HEADS OF FAMILIES.)

MALES

FEMALES

Daniel Peters
Mrs Prudence Noyes
George W. Williams
Joseph Peters
Nicholas Noyes
Miss Judith Wood
Isaac Cazneau
Mrs Lydia Phillips
Timothy Osgood
Isaac Osgood
Samuel G. Woodbridge
Mrs Mary Osgood
John Barnard Jr.
Miss Polly Stevens
Simeon Stevens
Osgood Barnard
John Wardwell
Daniel Mason
Mrs Deborah Hill
Samuel Frye
Stephen Frye
Enoch Frye
Isaac O. Barnard
William Perkins
Samuel Bailey Jr.
James Frye
Joseph Cummings
Joseph L. Long

FIGURE 4A. The left side of the double-page schedule showing the population schedule for "Free White Persons" at the Andover almshouse, listed under Joseph Cummings, superintendent (arrow). United States Census, *Population Schedules of the Fifth Census of the United States 1830, Roll 61, Massachusetts*, Vol. 3, Essex County. National Archives and Records Service, Microcopy No. 19, Roll 61, 166, courtesy Internet Archive.

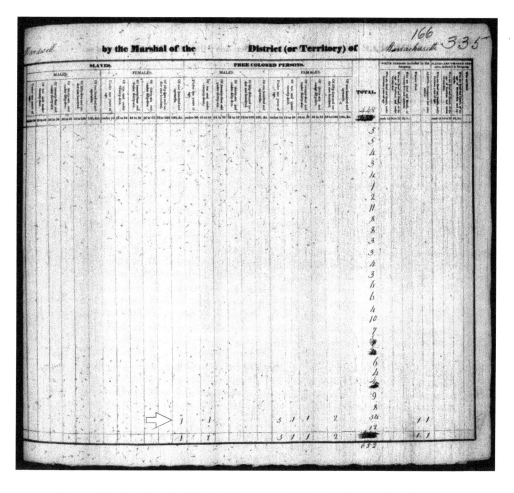

FIGURE 4B. The right side of the double-page population schedule for "Slaves" and "Free Colored Persons" showing the one female slave (arrow) whose age was "of one hundred and upwards" among the 54 total residents at the Andover almshouse. United States Census, *Population Schedules of the Fifth Census of the United States 1830, Roll 61, Massachusetts*, Vol. 3, Essex County. National Archives and Records Service, Microcopy No. 19, Roll 61, 166, courtesy Internet Archive.

Figures

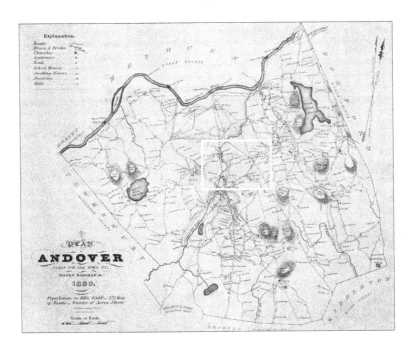

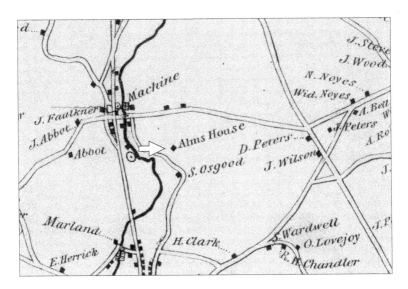

FIGURE 5. The Andover almshouse shown on Moses Dorman, Jr., "A Plan of Andover Taken for the Town," 1830, courtesy Harvard Map Collection, Harvard Library.

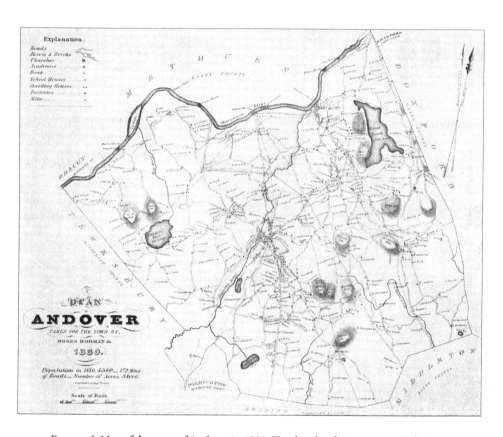

FIGURE 6. Map of the town of Andover in 1830. The then-bordering towns, clockwise from the top left, were Dracut, Methuen, Boxford, Middleton, Reading, Wilmington, and Tewksbury. The city of Lawrence was formed in 1847 from parts of Andover and Methuen; North Reading was created in 1853; and, North Andover was set off in 1855. Moses Dorman, Jr., "A Plan of Andover Taken for the Town," 1830, courtesy Harvard Map Collection, Harvard Library.

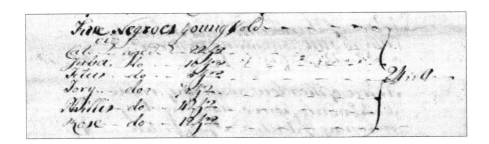

FIGURE 7. *Top*: The list of six "Negroes young & old" in the Sarah Frye estate inventory, May 1, 1781. *Bottom*: "To 6 Negroes appraised at £24—who have since taken their Freedom" in the estate distribution and accounting, September 7, 1790. Note that in the inventory, it appears that the word "Five" was first written, then the "ve" overwritten with an "x" to make the word resemble "Six". In the accounting, the numeral 6 was more heavily inked, possibly indicating it was changed from "5". Sarah Frye Probate file papers, Essex County, MA: Probate File Papers, 1638–1881, Case 10339, courtesy New England Historic Genealogical Society and Supreme Judicial Court Archives.

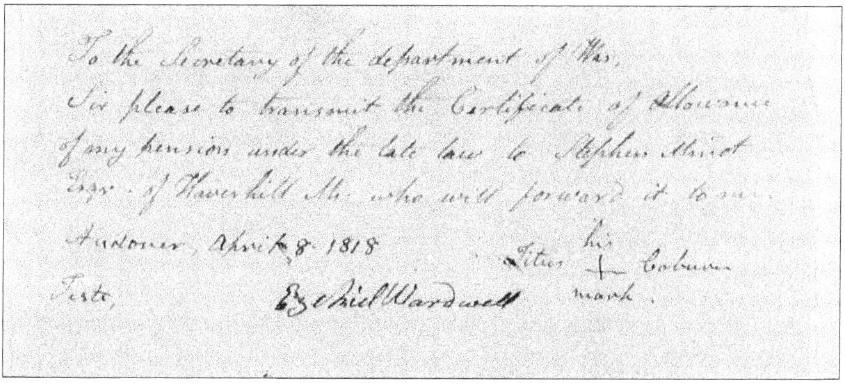

FIGURE 8. Titus Coburn's mark, April 8, 1818. Stephen Minot was a judge of the Essex County Circuit Court of Common Pleas for the Middle Circuit, Salem, Mass., who presided at Coburn's pension hearings on April 8, 1818 and on July 13, 1820. Titus Coburn did not adopt a consistent form for his mark: compare Figures 9–10. Titus and Rosanna Coburn Revolutionary War Pension Application File #W.6734, Revolutionary War Pension and Bounty-Land Application Files, Microfilm M804, Reel 589, courtesy National Archives and Records Administration.

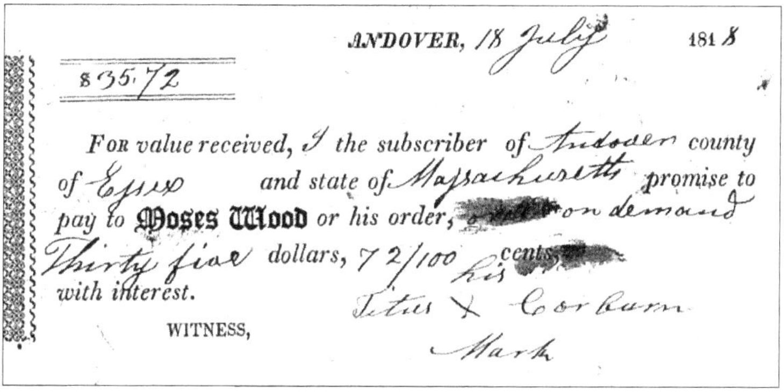

FIGURE 9. Titus Coburn's mark, July 18, 1818, on his promissory note to Moses Wood, a clerk at Shipman's store in Andover. Alpheus Gurney and Silvanus Packard v. Titus Coburn, Essex County Circuit Court of Common Pleas for the Middle Circuit, March 1819, file papers, courtesy Supreme Judicial Court Archives.

FIGURE 10. Titus Coburn's marks, Revolutionary War Pension Application File, July 13, 1820, Essex County Circuit Court of Common Pleas for the Middle Circuit, Salem, Mass. Collection of Essex County (Mass.) Court Records, EC 43, Box 2, Folder 5, details of digital images LIBMS0001448 (top), LIBMS0001447 (middle), and LIBMS0001450 (bottom), courtesy Phillips Library, Peabody Essex Museum, Salem, Mass.

FIGURE 11. Rosanna Coburn's mark, August 8, 1854. Likely copied by another hand, this mark lacks the distinctive shape of her other marks: compare Figures 12–16. Titus and Rosanna Coburn Revolutionary War Pension Application File #W.6734, Revolutionary War Pension and Bounty-Land Application Files, Microfilm M804, Reel 589, courtesy National Archives and Records Administration.

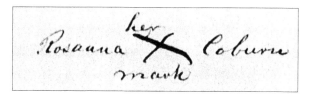

FIGURE 12. Rosanna Coburn's mark, August 8, 1854. Titus and Rosanna Coburn Revolutionary War Pension Application File #W.6734, Revolutionary War Pension and Bounty-Land Application Files, Microfilm M804, Reel 589, courtesy National Archives and Records Administration.

FIGURE 13. Rosanna Coburn's mark, August 8, 1854, from Titus Coburn Probate file papers, Essex County, MA: Probate File Papers, 1638–1881, Case 35592, courtesy New England Historic Genealogical Society and Supreme Judicial Court Archives.

FIGURE 14. Rose Coburn's mark on her will, December 23, 1854. Rose Coburn, Probate file papers, Essex County, MA: Probate File Papers, 1638–1881, Case 35590, courtesy New England Historic Genealogical Society and Supreme Judicial Court Archives.

FIGURE 15. Rosanna Coburn's mark, April 17, 1855. Titus and Rosanna Coburn Revolutionary War Pension Application File #W.6734, Revolutionary War Pension and Bounty-Land Application Files, Microfilm M804, Reel 589, courtesy National Archives and Records Administration.

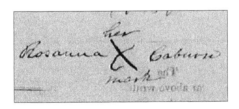

FIGURE 16. Rosanna Coburn's mark, April 17, 1855. Titus and Rosanna Coburn Revolutionary War Pension Application File #W.6734, Revolutionary War Pension and Bounty-Land Application Files, Microfilm M804, Reel 589, courtesy National Archives and Records Administration.

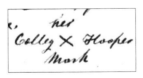

FIGURE 17. Colley Hooper's mark, August 8, 1854. Titus and Rosanna Coburn Revolutionary War Pension Application File #W.6734, Revolutionary War Pension and Bounty-Land Application Files, Microfilm M804, Reel 589, courtesy National Archives and Records Administration.

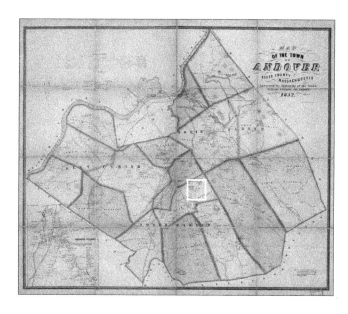

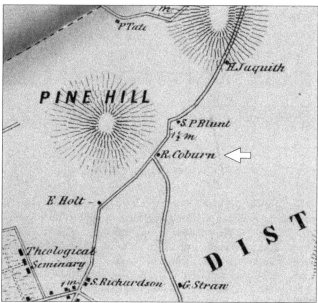

FIGURE 18. Rosanna Coburn and Colley Hooper's house in 1852 was located at the northeast corner of the intersection of present-day Highland Road and Woodland Road (the latter, running southerly from R. Coburn to "G. Stran", i.e. Straw, was then called Missionary Lane). Henry F. Walling, "Map of the Town of Andover Essex County Massachusetts," 1852, courtesy Harvard Map Collection, Harvard Library.

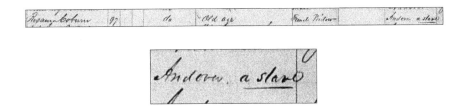

FIGURE 19. Rosanna Coburn's official state death record, written and submitted to
the state by the Andover town clerk. In the upper image, the column headers in which
writing appears are, respectively, name of deceased ("Rosanna Coburn"), age (97), place
of death (ditto, Andover), cause of death ("Old age"), "sex and condition" ("Female
Widow"), and place of birth ("Andover. a slave"). The abbreviation "do" means "ditto"
of what was written above in that column. The entry date and entry number are to the
left of the name, not shown in the image. The lower image is a more enlarged detail of
Andover town clerk Edward Taylor's nonconforming, additional notation ("a slave")
in the official state record. Rosanna Coburn death record, State Vital Records, Deaths
Register, Deaths 1859, vol. 129, 109, No. 16, March 19, 1859, Massachusetts Archives,
Genealogical Society of Salt Lake City, Ut., Microfilm Reel 960175, digital image 123
of 810, courtesy FamilySearch.

FIGURE 20. Rosanna Coburn's official town death record. Note the spelling "Rosana".
In the upper image, the column headers in which writing appears are, respectively,
name of deceased, age (97), place of death (ditto, Andover), "sex and condition"
("Female Widow"), place of birth (ditto, Andover "a slave"), cause of death ("old age"),
place of interment (ditto, Andover), informant or undertaker (ditto, "Henry Abbitt
2ᵈ" [i.e., Abbott]), and when registered (ditto, January 1860). The entry date and entry
number are to the left of the name, not shown in the image. The middle image is a
closer view of part of the entry. The lower image is an enlarged detail of Andover town
clerk Edward Taylor's nonconforming, additional notation ("a slave") in the column
for birthplace. The abbreviation "do" means "ditto" of what was written above in that
column. Rosanna Coburn death record, Town of Andover, Death Register 1855–1896,
9, No. 14, March 19, 1859, Town Clerk's Office, Andover, Mass., Genealogical Society
of Salt Lake City, Ut., Microfilm Reel 2358493, digital image 11 of 147, courtesy
FamilySearch.

44   *HISTORICAL SKETCHES OF ANDOVER.*

Here lies buried the body of
ROSE COBURN
Who died Mar. 19 1859 aet 92 years

She was born a slave in Andover and was the last survivor of all born here in that condition.

A pension was paid to her as the widow of a soldier of the Revolution.

She was a person of great honesty, veracity and intelligence and retained all her faculties in a singular degree to the last.

Also her daughter Colley Hooper died aged 58, who died first, neither of them leaving any descendants.

FIGURE 21. *Top*: Rose Coburn's epitaph quoted by Sarah Loring Bailey in *Historical Sketches of Andover* (1880), 44, courtesy Google Books. Bailey's transcription of "veracity" was an error for "vivacity" and there are other minor differences with the 1975 drawing (bottom) and with Coburn's 2002 replacement gravestone (next figures). *Bottom*: Jim Batchelder's 1975 drawing of Rose Coburn and Pomp Lovejoy's gravestones. The epitaphs were from transcriptions of his gravestone rubbings of the two stones. At the time the Rose Coburn gravestone rubbing was made, several words had eroded to be unreadable and the remainder of the original epitaph was buried. The drawing, provided courtesy of Jim Batchelder, was originally published in Eleanor Campbell's *West of the Shawsheen* (1975), 25.

Figure‌ 22. Rose Coburn and Colley Hooper's gravestones placed in 2002, South
Parish Cemetery, Andover. Rose Coburn's original gravestone was moved behind the
replacement stone; its back edge is barely visible in this photo to the left of Rose's new
stone. Both stones have "RPL 02" as the last line (obscured by vegetation in this photo),
indicating they are 2002 replacement stones. Previously Colley did not have a grave
marker: her grave location was indicated only by wording on her mother's original
gravestone. Cropped from photo by John Glassford © 2011, courtesy Find A Grave.

FIGURE 23. *Top*: Rose Coburn's original gravestone before restoration showing that most of the epitaph had eroded, South Parish Cemetery, Andover, cropped from photo provided by Charlotte Lyons, courtesy South Church. *Bottom*: Rose Coburn's gravestone placed in 2002. The last line at the bottom right partly obscured by vegetation is "RPL 02" indicating it is a 2002 replacement stone. Bottom photo by John Glassford © 2011, courtesy Find A Grave.

Notes

Abbreviations in Notes

ACHC	Andover Center for History & Culture (formerly the Andover Historical Society), Andover, Massachusetts
AHS	Andover Historical Society (since May 2018 known as the Andover Center for History & Culture), Andover, Massachusetts
DRCM	Daughters of the Revolution of the Commonwealth of Massachusetts
GSU	Genealogical Society of Salt Lake City, Utah
JA	Supreme Judicial Court Archives, Massachusetts Archives, Boston
MAC	Massachusetts Archives Collection (i.e., Felt Collection), M-Ar
M-Ar	Massachusetts Archives Division, Office of the Secretary of the Commonwealth, Boston
NAHS	North Andover Historical Society, North Andover, Massachusetts
RCEC	"Report of the Commissioners appointed under the Resolve of April 16th, 1846, to Examine the Claims presented to the Legislature of that Year for the Support of State Paupers" (by Massachusetts House of Representatives, published 1847)
RWPA	Revolutionary War Pension Application File
SFC	Suffolk Files Collection, JA
VRA	*Vital Records of Andover Massachusetts to the End of the Year 1849* (published 1912)

Editorial Conventions and Notes about Sources

[1] Brown, "Death-Defying Testimony," 131. Leonard, "The Instability and Invention of Racial Categories in the *Haverhill Gazette*"; Leonard, *Political Poetry as Discourse*. Results that paralleled Angela Michele Leonard's analysis of the *Haverhill Gazette* (1824–1827) were reported from Rhoesmary R.

Williams' linguistic study of the *Connecticut Courant* (1764–1827, later known as the *Hartford Courant*) a newspaper that also had a Massachusetts readership, Albakry and Williams, "Whitewashing Slavery in New England"; Williams, "Demonizing, Dehumanizing, and Whitewashing: Linguistic Examination of *The Connecticut Courant's* Coverage of Slavery."

[2] Konig, "Legal Fictions and the Rule(s) of Law," 107.

[3] Sanborn, *Middlesex County, Massachusetts Deponents*.

Chapter 1 Introduction

[1] Carter, et al., *Historical Statistics of the United States*, Vol. 2, 2-76 (Table Ba322), 2-375 (Table Bb7). United States Census, *Population Schedules of the Fifth Census of the United States 1830, Roll 61*, Essex County, 166. United States Congress, *Statutes at Large*, 22nd Cong., 1st sess., Res. 5, July 3, 1832, 606. United States Department of State, *Fifth Census; or, Enumeration of the Inhabitants of the United States, as Corrected at the Department of State*: the uncorrected data for Massachusetts indicating four slaves appear on pages 16–23. The errata sheet at pages 164–165 detailed the erroneous counts of slaves in Worcester County and in Hampshire County. As indicated at pages 21 and 165, the correct count for Massachusetts was one female slave in Andover, Essex County.

[2] Sarah Frye, Probate file papers, accounting and distribution, September 7, 1790.

[3] Similar notations were made by the town clerk in the official vital records for Cato Freeman (1858, parents were "Slaves"), Rosanna Coburn (1859, place of birth "a slave"), and Martha Matilda Henderson (1864, her and her father's place of birth "In slavery"), Death records, Town of Andover and State Vital Records; and for Robert Rollings and Julia C. Palmer (1863, both born "in slavery"), Marriage record.

[4] Bailey, *Historical Sketches of Andover*, 44.

[5] The research files of the Andover Center for History & Culture (hereafter ACHC, previous to May 2018 known as the Andover Historical Society [hereafter AHS], in the ACHC subject file for "African Americans") has an astounding sheaf of correspondence from 1948, about a research effort that endeavored to identify the Andover woman counted as a slave in the 1830 census. The letters were generated by the highly enthusiastic Texas historical documentary compiler Samuel E. Asbury (1872–1962), at the time a retired chemist. Collections of Asbury's vast assemblages of papers are preserved at several archival and research repositories. He styled himself "only a re-

search hunter, not a writer" (letter to AHS, July 9, 1948, 1), although he would later publish several narrative and musical works. During one of his applied research projects (on "the statistical and economic factors of County Reconstructions in the 16 ex-slave states, 1207 counties" [letter, May 25, 1948, 2]; "the great body of my work is statistical drudgery" [letter, July 21, 1948, 2]), he noticed among the national statistics the four slaves counted in the initial return for Massachusetts, and the corrected census figure of the one woman that had been counted as a slave in Andover. He commenced fervent inquiries about that matter to the United States Census Bureau, the Massachusetts Historical Society, the American Antiquarian Society, the clerk of the Massachusetts Supreme Judicial Court, Harvard College Library, the Essex Institute, and finally to the AHS, to which he sent typewritten copies of several of the replies he received. Asbury's handwritten letters to the AHS are ardent and marvelously lively. To convey a flavor: "This one lone slave mystery is like a brilliant spark from a blacksmiths hammering a large hot metal in his anvil" [letter, July 21, 1948, 2]. "The newspaper boys are always after me; and the editors don't like my non-publicity, non-writing ways. And they are half-right. Still, I must be just what I am. One can only live the way one was born to live" [letter, July 9, 1948, 3].

Asbury's July 9th letter to AHS conveyed that the Essex Institute (the letter from them is not included in the ACHC file, and the institutional records of the Essex Institute, stored at Phillips Library, Peabody Essex Museum, Rowley, Mass., had not been processed and were closed to researchers at the time I inquired) had referred him to L. Vernon Briggs' chapter, "White, Indian and Negro Slaves of Our Ancestors and Other Early Settlers, 1632–1830," in Briggs' *History and Genealogy of the Briggs Family*, 136. What Asbury spotted in that chapter, was the statement of "the compilers" quoted by Briggs (with very slight alteration) from the anonymous article, "Census of the Colored Population of the U.S.," *The Abolitionist*, January 1833, 10: "it is admitted on all hands that slavery cannot legally exist [...], we have thought it would be a misrepresentation to report any slaves as existing". Briggs had not identified that source, and Asbury was keen to locate it. Asbury (July 9, 1948, 3, italics mine) wrote that the statement by "the compilers" quoted by Briggs, "settles the mystery of the one lone slave of Massachusetts. *There wasn't one*." With penetrating perception, Asbury surmised in his May 25th letter that the only reason that the indigent woman was characterized as a slave was to substantiate that the town was not responsible for her economic support:

> [T]he existence of this old slave in Andover in 1830, was creditable
> to her mother or mistress, and local public opinion in Andover, they

were all opposed to slavery in 1830. But this Andover slave was already old (60 +) in 1790. Had she been given freedom at her age, she would have immediately become a charge on the community for the 40 + years of her life to follow. So I judge the Andover community ignored the judge made law in this instance. Had there [been] issue[d] a legislation law, they could not have ignored it. Moore [in *Notes on the History of Slavery in Massachusetts*, 242] makes the point that slavery was not abolished [by state statute in Massachusetts] until the [13th United States Constitution] Reconstruction Amendment was adopted.

Samuel Asbury conveyed his "reasonable [...] hope that local research may identify this Andover 'slave.' I shall be very glad to have any records of her life now extant" (May 25, 1948, 1–2).

[6] A mature free person (16 years or older), whether or not the head of household, provided the information about the household residents to the census enumerator. United States Department of State, *Fifth Census; or, Enumeration of the Inhabitants of the United States, as Returned by the Several Marshals*, v.

[7] Massachusetts House of Representatives, "Report of the Commissioners appointed under the Resolve of April 16th, 1846, to Examine the Claims presented to the Legislature of that Year for the Support of State Paupers" (hereafter, RCEC), 3, 5, 13, 14, 16–17. The report was dated February 1, 1847. It summarized their 1846 investigation of claims submitted during the fiscal year of 1845.

[8] Anonymous, "Sketches of Octogenarians" (about Rose Coburn's family); Anonymous, "Obituary" for Rosanna Coburn. The 1859 obituary included text slightly changed from the 1853 "Sketches" interview which conveyed, through a reporter, biographical and genealogical information that Rosanna provided.

[9] Minardi, *Making Slavery History*, 15.

[10] Rosanna Coburn (1859), Cato Freeman (1858), and Martha Matilda Henderson (1864), Death records, Town of Andover and State Vital Records; Robert Rollings and Julia C. Palmer (1863), Marriage record.

[11] Anonymous, "A Wind Fall," *Andover Advertiser* (Andover, Mass.), September 30, 1854, n.p. [2]; Anonymous, "Rose Coburn," *The Liberator* (Boston, Mass.), October 13, 1854, 163; Anonymous, "Gleanings of News," Rose Coburn note, *Frederick Douglass' Paper* (Rochester, N.Y.), October 20, 1854, n.p. [3]; Anonymous, Rose Coburn note, *The Anti-Slavery Bugle* (Salem, Ohio), November 4, 1854, n.p. [2].

[12] Anonymous, "The Black Patriot of Bunker Hill," *The Liberator* (Boston, Mass.), June 19, 1857, 100; Anonymous, "The Taney Hunt Against Colored Americans," *The Liberator* (Boston, Mass.), August 28, 1857, 139. Both sources must have relied on William C. Nell's *The Colored Patriots*, 21, which confused the Titus Coburn (1740 or 1756–1821) of Wilmington and later Andover who was granted a pension, with another man named Titus Coburn (1742?–1778), originally from New Hampshire, then Shirley, Harvard, and Littleton, Mass., who was a Minuteman on April 19, 1775, fought at Bunker Hill, and died at Valley Forge.

[13] Theodore Parker, Letter to George Bancroft, March 16, 1858, 235. The information that Bancroft was seeking about "Africans at the Battle of Bunker Hill," which Parker related to Bancroft, had been conveyed to Parker from his conversations with William C. Nell, author of *The Colored Patriots*. In his letter, Parker suggested that when Bancroft published his volume that included the information, "I wish you would send Nell a copy. Negroes get few honors." While Bancroft did not include all the particular and detailed information provided by Parker from Nell, which Parker anticipated in his letter that mentioned the forthcoming seventh volume of Bancroft's ten-volume *History of the United States*, Bancroft's seventh volume (which was the first volume of the part about "The American Revolution"), 421, does include an appreciative recognition of the "gallant band" of "free negroes" at the Battle of Bunker Hill who "took their place not in a separate corps, but in the ranks with the white man, and their names may be read on the pension rolls of the country, side by side with those of other soldiers of the revolution." For Nell's book interpreted alongside other antislavery and social reform projects, and about Revolutionary War pensions generally, see Jecmen, "Writing the Revolution," which at 180 referred to Titus Coburn's pension mentioned by Nell. Other historians have also considered Parker's March 16, 1858 letter and the Nell-Parker-Bancroft relations, e.g., Teed, "A Brave Man's Child.'"

[14] Anonymous, "Obituary" for Rosanna Coburn included text slightly changed from an earlier article, Anonymous, "Sketches of Octogenarians" (about Rose Coburn's family). Those sources reported that Booso first used the name Jubea. Abbott rendered Booso's earlier name as Jubah in "Historical Andover. No. 106. Africa to Andover" and "Historical Andover. No. 107. Africa to Andover.—(Concluded)."

[15] Knoblock, *African American Historic Burial Grounds*, 209, mentioned that Rose Coburn's original gravestone was replaced in 2002. Historical interest in Rosanna Coburn and Pompey Lovejoy, and the worn condition of her gravestone, was the impetus that commenced the ongoing historic cemetery survey, documentation, and preservation project at the South Parish Ceme-

tery, Piro, "Historic Undertaking: Repairing Stones is a Grave Undertaking";
Charlotte Lyons, email, August 7, 2017. Rose Coburn's gravestone—the first
of several stones that have been repaired or replaced during the preservation
project—was replaced in 2002 because it was severely eroded from the effects
of acid rain and the epitaph was unreadable. Colley Hooper (who predeceased her mother) did not originally have a separate gravestone. Rose's original gravestone epitaph indicated that she and her daughter were interred at
the same location ("Also her daughter Colley Hooper"). In 2002, a separate
grave marker was made for Hooper that stated she was the daughter of Titus
Coburn (she was in fact his stepdaughter, and his name did not appear in
Rose's original epitaph). The new marker for Colley also served to memorialize "Titus Coburn Buried Elsewhere". The 2002 gravestones for Rose Coburn, and for Colley and Titus, durably commemorate them and enhance interpretation of their local historical importance. The gravestone replacement
project was not intended to identically replicate Rose's single, eroded marble
grave marker, which would have been neither effective nor practical to meet
the project goals. Rose's original marble stone was retained and attached to
the back of her 2002 granite marker. The wording chosen for the 2002 markers for Rose and for Colley and Titus was conscientiously composed to commemorate, highlight, and interpretively expand their biographies.

The epitaph on the 2002 gravestone for Rose Coburn varies from that
which I quoted from Bailey, *Historical Sketches of Andover*, 44 (published
1880). An earlier, variant transcription of the original gravestone epitaph was
made circa 1863 to 1864 by Alfred Poore, "Andover Graveyards Old South
Andover Graveyards," n.p. [6] in "Cemetery Records of Andover, Mass.,"
n.d., MSS 0.424, Phillips Library, Peabody Essex Museum, Rowley, Mass.
(Poore added the "e" to his surname circa 1883, Perley, "Alfred Poore," 51.
For the reader's ease, in endnotes his surname is rendered "Poore." In the references cited, his works are listed serially under "Poor(e)" then "Poore.")

The version of the epitaph that appears on Rose Coburn's 2002 gravestone relied chiefly on a 1975 drawing of the original gravestone by Jim
Batchelder, published in Campbell, *West of the Shawsheen*, 25. The additional
information added to the epitaph in 2002 was from Campbell, ibid., 24, who
cited Bailey, ibid. Batchelder's drawing was based on a gravestone rubbing he
made of Coburn's and Pompey Lovejoy's stones for an educational program
at Camp Onway in Raymond, N.H. At the time the rubbing was made, several words had eroded ("in a singular" was no longer readable). The last two
lines about Colley's co-burial, that she predeceased her mother, and their lack
of descendants, did not appear in Batchelder's drawing because that portion
of the gravestone was below ground surface at the time he made the rubbing.
The campers transcribed the epitaph from the gravestone rubbing as a group

effort, and it was that transcription that was used for the wording shown in the 1975 drawing, Jim Batchelder, email, August 10 and 11, 2017.

As with the current stone, Batchelder's drawing does not include the word "veracity" that was in Bailey, ibid., 44, in the phrase *honesty,* veracity *and intelligence*. Poore read the word as "vivacity", which is more sensible and irredundant than Bailey's "veracity". The signification of "vivacity" was accordant with her buoyant character described in her obituary, and "vivacity" was the word transcribed by a *Boston Globe* reporter in 1896, Anonymous, "Andover's 250th Birthday," *The Boston Sunday Globe*, May 17, 1896, 40. The phrase is "honesty and intelligence" in Batchelder's 1975 drawing. Poore, ibid., and Batchelder's drawing spell "pention" (pension) identically.

Poore, Bailey, and the anonymous *Boston Globe* reporter all rendered the important characterization of Rose as *the last survivor of all born* here in *that condition* (i.e., the last slave born in Andover). Batchelder drew it as *born* with in *that condition* while the 2002 stone combined it as within, which conveys a slightly different sense. Indeed, the subtle shift from the specifically qualified, original characterization of Rose as the last slave *born* in Andover, to Rose as the last slave (to have *lived*) in Andover—which she was not—is seen and heard in present-day mentions of her. In one instance, the elision of Rose as the "last slave" was taken literally. An anonymous column, "Why Do They Call it That" in *The Andover Townsman*, September 3, 1942, 15, about the origin of the name of Pomp's Pond, explained that "Pompey was colored, and a slave—which needn't shock present-day residents, since slavery existed in Andover from the first quarter century after its founding [in 1646] until 1859, when Rose Coburn, Andover's last slave, died at the ripe old age of 92."

The last line on the original gravestone that referred to Rose and Colley—*neither of them leaving any descendants*—which bolstered the sense of finality of Rose as *the last survivor*, was not included in either Rose or Colley's replacement stones. Other minor and unimportant variations in the epitaph appeared among the transcriptions by Poore, Bailey, the *Boston Globe* reporter, Batchelder's 1975 drawing, and the 2002 stone—such as Poore's lack of commas in the phrase "honesty vivacity and intelligence" and his spelling of "surviver" that is unique among the transcriptions; and, the *Boston Globe* reporter's joined sentences about Rose's condition and the pension. Bailey, ibid., 43, through Campbell, ibid., 24, supplied the additional biographical details that appear on the 2002 stone after the epitaph: "Wife of Titus Coburn [/] Mother Phillis   Africa [/] Father Benjamin   W Indies [/] Servant of Joshua Frye". Charlotte Lyons, historian at the South Church in Andover, enthusiastically provided information, photographs of Rose Coburn's original and replacement gravestones, and facilitated my visit to the cemetery on

August 9, 2017. The long epitaph on the original gravestone is unreadable. Angela McBrien, ACHC Collections Manager, provided information and put me in contact with Jim Batchelder who conveyed the background and provided an image of his appealing drawing. Lyons joined me at Phillips Library on August 16, 2017 to read Poore's manuscript of Andover gravestone records.

The single name of Rosanna Coburn's father was spelled and rendered variously in documents: Booso, Boso, Booss, Booz, Boassee, Bussen, etc. The name has Dutch origins. Except in quotations, I used Booso, seemingly the fullest pronunciation of his name. "Benjamin" only appears in Anonymous, "Sketches of Octogenarians" (about Rose Coburn's family), n.p. [2] and Anonymous, "Obituary" for Rosanna Coburn, n.p. [2], which also asserted that Booso was called Booz Chickering. Bailey, ibid., 43, probably relied on the "Sketches" and "Obituary" as her source for the name Benjamin. Because the forms "Benjamin" and "Booz Chickering" do not appear in any other sources, while the town and court records and his one federal census entry referred to him by phonetically spelled variations of Booso, the other reported names may be examples of attempts to retrospectively regularize his unusual name. See O'Toole, *If Jane Should Want to be Sold*, 96–99, 131, for the practice of others later adding slave owner family surnames to names of servants or slaves who were actually only known by single names. They themselves may never have used or been known by that form.

Regarding the terms "servant" and "slave," see Benes, "Slavery in Boston Households," 15; Greene, *The Negro in Colonial New England*, 168, 218–223, 231–235; Matthews, "Hired Man and Help"; and, Warren, *New England Bound*, 32, 271 n50.

[16] Brown, "Memorial Narratives of African Women in Antebellum New England."

[17] Anonymous, "Obituary" for Rosanna Coburn, published April 2, 1859. Rose Coburn, Probate file papers, executor's accounting, June 11, 1861, Schedule B, cost of Rosanna Coburn's gravestone. Margot Minardi, in *Making Slavery History* and "Making Slavery Visible (Again)," 95–97, recognized idealization of Revolutionary War patriotism for "liberty" in nineteenth-century narratives that were linked with antislavery, abolitionism, and citizenship.

For antislavery and abolitionists, and the Civil War era in Andover, see Anonymous, "Auld Lang-Syne. Anti-slavery in Andover fifty years ago"; Anonymous, "Auld Lang-Syne. Anti-slavery Experiences in Andover" (both anonymous articles reprinting extracts from Bristol, *The Pioneer Preacher*, 40–55); Clements, "Abolitionism in Andover"; Goldsmith, *The Townswoman's*

Andover, 20–22; Greater Lawrence Underground Railroad Committee, *The Anti-Slavery Movement and the Underground Railroad in Andover & Greater Lawrence*; Grover, et al., "The Underground Railroad in Massachusetts 1783–1865"; Lima, "Bridging Town History"; Mofford, "The Underground Railroad Ran Through Andover"; National Park Service, *Poets, Shoemakers, and Freedom Seekers: Abolitionists and the Underground Railroad in Essex County*; Patrakis, *Andover in the Civil War*, 19–20; Schinto, "A Load of Hay," who researched and assessed the modern factoid that the Poor Family built wagons with hidden compartments to smuggle fugitive slaves, and traced it to a merely speculative suggestion by Juliet Haines Mofford in a paper that Mofford read to the AHS in 1999; and, Siebert, "The Underground Railroad in Massachusetts." Bessie Goldsmith, ibid., 15, summarized that in June 1835, Phillips Academy students held an abolition meeting at Indian Ridge in Andover (now Indian Ridge Reservation, a conservation area). Antislavery societies in Andover, with (unverified) membership figures reported for two of the groups, were mentioned in the abolitionist newspaper, *The Liberator*. A note published August 15, 1835 said that there were "more than 300 members" of the town antislavery society, Scobey, et al., "A Statement of the Circumstances which Induced Fifty Students of Phillips' Academy, Andover, To ask a Dimission from that Institution," 2 n. The same newspaper announced the 1836 establishment of a "Female Anti-Slavery Society" in Andover with "more than two hundred" members; the 1840 formation of an antislavery society "in *North* Andover"; and, that "a Female Anti-Slavery Society [...was in 1840] about to be formed in North Andover," Emery and Abbott, "Andover Female A.S. Society," 138; "Anonymous, "Another Society in Andover," 43. (The North Parish of Andover, created in 1709, was sometimes called "North Andover" before it was incorporated as the town of North Andover in 1855. For one view on the roots of the division, see Abbot, *Our Company Increases Apace*.)

Abolitionist members of several churches in Andover, members of antislavery societies, established the Free Christian Church in Andover in 1846, after years of disaffection and attempts at conciliation, Andover Free Christian Church, *The History of Free Christian Church*. Claude M. Fuess, *Andover: Symbol of New England*, 285–286, 313–318, provided a breezy overview of the matters that led to the founding of the Free Christian Church. Fuess has more interesting information about the strong personalities and activists in historical Andover's antislavery and abolition movement, and the town's political leanings leading up to the Civil War period.

For postbellum retrospectives of the history of slavery, abolition, and the Civil War, see Anonymous, "Dedication at North Andover [of the Johnson High School and Stevens Hall]. Address by Dr. George B. Loring," an undated and otherwise unidentified newspaper article published May 1867, pasted into the unique copy of Abbot, *History of Andover from its Settlement to 1829*, with "69 extra pages with newspaper clippings" once owned by Jonathan Clement and William G. Brooks, Accession No. 1991.140, ACHC, brought to my attention by Angela McBrien. Loring's address was reported in Anonymous, "Dedication of the Johnson High School House and Stevens Hall," *Lawrence American and Andover Advertiser* (Lawrence, Mass.), May 24, 1867, n.p. [2], which indicated that Loring's speech was "published in full in the Boston Journal of Wednesday" (i.e., May 22, 1867). Bailey, *Historical Sketches of Andover*, 530, reported that the dedication ceremony was held May 21, 1867. State Representative Loring used the occasion to recount slavery and the Civil War and to advocate for "universal suffrage", by which phrase he meant the right of men of color to vote, "to set aside the qualification of color" to achieve "manhood suffrage". Albert Poor, "The Oration," 82–83, delivered at Andover's 250th anniversary celebration in May 1896, and elsewhere in that same publication, 117, 134, 150, 170, addressed national antislavery, abolition, and emancipation in context of the Civil War. While he harkened also to enslavement practiced by signers of the Declaration of Independence, he elided about the practice of generational slavery in Andover.

The history of historical Andover's attentions to antislavery, antidiscrimination, women's suffrage, and related political reform efforts are fascinating. The historical information is vast, and has not yet been the subject of a detailed and focused study. For additional historical data on antislavery and abolition in Andover and North Andover, see the Abolition Visualized website that features animated maps, http://abolitionvisualized.com/tableview/, accessed July 16, 2017. Further research into Andover's antislavery, abolitionist, and colonizationist efforts should consider the many results mentioning the town in digital databases, such as Gale (a Cengage company), *Slavery and Anti-Slavery: A Transnational Archive*, and HeinOnline, *Slavery in America and the World: History, Culture and Law*. The Boston Public Library's Anti-Slavery Collection includes manuscript letters concerning Andover, digital images of which letters are available on the Digital Commonwealth website. Andover was mentioned in several letters to and from William Lloyd Garrison. In the volume of his letters edited by Louis Ruchames, *The Letters of William Lloyd Garrison, Volume II*, 238, 245, 300, 302–305, 323, 410, 453, 516, 726, 737, and possibly other pages, Andover appeared on many more pages than indicated in the volume index, and may be mentioned in other volumes in that published series.

Andover people's involvement with women's suffrage and women's rights movements in the nineteenth century arose from debates and activism in antislavery, etc., and a study should delve deeper into the relationships and connections of the people and topics involved. There was a thoughtful and eventually encouraging 1854 letter written from Andover by Antoinette Louisa Brown Blackwell to Elizabeth Cady Stanton that reiterated Brown's caution about "fastening theological questions upon the <u>woman movement</u>. It is not that I am horrified at your calling St Pauls writings 'human parchments'; but because I think when it is done officially that it is really unjust to the cause. It is compelling it to endorse something which does not belong to it. When you write for yourself say exactly what you please, but if you write as Cha'n [Chair(wo)man] Woman's Rights Con[vention] do not compel us to endorse anything foreign to the movement". In September 1853, Brown became the first woman in the United States to be ordained by a Congregational church. She left that ministry in July 1854. Brown's December 28, 1854 letter to Stanton followed up on a now-missing letter that she had written to Stanton to which Brown had not received a reply. Brown mentioned in passing that Lucy Stone might visit Andover and stay over for New Year's Day, Gordon, *The Selected Papers of Elizabeth Cady Stanton and Susan B. Anthony, Volume I: In the School of Anti-Slavery*, 289–290. Carol Lasser and Marlene Deahl Merrill, *Friends and Sisters*, 35, 73, 75, 82, 95–96, 99–102, 115, and possibly other pages, included transcriptions of several letters from and to Andover between Brown Blackwell (married in 1856) and Lucy Stone and that book has many more mentions of Andover than indicated in the book index. Brown Blackwell and Stone's husbands were brothers. I have not fully ascertained the occasions, durations, and reasons for Brown Blackwell's presence in Andover. Her brother, William Bryant Brown (1816–1902), was the minister at the Free Christian Church 1850–1855, Andover Free Christian Church, *The History of Free Christian Church*, 65. She preached at the Free Church on December 31, 1854 about the challenge of self-rule of the spirit (Proverbs 16:32) when "Anger, temptation, indolence, are all working against us", as an interested member of the church conveyed it, Anonymous, Diary of a woman, Andover, Mass., 1852–1855, n.p. [19–20, counting from the first handwritten page], Octavo Item No. 15 in "Diaries (unidentified) Collection, 1760–1855," Octavo vols. "D" Almanacs Collection, American Antiquarian Society, Worcester, Mass. Ashley Cataldo at the society provided digital images of the diary; Jessy Wheeler in the Research Services Department of the Boston Public Library assisted my research.

[18] Anonymous, Note about resetting gravestones at the Andover South Parish Cemetery, 5.

[19] McCaskill, *Love, Liberation, and Escaping Slavery*, 12.

[20] Ibid., 91.

[21] Ibid., 12. In parallel manner, Lois Brown, "Memorial Narratives of African

Women in Antebellum New England," 57, reflected on the ordinary "inconsistencies and elisions" in "incomplete and elusive histories [...] plagued by unruly chronologies, unattributed facts, and incomplete profiles of the subjects." Similarly, Julia Laite, "The Emmet's Inch: Small History in a Digital Age," 10, 24 n52, quoted Giovanni Levi, "The Uses of Biography," 62, about constructing biography from "disorderly evidence for the words and deeds of daily life." Laite's article, ibid., 10, 12, included penetrating analysis of method, theory, and technique used to construct narratives of historical biography, conscious about conveying "interiority and voice" whenever possible. When lacking documents composed by an individual with "richness, detail, context, and agency"—Laite's "voicelessness"—historical biography might reductively transform lived experiences of historical persons to be mere "synecdoche", "exemplars [...,] or cyphers", "deployed as symbol".

DoVeanna S. Fulton in *Speaking Power*, and DoVeanna S. Fulton Minor and Reginald H. Pitts, "Introduction. Speaking Lives, Authoring Texts," considered published texts derived from oral narratives, and the interplay between speaker and amanuensis. In the latter work, the coeditors examined Lucy Susan Thompson's *The Story of Mattie J. Jackson* (1866) about Martha Jane Jackson Dyer (1847–1910) that was related by her stepmother Lucy Susan Prophet Schuyler Thompson. Thompson was a Massachusetts botanical medical doctor of Native and African descent and an antislavery activist living in Lawrence, Mass. As Lucy S. Schuyler, she was instrumental in bringing a habeas action for an enslaved woman traveling from Tennessee with her owners who were at the time staying in Lawrence. Betty's Case was heard by Chief Justice Lemuel Shaw at the Supreme Judicial Court in 1857. Betty was aware she could be freed by her presence in the state, but she desired to remain with her owners and to return to Tennessee to her husband and other relatives there. Shaw's in-chambers decision adjudged that Betty was free to do what she wished and that neither Schuyler nor any other person should interfere with Betty's "personal liberty" to decide what she wanted to do (Betty's Case, Supreme Judicial Court, November 9, 1857, Shaw, C.J., in chambers, 20 [new series 10] Monthly Law Reporter 455 [1858], at 458). For significant further details about Betty's Case and her later biography— she escaped enslavement through the Underground Railroad to Ohio where her husband then arrived to her—see Han, "Slavery as Contract" and sources cited, particularly Soifer, "Status, Contract, and Promises Unkept" and Wong, *Neither Fugitive Nor Free*.

Chapter 2 *Slaves in the 1830 Census Returns for Massachusetts*

[1] A preliminary abstract of the 1830 federal census noted four female slaves in Massachusetts, all 55 years old or older, two in Hampshire County, and one each in Worcester and Essex Counties. United States House of Representatives, *Abstract of the Returns of the Fifth Census*, 5, 51. Nicole Topich brought the 1830 census matter to my attention, and provided me the link to the digital version of the 1832 congressional document (http://www2.census.gov/prod2/decennial/documents/1830a-01.pdf, accessed December 3, 2014). Probably referring to these same individuals, Anonymous, Letter to Daniel O'Connor, 96, wrote, "In Massachusetts there are three or four superannuated slaves."

[2] Price, *Slavery in America*, 14 (quotation). Bowen, *The American Annual Register for the Year 1830–31*, 375–376. Buckingham, *America: Historical, Statistic, and Descriptive*, Vol. 3, 291: "These four slaves were the personal servants of individuals coming up from the south, and returning again from the slave State from which they originally came, as no slaves exist among the permanent residents of Massachusetts."

[3] Anonymous, "Census of the Colored Population of the U.S.," 10. In fact, the 1830 United States Census was the only federal enumeration that reported slaves in Massachusetts. The absence of any slave counted in the first United States Census of 1790 for Massachusetts was once relied upon, but is now doubted as reliable evidence that slavery had ended by then in the Commonwealth. Blanck, "Seventeen Eighty-Three," 30–31 n15; Blanck, *Tyrannicide*, 124, 126–127, 194 n40; Cover, *Justice Accused*, 38, 45; Higginbotham, *In the Matter of Color*, 99; Knoblock, *African American Historic Burial Grounds*, 9; Lemire, *Black Walden*, 111; MacEacheren, "Emancipation of Slavery in Massachusetts," 304 n3; Melish, *Disowning Slavery*, 76; Melish, "Northern Slavery and Its Legacies," 124; Menschel, "Abolition Without Deliverance," 183, 184 n3; Minardi, *Making Slavery History*, 18–19; Moore, *Notes on the History of Slavery in Massachusetts*, 247 n2; Parker, "Making Blacks Foreigners," 95–96; Romer, *Slavery in the Connecticut Valley of Massachusetts*, 214–216, 223–225; Spector, "The Quock Walker Cases," 25; Sweet, "'More than Tears,'" 147; Sweet, *Bodies Politic*, 248–249; Whiting, "Emancipation Without the Courts or Constitution," 4–5, 16–17 n19–n21.

In research writings in progress, I compiled information about the persistence of slavery or slave-like situations in Massachusetts places after the 1781 and 1783 judicial decisions on the "Mum Bett" and on the "Quock Walker" cases. The "Mum Bett" case was Brom and Bett v. John Ashley, Berkshire County Court of Common Pleas Records, August 1781, 55; Supreme Judicial Court Records, Berkshire County, October 1781, 96, both at Supreme Judicial Court Archives, Massachusetts Archives, Boston (hereafter JA). The "Quock Walker" cases were three (for a total of five court actions, as two of the cases were first brought in the Court of Common Pleas then both appealed to the Supreme Judicial Court and one case was heard in original jurisdiction at the high court): the first case was Quock Walker v. Nathaniel Jennison, Worcester County Court of Common Pleas Records, June 1781, 215; Supreme Judicial Court Records, Worcester County, September 1781, 79, 84; the second case was Nathaniel Jennison v. John Caldwell and Seth Caldwell, Worcester County Court of Common Pleas Records, June 1781, 203; Supreme Judicial Court Records, Worcester County, September 1781, 79; and, finally, the third case was Commonwealth v. Jennison, Supreme Judicial Court Records, Worcester County, April 1783, 85, all at JA.

Despite popular belief, in point of fact the "Mum Bett" and "Quock Walker" cases did not abolish chattel slavery in Massachusetts, neither instantly nor effectively. A. Leon Higginbotham, Jr., ibid., 90–91, quoted a 1781 taxation statute used until 1793 that "recognized that some nonwhites were still enslaved". Joanne Pope Melish, "Northern Slavery and Its Legacies," 124, indicated that "Massachusetts continued to tax slaves as property through 1785." A comprehensive study of preserved state tax records for slaves has not yet been undertaken statewide or for Essex County particularly, but both Joseph Carvalho, III, and John Wood Sweet discussed the implications of the "startling" 1784 tax valuation of 92 "blacks" on the 82-acre farm of Benjamin Swetland in Longmeadow, Mass., (then in Hampshire Co., now Hampden Co.) in the Connecticut River Valley. Evidently Swetland was speculating in slavery, and those people may have been sold "down-river," presumably in Connecticut, or in Long Island, New York, or shipped to far more distant places. Carvalho, "Uncovering the Stories of Black Families in Springfield and Hampden County, Massachusetts," 68–69 ("startling"), 92 n27; Sweet, "'More than Tears,'" 164 n59 ("down-river").

Among the many Massachusetts examples of persistence of enslavement and slave-like conditions, there are several from Essex County that have been noticed by researchers. In Andover, local tradition maintained that Cato Phillips (1768–1853, later Cato Freeman) remained with the Phillips family as their enslaved servant until 1789. To express that Cato's enslavement to 1789 was anomalous, nearly all sources mentioned (the mistaken idea) that slavery was suddenly and universally abolished in Massachusetts with the adoption of the state constitution in 1780, e.g., Anonymous ["C." and "Mrs. P.F.C."], Letter to the editor about Cato Freeman; Bailey, *Historical Sketches of Andover*, 42; Brooks ["B."], Letter to editor about Cato Freeman; Clements, "Cato Freeman"; Forsyth-Vail, "African Americans and the North Parish and

Church of North Andover"; French, "Parson Phillips's Slaves – Also, Pomp and Rose"; Gohn, "Andover Stories: Cato Freeman, slavery and prejudice in early Andover"; Greater Lawrence Underground Railroad Committee, *The Anti-Slavery Movement and the Underground Railroad in Andover & Greater Lawrence*, 1; Knoblock, ibid., 209; Liffmann, "From Our Archives"; Malloy and Malloy, "Slavery in Colonial Massachusetts as Seen Through Selected Gravestones," 119; Mofford, *The History of North Parish Church of North Andover*, 109; Pike, *The History of South Church in Andover*, 21.

Cato emancipated himself on May 24, 1789, two days after his 21st birthday, and was distinguished in Andover in leaving enslavement by letter. The addressee of Cato's letter was not indicated, but tradition holds that it was written to his then-owner, Hon. Samuel Phillips, Esq. (1752–1802). The original manuscript preserves his compositional work and shows careful attention to implement precise revisions to achieve his particular intentions. Cato's letter graciously thanked the family for his upbringing, but he pointedly wrote "I hope; you not only having the name but the Disposition of Christians and wishing to have your own impe[^]r[^]fections overlookt; will I trust Do the Same by me. […] I hope that [^]I[^]myself […] may be admitted [^]with you[^] into that haven of rest [i.e., heaven], where there is no Di[^]s[^]tinction." Brooks, ibid., indicated that his transcription of Cato Freeman's letter was made from the original manuscript, but the published version differs. Bailey, ibid., 42–43, also has a transcription of Cato's letter that varies from the manuscript, as do the numerous other published quotations of the letter. The original manuscript letter is in the collections of the North Andover Historical Society, North Andover, Mass. (hereafter NAHS), Liffmann, ibid. (an unattributed copy of that article is in ACHC research files, "African Americans," accompanied by an unidentified, undated, typed transcription of Cato Phillips' 1789 letter that also differs from the manuscript).

Within seven months after Cato wrote his letter of departure, he had a new surname that conveyed his emancipated status. Cato Freeman married Lydia Bristow (1765–1854) on December 24, 1789, *Vital Records of Andover* (hereafter, *VRA*), Vol. 2, 356, 357 ("Negroes"). Sarah Loring Bailey, ibid., 450, related an anecdote that may be about Cato Freeman and Lydia Bristow's wedding ceremony, performed by Rev. Symmes at the North Parish church. The humorous anecdote was captured by Bailey from local oral tradition. It has aspects that were tinged with the stereotypical thinking of the storyteller, who was not entirely certain that the bridegroom's name was Cato but thought that it was.

Cato Phillips/Freeman and his family members appeared in several entries in day books kept by Andover physicians Joseph Osgood (1719–1797) and his son George Osgood (1758–1823) who lived in the North Parish. When Cato was enslaved by Hon. Samuel Phillips, Esq., he had a serious facial injury that was treated over three months. Three entries include charges for treating and bandaging Cato's chin, medicine, and lastly removing a tooth, Osgood and Osgood, Day Books, n.p., Vol. 2, August 7, 1788, https://iiif.lib.harvard.edu/manifests/view/drs:424481342$29i, digital image seq. 29; Vol. 2, September 20, 1788, https://iiif.lib.harvard.edu/manifests/view/drs:424481342$37i, seq. 37; Vol. 2, November 13, 1788, https://iiif.lib.harvard.edu/manifests/view/drs:424481342$42i, seq. 42. Within seven months of taking his freedom, Cato Freeman labored for one of the doctors, hauling by sledge with draft animals ("By one days Sleding from hemlocks for me") in exchange for "1 Bushel Potatoes". The cash value of his labor was not recorded, Vol. 2, January 9, 1790, https://iiif.lib.harvard.edu/manifests/view/drs:424481342$93i, seq. 93. One of the doctors visited Cato's house for "Delivering his wife of a Daughter" and his wife Lydia was prescribed medicine, Vol. 2, December 6, 1790 (page headed November 30,1790),https://iiif.lib.harvard.edu/manifests/view/drs:424481342$147i, seq. 147. Their daughter Mahala was born December 5, 1790, *VRA*, Vol. 1, "Negroes", 390. Cato's son (perhaps James Honestus Freeman, ibid., born September 1, 1793) was visited for a surgical procedure: "opening an Abscess", Osgood and Osgood, Day Books, n.p., Vol. 3, October 14, 1795, https://iiif.lib.harvard.edu/manifests/view/drs:424481566$132i, seq. 132. Bristow/Brister ("Bristol") was charged 7s. 1p. for a doctor's visit and medicine while he was at Cato's (presumably his son-in-law and daughter's home), Vol. 3, April 18, 1795 (page headed April 15, 1795), https://iiif.lib.harvard.edu/manifests/view/drs:424481566$99i, seq. 99, accessed October 19, 2019.

Cato Freeman was a skilled musician, but historical sources variously described his instrument as either a bass viol or a violin. Perhaps he played both. His father Salem may have also played the violin, if by "fiddling" was meant the instrument and not distracted trifling, Abbott, "Historical Andover. No. 107. Africa to Andover.—(Concluded)," 3. Talented musicians, famous historically, were among the Lew family to whom Cato was related by marriage to Lydia Bristow, so the intermarried families had musicianship in common. Forsyth-Vail, ibid., 11–13, quoting from Mofford, ibid., 112–114, reprinted the anonymous and undated poem that described the collapse of the choir loft at the church while Cato was performing, an event that Mofford dated after 1798, ibid., 109. (The Phillips Library catalog identified the poem's author as George Francis Chever and suggested it was published in 1849.) As with several anecdotal narratives about people of color in Andover and Essex County generally, the poem obviously reflected its author's stereotypical attitudes. That poem arose out of local tradition that implausibly blamed the collapse of the interior church structure on the literal tone and tenor of Cato's playing.

Cato Phillips/Freeman's parents, Salem and Rama (Rema, Remy, Rhena), were enslaved by the Rev. Samuel Phillips (1689/90–1771) of South Church. They married on October 16, 1760, and the now well-known conditional vows written by Rev. Phillips, "A Form for a Negroe-Marriage," expressed Phillips' ideas that repeatedly reminded them of their roles and duties as slaves to him and Mrs. Phillips, Moore, "Slave Marriages in Massachusetts"; *VRA*, Vol. 2, 358 (marriages, Negroes). For more about the vows, see chap. 4, note 10. A visually arresting image of how Rev. Phillips proceeded weekly to South Church "in a slow and stately procession" was conveyed by Claude Fuess, *Andover: Symbol of New England*, 156, who drew that depiction, uncredited, from that one "remembered now [1856] by eye-witnesses" and written by the Andover Rev. John L. Taylor, *A Memoir of His Honor Samuel Phillips*, 9. Fuess related that Rev. Phillips walked "each Sunday morning from the parsonage to the meeting house, his Negro servant [Salem] on his left and his wife [Hannah], with her maid [Rama], on his right." Rev. Phillips publically displayed his slaves to convey genteel status and position characteristic of wealthy or prominent individuals who enslaved multiple people in their households. Perhaps Rev. Phillips used his own money to purchase and support Salem and Rama, but maybe there are entries in the South Parish financials or the vast Phillips Family papers that indicate otherwise.

Rev. Phillips' will, written May 25, 1763, devised as his property two enslaved persons. Salem and Rama's three sons, Cato, Cyrus, and Titus, were not yet born when the will was composed, and Titus was not yet born when the estate was administered in 1771. In the 1763 will, Rev. Phillips directed that his wife was to have her choice of which of his two slaves she would have. The other enslaved person was devised to his three sons, impossibly to be "Equally Divided" among them, requiring in practical terms sharing the slave, one purchasing the slave from the other two, or selling the slave and dividing the proceeds. However, the probate file papers of Rev. Phillips do not include an inventory or other administration records that mentioned distribution of his slaves. By 1771, the slaves belonging to Rev. Phillips' estate were four in number, including Cato born in 1768 and his brother Cyrus born in 1770. (The images of Phillips' will show it to be fragmented, its pieces were poorly arranged before it was scanned, and an image of a portion of the last page of the will appears later in the sequence, partly obscured by another paper. The probate court records—i.e., the copied texts of the file papers made by the clerk for the probate court's official records—should have a transcription of Rev. Phillips' will, and any other mentions of his slaves might be apparent.) Two bills to the estate of Rev. Phillips regard payment to Miss Rose Holt for schooling Cato in 1772, and cotton for Cato's shirts in 1773, William A. Trow Collection, Ms S 556, Sub-group IV, Phillips Family, Series A, Rev. Samuel Phillips, 1689/90–1771, Bills, ACHC; Joan Patrakis, email, August 6, 2019, provided the data on the two bills.

After Rev. Phillips' death, his slaves (with the exception of Cato) came to be with his successor, the Rev. Jonathan French (1740–1809), ordained at South Church in 1772. Cato was taken to North Andover, while his parents and two brothers Cyrus and Titus stayed at the South Church parsonage with the family of Rev. French. Local tradition believed that Cato Phillips remained with the Phillips family as their enslaved servant, and at one time worked for Benjamin Phillips Jr. The widow Hannah White Phillips died in 1773 when she was 81 years old, *VRA*, Vol. 2, 525. When Titus was born in 1774 his parents were indicated to be "Servants of Rev. Jona[than] French," *VRA*, Vol. 1, "Negroes," 391, brackets in original. The fates of Cato's two brothers are undetermined. Charlotte Helen Abbott, ibid., 3, asserted that Cyrus' name changed to "Caesar" and as with his brother Cato, adopted the surname Freeman. Anthony F. Martin, "On the Landscape for a Very, Very Long Time," 142, wondered if Abbott was mistaken that Cyrus and Caesar Freeman were the same man. She acknowledged that some of her information about Salem and Rama was from Rev. French's granddaughter "Mrs. Abbott".

The means by which Salem, Rama, and their sons Cyrus and Titus came to be in Rev. Jonathan French's household is uncertain. The remaining members of the enslaved family may have been gifted by the Phillips family to the French family. Rev. French may have had to support everyone on his minister's salary. They may not have been legally church property, but in another sense the practice of slavery was unmistakably associated with the church through Rev. Phillips and Rev. French's positions, and by the presence of an enslaved family at the parsonage. Salem and Rama and their children may have been considered to accompany the office and household of the ministry, as Abbott, ibid., 3, put it, "like Russian serfs, passed with the parsonage to the successor". When Rev. French was ordained, he got the slaves that went with the parsonage as part of his compensation and in recognition of his status and position. Obviously, as they did for Rev. Phillips' household, multiple servants evoked power, authority, and prestige, and relieved Rev. French, Mrs. French, and their children from decades of tasks and labor other people had to do themselves. Correspondence to the church from Phillips and French about their salaries and information about parish support of the ministry is in Mooar, *Historical Manual of the South Church*, 41–55. For all the discussion about their income and expenses, the cost of multiple servants the ministers supported was not mentioned in the information that Mooar published.

Long after Cato Phillips/Freeman departed the residence of Hon. Samuel Phillips, Esq., there were servants in that North Parish household, but their status as free persons or slaves and their laboring arrangements are undetermined. On February 6, 1792, "Scipio" was visited by a doctor and medicine was administered, Osgood and Osgood, Day Books, n.p., Vol. 2, https://iiif .lib.harvard.edu/manifests/view/drs:424481342$202i, digital image 202, accessed October 19, 2019. Hon. Samuel Phillips, Esq. was charged for one or more visits and medicine for "Phillis Negro Girle", Vol. 2, under the page headed January 21, 1793, but marginal notes date the entry to March 20, 1793 (either a date of visit or the date paid). Notably, the balance for that entry (12s. 5p., which included medicine for "Mis Sarah Abbot") was paid for with "2 quarts of W: I: [West Indies] Rum" and "1 Gallon of Molasses", https://iiif.lib.harvard.edu/manifests/view/drs:424481342$208i, seq. 208, accessed October 16, 2019.

Salem and his wife Rama remained at the South Church parsonage in a dependent and servile relationship with Rev. French's family. When Salem and Rama's abilities declined, Rev. French decided that the couple should move to a separate house. Rev. French's daughter Abigail wrote to her brother in 1794 or 1795 that "papa proposes building a small house for Salem and she [Rama] such as Mr. Nehermiah Abbot [i.e., Nehemiah (1731–1808 or 1756–1822)] has for Ceasar [1722–1807] he thinks they are gro[w]ing old & in case of sickness it would be clever", Anonymous, "Auld Lang-Syne. More Old Letters," 2; *VRA*, Vol. 2, Deaths, 367 (Abbot), 573 "Negroes," "Cesar, servant of Nehemiah Abbot," December 12, 1807, age 85. Abigail's intended meaning of "clever" would seem to be that putting them in separate housing was, in the sense of that word, convenient and agreeable (*Oxford English Dictionary*, s.v. "clever," sense A.III). Whether removing the elderly couple from the parsonage was more convenient and agreeable to the Reverend and his wife Abigail Richards French (1742–1821), or to his servants in debility, is difficult to parse. O'Toole, *If Jane Should Want to be Sold*, 129–133, wrote about servants passed down generations in families, with succeeding heirs taking more or less interest in the responsibilities as the servants became less serviceable and required care.

In her next letter to her brother Jonathan (undated, but either 1794 or 1795), Abigail French wrote that "papa has bought the schoolhouse on the plane it was taken down & brought here to-day Mr. Jacob Osgood & his neibours assisted in takeing it down & bringing it for nothing it is to be put over in the orchard and Remy is to move in as soon as it is done." An anonymous local history columnist explained that "the 'school house on the plane,' [i.e., plain] [...] was unquestionably an old school house in the Osgood district, and there may be some traditions about it still in the West Parish, or some remembrance of it as Remy's home 'over in the orchard'", Anonymous, "Auld Lang-Syne. More Old Letters," 2. The same author, in a follow-up article about the Osgood District schools, wrote that "The old school house, which was evidently too old to be longer used as such, was the building sold to Rev. Jonathan French, moved to the Parsonage orchard and fitted up for a home for 'Salem and Remy'", Anonymous, "Auld Lang-Syne. Old Times in Osgood District," 2. (For the replacement Osgood District school built in 1795, see also Andover Preservation Commission, et al., *Andover Historic Preservation* webpage for 149 Andover Street, https://preservation.mhl.org/149-andover-street, accessed August 13, 2019; and, Anonymous, "Auld Lang-Syne. More from the 'Old Red School-house,'" 2.) The structure that Rev. French provided was inadequate and had a leaking roof. Abbott, ibid., 3, recounted two local tales about Salem which have speech events attributed to Salem, one of which was about the leaking roof. Deeper beneath the stereotypical portrayal, Salem's protest of the condition of the housing is discernable, and it is plausible he intended word to spread. Abbott, ibid., 3, may have not meant it literally or assumed it was the case that Salem and Rama were "pensioned". Further research into the South Church, South Parish, and Andover treasurer/overseers of the poor financial records may determine whether or not Rev. French ever paid his servants any wages, whether or when during their lifetimes the former slaves were legally manumitted, and when they become the responsibility of the town and/or the state as paupers. Salem Phillips, as he became known, died at the almshouse in 1815 when he was 90 years old, *VRA*, Vol. 2, 525. A record of his wife's death has not been found.

Cato Freeman's death notice, Anonymous, "Deaths. Death of an Octogenarian," *Andover Advertiser*, August 20, 1853, n.p. [3], generated a letter to the editor written by William G. Brooks, published on August 27, 1853. In the newspaper the authorship was credited to "B.", but a clipping was hand-emended "W.G.B." and pasted into Brooks' own copy of Abbot's *History of Andover from its Settlement to 1829*, with "69 extra pages with newspaper clippings" once owned also by Jonathan Clement, Accession No. 1991.140, ACHC. In his 1853 *Advertiser* letter, William G. Brooks provided a transcription of Cato's May 24, 1789 letter. Cato Freeman's death notice and Brooks' letter then generated a note about Lydia (Bristow) Freeman in the local history column, Anonymous, "Sketches of Octogenarians" (about Lydia Freeman), *Andover Advertiser*, September 3, 1853, n.p. [2], that said she was never enslaved, and had 11 children of which three were then living. Immediately following that "Sketches" column was printed an anonymous letter to the editor (credited to "C.", a clipping hand-emended "Mrs. P.F.C." in Brooks' copy of Abbot's *History of Andover* at ACHC) that was written in response to Brooks' letter with additional biographical details about Cato. A notice of Cato Freeman's 1853 death appeared among that year's obituaries for "many active, useful and honorable citizens" in the *Massachusetts Register for the Year 1854*, 263, distributed throughout the state and nationally: "Cato Freeman, North Andover. Formerly a slave of Gov. Phil[l]ips. He was 85 years of age."

Anomalously, Cato Freeman's 1853 town and state death records, prepared in 1854 by Andover town clerk Henry Osgood, listed Cato's parents as "George Abbot & Remah Phillips Slaves", Cato Freeman, Death record, Town of Andover and State Vital Records. Presumably the information was provided to the town clerk by his widow, Lydia (Brister) Freeman, or by one of their children. Cato's original birth record, however, read "Cato son of Salem & Rhema Negroes" (May 26, 1768), Town of Andover, "Town Records, Births, Marriages, Intentions, Deaths, 1701–1800" (title from microfilm target; spine title is "Births, Marriages, Deaths and Intentions 1701–1800 Town of Andover"), 385, second volume on Genealogical Society of Salt Lake City, Ut. (hereafter GSU) Microfilm Reel 878780, digital image 202 of 266, https://www.familysearch.org/ark:/61903/3:1:3QS7-L97M-YRSB?i=269&cc=2061550&cat=143281, accessed October 25, 2019. It is uncertain which George Abbot(t) was indicated by the death record to be Cato's biological father, for there were many in Andover. The anomalous information is intriguing and mysterious.

Cato Phillips/Freeman has been mistaken for other similarly or same-named men who served during the Revolutionary War, when he was 7 to 15 years old (in Andover Cato Frye, the drummer Cato Foster, and Cato Negro who may be one of the others or yet another man with that common name). Another man named Cato Freeman "of Newburyport" was in Andover at least briefly in 1793 (marriage intention with Rose Parker on November 21, 1793, *VRA*, Vol. 2, "Negroes," 357, 359. They may not have married. The Newburyport Cato Freeman married Sally Smith in that town on February 10, 1796, *Vital Records of Newburyport*, Vol. 2, "Negroes," 531, 533). Cato Phillips/Freeman of Andover was confused with yet another man, from Cambridge, Mass., who for a time called himself or was known as Cato Liberty, Cato Freeman, and Cato Stedman, cf. Herndon, *Unwelcome Americans*, 100–103 and Quintal, *Patriots of Color*, 107; Inga Larson, email, August 16, 2019.

I thank Inga Larson and Carol Majahad at the NAHS for determining that Cato Phillips/Freeman did not likely join military service as a 7- to 12-year-old but could have assisted others who did, and identified the other Revolutionary War veterans with whom he was mistaken; for images of Cato's original manuscript letter and of an 1820 mortgage agreement between Freeman and Henry Osgood; for identifying the NAHS newsletter article about those documents and for determining that the article author was Dee Liffmann; to Larson particularly for inspiring discussion about Cato Freeman and his family and sharing with me the results of her research findings about them, including Freeman's anomalous death record that had been noticed by Charlotte Lyons in 2005, Inga Larson, emails, August 7–9, 16, 17, October 25, 2019.

Lise Breen's Cape Ann research pursued information about continued participation in the illegal slave trade by people and ships from that region into the nineteenth century. Breen, "Inculcated Forgetfulness at a New England Port," referred to "Judith Sargent Murray's own letters, copied for posterity, where she wrote that she sold her two enslaved 'lads' in Gloucester as late as 1783, and that she tried to recover her brother's Mississippi slave when he fled while visiting Boston in September of 1807."

Lise Breen shared information found in accounting records of Gloucester yeoman Benjamin Ellery at the Cape Ann Museum Archives, Gloucester. Ellery hired out Pomp as late as 1785 as a teamster driving oxen. Pomp and members of Pomp's family had been enslaved by the Ellery family, *Vital Records of Gloucester*, Vol. 1, 802–804 (Births, "Negroes"). Breen shared images of entries for hiring out "yᵉ Nigar & Oxen" in June 1769; of entries for Nathaniel Ellery, "To My Self 4 [for] pomp" at 6s./day and "To pomp" at 2s./day in July 1782; and, of entries for Joseph Sanders ("Sandres") in May, June, and November 1785 with variable rates (depending on whether oxen and a horse were hired and the nature of the work plowing or mowing), but one entry charged Sanders 1s. 6p. for a half-day of Pomp's labor equivalent to a rate of 3s./day. Lise Breen made the point that while Ellery charged others for Pomp's labor, it is impossible to know if Pomp was paid. In any case, Ellery appears to have arranged Pomp's laboring assignments, profited from Pomp's labor, and controlled the accounting and payments.

In Ellery's 1769 entry, notice especially that in this context "Nigar" obviously connoted "slave." The term "Negro" was also a loaded term, in some contexts confounding "race" with legal status as a slave, as in "proper Negro servant" in freedom suit pleadings and jury findings, and in an example from a 1763 inventory cited by Gloria McCahon Whiting, "Emancipation Without the Courts or Constitution," 6, 17 n27 that referred to a "man's bondspeople as 'negroes,' 'servants,' *and* 'slaves' as if to make triply sure that nobody would mistake them for freeborn laborers." The metaphoric and literal textual proximity of references to enslaved people and to livestock has been interpreted as evidence of dehumanization, while it also expressed commodified market value of human beings as property, Berry, *The Price for Their Pound of Flesh*, 7. On the contradictory duality of slaves as persons and property, and the metaphorical entanglement with livestock, see Davis, *Inhuman Bondage*, 30–33, 52 and Melish, *Disowning Slavery*, 25–26. Nicholas T. Rinehart, "The Man that was a Thing: Reconsidering Human Commodification in Slavery," supplied a more generalized and theoretical critique of too-abstract historiographic treatments of dehumanization, objectification, and commodification of enslaved people. Marjory Gomez O'Toole, *If Jane Should Want to be Sold*, 94, considered that the listing in probate inventories of slaves near livestock showed recognition of difference and value. Evidence related by Whiting, ibid., 6, 8–9, from historical Suffolk County inventories is discomfitingly persuasive that enslaved people and animals were conceived "in the same frame" (8).

For supplementary information about persistent enslavement or slave-like relationships, Lise Breen and Jeanne Pickering were interested in tracing the latest use of quoted phrasing in published vital records that conveyed possession and dependence, such as a person being "of" (sometimes as in "servant of") or "belonging to", etc., understanding that the data in the published records were not consistently and representatively expressed. In Manchester, Mass., for example, Breen saw that the town clerk recorded "Tytas, 'a Molato boy Belonging to the Wid[o]w Sarah Cheever,' Oct. 19, 1788" and "'Pela, a Negro Garl Belonging to Mrs. Sarah Cheever,' June 12, 1793", *Vital Records of Manchester*, 128 (Births, "Negroes," brackets in original). Breen shared the Manchester town clerk entry for the death of "Taft, 'slave of Mrs. Lydia Lee,' Nov. 1, 1803, a. 76 y.", ibid., 296. Taft (also "Taff"), a female, was probably the same person in Lydia Lee's household in 1790, then counted as a non-"white" free person, United States Bureau of the Census, *Heads of Families at the First Census [...] 1790*, 80. Taff had been named in Mrs. Lee's late husband Samuel Lee's 1765 will with a "Molatto boy Called Troy".

Also remaining in the Manchester household of Lydia Lee for a long while was the enslaved man Christopher Lee (1756 or 1762–1834, also known as Greace/Grease/Grece/Greeas/Greece). Breen found Christopher Lee's obituary published in the *Salem Gazette* (September 23, 1834, 3) that asserted "He was a slave until 1787, and the only person of that class residing in the town." Breen noted that the 18- to 24-year-old "Negro boy Grece" had been named in the 1780 inventory of the estate of Samuel Lee (Lydia's husband) after the "Negro Woman" "Taff" and the "Negro girl Sarah". Entries for him, his wife Rachael, and their children were made in *Vital Records of Manchester*, "Negroes," 128, 228, 296: "Greace" and "Rachal Clark" married in 1788, and had a daughter "Judath" in 1790 and a son George in 1793. "Greece Black" was in a household of three free people of color in 1790 that presumably included his wife and their infant daughter, United States Bureau of the Census, ibid. Breen found Rachel Lee's obituary (*Salem Register*, November 28, 1857, 97 years old) that indicated she and her brothers Antony (the Troy named in Samuel Lee's 1765 will?) and Caesar had also been enslaved by Samuel Lee. I noted that Christopher Lee's household of three individuals was enumerated in the 1830 federal census, including a male indicated to be 10–24 years old, younger than expected if he were their 37-year-old son George. They were the only people of color enumerated in town. No person of color was indicated in 1840 population schedules in Manchester (suggesting that "the only person of that class residing in the town" asserted in his obituary meant that no other people of color lived in town at that time). Christopher and Rachael Lee's obituaries, Samuel Lee's probate file papers, and the Manchester 1830 and 1840 federal census population schedules are not included in the references cited. Breen, emails, October 21–22, 2016, November 1, 2016, August 20–21, 2019; Breen and Jeanne Pickering, emails, December 22, 2017.

Jeanne Pickering brought to my attention the 1786 will of Deacon Thomas Chadwick (1712–1788) of Boxford, approved and allowed in 1788 by Probate Judge Benjamin Greenleaf, that indicated that Chadwick's slave Dinah Chadwick (1759–1839) remained enslaved: "7^{ly} [i.e., 7th clause] I Give to my Negro Woman, Named Dina, at my decease Her freedom, to act for herself, if she may see fit to accept of it, I also Give to her, her Bed & Bed[d]ing b[e]longing to the same, so long as She may want it for her own Lodging and at her decease, I Give the same to my two Sons Thomas and Samuel Chadwick to be equally divided between them". Note how Deacon Chadwick ostensibly devised to Dinah the bed and bedding that belonged to her, but then asserted control over its subsequent devise after her death. Chadwick only granted its use to Dinah for her lifetime, not the legal title to the bed and bedding. The internal logic of that reversion of possession was that Dinah would remain enslaved "Lodging" in the Chadwick household. Dinah herself was vendible chattel who possessed no legal autonomy. [Deacon] Thomas Chadwick, Probate file papers; Jeanne Pickering and Lise Breen, email, December 22, 2017. Sidney Perley, *The History of Boxford*, 158, wrote that "The families of Chadwick and Porter probably owned most of the slaves, though several families held them as servants." "Dinah, born about 1759, was a slave of Deacon Thomas Chadwick from four years of age. About 1800 she went to live with her sister" Flora Chandler in Andover. Flora Chandler's death is not recorded, but Mooar, *Historical Manual of the South Church*, 140, indicated her death "after 1839." Mooar's estimate is unsure, but Flora Chandler died sometime after September 4, 1839. A notation for a wood delivery to "Flora + Dinah" on September 4, 1839 was made by David Gray, Account book, census and appraisal of townspeople's farm animals (and other property for tax purposes), May 1, 1838–October 11, 1839 (and later), n.p., Taft Collection, Ms S 134, Sub-group I, Series A, David Gray 1762–1844, Folder 9, ACHC. Flora Chandler's death, chief among other reasons, could have prompted the living arrangement of Dinah Chadwick with Harriet Dole. Chadwick, who had gone blind, died on December 16, 1839 while she was living with Harriet Dole, under Dole's care, Abbott, ibid.; Anonymous, "Auld Lang-Syne. A Snow-Storm Incident of Fifty Years Ago"; Dinah Chadwick, December 16, 1839, "lost by reason of insanity of H[arriet] D[ole]", *VRA*, Vol. 2, 407, brackets in original, Dole, "insane and perished in the snow", ibid., 424. For more about the sisters Dinah Chadwick and Flora Chandler, see chap. 3, notes 5 and 18.

Christopher Challender Child, "Chance Bradstreet (1762–1810)," investigated the biography of that man who, as a 15-year-old enslaved "Negro Boy", was leased in 1777 from Isaac Story of Marblehead to Abraham Dodge of Ipswich. To be clear, the lease agreement was a transfer of property for a term. It was not written as an indenture. It was not agreed to by Chance's parent as was required for a contract involving a minor, and it was not approved by town officials or the probate court as was required for indentures in loco parentis or guardianships. The 1777 lease agreement transferred for a term "all right & Title to my Negro Boy Chance & his Services" for £30. The term of the lease was for 12 years and four months to 1789 when Chance would be 27, long past the ordinary age of 21 when indentures customarily concluded. The remaining term of Bradstreet's service to Dodge was transferred to Dodge's widow Bethiah by his will signed May 4, 1786 that conveyed to her "all my Right to the Service of my Negro Man Chance". Probate Judge Benjamin Greenleaf allowed and approved the will on July 3, 1786. Bradstreet may have remained enslaved or in some other arrangement until the end of the lease term in September 1789. (The estate, with a tremendous list of creditors, was still being administered to 1808.) In the interim, Bethiah Dodge controlled Chance's labor, and arranged for him to work at "making fish", processing cod for export such as to sugar plantations in the West Indies. By 1794, Chance was a free man in Marblehead, occupying a residence with another person, possibly his mother. A memorial note reporting the death of Chance Bradstreet's mother, Phillis Bradstreet (1739–1815), "a very respectable black lady, once a Princess in Africa," was published in 12 New England newspapers. She died at the Marblehead "poorhouse." The house where Bradstreet was enslaved in Ipswich was dismantled in 1963, and moved to Washington, D.C., where it is displayed as the largest object in the American Museum of National History, Smithsonian Institution, in the exhibition "Within These Walls." Adams and Pleck, *Love of Freedom*, 255 n38; Child, "Chance Bradstreet (1762–1810)," 41–43, 43 n8, n10, for sources of quotations. For the evolution of indenture and apprenticeship practices in relation to Massachusetts enslavement, manumission, and abolition see writings by Ruth Wallis Herndon, including Herndon, *Unwelcome Americans*, Herndon, "'Proper' Magistrates and Masters," especially page 43 on "[t]he trajectory of pauper apprenticeship influenced [...] by the decline of slavery," Herndon, "Children of Misfortune" (a paper drawn from her forthcoming book by that title), and other chapters by her and by others in Herndon and Murray, *Children Bound to Labor*; Minardi, *Making Slavery History*, 118; Nickles, "Finding New Stories in an Old House"; *Vital Records of Marblehead*, Vol. 2, 707, "Negroes," deaths of Chance Bradstreet and Phillis Bradstreet. I thank Christopher Challender Child for providing me images of Abraham Dodge's will, and Lise Breen for directing my attention to the entries in the published vital records.

Another example of Essex County people remaining in enslavement and slave-like arrangements derives from documents noticed by several researchers, but Robert H. Romer, *Slavery in the Connecticut Valley of Massachusetts*, 215, was first to address it as a late example of continued enslavement. The May 23, 1787 will of the Andover-born Rev. James Chandler (1706–1789) of Rowley conveyed his slave Sabina to his wife. Sabina had previously been enslaved by Deacon Stephen Mighill. Chandler's will also included a provision about his other slave Phillis (Sabina's daughter) who he had manumitted in 1774. But Phillis' labor continued unpaid despite Chandler's promise to pay her an annual salary of £1 6s. 8p. Phillis had a child who also lived in the Chandler household. Phillis had married Cicero Green of Newburyport on March 11, 1783, likely the same man as Cicero Haskell, a Newburyport Revolutionary War veteran who served 1779–1781. Rev. Chandler died in April 1789, and his will was approved by Probate Judge Benjamin Greenleaf on May 5, 1789. The estate administrator, Chandler's nephew John Tenny, Jr., reported on May 3, 1791 that he had paid Phillis £20, probably for a part of the 15 years of unpaid back wages mentioned in the will. In Newburyport, Phillis Green remarried to Titus Odiorne on March 14, 1793. Just over a year before, Odiorne and Nancy Weed had published a marriage intention. The two separate provisions in Chandler's will about his slaves have been quoted by several, but the following transcription was adapted from that prepared by John C. MacLean, "Resources for Researching Massachusetts Slaves and Slaveholders," that I compared to the images of the 1787 will in James Chandler, Probate file papers.

> I commit to my said Wife my negro woman Sabina, not to be by her Sold out of the House, but to Serve her, and to be provided for by her, as is mete. But if Said Sabina Shall live to be a Burden, which my Said Wife Shall think too Heavy for her to bear, my Will is – that my

Executor assist in providing for her, as is fitting for an aged Servant
that has been faithful.

[....]

To My Negro Woman Phillis I give her Manumission or Freedom
and five Pounds lawful Money, a Chest, & Such other Things in my
House, as are known by the Family to be her Things. I give her also
the Bed that her Mother [Sabina] & She Lodge in and all the Bedding belonging to it. And I hereby testify that I gave her her Freedom
when she was eighteen years old [in 1774], and covenanted with her
that If she would live & Serve in my Family I would give her one
Pound & Six Shillings & eight Pence pr year for her Service & find
her her Clothes. She has lived with, and Served me ever since and I
have paid her Nothing of the Money that I promised as her wages &
therefore I owe it to her and Order my Executor to pay it to her. I
Suppose that my keeping her Child more than answers for Interest,
but I release what more it might be reckond of.

Sources that I used for the late practice of slavery by Rev. Chandler are
Bradford, "James Chandler," 94; Chandler, *The Chandler Family*, 102–103
(will); James Chandler, Probate file papers; MacLean, ibid. (will); Massachusetts Secretary of the Commonwealth, *Massachusetts Soldiers and Sailors of
the Revolutionary War*, Vol. 7, 425 ("Haskel, Cicero"), 433 ("Haskell, Cicero"); Nelson, "Georgetown," 817 (Sabina formerly owned by Mighill, will
mentioned); Romer, ibid., 215 (will); Shipton "James Chandler," 375–381
(will, 380–381); Spaulding, "James Chandler," 59–61 (will, 59); *Vital Records of Newburyport*, Vol. 2, 531, 532 (Marriages, "Negroes," Phillis Green
married Titus Odiorne, March 14, 1793); ibid., 532, 533 (Titus Odiorne
and Nancy Weed, marriage intention, January 7, 1792); *Vital Records of Rowley*, 237 (Births, "Negroes," "Phillis, d. [Cesar and Sabina, "negroes joined in
wedlock and servants to James Chandler." C.R. 2.], Mar. 13, 1756. P.R. 2.",
brackets and internal quotation marks in original, C.R. 2="church record,
Second Congregational Church, now in Georgetown", ibid., 5; P.R. 2="Record kept by Rev. James Chandler and Rev. Isaac Brayman, pastors of the
Second Church", ibid., 6; ibid., 434 ("Philis" Chandler married Cicero Green
of Newburyport, March 11, 1783). Lise Breen noticed that Bradford and
Spaulding did not include the part of the will about Phillis, and Chandler did
not include the part about Sabina.

There were slaves in Newburyport in 1793 and 1795. A "Negro" boy
about 13 years old named Calestin ran away from Louis Daniel DuPatty
in Newburyport, according to an advertisement dated June 29, 1793 in the
Essex Journal and in the *Impartial Herald*. Six months later Felix, a 20-year-
old described as a "Negro Boy," ran away from DuPatty on December 18,

1793, with "some property not his own." The notice for Felix appeared in the *Impartial Herald* on December 27, 1793. DuPatty (also spelled Dupaty) was a French émigré. Perhaps Calestin, who spoke "very little English", accompanied DuPatty from France as a servant or in some other role. The ad for Calestin in the *Essex Journal* was reproduced in classroom teaching materials prepared by Zimmerman, "Secretive Slavery in Essex County," and Lise Breen found the *Impartial Herald* ads for Calestin and Felix (the advertisements are not included in the references cited). In Newburyport in 1795, Nicholas Cools Godfroy arrived with "about twenty Negro slaves, house servants, and families from his plantation" on St. Lucia. Emery, *Reminiscences of a Nonagenarian*, 187, noted in Uscilka, *The Newburyport Black Heritage Trail*, 18, 34 n18.

The 1793 runaway advertisements in Essex County newspapers for Calestin and Felix prompted Lise Breen to also send me the webpage for National Park Service, Boston African American National Historic Site, *Slave Advertisements*, https://www.nps.gov/articles/slave-advertisements.htm, accessed March 14, 2019. That webpage reported on what were said to be the last two slave-for-sale advertisements that appeared in the *Boston Gazette* (December 10, 1781). Breen located a runaway advertisement reporting that on August 9, 1783, the 24-year-old Phillis had left Jacob Hooper in Manchester: it was published in the *Salem Gazette* on September 18, September 25, and October 2, 1783 (the advertisements not included in the references cited). Efforts continue to document Massachusetts newspaper advertisements for slaves-for-sale and escapees that were the public face of the practice and the trade, in contrast to clandestine operations of smuggling, the knotted rope that continued to tie New England industry and economy to slavery, and the continuance of generational servitude with Massachusetts families.

Lise Breen conveyed information about Else (Elsey) (circa 1763 or 1769–1838), purchased in 1776 for £20 when she was 7 to 13 years old, who as late as 1830 was still living with the Gloucester woman who became her owner. Else was presumably the "free colored" female aged 55–100 years old counted in the household of Mary (Norwood) Baker (1741 to 1743–1832), United States Census, *Population Schedules of the Fifth Census of the United States 1830, Roll 61*, Essex County, 574. As an example of generational slavery, Else was the daughter of Dick (servant of Capt. William Norwood, Mary's father) and Philis (servant of Anne Baker, presumably another relative of Mary). Else's purchase and presence in the widow Baker's household was described in a 1923 article by Leila Norwood Adams, "Old Norwood Homestead." Adams used Mary Baker's diary (which has not been located) to convey the farm and domestic labor that was managed by the two women, I expect with help from Mary's relatives, neighbors, and hired day laborers. Adams, ibid., 22, quoted from Baker's diary entry of May 25, 1825 to relate that a neighbor, "Mrs. Marthy Riggs [...] has been here taking care of me some 10 or 12 days. I have been sick." Although Adams, ibid., surmised that "Mary Baker lingered on, alone in the partly closed house until her death", Else may have attended to Baker as well. Perhaps the neighbor assisted in nursing Baker while Else managed the farm and house chores, perhaps Else was away at the time, or perhaps Else had left Baker entirely. Although Mary Baker's will devised real estate, livestock, and many particular household and farm items to her family, and her will established a trust fund for the local school, Mary Baker left nothing to her family's lifelong servant. Consequently, Else (Elsey) ended impoverished and homeless, and died six years later. Elsey, with no surname, died at the Gloucester workhouse in 1838. Again, this is another example of practically lifelong servants passed down generations in families, succeeding heirs taking more or less interest in the responsibilities, O'Toole, *If Jane Should Want to be Sold*, 129–133. Mary Baker, Probate file papers (will, April 21, 1826); *Vital Records of Gloucester*, Vol. 1, 495 (Births, Mary Norwood, daughter of William and Judith Norwood, May 6, 1743), 803 (Births, "Negroes," Else, baptized March 12, 1769); Vol. 2, 602, 604 (Marriages, "Negroes," Dick and Philis, June 28, 1763); Vol. 3, 67 (Deaths, Mary Norwood Baker, June 13 or 15, 1832, 82 [89–91] years old), 337 (Deaths, "Negroes," Elsey, September 21, 1838, 75 years old).

A secondary source purported continued enslavement long into the nineteenth century, but further investigation showed that it was mistaken. In Ipswich, a family genealogist asserted that Ned and Sabina (Binah) "remained slaves until 1845, when Mr. Francis Choate gave them their freedom if they wished to take it, otherwise they were to be supported. They chose to remain with the family, and accordingly were cared for as long as they lived." Jameson, *The Choates in America*, 11 (quotation), 37. However, Lise Breen determined that the late date was an error because Francis Choate died in 1777; Ned died in 1800 (as indicated by Jameson, ibid., 11, 37); and, Binah died in 1826, *Vital Records of Ipswich*, Vol. 2, 522 (Deaths, Francis Choate, Esq.), 719 (Deaths, "Negroes," Binah and Ned Choate). Francis Choate's 1775 will proposed only the conditional possibility of freedom for his male slaves, if they could obtain bonds to indemnify the town of Ipswich and the Choates from poor relief that the men might require. Otherwise the male slaves were to serve his sons who were to support them if the men's "Earnings shall fall short of supporting them in Sickness or old age". Francis Choate did not extend even a possibility of freedom to his "Negro Girl called Peggy," who he bequeathed to his daughter. None of the slaves, however, were listed in Choate's 1777 inventory. Francis Choate, Probate file papers (will, December 22, 1775; inventory, December 16, 1777). Erik Seeman, "'Justise Must Take

Plase," 396–399, 407–411, considered the Choate's slave Flora's religious confession testimony, and investigated her biography. Biographical moments of the many enslaved people with the Choate family have been considered by several, but an applied researcher would benefit from documents (e.g., the 1759 "Bill of Sale for Negro boy" and the 1778 "Passing obligation to support two Negro men" noted in the finding aid) in the Choate Family Papers at Phillips Library, Peabody Essex Museum, Rowley, Mass., and from study of the notes of reminiscences about the Choate family's slaves at the Essex Shipbuilding Museum, Essex, Mass. I thank Lise Breen for noticing the Ipswich *Vital Records* entries, discerning slave-owning family connections, and for sharing and discussing these sources and corrective information about the Choates and their slaves in Ipswich.

In the nineteenth century, Massachusetts citizens of color, free people, were vulnerable when traveling to slave states. Louisiana presumed any unaccompanied person of color was a fugitive slave. They were arrested on sight and imprisoned. Those prisoners were put to work on chain gangs to do highway repair and could be sold into slavery to pay their jail fees that accrued from arresting, imprisoning, and forcing them to labor. Under color of law in the Carolinas, mariners were forcibly removed from vessels, and the captains were extorted to pay for their release and post bonds before the ships were allowed to get underway. Corruption by "fees" was notorious. Several slave states had similar systems of "slavery by another name" to generate revenue with unfree labor. Bell, "Freeing Eral Lonnon"; Fladeland, *Men and Brothers*, 187–189, 319–321, cited by Davis, *The Problem of Slavery in the Age of Revolution*, 522 n92; Massachusetts General Court, *Special Joint Committee Report on the Deliverance of Citizens, Liable to be Sold as Slaves*, House No. 38, March 1839, which report Lise Breen brought to my attention. Calvin Schermerhorn, *Unrequited Toil*, 73, concluded significantly that the "slave security state" which developed in the southern states in the 1830s followed rebellions and insurgency by enslaved people in that region. "Southern whites traded liberty for security, [...] sacrificed economic diversity and democracy to the imperatives of slave labor production [..., and implemented] a repressive regime that squashed economic vibrancy in the service of war capitalism. It was that move to a society of suspicion and the overriding imperative of protecting enslaved property that divided the Slave South from states in which slavery was prohibited."

Helen Tunnicliff Catterall, *Judicial Cases concerning American Slavery and the Negro*, has summaries of nineteenth-century state and federal court cases about: slaves brought to Massachusetts from slave states; free people of color who were Massachusetts residents that were kidnapped to be enslaved in other states; a case of an ostensibly free person of color, an orphaned girl born of a slave being raised by a "white" Massachusetts couple, who was kidnapped then kept by people of color in Boston; mariners and their vessels involved in the slave trade; probate of estates that owned slaves in slave states; apprehension of fugitive slaves present in Massachusetts; and, about a dispute to property (contents of a trunk) once owned by a former slave. Catterall, ibid., also included several cases about due process and equal protection in nineteenth-century Massachusetts that did not involve slaves.

[4] United States Congress, *Journal of the House of Representatives*, 22nd Cong., 1st sess., January 25, 1832, 240; January 26, 1832, 242–243. There were several previous and subsequent legislative actions relating to investigating, correcting, and publishing the 1830 census data in 1831 and 1832, ultimately enacted by the United States Congress, *Statutes at Large*, 22nd Cong., 1st sess., Res. 5, July 3, 1832, 606. Livingston, "Erroneous Return of Slaves," 1. I thank Nicole Topich for bringing United States Secretary of State Livingston's report to my attention. Livingston's report was noted in a short article, Anonymous, "Errors in the Census," 167 in the March 1830 issue of the abolitionist newspaper, *The Genius of Universal Emancipation*: "The few slaves, who still remain in the Eastern States and other states, where slavery is not allowed, are those who are unable, through age or infirmity, to provide for their own support, and are allowed to depend upon their masters. There have been no slaves in Massachusetts for more than fifty years."

[5] The 1781 and 1783 "Quock Walker" cases were only retrospectively asserted to have judicially abolished slavery in Massachusetts, but did not actually do so. People remained enslaved and in slave-like circumstances decades after. Despite popular belief and the endless repetition of the historical myth by otherwise careful and circumspect historians, even while some make effort to qualify their characterization of its supposed immediate impact and statewide effects, no decision of record issued from the Supreme Judicial Court for the "Quock Walker" cases that instantly freed anyone else in Massachusetts but Quock Walker. Quock Walker v. Nathaniel Jennison; Nathaniel Jennison v. John Caldwell and Seth Caldwell; Commonwealth v. Jennison. Gloria McCahon Whiting, "Emancipation Without the Courts or Constitution," 5, established "with unprecedented precision and certainty" that in historical Suffolk County (then also including most of what is now Norfolk County) slave ownership indicated in probate records precipitously declined at the commencement of the Revolutionary War in 1775, but also persisted there (albeit in greatly reduced numbers) long after the "Quock Walker" cases, ibid., 11, 17 n21, 18 n38. Whiting's highly important research findings drawn from probate records dating 1760 to 1790 for "the wealthiest county in the Bay State, and the county with the highest proportion of black people"

(5) prove that neither the 1780 state constitution nor the "Quock Walker" cases were direct and instant causes of Massachusetts abolition.

[6] The manuscript 1830 population schedules for Worcester County, in the totals for the town of Barre, summarized that one female slave over 100 years old was counted in the town. However, no slave was counted in the household of Prince Walker, nor in any other Barre household, nor in any other Worcester County household. United States Census, *Population Schedules of the Fifth Census of the United States 1830, Roll 68*, Worcester County, 585 (Walker household), 596 (Barre totals). I viewed all the images of the pages where slaves would be counted for all Worcester County towns, and none were indicated, except on page 596. I thank Cheryll Toney Holley for locating the entry for Prince Walker's household in the manuscript volume. For Prince Walker, who escaped back to Massachusetts after Nathaniel Jennison sold him in East Windsor, Conn., see Cushing, "The Cushing Court and the Abolition of Slavery in Massachusetts," 144 n38; Knoblock, *African American Historic Burial Grounds*, 201–202; McCarthy and Doughton, *From Bondage to Belonging*, xxxi n16; Malloy and Malloy, "Slavery in Colonial Massachusetts as Seen Through Selected Gravestones," 136–139; O'Donovan, "The Descendants of Mingo and Dinah"; O'Donovan, "The Mormon Priesthood Ban and Elder Q. Walker Lewis," 53–54; Stevens, *Anthony Burns*, 288; and, Walker, "Barre," 352. Prince Walker (1774–1858) was either Quock's son or brother. Quock Walker was born about 1753 and married Elizabeth Harvey in 1786. The family tree and family group sheets prepared by O'Donovan, "The Descendants of Mingo and Dinah," indicate that Prince was the son of Quock's father Mingo and either his first wife Dinah or his second wife Elizabeth Harris. Stevens, ibid., 288, derived his information that Prince was Quock's brother from Seth Caldwell, Esq. of Barre, the grandson of the co-defendant/appellant John Caldwell in the second "Quock Walker" lawsuit, Nathaniel Jennison v. John Caldwell and Seth Caldwell. Stevens, ibid., wrote that Prince Walker "is still living (August, 1856), at a very advanced age. He is, perhaps, *the last survivor of the Massachusetts slaves*." I thank John Hannigan for sharing information about Prince Walker. Hannigan directed me to Worcester County Deeds, Book 274, pg. 11, where Prince Walker was among the heirs of "Quacko" Walker, which deed was also referred to by O'Donovan, "The Mormon Priesthood Ban and Elder Q. Walker Lewis," 53–54 n14. Mayo, "The Quork-Lewis Family (1754–1954)," has additional information about the family. Secondary sources give conflicting information about the genealogical relationship of John and Seth Caldwell to each other (some say father and son, others say they were brothers) and to their relation to Nathaniel Jennison's late wife Isabel/la Oliver Caldwell Jennison who once owned Quock Walker (some say her brother and nephew, others say her brothers, and yet others say they were her sons). The accurate and

precise biographical details of the individuals involved in the "Quock Walker" cases, a correct documentary analysis and accounting of the legal history, and a bibliography of the historiography await the efforts of a thorough scholar.

A different man named Prince Walker was in Andover who married a woman named Phillis. She died in 1811, then he married Rose Parker in 1812, *VRA*, Vol. 2, "Negroes," 358, 359, 575. That Prince Walker was a free man who had arrived in Andover from Concord, N.H. He and his wife were warned out of Andover by the selectmen on January 30, 1792, Town of Andover, "Town Records, Town Meetings, Persons Warned to Leave Town 1790–1793" (untitled volume, title from microfilm target), n.p., second volume on GSU Microfilm Reel 887742. Cutter, "Longevity in Woburn," 155, 158, cited sources with anecdotes about the Andover Prince Walker, born and sold in Woburn, Mass., to Rev. Timothy Walker of Concord, N.H. Prince Walker, Jr. died in Andover in 1815, *VRA*, Vol. 2, "Negroes," 575. The 1816 Andover treasurer/overseers of the poor records have entries reimbursing Andover residents for supporting "Prince Walker Jr in his last sickness" and for "digging a grave for Prince Walker Jr". The father's name appeared for years after in the town poor relief records. Town of Andover, "Town Records, Tax Records 1799–1822" (untitled volume, title from microfilm target but actually treasurer records of payments for orders drawn by the overseers of the poor), n.p., first volume on GSU Microfilm Reel 878782, April 23, 1816 (Nos. 10–12). Cutter's sources mistook the Andover Prince Walker for yet another man by the same name (possibly another one of the Andover man's sons, or not) who died at the Woburn almshouse in 1825, Johnson, *Woburn Records of Births, Deaths, and Marriages*, 201. Additional research is needed to sort the biographies of these same-named men.

[7] United States Department of State, *Fifth Census; or, Enumeration of the Inhabitants of the United States, as Returned by the Several Marshals*, v.

[8] For the manuscript population schedule showing the count of the enslaved woman at the Andover almshouse among the 54 residents enumerated under Superintendent Joseph Cummings, see United States Census, *Population Schedules of the Fifth Census of the United States 1830, Roll 61*, Essex County, 166. Mooar, *The Cummings Memorial*, 294, indicated that Cummings was the almshouse superintendent. The Andover treasurer and overseers of the poor used the title *master of the almshouse* for Cummings from at least 1817. They capitalized "Master of Almshouse" in 1830, Town of Andover, "Town Records, Tax Records 1799–1822" (untitled volume, title from microfilm target but actually treasurer records of payments for orders drawn by the overseers of the poor), n.p., first volume on GSU Microfilm Reel 878782, October 6, 1817 (No. 74: "master of the almshouse"); Town of Andover,

"Town Records, Tax Records 1823–1847" (untitled volume, title from microfilm target but actually treasurer records of payments for orders drawn by the overseers of the poor), n.p., ninth volume on GSU Microfilm Reel 878782, October 18, 1830 (No. 48: "goods delivered Mr Cummings Master of Almshouse"). The title *master* was synonymous with *superintendent*. At other times and places in Massachusetts, an alternate term used for the position was *warden*. (Usually there was a female authority figure also present called *matron*, and there was metaphoric use of the term *family* in Andover as at other almshouses to fictively and paternalistically refer to the aggregation of the supervisors and inmates together.) Bell, *Historical Archaeology at the Hudson Poor Farm Cemetery*, 22–24 and sources cited; Rothman, *The Discovery of the Asylum*, 43, 55, 151–152; Spencer-Wood, "A Feminist Approach to European Ideologies of Poverty and the Institutionalization of the Poor in Falmouth, Massachusetts," 119; Spencer-Wood, "Feminist Theoretical Perspectives on the Archaeology of Poverty"; Wiesner, "Spinning Out Capital," 221 ("family" metaphor at European hospitals). For the metaphoric use of "family" for the Andover almshouse residents, see Fay, *Pauperism*, 1, quoted in Reef, *Poverty in America*, 36: in the words of an Andover overseer of the poor, females inmates at the almshouse were "employed in spinning, weaving, making clothes for the family [i.e., the almshouse inmates and the staff], taking care of the sick, &c. [etc.]" The quotation by Fay was in a publication issued in 1827, and was slightly modified from a nearly identical sentence in an 1820 letter: "The females are imployed in spinning weaving making cloaths for the family taking care of the sick +c. [etc.,]" Town of Andover, Overseers of the Poor, William Johnson, David Gray, and Stephen Abbot letter to Alden Bradford, Massachusetts Secretary of the Commonwealth, September 22, 1820, Ms. S 202, ACHC. Crane, *Ebb Tide in New England*, 119, considered that spinning required of or taught to women at institutions for the poor "exacerbated rather than mitigated [...the] dependence" of "ailing or impoverished women," because spinning "was still gender based and effectively relegated women to an employment that provided little income." The official names of the town institution evolved significantly: *almshouse, workhouse, poor farm, town farm, infirmary*, and finally *rest home*. For a summary history of the several Andover almshouses, see Meltsner, *The Poorhouses of Massachusetts*, 123–125.

An 1833 state legislative report noted that the brickyard established at the Andover almshouse brought in "extraordinary revenue", Massachusetts House of Representatives, *Report of the Commissioners appointed by an Order of the House of Representatives, Feb. 29, 1832, on the Subject of the Pauper System*, 26. Yet, only three males and five females were able to labor half a day each, either in farm work, at the brickyard, picking wool, or spinning. The

1833 report, ibid., 55, conceived that "Considerable evils result from the impracticality of separating and classifying its inmates." Throughout the report, "evil" and "evils" occurred frequently (ibid., 7, 8, 10, 12, 13, 22, 27, 33, 35, 38, 39). The meaning in those contexts was that providing support to the poor had the unintended consequence of encouraging dependence ("pauperism") as people were "lured [...] by the inviting paths of indolence and dissipation", ibid., 37. The attendant rising costs of supporting the poor was itself an "evil" as was the effects of impoverishment on the "morals" and demeanor of the poor that could, the legislators feared, lead to civil unrest. The report, ibid., 42–43, advocated for "classification" of inmates, and physical separation of the classes within almshouses, seemingly to prevent bad "moral" influences on attitude and behavior: "classification [...] should be made and maintained, at once from sympathy with the virtuous and impotent poor, for the restraint of the vicious poor, and the prevention of pauperism." The report recommended obtaining plans of the internal configuration of the institutions "to supply towns and counties with a knowledge of the most effectual, and at the same time the most economical modes, of separating, classifying, and in other respects providing for, the poor inmates of these institutions."

In regards to the mention of "evils" at the Andover almshouse (as also at Boston, ibid., 45; Lynn, 48; Gloucester, 50; and, Malden, 60), the meaning was the general concern of bad influence on attitude and behavior. If the 1833 legislative report authors were making oblique reference to sexual activity, it is difficult to discern (unlike in Dorthea Dix's 1843 *Memorial to the Legislature*, e.g., 7–8, 12, 24, which did not mention Andover among the places she reported upon). For Boston, the 1833 legislative report, ibid., 45, indicated that "It is a great evil of the institution, that the children who are in it cannot be kept apart from its adult inmates." For Gloucester, the 1833 report stated that "Great evils have resulted from the impracticality of separating the sexes, and of classifying the poor, which, it is thought, may now be prevented", ibid., 50. In contrast, at the almshouses in Roxbury, ibid., 68, 69 and Northampton, ibid., 81, the report noted that sexes were separated. At Roxbury, ibid., 68, "Husbands and wives are not allowed to live together" and that rule "brought the house into disfavor with some who would otherwise have taken up their abode in it." In places that separated males and females, a decline in the number of inmates and consequently a reduction in costs were reported.

The 1845 issue of the Town of Andover, *Annual Town Reports*, had commentary by the auditors who prepared the financial report, which reflected concern for the presence of children in the town almshouse (which in the reports for 1843, and 1845–1848 was called, significantly, *Workhouse* [Work-house, Work House] but in 1846–1848 variants of *almshouse* were used interchangeably): "The number of children in the Workhouse, and other circumstances, well known to the Town, have induced the Overseers [of the Poor] to employ a female teacher to take charge of the children there." The auditors prefaced that statement by recounting that from March 1844 to February 1845, there were 60 persons in the almshouse: 20 males, 40 females, of whom 47 were adults, and 13 were minors. While perhaps the auditors were alluding to the almshouse murder of Mehitable Long in 1842 (Patrakis, "Who Killed Mehitable?"), as with "evils" used elliptically by the 1833 legislative report authors, the Andover auditors were not explicit about what the "other circumstances, well known to the Town" were that they expected could be ameliorated by a female teacher. Gendered idealization of a probably unmarried female teacher would bring expectations for her to exhibit and instruct moral norms, exercise discipline appropriately, encourage a work ethic, and provide the children practical educational content in a scheduled structure that would benefit their future employability and citizenship.

9 My applied efforts were unsuccessful to identify the woman at the Andover almshouse characterized as a slave in the 1830 United States Census. In the town annual reports for 1829 and 1831, names were not specified for individuals that were living at the almshouse in the report for the period from March 2, 1828 to March 2, 1829, nor were names specified for almshouse inmates nor for others who were "State Paupers and Poor belonging to other Towns" in the report for the period from March 1, 1830 to March 4, 1831, Town of Andover, *Annual Town Reports*, 1829, 1831. The intervening 1829–1830 town report is not in the ACHC collection. In Massachusetts *Acts and Resolves*, female state paupers for whose support Andover was reimbursed were named (sometimes only as wives of named men) in three state pauper account rolls: January 1830 (Roll No. 102), January 1831 (Roll No. 104), and June 1831 (Roll. No. 105). Andover names were not specified or not reimbursed in 1829 (Roll No. 100, 101) and Andover was not reimbursed in June 1830 (Roll No. 103).

Female state paupers in Andover in January 1830 (Roll No. 102) included Sukey Hornsby (not a centenarian in 1830; she was 46 in 1830; listed in 1833 as "Sukey Ornsby" "about 58" years old, a "white" woman in the almshouse since "about 1815", "lunatic", Town of Andover, Overseers of the Poor, "Return of the Poor in the Town of Andover during the year ending on the last Monday of December, 1833," Ms. S 203, ACHC; indicated as 65 years old in an insane asylum in 1849, Massachusetts Secretary of the Commonwealth, *Abstract of Returns of the Keepers of Jails and Overseers of the Houses of Correction*, 31), Martha Wright, "Lavinia" Bean, and the wife of Peter "Sigorney", Massachusetts *Acts and Resolves* (1828–1831), 312. Sigourney's wife was the only female identified as "colored" among the Andover state paupers on Roll

No. 102. However, I discounted her as the "slave" in 1830 because there is evidence that she was enumerated in her husband's household that year, rather than at the almshouse, as explained further in this endnote, below.

In January 1831 (Roll No. 104), female state paupers were Sukey Hornsby, Hannah Highland (born 1827, *VRA*, Vol. 1, 194; mother Ann died January 3, 1828, *VRA*, Vol. 2, 462; in 1833 listed as "Hannah Highlands", a 6-year-old "white" child in the almshouse since birth, Town of Andover, Overseers of the Poor, "Return of the Poor in the Town of Andover during the year ending on the last Monday of December, 1833," Ms. S 203, ACHC), "Lavina" Bean, Peter "Sigourney's" wife, Rosanna Coburn (not at the almshouse in 1830), and Dinah Chadwick (not a centenarian in 1830, she was 69 to 71 years old in 1830 probably then living with her sister Flora Chandler, United States Census, *Population Schedules of the Fifth Census of the United States 1830, Roll 61*, Essex County, 183 [Flora Chandler household, 2 free colored females 55–100 years old; 1 ditto 24–36 years old]; Dinah was 78 years old at death in 1839, *VRA*, Vol. 2, 407), Massachusetts *Acts and Resolves* (1828–1831), 535.

In June 1831 (Roll No. 105), female state paupers included Sukey Hornsby, Hannah Highland, Mary Maloney, possibly an "Esther" Benson ("William [and ?] Esther Benson"), and James Graham's wife, Massachusetts *Acts and Resolves* (1828–1831), 637.

The woman characterized as a slave in 1830 was not Rosanna Coburn's mother Phillis because she died prior to January 5, 1829. The centenarian woman may be one of those whose names appear in the 1830–1831 state pauper lists and who cannot be discounted based on age or residing outside the almshouse around June 1830. The records of the Andover overseers of the poor and treasurer include notations for adult females, but their ages, whether they resided at the almshouse around June 1830, were persons of color, or former slaves is not discernible. Further biographical research for each of them could preclude more names to arrive at a shorter list of possible candidates for the slave. No woman who died after 1830, over 100 years old, is listed in *VRA*, Vol. 2, 573–575, in the section for "Negroes." I also searched throughout that volume for the names of the women listed as state paupers 1830–1831, and for other women who were indicated to have died at the almshouse in or after 1830, but with no compelling results. Almshouse intake records may yet be rediscovered in the Andover town clerk vaults that would, finally, identify the centenarian woman characterized as a "slave" in 1830. Barbara Brown, "Black Lucy's Garden," made intriguing reference to "Andover Infirmary Records," but no records by that title were located by the Andover town clerk (Austin Simko, email, April 26, 2019). Brown may have been referring to different records or to the same "Andover Overseers

Records 1815–1839" that Joan Patrakis identified in the town clerk vaults (Patrakis, email, April 20, 2019).

Because the wife of Peter Sigourney (surname spelling varies) was the only woman listed as "colored" among the state paupers in January 1830 (Roll No. 102), Massachusetts *Acts and Resolves* (1828–1831), 312 ("Peter Sigorney and wife, (colored)"), I especially considered if she might be another candidate for the slave counted at the almshouse in the 1830 census. However, in the 1830 census, in the separately enumerated Andover household of "Peter Siginy" there was counted two "free colored" males (36 to 55, and 55 to 100 years old) and two "free colored" females (24 to 36, and 55 to 100 years old)—the older female was probably Peter's wife, and if so, thus not at the almshouse, United States Census, *Population Schedules of the Fifth Census of the United States 1830, Roll 61*, Essex County, 182. On the other hand, it is impossible to know for sure that the older woman in the 1830 Sigourney household was Peter's wife. The Sigourney family does not appear in the 1800 or 1810 population schedules, and the 1820 schedules for Andover did not enumerate heads of households for people of color. I hesitate to speculate that Sigourney's wife was counted twice in 1830, once at home (in the 55- to under 100-year-old category) and again at the almshouse (in the 100-year-old and greater category). Many entries for support of the Sigourney family were made in the Andover treasurer/overseers of the poor records.

Pertaining to Mrs. Sigourney, she died on September 1, 1830. The town and state poor relief records, and the town and South Church death records, did not indicate Mrs. Sigourney's forename or age. Two entries for her death appear in *VRA*. The editors of *VRA*, Vol. 2, 543, referred to South Parish Congregational Church records for their source of Mrs. Sigourney's death date, but unlike her husband, her place of death was not indicated: she may have died at home, at the almshouse, or somewhere else. Peter died "at the almshouse" three years to the day of his wife's death, *VRA*, Vol. 2, 543. In *VRA*, Vol. 2, 575, under "Negroes" there appeared a death record for "Sidney, ___, w. Peter, Sept. 1, 1830." (Joan Patrakis noticed that entry, email, September 15, 2017.) The surname "Sidney" was another variant of Sigourney. The editors of the *VRA* probably got that information from the recopied town death records, Town of Andover, "A Record of Deaths in the Town of Andover (Including North Andover), Essex County, Massachusetts, from 1650 to 1844 Covering a Period of 194 Years Chronologically Arranged and Transcribed from the Original Records Verbatim et Literatim by Samuel W. Blunt and Completed March 1, 1879," 167: "_____, Consort of Peter Sidney, a Color'd woman." The Andover overseers of the poor issued orders to pay for "a grave for [...] Peter Signeys wife" and a "Coffin for Sigourney's wife" on October 10, 1830 (No. 45, grave) and on October 18, 1830 (No.

46, coffin), Town of Andover, "Town Records, Tax Records 1823–1847" (untitled volume, title from microfilm target but actually treasurer records of payments for orders drawn by the overseers of the poor), n.p., ninth volume on GSU Microfilm Reel 878782. While I have not found information that Sigourney's wife was formerly enslaved, it is probable; but that research avenue is impeded because her given name is not known. While they may have married in another town (the Peter Sigorney who married Celia Loring in Boston in 1769 was not them), the *VRA* provided no suggestive identity for her in the "Negroes" sections for births, marriages, and deaths for "Peter" or in other parts of the *VRA* under any spelling of Sigourney, McConnell (the name that Peter used when he first arrived in Andover), or Abbot (the name of the family with whom Peter first resided). Peter Sigourney was the same man as "Peter McConnell alias Sigine a Negro Man" in the Andover household of Capt. John Abbot, Jr. in 1783. Peter had been a slave in Pembroke, N.H., and had arrived in Andover from Bradford, Mass. (originally Rowley, now Haverhill, with part annexed to Groveland). The record of Peter's arrival was not made in the town records until February 23, 1785, when he was then 25 years old, Town of Andover, "Records of Information of Persons Taken into Town – Since the last Act of Court in Regard of the Maintenance of poor persons," n.p. Peter Sigourney appeared in Town of Andover, Overseers of the Poor, "Return of the Poor in the Town of Andover during the year ending on the last Monday of December, 1833," Ms. S 203, ACHC, which has a clerk's endorsement of January 18, 1834. The list indicated that he was "about 71" years old, "colored", his birthplace was "unknown", that he could neither read nor write, that he had two children, had been a laborer, was lame, was intemperate, and that he had been an almshouse resident from 1831 until his death on September 1, 1833.

[10] A household harboring a fugitive slave would be disinclined to identify the escapee to federal census enumerators. But two "slaves" from Charleston, S.C., Elvinah and Jack, were married at the West Parish Church in Andover in June 1835, Patrakis, *Andover in the Civil War*, 19; *VRA*, Vol. 2, 357 (Marriages, "Negroes"). Wilbur H. Siebert, "The Underground Railroad in Massachusetts," 51–52, conveyed that "[a]mong the last runaways to pass through Andover were a man and his sister [...] from Virginia," as reported in a note published in the *Andover Advertiser* (Anonymous, "A Fugitive," July 7, 1860, n.p. [2]). Robert Rollings and Julia C. Palmer, whose Andover marriage was officiated on November 29, 1863, may have been escaped slaves. Their marriage record indicated, in the column for place of birth, that he was born in "Maryland—in slavery" and that she was born "South—in slavery". In the column for "What Marriage—Whether First, Second, Third, &c. [etc.,]" Andover Clerk Edward Taylor wrote that Rollings and Palmer had

previously "married south according to the slave laws." Rollings and Palmer, Marriage record. Julia C. (Palmer) Rollings' sister, Mrs. Martha Matilda (Palmer) Henderson, who died in Andover on December 3, 1864, might have been an escaped slave. "In slavery" was written for her place of birth in her town and state death records. Under occupation was written, in parentheses, "(african)". Martha Matilda Henderson, Death record, Town of Andover and State Vital Records. Allen Hinton (1835, 1837, 1844, or 1847–1912), a former and apparently escaped slave from North Carolina, moved to Andover in 1864. In 1867, Hinton married Mary Jane (Patmore) Johnson (a widow with a son, also said to be a sister of Robert Rollings' wife Julia, but the Hinton-Johnson marriage record indicated she was born in Connecticut, and he in South Carolina). In 1877 he established a family ice cream business in Andover, AHS, "Allen Hinton", http://www .andoverlestweforget.com/faces-of-andover/gleason-holt/allen-hinton/, accessed August 25, 2017; Balboni, "Andover Stories: Hinton's Ice Cream was Sweet Success of Former Slave"; Hinton and Johnson, Marriage record; Patrakis, ibid., 65–68.

[11] I thank John Hannigan for sharing information about the Coburn family, for alerting me to Titus and Rosanna Coburn's Revolutionary War pension application records, and for tentatively proposing that Phillis could be the slave counted in the 1830 census. Hannigan's suggestion was based on Phillis' stated age of 90 in 1820, that she had been a slave, and that the family "had assistance from the town for many years past", Titus Coburn, July 13, 1820, in Titus and Rosanna Coburn, Revolutionary War Pension Application File (hereafter RWPA). The records cited to and quoted from RWPA are the federal government's files held by the National Archives, unless otherwise specified. The Essex County Circuit Court of Common Pleas for the Middle Circuit, RWPA file for Titus Coburn, July 13, 1820, is in Collection No. EC 43, Box 2, File 5 pension applications, "Collection of Essex County (Mass.) Court Records, 1628–1914," Phillips Library, Peabody Essex Museum, Rowley, Mass.

[12] Titus Coburn, July 13, 1820, in Coburn and Coburn, RWPA, indicated that Phillis was 90 (thus born 1730). Anonymous, "Sketches of Octogenarians" (about Rose Coburn's family) and Anonymous, "Obituary" for Rosanna Coburn, derived from "Sketches," indicated (mistakenly) that Phillis died about 1836 when she was 101 years old (thus born 1735). Ages and dates specified in both sources are problematic. Phillis died before January 5, 1829. If Phillis died late 1828 at 101, she was born about 1727.

In preparing the July 13, 1820 pension application, Coburn and Coburn, RWPA, which is the federal version of the pension application—a copy

made from the original county court records—the copyist misread Phillis'
name and it was written as "Chillin" in the federal copy, the flourished letters
P and *s* in the original having been misread by the copyist as *C* and *n*. The
federal and county court versions were each written by different hands, and
the federal version was a later copy. Titus Coburn, RWPA, July 13, 1820,
Essex County Circuit Court of Common Pleas for the Middle Circuit,
Collection No. EC 43, Box 2, File 5 pension applications, "Collection
of Essex County (Mass.) Court Records, 1628–1914," Phillips Library,
Peabody Essex Museum, Rowley, Mass.

[13] Town of Andover, "Town Records, Tax Records 1823–1847" (untitled
volume, title from microfilm target but actually treasurer records of
payments for orders drawn by the overseers of the poor), n.p., ninth volume
on GSU Microfilm Reel 878782, January 5, 1829 (No. 36, $3.00: "An order
to Stephice [Stephen] Holt for a coffin for Phillis Wid[ow] of Boos").

[14] United States Census, *Population Schedules of the Fifth Census of the United
States 1830, Roll 61*, Essex County, 181 (Mrs. Rosanna Coburn). Colley
Hooper, Death record, Town of Andover and State Vital Records.

[15] United States Secretary of Commerce and Labor, "Useless Papers in
Commerce and Labor Department," 2, listed "2 bound volumes [of]
letters sent and received" pertaining to the Fifth Census, as having "no
permanent value or historical interest" and recommended to be discarded.
The destruction was approved in 1908 by the United States House of
Representatives, Joint Select Committee on Disposition of Useless Papers
in the Executive Departments, "Disposition of Useless Papers in the
Department of Commerce and Labor." For the Congressional procedure
authorizing destruction, see Wells, et al., "Historical Development of the
Records Disposal Policy of the Federal Government Prior to 1934," 188–
189.

[16] United States Congress, *Statutes at Large*, 22nd Cong., 1st sess., Res. 5,
July 3, 1832, 606. The corrected edition of the 1830 aggregate statistics
is United States Department of State, *Fifth Census; or, Enumeration of
the Inhabitants of the United States, as Corrected at the Department of State*,
published in 1832. The uncorrected data for Massachusetts indicating four
slaves appear on pages 16–23. The errata sheet at pages 164–165 detailed the
erroneous counts of slaves in Barre (Worcester County) and in Worthington
and Westhampton (Hampshire County). As indicated at pages 21 and
165, the correct count for Massachusetts was one female slave in Andover,
Essex County. The United States Bureau of the Census, *Bureau of the
Census Catalog of Publications*, 6–7, described discrepancies with the various
editions of the publications of the 1830 statistics: "The [corrected] edition

was published the same year as the first print[ing] of the census results upon direction of Congress. The two editions, of which the corrected one contains the statistics ultimately used as a basis for Congressional reapportionment, were bound in one volume and preceded by a summary of the results of the enumerations of 1790–1820 inclusive." It is that second, corrected edition (the third part of the bound volume, each part independently paginated) that I cited above as United States Department of State, *Fifth Census [...] as Corrected*, etc. The corrections, however, were only indicated in the errata sheet at the end of that third part of the volume. The corrected information was the source for the one Massachusetts slave reported by the United States Bureau of the Census in 1909, "Statistics of Slaves," 133, Table 60, and the 1918 publication United States Bureau of the Census, *Negro Population 1790–1915*, 57, Table 6. The 2006 edition of *Historical Statistics of the United States*, edited by Carter, et al., Vol. 2, 2-76 (Table Ba322), 2-375 (Table Bb7), listed one slave in Massachusetts in 1830. Angela Michele Leonard, *Political Poetry as Discourse*, 145, also noticed discrepancies in tabular reporting of the 1830 census data.

Chapter 3 The Persistence of "Slave" Denotations in Historical Andover

[1] Jeremy Belknap, "Queries Respecting the Slavery and Emancipation of Negroes in Massachusetts," 203, said that "Some of the aged and infirm thought it most prudent to continue in the families where they had always been well used." Slave owners were required to support their slaves in sickness and in old age, but were not required to do so after their manumission. Theophilus Parsons [Jr.], *Memoir of Theophilus Parsons*, 16, 17, (written by the same-named son of the late Chief Justice) related an example from his own Essex County family involving their slave Violet who adamantly refused Rev. Moses Parsons' offer of manumission. Roger N. Parks, "Early New England and the Negro," provided several more examples, emphasizing "the retention of what was essentially a master-slave relationship after the slave had legally become free". (Subsequent editions appeared of Park's 1969 writing with the subtitle "Revised edition. A Teaching Background Paper," published in 1973 and 1978 by the Museum Education Department, Old Sturbridge Village, Sturbridge, Mass.) Historian Elise Lemire explained that decades after slavery was no longer legally tenable, many laboring servants in Concord, Middlesex County, Mass., nevertheless chose to remain in a condition of enslavement and were treated as slaves, being transferred as property in wills. Those that "stayed on" with families seemed to do so for the security of room and board; one eventually received "nominal" pay, but others were not paid. Other former servants in Concord chose to become independent: at least

three owned property, and others occupied agriculturally marginal land, doing what labor they could to subsist. Lemire, *Black Walden*, 10, 12, 109, 110 (quotations), 111, 117–118, 128–129, 131–132, 137–138, 151, 180 (landowners). Claude M. Fuess, *Andover: Symbol of New England*, 311, without specifying to whom he was referring, asserted that "several former slaves stayed on by preference in the households of their former masters." It was in those kinds of uncertain arrangements where actual slavery (among other oppressions, work for no wages) or slave-like servitude persisted in Massachusetts—however the situations manifested, and to whatever sense and degree they were negotiated. As Gloria McCahon Whiting and her research assistants did for historical Suffolk County, intensive searching, recordation, and analysis of probate files among other archival sources for data about people of color treated as property in other Massachusetts places could finally clarify the murky devolution of slavery in this state.

[2] Massachusetts Chapter 1 of the Acts of 1703 required owners to post bonds with towns for their manumitted slaves. George H. Moore, *Notes on the History of Slavery in Massachusetts*, 53, 54, 219, miscited the 1703 law as "Chapter 2" of the Acts. Kunal M. Parker, "Making Blacks Foreigners," 97 n46, misunderstood Moore, ibid., 54, who actually indicated that the 1703 law "was still in force as late as June 1807 when it was reproduced in the revised laws". I have not been able to identify Moore's source, but the Commonwealth of Massachusetts, *Perpetual Laws*, Vol. 3, 164–165 (published March 1801) included the law in the Appendix as Chapter 24, and noted it was "Revised." Despite that, Emily Blanck's applied research effort, *Tyrannicide*, 117–118, 191 n3, n4, 192 n12, n14, showed that posting bonds was not routinely practiced. Jeremy Belknap, "Queries Respecting the Slavery and Emancipation of Negroes in Massachusetts," 203, reported "that in some of the country towns, votes were passed in town-meetings [...] that they would not exact of masters, any bonds for the maintenance of liberated blacks, if they should become incapable of supporting themselves." Belknap's source was Thomas Pemberton, "Thomas Pemberton to Dr. Belknap, Boston, March 12, 1795," 392–393, who related, "There was a manifest inconsistency in holding any of their species in bondage whilst they were contending for their own liberty. This sentiment seems to have operated on the minds of the citizens of this State, and in some of the country towns they voted to have no slaves among them, and to indemnifie their masters (after they had given them freedom) from any expence that might arise by means of their age, infirmities, or inabilities to support themselves." While they may be yet undiscovered, in the Andover town records that I viewed, I noticed no entries for such bonds and no town meeting vote on the matter.

The town of Wilmington, Mass., where Titus Coburn was manumitted (by Edward Hircom's will, Edward Hurcum, Probate file papers, will, July 14, 1781), voted on March 3, 1777 to support any poor former slaves who were manumitted within one month: "Voted to Accept of all the Negroes belonging to said Town of Wilmington Whose masters are willing to give them their Freedom in One month from this Date, and [^]in[^] Case said Negroes Should not be able to Support themselves to Support them as yᵉ Towns [^]poor[^]", Town of Wilmington, "Town Meetings, etc. 1730–1807," 164 (quotation). Several writers have described the vote, but none mentioned the 30-day sunset clause, Meltsner, *The Poorhouses of Massachusetts*, 66; Noyes, *1730–1880. Wilmington. Historical Addresses*, 46; Smith, *Morrill Kindred in America*, 58 (Cadwallader Ford, Jr., son-in-law of Rev. Morrill), 60. Wilmington historian Larz Neilson featured information about the 1777 vote in several local history articles, as if it were chiefly an emancipative action, which it was not directly. However, by offering slave owners a month to free their slaves to avoid the requirement to post a bond prior to manumitting—the town only agreeing to support any former slaves who required poor relief who had been manumitted during that time—the town vote encouraged at least two owners to manumit two enslaved women within the month. Neilson, "The Wilmington Resolves on Civil Rights"; "Wilmington voted to free slaves in 1777"; "Wilmington black man served in Revolution"; "The day the slaves were freed" (misstated the year of the town vote as 1779); "Wilmington's first town meeting" (corrected year of the town vote to 1777); and, "Freedom for the slaves of Massachusetts."

As a consequence of the March 3, 1777 vote, the Wilmington town clerk recorded three related entries, serially and in short order. On the same day as the vote, a statement of mutual objections of Cadwallader Ford, Esq. (1703–1790) and Cadwallader Ford, Jr. (1743–1804) was recorded by the latter who was also the town clerk and the son-in-law of Rev. Isaac Morrill (1718–1793). The father (who had been elected moderator at that meeting) and the son stated that they "Oppose and protest against sᵈ Vote, and proceeding of said Town Thereon &c. [etc.]" "Respecting the Negroes [...] which was to see if yᵉ Town would Accept of all such Negroes whose Masters should see cause to give them their Freedom – and in case sᵈ Negroes should Come to want [i.e., to need assistance] to support them as yᵉ Towns poor". The record of that town meeting had no indication of any procedural objection (at another meeting such a notation was made that a previous meeting was decided to have been improperly conducted). The clerk duly recorded the results. On the following page was recorded the March 10, 1777 manumission of Rev. Isaac Morrill's "Negro Woman Dinah" (and what may be the original manumission paper is attached at that page). Morrill wrote that Dinah "has for some time past had a desire for her freedom, and as this Town did at their Last meeting Vote that Such Negroes as were within one month freed by their Masters Should be Supported by the Town in Case of Necessity; [...] in Consequence of Said Vote of this Town, and the desire of y^c Said Dinah I have given her her Freedom and she is at free Liberty to Leave my House and Service when She pleases". Then, on the next page, the town clerk recorded Violet's manumission on March 29, 1777 from Benjamin Thompson. Thompson's action would also appear to have been prompted by the March 3, 1777 town meeting vote. Before the town clerk, Thompson (spelled "Tompson") "Declared that he had given his Negro Girl Named Vilot her Freedom – & Desired that I would Enter it upon Record", Town of Wilmington, "Town Records Town Meetings Intentions 1762–1834" (title from microfilm target; spine title "Town Meetings Etc. 1807–1834 Intentions Town of Wilmington"), 343, 344, 345, first volume on GSU Microfilm Reel 887763, digital image 189 and 190 of 430, https://www.familysearch.org/ark: /61903/3:1:3QS7-9979-M9D6-G?i=188&cc=2061550&cat=146917; and, https://www.familysearch.org/ark:/61903/3:1:3QSQ-G979-M9D8 -R?i=189&cc=2061550&cat=146917, accessed February 16, 2019. I thank Keith S. Blake for noticing the sunset clause "as were within one month" in Rev. Morrill's words.

[3] Minardi, *Making Slavery History*, chapter 2. The Massachusetts House of Representatives, RCEC, 8–12, summarized their understanding of the evolution of the settlement laws and the eligibility of persons for state reimbursement. See Parker, "Making Blacks Foreigners," 84–91, 111–117 and the sources he cited for details of the progression of the statutory settlement laws, and the court-decided common law of settlement and poor relief pertaining to former slaves.

[4] I have completed comprehensive documentary research about Nancy Parker (fl. 1752–1825, also called Nancy Poor during her lifetime), her husband Salem Poor (1744–1802, died in Boston, Mass.), and their son Jonas (baptized 1776–?). Nancy Parker has been featured and transformed legendarily in local oral and written traditions, but her factual biography was uninvestigated beyond tantalizing notes in a genealogical article about her owner's family, Fitzpatrick, "Joseph Parker of Andover," and in a brief but powerful AHS newsletter article, Patrakis, "Nancy Parker." Like Rosanna Coburn remembered as "the last slave" in Andover, Nancy Parker was curiously, inaccurately, and purposefully remembered in local history narratives as "the last Indian" of Andover, e.g., Bailey, *Historical Sketches of Andover*, 27 n2, among numerous other writers. (The adjoining city of Lawrence, Mass., created from a part of Andover, also claimed her by that shibboleth.) "The last Indian" is a

fallacious and pernicious trope of Native extinction, ubiquitous in New England history projects, which was applied to explain and justify the dislocation of Native people and the dispossession of Native homelands by settler-colonists. As with "the last slave," the sentimental cliché of "the last Indian" also functioned to contrast historicalness with modernity and social reform, O'Brien, *Firsting and Lasting*, 136–137; Minardi, *Making Slavery History*. By "historicalness," I mean perceptively "of history," the perceived quality of being an antiquity or a relic, in contrast to historical factuality denoted in "historicity."

In its application to Nancy Parker and to Andover, the stock phrase "the last Indian" is false because she had a son (although he tragically predeceased her), there were Native people with their children in town before, during, and after her lifetime, Native people are still connected to their ancestral homelands of the Merrimack River watershed there, and 2010 federal census data indicate Native American residents in town. Only after her death was Nancy Parker's evidently multiple ancestries abridged to "Indian." During her life she was called "Negro" or "Molatto". Nancy Parker's death record in the published *VRA*, Vol. 2, 519, was listed by the editors among the Parkers, not among "Negroes." (There was no separate section for deaths of "Indians" in *VRA*: that category was created only for births and marriages.) While the editors of *VRA* were not aware that Nancy Parker was the same "mulatto" person of color who married the "negro" Salem, ibid., 358, the inconsistent editorial decisions underscored the problematic and shifting racialization assigned to people of color during and after their lives.

A significant achievement of Nancy Parker had been forgotten: in 1771 Nancy ended her 19-year enslavement in Capt. James Parker's family by winning a freedom suit against Parker's widow and son, Nancy v. James Parker, Jr. and Dinah Parker, Essex County Court of Common Pleas Records, September 1771, 147; December 1771, 197, JA. (The freedom suit was heard September 1771; a follow-up suit against James Parker, Jr., who did not pay her court costs and damages as he promised, was heard December 1771.) In her first lawsuit, Nancy's attorney stated she was freeborn, and the Parkers acceded to that assertion. If Nancy was freeborn in fact, and the Parkers knew that Nancy was freeborn—rather than that assertion being merely a legal fiction and the Parkers merely capitulated to that legal fiction because doing so was necessary to resolve the suit through arbitration—then Nancy's ancestry can be discerned. If Nancy were in fact freeborn, then her mother was of Native or "white" ancestry and thus not legally enslaveable, *partus sequitur ventrem*.

Nancy Parker is frequently mentioned in modern histories about Massachusetts African Americans and Native Americans during and after the Revolutionary War, but only because of her marriage to Salem Poor. Nancy became mentioned with Salem, typically and imprecisely styled as Poor's "Indian" wife. He has been celebrated in innumerable historical, nationalistic, heroic narratives, because of his distinguished exploits during the Battle of Bunker Hill. Nevertheless, commonly surmised speculations advanced to fill out Salem Poor's scant biography, erroneous factoids, and misinterpretations, are rife and recurrent in popular historical narratives created about him. Muddling matters further, Salem Poor has been often confused with two other African American Revolutionary War soldiers, Peter Salem (circa 1750–1816, died in Framingham, Mass.), and Salem Middlesex (died November 4, 1799, in Weston, Mass.). My long-term research and writing project about Nancy Parker continues to progress. Early notice of her was in Bell, "Archaeology and Native History of the Den Rock Area" and in "Discerning Native Placemaking." I conveyed research highlights for an educational conference in "Obtaining Her Liberty."

[5] Several Andover woman of color named Rose have been often confused and their biographies conflated. Pompey Lovejoy's (1724–1826) wife Rose (1727–1826) was enslaved by John Foster when they married in 1751, according to *VRA*, Vol. 2, 358 ("Negroes"). Charlotte Helen Abbott, "Historical Andover. No. 107. Africa to Andover.—(Concluded)," 3, however, wrote that Pompey married "Rose Chadwick of a Bradford house [originally Rowley, now Haverhill, with part annexed to Groveland] in 1751." Alfred Poore, "A Genealogical-Historical Visitation of Andover, Mass., in the Year 1863," *Essex Institute Historical Collections* 51 (4) (1915): 306, similarly asserted that Rose "was servant of Mr. Chadwick in Boxford." Poore, ibid., 48 (3) (1912): 289, intriguingly declared that "Pompey Lovejoy was a slave to his [Sylvester Abbott's] grandmother's father, Henry Abbott". Where Charlotte Helen Abbott and Alfred Poore obtained their information regarding Chadwick is unknown, but the original 1751 marriage intention and marriage record (not included in my references) indeed indicated that Pompey was enslaved by Capt. William Lovejoy, and that Rose was enslaved by John Foster, all of Andover. Pompey Lovejoy was manumitted by Capt. Lovejoy's will written January 14, 1762, approved and allowed on April 5, 1762 by Probate Judge John Choate, Esq., William Lovejoy, Probate file papers, will, fourth clause: "I give [^] my [^] Negrow man Named Pompy his Freedom from all Slavery and Servitude."

Jonathan French (1805–1895), "Parson Phillips's Slaves – Also, Pomp and Rose," recorded a local oral tradition that "Pomp Lovejoy was bought in Boston of a Baker. [...He] was famous for his Bakery near Pomp's Pond – named for the honest baker[^].[^] ~~assisted by his~~ Rose his respectable wife. is remembered by aged persons in Andover". In the handwritten manuscript,

French had first begun to convey that Pompey was "assisted by his" wife Rose and had ended the sentence at that thought. But then French struck-through those words and adjusted punctuation to create two sentences, which in effect concealed Rose's labor. French's initial idea supports several other accounts that Pompey and Rose worked together to prepare food and beverage for sale. Cooperative labor was a practical strategy. Abbott, ibid., wrote that Rose "was a good cook and Pomp drove a bake cart" and that he also butchered cattle. Abbott, ibid., related several interesting anecdotes about the couple, including one when her aunt visited their home and saw the cakes the couple had prepared for Election Day. Regarding the frequent references to Pompey and Rose preparing "'Lection Cake" and root beer or beer or ale for "Election Day" (so-called), the public festival was held customarily in April or May, Abbott, ibid.; Fischer, *Albion's Seed*, 164; Old Sturbridge Village, "Celebrations in the 1830s." Both Anthony F. Martin and I independently considered whether the references were actually to "Negro Election Day" festivities, but have so far found no corroborative documentation that any were held in Andover, although they were in other Essex County places. The couple could have traveled to those gatherings to sell their food, Martin, "On the Landscape for a Very, Very Long Time," 116–121, 170–171 and sources cited. Martin, "Homeplace Is also Workplace,"109–110, suggested other occasions when people of color might have gathered in Andover homes, such as after church services or funerals. Pam Smith, "Andover Stories: Pompey Lovejoy," related that "Pompey and his wife would host gatherings at their cabin in the woods, and they were in charge of making the 'lection cake and ginger root beer. [...] It was said 'Pity the town meeting house crowd on election day if Pompey was not custodian of the cake and beer. Woe to the funeral wake if Pompey did not mix the grog and serve it.'" Pompey's travel between Andover and Milton, Mass., was documented by Peter Hopkins, "Pomp Lovejoy and 'lection cake," citing to the manuscript volumes, Vose, Lewis and Crane, Ledger of Liberty Paper Mill, Milton, Mass., 1770–1793, Crane Museum and Center for the Paper Arts, Dalton, Mass.: "Pomp Lovejoy visited the Liberty Paper Mill twice. In May of 1781 he purchased 1¼ dozen press papers, and in May of 1782, bought one dozen press papers. He paid with 121 pounds of rags from Andover."

Pompey Lovejoy's advanced age while he was alive, then at his death, and his wife Rose's death, were reported and republished in many local, regional, and national newspapers. An anonymous article, "Longevity," originally published in the *Salem Gazette* (Salem, Mass.), November 1, 1825, 2 (Pompey Lovejoy, "oldest man in Essex County," 102 years old, wife 93 years old; "attended in their family by two unmarried nieces" 78 and 50 years old) was reprinted widely. Anonymous, "Longevity," appeared in the *Independent*

Chronicle and Boston Patriot (Boston, Mass.), November 2, 1825, 2; *Essex Register* (Salem, Mass.), November 3, 1825, 3; *Boston Traveler* (Boston, Mass.), November 4, 1825, 2; *Salem Observer* (Salem, Mass.), November 5, 1825, 3; *Haverhill Gazette* (Haverhill, Mass.), November 5, 1825, 2; *Niles' Weekly Register* (Baltimore, Md.), November 12, 1825, 176 ("Pompey Lovejoy, aged 102 years, with his wife, in her 98th year, and his two neices [*sic*], aged 78 and 50 respectively, are all living together"); *Alexandria Gazette* (Alexandria, Va.), November 15, 1825, 3; *Massachusetts Spy* (Worcester, Mass.), November 16, 1825, 2; *Ladies Museum* (Providence, R.I.), November 26, 1825, 72, and likely in several other places. The original *Salem Gazette* article, as republished by the *Boston Traveler*, included that Pompey "was born a slave. He has lived to enjoy the blessings of Liberty; and the decays of nature are alleviated by glorious visions of 'the march of mind,' 'the spirit of the age,' 'the reign of liberal ideas,' 'and the perfectibility of man.'" Those quoted phrases referred to intellectual and political themes of the time. Death notices and notes about the deaths of Pompey and Rose Lovejoy were also far-reaching. Anonymous, Note about death of Pompey Lovejoy, appeared in the *Salem Gazette*, February 28, 1826, 2; *Boston Patriot and Daily Chronicle* (Boston, Mass.), March 2, 1826, 2; *Salem Observer*, March 4, 1826, 3; *Portsmouth Journal of Literature and Politics* (Portsmouth, N.H.), March 4, 1826, 3; *The Christian Watchman* (Boston, Mass.), March 10, 1826, 3; and, in the *Boston News-letter and City Record* (Boston, Mass.), March 11, 1826, n.p. [4] (death at 102 years and oldest resident of Essex County; survived by his wife who was 98 years old; two unmarried nieces aged 68 and 50, "whom it is customary with them to designate as the *children*, live in the family"). Short death notices were published, Anonymous, "Deaths" (Pompey Lovejoy), in the *New-Hampshire Statesman and Concord Register* (Concord, N.H.), March 11, 1826, n.p. [3]; and, Anonymous, "Deaths" (Rose Lovejoy), in the *New-Hampshire Statesman and Concord Register*, December 2, 1826, n.p. [3]. Anonymous, Note about death of Rose Lovejoy, appeared in the *Haverhill Gazette*, November 25, 1826, 3; and, the *Salem Observer*, November 25, 1826, 3 (Rose death at 100 years old, Pompey at 111 years old). I thank Lise Breen for finding many of these articles and providing the particular bibliographic data.

An anonymous ("G.") article, "Pomp and Pomp's Pond," published in the *Andover Advertiser*, October 30, 1858, n.p. [1], indicated that "*Flora* and *Dinah*" were Pompey and Rose Lovejoy's "companions", and attributed the ale-making and cake baking to Flora. If the news stories were true, Flora had assumed cooking for her elderly aunt and uncle and her nearly blind sister, and continued the Lovejoy's provisioning business. If the news accounts were accurate about the family relationship, and that the sisters Flora Chandler and Dinah Chadwick lived with Pompey and Rose, then the sisters were

Rose Lovejoy's nieces. Flora was the older sister, and the ages reported in the newspapers are not out of line with ages estimated from other sources. Flora's son was named Pomp Chandler, possibly honoring Pompey Lovejoy, *VRA*, Vol. 1, 389 ("Negroes," Pomp Chandler, son of Flora, baptized July 5, 1778). Flora's daughter Damon Chandler was baptized the same day as her brother, *VRA*, Vol. 1, 95, not listed under "Negroes." Yet, the 1790–1810 census population schedules for Pompey Lovejoy's household only ever counted three individuals, United States Census, *Population Schedules of the First Census of the United States 1790*, 19; *Population Schedules of the Second Census of the United States 1800, Roll 14*, Essex County, 200; *Population Schedules of the Third Census of the United States 1810*, 253. Joan Patrakis (emails, March 29, and April 2, 2019) shared the 1858 Andover newspaper source with me, noticed the entries in *VRA* for Flora's children, and encouraged my research to consider if or when Flora and/or Dinah resided with Pompey and Rose, and if they were the unnamed nieces mentioned in the sources. For related information about Flora and Dinah, see chap. 2, note 3, and chap. 3, note 18.

In addition to confusing Rose Lovejoy with other Andover women named Rose, some sources insist that Pompey Lovejoy's wife was named Dinah. It seems that the many misattributions were to Dinah Chadwick, inferred to be Rose Lovejoy's niece. For example, Sarah Stuart Robbins (1817–1910), in her 1908 memoir *Old Andover Days*, 140, conveyed childhood memories and dialogue of "Old Pomp and Dinah". Also mistaking Dinah Chadwick for Rose Lovejoy, Wilson Flagg (1805–1884), the naturalist, writer, and conservationist who attended Phillips Academy, in his essay "Rural Architecture" (first published 1876 in *The Atlantic Monthly*, 433–434, and republished 1881 in his book *Halcyon Days*, 16–18), provided an astonishingly detailed recollection of the architecture, layout, and appearance of Pompey and Rose Lovejoy's cabin and its grounds. Sarah Loring Bailey, *Historical Sketches of Andover*, 39, 43, 302, wrote of the historical association of the name of Pomp's Pond (formerly Ballard's Pond), transcribed a 1779 letter from Prince Proctor to Pompey Lovejoy, and noted Lovejoy's Revolutionary War service. Some sources asserted that Pompey Lovejoy received a Revolutionary War pension, but I have found no record. Pompey Lovejoy has been confused with other men by several historical writers. William C. Nell, in *Services of Colored Americans in the Wars of 1776 and 1812*, 11, and identically in *The Colored Patriots of the American Revolution*, 44, mistakenly wrote that descendants of Pomp Jackson (circa 1728–1822, formerly in Newton, Mass., and then Newburyport) resided near Pomp's Pond in Andover. Nell mistook Pomp Jackson for Pompey Lovejoy, but Nell seemingly knew that the war veteran Pomp Jackson that he wrote of—"instead of 'cutting his master's throat,' he only slashed the throats of his country's enemies"—was not the indentured servant Pomp (circa 1767–1795) who murdered his Andover master, Charles Furbush. Theophilus Parsons [Jr.], *Memoir of Theophilus Parsons*, 176 n, also confused Pompey Lovejoy with Pomp Jackson. Nell and Parsons appear to be sources of that confusion repeated in many nineteenth- and twentieth-century works. Harriet Beecher Stowe, in her 1891 book *Sam Lawson's Oldtown Fireside Stories*, 252–253, inauthentically imagined that Pompey Lovejoy's Revolutionary War service consisted only of him serving apple cider he brought to "our men." Stowe's intentions were to portray Lovejoy as an enthusiastic contributor to the cause, giving "all the cider he had" (253), but the character of Pompey Lovejoy that she drew has uncomfortable parallels with the emasculated and servile Uncle Tom. In actuality, Pompey Lovejoy mobilized with other Andover men who responded to the Lexington alarm on April 19, 1775, and was credited for 1½ days service, Massachusetts Secretary of the Commonwealth, *Massachusetts Soldiers and Sailors of the Revolutionary War*, Vol. 9, 996 ("Lovejoy, 'Pompe'").

At the South Parish Cemetery, the graves of Pompey and Rose Lovejoy are in the same row adjoining the graves for Rose Coburn and Colley Hooper. Presently, there is a space of about eight feet with no grave markers between the two gravestones for the Lovejoys and the gravestones for Coburn and for Hooper. The stones for Rose Lovejoy, Rose Coburn, and Colley Hooper were created and placed in 2002. Pomp's Pond, where the Lovejoys lived, is now a town recreation area and the associative history with the couple is interpreted on the town's website http://www.andoverrec.com/pompspond/history, accessed August 11, 2017. I thank Lauren Kosky-Stamm for sharing her observation that even before Pompey Lovejoy died in 1826, the pond associated with him was called "Pompeys Pond", Hales, "The County of Essex" (map engraved June 19, 1825). I thank Anthony F. Martin for sharing and discussing information about the Lovejoys. Martin's dissertation, ibid., 134–135, 166, 167, 176, included biographical summary of the Lovejoys, citations to important sources, and linked them with other Andover people.

A vast body of primary and secondary sources—and artifacts associated with them that are preserved at the ACHC—await a biographer of the Lovejoys. The ACHC has a roundabout chair (named for the rounded back, also called a corner chair) said to have been made by Pompey Lovejoy. Measuring only 72 cm in height (just over 2' 4"), the characteristically low chair style was particularly suited to be used with a desk or writing table. Jennie Killorin, "Pompey's Corner Chair," n.p. [4], in a 1977 article published in the AHS newsletter about the donation (Accession No. 1977.001.1), indicated that the chair is made of apple wood "with a simple box stretcher and one ambitious turned leg." It has "a splendid, continuous back and arm" with a board seat that replaced an earlier woven rush seat. It was painted "soft, grey-blue", then later "reddish-brown". Provenance information in the ACHC accession record indicated that from 1910–1952 the chair was kept by Harry Ames Ramsdell (1867–1955) at 16 Summer Street, Andover. The chair may have come to Ramsdell from his mother, Georgette Russell (born circa 1836), who was the daughter of Frances F. Wardwell (1804–1892), all born in Andover. The ACHC also preserves swatches from what local tradition identified as Rose Lovejoy's beautifully colorful wedding dress. The fabric pieces were received as three separate accessions (Accession No. 1924.014 [Mary Ballard Estate], 1936.009 [Alice Carey Jenkins], and 1945.037 [Dr. Edward D. Lovejoy]). The textile is handwoven linsey-woolsey, with wide and narrow stripes of red, green, blue, and yellow. The wide red and green bands have an intricate and delicate white design.

The preservation, as meaningful heirlooms, of the circa 1740 chair and the circa 1751 cloth pieces into the early to late twentieth century by Andover families conveys the persistent devotion to remembering Rose and Pompey Lovejoy, and by association, Andover's former slaves and its antislavery movement. The fragment of the dress kept by Mary Ballard was exhibited in 1896 for Andover's 250th anniversary celebration, Andover *Catalogue of a Loan Collection at Punchard Hall*, 19 (Item 525, "piece of wedding dress of Pomp Lovejoy's wife" lent by Miss Mary A. Ballard). The following year, the sample of the wedding dress was exhibited in Boston among other artifacts gathered by the Andover Phoebe Foxcroft Phillips Chapter of the Daughters of the Revolution of the Commonwealth of Massachusetts (hereafter, DRCM), and the objects were listed in DRCM, *Catalogue of a Loan Collection of Ancient and Historic Articles*, 101, 102 (credited loan of that and other objects to Miss Mary A. Ballard), 105 (quotation, "Piece of wedding dress of Dinah, wife of Pompey Lovejoy. 'They were born slaves but died free'", ibid., perhaps paraphrasing from Pompey Lovejoy's gravestone epitaph, "Born in Boston, a slave: died in Andover a freeman", and mistaking Dinah for Pompey's wife Rose). Angela McBrien provided me the accession data and allowed me to see the chair and fabric pieces. The DRCM was a separate organization from the Daughters of the American Revolution. Records of the Andover chapter of the DRCM (1895–1932) are at ACHC, Ms S 619; Morgan, "Inventory, Daughters of the Revolution Records in Andover Historical Society." The wedding dress fragments were considered by Anonymous, "Born into Slavery and Brought to Andover: Four Pieces of Cloth are all that Remain of her Story of Slavery and Freedom" and by Clements, "The Story of Rose Lovejoy's Wedding Dress." On the role of objects in telling stories about enslavement and emancipation, see Minardi, "Making Slavery Visible (Again)."

[6] Davis, "Reflections on the Black Woman's Role in the Community of Slaves," 86–87 (quotations). Angela Yvonne Davis' discerning article—written and published while she was imprisoned in 1971 and reprinted many times—arrived at significant insights about labor and family life during and after enslavement that confronted then-prevailing presentist interpretations, and perceptively prefigured themes and conclusions revived decades later under the rubric of Black feminist theory, Davis, "The Legacy of Slavery." Nedra K. Lee, "Boarding: Black Women in Nantucket Generating Income and Building Community," 91–92, examined how "Black women [...] engaged in diverse domestic economies that both generated income and created a network of social support that sustained a growing free Black community in the North that faced racism and economic exploitation." Lee, ibid., 92, ascertained that "Black women's domestic chores and responsibilities [...] not only helped Black people maintain a connection to place but also provided income [such as by taking in boarders, and laboring for others inside and outside their homes] and deepened conventional social networks by incorporating other Black diasporic peoples." On women's role in "making community" "through the building and shaping of [...] culture," see Darlene Clark Hine, *Hine Sight*, xxii. Jacqueline Jones, "Race, Sex, and Self-Evident Truths," 303, summarized "several factors that determined the well-being of slave women: their material standard of living (defined by the adequacy of their food, clothing, and shelter); their ability to form kin relationships and then to preserve them; the amount of control they exercised over their own productive energies; and the arduousness of, or physical danger associated with, their labor." Whether slave or free, Jones, ibid., 332, most women of color were limited in their labor choices, undertaking the same tasks for other families as they did for their own: "cooking, washing clothes, cleaning, serving, and tending [...] children." See also Jones, "'Domestick Enemies.'" Felicia Y. Thomas, "Entangled With the Yolk of Bondage," has a chapter on labor, including textile work and laundry, with information drawn mostly from slave-for-sale newspaper advertisements.

For Nancy Parker's paid labor, see Anonymous, *Lawrence Up to Date*, 24; Dorgan, *Lawrence Yesterday and Today*, 9; French, Manuscript about Nancy Parker; Patrakis, "Nancy Parker," n.p. [3]; Robert H. Tewksbury, "Lawrence," 211 (quotation, "champion spinner"). After the importation boycott in December 1774, "Spinning bees were held at the [North Parish church] parsonage, which made for some diversion and sociability during these tense times." Mofford, *The History of North Parish Church of North Andover*, 97. There may be where Nancy Parker earned her reputation as a champion spinner. Many New England ministers hosted spinning meetings before and after the boycott. For 46 other spinning meetings held at New England ministers' homes, 1766–1770, see Ulrich, "'Daughters of Liberty,'" 216–217 (Table 1). For Dinah Simpson's and Lucy Foster's textile processing for cash and barter, see Samuel Abbot Business Papers, 1754–1819, Series I, Financial records, "Samuel Abbot's Waste Book, & Memorandum Book, & Petty Ledgger, Began May 11ᵗʰ: 1768," (i.e., 1768–1812), n.p. in parts, Mss:761 1754–1819 A122, Vol. 3A, https://hollisarchives.lib.harvard.edu/repositories/11/archival _objects/168654, digital images seq. 4, 13 (Caesar and Dinah "Sibson"); digital images seq. 6, 13 (Lucy Foster and Lucy "Chandler"); and, Receipted bills, spinning, Mss:761 1754–1819 A122, Box 73, Folder 13, Baker Library Historical Collections, Harvard Business School, Boston, Mass., https://hollisarchives .lib.harvard.edu/repositories/11/archival_objects/168825, digital images seq. 1–seq. 5 (Lucy Foster and Lucy "Chandler"), accessed August 13, 2019. For Rosanna Coburn trading and brokering, see Carpenter, "Glimpses of Life in Andover Eighty Years Ago, from an Old Family Expense-book," 3.

[7] Nash, "African Americans in the Early Republic," 14 (quotation). Lorenzo Johnston Greene, *The Negro in Colonial New England*, 298, bluntly generalized that "The condition of free Negroes in New England was probably no more favorable than elsewhere in colonial America. Strictly speaking, they were not free for they were proscribed politically, economically, and socially." Barbara McCaskill, *Love, Liberation, and Escaping Slavery*, 42, recognized "the precariousness of nominal northern freedom". Julie Saville, in "Rites and Power," 81, also understood the capricious nature of degrees of freedom: "Reversible, contingent changes in labour and property relations, in rule and resistance, and in the political standing of individuals no less than of states mark the trail of slaves' emancipations". Stephen Kantrowitz, "Fighting Jim Crow in the Cradle of Liberty," gave vivid examples of common, undignified affronts and assaults when traveling by railroad or on foot. Compare Walter Johnson, "On Agency" and Jessica Millward, "On Agency, Freedom, and the Boundaries of Slavery Studies," 195: "For recently manumitted and freeborn black women," particularly those who had brought freedom suits and had won, their awareness of their own legal freedom cannot be doubted—but neither can the nature of the culturally constructed "realities" of social and economic structures and processes of power and powerlessness that were present in their specific times and places. For Phillis and her children, their "agency" is evident in the wording used by the administrator of Sarah Frye's estate, writing off £24 of value after all the slaves had "taken their Freedom". I surmise that they had obtained "legal consciousness" and became aware that they could consider themselves free, of their own accord, without having to sue, or purchase themselves, or flee. Rather, they stayed in Andover, possibly even at the Frye farm and hat-making workshop for an interval, before setting up their own independent households.

[8] On the theoretical term, see Kathy Davis, "Intersectionality as Buzzword." I thank Patrick R. Grzanka for bringing Davis' article to me. Grzanka, et al., "Intersectionality, Inc.," 19, 21, 22, stressed the importance of remembering that the theoretical concept of intersectionality was initially developed in Black feminism by Kimberlé Crenshaw, "Mapping the Margins," in critique of systemic oppression in law "as a justice project." Intersectionality is distinct from identity theories and includes "a critique of structural inequalities [...] theorize[s] a matrix of domination [..., and] imagine[s] the historicity of shifting oppressions" in a program of social activism, Grzanka, et al., ibid., 21.

[9] Information about the range and frequency of travels of Andover people of color was sometimes captured in documentary sources. Peter Hopkins, "Pomp Lovejoy and 'lection cake," noticed that the Andover man traveled to the Liberty Paper Mill in May 1781 and in May 1782, hauling 121 pounds of rags from Andover to Milton, Mass., to exchange for paper. Military rosters and diaries placed men of color as soldiers and others as servants, marching, couriering, encamping, and fighting in many places throughout the Northeast. Lawyers' records show visits by clients to their Essex County offices. Records of trial appearances, probate actions, pension applications, land deeds, and a manumission paper, trace visits to Essex County courthouses and registries. Federal pension payment records indicate that Titus Coburn visited the federal bank in Boston. Account books document their labor at local farms. The published *Vital Records* of several towns indicate out-of-town marriages of Andover people of color, and so there were travels for courtship. Mariners of color from Andover are not yet identified, but sea journeys can be presumed. Phillis was stolen from her people in Africa and Booso was captured and forced from his wife and children in the West Indies: they were presumably among several people born in distant lands and brought terrified across oceans before arriving to the Merrimack River valley town.

"Bristow" and "Brister" (in other sources also rendered as "Bristo" and "Bristol") are the same man, a slave of "Col. Osgood", mentioned in Stephen Peabody's (1741–1819) diary in December 1767 and March 1768, Wright, *Pedagogues and Protesters*, 122, 167–168. Bristow/Brister traveled from Andover to Brighton and Roxbury with oxen and sheep, probably for market, and he couriered letters to and from Andover for Harvard College students in Cambridge. Wright, ibid., xxxiii–xxxiv, appreciated the geographic data encoded in Peabody's diary for tracking Peabody's extensive travels and the locations of his familiars that extended throughout northeastern Massachusetts into Maine. Peabody's visits among residents in his hometown of Andover, including the Fryes, were well-represented in his diary, and during those visits he would have seen and been seen by the people of color living in the households. James Stevens (1749–1834), Andover carpenter and Revolutionary War diarist, saw Joshua Frye arrive in Cambridge on September 26, 1775. The next morning Stevens rode Frye's horse to Andover, arriving in the middle of the afternoon at Sarah Frye's, and from there walked home. As in Peabody's diary, Stevens did not mention the Frye's slaves in his brief journal entries, but expectedly both men encountered them and were familiar with them, Stevens, "The Revolutionary Journal of James Stevens," 57.

The same "Molatto Fellow Named Brister" was listed in the inventory of the estate of Deacon John Osgood (1683–1765) of Andover, dated April 5, 1766. In that inventory, Brister was itemized before "a Negro Woman Called Nancy" and "A Negro Boy", John Osgood, Probate file papers. Over a decade earlier, in 1755, Nancy, then enslaved by Capt. Joseph Osgood, married "Primas" who was enslaved by Maj. John Osgood, *VRA*, Vol. 2, 358 (Marriages, "Negroes"). A transcribed record of the Andover town meeting of September 5, 1769 documented a vote that directed the town treasurer to "take all legal measures to recover the cost of the charge that hath arisen for the support of Dorkis (?) [i.e., Dorcas], the wife of Bristo, formerly a molatto servant of John Osgood, Esq. and their children", Town of Andover, "Andover, Massachusetts, Town Meeting Records, 1709–May 21, 1776," Microfilm Frame 5215, question mark in the typed transcript. After enslavement by John Osgood's family, Bristow/Brister was still enslaved when he was listed as "Servant to Dudley Woodbridge", Osgood and Osgood, Day Books, n.p., Vol. 1, June 24, 1771, https://iiif.lib.harvard.edu/manifests/view/drs:424481266$49i, digital image seq. 49, accessed October 18, 2019. Bristow/Brister may have been leased by the Osgood family as a slave to Woodbridge, but the arrangement did not last. Just over two years later, prior to December 1773, Bristow/Brister commenced legal action to obtain his freedom.

Salem lawyer William Pynchon was consulted by several enslaved clients seeking freedom: in November 1773, men named Bristoe, Cato, and Jack met with Pynchon for advice on that subject. Pynchon, "William Pynchon Papers, 1746–1789," I. Legal Records, Box 1, Folder 2, Court Fees, 1761–1773/Miscellaneous Legal Fees 1764–1771 (bound manuscript volume), Mss. 236, Phillips Library, Peabody Essex Museum, Rowley, Mass. The identities of those men are not determined, but the Bristoe who met with Pynchon may be the same Andover man Bristow/Brister who brought the freedom lawsuit Bristol v. John Osgood, Essex County Court of Common Pleas Records, December 1773, 38, JA. In that matter, both parties defaulted, and their failure to appear might suggest that the case was settled out of court. (Despite the parallels of the names, the Cato and Jack who met with Pynchon in 1773 were probably not the Andover men later called Cato Frye and Jack Booz enslaved by Sarah Frye. If their ages were correctly stated in Sarah Frye's 1781 estate inventory, they would have been 14 and 2 years old, respectively. In any regard, Cato Frye and Jack Booz [called Juba in 1781] did not pursue freedom suits, but took their freedom between May 1781 and September 1790, Sarah Frye, Probate file papers, inventory, May 1, 1781; accounting and distribution, September 7, 1790.) Precisely when Bristow/ Brister became legally free is not determined. His leaving enslavement may have occurred soon after his legal action against John Osgood.

Bristow/Brister and his family members appeared in more entries than any other persons of color in the day books kept by the Andover physicians Joseph Osgood and his son George Osgood who lived in the North Parish. Bristow/Brister's name was rendered in the day books as "Bristo" and "Bristol" and he was described as "Molatto", Osgood and Osgood, Day Books, n.p., Vol. 1, November 3, 1770, digital image seq. 25; Vol. 1, April 23, 1771, seq. 42. (Image-specific URLs for each entry referenced in this endnote are not further provided due to space considerations. Interested researchers can locate the digital images of the entries from the webpage for the main catalog record of the three volumes—http://id.lib.harvard.edu /alma/990065550010203941/catalog—by using the volume number and digital image sequence number provided.)

Entries in the Osgoods' day books credited Bristow/Brister's labor that he performed at their farm. He was skilled at animal slaughtering (Osgood and Osgood, Day Books, n.p., Vol. 1, November 3, 1770, seq. 25; Vol. 2, August 30, 1788, seq. 34; Vol. 3, November 24, 1794, seq. 75; Vol. 3, December 22, 1794 [on page headed December 16, 1794], seq. 79; Vol. 3, December 15, 1795, seq. 142). He shoveled gravel, hauled wood ("sleding" using draft animals), and performed other unspecified farm labor (Vol. 2, September 20, 1788, seq. 37; Vol. 2, February 2, 1789, seq. 49; Vol. 2, January 9, 1790, seq. 93; Vol. 3, August 16, 1794 [two days work credited to a 3s. bill for doctor's visit and medication for Susanna Mac(?)], seq. 57). He purchased meat and received corn from the Osgood farm (Vol. 2, September 29, 1794, seq. 206; Vol. 2, February 27, 1790 [loose receipt, imaged at page headed April 3, 1790, order from Col. Samuel Johnson requesting that Bristol have a bushel of Indian corn and charge Johnson's account], seq. 103). Samuel Frye of the South Parish was charged 2s. 8p. for "Colouring + Pressing a piece of Cloth for Dorcas Bristos Ware", presumably labor performed by women in the Osgood household (Vol. 2, February 16, 1789, seq. 51). It is uncertain whether that dyed and ironed textile was for Bristow/Brister's first wife or daughter.

Bristow/Brister, his first wife Dorcas, and their daughters Annah, Dorcas, Olive, and Lydia, were visited and treated for medical issues on many occasions (Vol. 1, April 23, 1771, seq. 42; Vol. 2, March 31, 1788, seq. 7; Vol. 2, May 12, 1788 ["Calling to see Daughter Annah", to bleed him, and medicine for both], seq. 13; Vol. 2, June 22, 1788, seq. 22; Vol. 2, July 23, 1789 [Bristo charged "to Bleeding your Wife" and medicine], seq. 72; Vol. 2, November 18, 1789 [Lydia Bristo, "Extracting a tooth for you" but the entry had no cost and was marked "void"], seq. 87; Vol. 2, December 23, 1789 [Bristo charged for visit and medicine "for your Wife"], seq. 91; Vol. 2, February 5, 1790, seq. 95; Vol. 2, July 5, 1790, seq. 128; Vol. 2, August 2, 1790, seq. 132; November 2, 1791, Vol. 2 [Olive Bristo charged "to Visit to you at your Fathers" and for a second visit and medicine listed in that same entry], seq. 194; and again Olive Brister was charged for visits to her on November 25 and December 1, 1791 [both entries on same page headed November 25, 1791], Vol. 2, seq. 197; Vol. 2, May 23, 1792, seq. 203 [Bristo charged for visits and medicine for his wife]; Vol. 2, July 4, 1794 [under page headed that date, but marginal entries might indicate visit on September 14, 1794; Jonathan Tyler charged for doctor extracting tooth for Dorcas Bristo, probably Bristow/Brister's daughter], seq. 216; Vol. 3, August 16, 1794 [Bristo charged for visit and medicine for Susanna Mac(?)], seq. 57; Vol. 3, April 18, 1795 ["at Cato's", page headed April 15, 1795], seq. 99, accessed October 19, 2019).

Bristow/Brister's family and descendants bear further research and documentation. Charlotte Helen Abbott, "Historical Andover. No. 107. Africa to Andover.—(Concluded)," 3, provided some intriguing information about "Old Bristoe" and his descendants, but she may have conflated individuals and generations. Abbott indicated that Bristow/Brister used the surname Richardson, that his second wife was Eunice Pickett of Middleton, Mass., and that their daughter "possibly was called Eunice Freeman and married Moses Richardson" (cf. *VRA*, Vol. 2, Marriages, 65, "Brister, Eunice [Freeman. int.] and Moses Richardson, July 25, 1819", brackets in original; ibid., Marriages, "Negroes," 357 for "Bristo" Freeman and "Eunice Picket of Middletown" [*sic*], July 19, 1795). The descendants of Bristow/Brister and Dorcas married with members of the distinguished Lew family after the Lews were in Dracut, Mass. The family relationships of Bristow/Brister and Dorcas' line with the Dracut Lew family had not been previously identified in published genealogical sources I have seen, although the Lew family's dedicated interest in their genealogy may have ascertained the connection to those two Andover ancestors, Dorman, *Twenty Families of Color in Massachusetts*, v (dedication to genealogy), 276, 277 (e.g., did not identify Bristow/Brister and Dorcas of Andover as the parents of Sarah Brister and Dorcas Brister), 329 (Lew family descendants interviews, correspondence, papers); Morrison, "Negroes Who Fought at Bunker Hill" (Lew family descendants, genealogy research, and oral history in the 1960s). Under surnames of Bristo(w)/Brister, etc. and Lew/Lue, etc. are many entries in the *VRA* (as well as in the published *Vital Records* of other towns, such as Dracut) that appear both in the main sections as well as in the births, marriages, and deaths sections for "Negroes" and "Surname Missing." Lydia Bristow born December 26, 1765, *VRA*, Vol. 1, 80 was Bristow/Brister's daughter. She married the locally famous Cato Freeman (1768–1853, formerly Cato Phillips) on December 24, 1789, *VRA*, Vol. 2, 356, 357 ("Negroes"). Sarah Loring Bailey, *Historical Sketches of Andover*, 450, related an anecdote that may be about Cato Freeman and Lydia Bristow's wedding ceremony, performed by Rev. Symmes at the North Parish church. A note about Lydia (Bristow) Freeman in the local history column, Anonymous, "Sketches of Octogenarians" (about Lydia Freeman), *Andover Advertiser*, September 3, 1853, n.p. [2], said she was never enslaved, and had 11 children of which three were then living. Lydia (Bristow) Freeman died 1854.

Many children of Cato and Lydia (Bristow) Freeman are noted in the *VRA* (Vol. 1, Births, and Vol. 2, Deaths, both under "Negroes"), and Martin, "On the Landscape for a Very, Very Long Time," Chapter 5, devoted several pages to the family and prepared a genealogical chart. The 51-year-old son of Lydia (Bristow) and Cato Freeman, Zadock Lew Freeman, a widower and a laborer, died of a "fit" on July 13, 1849, *VRA*, Vol. 1, 390 ("Negroes," birth of "Zadoc Lew" Freeman, August 5, 1797); Vol. 2, 137, 258, 443 (his wife Judith A. Page, died 1834), 574 ("Negroes," death of Zadock). Zadock Lew Freeman was named after Zadock Lew—the son of Barzillai Lew [Sr.] and the husband of Sarah "Bristo" Lew, the daughter of Bristow/Brister and Dorcas, *VRA*, Vol. 2, Marriages ("Negroes"), 356, 357. Zadock Freeman was paid by Andover for building a wall along a road in 1832, and his burial was paid by the town in 1850. The amount paid by the overseers of the poor for Zadock Freeman's burial ($11.50) was considerably more than what was paid for burials of four other individuals ($2.50–$3.00), Town of Andover, *Annual Town Reports*, 1832 (wall), 1850 (burial). Zelew, a four-month-old child of "Zadoc" (from the name Ze*lew*, and date, probably Zadock and Lydia Lew's son, but also possibly a Freeman), died May 29, 1813, *VRA*, Vol. 2, 575 ("Negroes"). Another likely daughter of Bristow/Brister and Dorcas, Olive Bristor/Brister of Andover, married Samuel Barker in Dracut on August 17, 1794, *Vital Records of Dracut*, 138, 145. Yet another daughter of Bristow/Brister and Dorcas, Dorcas Bristor/Brister, was Barzillai Lew [Jr.]'s first wife, married in Dracut on September 30, 1801, *Vital Records of Dracut*, 145, 207. Dorman, ibid., 277, did not indicate that the Dorcas (Brister) Lew who died in Andover January 24, 1819, was at the time of her death the wife of Zadock Lew, which supposes that Zadock Lew married his former sister-in-law (his brother Barzillai Lew [Jr.]'s first wife), *VRA*, Vol. 2, 490. Lillian Ashcraft-Eason, "Freedom among African Women Servants and Slaves," 68, recognized "a system of levirate" "[i]n many parts of Africa" of brother- and sister-in-law marriages, a tradition that might have figured in Zadock Lew and Dorcas (Brister) Lew's arrangement. "Mrs. Lew", who died in Andover on January 2, 1837 at 96 years old, *VRA*, Vol. 2, 574 ("Negroes"), was Dinah Lew, Barzillai Lew [Sr.]'s widow, Dinah Lew, Probate file papers, which indicated in one place that Mrs. Lew died on January 1, 1837. For more on the Lew family history, see Coburn, *History of Dracut*, 322, 332–336; Dorman, ibid., 271–329; Martin, ibid., 135–136; Mayo, "The Lew Family"; and, Morrison, ibid. Notably in these genealogical records, there are African-derived naming practices evident, where a father's forename became a child's surname and names of relatives were adapted. Barzillai Lew [Sr.]'s same-named son was a close acquaintance of Titus and Rosanna Coburn.

[10] Jones, "'Trifling Patriots and a Freeborn Pepel'"; Leonard, *Political Poetry as Discourse*, 153; Melish, "The 'Condition' Debate and Racial Discourse in the Antebellum North"; Stewart, "Modernizing 'Difference.'" Elise A. Guyette, *Discovering Black Vermont*, 2–5, summarized evolving vernacular ideas about "race" among New Englanders. Patrick Rael, *Black Identity and Black Protest in the Antebellum North*, 418–419 (s.v. "Racial labels") has considerable information about these ideas and the evolving meanings of racial terms used in this region into the nineteenth century. Elizabeth Stordeur Pryor, "The Etymology of Nigger," effectively traced that term. Regarding the historical meanings, semantic contexts, and evolution of the terms "servant" and "slave" in New England, see Benes, "Slavery in Boston Households," 15; Greene, *The Negro in Colonial New England*, 168, 218–223, 231–235; Matthews, "Hired Man and Help"; and, Warren, *New England Bound*, 32, 271 n50. Familiar racialized terms are ubiquitous in the records and writings about people of color in historical Andover and the region generally. Ironically, the evident effort made in historical writings to especially designate people of color (what is called *marking* [i.e., "markedness"] in linguistic theory and which, axiomatically, consciously and unconsciously conveyed subjects of heightened interest and concern to writers and speakers) proves useful to identify people of color and to further investigate moments of their biographies. A linguistic study of the practice and evolution of racialized terms, along the lines of Leonard's methods for Haverhill newspapers, is possible with this area's rich documentary heritage.

[11] The information about Andover is drawn from my research. Elise Lemire, *Black Walden*, conveyed parallel findings for Concord, Mass., and demonstrated how a local, microhistorical focus on people of color in Massachusetts towns reveals specific, factual information about the protracted process of the transition from enslavement to freedom and independence. Anthony F. Martin undertook a vast survey and analysis of archaeological collections from Massachusetts African American sites and examined the African Amer-

ican community in Andover in his dissertation, "On the Landscape for a Very, Very Long Time," and in his article, "Homeplace Is also Workplace."

[12] Massachusetts House of Representatives, RCEC, 3, 5, 13, 14, was dated February 1, 1847. It reported on their 1846 investigation of claims submitted during the fiscal year of 1845. In addition to Andover, the towns of Topsfield and Cummington also submitted state pauper claims for former slaves who were determined to be legal town residents, ibid., 16, 35, 91–92. The towns of Andover, Stoneham, New Braintree, Monson, Pittsfield, and Scituate submitted claims for nonresident former slaves; some charges were allowed, others disallowed, but based only on whether or not the individual had received "entire" support at the almshouse, ibid., 52, 65, 82, 130, 173. The members of the two-person commission, ibid., 13, were state representatives Thomas Kempton (New Bedford, elected 1844–1846, 1850–1851) and John Sargent (1799–1880, Cambridge, elected 1844–1848).

[13] Ibid., 7–8.

[14] Ibid., 16–17; Massachusetts *Acts and Resolves* 1845, 654 (Roll of Pauper Accounts, "Andover, for support of State Paupers").

[15] Town of Andover, Overseers of the Poor, Nathan W. Hazen, draft letter to State Commissioner John Sargent, November 18, 1846, regarding Rosanna Coburn and daughter Elizabeth (Colley Hooper), in Town of Andover, "Town Records, Selectmen Records 1841–1861" (untitled volume, spine title "Letter Book", title from microfilm target but actually orders for payments drawn by the overseers of the poor, and letters written and received regarding poor in Andover), n.p., third volume on GSU Microfilm Reel 887743. I preserved original layout, indentation, line breaks, hyphenated word divisions, and other compositional elements in this transcription of the entirety of Hazen's letter. Hazen was an overseer of the poor in at least 1846 and 1847, Town of Andover, *Annual Town Reports*, 1846, 1847.

[16] Eight years after this letter was drafted, Nathan W. Hazen (1799–1887) witnessed Rose Coburn's will (1854). Hazen was also appointed (1859) as one of three appraisers of Rose Coburn's estate, which consisted only of savings in a bank account. Hazen also acted as attorney to Coburn's executor John Parnell during the probate process (1859–1861) and also in his role as a Justice of the Peace, took Parnell's sworn oath to the final accounting of the estate. Rose Coburn, Probate file papers. Hazen authored several publications during his long life, among them the open letter of 36 printed pages to deny assertions he was self-dealing in real estate while representing the Essex Company in Lawrence, Hazen, *A Letter to the Inhabitants of Andover and North Andover* (1856).

[17] Town of Andover, *Annual Town Reports*, 1847. Massachusetts Chapter 119 of the Resolves of 1844, 333. Massachusetts House of Representatives, RCEC, 6 ("overcharges"), 7, 8, 11 ("not aware"), 12 ("actually and entirely"), 17 (Andover accounting). To counter the town of Andover's claim that Rose and Elizabeth Coburn were state paupers rather than settled residents, the commissioners' report, ibid., 16, cited three Supreme Judicial Court decisions about claims for supporting formerly enslaved paupers: Winchendon v. Hatfield (4 Mass. Reports 123 [March 1808]); Dighton v. Freetown (4 Mass. Reports 539 [October 1808]); and, Andover v. Canton (13 Mass. Reports 547 [November 1816]). The commissioners glossed the case law that "if born a slave, [she] would take the settlement of her master." The three court decisions were actually more nuanced. The commissioners ignored attorney Hazen's referenced case of Lanesborough v. Westfield (16 Mass. Reports 74 [September 1819]) that decided that a daughter of slaves and their granddaughter were born free, but obtained no settlement either from the daughter's enslaved parents or their master's residence: they were state paupers. The 1816 case of Andover v. Canton was legally and historically significant. The Andover overseers of the poor paid for support of Lewis Elisha (a man of Ponkapoag Indian and African ancestry from Canton, Mass.), his wife Hannah Richardson Elisha (whose father was "mulatto" and mother "white"), and their children. Lewis and Hannah Elisha were married and settled in Andover in 1803, *VRA*, Vol. 2, 111, 285. I noticed but did not record the many pages of the town records that indicated support of that family, the pursuit of reimbursement from Canton, and prosecuting the lawsuit. Daniel R. Mandell, *Tribe, Race, History*, 51–53, 294, and Amber D. Moulton, *The Fight for Interracial Marriage Rights in Antebellum Massachusetts*, 39–40, considered Andover v. Canton among other nineteenth-century cases involving disputes between towns about support of poor people of color. Both scholars examined the legal complications for people of color to establish legal residency and evolving notions of illegitimacy and multiple heritages.

[18] Joan Patrakis, "Who Killed Mehitable?" described the 1842 murder of Mehitable Long at the Andover almshouse. Laurel Daen, "'To Board & Nurse a Stranger,'" 17, recognized the diminishment of "freedom, autonomy, and personalized care" in almshouses. But people in need of care living outside the almshouse were also vulnerable.

Neither Dinah Chadwick nor Harriet Dole were ever almshouse residents—Chadwick was a state pauper who resided in Dole's home under her care—but both died "in the snow" on December 16, 1839. Chadwick was "lost by reason of insanity of H[arriet] D[ole]", and Dole was "insane and perished in the snow", *VRA*, Vol. 2, 407 (brackets in original), 424; Massachusetts *Acts and Resolves* (1828–1831), 535 (Dinah Chadwick, state pauper). On that December night, Harriet Dole was delusional. Apparently thinking she needed to remove Dinah Chadwick from a perceived threat, Dole brought the blind woman outside during a snow storm where she concealed her. Harriet later ventured outside again, and wearing little she died of exposure as well. Dole was buried at the almshouse cemetery. Dinah's body was not found until mid-February, and it is likely that she too was buried at the almshouse cemetery, *VRA*, Vol. 2, 407 (death on December 16, 1839, burial on February 18, 1840). A compelling account of the tragedy was published anonymously in *The Andover Townsman* local history column called "Auld Lang-Syne," Anonymous, "Auld Lang-Syne. A Snow-Storm Incident of Fifty Years Ago." Charlotte Helen Abbott, "Historical Andover. No. 107. Africa to Andover.—(Concluded)," 3, drew from that column and from "a very correct account […] preserved by the late Mrs. Joshua Ballard" to convey the story.

Harriet Dole had worked for Dr. Abiel Pearson (1756–1827), for James Howarth (1783–1832), and for several other Andover families. Dole had purchased a small house with ½ acre of land in 1829, then purchased a contiguous parcel of about two acres in 1830, Andover Preservation Commission, et al., *Andover Historic Preservation* webpage for 141 Elm Street, http://preservation.mhl.org/141-elm-street, accessed August 23, 2017. Both Dinah Chadwick and Harriet Dole were women of color. Dinah Chadwick, her sister Flora Chandler, and members of Harriet Dole's family, were well-known to the Andover overseers of the poor, having received support for decades. The placement of Dinah at Harriet's home may have been arranged by the overseers. Receiving Chadwick into her home supplemented Dole's income. Selecting poorer households to board the needy poor provided income to those households, reduced the number of almshouse inmates, and in part lessened town expenses for poor relief. Decisions to board people of color with people of color were based in ideologies about "gender, race, class, and capacity", Daen, ibid., 3, 13 (quotation), 14, 16, 18. Dinah Chadwick's vulnerability and her fate laid at intersections of poverty, disabilities, age, gender, and ideas about "race."

Dinah Chadwick had been enslaved from the age of four by Boxford Deacon Thomas Chadwick, and not manumitted until his death in 1788. Her sister Flora Chandler had been enslaved in Andover by Nathan Chandler. Flora ("servant of Nathan Chandler") was received into the South Parish church congregation on May 22, 1774. Flora had two children, a daughter Damon, and a son Pomp, both baptized at South Parish church in July 1778. Nathan Chandler's October 14, 1778 will conveyed Flora to his wife, Priscilla (Holt) Chandler: "I give to my said wife the time and improv[e]ment of my Negro woman Named Flora as long as my wife continues in Life". The 1790

United States Census indicated that widow Priscilla Chandler's household included a person of color who may have been Flora. Priscilla's grandson, Nathan Chandler, had one person of color living with him as well who may have been one of Flora's children. The widow, born about 1709, was buried 1803, Abbott, "Early Records and Notes of the Chandler Family of Andover," 13, which study referred to an unidentified South Church record of November 25, 1803 that indicated that Priscilla Chandler was then 95 years old; *VRA*, Vol. 2, 410 (burial). Dinah Chadwick moved to her sister Flora Chandler's place in Andover about 1800, and may have also worked for local families. By 1826 Dinah had been "almost blind for some time." If newspaper articles were accurate, in 1825–1826, Flora and Dinah, then respectively 78 or 68 years old and 50 years old, were living with their 98-year-old aunt Rose Lovejoy and her 102-year-old husband Pompey Lovejoy.

In 1830, Flora and Dinah probably lived together with a younger woman of color, 24–36 years old. Flora's daughter Damon Chandler would have been at least 52 years old, *VRA*, Vol. 1, 95 (baptized 1778). In December 1833, Flora Chandler (age 84) and Dinah Chadwick (age 72) appeared sequentially on the list of the town poor, so seem to have lived together. The sisters were indicated to have been born in Charlestown, Mass., and both had been unmarried. Flora was indicated to be "colored", able to read, had one child, and was experiencing "general debility". The expense of her support paid by the town was $22.14. Dinah was indicated to be "colored", unable to read or write, and experiencing rheumatism but there was no mention of blindness. The expense of her support paid by the town in 1833 was $7.10. Financial support provided to the women by Andover was indicated in the printed *Annual Town Reports*: Flora Chandler (1832, 1836—Dinah Chadwick was not indicated, but names for some years seem to have been for heads of households), "Flora and Dinah Chandler" (1835, 1837, 1838), and seemingly they were so well-known that their listing for 1839 was simply "Flora and Dinah". A notation for a wood delivery to "Flora + Dinah" on September 4, 1839 was made by David Gray, Account book, census and appraisal of townspeople's farm animals (and other property for tax purposes), May 1, 1838–October 11, 1839 (and later), n.p., Taft Collection, Ms S 134, Sub-group I, Series A, David Gray 1762–1844, Folder 9, ACHC. Flora Chandler's death is not recorded, but Mooar, *Historical Manual of the South Church*, 140, indicated her death "after 1839." Mooar's estimate is uncertain. Dinah Chadwick could have left Flora Chandler's household for any number of reasons, but she would have had to move when Flora died after September 4 and before December 16, 1839. Most likely it was her sister's death that prompted the living arrangement with Harriet Dole in whose care Dinah died that winter night.

Flora Chandler and Dinah Chadwick were each due a small legacy from a former Reading man Timothy Russell after he died in 1818 at Boxford. Flora was due $5 in 1820 and Dinah was to be paid $3 in 1821, so perhaps, like their brother Anthony Ballard, they also labored for Timothy Russell. Anthony Ballard (sometimes rendered as "Antony" and "Toney"; died March 17, 1818) had been a "servant" of Timothy Russell, and by a 1796 will was to receive half of Timothy Russell's estate, but Ballard predeceased Russell. Ballard was previously in Andover, enslaved by William Ballard (1723–1782). As an enslaved man, "Toney Ballard" served three months at West Point, N.Y. in 1780 as a Private in Capt. John Abbot's Company from Andover, Col. Nathaniel Wade's Regiment of Militia. William Ballard included a provision in his 1781 will to manumit Anthony: "8.^{ly} [i.e., 8th clause] my Will is that my Negro Servant Tony when he shall arrive to the Age of Twenty five Years (in Consideration of the good Services I have received from him,) shall be free from any Claims or Demand my Heirs or any other Person may suppose to have over him". By the time of his death, Anthony Ballard had become a prosperous yeoman farmer in Reading who died intestate. His only heirs were his two sisters Flora Chandler and Dinah Chadwick. Ballard owned land in Reading, Wilmington, Peterborough, N.H., and Albany, Me. His livestock included a horse, pairs of oxen and steers, five cows, a "swine", a "hog", and eight hens. His inventory listed many items including agricultural and husbandry equipment and tools, a table, four chairs, other furniture, cooking equipage, serving and storage vessels (23 plates, six tumblers, a pitcher and mug, two decanters, several bottles, a tea pot and a coffee pot, a "sett of Tea cups & saucers", 19 tin pans [the pans evidently borrowed from and later claimed by Timothy Russell]), an impressive store of foodstuffs, and more. Altogether, Ballard's personal property gives the impression that he may have been a caterer, ran a boardinghouse or tavern, or otherwise hosted social gatherings, along the lines inferred for Lucy Foster of Andover by Whitney Battle-Baptiste, *Black Feminist Archaeology*, 130 and by Anthony F. Martin, "Homeplace Is also Workplace," 108–110, and more generally considered by Nedra K. Lee, "Boarding: Black Women in Nantucket Generating Income and Building Community."

Anthony Ballard was indebted to an incredibly long list of people, not unexpected at the time, which reflected Ballard's expansive social and business interactions in the regional barter and credit economy. Ballard's complicated estate would appear to have been conscientiously administered by Edmund Damon, a Reading man who was at one time a Reading overseer of the poor. The estate administration lasted from 1818 to 1822. At one point, Damon calculated that Ballard's estate was worth $1,590.67 before sale of real estate. However, the estate was in debt to the amount of $1,815.16.

Again, the proportion of assets to debt was managed during Ballard's life, but during the estate administration his goods and real estate were auctioned to repay his creditors and to cover the ordinary costs of a highly complicated estate administration. When Anthony Ballard's estate was finally settled on March 27, 1822, Flora Chandler and Dinah Chadwick received only $16.45 each. Anthony Ballard's probate file papers include two documents (March 20, 1818, March 27, 1822) bearing the marks in lieu of signatures of Flora and Dinah, which are their only presently known writings and thus particularly significant artifacts.

In addition to the sources noted above, I found information in Abbott, "Early Records and Notes of the Chandler Family of Andover," 13 (Flora, age 95 on November 25, 1803); Abbott, "Historical Andover. No. 107. Africa to Andover.—(Concluded)," 3 (several errors, quotation, Anthony "servant" to Timothy Russell); Town of Andover, *Annual Town Reports*, 1832, 1835–1839 (Flora and/or Dinah received town support); Town of Andover, Overseers of the Poor, "Return of the Poor in the Town of Andover during the year ending on the last Monday of December, 1833," Ms. S 203, ACHC, bearing clerk's endorsement of January 18, 1834 (Flora Chandler and Dinah Chadwick); Anonymous, "Longevity," *Niles' Weekly Register* (Baltimore, Md.), November 12, 1825, 176 ("Pompey Lovejoy, aged 102 years, with his wife, in her 98th year, and his two neices [*sic*], aged 78 and 50 respectively, are all living together"); Anonymous, Note about death of Pompey Lovejoy, *Boston News-letter and City Record*, March 11, 1826, n.p. [4] (two unmarried nieces aged 68 and 50, "whom it is customary with them to designate as the *children*, live in the family" with Pompey and Rose, 102 and 98 years old, respectively); Anonymous ("G."), "Pomp and Pomp's Pond," *Andover Advertiser*, October 30, 1858, n.p. [1] ("*Flora* and *Dinah*" "companions" of the Lovejoys, Flora making ale and baking); Bailey, *Historical Sketches of Andover*, 386 ("Toney Ballard" military service); Anthony Ballard, Probate file papers; William Ballard, Probate file papers (will, November 21, 1781, approved April 1, 1782 by Benjamin Greenleaf, Judge of Probate); [Deacon] Thomas Chadwick, Probate file papers; Chandler, *The Chandler Family*, 154 (Nathan Chandler's will regarding Flora Chandler); Nathan Chandler, Probate file papers (will, October 14, 1778, approved and allowed October 5, 1784 by Benjamin Greenleaf, Judge of Probate); Farlow, *Ballard Genealogy*, 94 (William Ballard and Tony in his will); Martin "On the Landscape for a Very, Very Long Time," 160–161, and Martin, "Homeplace Is also Workplace," 109, surmised that Dinah Chadwick may have been living with Flora Chandler in 1833, based on their sequential listing in Town of Andover, Overseers of the Poor, "Return of the Poor in the Town of Andover"; Massachusetts Secretary of the Commonwealth, *Massachusetts Soldiers and Sailors of the Revolutionary*

War, Vol. 1, 552 ("Ballard, Toney"); Mooar, *Historical Manual of the South Church*, 140 ("Flora (servant of Nathan Chandler)" on May 22, 1774, death after 1839); Perley, *The History of Boxford*, 158 (quotation, "almost blind"); Timothy Russell, Probate file papers; United States Census, *Population Schedules of the First Census of the United States 1790*, 20½ (Nathan Chandler and Priscilla Chandler households); United States Census, *Population Schedules of the Fifth Census of the United States 1830, Roll 61*, Essex County, 183 (Flora Chandler household, two free colored females 55–100 years old; one ditto 24–36 years old); and, *VRA*, Vol. 1, 95 (Damon Chandler, daughter of Flora, baptized July 5, 1778), 389 ("Negroes," Pomp Chandler, son of Flora, baptized July 5, 1778); Vol. 2, 410 (Priscilla Chandler, buried November 25, 1803, age 95 years, 7 months). See chap. 2, note 3, and chap. 3, note 5 for related information about Flora and Dinah.

[19] Town of Andover, *Annual Town Reports*, 1845–1846. Kunal M. Parker, "State, Citizenship, and Territory," 619 n99, 620 n100, cited the 1847 Massachusetts House of Representatives, RCEC, to exemplify "numerous attempts [by towns] to shift the costs of supporting town paupers onto the Commonwealth" (620). In that broader article, I think Parker overstated that practice as "corruption" (603, 617–620), as he also did in *Making Foreigners*, 109, when referring to it as "a species of cheating or corruption". In 1849, a state office of Auditor of Accounts was created to ferret out malfeasance, and even the archival collection description for the Massachusetts General Court Committee on Accounts, Account roll submissions, 1786–1860 (CO6/9x, Massachusetts Archives Division, Office of the Secretary of the Commonwealth, Boston, hereafter M-Ar), recognized that the "expense and attendant corruption" in the state pauper reimbursement system led to its collapse. The state commissioners (Massachusetts House of Representatives, RCEC, 12) indeed deduced "several instances" of false claims that occurred in the fiscal year 1845: "the commissioners regret to say, that in several instances they found the State charged for the support of persons who had received no assistance whatever for the town making such claim." Yet, the impression is that knowingly false claims were neither numerous nor common in the charges submitted by towns for 1845, and none were made by Andover. The state commissioners were more circumspect and considered that, firstly, overburdened town officials (who were not usually legal professionals) misunderstood the complexities and transformations of the statutory and common law of settlement and poor relief that required tedious case-by-case application to details of a pauper's genealogy and history of inhabitancy; and, secondly, that many town officials were "not aware" of an 1844 law that the commissioners novelly interpreted as requiring any state support to be provided only to paupers residing at the town almshouse. Massachusetts House of Repre-

sentatives, RCEC, 6–8, 11 (quotation, "not aware"), 12. The wording of the 1844 law did not specify that state paupers had to reside at a town almshouse if the town were to be reimbursed, only that state paupers be supported "actually and entirely […] the whole number of days" that were claimed, Massachusetts Chapter 119 of the Resolves of 1844, 333. Conceivably the town overseers who did read the 1844 law could have interpreted that provision differently than the commissioners. The Joint Special Committee to which the report was referred accepted the commissioners' interpretation, which reinforced the limited scope of state reimbursements to towns for support of state paupers, Massachusetts Senate, Document No. 66, Report on the Report of Commissioners on Claims for Support of State Paupers, March 22, 1847 (document title from volume index, vii; each document independently paginated).

Detailed legal guidebooks published for Massachusetts town officials, which appeared in several editions during the period, summarized the then-current statutory and case law as it applied to their responsibilities, including as overseers of the poor. All of the guidebooks had ponderous titles, but were generally known as *Town Officer*. I have not fully traced the publishing history of the various editions (nor do I include them in the references cited but they are digitized and available at Hathitrust.org). They included John Bacon's *The Town Officer's Guide* (Haverhill, Mass.: E.W. Reinhart, 1823); Isaac Goodwin's *Town Officer* (second edition, revised and enlarged, Worcester, Mass.: Dorr and Howland, 1829; third edition, revised and enlarged, Worcester, Mass.: Dorr, Howland and Co., 1834); Benjamin F. Thomas' *The Town Officer* (new edition, revised and corrected, Worcester, Mass.: Warren Lazell, 1849); and, Dwight Foster and James E. Estabrook's *Thomas' Town Officer* (new edition, revised to the present time, Worcester, Mass.: Enos Dorr and Co., 1856). I have not determined if Andover officials owned any of the *Town Officer* guidebooks. Andover attorney Nathan W. Hazen was an overseer of the poor in 1846 and 1847, and he argued legal issues with the state commissioners. Town of Andover, *Annual Town Reports*, 1846, 1847; Town of Andover, Overseers of the Poor, Nathan W. Hazen, draft letter to State Commissioner John Sargent, November 18, 1846, regarding Rosanna Coburn and daughter Elizabeth (Colley Hooper), in Town of Andover, "Town Records, Selectmen Records 1841–1861" (untitled volume, spine title "Letter Book", title from microfilm target but actually orders for payments drawn by the overseers of the poor, and letters written and received regarding poor in Andover), n.p., third volume on GSU Microfilm Reel 887743.

Understandably motivated to reduce their own town's expenses, overseers of the poor ordinarily sought reimbursement of poor relief costs from other towns or the state. From their investigations, town overseers ascertained that others were instead responsible for the costs of supporting people who they deemed —rightly or wrongly—to be nonresidents. Despite Parker's broad characterization of "various kinds of misrepresentation, cheating, and corruption" ("State, Citizenship, and Territory," 603) that he applied to the entire history of the system of state pauper reimbursements, he provided documentation of few discernible examples of evidently deliberate and knowing false claims, and cited only two lawsuits brought by the state against towns to recover money: ibid., 619 n95 (Cambridge 1838 on a complicated matter involving earnings of state paupers put to paid labor, that should have been deducted from the total state reimbursement to the town if the town's total costs of supporting state paupers was more than the reimbursement) and ibid., 635 n152 (Dracut 1857 on town residents supported at a state almshouse).

In their 1847 report, the commissioners made few findings of "overcharges" for former *slaves* determined to be legal town residents (Massachusetts House of Representatives, RCEC, Andover, 16; Topsfield, 45; Cummington, 92). Reimbursements for two other former slaves were disallowed but only because the support was not provided entirely at the almshouse (ibid., Andover, 17, support disallowed except for the two weeks Lucy Foster was at the almshouse; New Braintree, 65, support disallowed for a woman "supposed to be an absconded slave" and for her child living with a family). Providing support to any poor person living outside the almshouse was a common reason for disallowing state reimbursement.

As a result of the commissioners' investigation and report, the General Court (the legislature) passed two acts regarding state reimbursements that were determined by the commissioners to be "overcharges": the state treasurer was to reserve "all sums of money which have been overpaid [...] for State pauper charges" from any state funds due to municipalities, Massachusetts Chapter 54 of the Resolves of 1847, 523; and, "cities and towns [...] shall respectively refund, to the Treasurer of the Commonwealth, such sums as shall be found to have been illegally charged in the [pauper] accounts", Massachusetts Chapter 100 of the Resolves of 1847, 540, also cited by Parker, "State, Citizenship, and Territory," 619–620 n99. Drawing from that second resolve, Parker, ibid., 619–620, twice used the phrase "'illegal' charges", but "sums [...] illegally charged" did not denote a criminal act per se, nor does it establish "corruption." The meaning of "illegally" should be understood generically: that reimbursements were rejected because they were not in accordance with law. Parker provided no research findings on the matter, and I also did not pursue the topic, of whether or not any criminal prosecution resulted because of false claims or other sorts of "corruption" by town officials. The 1847 resolves indicated only that state-rejected claims were expected to be resolved administratively with the state treasurer. Further research could detail the specific tensions and resolutions between towns and the state in the history of town support for the poor and the state reimbursement system.

While he expressed it differently, Kunal M. Parker, ibid., 620, understood that the attention and efforts that town overseers of the poor made to investigate and document responsibility for supporting indigent persons showed that "citizenship, settlement, and other markers of belonging [*very much*] mattered to local poor relief officials" and not only because of public financial implications. Decisions of municipal and state officials about which indigents belonged and which were "foreigners" were delimited deliberately in practice and law. They constrained options of settlement and mobility. Parker's interest was to address even broader and still current issues in immigration history and law, Parker, ibid., 586. The findings of the 1847 Massachusetts House of Representatives, RCEC, were leveraged during consideration of citizen petitions against public funding for foreign immigrants ("alien passengers," of course at that time chiefly the Irish) to propose eliminating all state reimbursements to towns to support state paupers: "the small contribution paid by the State towards the support of this class of paupers ["citizen State paupers" in contrast to "alien paupers"] renders the towns extremely inefficient in the investigation of settlements; which, together with the frequent changes in the board of overseers of the poor, and the reluctance with which pauper settlements are usually examined, often causing much expense and litigation to the towns, induces them to be satisfied with the State allowance, and pay the additional expenses from their own funds. If all the expenses of supporting such paupers were thrown upon the towns, it would undoubtedly stimulate them to the investigation of settlements, and the paupers would be rightly supported in their own towns", Massachusetts Senate, Document No. 109, Report and Bill concerning Alien Passengers and Paupers, April 21, 1847, 10 (title from volume index, iii).

For the evolution of historical ideologies and intersectional social constructions of poverty and social alerity—satisfyingly considered in specific cultural, geographic, and temporal contexts—see Herndon, *Unwelcome Americans* (particularly for impoverished people in Rhode Island who were formerly enslaved or descended from enslaved people in Massachusetts); Herndon, "'Proper' Magistrates and Masters," especially 43 on "[t]he trajectory of pauper apprenticeship influenced [...] by the decline of slavery"; Herndon, "Children of Misfortune" (a paper drawn from her forthcoming book by that title); Herndon and Murray, *Children Bound to Labor*; Jones, "The Transformation of the Law of Poverty in Eighteenth-Century Massachusetts"; and, Spencer-Wood and Matthews, "Impoverishment, Criminalization, and the Culture of Poverty," as well as the sources cited in all those works.

[20] Massachusetts *Acts and Resolves*; Town of Andover, *Annual Town Reports*. The state pauper accounts for Andover printed in the Massachusetts *Acts and Resolves* series include reimbursements to Andover for Rosanna Coburn (sometimes rendered "Rosannah"), from 1831 to 1843, and for "Elizabeth C. Coburn" (so rendered twice; as "E.C. Coburn" once, and as "Elizabeth Coburn" twice), from 1839 to 1843. Searching for their names, I noticed Lucy Foster's name as well but did not also catalog all those entries. "Roll" refers to the numbered state financial account rolls. The page number provided after the date of the roll refers to the page of the relevant printed volume for that year in the *Acts and Resolves* series. Volumes in that series sometimes spanned multiple years. In the summary below, "id." indicates that the name was rendered identically as the previous quoted entry.

> Roll 104, January 1831, 535 ("Rosanna Coburn"); Roll 108, January 1834, 670 (id.); Roll 109, January 1835, 150 (id.); Roll 110, January 1836, 325 ("Rosannah Coburn"); Roll 111, January 1837, 505 (id.); Roll 112, January 1838, 672 ("Rosanna Coburn"); Roll 113, 1839, 114 ("Rosannah Coburn" and "E.C. Coburn"); Roll 114, 1840, 268 ("Rosanna Coburn" and "Elizabeth C. Coburn"); Roll 115, 1841, 439 ("Rosannah and Elizabeth C. Coburn"); Roll 116, 1842, 576 ("Rosannah and Elizabeth Coburn"); Roll 117, 1843, 89 ("Rosanna and Elizabeth Coburn").

Among the named Andover paupers in the Massachusetts *Acts and Resolves*, neither Rosanna nor Colley (Elizabeth) appeared in 1831 (Roll 105, June 1831, 637) or in 1832 (Roll 106, January 1832, 190). The 1833 list (Roll 107, January 1833, 498) had no individual names for Andover. The notations each year were for "supplies to" (1831), then for "support of" the named paupers. I searched the printed state pauper accounts in the *Acts and Resolves* series from 1786 forward for any mention of members of Phillis' extended family. For some intervening years, individual names were not specified in the printed state pauper accounts, the reimbursement made to Andover for support of, e.g., "sundry paupers." After 1843, the printed state pauper accounts did not include individual names for Andover state paupers. Because Rosanna and Colley were noted in the Massachusetts House of Representatives, RCEC, 16–17, the town of Andover also submitted claims for them for the state fiscal year of 1845. Presumably, claims for their support were submitted to the state for other years, but their names were not specified in the state accounts. In the Town of Andover, *Annual Town Reports*, when Rosanna and Colley together or separately were characterized as state paupers (1832, 1843, and 1845–1847, 1851), then presumably the town submitted claims to the state for those years. Differences between the state and town fiscal year accounting and reporting, and delays in submitting claims and receiving state reimbursements may account for the lack of agreement between state and town printed financial reports.

Stephanie Dyson and Caitlin Jones at M-Ar guided me to determine that beyond what appeared in the printed Massachusetts *Acts and Resolves*, for the years that Rosanna and Colley were named there was no additional pertinent information in the two related archival series, Massachusetts General Court Committee on Accounts, Account Rolls, 1786–1862 (CO6/2268x) and Account Roll Submissions, 1786–1860 (CO6/9x), M-Ar. Finding aids to the related archival series include descriptions of the archival series; a box of photocopies of the itemized account rolls from the Massachusetts *Acts and Resolves* series that include the pauper accounts which I used to compile this information; as well as the analyzed tables and container lists included with the CO6 archival series finding aids that indicate what if any related and supplemental records are preserved for the printed accounts for state expenditures. However, I was not able to comprehensively search each of the account roll submissions made by Andover, which does include information about people of color, and may have additional information about Phillis' extended family. Daen, "'To Board & Nurse A Stranger,'" 10, 13, 24 n23, 25 n29, made use of these records, and indicated information about the 1791 Andover account roll submission.

[21] Massachusetts House of Representatives, RCEC, 16–17, which also indicated the state-set daily rate. Kunal M. Parker, "State, Citizenship, and Territory," 615 n84, provided that the state rate that prevailed since 1820 was reduced by half in 1835. In 1820 the rate was set at $1 per week for adults and 55¢ per week for children. In 1835 it was halved to 7¢ per day for everyone except for those under 12 years old who were granted only 4¢ per day: there it remained a decade later despite the amount not being sufficient to meet the actual, greater costs borne by towns for supporting state paupers, ibid., 619.

Lucy Foster's warning out was issued February 9, 1791, and provided important biographical facts. "Lucy (a Negroe Woman) formerly a Servant to Job Foster late of said Andover decd an Native of Boston" indicated that she was born in Boston, and at least to the clerk and constable, she was at that time known only by her single name. The phrase "formerly a Servant to Job Foster" was included chiefly to identify her, but it concurrently implied that by that date she was no longer enslaved. The same day as Lucy's warning out, the selectmen issued the warning out for Prince, "a Negroe Man formerly a Servant of Jonathan Cummings". Just as with Lucy, Prince was born in Boston and was a longtime Andover resident. He was brought into Andover as a slave "when an infant" and baptized in October 1769, Town of Andover, "Town Records, Town Meetings, Persons Warned to Leave Town 1790–

1793" (untitled volume, title from microfilm target), n.p., second volume on GSU Microfilm Reel 887742 (quotation, February 9, 1791 warning out for Prince); Mooar, *Historical Manual of the South Church*, 148 (Lucy Foster, joined September 22, 1793); *VRA*, Vol. 1, Births, "Negroes," 390 (Peter Foster, son of Lucy Foster, baptized October 20, 1793 at South Parish church), 391 (Prince, infant belonging to ["of"] Jonathan Cummings, Jr., baptized October 1, 1769 at South Parish church).

An ornate archive about Lucy Foster and her contemporaries exists, and some records are unexamined. The whole primary and secondary writings about her and her cohorts, including scholarship, the curated archaeological collection of artifacts and records, and related documentation of the several historical and archaeological investigators of her biography, have not yet been entirely and contextually considered, nor are the primary sources adequately documented. In publications and research files about Lucy Foster and her social group appear imperfect transcriptions of town and church manuscript record entries; miscitations of town records as ecclesiastical records (which also, with incomplete and nonspecific citations to original manuscript sources, make it needlessly tedious to relocate and reexamine particular documents); and, misunderstandings of information appearing in primary and secondary sources. The original excavators of "Black Lucy's Garden" homestead site were the first to notice inconsistencies in historical sources about Lucy Foster and her cohorts, Bullen and Bullen, "Black Lucy's Garden," 26, 28, then committed several errors themselves. Imprecision and lacunae in referencing source materials, and matters of compounding errors with misinterpretation and speculation, are part of a woeful tradition of confusion in writings about Lucy Foster and of Sarah Gilbert.

Sarah Gilbert came to Andover from the adjoining town of Tewksbury as a child to live with Job and Hannah Foster. Sarah was a relative, boarder, or an indentured servant of the Fosters, and lived in their household with Lucy. The absence of racial qualifiers in records about Sarah Gilbert would indicate that she was not a person of color. Sarah and Lucy (both were children) were baptized the same day, July 14, 1771: "Sarah a Child given to Job Foster & Lucy a Negro Child was Baptd." Their concurrent baptism records joined in a single line in the church manuscript book—and several variants of erroneous transcriptions have been published that added punctuation and made other changes to the text that do not appear in the original manuscript writing—led the Bullens and then others to misapprehend that Sarah Gilbert was Lucy's child by Job Foster. Sarah was not, of course, the four-year-old Lucy's daughter. The father of Lucy's son Peter is unknown. Despite established historical fact to the contrary, and multiple efforts over decades to convey the correct information by Andover historians Joan Patrakis and Barbara Brown and by archaeologists Eugene Winter, Whitney Battle-Baptiste, Elena Sesma, and Anthony F. Martin, the libelous error that Lucy was raped by Job Foster has been continually and uncritically repeated in derivative archaeological writings that I do not see fit to cite. That error distracts historical investigation of actual sexual assault of women of color for which there is evidence in this area, e.g., Flora's 1758 complaint against Nathaniel Perley of Boxford (1735–1810, "Cooper Nat" as he was known colloquially), Allis, *Youth from Every Quarter*, 11–12, 701 n19 (Flora and Nathaniel Perley); Perley, *Dwellings of Boxford*, 43–44 (Cooper Nat visiting other "girls"); *Vital Records of Boxford*, 274 (Deaths, "Negroes," Flora, January 1, 1815).

At the time that the two girls Sarah and Lucy lived in the Foster household, there was also an enslaved boy there. Twelve days after Sarah and Lucy were baptized, an Andover doctor made an entry in his day book for Job Foster, charging 5p. for medicine "and Dressing y^r Negro Boys shoulder", Osgood and Osgood, Day Books, n.p., Vol. 1, July 26, 1771, https://iiif.lib.harvard.edu/manifests/view/drs:424481266$53i, digital image seq. 53, accessed October 16, 2019. Whether by overwork, accident, or violence, the child's injury was serious enough to require a doctor's treatment, and the entry conveyed the physical dangers that enslaved children faced.

Additional historical sources for the information in the section above include Andover South Church, "A Book bought by the Chh in the south part of Andover for their use 1711," 95 (Sarah and Lucy's baptism); Baker, *Historical Archaeology at Black Lucy's Garden*; Baker, "Archaeological Visibility of Afro-American Culture"; Battle-Baptiste, *Black Feminist Archaeology*, 124, 126; Douyard, "Property, Capital, and Race," 190–191; Martin, "On the Landscape for a Very, Very Long Time"; Martin, "Homeplace Is also Workplace"; Patrakis, "Recent Research Clarifies Black Lucy's Life Story"; Sesma, "Creating Mindful Heritage Narratives," 51–57; Tarbox and Patrakis, "Andover Stories: Digging into a life, a garden"; Winter and Brown, "Black Lucy's Garden – Amendments." I thank Anthony F. Martin for providing me a copy of Winter and Brown's research paper, which included references to and reproductions of important documents about Lucy Foster and her son Peter. A three-page typed research paper by Barbara Brown, "Black Lucy's Garden," summarized documentary and archaeological findings. While Brown's paper made intriguing reference to "Andover Infirmary Records," no records by that title were located by the Andover town clerk (Austin Simko, email, April 26, 2019). Brown may have been referring to different records or to the same "Andover Overseers Records 1815–1839" that Joan Patrakis identified in the town clerk vaults (Patrakis, email, April 20, 2019).

In a 1901 newspaper article, Andover historian and genealogist Charlotte Helen Abbott, "Historical Andover. No. 107. Africa to Andover.— (Concluded)," 3, provided appealing biographical details about Lucy Foster: "Lucy had a wonderful singing voice that would carry her songs for half a mile." In that article, Abbott also surmised that Sarah Gilbert was "a white child" and indicated that Lucy was Sarah Gilbert's servant at "Henry Haywards" until 1812. Abbott suggested that Sarah Gilbert was the same person as "Sarah Dunklee," the wife of Nathaniel Dunklee of Wilmington, Mass., named as a beneficiary of $40 in a clause of Hannah Ford Foster Chandler's will. The clause for Sarah Dunklee appeared immediately after the clause for the bequest to Lucy Foster, and before the clause for Hannah's son Joseph Foster. Hannah Ford was born in Wilmington on May 27, 1738, and there married Job Foster in 1760; so, it may be that Sarah Dunklee of Wilmington was Hannah Ford's sister, the Sarah Ford born in Wilmington on March 2, 1731, Hannah Chandler, Probate file papers (will, December 15, 1812); Kelley, *Wilmington Records*, 37 (Ford births), 131, 132 (marriage to Job Foster); *VRA*, Vol. 2, 129, 133 (Wilmington marriage to Job Foster). I have not found a marriage record for Sarah and Nathaniel Dunklee, but his surname may have been rendered differently in their marriage record. I also searched with no conclusive results for additional information about Sarah Gilbert, whose biography remains elusive.

Exactly when Lucy became a contingently free woman is unknown. There is no reason to propose, as has been asserted, that Lucy was freed when she was 16 in 1783. That assertion seems to have been only predicated on the mistaken notion that statewide abolition instantly occurred that year as a result of one of the "Quock Walker" cases. The 1791 "warning out" stated that Lucy was "formerly a Servant" and by implication indicated that she was no longer enslaved by then. The 1791 "warning out" for Lucy did not effectuate her leaving town (which would have required further judicial process and court order), and other records indicate that she stayed. The bureaucratic legal record was primarily created by the town to legally establish that Andover did not consider her to be a legal resident. The record of the warning out was intended to be legal evidence that Andover would not be financially responsible for any support she might require while she was in Andover, but particularly in the event that another town made a claim against Andover for her care if she had traveled to another place. The assertion by town officials that Lucy Foster was not an Andover resident also allowed the town to seek reimbursement for her support from the state, which it did. Town of Andover, "Records of Information of Persons Taken into Town – Since the last Act of Court in Regard of the Maintenance of poor persons," n.p., May 2, 1771 (Sarah Gilbert from Tewksbury); Dayton and Salinger, *Robert Love's Warn-*

ings, for the legal purpose of records of warnings out, and especially page 15 for their ordinary ineffectiveness as a mechanism of physical removal. Jones, "The Transformation of the Law of Poverty in Eighteenth-Century Massachusetts," recognized that prosecution for transiency and the enforcement of removal was not commonly undertaken.

Eugene Winter and Barbara Brown, "Black Lucy's Garden – Amendments," 3, noticed an 1807 death record for "*Peter, a Negro Man*" who they suggested may have been Lucy Foster's son. Peter ("Son of Lucy Foster negro woman") was baptized at South Church on October 20, 1793 (ibid., 3, mistakenly substituting the date September 22, 1793, which was the date that Lucy Foster became a member of the South Church and that then allowed her to have her son baptized there, Mooar, *Historical Manual of the South Church in Andover*, 148, cited by Winter and Brown, ibid., 2). Winter and Brown's citation to their source of the death record for Peter (cited to "Book of Vital Statistics at the Andover Historical Society") was obscure, but it was summarized as an entry in *VRA*, Vol. 2, 574 (Deaths, "Negroes," "Peter, Jan. 26, 1807"). I located both the original and copied manuscript death records for that individual. The image of the death record provided by Winter and Brown (in the illustrations following the paginated typed pages) was of the original record, Town of Andover, "Births & Deaths from 1800 to May 1844 Andover, Mass." (spine title), n.p., third volume on GSU Microfilm Reel 767599, January 26, 1807 ("Peter a Negroe Man"). The copied manuscript death record appeared in Town of Andover, "A Record of Deaths in the Town of Andover (Including North Andover), Essex County, Massachusetts, from 1650 to 1844 Covering a Period of 194 Years Chronologically Arranged and Transcribed from the Original Records Verbatim et Literatim by Samuel W. Blunt and Completed March 1, 1879," 107 ("Peter, – 'a negro man[']").

I noticed that Lucy Foster's name appeared in several additional historical records that supplement the many record entries described by other researchers. In 1798 and 1799, "Lucy Chandler" (also rendered at the same time as "Lucy Foster") had business with local merchant Samuel Abbot. She borrowed cash, purchased tea, sugar, and (appealing for archaeologists) "2 sets of cups & saucers". She paid off her loans and purchases through her labor by spinning wool, picking wool, washing wool ("grees" noted by Abbot seems to refer to grease wool, as shorn, before it is cleaned) and/or washing yarn, and either washing more wool/yarn or laundry. The value of her labor was only partly recorded: for spinning yarn, she charged 5p./skein; for picking wool, 4p.; for washing wool, yarn, laundry, and/or other unspecified work her rate was 1s. 6p./day. A bill from Foster to Abbot for her labor and products may be in Foster's handwriting or written by another on her behalf. Samuel Abbot Business Papers, 1754–1819, Series I, Financial records, "Samuel Abbot's

Waste Book, & Memorandum Book, & Petty Ledgger, Began May 11th: 1768,"
(i.e., 1768–1812), n.p. in parts, Mss:761 1754–1819 A122, Vol. 3A, https://
hollisarchives.lib.harvard.edu/repositories/11/archival_objects/168654, digital images seq. 6, 13; and, Receipted bills, spinning, Mss:761 1754–1819
A122, Box 73, Folder 13, Baker Library Historical Collections, Harvard Business School, Boston, Mass., https://hollisarchives.lib.harvard.edu/repositories
/11/archival_objects/168825, digital images seq. 1–seq. 5, accessed August
13, 2019. There may be additional entries, bills, and receipts for Lucy Chan-
dler/Foster in separate volumes and papers in Abbot's financial records. Other
financial records kept by other Andover residents quite likely captured parallel
information about laboring and exchanges with Lucy Foster and other people of color in the region. Lucy Foster continued to labor for others as part
of her economic strategy late in her lifetime. In circa 1821–1822, toward the
end of her life, Foster worked for Andover farmer Isaac Chandler, related
to Philemon Chandler who Lucy's mistress, Hannah Ford Foster Chandler
(1738–1812), had remarried. Isaac Chandler, Account book (bound volume), n.p., Chandler-Hidden Family Papers, 1678–1866, Ms. N-358, Massachusetts Historical Society, Boston. What Anthony F. Martin taught us in
"Homeplace Is also Workplace", and in "Haven to the East, Haven to the
North," 318 (quotation), was that "with many African Americans, homeplace
was also workplace, especially for women of color who did income-based jobs
in their homes for White families, including laundry and the mending and
making of clothing", as they also did for themselves and for or with their family members in their own time. Lucy's sewing was long recognized, but her
skills in textile production for income had not been previously documented.

In the posthumously published, multipart series drawn from his manuscript notebooks, Alfred Poore, "A Genealogical-Historical Visitation of
Andover, Mass., in the Year 1863," *Essex Institute Historical Collections* 49
(1) (1913): 54, conveyed what he learned from residents who remembered
"Black Lucy Foster" and her 30-year occupation of her cottage. The same author, Alfred Poore (1818–1907), then spelling his surname Poor, wrote the
1863 *Andover Advertiser* newspaper article (published anonymously) that
Bullen and Bullen, "Black Lucy's Garden," 26, and that also Flagg, *A Guide
to Massachusetts Local History*, 49, credited to him, which newspaper article,
Poore, "History of Andover. Woburn street, continued," n.p. [2], was the
source that gave the site location its name, "a sand bank called Black Lucy's
garden". The 1863 newspaper article provided more details about Lucy's biography and the site's history than did the brief note in Poore's posthumously
published series. Flagg's bibliographic entry, and the anonymous introductory note to Poore's posthumous series (*Essex Institute Historical Collections* 48
[3] [1912]: 276), both refer to Poore's manuscript notes that if located might

yield additional information. Poore's notes and transcriptions of gravestone inscriptions in Andover cemeteries (*VRA*, Vol. 1, 3, indicated made in October 1864, but Poore's genealogical visit to Andover occurred in 1863) are the "Cemetery Records of Andover, Mass.," n.d., MSS 0.424, Phillips Library, Peabody Essex Museum, Rowley, Mass. On Alfred Poore and his productive history methods, products, and informational legacy, see Anonymous, *The Poor-Poore Family Gathering at South Church, Andover, Massachusetts*, 16–18, 71, 85, and Perley, "Alfred Poore," which indicated (at 51) that Poore added the "e" to his surname circa 1883.

Searching for other matters, I noticed that Lucy Foster appeared several times in the early nineteenth-century Andover overseers of the poor/treasurer records (Baker, *Historical Archaeology at Black Lucy's Garden*, 115–116, lists some examples); in the itemized "pauper accounts" in the Massachusetts *Acts and Resolves* series; and, in the Town of Andover, *Annual Town Reports*, 1832–1846. The annual town reports indicated that Lucy Foster was considered by the town to be a state pauper in 1832, 1843, 1845, and in 1846, when her death was noted in the report for that last year, being among the five people named who died at the almshouse between March 1845 and February 1846. I leave it to another researcher to locate and catalog all those entries in the state and town records, and to investigate the several suggestive record entries for people named Lucy Foster, Peter Foster, Sarah Gilbert, and alternative spellings of the name of "Sarah Dunklee" (Dunclee, Duncklee, Duntclee, Duntlee) in reliable genealogical databases at americanancestors .org, familysearch.org, and in digitized historical publications.

The AHS and Peabody Museum of Archaeology at Phillips Academy collaborated on a 2003 exhibition at AHS called "Lucy's Acre: A Place in Time" that exhibited artifacts, original documents, and dioramas created by Eugene Winter, and developed a traveling educational kit for schools, Ciolfi, "*Lucy's Acre: A Place in Time* Exhibit Shows Life of Former Slave." In 2018, artifacts from Lucy Foster's homestead were loaned by the renamed Robert S. Peabody Institute of Archaeology at Phillips Academy, for exhibition in the newly opened Smithsonian Institution's National Museum of African American History and Culture, Washington, D.C., Taylor, "Peabody at the Smithsonian." The opening exhibition labels about Lucy Foster incorporated three mistaken or merely speculative ideas that she was emblematic of live-in enslaved domestic workers who were "frequently subjected to sexual violence", that "Massachusetts abolished slavery in 1783", and that Foster "possibly" ran "a tavern for travelers to Boston." The echo of the misconstrued baptism record for Lucy Foster and Sarah Gilbert, and the myth of instant statewide abolition are evident mistakes. The speculation that Lucy ran a tavern was prompted by the relatively great number of ceramic vessels in the archaeological collection from the Lucy Foster homesite. The majority of the ceramic vessels, however, were recovered from a dump immediately adjacent to the dwelling and from the well. Those deposits may have been created after Foster's residence burned, and may include objects discarded from Foster's ruined home as well as trash from other nearby households. The Ballard Tavern was a short distance from the Foster homestead, and the small size of Foster's domestic structure also argue against the speculative idea that Foster engaged in the public tavern business. A tavern would have required approval and regulation by the town, for which there is no documentary evidence, Bullen and Bullen, "Black Lucy's Garden," 17 (Figure 1, E), 18 (Figure 2), 20.

More sensibly, Whitney Battle-Baptiste and Anthony F. Martin suggested that Lucy Foster's home was an occasional and popular gathering place, especially for Andover's people of color. For the Boston-Higginbotham House on Nantucket, owned by generations of people of color, Nedra K. Lee, "Boarding: Black Women in Nantucket Generating Income and Building Community," 92, joined census data that indicated "paying lodgers" were present there, with the large number of tablewares and teawares recovered archaeologically from that property, to appreciate that the strategy of taking in boarders provided household income, but more provocatively and meaningfully "was also a form of politicized community work. Black women formed relationships with boarders that also expanded their familial and social networks." Lucy Foster's purchases from Samuel Abbot of ¼ lb. tea and "2 sets of cups & saucers" the last week of June, and then 1 lb. sugar the next week in July suggests that she might have anticipated hosting a mid-summer 1799 social event, or perhaps she was planning to have boarders (either as lodgers or only for meals). The two "sets of cups & saucers" would serve 12, as ordinarily a "set" consisted of six teacups and six saucers, although sets of twelve and "the potter's dozen" of eighteen were also produced, Miller, "Common Staffordshire Cup and Bowl Shapes," 6. Lucy Foster's investment in durable household goods further suggests she expected to host group gatherings in future, conceivably as familiar restorative rituals of sociability and comfort. Alternatively, one or both sets of teaware could have been purchased for a gift.

Beyond ideas that personal comportment and complicated symbolic perceptions about material culture reflected participation in the bourgeois "cult of domesticity" and respectability politics (the "cult of respectability"), Nedra K. Lee, ibid., 92, stressed that it cannot be "assumed that women of color shared the same middle class roles, responsibilities, opportunities, and expectations of white women". Anthony F. Martin, "Haven to the East, Haven to the North," 318, provided an especially suitable conceptual perspective to approach documentary references about Lucy Foster's consumer choices, and to further appreciate the singularity and relatedness of the archaeologically excavated sample of artifacts from her Andover homeplace:

> What can be seen in these [archaeological] assemblages is resistance against the dominant society's relegation of people of color to second-class citizenship. Additionally, moral uplift can be seen [such as with Lucy Foster's church membership, with her hosting gatherings, with her providing friendship, comfort, nourishment literally and musically, and with her offering consolation and support to her son and her familiars as needed, when she could]. Because they are "American" households and because of the racialized context of their lives, their consumer choices amount to a form of resistance against the dominant culture's attempts to deny them full social equality and citizenship. Through consumption of mass-produced and mass-marketed products, these Black Americans pushed themselves into White space [...]. This does not mean African Americans bought into the same meaning and consumed the same products in the same way that members of the dominant cultures did. It illuminates other forms of resistance and the multivalent character of material culture. Key concerns of African Americans were full citizenship, abolition of enslavement, and advancement of the race through moral uplift. If these were concerns at all, they were not of the same magnitude of importance in White households [but rather, such concerns were especially in mind of women of color in the situated and protective spheres of their domestic spaces as homeplaces. See also Battle-Baptiste, *Black Feminist Archaeology*, and Martin, "Homeplace Is also Workplace," mutually inspired by biographical theorizing of "homeplace" by writer bell hooks, *Yearning*].

A modern cenotaph for Lucy Foster, a slate stone carved by Michael Updike and placed in the South Church cemetery, was dedicated on May 11, 2019. The epitaph reads, "Born into captivity in Boston [/] Came to her freedom in Andover". The epitaph was obviously inspired by Pompey Lovejoy's epitaph ("Born in Boston, a slave: [/] died in Andover a freeman"). As a resident of the South Parish and a member of the South Church, it is possible that Lucy's body was interred in an unmarked grave in that cemetery. Alternatively, because Lucy Foster died an indigent at the almshouse in 1845, she might have been buried in the almshouse cemetery. If so, then her remains were exhumed in 1923 from the almshouse cemetery and reinterred at Spring Grove Cemetery, Anonymous, "A Fitting Memorial"; Anonymous, "Local News Notes"; Crimaldi, "'She deserves her place'"; Goldsmith, "Siftings."

22 The notability of the archaeological study of Lucy Foster's residence—both for its substantive and significant historical and archaeological information,

as well for its influence in the history of the discipline of American historical archaeology—is reflected in its meaningful treatment and reexamination in a multitude of internationally disseminated scholarly articles, books, bibliographies, textbooks, and encyclopedias on the history and archaeology of the African diaspora and on historical archaeology generally.

In terms of understanding the historical position of the Bullens' archaeological investigation, it bears remembering that the Black Lucy's Garden Site was excavated in 1943 only incidentally to archaeological study of the ancient Native American Stickney Site at that same location. The Stickney Site excavation was part of a regionally significant five-year survey of ancient sites in Northeastern Massachusetts. The local focus of the study was in part a result of wartime restrictions on gasoline that limited travel to places close to the Robert S. Peabody Foundation for Archaeology (as the Institute of Archaeology was then called), Bullen, *Excavations in Northeastern Massachusetts*, v. The presence of historical ceramics in apparent stratigraphic but not depositional association with ancient artifacts was what prompted the investigation of Lucy Foster's homesite. The goal of excavating at the house cellar was to resolve the source and age of the contextually anachronistic historical period artifacts at the ancient site, Bullen and Hofman, "The Stickney Site," 20, 25. At the time of its excavation, it would appear that the association of the historical period site with Lucy Foster was not known to the investigators: as that information was learned, the research developed to focus on her. Indeed, it is not until nine pages into the 12-page article by Bullen and Bullen, "Black Lucy's Garden," 26— not until after the capable description of features, stratigraphy, and comparatively avant-garde identification and dating of the historical artifacts—that it was only then revealed that "The story of this site is really the biography of Lucy Foster, a negress." The documentary and oral history research findings followed and only then informed the "biography" represented in the material culture at the site. What is also characteristic of the published historical archaeology of its time is that the article thrice highlighted supposed antiquarian shadows: it made visible "life in Andover of one hundred years ago", "sheds some light on the Andover of 100 to 200 years ago", and gave "a glimpse of old Andover", ibid., 17, 26, 28. Local knowledge, however, had preserved remembrance of the historical place, ibid., 28: "Miss Ethel Howell, of Andover, whose mother was born on the Foster farm (then the Howell farm) was told by her great-aunt that a negro couple used to live where the cellar hole is."

The serendipitous archaeology of the homesite of a contingently free woman of African ancestry, formerly enslaved in New England, continues to enthrall and inspire generations. The modern, international knowledge and continued remembrance of Lucy Foster is extraordinary—as also of several other familiar and ordinary people in historical Andover who were each nearly forgotten but are now broadly known. Among them, famously, is Salem Poor. Through the writings of the "Early Black Historians," Salem Poor became a nationally significant figure representatively for his valor and gallantry at the Battle of Bunker Hill, after the discovery in the M-Ar of the 1775 recommendation to the legislature extolling his battlefield heroism signed by 14 officers (a fifteenth signature was effaced), Brewer, et al., "Recommendation of Salem Poor a free Negro for his Bravery at ye Battle of Charlestown," December 5, 1775, Massachusetts Archives Collection (hereafter MAC), Vol. 180, 241–241a, M-Ar. Later, by interest of broader historical inclusiveness, Nancy Parker became mentioned with him (typically and imprecisely styled as Poor's "Indian" wife). During their lifetimes, Pompey and Rose Lovejoy, Rosanna Coburn, and Cato Freeman were featured in newspaper articles that circulated statewide and nationally. Locally, all the more broadly known individuals, along with Barzillai Lew [Jr.], Allen Hinton, Alice Hinton and others, are remembered because their names appear again and again in historical projects through the efforts of public historians in Andover, North Andover, and Lawrence.

[23] Sarah Frye, Probate file papers. The legal heritability of slave or free status varied in different Atlantic World places at different times. By custom in Massachusetts, not statute, the free or enslaved status of the mother determined the legal status of the child, *partus sequitur ventrem*. Greene, *The Negro in Colonial New England*, 126, 294, 322. Occasionally in New England, the free status of the father was considered in determining freedom for his child, *partus sequitur patrem*. Whiting, "Endearing Ties," 95 n42, cited Adams and Pleck, *Love of Freedom*, 45–46, 48, about a 1702–1703 Connecticut case that successfully argued freedom for Abda Duce also known as Abda Jennings, the son of an Englishman and an enslaved African, because of his "English blood", Fowler, *The Historical Status of the Negro in Connecticut*, 117–121 (quotation at 121); Greene, ibid., 182–183. Newell, *Brethren by Nature*, 248, provided further information about Abda's case: while it was successfully appealed to the Connecticut General Assembly, Hartford town officials "refused to compel" Abda to return to his master. Adams and Pleck, ibid., 48, noted that Abda died in 1708 as a propertied free man. I noticed a 1720 Massachusetts case that successfully won freedom for the enslaved daughter of a "white" man, but on what basis the jury was swayed is not known. A deposition in the case file papers described the mother as an enslaved "Spanish Indian" from the West Indies; the father was "a Privateer [^]a[^] white Man" who lodged in the household. Thomas Messinger, Deposition, April 5, 1720, Suffolk Files Collection (hereafter SFC), File #13991 (file papers for the case of Mary Auter Note v. Sarah Tomlin), JA; in the references cited, the

reference to the record of the court decision is placed under the reference to Messinger's deposition.

[24] Massachusetts House of Representatives, RCEC, 16.

[25] Ibid., 14 (specifying claims submitted for 1845), 17.

[26] Commonwealth v. Aves (18 Pick. [35 Mass. Reports] 193, at 208, 210, 217 [March 1836]). Booso v. Samuel Chickering (Essex County Court of Common Pleas Records, July 1778, 476, JA, defendant defaulted). Konig, "Legal Fictions and the Rule(s) of Law," 107. Nelson, *Americanization of the Common Law*, 102. Sarah Frye, Probate file papers, accounting and distribution, September 7, 1790.

During my years of research I noticed and passed over assertions in antiquarian writings that contended Massachusetts emancipated its slaves before, during, or soon after the Revolutionary War, knowing that slavery in fact persisted in the state long after the Treaty of Paris (September 3, 1783). Thomas Pemberton, "Thomas Pemberton to Dr. Belknap, Boston, March 12, 1795," 392, informed Jeremy Belknap that "This business of importing and selling negroes continued till nearly the time of the controversy with Great Britain. The precise date when it wholly ceased I cannot ascertain; but it declined and drew towards a period about the time the British Parliament attempted to enslave the colonists by arbitrary acts." Margot Minardi, *Making Slavery History*, 38, saw that while nineteenth-century historians most frequently attributed emancipation to the 1780 state constitution or the "Quock Walker" cases, they also subtly and representatively linked Massachusetts abolition with popular ideologies they associated with the Revolutionary War. One other trope that appeared again and again in a variety of secondary sources was the absurd assertion that slavery was always marginal to the Massachusetts economy. I dismissed those as part of a narrative of regional exceptionalism, knowing that slavery was integrated at all economic scales from the earliest colonial years and that the internal and external slave trade was pursued with vigor, even clandestinely after the trade was outlawed in 1788, Massachusetts Chapter 48 of the Acts of 1787 (passed March 26, 1788). Now I ponder if those published assertions contained kernels of truth derived from memories and oral traditions about events spanning the war. Gloria McCahon Whiting, "Emancipation Without the Courts or Constitution," recently established (in 2019) that in historical Suffolk County (then also including most of what is now Norfolk County) slave ownership indicated in probate records precipitously declined at the commencement of the Revolutionary War in 1775, but also persisted there (albeit in greatly reduced numbers) long after the "Quock Walker" cases of 1781 and 1783, ibid., 11, 17 n21, 18 n38. As slavery attenuated rapidly during and following the war, its economic importance diminished proportionately and so perhaps that period was what was most remembered, rather than when slavery and the slave trade figured more importantly in the Massachusetts economy. Applying Whiting's methods that consisted of a "page-by-page perusal of all the probate records from Suffolk County between 1760 and 1790" (17 n22) for other Massachusetts counties and expanding the temporal range and archival sources could finally bring the same "unprecedented precision and certainty" (5) to definitively trace slavery and emancipation throughout the state.

Contrary to Chief Justice Shaw's assertion in the March 1836 decision of *Aves* (18 Pick. [35 Mass. Reports] 193, at 210, italics mine) there was no "unbroken series of judicial *decisions*" on that point, that slavery was judicially abolished (retrospectively) from the adoption of the state constitution in 1780 going forward in time. The 1836 decision was the first instance of that notion that appeared in a judicial decision of record, with instant, statewide applicability and with the power of reliable precedential authority. Prior to *Aves* there were four matters in the orbit around the central point of the legality of slavery in the Commonwealth, but none of which ever articulated the common law in a form and manner that could be depended upon as binding precedent in a judicial decision of record.

First, there was Chief Justice William Cushing's "Legal notes" about the third "Quock Walker" case, Commonwealth v. Jennison (1783), with seemingly contemporaneous trial notes and what appear to be his jury instructions, and his separate "Notes of Cases" prepared after 1789 with revised case notes and a more elaborated jury charge (Cushing, "Legal Notes"; Cushing, "Notes of Cases"; Hamburger, *Law and Judicial Duty*, 482–483 and n12–n15). John D. Cushing, "The Cushing Court and the Abolition of Slavery in Massachusetts," 127 n12, 132 n20, observed that in the "Legal notes," the assertion that was added to a page that followed the apparently original trial notes and charge to the jury ("The preceding Case was the one in which, by the foregoing Charge, Slavery in Massachusetts was forever abolished", Cushing, "Legal Notes," 99) was not in the Chief Justice's handwriting, and appears to me to be a nineteenth-century writing style. The separate revised and elaborated "Notes of Cases" (34, quotation) was made after 1789 by yet a different hand that added much but pointedly that "slavery is [^] in my judgment [^] as effectively abolished as it can be". Philip Hamburger, ibid., 483 n15, referring to Chief Justice Cushing's "Legal notes," and to the revised and elaborated "Notes of cases," honed in on the historical problem created when someone "rewrote his instructions about Jennison's indictment to reach a more dramatic conclusion [....] No longer merely an opinion about the common law that could be discerned 'by our own conduct & Constitution,' this was now an opinion about what the Constitution had 'abolished.' It was part of a broader rewriting of history that would gratify many nineteenth-century inhabitants of Massachusetts, that would annoy many twentieth-century historians, and that would in both ways distract attention from what actually happened." While Cushing's notebooks were unknown to Chief Justice Shaw at the time of *Aves*, a judge's notes are not equivalent to an official record of decision, and they carry only limited evidentiary value in subsequent judicial consideration. However, Chief Justice Cushing's notes and jury charge in Commonwealth v. Jennison figured importantly in the much later historical misremembrance of the effects of the "Quock Walker" cases. Rather than investigating the official judicial records for the "Quock Walker" cases, attorneys and jurists may have accepted the characterization of the reasoning and effects of the judicial decision for *Jennison* that was published in 1795, Belknap, "Queries Respecting the Slavery and Emancipation of Negroes in Massachusetts," 203. Belknap derived his idea that the Declaration of the Rights in the 1780 state constitution was instrumental to deciding the 1783 *Jennison* case from James Sullivan. A transcription of his letter to Belknap was published in 1877 as "James Sullivan to Dr. Belknap. Boston, April 9, 1795." The historical idea that the 1783 *Jennison* case instantly abolished slavery in Massachusetts by reliance on the 1780 state constitution was reinforced by a 1874 lecture to the Massachusetts Historical Society by Supreme Judicial Court Chief Justice Horace Gray, Jr., during which Cushing's "Legal notes" manuscript was exhibited (Gray, *The Case of Nathaniel Jennison*; Gray, *The Abolition of Slavery in Massachusetts*; Gray, "Note by Chief Justice Gray," 292–293, quotation): "Chief Justice Gray submitted for the inspection of the members of the Society Chief Justice Cushing's original note-book [..., i.e., the "Legal notes"] (which had been intrusted to him for the purpose by Mr. William Cushing Paine, the namesake and great grand-nephew of Chief Justice Cushing), and read therefrom the minutes of the trial at April Term 1783 of the case of *The Commonwealth v. Nathaniel Jennison*, in which it was established that slavery was wholly abolished in this Commonwealth by the Declaration of Rights prefixed to the Constitution of 1780." Evidence indicates, however, that the constitutional declaration of freedom, equality, and liberty figured in an earlier "Quock Walker" case, probably Jennison v. Caldwell and Caldwell (1781), and most probably earlier still in the "Mum Bett" case (1781) that had been judicially forgotten. The official judicial documentation of the "Mum Bett" and "Quock Walker" cases that Chief Justice Shaw did not investigate (18 Pick. [35 Mass. Reports] 193, at 209–210) and Cushing's apparently contemporaneous notes and jury charge for *Jennison* are further considered below in this note.

Second, there was Chief Justice Theophilus Parsons' obiter dicta in March 1808, Winchendon v. Hatfield (4 Mass. Reports 123, at 128–129, judicial history of abolition), recollecting and differently characterizing the unpublished decisions of Commonwealth v. Jennison (1783, the third of the three "Quock Walker" cases) and of Littleton v. Tuttle (1796). The complicated matters of *Littleton* are examined in detail further below in this note as its misremembrance came to be relied upon in subsequent decisions of record.

Third, there was Associate Justice Theodore Sedgwick's historic dissent in March 1810, Greenwood v. Curtis (6 Mass. Reports 358, at 362–374 n): a contractual matter involving slavery was "*malum in se* [wrong in itself] and not sustainable at common law in Massachusetts" (Welch, "Mumbet and Judge Sedgwick," 18). In his dissent, Judge Sedgwick only alluded to the "Quock Walker" cases. Justice Sedgwick wrote: "In less than a year after the [state] constitution was adopted and went into operation, it was solemnly adjudged by this Court, that negro slavery did not exist in the commonwealth, and that, had it previously existed, it would have been abolished by [...] the constitution" (6 Mass. Reports 358, at 370 n). Justice Sedgwick's dissent in *Greenwood* was cited in *Aves* in arguments to the court, and so that presumably informed Chief Justice Shaw, but in his decision in *Aves* he did not cite that case decision or the dissent (18 Pick. [35 Mass. Reports] 193, at 196, 202). In any regard, a dissent does not carry precedential authority nor does it affect common law.

And finally, there was a case that came before Chief Justice Shaw as a single-justice matter that he decided December 4, 1832, In re Francisco (9 American Jurist 490 [1833], Finkelman, *An Imperfect Union*, 101–102). The decision was not published in *Massachusetts Reports*. The report of Shaw's opinion that appeared in *American Jurist* was derived from a newspaper story (that cautiously expressed it was "a very imperfect sketch") published in the *Boston Atlas* (December 5, 1832, according to Levy, *The Law of the Commonwealth and Chief Justice Shaw*, 61 n4, who noticed that the news article was reprinted verbatim in several publications). The case was similar to *Aves* in that it involved a child, "Francisco, a colored boy, twelve or fourteen years of age," who was purchased by a Mrs. Howard as a slave in a place (Cuba) where slavery was permitted, and who was then brought by her into Massachusetts. Before she departed Havana with her enslaved servant, Mrs. Howard "was admonished that he would become free upon being brought into this country" (9 American Jurist 490, at 491). Unlike in *Aves*, the minor was asserted by Mrs. Howard to be a free servant. Shaw decided the case, not as a matter of illegal enslavement, but rather as a matter of guardianship and personal autonomy in consideration of Francisco's wishes to remain with Mrs. Howard that Shaw ascertained from an in camera interview with the boy. Importantly, however, even the "imperfect sketch" conveyed Shaw's view of the common law that slavery was illegal in Massachusetts, but the view was expressed only as obiter dicta: "If Mrs. Howard [...] had claimed the boy as a slave, I should have ordered him to be discharged from her custody. But it appears from her return to the writ, that she does not claim him as a slave. The boy, by the law of Massachusetts, is in fact free; and Mrs. Howard having, by her return to the writ, disclaimed to hold him as a slave, has made a record of his freedom, and cannot make him a slave again in the Island of Cuba" (ibid., at 491–492). In any regard, none of those four previous matters were judicial decisions of record that perspicuously established the particular legal point of Massachusetts abolition. While instructive, none were legally withstanding as binding precedent on that precise legal issue of the judicial abolition of Massachusetts slavery.

The unpublished 1796 decision of Littleton v. Tuttle (Supreme Judicial Court Records, Middlesex County, October 1796, 302, JA) was featured in a number of Massachusetts poor relief cases involving former slaves, but the information relied only on an abstract in a note added by the reporter to the published 1808 decision of Winchendon v. Hatfield (4 Mass. Reports 123, at 128 n). The abstract of *Littleton* in the reporter's note asserted that "*The Court*, stopped the defendant's counsel from replying, and *the Chief Justice* charged the jury, as the unanimous opinion of the Court, that *Cato* [Jacob], being born in this country, was born free; and that the defendant was not chargeable for his [Jacob's] support after he [Jacob] was 21 years of age" (4 Mass. Reports 123, at 128 n). Chief Justice Parsons in *Winchendon* (ibid., at 129, italics mine) had similarly characterized the *Littleton* decision: "the Chief Justice [Francis Dana], in directing the jury, stated, as the unanimous opinion of the Court, that a negro born in the state *before* the present [state] constitution, was born free, although born of a female slave." Chief Justice Isaac Parker followed the abstract about *Littleton* in his 1816 decision of Andover v. Canton (13 Mass. Reports 547, at 551–552): "the Court, early after the adoption of our [state] Constitution, deciding, not only that slavery was virtually abolished by that Constitution, but that the issue of two slaves [i.e., their child Jacob], born in wedlock in the year 1773, was born free; probably upon the principle, that, although slaves acquired in a foreign country might remain bound during their lives; yet, that, in a free country, they could not transmit their slavery to their posterity. This was settled in the case of *The Inhabitants of Littleton* vs. *Tuttle*." But Chief Justice Parker doubted that (ibid., 552). In his *Andover* decision, Parker conveyed that Parsons (in *Winchendon*, 4 Mass. Reports 123, at 129) had pointed out that, contra *Littleton*, before and after the 1780 state constitution, slaves were conveyed as property and children of slaves became enslaved. Parsons knew that, because as a practicing attorney he had represented enslaved plaintiffs in their freedom suits, as he also at least once appeared as counsel for a purported slave owner (Silas Royal

v. Joshua Wyman [on appeal, so captioned in the appellate record of decision as "Wyman vs Royall"], Superior Court of Judicature Records, Middlesex County, October 1778, 42, JA; see pleadings for that case by Theophilus Parsons representing appellant Wyman in SFC, File #148316, JA.)

Parenthetically here, Helen Tunnicliff Catterall, *Judicial Cases concerning American Slavery and the Negro*, Vol. 4, 456 n10, 485 n2, 486, 496 n5, overstated Parsons' obiter dicta that did *not* aver that there was "no foundation in law, as there was none in fact" to suppose that children born of slaves were born free (ibid., 456 n10). Parsons' obiter dicta did not go as far as that: Parsons only recollected that, in custom and practice, children of slaves were in fact enslaved. Catterall (ibid., 496 n5) was mistaken that Parker "omits to state that Chief Justice Parsons [...raised *Littleton's* holding of supposed pre-constitutional emancipation] only to disapprove" of that wrong notion in *Littleton* that children of slaves were not enslaved. Parker had indeed stated (in Andover v. Canton, 13 Mass. Reports 547, at 552) Parsons' contrarian obiter dicta in *Winchendon* (Parsons in *Winchendon*, 4 Mass. Reports 123, at 129: "It is, however, very certain that the general practice, and common usage, had been opposed to this opinion", i.e., contra *Littleton*, children of slaves were in fact enslaved). Parker, in summarizing Parsons' point—that contrary to *Littleton* children of slaves were indeed enslaved—wrote that children of slaves were, in fact, "the property of the master of the parents, liable to be sold and transferred like other chattels, and as assets in the hands of executors and administrators" of estates (Parker in *Andover*, 13 Mass. Reports 547, at 552).

Chief Justice Parker in the 1819 decision of Lanesborough v. Westfield unaccountably stated that "in the year 1796, it was solemnly and unanimously decided by the Court, that the issue [i.e., children] of slaves, although born *before* the adoption of the [Massachusetts] constitution, were born free" (16 Mass. Reports 74, at 75–76, citing to the note in *Winchendon* about *Littleton*, italics in the quotation mine). William E. Nelson, *Americanization of the Common Law*, 101–102, 228 n166, quoted from Chief Justice Francis Dana's "Minute Books" which are in a subseries of the Dana Family Papers, Ms. N-1088 at the Massachusetts Historical Society, Boston. The extract from Dana's notebook that Nelson quoted indicated that while Jacob was bought in 1779 and held as a slave, "at the time all Negroes were considered in fact as Free: although they had been imported from Africa & Sold here as Slaves." James Kent's influential *Commentaries on American Law* (1827), Vol. 2, 205, referred to the reporter's note about *Littleton* to state that "In Massachusetts, it was judicially declared, soon after the revolution, that slavery was virtually abolished by their constitution, and that the issue of a female slave, though born prior to their constitution, was born free."

Nevertheless, for Littleton v. Tuttle, the Supreme Judicial Court record of decision, the docket entries for the case, and the appellate case file papers provide no indication that the court reached any decision of retrospective pre- or post-constitutional or common law abolition, Middlesex County Court of Common Pleas Records, September 1794, 486; Supreme Judicial Court Records, Middlesex County, October 1796, 302; Supreme Judicial Court Docket (Minute Books), n.p., October 1795 (#29), April 1796 (#16), October 1796 (#9); SFC, File #150987, JA. The case decision indicated, rather, that Tuttle made no promise to the town that he would pay to support his former slave. George H. Moore, in his *Notes on the History of Slavery in Massachusetts*, 20, 22–24, first relied on the reporter's published note about *Littleton* (4 Mass. Reports 123, at 128 n), and accepted that characterization of *Littleton* as the only positive evidence of a judicial order that children born of slaves in Massachusetts were born free. But in Moore's "Slavery in Massachusetts. Mr. Moore's Reply to His Boston Critics," 190–191, 193–194, he reviewed the unpublished *Littleton* decision (190) and realized the discrepancy of the case record versus its characterization by Chief Justices Parker and Parsons and by the reporter of the published abstract. Moore, ibid., 191, also saw discrepancy in another published case summary of *Littleton* that Moore attributed to the town's attorney, Attorney General James Sullivan, "Law Cases," 47, published anonymously two years after the Supreme Judicial Court decision in the *Collections of the Massachusetts Historical Society* in 1798. (Sullivan was the first president of the society, and was listed in that volume, 291, as a "resident member" of the society. See Sullivan, "James Sullivan to Dr. Belknap. Boston, April 9, 1795," 404 n, where in an editorial note Sullivan was identified as the first society president.)

Matters of legal consequence and precedent were asserted in the reporter's published abstract for *Littleton* (4 Mass. Reports 123, at 128 n), and in Sullivan's summary in "Law Cases," that are at variance with the appellate court record of decision, the docket entries, and the file papers for *Littleton*. There are also legally inconsequential matters, biographical details, in the reporter's note and Sullivan's article that are supported in the *Littleton* court documentation and in published town records. Rather than "born free", Jacob was born a slave in 1773, and assigned a slave name of "Cato." Jacob was the son of Ziphron (the initial letter appears to be *Z* not *S*, consistent with the Biblical placename mentioned in Numbers 34:9 KJV). "Scipio", as the reporter wrote, was a slave name assigned to Ziphron who named his son Jacob, Old Testament-style. Sanderson, et al., *Records of Littleton*, rendered it "Sipporon", 269 (marriage intention, September 13, 1766) but also rendered it "Scipio", 339 (death of child of Scipio and Violet, May 16, 1788; death of Scipio, June 15, 1788). Ziphron and Violet were "lawfully married" when

Ziphron was enslaved by Nathan Chase and Violet was enslaved by Capt. Joseph Harwood. The reporter was correct that it was Harwood who sold Jacob when he was six years old to William Tuttle. When Jacob was 21 years old in 1794, Tuttle told the town of Littleton to "immediately provide a place for and remove him, or I shall of Necessity be Obliged to visit you with him". The reporter would seem to have inferred correctly that Jacob was (in the language used in those times) "a cripple, and unable to labor" and Tuttle's 1794 request to the town indicated that Jacob was "unable to support himself". Deposition of Eleanor Wright, October 19, 1795; and, William Tuttle to Littleton Selectmen, April 9, 1794 in SFC, File #150987, JA. Sullivan, ibid., also concurred that Jacob "became lame, and unable to labour" and that Tuttle "carried him, and left him with the overseers of the poor, for support." On matters of disabled enslaved people, see Warren, "'Thrown upon the world': Valuing Infants in the Eighteenth-Century North American Slave Market," 630–631, and cited scholarship at 640–641 n44 and n45.

While of course there is no transcript of the court proceedings for *Littleton*, there is no indication in the appellate decision, in the docket entries, or in the file papers that an en banc opinion about constitutional or common law abolition was made, nor do the judicial archives indicate that a directed verdict issued from the bench, nor that the case involved a special verdict (when a jury defers to judges to determine issues of law). Sullivan's summary of the proceedings does not mention that supposed declaratory outcome, and he himself attended trial as Attorney General representing the town. Surely, if such a momentous decision had been made, Sullivan would have noted that in his article published by the august historical society long-interested in that topic. Curiously, however, Sullivan's summary indicated that "The judges were of opinion" that a slave born in a town gained inhabitancy "Whereupon the plaintiffs became non-suit." While Sullivan may have used the word in a figurative sense, a nonsuit result was not indicated in the decision, docket entries, or file papers, either: the trial did not end but proceeded to a jury verdict. The docket entries show the progression of the appellate case. It was first entered in October 1795 (entry #29), and the case was continued because an identical controversy was not yet then decided: "First Jury—There being an action contin[d] for advisem[te] [advisement] from the last Term of this Court held at Northampton, wherein the same point came in question as arrives in this cause, the same is contin[d] by order of Court to await their Judgm[t] thereon". (The action was Shelburne v. Greenfield, Supreme Judicial Court Records, Hampshire County, September 1796, 252, JA, plea of review of special verdict, residency of former slaves and their children was in the town of their former master.) *Littleton* was continued again in April 1796 (#16). At the October 1796 term, the case proceeded to trial and was decided.

As the record of decision indicated, the jury found that William Tuttle "never promised" to pay the town of Littleton to support his then 21-year-old "negro man" and the court awarded Tuttle his costs of the lawsuit. The docket for October 1796 (#9) summarized the jury finding and indicated that Tuttle's costs were $24.43. The town did not initially pay that judgment, so on November 26, 1796 the court issued an execution (i.e., an order to the sheriff to execute—carry out—the court's judgment, to obtain the money due and pay the winning party). It was an ordinary outcome for an action brought on a plea of trespass on the case on promises (shortened as "case"). (Another error in the published *Littleton* abstract was that assumpsit—a related but distinct form of action—was the plea used in *Littleton*, which it was not: that too was repeated by others to become a factoid.) To repeat what George H. Moore said in frustration when confounding assertions were revealed by original records to be erroneous, "So distinct and positive an assertion should have been fortified by unequivocal authority," *Notes on the History of Slavery in Massachusetts*, 22. Moore, in "Slavery in Massachusetts. Mr. Moore's Reply to His Boston Critics," 190–191, 193–194, expressed the same amazement with the judicial declarations that (fictively and legally) characterized differently what had been actually decided in those earlier cases.

Unlike Chief Justice Parsons' creative characterizations in *Winchendon* in 1808 of the *Jennison* and *Littleton* cases that were merely within obiter dicta of historical background, Chief Justice Parker's legal fiction in the 1819 *Lanesborough* decision—that retrospective, *pre*-1780 judicial emancipation was ordered by the Supreme Judicial Court in *Littleton* in 1796—was essential to his finding in *Lanesborough* and so that decision carried precedential authority. In *Aves* (18 Pick. [35 Mass. Reports] 193, at 209), Chief Justice Shaw referenced *Winchendon* and *Littleton*, but not *Lanesborough*, to make his legal finding of *post*-1780 emancipation. Regardless, Parker's, Parson's, Sullivan's, and the reporter's mischaracterizations of *Littleton*, and Shaw's "unbroken series of judicial decisions", were all part of a proud legal and popular historical tradition in Massachusetts of "purposeful misunderstanding" of the indistinct history of judicial abolition. That tradition insists to this day that slavery was abolished in 1781 or 1783 by the still-differently remembered decisions of the "Mum Bett" and "Quock Walker" cases, Hunter, "Publishing Freedom," 9 ("purposeful misunderstanding") and 150 (the "Quock Walker" cases).

Among several others, Wiecek, "Somerset," 124, perceptively observed that "[t]he Quock Walker story can be seen as an American counterpart of *Somerset*, especially in its ambiguity and in the resultant misunderstanding about its impact." The English case of *Somerset* (James Somerset v. Charles Stewart, King's Bench, 12 Geo. 3, Easter Term 1772, 98 Eng. Rep. 499 and 20 Howell's State Trials 1), in an opinion issued by Lord Mansfield, held that slavery cannot be maintained legally without explicit law to authorize it. But in both legal and popular minds, the legal effects of *Somerset* were misconstrued and enlarged beyond its actual and particular holdings. See Cotter's clarifying article for "The Somerset Case and the Abolition of Slavery in England." Cotter reminded me that the only known explicit reference to *Somerset* in a Massachusetts freedom suit was made by attorney John Lowell during oral arguments in the trial of Caesar Hendrick v. Richard Greenleaf (Essex County Court of Common Pleas Records, September 1773, 8, JA). Lowell expanded the English decision by stating, "Somersett case shews every one setting his foot on English ground to be free, wherever he came from", Wroth and Zobel, *Legal Papers of John Adams*, Vol. 2, 65. The lack of notes of arguments for most other Massachusetts freedom suit trials that date after the *Somerset* decision makes it impossible to determine when *Somerset* was invoked by attorneys or judges during trial. Davis, *The Problem of Slavery in the Age of Revolution*, 508, recognized that Levi Lincoln, "Brief of Levi Lincoln in the Slave Case Tried 1781," 439, paraphrased arguments in *Somerset* during Jennison v. Caldwell and Caldwell. Chief Justice William Cushing echoed Lord Mansfield's holdings in *Somerset* in what seem to be his contemporaneous jury instructions in his "Legal notes," expanded in his "Notes of cases" pertaining to Commonwealth v. Jennison.

In *Aves*, the *Somerset* decision was raised in oral arguments (18 Pick. [35 Mass. Reports] 196–204, passim) and so *Somerset* was considered by Chief Justice Shaw (ibid., 209, 210–211, 212, and at 224 citing to a note about French law that had appeared in 20 Howell's State Trials 1, at 15). Shaw did not find *Somerset* to be completely persuasive to decide *Aves*. Interestingly, Shaw extended Lord Mansfield's evident meaning of "positive law" (i.e., explicit, statutory law being required to authorize enslavement) to also mean that slavery might be permitted by custom (customary law, not common or statutory law) and "tacit acquiescence" (ibid., 212; cf. Finkelman, *An Imperfect Union*, 113, who concluded differently that "Shaw's decision was virtually a total application of Somerset to Massachusetts"). Among several scholars, Thea K. Hunter, "Publishing Freedom," considered newspaper reporting of the 1772 *Somerset* case that popularized its misunderstanding, and the *Somerset* arguments in the "Quock Walker" and *Aves* cases; see also Hunter's considerations of *Aves* and *Somerset* in "Geographies of Liberty" and in "Transatlantic Negotiations." Patricia Bradley, *Slavery, Propaganda, and the American Revolution*, Chapter 4, "The Somerset Case," detailed its reception and reporting in newspapers. Supplemental to newspaper reports, information about *Somerset* reached the reading public through pamphlets published in London in 1772 and 1788, one reprinted in Boston in 1774, one reprinted in Newport, R.I. in 1788, Finkelman, *Slavery in the Courtroom*, 18, 21–25.

The "Mum Bett" and "Quock Walker" cases have become in modern heroic narratives the defining moments of agency and determination by enslaved people themselves to force courts to abolish Massachusetts slavery—paradigmatically shifting credit from Jeremy Belknap's vague "publick opinion" to direct action by the enslaved and their allies. As sketched here, the legally obscure case of "Mum Bett" was judicially forgotten and the "Quock Walker" cases were only alluded to in what Chief Justice Shaw glossed in *Aves*, 210, as an "unbroken series of judicial decisions". William O'Brien, "Did the Jennison Case Outlaw Slavery in Massachusetts?" 220, captured the "certain disquieting obscurity [...that] has always hung over this page of history" and similarly Robert M. Cover, *Justice Accused*, 38, characterized the history of Massachusetts judicial emancipation as "decidedly murky." Particular to this *legal* point, until 1867 the "Quock Walker" cases were only referred to allusively in judicial decisions and not explicitly cited in published opinions of the Supreme Judicial Court, Blanck, *Tyrannicide*, 126, 127; O'Brien, ibid., 220 and n4; Romer, *Slavery in the Connecticut Valley of Massachusetts*, 215 n26.

The "Mum Bett" and "Quock Walker" cases were heard as jury trials with party-particular outcomes. The decisions of the Common Pleas courts and Supreme Judicial Court were unpublished, and only existed in original manuscript form. In eighteenth-century legal circles, which depended on memory of judicial decisions and bench rulings to invoke case-made common law principles, the cases were soon forgotten. Practicing legal professionals in at least Berkshire and Worcester counties remembered the outcomes for a time, and advised their slave-owning clients of the futility of defending or appealing lawsuits for liberty in a changed legal landscape. Historian Arthur Zilversmit, "Quock Walker, Mum Bett, and the Abolition of Slavery in Massachusetts," 618, 622, discovered that Col. John Ashley (the same-named father and son were both titled Esq., and historians refer to them as the Colonel and the General, respectively) who was the defendant in "Mum Bett," was the defendant in another freedom suit, Zach Mullen v. John Ashley, Berkshire County Court of Common Pleas Records, April 1781, 24; August 1781, 53; February 1782, 237, JA. *Mullen* was brought and continued from the April 1781 to the February 1782 terms, then dismissed when neither party appeared. Zilversmit, ibid., discerned that the "Mum Bett" and "Quock Walker" case decisions were instrumental to the *Mullen* outcome, as the first two "Quock Walker" case outcomes were to "Mum Bett." Similar examples are apparent in records for Worcester County freedom suit cases near-contemporary to the "Quock Walker" cases, but as also with *Mullen* the timing of legal events and the correspondence of the outcomes require further research and documentation.

The record of the Common Pleas decision for the "Mum Bett" case specifically, narrowly, and particularly adjudged that Brom and Bett were not "legal Negro" servants and awarded the plaintiffs 30s. damages and their court costs of £5 14s. 4p. Brom and Bett v. Ashley, Berkshire County Court of Common Pleas Records, August 1781, 55, quotation at 57; see also the jury verdict in the case file papers: "Brom & Bett are not [...] legal Negro Servants", SFC, File #159966, JA. Notice especially that "legal Negro Servants" connoted "slaves," confounding a racialized term with legal status and implicating assumptions that African ancestry supposed a destiny of servitude unless formally declared otherwise. That conception is apparent in many Massachusetts freedom suits. Ashley's appeal to the Supreme Judicial Court was abandoned and that court awarded Brom and Bett 30s. in damages and their legal costs: the appellant Ashley "confesses Judgment", Supreme Judicial Court Records, Berkshire County, October 1781, 96, captioned as "Ashley apl Brom et al.", JA.

No near-contemporary evidence has been found and brought forth that documents exactly what issues were raised at trial in "Mum Bett." Arthur Zilversmit assembled convincing evidence that supported historical traditions that the plaintiffs' attorneys, Tapping Reeve (1744–1823) and Theodore Sedgwick (1746–1813), strategized their approach to prosecute the case, in mind that the freedom and equality guarantees of the Declaration of the Rights in the then-fresh Massachusetts Constitution (1780) could be employed in freedom suits to legally emancipate enslaved people. While neither the Berkshire Court of Common Pleas nor the Supreme Judicial Court "rule[d] on the constitutionality of slavery" (Zilversmit, ibid., 622), the Common Pleas jury likely were swayed by the plaintiffs' talented attorneys who it would be expected had raised the principles in the Declaration of the Rights in their opening statements and closing arguments. After so many decades of scholarly and historical review and conclusion, both the "Mum Bett" and "Quock Walker" cases should be regarded, not with false historical consciousness as instantly abolishing slavery in Massachusetts, but rather as significant in the long history of the demise of legal slavery (to paraphrase Paynter, et al., "Excavating the 'Garden of the North,'" 242). Gloria McCahon Whiting, "Emancipation Without the Courts or Constitution," 20 n63, referring to the perceived outcome of Commonwealth v. Jennison, concluded that "the significance of the 1783 high court ruling lies not in bringing about a broad-based emancipation, but instead in legally acknowledging an emancipation that had already [largely] taken place [...by 1775] at least, for [historical] Suffolk County" but probably also in other counties, while conclusively enslavement and its similar circumstances continued for decades in this state, seemingly into the early nineteenth century. As developed in common law through freedom suits, the constitutional arguments presumably raised first in "Mum Bett" and then two years later in *Jennison* provided enslaved people and their captors with the vague but ineffaceable "sense that slavery was defunct in Massachusetts" (Minardi, *Making Slavery History*, 15, also quoted by Paynter and Battle-Baptiste, "Contexts of Resistance in African American Western Massachusetts," 332), that "at some critical moment in the history of Massachusetts, emancipation became common sense" (Breen, "Making History," 95, also quoted by Whiting, ibid., 21 n70).

Arthur Zilversmit, ibid., 630 n17, discerned a significant legal detail of the "Mum Bett" case: that it finally commenced on a "pluries" writ that characteristically included the distinctive phrase, "When we have often commanded you". A pluries writ was issued when a first (original) writ and then a second (alias) writ were ineffective to implement the court's order, in this case for the sheriff to take protective custody of (to replevy) Brom and Bett and to direct Ashley to appear in court. It is the only Massachusetts freedom suit thus far identified that required a pluries writ. Defendants in the other identified lawsuits complied with original writs. The pluries writ, recited in the Common Pleas record, stated that Col. John Ashley "did not permit a delivery" of Brom and Bett to the sheriff, indicating that the Colonel evaded service and process and was recalcitrant to the court and the sheriff. Col. Ashley's obstinacy was all the more curious because he was a member of the bar (Hampshire County, 1732), had been a Hampshire County sheriff (1755), served as a state representative (intermittently 1750–1780), and was a judge at the Berkshire County Court of Common Pleas (appointed 1761 and served to 1774, when the court closed until 1781). (Information varies in secondary sources about Col. Ashley's appointments and their duration, cf. Piper and Levinson, *One Minute a Free Woman*, 42; Schutz, *Legislators of the Massachusetts General Court*, 151; Taft, "Judicial History of Berkshire," 104–105; Trowbridge, *The Ashley Genealogy*, 55–58; and, Washburn, *Sketches of the Judicial History of Massachusetts*, 394. For closure of the Berkshire county court 1774–1781 during the Revolutionary War period, see Raphael and Raphael, *The Spirit of 74*, 54–64, and Wright, *Report on the Custody and Condition of the Public Records*, 334 n2.)

That it took three writs to get Col. Ashley to comply raises the issue that if in fact Brom and Bett had not already fled their captivity (local tradition related that Bett had left the Ashleys, then filed suit), then they would have been increasingly in danger of retribution and being secreted away from the area. Mum Bett and another slave, probably her daughter Betsey, had been victims of domestic violence in Col. Ashley's house, legendarily by his wife Hannah (Annetje). The clues in the writ provide opportunity to consider that the decision by an enslaved person and their allies to bring legal action against a captor arrived after internal deliberation of alternatives and their potential consequences, careful planning, and logistical preparation. If they had not already made their moves and left, the sudden appearance of the sheriff that disclosed what the enslaved person had done instantly created a domestic situation fraught with uncertainties and danger for the captive and their loved ones. Banks, "Dangerous Woman," 821, n122; and VanderVelde, *Redemption Songs*, 4–6, 199.

Recognition of the distinctive legal language only used for a pluries writ, realizing its legal meaning and purpose, and further considering the legal case documents and historical information, challenge elements of some local traditions about the Ashleys. Col. Ashley did not resign as a judge of the Berkshire County Common Pleas when *Brom* came before the court, in a supposed demonstration of honor and judicial ethics. He was not on the bench when the court reopened in 1781, so had resigned or not been reappointed during the interregnum. Ray and Marie Raphael, *The Sprit of 74*, 62, indicated that Col. Ashley effectively resigned when the county courts closed in August 1774. The legal resolution of "Mum Bett" occurred when Col. Ashley finally capitulated, but only after he had appealed the case to the Supreme Judicial Court and had his lawyer announce that he accepted the judgment of the Court of Common Pleas. Particular legal details of "Mum Bett" counter local historical traditions that deemphasize the leading role of enslaved people themselves and their allies to effectuate emancipation on their own volition by resistance and protest through legal authorities. Historical traditions can simultaneously misremember and then forget the activities of slave owners to preserve the institution by legal, illegal, and legally ambiguous activities. In spite of the outcome of "Mum Bett," the Ashley family persisted in the slave trade and protracted the institution if not de jure than de facto by one method "whose legality seems dubious at best". In 1789 Gen. John Ashley purchased an enslaved woman in New York, and transformed her laboring arrangement into an ersatz 10-year indenture that "was obviously calculated to extend the slave relation rather than to mitigate it," Melish, *Disowning Slavery*, 96, 97 (quotations), 101. Mary's indenture with Gen. John Ashley was also considered by Blanck, *Tyrannicide*, 141–142; Drew, *If They Close the Door on You*, 47; and, Piper and Levinson, *One Minute a Free Woman*, 74.

Even though the Ashley family owned many slaves, generous speculation was that they relented to Mum Bett's desires for emancipation because they were expansive to notions of liberty and individual rights, particularly as the Colonel helped draft the 1773 Sheffield Resolves. Similarly, local tradition offered that abandoning the Supreme Judicial Court appeal showed that Col. Ashley surreptitiously cooperated to effectuate Brom and Bett's emancipation. These speculative traditions trivialize Brom and Bett's agency and resolve to demand and obtain their freedom. Subtly and explicitly rehabilitating Col. Ashley ignores that he and his son had their own and broader interests and motivations to evade the sheriff's process to commence the lawsuit, to delay releasing Brom and Bett from enslavement after the Common Pleas decision, to protract the lawsuit by appeal, and to persist in the slave trade as late as 1789. Doing so maintained the status quo of slavery and the slave trade that served not only the Ashley family but also their social and economic equals. Revisionist traditions frequently reflect an effort to retrospectively resolve conflicting and upsetting historical information while presaging later views and values, Minardi, *Making Slavery History*; Minardi, "Making Slavery Visible (Again)." Munificent speculation about the Ashleys as incongruously protoabolitionist, as local traditions aver, reflects linkage of later developments in abolition, anti-discrimination, enfranchisement, and better economic opportunity for people of color with idealization of Revolutionary period rhetoric for "liberty" that was in actuality contradictory and cabined to mean profit and legislative representation.

The Ashley family was regionally powerful and wealthy with achievements in politics, industry, and the military. What was cognitively troubling was their involvement in the slave trade, their possession and captivity of enslaved laborers, the violence that occurred against Mum Bett and the other enslaved female at their historic and well-appointed residence, and their contestation of the long-remembered and celebrated freedom suit that freed Mum Bett (and Brom who is less frequently mentioned). Her emancipation led to her choosing her new name, Elizabeth Freeman, and to becoming a propertied woman who lived a full and long life with family and friends, as related by so many and so well-documented by Emilie Piper and David Levinson in *One Minute a Free Woman*. By undeservedly attributing pre-emancipationist and other anachronistic liberal values to the Ashley ancestors, such speculation was intended to prefigure and heighten the importance of the Berkshires in becoming a demonstrable locus of contingent freedom, opportunity, and achievement for people of color. The Berkshire region was geographically positioned to draw escapees from the adjoining states of Connecticut and New York that legislatively enacted a gradual manumission scheme that lasted into the nineteenth century, and also drew people from more distant slave states. Just like in other regions of the country, people of color in the Berkshires vividly recollected everyday experiences of oppression, discrimination, segregation in housing and restaurants, and not only "structural" violence (there were there, as in other Massachusetts places, Ku Klux Klan meetings). Robert Paynter and Whitney Battle-Baptiste, "Contexts of Resistance in African American Western Massachusetts," with their students, colleagues, and regional historians, have long educated us in their expansive studies centered from the W.E.B. Du Bois Boyhood Homesite in Great Barrington (see also Paynter, et al., "Excavating the 'Garden of the North'" and the other articles about western Massachusetts in that same journal issue and their cited references, and especially Drew, ibid.; Elder, *African American Heritage in Massachusetts*; and, Levinson, et al., *African American Heritage in the Upper Housatonic Valley*). Visitors to the Col. Ashley property owned and managed by The Trustees of Reservations, and to their website, are now presented an explicit interpretation and context of the Ashley family's domestic and industrial slave labor and their involvement in the slave trade, The Trustees of Reservations, *Elizabeth Freeman: Fighting for Freedom*, https://web.archive.org/web/20181215115229/http://www.thetrustees.org/what-we-care-about/history-culture/elizabeth-freeman-fighting-for-freedom.html, accessed August 3, 2019.

The Supreme Judicial Court records of the decisions for the "Quock Walker" cases only plainly show that in Walker v. Jennison, the appellant (Jennison) was found to be in default for not having presented attested copies of the Common Pleas file; in Jennison v. Caldwell and Caldwell that the appellants (the Caldwells) were not guilty of trespass on the case; and, in Commonwealth v. Jennison, that he was guilty of assault and imprisonment of Quock Walker for which he was fined the nominal sum of 40s. plus costs of prosecution and court costs. Furthermore it should be remembered, that at that time, cases appealed to the Supreme Judicial Court were heard as full new jury trials (trials *de novo*) with outcomes that were particular to the case-specific issues and parties. At that time, decisions were unpublished and common law precedent depended on indifferent memories and trial notes of attorneys and jurists. Unlike with today's appellate law trials, the Supreme Judicial Court was not then focused only on narrow and residual appellate issues, with published decisions (in what became the *Massachusetts Reports* series) that had instant and binding statewide consequences. (On that matter of earlier, narrow, party-specific unpublished decisions in contrast to later statewide pronouncements of law that were published as opinions of the court, and generally about historical development of the court's practices and procedures, see e.g., Bellefontaine, "Theophilus Parsons as a Legal Reformer," 16–17; Cushing, "The Cushing Court and the Abolition of Slavery in Massachusetts," 125–126 n10; and, Grinnell, "The Constitutional History of the Supreme Judicial Court," 474–479, 533.) To emphasize, the manuscript records of the "Mum Bett" and "Quock Walker" court decisions do not convey that the cases were momentous at the time that they were decided. No coetaneous newspaper reporting of the cases has been found, Blanck, *Tyrannicide*, 124; Romer, *Slavery in the Connecticut Valley of Massachusetts*, 214 n26; Whiting, "Emancipation Without the Courts or Constitution," 20 n63.

The seemingly contemporaneous trial notes and what appears to be his jury charge for Commonwealth v. Jennison, written by Chief Justice William Cushing ("Legal notes," 92–98, quotation at 97–98), document that the freedom, equality, liberty, and property provisions of the Declaration of the Rights of the Massachusetts Constitution figured in his views about where the common law had already arrived, that slavery for life was not sustainable in law in Massachusetts: "I think y^c Idea of Slavery is in consistent [i.e., inconsistent] with our own conduct & Constitution & there can be no such thing as perpetual servitude of a rational Creature, unless it [^]his Liberty is[^] forfeited by [^]Some[^] Criminal Conduct or giv given up by personal Consent or Contract." Gloria McCahon Whiting, "Emancipation Without the Courts or Constitution," 8, precisely determined that slaveholding declined significantly and rapidly in historical Suffolk County with the outbreak of the Revolutionary War in 1775: entries in "[i]nventories listing enslaved people virtually disappeared". The rapid and widespread demise of household and workspace slavery occurred there at that chaotic time through individual decisions of enslavers and the enslaved, seemingly based in personal and business financial reasons and in consideration of popular Revolutionary sociopolitical rhetoric that expanded notions of individual "liberty" above and beyond its allusive economic meaning. Another of Whiting's key findings, ibid., 2, 12, 16 n15, 18 n38, 20 n59 and n63, 21 n70, is that by the time Chief Justice Cushing expressed his views of the common and constitutional law about enslavement in 1783, social and economic practices and popular sentiments had already largely changed to disfavor slavery in that vast area of the state that previously had the most slaves. By the legal actions of enslaved people and their allies, the common law had already evolved over a century as juries in the county and appellate courts decided case-after-case that nearly always freed enslaved plaintiffs. Cushing's statement to the *Jennison* jury about the common law was consonant with judicial tendencies to avoid making radical and controversial decisions that were not generally supported by the public. With the new information now brought forth by Whiting, the phrase "our own conduct" in Cushing's jury charge can be understood to indicate that customary law had by then already shifted. Cushing's view of where the common law had arrived and what the constitutional law meant, was consistent with the significant and then still-ongoing social, economic, political, and legal transformations that eroded slavery in the Commonwealth. Evidence from Levi Lincoln's "Brief of Levi Lincoln in the Slave Case Tried 1781," for Jennison v. Caldwell and Caldwell (noted above), and from Nathaniel Jennison's legislative petition (discussed below), further indicate that Cushing's jury charge in Commonwealth v. Jennison followed pronouncements made *earlier* in the "Quock Walker" cases that had already established the common and constitutional law that slavery in Massachusetts was illegal per se. The auspicious preservation of Cushing's seemingly contemporaneous notes and jury charge for Commonwealth v. Jennison, and its subsequent historicizing that occurred after 1874 when the notebook was brought forth by Chief Justice Gray in his presentation to the Massachusetts Historical Society, were instrumental to later beliefs about which of the "Quock Walker" cases had supposedly judicially abolished slavery.

Even while the official court decisions of record in "Mum Bett" and "Quock Walker" made no broad, statewide declaration of abolition, Nathaniel Jennison himself asserted that the first two "Quock Walker" cases were broadly consequential, and according to him, all his slaves thought that the cases freed them too. Before or in June 1782 (so, after he lost the first two cases, but before his conviction in the third), Jennison petitioned the legislature to absolve former slave owners from economic responsibility for their emancipated slaves: "by the Determination of the Supreme Judicial Court [...] the Bill of Rights is so to be construed, as to operate to the total discharge & manumission of all Negro Servants". (By "Bill of Rights", Jennison was referring to the Declaration of the Rights in the state constitution. His mention of that "Determination" is further evidence that the Supreme Judicial Court had, previous to Commonwealth v. Jennison and most probably in the appeal of Jennison v. Caldwell and Caldwell, arrived at the view that slavery was unsustainable in common law.) Jennison petitioned that "if you shou'd be of opinion that they are Free by the [state] Constitution, that you wou'd repeal the Law which binds the Master to support them, & thus give the Master his freedom as well as the Servant—if your Mem:° [Memorialist] is bound to support his Ten Negroes while they run about living in pleasure & Idleness, he is the most abject Slave that ever existed". Jennison, Petition of Nathaniel Jennison, n.d., before or in June 1782, House Unpassed Legislation 1782, Docket 956, SC1/230, M-Ar, digital images in Carpenter, et al., *Digital Archive of Massachusetts Anti-Slavery and Anti-Segregation Petitions, Massachusetts Archives, Boston MA, 2015*, https://dx.doi.org/10.7910 /DVN/3TZYJ, accessed August 15, 2017. For that and other legislative petitioning by Jennison regarding the "Quock Walker" case decisions and the legislative history of their consideration, see Moore, *Notes on the History of Slavery in Massachusetts*, 215–220.

The "Quock Walker" cases were later remembered in legal circles as having had different common law effects (e.g., by Parsons in *Winchendon* who alluded to the "Quock Walker" cases but did not name the parties or even give the year of the decision, O'Brien, ibid., 220 n5). Again, consider Hunter, "Publishing Freedom," 9, 150, for "purposeful misunderstanding" of the "Quock Walker" cases in legal contexts, and its interpretive "ambiguity" used "cannily" as a legal "tool". In his legislative petition quoted above, Jennison too may have purposefully mischaracterized the instant emancipative effects of the court decisions to make his polemical points. In *Aves* (1836), Chief Justice Shaw's sweeping and unequivocal legal decision on liberty and freedom in Massachusetts was immediately appreciated, more so of course for its findings about the limits of interstate comity, Finkelman, *An Imperfect Union*, 41, 113–114 and n46; Schermerhorn, *Unrequited Toil*, 173–177 for subsequent state and federal cases and laws; Soifer, "Status, Contract, and Promises Unkept"; Wong, *Neither Fugitive Nor Free*, 81–93 and passim. Karen Woods Weierman, *The Case of the Slave-Child, Med*, considered the neglected biography of the subject of *Aves* in the context of Boston abolitionist politics. Med was renamed Maria Sommersett, in honor of Lydia Maria Child and Maria Weston Chapman who championed Med's case, and of James Somerset, ibid., 76. The Boston Female Anti-Slavery Society, which championed Med's case, drew closer parallels with *Somerset* than did Shaw's decision.

While there are now excellent treatments of the issues and personalities involved with *Aves* and the "Mum Bett" cases, it is surprising that for the "Quock Walker" cases—among the most popularly significant cases in the state's judicial history— no scholarly, contextualized, historiographic, book-length treatment has appeared. With few exceptions, innumerable writers seem unable to wholly wrest themselves from the tenacious legacy of the prevailing myth that the "Quock Walker" cases resulted in a "decision" (*sensu* an *opinion* of the court) that rendered instant and universal abolition in Massachusetts. Once again, John D. Cushing, "The Cushing Court and the Abolition of Slavery in Massachusetts," 125–126 n10, explained that the particular and party-specific unpublished case decisions made in Supreme Judicial Court jury trials at that time (trials *de novo* held in each of the counties), were "not comparable to decisions in other tribunals where no jury was used". They were not equivalent to the later, now-familiar published opinions of the court that decided general matters of law and that had immediate and statewide effect: that practice developed in the early nineteenth century. Historical treatments of the "Quock Walker" cases have not adequately investigated and thoroughly and precisely documented the biographies of the dramatis personae. Many writings about the "Quock Walker" cases have troubling factual errors, even in relating genealogical relationships of the involved persons. Historical legal processes and practices are misunderstood, confusing and presentist speculations are rife about motives, events, decisions, and outcomes, and there are disappointing lapses in transcribing and documenting primary manuscript sources.

[27] The 1,500 likely pre-1800 graves at the cemetery were derived from the lists of church members in Mooar, *Historical Manual of the South Church in Andover*, and information in *VRA*. Charlotte Lyons (pers. comm., August 9

and 16, 2017) referred me to the Andover South Church, *South Parish Burial Grounds Cemetery Database* webpage with the statistics for preserved gravestones there, https://southchurch.com/cemetery-information/, accessed August 10, 2017. Indeed, throughout the world, the relatively small number of surviving gravestones compared with known decedents, and the few with any indication of gravestone purchase in probate records, has been long recognized by cemetery scholars internationally to indicate that the majority of our forebears are in unmarked graves, Bell, *Vestiges of Mortality and Remembrance*, 28.

[28] Andover's seventeenth-century religious history (particularly the Witchcraft Hysteria), and historical and theological developments at the theological seminary are well-studied. Helpful introductions to Andover's major eighteenth- and nineteenth-century religious matters were provided by Philip J. Greven, Jr., "Youth, Maturity, and Religious Conversion," and by Richard D. Shiels, "The Scope of the Second Great Awakening." Jon Butler, *Awash in a Sea of Faith*, particularly his provocatively titled chapter, "Slavery and the African Spiritual Holocaust," was among many who have critiqued the entangled historical relationship of Christian churches with slavery, and the tensions with African and African-derived, as well as indigenous (Native American) religious belief systems and practices. Lillian Ashcraft-Eason, "Freedom among African Women Servants and Slaves," 64–65, 69, conceived that seventeenth-century Africans saw contextual parallels in Christian hierarchical structures, discipline, and communal ceremonies with the varieties of their African religious and social traditions. Heather Miyano Kopelson, *Faithful Bodies*, was a more recent and more detailed consideration of hybridized ritual systems, and while focused on the seventeenth century, included eighteenth- and nineteenth-century information. Linford D. Fisher's seminal article, "Native Americans, Conversions, and Christian Practice in Colonial New England, 1640–1730," 107–108, concluded that during that period in this region "Native Americans [...] did, in some fashion, choose to adopt certain forms, rituals, and beliefs of European Christianity—including all the ambiguity, mixed elements, surprising Native appropriation, and range of responses that their practice of Christianity entailed. These appropriations eventuated in the formation of a hybridized indigenous Indian Christianity that remained simultaneously Native and Christian". Fisher, in *The Indian Great Awakening*, extended his period of review into the nineteenth century. Both cited works by Fisher provide references to additional pertinent scholarship. First Great Awakening evangelicals had "promoted religious conversion of slaves as a means of ensuring meekness, docility, and obedience" to authorities, Davis, *The Problem of Slavery in the Age of Revolution*, 277. On the other hand, in Andover people of African and Native ancestry were baptized

(albeit some as enslaved infants or children by their then-owners), had their children baptized, attended churches, and some became covenant members. Their participation assumes that they sought comfort, community, hope, and communion in the churches. Erik R. Seeman, "'Justise Must Take Plase,'" emphasized particular and individual religious experience. Jared Ross Hardesty, "An Angry God in the Hands of Sinners," considered how enslaved people in Boston advantaged knowledge learned in churches, particularly reading, writing, and rhetoric.

Greene, *The Negro in Colonial New England*, 61–62, 285–289, 330–331, made the point that ecclesiastical authorities invoked scripture selectively to justify enslavement: many owned slaves. Religious leaders and their congregants, including church attendees who were people of color, variously enforced, participated in, and acquiesced to the disparate treatment of people of color in secular and religious settings generally. Such was custom and practice in this and other regions, but it did not go unnoticed or uncontested. "[T]he manner in which Christianity was interpreted to Negroes tended to set up within them a cultural resistance to the religion of their masters [... and to...] the duplicity of the ministers" (330). Religious leaders, their congregants generally, and the people of color who attended services or became church members, witnessed and bore the entrenched, institutionalized segregation and discrimination. Some religious leaders and laity both subversively and explicitly resisted those notions, attempted or achieved change within, while others later formed their own churches that were more comfortable to them. After years of dissention and efforts toward conciliation, the Free Christian Church was established in 1846 by disaffected abolitionists from several Andover churches, many of whom were also members of antislavery societies, Andover Free Christian Church, *The History of Free Christian Church*.

Segregated seating was once common in New England churches, Benes, *Meetinghouses of Early New England*, 67, 70; Dinkin, "Seating the Meetinghouse in Early Massachusetts," 457–458; Greene, ibid., 282–284. The North Parish church had segregated seating for people of color, first in the small upper gallery then at the side galleries. Mofford, *The History of North Parish Church of North Andover*, 84 (quotation), 114, 158, described the location where people of color sat in the fourth meeting house constructed 1753 as "a small, upper gallery, close under the eaves." Evidently what Frederick Douglass and then W.E.B. Du Bois called "the color line" was traversed in Andover. On March 17, 1766, the North Parish, at an official "town" meeting, "Voted that all the English women in the Parish who Marry or Associate with Negro or Melatto-men be Seated in the Meeting-house with the Negro-women". The marginal index note for that vote called it "Negro's wives &c: Seated" and the use of the plural throughout suggests that the vote was not intended for a single couple. On November 21, 1803, at an official "town" meeting, "it was put to Vote to see if the parish would provide a Seat in the Meeting House for the Negroes and pas[se]d in the Negative" (i.e., it did not pass). At an official "town" meeting held on March 9, 1797, adjourned to March 27, 1797, then adjourned again to reconvene June 26, 1797, the North Parish freeholders "Voted to have white people purchase the pews Built in the year 1797 and no others & occupy the [^]same[^.]" On March 10, 1825, the North Parish "Voted that 10 feet of the East end of the side Gallerys be appropriated for the use of coloured People." Andover North Parish, "A Booke of Records for the North Precinct in the Towne of Andover There Being a division in the Towne By His Excelency the Governer and Generall Assemblys Order and Apointment Anno 1708," n.p. (not consistently paginated), also called "North Parish Records 1710–1827," object 1977.004.002 at NAHS. The microfilm target titled that same volume "Andover North Parish Church Records Meetings 1710–1827," digital images of NAHS Microfilm Reel 11, provided courtesy of the North Andover town clerk. The votes on segregated seating were recounted, with slightly different renderings of the manuscript entries, by Bluemel, "Stepping Up to Our Past: Black History at North Parish," n.p. [3, 5, 6, 10]; Bluemel, "Invisible History," 7; Forsyth-Vail, "African Americans and the North Parish and Church of North Andover," 7, 14; Fuess, *Andover: Symbol of New England*, 311; and, Mofford, ibid., 84, 114, 158.

The votes on segregated seating were among many other ecclesiastical matters considered, I emphasize, in several official "town" meetings by the legal (male) voters of the parish. The North Parish records include both ecclesiastical matters of the North Parish church as well as government matters of the North Parish section of the town of Andover. Records of civic matters include, e.g., minutes of official parish meetings (i.e., records of official, legal, government "town" meetings of the North Parish section of the then-town of Andover; the North Parish became the town of North Andover in 1855), official tax assessments, etc. At the time, official government actions by the North Parish section of the town supported and maintained the North Parish church buildings, lands, ministers, etc. Records of North Parish (government) tax assessments include exemptions granted to persons who were members of other churches. What are now wholly official government duties of record-making (such as vital statistics of births, marriages, and deaths in town clerk's records), were then (sometimes only, sometimes also) made in ecclesiastical records of baptisms, marriages, and deaths. Likewise, now wholly ecclesiastical concerns such as payment of ministers' salaries and maintenance of church buildings and grounds also appeared in records created for civic administrative purposes ("town" meetings and tax records).

The Fryes, who owned Phillis and her children, were members of the

North Parish church. The Osgoods and Chickerings may have attend-
ed North Church when the intermarried families owned Booso. Booso
(Boassee/Bussen) married Moriah by the Rev. John Barnard at the North
Church in Andover (now North Andover), *VRA*, Vol. 2, 356, 358 ("Negroes," February 13 or 15, 1755); Bailey, *Historical Sketches of Andover*, 438
(Barnard ministry). I have not been able to comprehensively search the
North Parish and South Parish church records for baptisms, membership,
marriages, or deaths of Phillis and her children. The microfilm of the North
Parish records, the printed images from that microfilm, and the digital images made from the microfilmed church records are indistinct. The filmed
manuscript records show them to be fragmentary, worn or faded in parts,
chronologically disorganized, and seemingly in part recopied from even
earlier records. Andover North Parish Church, "Andover North Parish
Church Records 1686–1810" (the original manuscript volume is object
1977.004.001 at NAHS). Absence of any obvious entries for Phillis and her
children in *VRA*, which incorporated information from Andover church
records, strongly suggests that no entries for them appeared in the surviving
North Parish or South Church records of baptisms and marriages, but they
might have appeared in the records about communicants (church members
who joined, were disciplined, or left). The South Church records are at the
ACHC, and at least some were imaged in the circa 1960 NAHS microfilm
series.

Titus Coburn was baptized (with Edward Hircom's other slave, as "Peggy
& Titus} Negro Ser[van]ᵗˢ of Capᵗ Hircom") at the Second Church of Christ
in Reading on August 23, 1767, Reading, Mass., Second Church of Christ Re-
cords, 1720–1806, RG5021, n.p., The Congregational Library & Archives,
Boston, Mass., http://nehh-viewer.s3-website-us-east-1.amazonaws.com/#
/content/ReadingSecond/viewer/Church20Records2C2017201806/64,
digital image 64. Titus Coburn and Violet Noble were married by Rev. Isaac
Morrill at the First Church in Wilmington, Town of Wilmington, "Vital
Records Cattle Records 1716–1851" (spine title), n.p., first volume on GSU
Microfilm Reel 761324, https://familysearch.org/ark:/61903/3:1:3QSQ
-G97M-59T2-G?i=120&cc=2061550&cat=146741, accessed August 12,
2017, digital image 121 of 288, "Titus Cober & Vilot Noble" (August 28,
1785); Smith, *Morrill Kindred in America*, 50–67 (Morrill's church). Titus
Coburn's will, written the day he died, began with "In the name of GOD
amen" and also included "blessed be almighty GOD", Titus Coburn will,
May 5, 1821, in Coburn and Coburn, RWPA (copy by Essex County register
of probate, August 8, 1854), and in Titus Coburn, Probate file papers (copy
of will, August 8, 1854).

Rosanna Coburn received a small annual stipend (1824, 1836–1854) from a charitable fund administered by the South Church because she was a poor person residing in the South Parish part of Andover. At least one other person who received the dole—Nancy Parker—was not a member of the South Church, and also the wording of the trusts that established the fund do not indicate that the fund was reserved for South Church members. Andover South Church, Records of the Samuel Phillips and Samuel Abbot Funds for the Relief of Indigent Persons in the South Parish (untitled, bound volume, n.p.), Andover South Parish Church I Records, Ms S 665, Subgroup IV, Series B, Subseries 1, ACHC, which also recited the trusts.

In ecclesiastical records, Colley Hooper's death was noted ("Collie Coburn Colored Woman age 70"), as was Rosanna Coburn's death (but the latter who died in 1859 was mistakenly put among the entries for 1858), in another manuscript volume of North Parish church records, called the "Minister's Book" (the original is object 1977.004.010 at the NAHS), Andover North Parish Church, "Andover North Parish Church Records Minister's Book 1810–1850 [i.e., 1848–1937] Baptisms Admissions to Membership Marriages Deaths," 79. The information about Colley and Rosanna's deaths recorded in the "Minister's Book" is in a section of that manuscript volume that appears to have been created from other records made by the Rev. Charles C. Vinal, whose records were copied into the "Minister's Book." Rev. Vinal served the North Parish (Unitarian) church from 1857–1870, ibid., 77. The recording of their deaths in the "Minister's Book" could, but does not necessarily indicate that Rosanna and Colley had been members of the North Parish (Unitarian) congregation. But perhaps the Rev. Vinal only noted their deaths because he knew of them, although Colley's variant surname (Coburn, rather than Hooper) and Rosanna's wrong year of death suggests he did not know them well. Perhaps he officiated at or attended their funerals or burial services, although their graves are at the South Parish Cemetery maintained by the South Church. The now disbound manuscript volume of the "Minister's Book," which was not consistently paginated, had been microfilmed circa 1960 in two consecutive parts. The first part of the volume (entries dated 1810–1860, pp. 7–69) appears on NAHS Microfilm Reel 10; the second part (1848–1937, pp. 70–end—there was mispagination, but the last page was once misnumbered "76" and then renumbered "171") appears on NAHS Reel 11. Digital files created from the two microfilmed parts of the "Minister's Book" were named, respectively, "N. Parish Vitals 1810–1850" (i.e., 1810–1860), and "North Parish Church 1810–1850" (i.e., 1848–1937). The circa 1960 microfilming of North Andover and Andover records was a project undertaken by the two town historical societies; microfilm reels and typewritten guides are available, variously, at NAHS, at Stevens Memorial Library (North Andover), and at Memorial Hall Library

(Andover). Digitization of parts of the microfilmed records was an historical records preservation and access project of the North Andover town clerk's office. I thank Inga Larson and Carol Majahad of the NAHS for their direct assistance to identify and to help me resolve the relationship of the manuscript, microfilmed, printed photoreproduced, and digital versions of the North Parish records. Joyce Bradshaw, North Andover town clerk, kindly provided me digital files created from the circa 1960 NAHS microfilm series.

The information in the North Parish of North Andover Unitarian Universalist Church's acknowledgement by sermon about the historical treatment of people of color in the North Parish church, written by Rev. Lee Bluemel, "Stepping Up to Our Past: Black History at North Parish" (February 21, 2010), was drawn from Gail Forsyth-Vail's research, "African Americans and the North Parish and Church of North Andover." Forsyth-Vail was former Director of Religious Education at the church. See also, Bluemel, "An Invisible History," a sermon preached in 2016. At South Church also, acknowledgement has been made and also continues to be conveyed, Lyons, "South Church: Founding History and Abolitionism"; Lyons, "How is it that Two Andover Slaves are Buried Next to One Another in the South Church Burial Yard?"; Walsh, "'Bear Witness.'" For the South Church history generally, see Mooar, *Historical Manual of the South Church in Andover*, and Pike, *The History of South Church in Andover*.

[29] Anonymous, "Sketches of Octogenarians" (about Rose Coburn's family) and Anonymous, "Obituary" for Rosanna Coburn reported that Booso first used the name Jubea. Abbott, "Historical Andover. No. 106. Africa to Andover" and Abbott, "Historical Andover. No. 107. Africa to Andover.—(Concluded)" rendered Booso's earlier name as Jubah. Jack Booz was mentioned in the "Sketches" article; Hepzabeth Boose's death at the almshouse on August 17, 1814, age 40, was listed in *VRA*, Vol. 2, among "Negroes," 573. Handler and Jacoby, "Slave Names and Naming in Barbados" (and the sources they cited) provided that Juba is a West African day name meaning "born on Monday," traditionally given to females, 697, 698, 699 n2, but indicated (697) the practice of flexibility with other traditionally gender-specific names. Odu's "Note on the Title" of the 2015 novel *Ah Juba!*, gives a broad overview of the word "Jubah" and its variants used in East Africa, West Africa, the Caribbean, and the Americas, and emphasized its evolution in multiple, meaningful contexts, as Handler and Jacoby, ibid., also concluded about African and African-derived names and naming practices. For African-derived traditions of using the paternal name as a surname, see Whiting, "Endearing Ties," 117–120 and sources cited, and for variant surname practices see Handler and Jacoby, ibid., and Sachs, "'Freedom By A Judgment,'" 179 n13 and 195

n71 and sources cited.

[30] Robert H. Tewksbury, "Lawrence," 237, drew on local oral traditions to prepare his historical narratives, and recounted the story about Boise. Charlotte Helen Abbott, "Historical Andover. No. 107. Africa to Andover.—(Concluded)," 3, provided clues that appear to identify Booso as the same man as Boise/Bowser: "Boise alias Bowser [...] was found to be, with wife Maria, of the household of Samuel Chickering, Jr." Boise/Bowser ("with wife *Maria*") could be another man, or the same as Booso, the Boassee/Bussen who married *Moriah*, emphasis added, *VRA*, Vol. 2, 356, 358 (Marriages, "Negroes," Boassee/Bussen and Moriah). The symbolic action in Tewksbury's account about Boise has parallels in magic and ritual traditions involving trees and knives described in Murrell, *Afro-Caribbean Religions*.

The anthropological literature on African, Caribbean, and African American religious traditions is vast. Paul E. Lovejoy, "The African Diaspora," n.p. [9–11] pressed several points about historical analysis of religious customs and practices, rejecting "ahistorical generalizations" [9] which apply modern ethnographies of diverse contemporary peoples in African places to diverse historical peoples in American places; which do not account for historical change in religious systems, beliefs, and practices; which invoke a "meaningless" monolithic, pan-African "tradition" [10]; which do not investigate "religion and culture [...in relation to] the lived experiences of enslaved Africans themselves" [10]; which do not consider "how religion was related to ideology and political structure" [10]; and, which may not perceive the influences and effects of Christianity and Islam on indigenous religious systems in African places, on those Africans who converted before they were transshipped, and their contributions after arriving "in spreading the faith among slaves in the Americas" [11].

Alongside considering if Boise/Bowser's "furious attacks upon the trees" was a performative ritual based in his traditional knowledge, in the moment when he "would grow wild when recounting the history of his capture by slavers", he may have shifted his perceptions to another cultural conception of temporality, of time as recurrent or cyclical that differed from European-derived temporal linearity. Historian Walter Johnson framed it as "[w]orking [...] up and down scales of time—metaphysical, political, local, psychological". As one can flexibly alter their linguistic register when needed (e.g., from patois to formality and back again), it is conceivable that Boise/Bowser shifted temporalities to be (again) at the time of his capture. Perhaps he was only conscious of *remembering* his capture as a past event in linear time. But whether or not he consciously accessed a culturally different view of time, his speech and actions were part of "a dimension of that confrontation [with having been enslaved], a way of being in time—a temporality—according to which historical actors made sense of what it was that was happening [...] and how they would respond at any given moment. These temporalities were layered, intertwined, and mixed through the process of the slave trade, running sometimes concurrently, sometimes oppositionally, tangled together by a historical process", Johnson, "Time and Revolution in African America," 204, 214.

For Phillis as a community historian, see Anonymous, "Sketches of Octogenarians" (about Rose Coburn's family) and Anonymous, "Obituary" for Rosanna Coburn. Loren Schweninger, "Freedom Suits, African American Women, and the Genealogy of Slavery," revised and updated in his book *Appealing for Liberty*, understood that oral histories about community lineage preserved by African American women in memory, brought forward as evidence in Maryland freedom suits, were examples of broader and long-standing cultural traditions. Honor Sachs, "'Freedom By A Judgment,'" 192–193, 199–203, uncovered how Virginia courts eventually became unwilling to accept oral testimony of African American genealogy as evidence in freedom suits, regarding it as hearsay. The Virginia court's "retrenchment into strict legalism" (200) disclosed "the consolidation of a legal regime that secured white power by systematically denying the validity of family histories" (202). On African American traditions of oral history and social memory, see Fulton, *Speaking Power*, and for how those informed published histories of the American Revolutionary War, see Hancock, "'Tradition Informs Us.'"

Chapter 4 Phillis

[1] Anonymous, "Sketches of Octogenarians" (about Rose Coburn's family); Anonymous, "Obituary" for Rosanna Coburn. While those sources asserted that her mother was called Phillis Frye, I have not noticed that form in records. The precise dates regarding Phillis that can be calculated from the information in the 1853 interview, which was the basis for the 1859 obituary, are obviously doubtful. Phillis died probably late 1828, Town of Andover, "Town Records, Tax Records 1823–1847" (untitled volume, title from microfilm target but actually treasurer records of payments for orders drawn by the overseers of the poor), n.p., ninth volume on GSU Microfilm Reel 878782, January 5, 1829 (No. 36, $3.00: "coffin for Phillis Wid[ow] of Boos"). The dates that can be calculated from Rosanna Coburn's 1853 interview and 1859 obituary are also inconsistent with the assertion in 1820 that Phillis was then 90 years old (thus born 1730, thus arriving 1740, and if she died at 101 years old, death in 1831), Titus Coburn, July 13, 1820, in Coburn and Coburn, RWPA. Recall that Lois Brown, "Memorial Narra-

tives of African Women in Antebellum New England," 57, vividly depicted the ordinary "inconsistencies and elisions" in these sorts of "incomplete and elusive histories [...] plagued by unruly chronologies, unattributed facts, and incomplete profiles of the subjects."

The 1853 interviewer reported that Phillis "was brought from Africa and arrived in Charlestown one hundred and eight years ago [1745]; she was then ten years old. [...] She [...] died about seventeen years ago [1836], at the age of one hundred and one years." There are other chronological confusions in that account. "Joshua Frye, of this town," was not yet "a Representative to the General Court at that time, [when he] bought her" (if "at that time" referred to Phillis' arrival between 1737 and 1745). Frye served in the state legislature from 1755–1756. Alternatively, while the chronology drawn from other sources becomes less aligned, the interviewer may have meant that Frye purchased Phillis a decade or more after she landed in Charlestown. Joshua Frye's 1764 will and 1767 tax valuation indicated only one slave in his household: a boy named Cato was devised in Frye's will and was probably the same individual counted in the tax valuation. However, the presence of Phillis in the Frye household prior to 1767 cannot be discounted by her absence in Frye's 1767 valuation. The 1767 tax records tallied far fewer slaves in Andover than expected, based on earlier counts. Anonymous, "Number of Negro Slaves in the Province of the Massachusetts-Bay, Sixteen Years Old and Upward, Taken by Order of Government in the Last Month of the Year 1754, and the Beginning of the Year 1755," 95 (Andover 1754–1755 "Negro Slaves" 16 years old and above, n=42; 28 male, 14 female); Benton, *Early Census Making in Massachusetts*, 11, 12, section n.p. [76–77] (Andover 1764 "Negroes" in the same age cohort, n=86; 56 male, 30 female); Joshua Frye, Probate file papers, will, March 14, 1764; Greene, *The Negro in Colonial New England*, 340; Greven, *Four Generations*, 176; Massachusetts Valuation of Towns, Andover 1767, MAC, Vol. 130, 40 (Joshua Frye household, "Negros", n=1), 34–49 (Andover 1767 "Negros" counted as property in households, n=40), 70, 74, (tax of 40s. for each slave [called "servants for life"] that was 14–45 years old, but no mention of gender distinction for taxation purposes), 106 (Andover 1767 aggregate total of slaves 14–45 years old, n=26), M-Ar. Further regarding provincial tax assessments and population estimates of slaves, see chap. 4, notes 5 and 7.

I conducted a search of the online *Trans-Atlantic Slave Trade Database* for ship voyages that brought captives to Massachusetts from 1737–1745. The database listed seven voyages, all departing from and arriving back at the port of Boston. Intermediate stops, such as the West Indies, mid-Atlantic, or southern ports may have occurred that are not indicated in the database. Three voyages obtained slaves at Gambia, and four at unspecified African ports: Voyage ID 25161 (Arrived in Boston 1737), 39100 (1737), 25180 (1739), 25179 (1740), 25186 (1743), 25187 (1743), and 25189 (1744), https://www.slavevoyages.org/voyage/database#searchId=aFMVPPZp, accessed July 10, 2019. I did not further pursue the sources that were specified for the information in the database about each of the seven voyages. The specified primary and secondary sources may have information to identify which vessel carried Phillis, but that possibility seems remote. Because the database is an ongoing compilation project, additional data about those or other voyages may be added in future.

[2] Hardesty, *Unfreedom*, 22–23. Slaves who spoke "good English" (as a 1712 Boston newspaper advertisement enticed, ibid., 23, 189 n37) and who were familiar with other European-derived cultural practices were more appealing to potential buyers. Lillian Ashcraft-Eason, "Freedom among African Women Servants and Slaves," conceived how arriving African women understood and made their own sense of colonial English practices in terms of their cultural knowledge, traditions, and cosmologies. Benjamin N. Lawrance, *Amistad's Orphans*, 69, considered "the plasticity of childhood and the malleability of child identities" in terms of learning cultural knowledge and establishing and changing identities ("ethnicity"). Paul E. Lovejoy, "The African Diaspora," n.p. [7, 14], twice invoked the connotatively problematic word "deracination" (etymology traces the word to the Latin *radix* ["root," from even earlier tongues] not to "race") in its strictly correct technical sense to convey that while Africans were uprooted from their homelands and separated from their familiar people, their retention, continuation, adaptation, and transformation of African-derived cultural forms were not static African fossils as the term "survivals" might suggest [4, 5, 7, 8, 15, 16, 19 n10, 20 n16]. See also Lovejoy, *The "Middle Passage"* and Rawley, "The American Dimensions and the Massachusetts Contribution." Wendy Warren, "'Thrown upon the world': Valuing Infants in the Eighteenth-Century North American Slave Market," 626, 639 n20 (quotation), conveyed that "children were a significant proportion of the slave population that traveled across the Atlantic in the eighteenth century, and that in fact more African children came to North America than did European" children. Of all the children that arrived in North America before 1800, over 90% were not from Europe. Lawrance, ibid., 36–37, emphasized that children were more "coercible" than adults, and when raised as slaves were "more controllable and less likely to rebel", Hollander, Review of *Amistad's Orphans* by Benjamin N. Lawrance, 847 (quotation). In that same regard of coercion and control, following Metacom's Rebellion (King Philip's War, 1675–1676), official genocidal policies of New England colonial government authorities placed Native children (and women) in English households as slaves ("servants" for a term that in cases became de facto slavery for

life). The policies established spans for servitude based on age: the younger the person, the longer the term of enslavement, Fisher, "'Why shall wee have peace to bee made slaves': Indian Surrenderers during and after King Philip's War." Linford D. Fisher also noticed examples of captured Indian children made servants in households of Indian leaders and in 1676 an Indian child was sold in Connecticut by a prominent Pequot man to an enslaved African woman. See also Newell, "The Changing Nature of Indian Slavery"; Newell, "Indian Slavery in Colonial New England"; and, Newell, *Brethren by Nature*. Enslaved people with Native ancestry in Andover following the later colonial wars (1689–1763), such as Dido and Nancy Parker both also of African descent, might have been separated from their extended families as a result of the conflicts.

3 Farnham and Abbot, "A plan of the Town of Andover," (1795) indicated that the distance from the North Parish meeting house to Boston was 25 miles. From the South Parish meeting house to Boston was 22½ miles and to Salem was 17 miles. Charlestown is a couple miles closer to Andover. A horse walks slowest at about four miles per hour, trots at 8 to 12 miles per hour, and gallops at about 25 to 30 miles per hour, according to Reisner, *Speed of Animals*, http://www.speedofanimals.com/animals/horse, accessed May 28, 2017.

4 Abbott, "Historical Andover. No. 47. Some Old Residents"; Barker, *Frye Genealogy*, 54; Caulfield, "A History of the Terrible Epidemic"; Caulfield, "The 'Throat Distemper' of 1735–1740," 289 n105 ("Fice" is a typographic error for Frie [Frye], named among several other afflicted Andover families).

5 In 1754–1755, 42 slaves that were 16 years old and older (28 males, 14 females) were counted in Andover. In 1764, 86 "negro slaves" in the same age cohort (56 males, 30 females) were counted in Andover. In 1767, 40 "Negros" were counted as property in Andover households, which was fewer than expected. Anonymous, "Number of Negro Slaves in the Province of the Massachusetts-Bay, Sixteen Years Old and Upward, Taken by Order of Government in the Last Month of the Year 1754, and the Beginning of the Year 1755," 95; Benton, *Early Census Making in Massachusetts*, 11, 12; Greene, *The Negro in Colonial New England*, 340; Greven, *Four Generations*, 176; Massachusetts Valuation of Towns, Andover 1767, MAC, Vol. 130, 34–49 (Andover count, n=40), 40 (Joshua Frye, "Negros"=1), 106 (Andover aggregate total of slaves, n=26), M-Ar. Despite what would seem to have been the rule to tax both male and female slaves, perhaps only male slaves were considered for taxation in 1767 (ibid., 70, 74, included minutes of a committee decision setting the tax of 40s. for each slave that was 14–45 years old, but no mention of gender distinction for taxation purposes). Lemire, *Black Walden*, 75,

198 n3, also ascertained the presence of enslaved women in particular Concord, Mass., households, despite their absence in tax or inventory records. Moore, *Notes on the History of Slavery in Massachusetts*, 62–65, indicated that female slaves were ordinarily counted and taxed. Male and female slaves were counted separately in the 1755 and 1764 valuations. The 1770 valuation did not count slaves for Andover, and the 1771 valuations for Andover were not preserved. For the evolution of taxation of slaves in Massachusetts, see Einhorn, *American Taxation, American Slavery*, 72, and Rabushka, *Taxation in Colonial America*.

[6] Barker, *Frye Genealogy*, 54; Joshua Frye, Probate file papers, will, March 14, 1764. Charlotte Helen Abbott, "Historical Andover. No. 106. Africa to Andover," 3, identified Cato as "Cato Frye in War Records, a veteran." I have not been able to further pursue Cato's biography. During his lifetime he may have used or been known by other names.

[7] For Joshua Frye's political offices, see Schutz, *Legislators of the Massachusetts General Court*, 227 and Barker, *Frye Genealogy*, 54 ("1775–1776" is a typographic error for 1755–1756). Joshua Frye's same-named son was assigned only minor civic duties in Andover (Field Driver and Hog Reeve) in 1781 and 1782, Hammond, "A List of Town Officers." Philip J. Greven, Jr., *Four Generations*, 233, 234 n11, mentioned the Frye family's "hatter's trade" and noted the senior Joshua's probate records.

Sarah Frye, Probate file papers, will, June 1, 1776, repeatedly used the first person possessive case "my" rather than the definite article "the": "my oxen (if I should leave any) all my Husbandry utensils of every Sort, also all my utensils for managing the Trade of hat making of every Sort [...] my Pasture Land [...] my woodland [...] my Lands and buildings", etc. Rather than a passive role, Sarah Frye's active and involved supervision and management of her household, her farm with her livestock and her tools, her hat-making business, and her slaves may be inferred by her grammar and syntax, along with her forethought and contingency that previous to her death, she herself may have already sold the oxen ("if I should leave any") and she herself may have sold two of her slaves: "my Negro Servants namely Rose & Juba (except [if] I should, in my life time otherwise dispose of them)". If Sarah was indeed the mistress she comes off as in her will, her son Joshua may have been under his mother's bidding, assisting her in management, supervision, and business dealings as and when he could. In Joshua's or Sarah's absence, Cato may have taken on those roles. Cato would have implemented Sarah's directives in agriculture, husbandry, building maintenance, and other suitable labor; alternatively, he could have been mostly or exclusively an indoor servant. The female servants would be involved in some agricultural and livestock chores, and all the skilled and semiskilled household tasks of child-care, housecleaning, laundry, sewing, cooking, serving, production such as preserving food, making soap and candles, etc.

Both males and females cooperated to accomplish projects, whether the tasks or they themselves were male-gendered or female-gendered. Sarah may have employed other male and female laborers and servants sporadically and seasonally. Periodically, neighbors, and their slaves, servants, and children participated in reciprocal sharing of labor, task-animals, and tools. Both males and females could have been employed in Sarah's hat-making business. Considerable research results are available for New England straw and palm leaf hat-making, chiefly in the early to mid-nineteenth century, but not for the small-scale industry of what I presume to have been the felt hats that Sarah Frye manufactured in the late eighteenth century. Her inventory (in Sarah Frye, Probate file papers, May 1, 1781) listed "Hatters Tools" (£12) between her farming implements and her "Bound Books" and "Pamphlets" so it is not certain where the hatter's tools were stored or used, perhaps in "The old Shop" (£1 10s.). Sarah Frye's inventory counted no sheep but many Andover farmers raised them. Bailey, *Historical Sketches of Andover*, 577–580, described the town's fulling mills including one built in 1718 by Col. Samuel Frye (1694–1761) and "added to" (580) by his son Samuel Frye, Esq. (1729–1819), Barker, *Frye Genealogy*, 48, 52, 59. Towner, in the posthumously published book *A Good Master Well Served*, 42–43 n13 and 122 n65, noted the English Hat Act of 1732 (5 Geo. II. c. 22) that "forbade using Negroes in hat making" but "found no evidence indicating compliance". "The old-fashioned apparatus [and procedure] of making felt hats by hand" was a skilled and complicated process; the materials, tools, and processes were described in the 1881 edition of Barnard and Guyot, *Johnson's New Universal Cyclopaedia*, Vol. 2, Part 1, 822–823. Unlike with hats made of consolidated fur felt such as from beaver, wool felt hat-making did not involve "carroting" furred pelts with a solution containing toxic mercury that infamously poisoned hat makers who handled consolidated fur felt.

The official inventory of Sarah Frye's estate that listed the six slaves was dated May 1, 1781 and was accepted on June 5, 1781 by Benjamin Greenleaf, Probate Judge, Sarah Frye, Probate file papers. It was prepared by John Farnham, Moody Bridges, and Nathaniel Lovejoy, and may have been written by the latter. I identified an earlier draft of this inventory. The draft inventory was undated and unsigned, but it was written by the same hand as the official inventory. While there are several differences between the draft and official inventory, the significant difference is that the draft did not include the six "Negroes young & old" (valued at £24 in the official inventory). In the draft inventory, the total value of the estate was £790 which is £24 less than the total of £814 in the official inventory. Sarah Frye draft estate inventory, n.d., in "Collection of Essex County (Mass.) Court Records, 1628–1914," Collection No. EC 43, Box 13, Folder 3 "Estate papers of various individuals," fourth item in file, Phillips Library, Peabody Essex Museum, Rowley, Mass. A penciled note on the draft document indicated its provenance, that it came to the former Essex Institute (now the Peabody Essex Museum) as a gift from "Haverhill Pub[lic]. Lib[rary]. (thro[ugh]. Miss Pauline Pulsifer) Ja[nuary] 28, 1942". How the manuscript draft inventory came to be initially at the Haverhill Public Library is unknown. Pauline Feodora Pulsifer (1890–1979) was an assistant at the Haverhill library, worked in cataloging, and facilitated transferring other materials, such as historical newspapers, from the library to Essex Institute and to the Haverhill Historical Society.

Ascertaining the comparative economic position of Sarah Frye's household at the time of her death, in relation to other households in Andover, in Essex County, in Massachusetts, and generally in New England would involve extensive research in probate and tax records, and intensive statistical analyses corrected and weighted for many factors such as fluctuating currency and land values, as done in the many well-known publications of Gloria L. Main and Winifred Barr Rothenberg, which I do not include in the references cited. Richardson, "Slavery, Trade, and Economic Growth in Eighteenth-Century New England," provided an exceptional analysis and synthesis for the region with specific information about Massachusetts, and Salem in particular. For relative economic positions of Essex County residents generally, see Vickers, *Farmers & Fisherman*, which includes citations to works of Main and Rothenberg. Reliable comparison to the economic data in Greven, *Four Generations*, is difficult because of the format of the data, oriented chiefly prior to the relevant period of Sarah Frye's estate administration from 1781 to 1790, and the shifting values of currency and land during that nine year period. Consistent with Greven's findings, Sarah Frye's wealth was predominantly in real estate.

For slave owning among the wealthier, consider that in 1764, 12.8% of the 40,876 Massachusetts households held the 5,235 slaves living in the colony, Greene, *The Negro in Colonial New England*, 320. The statewide data of course are less revealing than estimates for the town. In 1754–1755, Andover's population was estimated to be 2,135, among which there were 42 "Negro slaves" over 16 years of age consisting of 28 males and 14 females. Anonymous, "Number of Negro Slaves in the Province of the Massachusetts-Bay, Sixteen Years Old and Upward, Taken by Order of Government in the Last Month of the Year 1754, and the Beginning of the Year 1755," 95; Benton, *Early Census Making in Massachusetts*, 11, 12; Greene, ibid., 340; Greven, ibid., 176. In 1764, there was a total estimated "white" population in

Andover of 2,356 and 86 "Negroes" consisting of 56 males and 30 females; no "Indians" were enumerated but people of Native ancestry were present, Benton, ibid., section n.p. [76–77], Greven, ibid., 176. Valuation data collected only three years later counted fewer slaves by more than half, suggesting that the actual number of enslaved persons was concealed to avoid taxation. Inexplicably, while 40 "Negros" were counted as property in Andover households in 1767, the aggregate total for the town that year only indicated 26 slaves. Massachusetts Valuation of Towns, Andover 1767, MAC, Vol. 130, 34–49 (Andover counts, n=40), 70, 74 (taxation committee minutes regarding rates for slaves 14–45 years old, taxed at 40s. each), 106 (Andover aggregate total, n=26), M-Ar.

[8] Lovejoy, *The "Middle Passage."* Rawley, "The American Dimensions and the Massachusetts Contribution." Richardson, "Slavery, Trade, and Economic Growth in Eighteenth-Century New England." Joanne Pope Melish, *Disowning Slavery*, 8, 16–23, synthesized and further considered the economic, social, and political benefits of slave ownership. The economic necessity of women's productive labor counters popular notions that New England household slavery was primarily a symbolic and aspirational ploy by slave owners. The goods and services that woman—free and enslaved women—produced were literally vital. Drawing on the 1688–1710 account book of Thomas Barnard of the Andover North Parish, James E. McWilliams, "Butter, Milk, and a 'Spare Rib': Women's Work and the Transatlantic Economic Transition in Seventeenth-Century Massachusetts," 14, 23, discerned "the essential role that women played in maintaining networks of local exchange." "As merchant and farmer account books prove, women filled direct, niche-oriented roles in fostering Massachusetts' integration into the transatlantic economy. In doing so, they preserved local-external bridges that would prove integral to the growth and development of the New England economy as a whole." In the development of merchant capitalism, "as early as the fifteenth century," women were "an important human link between the rural and urban economies" and thus to global markets, Wiesner, "Spinning Out Capital," 212. Seth Rockman, "The Unfree Origins of American Capitalism," was also influenced by Melish's considerations, and Melish, Rockman, and others informed Jared Ross Hardesty's *Unfreedom*. Margaret Ellen Newell, *Brethren by Nature*, 5, 260–261, n11, n13, drew my attention to remember the utility of Melish's treatment of the many competing interpretive perspectives of New England slavery as honorific vs. economically important. Newell, beginning in "The Birth of New England in the Atlantic Economy," in other writings not cited here, and further in *Brethren by Nature*, documented that enslaving Indians and Africans to labor was figured deliberately in the earliest development of the settler-colonists' capitalist system. Massachusetts slaves labored

in households, on farms, with artisans, in shops and taverns, in manufacturing and industry, in the maritime trades, on ships based from New England ports, and on vessels that arrived here for trade.

Hardesty, "Creating an Unfree Hinterland," incorporated Melish's argument of the economic importance of New England slavery, and drew together evidence of early eighteenth-century slave labor on Massachusetts country estates used to create agricultural surplus to supply plantations in the West Indies. Wendy Warren, *New England Bound*, drew broad and focused pictures of the inexorable ties of New England-based families with slavery and colonization projects here and abroad. The vast generational wealth enjoyed by the most socially and politically prominent intermarried New England families and their businesses was derived from entanglements in the domestic and global slave trade from the seventeenth to the nineteenth century; from business at and with Mid-Atlantic, Southern, and Caribbean plantations from the seventeenth to the nineteenth centuries; from profits made in textile and shoe manufacturing that used raw materials from, and which in turn supplied finished products to, slave-holding plantations in the nineteenth century; and, from participation in the lucrative nineteenth-century drug cartel of the opium trade, which also involved unfree labor, Bailey, "The Slave(ry) Trade and the Development of Capitalism in the United States: The Textile Industry in New England"; Kimball, "'What have we to do with slavery?': New Englanders and the Slave Economies of the West Indies." Historian Marisa J. Fuentes, "A Violent and Violating Archive: Black Life and the Slave Trade," n.p., directed "our attention to the lingering legacies of black commodification and subjection [...to] force an acknowledgement of how black bodies, labor and death produced markets, wealth and global networks for much of the West" as that did for the places of their origins and exchanges.

The paradigmatic shift among contemporary historians of New England to adopt Atlantic World and global perspectives, yet grounded in microhistorical focus of individual biographies, brings understandings about the identifiable regional origins of enslaved people in Massachusetts (but seemingly also unpaid laborers for terms with or without a written contract) from central and western Africa, Madagascar, northern Africa, the Middle East, or other places in the northern Indian Ocean region. People brought to Massachusetts from those places had been transferred among slave traders from African nations, Portugal, Spain, the Netherlands, England, and New England. Additional to business records that identified origins of named individuals among the cargo, clues in rendered names can suggest derivations from Dutch, Portuguese, Spanish, or French, from the multitudinous languages spoken in Africa, or from the several Caribbean Creole languages. Gallio Nota, a "Negro" slave in Maj. Dudley Bradstreet's house, had a distinctive,

Portuguese-sounding surname, while the Biblical origin of her forename allusively denoted "indifference." One genealogical website indicated that the surname Nota is most prevalent today in the former Portuguese colony of Mozambique, *Forebears* (website), https://forebears.io/surnames/nota, accessed September 15, 2019; *Oxford English Dictionary*, s.v. "Gallio"; Pleck, "Slavery in Puritan New England," 311; *VRA*, Vol. 1, 391 "Negroes" (birth of son Stasie, June 24, 1687), Vol. 2, 575 "Negroes" (death of Stacy, "a mallatoe", May 7, 1696). The rendering of Stasie's birth record in *VRA* was not consistent with the original record that made clear that an African-derived naming system was used for the child, whose father would seem to have not been a person of color, and that in this possessive context the term "Negro" was synonymous with "slave": "Stasie Gallio yᵉ son of John Stasie & Gallio Nota Negro – yᵉ Negro of Mʳ Dudley Bradstreet borne yᵉ 24 June 1687", Town of Andover, "Town Records, Births Marriages Deaths 1651–1700" (title from microfilm target), first volume on GSU Microfilm Reel 878780, digital image 30 of 515, https://www.familysearch.org/ark:/61903/3:1:3QSQ-G97M-YR6Q?i=29&cc=2061550&cat=143281, accessed September 15, 2019.

Generic-seeming terms such as "Moor" ("Black-moore," "blackamoor"), "Angola", and "Guinea" were used in historical Massachusetts. If their connotative sense was merely a gloss and not intended to be precise as it seemed, they conceal and complicate true origins and connections. Nedra K. Lee, "Boarding: Black Women in Nantucket Generating Income and Building Community," 97, noted that "Guinea" and "New Guinea" were common placenames for enclaves of people of color in New England that "obscured the [multiple] geographic [origins] and cultural diversity of Black people captured during the transatlantic slave trade and disregarded the new identities that emerged from the commixture of Black and indigenous peoples" in this region. Melinde Lutz Sanborn, "Angola and Elizabeth," and Linda M. Heywood and John K. Thornton, "'Canniball Negroes,' Atlantic Creoles, and the Identity of New England's Charter Generation," delved into such terms and considered African and early New England history (including the Providence Island colony in the West Indies) to identify regions in Africa where enslaved people were from originally, how they came to be taken captive in Africa, and the routes by which they were transported to New England. Significantly, Heywood and Thornton, ibid., 84 (quotations), 93, estimated that prior to the mid-1640s, most enslaved Africans that landed in New England "had central African origins" and were processed through "the port of Angola". Later, the West African region became the predominant source of slaves to New England. Marisa J. Fuentes, ibid., n.p., emphasized that "a focus on markets and slavery can implicitly [put] the lives of the enslaved in aggregated abstraction much like the contests [and contestations] over how many captives were transported that [...was] characteristic of some of the early historical work on the transatlantic trade in human lives." The attentions of contemporary historians of New England have largely shifted from historiographic inheritances of purposeful denial, apologia, contrarianism, and regional exceptionalism, to focus on individual lives while considering entanglements and impacts of New England's slavery and other unfree labor practices in global view beyond the Atlantic World, especially evident in writings by, e.g., Lillian Ashcraft-Eason, Ronald Bailey, Ira Berlin, David Brion Davis, Jared Ross Hardesty, Linda M. Heywood, Heather Miyano Kopelson, Kerima Marie Lewis, Paul E. Lovejoy, Margaret Ellen Newell, Melinde Lutz Sanborn (now Byrne), John K. Thornton, Wendy Warren, Gloria McCahon Whiting, among others. (Only some works by those authors are included in the references cited, and I encourage readers to seek more of their significant oeuvre.)

[9] Harvard Law School Shield Committee, "Recommendation to the President and Fellows of Harvard College on the Shield Approved for the Law School," 2 (quotation).

[10] Smith, "George H. Moore, 'Tormentor of Massachusetts.'" Moore's *Notes on the History of Slavery in Massachusetts* was written as an historical exposé; it remains a fundamentally important source. Moore, "Slave Marriages in Massachusetts," was a transcription of the undated Andover manuscript, "A Form for a Negroe-Marriage" written by Rev. Samuel Phillips, minister of the South Parish Church in Andover from 1710 to 1771, Mooar, *Historical Manual of the South Church in Andover*, 96. The individuals denoted in Phillips' conditional vows were given initials S. and R. They would appear to be Phillips' own slaves, Salem and Rama (Rema, Remy, Rhena) who were married on October 16, 1760, Anonymous, "Auld Lang-Syne. More Old Letters"; French, "Parson Phillips's Slaves – Also, Pomp and Rose"; *VRA*, Vol. 1, 389 (Births, "Negroes," baptism of Cyrus, son of "Salem and Rama, servants [of Rev. Samuel Phillips]," brackets in original), Vol. 2, 358 (Marriages, "Negroes," Salem and Rama). For a biographical sketch of Salem and Rama, see chap. 2, note 3. Whether the vows were used only for that couple, or if he used the same "Form" for other marriages of slaves in Andover, is unknown. Similar conditional vows had been used in Massachusetts and other places at other times, Sword, "Wayward Wives," 218–220. The vows have been considered by many historians: unaccountably, some reprinted versions replaced the initials S. and R. with "Bob" and "Sally". I thank Jared Ross Hardesty for introducing me to the document.

The editor of the journal where Moore's transcription of the Andover manuscript appeared, Henry B. Dawson of *The Historical Magazine*, used Moore's newly found document to castigate the "hypocrisy" of popular historical traditions that suggested slavery in Massachusetts was benign. In a scathing 1869 review, Dawson, "Books," 280, charged that Moore's finding was "CONCEAL[ED]" by Massachusetts historians. Dawson's vitriolic review was quoted in an anonymous column, "Notes," published in the July 1, 1869 issue of *The Nation*, 11, in which that publication criticized both Moore and Dawson, who "have for some years troubled the historical societies of New England." In an anonymous article, "A Relic of Slavery in Massachusetts," published May 21, 1869 in the African American newspaper, *The Elevator* (San Francisco, Calif.), the publication of the Andover manuscript was treated in a more balanced manner as evidence of the nature of slavery in New England, "which is not a matter of surprise to any one who knows how long it contin[u]ed to affect public sentiment at the North as well as the South". In November 1872, three years after Moore's transcription of the Andover vows appeared, *The Southern Magazine* reprinted the document text to counter the historical theme that New England slavery was benign, and sharply pointed out revisionism in postbellum historical writings: "Massachusetts historians take good care to make history to suit themselves; and if the facts are against them, 'so much the worse for the facts.'" Anonymous, "The Green Table," 637.

A similarly chastising account is William B. Weeden's (1888) "The Early African Slave-Trade in New England," e.g., 109: "Massachusetts writers have always been especially sore, at the point where the trade in African negroes is touched. If they had admitted that in fact, none knew at the time the enormity of the offense and that Massachusetts partook of the common public sentiment which trafficked in Indians or Negroes as carelessly as in cattle, their argument would be more consistent. Massachusetts attained enough in her history that is actual and real; it is not necessary to prove that she was endued with superhuman forecast, or a pragmatic morality."

[11] Modes of resistance and defiance, linguistic dexterity, distinctive speech and appearance, etc. can be discerned in anecdotes transformed from oral traditions in Andover, such as those reported by Abbot, "A Massachusetts Slave," 234–235; Abbott, Manuscript about Nancy Parker; Abbott, "Historical Andover. No. 106. Africa to Andover"; Abbott, "Historical Andover. No. 107. Africa to Andover.—(Concluded)"; Bailey, *Historical Sketches of Andover*, 41–46; Forsyth-Vail, "African Americans and the North Parish and Church of North Andover" and in the sources Forsyth-Vail cited. A personally favorite example was related by Charlotte Helen Abbott in 1901, "Historical Andover. No. 107. Africa to Andover.—(Concluded)," 3: when Pompey Lovejoy requested a marriage license in 1751, "there was some undignified joking on account of his color. The town clerk himself (probably a brunette Barker) was very dark and when Pomp had swallowed more than he could

hold, he burst forth, 'And who in the d— [devil] married you anyway?[']".

An 1899 account of a bicycle tour in Andover, Anonymous, "Ten Miles Awheel," 5, recollected that, "At the corner of the back road or 'Dinah's road,' as it is variously called, we turned our wheels to the left and rode down this almost lane to Highland road. It is told by the residents of that section of the town that many years ago there lived on this back road, an aged colored couple—Dinah, for whom the road was named, and her husband who lived to be over a hundred years old, it is said. Dinah kept pigs and one of her sayings, which is repeated by the aforesaid residents of that section who do not vouch for its veracity, however, is that she "hope dat dar'll [there will] be shoats a' runnin roun in der nex wurl what'll be all roasted, an a cryin 'com eat me, com eat me,' and ther taters'll be so thick ther that they'll say 'lay over, lay over.'" By "lay over," she may have meant, in cookery, to encrust the potatoes, or to cover the potatoes with another ingredient such as juicy slices of roast pork, or to set ("lay") a table ready for a meal, meanings of which I draw from several late eighteenth- and nineteenth-century dictionaries, cook books, and domestic advice books not included in the references cited. Notably, the story about Dinah Simpson and a recollection of her speech was preserved in oral traditions 90 years after her death. In her circa 1938 memoir, Alice Hinton, "Memory Pictures," 1, stated that she was born in "Dinah's house" on Missionary Lane (now Woodland Road). Hinton's knowledge of Dinah Simpson evidences long-term persistence of local historical traditions about people of color in the town.

Additional biographical information about Dinah Simpson and her husband was noticed during this research, and more awaits an applied researcher. Dinah's husband was identified as Caesar Simpson, "from Africa" who "lived where James Brown now resides," Poore, "A Genealogical-Historical Visitation of Andover, Mass., in the Year 1863," *Essex Institute Historical Collections* 51 (4) (1915): 306. Abbott, "Historical Andover. No. 107. Africa to Andover.— (Concluded)," 3, also mentioned the couple and "the back street still called the Dinah road by Salem street folks though the cellar hole has disappeared."

Dinah and Caesar "Sibson" had business with local merchant Samuel Abbot. Although Abbot's accounting records for the couple are chiefly under Caesar's name, notations indicate that it was Dinah who mostly interacted with Abbot. Abbot noted that raw and initially processed flax was "Deliver^d Dinah his Wife" (May 10, 1798). When she appeared on May 31, 1798 to borrow 6s. cash, Abbot initially wrote "To Cash pd her self" (meaning a loan), but later wrote over the entry so that it read "To cash pd his [^]Wife[^]". Between May 10 and June 12, 1798, and between June 22 and September 22, 1798, Dinah took green flax (unbroken straw with seeds) and flax tow (coarse broken fibers after hackling) to spin. Abbot differentiated spinning, doubling and twisting yarn to make linen sewing thread, and boiling yarn. Dinah returned to Abbot with the linen products. In exchange Abbot applied the value of her labor and products to settle accounts. Samuel Abbot Business Papers, 1754–1819, Series I, Financial records, "Samuel Abbot's Waste Book, & Memorandum Book, & Petty Ledgger, Began May 11th: 1768," (i.e., 1768–1812), n.p. in parts, Mss:761 1754–1819 A122, Vol. 3A, Baker Library Historical Collections, Harvard Business School, Boston, Mass., https://hollisarchives .lib.harvard.edu/repositories/11/archival_objects/168654, digital images seq. 4, 13, accessed August 13, 2019. Additional to those entries, there may be other entries and related papers mentioning the Simpsons in other volumes and files in that collection.

"Cesar Simpson" brought a civil action (called a *process of confession*) against Catherine Timan, identified as an Andover "Negroe Woman" (and possibly the daughter of Timon Chadwick/Freeman who had sued Peter Osgood, Jr. and won his freedom in 1777). Simpson's case against Timan was heard by the Andover Justice of the Peace on April 9, 1798. The nature of the dispute was not specified (for the specific detail of the complaint, the hearing record referred to a writ and note on file that was not preserved with the hearing record), but most likely was for debt owed for goods or services. Timan defaulted (did not appear) and Simpson was awarded $36.58 in damages and $2.58 in costs of bringing the action, Nathaniel Lovejoy, "Processes of Confessions," 1797–1800 (Justice of the Peace Records, Andover, Mass.), n.p., Case No. 26, Collection No. EC 43, Box 6, File 4, "Collection of Essex County (Mass.) Court Records, 1628–1914," Phillips Library, Peabody Essex Museum, Rowley, Mass.

"Cesar Sibson" appeared on one manuscript list of expenses for the poor, 1802–1803, seemingly prepared by Joshua Chandler (1758–1817) as an Andover overseer of the poor. The absence of his name from the previous 1801–1802 list could mean he did not receive any support during that period. However, the 1801–1803 compilation that did not list his name indicates the compiled list was not carefully prepared, so perhaps the earliest list was not either. Town of Andover, Overseers of the Poor, "An Account of the Expence of Supporting poor of Andover from the first of March 1801 to the first of March 1802"; "An account of the Expence of Persons Supported by the Town; also of Persons in part Supported Viz. from the first of March 1802 to the first of March 1803" ("Cesar Sibson" $4.25); and, "A List of Persons to be Let out for the present year Viz Expences for 1803 1802 1801", all in Joshua Chandler (1758–1817) Papers, Ms S 52, Sub-group I, Joshua (7) Chandler, Series C, Official Town Documents, Sub-series 2a–2c, Overseers of the Poor, ACHC.

"Cesar Sibson W^d" seemingly indicating "widow of" and as he prede-ceased her, thus referring to Dinah, appeared on the list of inhabitants of the Holt District (in 1852 the district was in southeast Andover between Phillips Academy and what is now North Reading), Anonymous, "Memorandum of the Names of the Families in each District in the South Parish in Andover 1805 Taken in January 1805," n.p. [page 12 when counting, not the cover, but the first text page as page 1], Ms S 56, ACHC; despite the date in the title of this notebook, it is apparent that names were added later. "Cesar" "Sibson" was buried November 5, 1805, age about 80 years, and Dinah "Sibson" was buried August 23, 1809, age 78, *VRA*, Vol. 2, 574 (Deaths, "Negroes").

Robert H. Tewksbury's distressing account, "Lawrence," 237, of Boise (possibly the same man as Booso) remembering "his capture by slavers; and, drawing a huge knife, [he] would make furious attacks upon the trees, thus taking revenge upon an imaginary foe" embedded resistant struggle to being captured, symbolic retribution for persistent frustration and unhappiness of enslavement, and possibly African and/or Caribbean magic or ritual prac-tices and a conception of temporality that differed from European-derived ideas.

Folklore research to gather and analyze "texts" about people of color recorded in historical Andover and in Essex and Middlesex counties gener-ally would be revealing. Catherine Besteman, "Public History and Private Knowledge," 567 (quoted by Bonacci and Meckelburg, "Revisiting Slavery and the Slave Trade in Ethiopia," 16 n77), conferred that "Much historical information about ex-slaves and the transition to freedom is recoverable only in informal oral and life histories, or in uncovering symbolic or significant tidbits in daily conversations." Geographic information on residence, work, travel, and social aggregation are encoded in these narratives, e.g., Martin, "On the Landscape for a Very, Very Long Time"; Martin, "Homeplace Is also Workplace"; Poore, "A Genealogical-Historical Visitation of Andover, Mass., in the Year 1863"; Wright, *Pedagogues and Protesters*. For the ancient and historic Native American cultural traditions in the Shawsheen–Merrimack area of Andover, North Andover, and Lawrence, see Bell, "Discerning Na-tive Placemaking" and sources cited. For examples of perceptive analysis of problematic texts, see Bly, "Pretty, Sassy, Cool: Slave Resistance, Agency, and Culture in Eighteenth-Century New England"; Brown, "Memorial Narra-tives of African Women in Antebellum New England"; Brown, "Death-De-fying Testimony"; Prude, "To Look Upon the 'Lower Sort': Runaway Ads and the Appearance of Unfree Laborers in America"; Pryor, "The Etymology of Nigger"; and, White and White, "Slave Clothing and African-American Culture in the Eighteenth and Nineteenth Centuries." I thank Leon Jackson for mentioning Prude's article.

[12] Slaves at the same meal table as the owner's family is a persistent trope intended to suggest that slavery in New England households was paternalistic. Sarah Kemble Knight, *The Journal of Madam Knight*, 37–38, infamously commented in 1704 that the practice was "too Indulgent (especially ye farmers) to their slaves: suf[f]ering too great familiarity from them, permitting y^m [i.e., them] to sit at Table and eat with them, (as they say to save time,) and into the dish goes the black hoof as freely as the white hand." Theodore or Henry Dwight Sedgwick (authorship of the anonymous 1831 work has been attributed to each of them), in *The Practicability of the Abolition of Slavery*, 14, referring generally to Northern states, believed that "slavery existed in a very mitigated form [....] The slaves were precluded from the table in but few families."

[13] Benes, "Slavery in Boston Households," 15 ("vendible property"). Philip D. Morgan, "African Americans," 152, summarized varied perspectives on the historical problem of paternalism of slave owners toward their enslaved property. The historical trope of paternalism in New England undoubtedly derived from "an authentic, but deeply flawed, worldview" in this society with slaves, which was not inconsistent with capitalist interests. Even when joined with fictive kinship metaphors, paternalism was a rationalization that "offered no guarantee of benevolence." Even among those opposed to enslavement, "antislavery sentiment did not imply an inclusionary worldview", Warren, *New England Bound*, 237. See and compare also, Davis, "Reflections on the Black Woman's Role in the Community of Slaves"; Davis, "The Legacy of Slavery"; Faucquez, "L'esclavage en milieu urbain," English abstract; Fitts, "The Landscapes of Northern Bondage," 56–61; Hancock, "'The Law Will Make You Smart'"; Hardesty, *Unfreedom*; Hardesty, "Social Networks and Social Worlds," 240 and n12; Lewis, "Fires of Discontent"; Newman, "The Grammar of Emancipation"; and, Twombly, "Black Resistance to Slavery in Massachusetts," 26–31. Gail Forsyth-Vail, "African Americans and the North Parish and Church of North Andover," discussed years of debates about desegregating the seating of African Americans in Andover churches. See also, Mofford, *The History of North Parish Church of North Andover*, 84, 114, 158; and, Hardesty, "An Angry God in the Hands of Sinners." Mysteriously, Mary Grant of Middleton, Mass., described as a "stranger" in town, died suddenly at Moses Richardson's in Andover, on December 23, 1827, when she "received a blow in an affray with Blacks." *VRA*, Vol. 2, 454, citing North Parish Congregational Church records. The explicit racial marking, in the church records, of the description of that public fight "with Blacks" implicates the racial tensions at that church explained by Mofford, ibid. and by Forsyth-Vail, ibid.

[14] Sarah Frye, Probate file papers, will, June 1, 1776; inventory, May 1, 1781; accounting and distribution, September 7, 1790. In the 1781 inventory list-

ing of the six slaves, the word for the number of slaves appears to have been first written as "Five", then the "ve" overwritten with "x" to make it only resemble the word "Six". Comparison of the formation of the initial capital letter of the word meant to convey "Six" with other examples of capital *F* and *S* on that same page confirms that impression. In the 1790 accounting of the "6 Negroes", the numeral "6" is more heavily inked, possibly indicating that the numeral was first written as "5". Anonymous, "Sketches of Octogenarians" (about Rose Coburn's family) (quotation about Jack Booz). Taking one's father's forename as a surname followed African-derived traditions, Whiting, "'Endearing Ties,'" 117–120 and sources cited. See Handler and Jacoby, "Slave Names and Naming in Barbados" and Sachs, "'Freedom By A Judgment,'" 179 n13 and 195 n71 (and the sources they cited) for African and African-derived naming practices generally. Of Phillis' 14 children, Abbott, "Historical Andover. No. 106. Africa to Andover," 3, could "not fully account" for all of them either because of a lack of vital records.

[15] Sarah Frye, Probate file papers, will, June 1, 1776. Andover historian and genealogist Charlotte Helen Abbott noted Frye's "Justice & Humanity" phrase. Abbott's only comment was that "I do not find a case where the Fryes set their servants free so far." Abbott, "Historical Andover. No. 47. Some Old Residents"; "Historical Andover. No. 106. Africa to Andover," 3 (quotation); Abbott, "Early Records of the Frye Family of Andover," 45. Sarah Frye's son John Frye (1750–?) had attended Harvard College until December 1767 when he was sent away for misbehavior; he returned to school briefly in 1770. John was mentioned frequently in Stephen Peabody's (1741–1819) college diary, as were John's parents with whom Peabody visited and dined, Wright, *Pedagogues and Protesters*. John Frye's lively, scandalous, and unsuccessful period at the college was summarized by Shipton, "John Frye," 158–159 and by Chase, "Harvard Student Disorders in 1770." Leon Jackson, "The Rights of Man and the Rites of Youth," 30 n15, pointed to John Frye's behavior as an example of outward expressions of liminal experiences of early adulthood.

[16] Davis, "Re-Examining the Problem of Slavery in Western Culture," 263, 266. That magnificent essay distills Davis' career-long examination of the ideological problems of slavery. Especially pertinent to Massachusetts, in view what we now call the Atlantic World, is his masterful book published in 1975, *The Problem of Slavery in the Age of Revolution*. With all due respect for his superior intellect and synthetic compositional talent, I did wonder if his own analytic anxieties were at play when he critiqued "historians [who] tend to exaggerate the autonomous power of ideas", ibid., 274 n31 (quotation), 288 (similarly, that "millennialism cannot be quite thought of as an autonomous force or 'influence'"). For example, it is conceptually difficult to specifically locate a place and discern a time when "American colonists felt

[*sensu* thought] that they were uniquely qualified for republican life", ibid., 282. Sweeping normative ideological summary rather too neatly packages nuances of variation and dissention. Consequently it is challenging to always precisely match broadly stated ideals with forceful evidence found in historical expressions in places such as Andover. Davis privileged evidence of action, but did not always specify the sources of all his evidence. Without providing reference to any particular documentary sources, he detected the shift in moral perception "in the antislavery resolutions of New England town meetings" and "in individual wills that manumitted slaves", ibid., 285. Litwack, *North of Slavery*, 9 n11, gave particular examples from Worcester in 1767 and the adjoining town of Leicester in 1773 that he noticed among other instructions to their state representatives. Salem town meeting likewise directed its representative in 1773, Perley, "Essex County in the Abolition of Slavery," *Essex-County Historical and Genealogical Register* 1 (3) (1894): 37–39.

Perhaps there may be found expressions of such humanistic and liberalistic ideas about enslaved people (which Davis, ibid., 285, stressed was *not* insincere "empty rhetoric") in the records of town meetings in Andover or surrounding towns. Judicial records indicate that Essex County jurymen and arbitrators were so inclined when they decided Andover freedom suits that freed enslaved plaintiffs. The Wilmington vote of March 3, 1777, "Town Meetings, etc. 1730–1807," 164, to support any poor former slaves who were manumitted within one month, seemingly ideologically aligns with Davis' shift in moral perception that enslaved people of color were a part of humanity upon whom misfortune might befall. Yet, though, the Wilmington offer to slave owners was temporary in effect and more cynically intended to prospectively absolve slave owners of financial duty. More in spirit of what Davis, ibid., 274 and n31, referred to as the "monstrous inconsistency" between revolutionary rhetoric and contradictory practice—infamously expressed in Samuel Johnson's biting "*yelps* for liberty among the drivers of negroes" (ibid., 275, italics do not appear in some editions of Johnson's 1775 pamphlet, *Taxation no Tyranny*, none of which editions are included in references cited)— were several Andover resolutions complaining about the duties imposed on tea, paper, and glass, and other obnoxious Parliamentary actions. The Andover resolutions seem, however, to be specifically worded to evade charges of logical contradiction. Thus, fascinatingly, the wording appears to reflect awareness in Andover of that rhetorical debate that also invoked theological worries about spiritual and temporal consequences for moral inconstancy (ibid., 283–284).

The Andover revolutionary resolutions adroitly cabined the civil rights and liberties they complained were being trampled on by king and Parliament, to be rights and freedoms that they themselves as free men had naturally, and had more exclusively attained as *freemen*, but that decidedly their slaves had not. In that hierarchical, hegemonic patriarchy, degrees of authority, power, and autonomy were pyramidically arranged, but assigned and experienced degrees of unfreedom were neither uncontested nor unnegotiated. Andover men with power and authority appealed to even higher power and authority in England. As they contested and negotiated with king, Parliament, and their colonial authorities—as defiant and obstreperous individuals below the status of freemen (women, children, indentured apprentices, slaves) otherwise did with them furtively or directly—the Andover resolution writers used narrative finesse to resolve any bothersome cognitive dissonance that naturally arose if they reflected on the humanistic implications of their reliance on slave labor and their profitable participation in the slave trade. At the May 21, 1770 meeting, "liberty and freedom" were specifically delimited to "free and natural born subjects" who had "rights […that they were] entitled to as men, and as Englishmen." At the May 31, 1773 meeting, it was the "bold invasions made upon our civil rights" to which they objected. It was voted at the Andover town meeting of February 3, 1774, to adopt the wording of the "Philadelphia Resolver": "that the disposal of their own property is the inherent right of Freemen; that there can be no property in that which another can, of rights, take from us without our consent", and that taxation without representation "introduce[s…] Slavery", Town of Andover, "Andover, Massachusetts, Town Meeting Records, 1709–May 21, 1776," Microfilm Frames 5218 (May 21, 1770), 5228–5229 (May 31, 1773), 5233 (February 3, 1774). Perceptively, Patricia Bradley, *Slavery, Propaganda, and the American Revolution*, xiv, saw invocation of the "slavery" metaphor in revolutionary rhetoric to have "encouraged, and even legitimized […] prejudices […] and may have served to delay a national solution to the American institution of slavery."

Sarah Frye's invoking "Justice & Humanity" about the slaves she held captive is a clear example of Davis' shift in moral perception that yet did not attain a pure benevolence nor accept a natural, equal right to liberty among all people, Sarah Frye, Probate file papers, will, June 1, 1776. In this monograph, I noted and quoted several examples of manumissions by will written by slave owners in Andover and surrounding towns. Sometimes wills indicated that freedom had been seemingly legally granted prior to the testamentary directions, not only ultimately upon the testator's death. Simultaneously, the same wills and estate administration papers proved that seemingly manumitted servants remained in ambiguous laboring arrangements with tenuous control over their persons and property that appear to have been comparable as slavery. To stress here, enslavement per se did not only involve involuntary work for no or little pay: slavery and other points along the continuum of "unfreedom" involved separation from kin and kith; degrees of subservience;

dependence for food, shelter, and medical care; constriction of movement and autonomy; treatment as vendible property; and other facets of, generically, "slavery." A comprehensive survey of the Essex County probate file papers could be accomplished that would finely trace the timing and details of modes of enslavement and emancipation in treatments of people as property, as linguistic study and interpretation would be able to discern ideological foundations in the sentiments and reasoning of testamentary compositions.

[17] Blanck, *Tyrannicide*, 66–68. After 1670 in Massachusetts, enslaved people had basic rights as "subjects of the king" that entailed legal protections from torts that abstractly "offended" the king's "peace" such as assault, wrongful imprisonment, etc. As the colonial common law (but not statutory law) developed, enslaved individuals had "the right to own property, write contracts, sue, petition, and witness", ibid., 18, including habeas corpus and due process in criminal cases. The ability of enslaved people to use the Massachusetts courts to obtain liberty derived from those legal rights established by common law and in legal customs, practices, and procedures, ibid., 111–112; Hancock, "'The Law Will Make You Smart.'"

[18] Breen, "Making History," quotations, in order, 67, 82, 76, 77, 72 (two quotations), 70, 71, 94. T.H. Breen, ibid., 72 n7, quoted "publick opinion" from Belknap, "Queries Respecting the Slavery and Emancipation of Negroes in Massachusetts," 201. Thea K. Hunter, "Geographies of Liberty," 320 n3 and sources cited, had considered the involvement of people of color in the 1747 anti-impressment Knowles riots in Massachusetts as influential in political consciousness-raising. Manisha Sinha, "To 'Cast Just Obliquy' on Oppressors," 152–153, saw in Massachusetts Revolutionary era petitions "the foundations of African American abolitionist ideology [...upon which] later generations of black abolitionists self-consciously built [...] their incipient ideas." Sinha, *The Slave's Cause*, expanded upon and detailed intellectual and strategic influences in the history of abolition and included bibliography of parallel scholarship.

[19] Minardi, *Making Slavery History*, 37–38 (quotation, "complex interplay"), 41–42. Political efforts faced legislative impediments to statutorily counter enslavement and discrimination. Protests and petitioning to abolish slavery and to secure civil rights by statute in Massachusetts and in other New England places met deliberate inaction in state legislatures. In her Epilogue, Margaret Ellen Newell, *Brethren by Nature*, 253, significantly construed that "republican state governments in New England resisted abolishing slavery, despite pressure from African American, Indian, and Euro-American petitioners and advocates. [...] The opacity of the law of slavery and its customary

basis in New England made it difficult—though certainly not impossible—to achieve abolition in statutory form. The unwillingness of legislatures to prioritize antislavery over property rights [...] also contributed to the delay. Instead, these states forced individual Indians and African Americans to free themselves one by one through lawsuits—or, with the support of neighbors, by simply walking away from masters." While Vermont famously but not altogether effectively outlawed slavery constitutionally in 1777, and other New England states passed gradual emancipation schemes that legally extended slavery into the nineteenth century, Massachusetts did not statutorily abolish slavery. For overviews of the long and uneven efforts by New England legislative bodies toward emancipation and legal equality, see, e.g., Greene, *The Negro in Colonial New England*; Hardesty, *Black Lives, Native Lands, White Worlds*; Melish, *Disowning Slavery*; Sherburne, *Slavery & the Underground Railroad in New Hampshire*; and, Whitfield, *The Problem of Slavery in Early Vermont*.

[20] Sinha, "The Mobile Resistance," n.p. (quotations). In her review of Julius S. Scott's *The Common Wind*, Manisha Sinha conveyed Scott's influential approaches and ideas that recognized the role of mariners of color in spreading news. Goldsmith, *The Townswoman's Andover*, 20–22; Greater Lawrence Underground Railroad Committee, *The Anti-Slavery Movement and the Underground Railroad in Andover & Greater Lawrence*; Hunter, "Geographies of Liberty"; Hunter, "Transatlantic Negotiations"; Mofford, "The Underground Railroad Ran Through Andover"; National Park Service, *Poets, Shoemakers, and Freedom Seekers: Abolitionists and the Underground Railroad in Essex County*; Patrakis, *Andover in the Civil War*, 19–20; Sachs, "'Freedom By A Judgment,'" 187 (quotation), 188 n46 and sources that Sachs cited for "the context of an emerging transatlantic conversation about slavery and emancipation."

[21] Melish, "Northern Slavery and Its Legacies," 127–128 (quotation). Jones, "'Trifling Patriots and a Freeborn Pepel,'" n.p. Generations of historians have been occupied with these problems in American revolutionary, constitutional, and sociological ideologies—not just particularly in regards to the "American Hypocrisy" during the Revolutionary era when slave owners complained about their "liberty" (as property, profit, and commerce) being trampled upon by king, Parliament, and their provincial minions. Peter H. Wood, "'Liberty Is Sweet,'" provided a consideration complementary to Jones' essay. Manisha Sinha, "To 'Cast Just Obliquy' on Oppressors," 152, pointed to the Massachusetts African American petitions that raised the hypocrisy issue. Sinha, ibid., and François Furstenberg, "Beyond Freedom and Slavery," provide references to the historiography of the intellectual matter. The first part

of the title of Rhett S. Jones' article ("Trifling Patriots") quoted the Baptist Rev. John Allen's pamphlet, *The Watchman's Alarm*, 27, published in Salem, Mass., in 1774:

> Blush ye pretended votaries for freedom! ye trifling patriots! who are making a vain parade of being the advocates for the liberties of mankind, who are thus making a mockery of your profession, by trampling on the sacred natural rights and privileges of the *Africans*; for while you are fasting, praying, non-importing, non-exporting, remonstrating, resolving, and pleading for a restoration of your charter rights, you at the same time are continuing this lawless, cruel, inhuman, and abominable practice of enslaving your fellow-creatures, which is so disgraceful to human nature; a practice which must redound to the eternal dishonor of any people much more to those who *wear* the christian name, and must surely make the heart of every feeling person shudder at the thought of being held in perpetual slavery, but shocking to relate, it is realized by millions of unhappy mortals in the world, a greater part of which I am sorry to say are dwellers in this *American* land of freedom!

Allen's political tracts that carried his evolving antislavery were popular reading, Davis, *The Problem of Slavery in the Age of Revolution*, 266–267 n16, 276–277 and sources cited. Bradley, *Slavery, Propaganda, and the American Revolution* has particular information that documented transmittal of political rhetoric in Massachusetts through newspapers.

In *The Watchman's Alarm*, 28 n, 29, Rev. Allen disclosed his knowledge of an Essex County freedom suit and conveyed his approbation for the men to whom the case had been referred for arbitration, who Allen believed "gave a verdict in favor of the negro, by which he obtained his freedom, there being no law of the province to hold a man to serve for life. Of those worthy patriots for liberty, those sincere friends to the rights and liberties of mankind, who, emulated with a spirit of liberty, have so nobly let public virtue triumph over sordid self-interest, and have released a number of valuable black servants who were held in bondage." Allen's note about the freedom suit was (in the modern parlance) "sinister wisdom" in that it advertised that legal option for emancipation as a revolutionary action. How Allen learned of that obscure legal case to note it in his 1774 antislavery tract is an intriguing mystery, but the incomplete and misleading case information in his footnote has confused innumerable scholars who ultimately relied on Allen's mischaracterization of it.

Allen's note of the freedom suit was quoted by George H. Moore (1866, *Notes on the History of Slavery in Massachusetts*, 119), but the case was brought to broader knowledge when Allen's note and Moore's notice of it was repeated by George Williams (1882, *History of the Negro Race in America*, 231 n4). The misinformation about that case from either or both nineteenth-century sources was restated by subsequent writers to the present day. After intensive searching, I finally identified the case as Sampson v. Caleb Dodge and Josiah Batchelder, Essex County Court of Common Pleas Docket, July 1774 (Case #2, "Rule issued July 20, 1774" adding Batchelder as a second defendant and referring the case for arbitration), September 1774 (Case #1/33, as "Samson"), December 1774 (Case #2/25), May 1775 (Case #3/20), July 1775 (Case #4/19 & #5/19, listed twice). The documentation of the case only appeared in the court docket, not the records of decisions. After July 1775 the case no longer appeared on the docket, which indicates that the case did not proceed and was thus a legal nullity. If the missing case file papers are ever located, they may provide information about its resolution, which may have occurred out of court. The case was not resolved by a formal decision of court-appointed arbitrators, as Allen averred, that would have been made in a report to the court (the "verdict" as Allen put it imprecisely), and which report would have been included in a decision of record by the court. Despite what Allen asserted, and what historian-scholars endlessly repeated, because the case was a nullity that never came to trial, there was no decision issued by the bench, by arbitrators, or by a jury verdict.

Rhett S. Jones located the "gradual coalescence of racist thought" in discredited literature in science, anthropology, sociology, history, and philosophy that confused ancestry ("race") with intelligence and capacity. Beyond ersatz intelligentsia, the vulgar terms and actions that were employed by legions of common non-intellectuals who ascribed to that racist "public fiction" affected the everyday experiences of people of color. Jones' point was that street-common racism influenced intellectuals whose defective and reinforcing scientist conclusions were reabsorbed by the bourgeoisie and canaille. Compare Jones, "In the Absence of Ideology," 33 ("following American independence even free Blacks found their liberties in jeopardy") and 35 ("the public fiction of Black inferiority" was misinformed by and was recursively reproduced in discredited literature). Rhett S. Jones (1940–2008) developed his ideas over decades of writing that exposed racial preconceptions and racist prejudice that lurked covertly and was expressed overtly in studies repudiated long ago, but which shaped and justified disparate treatment of African- and indigenous Native American-descendant people psychologically, socially, legally, politically, economically, graphically, and literarily. Jones' training in the sociology of his day heightened the polemical effectiveness of his arguments about general historical themes and issues as long-standing, unsolved *problems* to understand circumstances of people of color in contemporary society.

Lois E. Horton, "From Class to Race in Early America"; Joanne Pope Melish, "The 'Condition' Debate and Racial Discourse in the Antebellum North"; Melish, "Northern Slavery and Its Legacies," 126–128; James Brewer Stewart, "Modernizing 'Difference'"; and Elizabeth Stordeur Pryor, "The Etymology of Nigger," 210 (quotation), timed the "coalescence" that Rhett S. Jones had inferred "precisely at the moment when gradual abolition and emancipation began to free people of color in the North." Socially, demeaning language was employed with physical violence "to prevent black geographic mobility and social aspiration", ibid., 226. Petty rules combined with insulting language and physical assault enforced segregation in public spaces and privately owned public transportation such as railroad cars, Kantrowitz, "Fighting Jim Crow in the Cradle of Liberty"; Ruchames, "Jim Crow Railroads in Massachusetts." Pryor, ibid., 231, observed that in literary and graphic representations, among other forms and manifestations, "[t]his new iteration of anti-black cultural productions was largely a response to black freedom in the North and the interracial abolitionist movement." Leon Jackson emphasized that occupational opportunities also attenuated. His research into "tax records, property deeds, Debtor's Jail calendars, and Court of Common Pleas file papers" for the period 1810–1830, indicated a "dramatic contraction in both the range and status of jobs available to people of color in Boston" (Leon Jackson, email, September 29, 2019).

Padraig Riley, *Slavery and the Democratic Consciousness*, 18, conveyed that the coeval "official and informal discrimination" in New England toward free people of color was related to "an ideological accommodation with southern slaveholders" that supported "a political coalition that protected slavery at the national level." Regional economic interests that depended on plantation slavery influenced political positions. By the 1850s, the political strivings of radical abolitionists began to move some Massachusetts Whigs toward antislavery, including the industrialist and corporate merchant Amos Adams Lawrence (1818–1846, the nephew of Abbott Lawrence, "the chief financial backer of the textile manufacturing enterprise and early mills" of the city of Lawrence). Amos Lawrence "protested the Fugitive Slave Law and financed the passage of liberated slaves to the African colony of Liberia. Further, he became the primary supporter and treasurer of the New England Emigrant Aid [... Company] to send settlers to inhabit the territory of Kansas [...intending it to become] a Free State." Amos Lawrence was involved with shipping Sharps rifles to Kansas to confront incursions of proslavery elements from Missouri, but also implored individuals to obey federal authorities. Carter Jackson, *Force and Freedom*; Greater Lawrence Underground Railroad Committee, *The Anti-Slavery Movement and the Underground Railroad in Andover & Greater Lawrence*, 3 (quotations); Kansas State Historical Society and

University of Kansas, *Territorial Kansas Online 1854–1861*, search results for "Lawrence, Amos Adams, 1814–1886", accessed August 31, 2019.

[22] Leonard, *Political Poetry as Discourse*, 4 ("to disclose"; "subgroups"; "blacks"; "black referent newstexts"); 115 ("whites"); 134 ("multiple yet distinct"); 4 ("recurrent racial signifiers"); 4, 114 (the racial terms); 132 ("literally create[d] radical subgroups", italics mine); 135 ("did not nor could it mandate"); 136 ("units...coalesce[d]"); Leonard, "The Instability and Invention of Racial Categories in the *Haverhill Gazette*," 278 ("gradually spreading"); 280 ("colonizationist rhetoric"). Leonard's book, *Political Poetry as Discourse* was published in 2010, and followed the 1999 publication of her 1998 conference paper, "The Instability and Invention of Racial Categories in the *Haverhill Gazette*," which has additional and independent observations. Fortuitous to my interest in historical Andover, Leonard's study focused on a nearby Essex County locale. Similar analytic results were found studying historical newspaper texts from the *Connecticut Courant* (1764–1827) that also had a Massachusetts readership, Albakry and Williams, "Whitewashing Slavery in New England"; Williams, "Demonizing, Dehumanizing, and Whitewashing: Linguistic Examination of *The Connecticut Courant's* Coverage of Slavery." Rhoesmary R. Williams' academic thesis, and the article she coauthored with her professor Mohammed Albakry, demonstrated the historical subversion of memories of Northern slavery and the slave trade, the application of that revisionist history to contrastively disparage enslavement in Southern states, and by applying discourse analysis to racialized linguistic terms printed in that newspaper, traced the evolution of racist ideologies in the New England region.

Of the chapter in Leonard's book that focused on the Haverhill news articles, she wrote that "the decision to 'close-read' a four-year period of the *Haverhill Gazette and Essex Patriot* began as an interest in political voices in John Greenleaf Whittier's 'cultural context,' which may have informed his antislavery temperament. So this chapter began as a mission to excavate a political message about blacks in this local, discursive medium." The Haverhill-born poet and essayist was briefly editor of that paper when published as the *Essex Gazette* (Leonard, *Political Poetry as Discourse*, 111). Her historical lexical study was placed within a book that traced an arc from the political protest manifest in the nineteenth-century poetry of John Greenleaf Whittier and Ebenezer Elliott to that of modern Hip-Hop performers: all of them "poets who subvert oppressive structures of containment in their world with words" (ibid., 1). I pondered her choice of the present tense in her historical study. Assuredly her analysis and interpretations have broader historical and ongoing sociocultural implications. As Leonard explained (ibid., 5–6), "the purpose and mission" of her book was to teach her students about discourse analysis, "to read, listen, and observe closely the relationship between ideologies and the reproduction of power; that is, dominant and prevailing cultural practices, habits, and behaviors." "So when one considers the sociolegal history of 'free blacks' in the early nineteenth century, the un-boundedness of slavery for all blacks becomes pervasive" (ibid., 134).

I inferred a dual meaning of "slavery" in Leonard's phrase "the un-boundedness of slavery": literally as it existed in slave states, but also figuratively, as in the same entwined, oppressive, institutional and systemic practices of segregation and discrimination that were sanctioned officially and unofficially, along with the attendant legal and socioeconomic inequities that permeated the experiences of free persons of color and those in their orbit. That was termed "the *spirit* of slavery", in 1833 by David Tenney Kimball at the Andover Theological Seminary, in his sarcastically titled "Apology for Anti-Slavery," 153: "in reference to the colored people [it] is to be found in every portion of the union. The oppressive civil disabilities laid upon them in the non-slaveholding States, and the settled opposition to their education and elevation [...] are but glaring indications of the prevalent spirit of slavery. The same contempt of the black man—the same disposition to trample on his rights and to lord it over his person, follows him, whatever *degree* of emancipation he may have obtained, and in whatever part of the nation he takes his refuge." Racialized vocabulary persisted to "semantically recognize [..."blacks"] as transportable and marketable property" (Leonard, *Political Poetry as Discourse*, 110).

Kimball's "*spirit* of slavery" reflected and embodied powerful ideologies that persisted in postslavery societies and which continued to enforce, reinforce, and justify disparate treatment of formerly enslaved people and their descendants who were simultaneously known to be emancipated, yet were persistently and explicitly, linguistically and narratively linked to their former status as "slaves." Notwithstanding their emancipated condition, notwithstanding biographical and genealogical actualities that other people of color were, rather, descendants of contingently free people of color who were never enslaved, in postslavery societies people of color came to be primarily identified and characterized as if they were and remained "slaves" through nebulous and evolving notions of racial and racist ideologies that are always socially circumstantial, varying in time and place. The most common racial term used for the longest period in this area ("Negro") carried connotative assumptions about legal and social status. In specific contexts, "Negro" was synonymous with "slave." Defendants in several Massachusetts freedom suits responded that the plaintiff was their "own proper Negro slave."

By way of positioning myself, I acknowledge here "*meaning making* out of borrowed material" (Leonard, ibid., 146), an observation that Leonard made when referring to the editorial practice of newspapers to reprint articles from other news publications. As scholars do, I have selected from Leonard's cohesive narrative and editorially transformed her words. It is impossible, of course, to represent the subtle nuances and aesthetic cohesion of her original authorial intentions by reordering and recasting these quoted portions, but I have endeavored to fairly and reasonably convey her interpretive findings and pedagogic goals. In "The Instability and Invention of Racial Categories in the *Haverhill Gazette*," 282, Leonard emphasized, in conclusion, that her "study aims to assist the development of oppositional and resistant readers, who will challenge the ways in which thoughts and images are formed about members of different socially-identified racial groups."

[23] Leonard, ibid., 275 ("derogatory and negative"); 277 ("oxymoronic" used in another context); 279 ("Society's undesirables"); 281 ("stigmatization"). Rael, *Black Identity and Black Protest in the Antebellum North*, is informative for the history of many allied and competing ideologies. See Anonymous, *The Colonizationist and Journal of Freedom*, 32, 98, 140–143, 356, for people associated with Andover Theological Seminary in 1834, but also compare the names of "Messrs. Tracy, Baker, Hackett and McLane, from Andover" who "addressed the meeting" of the newly formed Methuen Colonization Society around March 1834 (ibid., 325, 356) with the online list of notable Phillips Academy alumni in the 1800s, https://web.archive.org/web/20170808005328/https://www.andover.edu/About/NotableAlumni/LongList/Pages/default.aspx, accessed November 17, 2019. For both the majority support and minority opposition of colonization, and diversity in antislavery views among students and faculty at the seminary, see Thompson, "Abolitionism and Theological Education at Andover," and Kimball's sarcastically titled, "Apology for Anti-Slavery"— written in opposition to colonization that was being advocated by the Anti-Slavery Society at the seminary—reprinted in *The Liberator*, September 28, 1833, 153–154.

For the recollections of a student at Phillips Academy during that time of antislavery and colonizationist activities, see Bristol, *The Pioneer Preacher*, 40–55, in parts reprinted in *The Andover Townsman* local history column, Anonymous, "Auld Lang-Syne. Anti-slavery in Andover fifty years ago" and Anonymous, "Auld Lang-Syne. Anti-slavery Experiences in Andover." A related research topic not yet sufficiently explored is the relationship and influences of the antislavery societies of Andover and North Andover with the students and faculty of the academy and seminary. Thompson, ibid., 245, for example, indicated that "townspeople" and Phillips Academy students attended a series of antislavery lectures at the seminary in 1835. By 1839, the Andover Colonization Society affiliated with the American Colonization Society had been established at the seminary with "more than one hundred" men, including "all the principals and teachers of the Latin and English schools, with one exception." Anonymous, Note about the Andover Colonization Society in *The African Repository and Colonial Journal*, 228.

Paul E. Lovejoy, "The African Diaspora," n.p. [6 (panyarring)], [14 ("there does not appear to have been a movement to abolish the slave trade or emancipate slaves in Africa before the nineteenth century")]. Mimi Sheller, "Beyond Post-Emancipation Studies?" (her review essay about *Beyond Slavery* by Frederick Cooper, Thomas C. Holt, and Rebecca J. Scott), 120–121 (quotation, "'Western' concepts [...] as tainted ideologies"). Walter Johnson, "Time and Revolution in African America," 208 (quotation, "take the temperature" and "a single story"). Walter Johnson was among several thoughtful historians who detected modern ideas and teleological themes interwoven in historical narratives about American slavery, emancipation, and citizenship (see Johnson's reference to "'liberal developmentalism' as a historical metanarrative immanent in the work[s] of Marxist and other scholars", ibid., 208 n29). Mimi Sheller, ibid., 122–123, conveyed that the extreme notion that "freedom" etc. is a "tainted" (121) concept had arisen in "certain strands of post-colonial theory" (123) that should now be considered faulty. Instead, Sheller apprised that the editors and authors of the book she reviewed "investigate[d] the contests over these ideologies and practices, the ambiguities within them, and the strategic (mis)appropriations of them both by colonial elites and by 'emancipated' peoples" (121). Sheller (121) did not discount the well-meant paternalism (as "beneficent despotism") that rode along with racist ideas that free people of color were incapable "to govern the private sphere of family life in a manner that would make them fit to act as public citizens." While Sheller was particularly referring to Britain in the later nineteenth century, she recognized that the same practice was apparent at the same time in the United States "and the wider Atlantic world" (121). Despite generations of historians and sociologists who have exposed and countered that erosive idea, it still rears in political debates and actions, Coates, "The Black Family in the Age of Mass Incarceration." Most significantly, Sheller, ibid., recognized in postslavery societies "new boundaries of citizenship and systems of colonial rule, of belonging and exclusion, autonomy and dependence, articulated in relation to gender ideologies and racial marking" (120) and that "the struggles that emerged in freedom's wake remain on our own horizon" (123). Among many significant points raised by Sheller was that intersectional oppression (particularly but not exclusively in gendered ideologies) was not relieved simultaneously by emancipative process.

Bonacci and Meckelburg, "Revisiting Slavery and the Slave Trade in Ethiopia," 20 (quotation, challenging "existing notions of abolition being a 'Western' endeavor" by their study of "the Ethiopian abolitionist agenda"). My introduction to the appealing research area of postemancipation and postslavery studies, traditions of enslavement and slave trading in African locales, and African and Caribbean histories of emancipation, included Ashcraft-Eason, "Freedom among African Women Servants and Slaves"; Bellagamba, "Freedom from Below"; Bellagamba, et al., "Introduction. Slaves and Masters"; Ben-Ur, "Bound Together? Reassessing the 'Slave Community' and 'Resistance' Paradigms"; Bonacci and Meckelburg, ibid.; Johnson, ibid., 200–205; Lovejoy, ibid.; Lovejoy, *The "Middle Passage"*; Newman, "The Grammar of Emancipation"; Rossi, "African Post-Slavery"; Rossi, "Preface to the Second Edition" of *Reconfiguring Slavery*; Rossi, "Dependence, Unfreedom, and Slavery in Africa"; Rossi, "Freedom Under Scrutiny"; and, Sheller, ibid. Giulia Bonacci and Alexander Meckelburg, ibid., 7, quoted Benedetta Rossi, "African Post-Slavery," 303, who defined "post-slavery" to mean "historical and social circumstances identifiable in 'contexts where slavery was a fundamental social institution and its legal abolition was followed by resilient legacies of past hierarchy and abuse.'" Bonacci and Meckelburg, ibid., stressed that to "inform the national discourse [...] would entail acknowledging the ways in which slavery frames today's social fabric, and in particular how it influences the interethnic relations between former slaves and their descendants on the one hand, and former masters and their descendants on the other." The lively research area of postemancipation and postslavery studies brings a refreshing intellectual rigor to global histories of slavery and abolition grounded in individual experiences and contextualized to place and time, as it informs about still-current socioeconomic and political issues arising from its legacies.

[24] Hardesty, *Black Lives, Native Lands, White Worlds*, 33–34, 123. In that and in his previous book, *Unfreedom*, Jared Ross Hardesty provided accessible summaries of eighteenth-century emancipative ideologies developed by literate people of color in protests and petitions. Joanne Pope Melish, "Northern Slavery and Its Legacies," 124, recognized that "the economic disruption of the [Revolutionary] war eroded the profitability of northern slavery".

Gloria McCahon Whiting, "'Endearing Ties,'" 281, 286, and "Emancipation Without the Courts or Constitution," 10, 20 n57 (quotation) summarized the trend for the historically larger Suffolk County (that then also included most of what is now Norfolk County) using numbers from probate records: "prior to the Revolution, decedents bequeathed enslaved people to their heirs [n=56] more often than they manumitted them [n=30]". After

1775, only four wills devised slaves, while 18 wills included stipulations that manumitted enslaved people. These statistics reliably demonstrate the temporal trend at the county scale for that large area in eastern Massachusetts, both urban and rural, that held the greatest number of slaves in the state. Whiting and her research assistants conducted a comprehensive research effort that consisted of a "page-by-page perusal of all the probate records from Suffolk County between 1760 and 1790" (ibid., 17 n22). That monumental research project obtained the best representation of slave-holding that we can expect for that vast area of eastern Massachusetts during that period.

In devising her research design and methodology, Whiting considered several factors inherent to the archival series of probate records that are important to understand her results. (For Whiting's methodological considerations in those regards, see also her dissertation, "'Endearing Ties,'" e.g., 88–89 n33 and sources she cited.) Those and other analytic issues matter to those who might plan similar time-series studies of probate records elsewhere in the state. Estates of all slave owners may not have gone through the probate court process, or might have been probated in other venues. Enslaved people who entered and then left households before the probate process of course would not appear in the court records. Bondspeople in households may not always have been mentioned in wills. There were intestate decedents (no will probated) and inventories were not always completed for all probated estates that may have had bondspersons. Slaves may have been brought into households after wills were composed, and in those instances when those estates were also not inventoried, bondspeople might not be indicated at all in probate documents. There were probably rare occurrences when valuable slaves were fraudulently concealed from inventory-takers. And there were probably even rarer scrivener's errors when probate court clerks prepared the records (which were ordinarily carefully copied from the file papers submitted to the probate court) and inadvertently did not copy over some mention of an enslaved person. Yet, the archival series of file papers itself suffered losses, and information from now-missing file papers are only preserved in the copied probate records. By their nature, probate documentation skews toward older and toward economically middling and more affluent decedents who over their lifetimes were more likely to have obtained sufficient resources to own slaves. Some people owned fractional shares (moieties) in slaves, or devised by will a single individual to multiple beneficiaries, Benes, "Slavery in Boston Households," 15 n8; Whiting, "Emancipation Without the Courts or Constitution," 6, 9. Other well-known archival series that can be specially studied for slaveholding and its decline, particularly at the household and individual level, which supplement probate documentation, include provincial and state legislative acts and treasurers records, tax assessments, ship manifests, private accounting records, deeds of purchase and manumission, notorial records, freedom suit documentation, military pension files, newspapers, diaries, oral traditions rendered in secondary historical narratives, etc., but as Whiting indicated in her dissertation those and other archival and published sources also have problematic analytic issues and at the broad county scale are less generally representative (temporally, geographically, demographically, etc.) than the well-preserved archive of probate records that she used suitably at the appropriate county-scale to meet the goals and purposes of the time-series study related in her article.

Different than my momentary economic attention at this juncture, in her distilled article that scoped at the county level, Whiting, "Emancipation Without the Courts or Constitution," 12, did not emphasize practical, individual- and household-scale financial reasons for the rapid decline in historical Suffolk County slave ownership that commenced with the outbreak of the war in 1775, when economic disruptions were experienced at many scales. It may be that the fallacious historical idea that slavery was *always* marginal to the Massachusetts economy was an impression actually particular to the time, beginning with the war, when slavery did become less economically important. At turns in her dissertation when Whiting viewed at the individual and household scale, Whiting considered economic decision-making and realized instances when purely financial concerns did not always prevail. That is an especially important point to temper simple economic calculus, as abstractions of so-called "rational" economic decision-making were not always withstanding. In her county-scaled article, ibid., she balanced interpretive scales by attending to both "the internal dynamics of slaveholding households" and to "the chaos of the war and changes in popular attitudes that made many question the utility and morality of slavery". Those changes in attitudes were greatly influenced by resistive and political actions of enslaved people and their allies. Writing more generally about the history of Massachusetts abolition, Whiting, ibid., accentuated that the process she deduced was "a bottom-up revolution in social relations" that *later* led to the better-known "political and legal changes enacted by prominent citizens—delegates to the [state] constitutional convention, lawyers, court justices, and juries". Rather than a consequence of later state constitutional and judicial actions, large-scale emancipation in the state actually occurred earlier than previously realized through "the actions of ordinary people: white people who chose to manumit their enslaved laborers and black people who managed to extricate themselves from bondage around the time of the Revolution's outbreak." See ibid., 18 n38 for a September 1784 inventory that listed a slave. See also MacEacheren, "Emancipation of Slavery in Massachusetts," 296 (Table 1), 299 (Table 2), for a much smaller and more temporally delimited (1770–1790) sample of Boston wills mentioning slaves, and for a manumission by a will written in 1787. The complementary information related in Peter Benes, "Slavery in Boston Households," 14, was "[b]ased principally on a survey of slavery from Suffolk County wills and inventories" dating 1647–1770 "undertaken in 1997 by Jane Montague Benes" (14 n4), and "supplemented by a review of published marriage lists, church records, and period advertisements in Boston newspapers offering the sale of slaves, rewards for catching runaways, and appeals to give away infant or newborn African-Americans."

[25] Robert Paynter and Whitney Battle-Baptiste, "Contexts of Resistance in African American Western Massachusetts," 331, considered "White working class" laborers' hostility and violence toward enslaved laborers, toward slave owners, and vandalism of (non-human) property, "harassments that contributed to making their [own] employers [and slave owners] interested in abolition [for the purpose of obtaining a larger labor pool of former slaves, depressing wages for everyone] and strengthening African-descent people's resistance to their captivity". On that point, Paynter and Battle-Baptiste cited Litwack, *North of Slavery*, 5–6, who had quoted John Adams' 1795 letter to Jeremy Belknap, a transcription of which was published in 1877 as "John Adams to Dr. Belknap. Quincy, March 21, 1795." Professor Paynter, a scholar of W.E.B. Du Bois, indirectly prompted me to the essay by Ta-Nehisi Coates, "Reporter's Notebook: 'A Species of Labor We Do Not Want,'" which considered the analysis and distilled synthesis by Du Bois in *Black Reconstruction*, and the related and even earlier sociopolitical and economic debates about wage labor and slavery (for which see also Davis, *The Problem of Slavery in the Age of Revolution*). These ideas expectedly took on even more urgency and relevance during the early to mid-nineteenth century, and then following the Civil War, as oppressive industrial-era laboring arrangements met up with rising working-class consciousness, organization, and active resistance to oppression along many perceived intersectional axes, such as gender binaries, racial binaries, ethnic nationalism, etc. Melish, "Northern Slavery and Its Legacies," 126–128, summarized the protracted, intersectional, recurrently reinforcing social and economic effects of bias and racism. Paynter and Battle-Baptiste, ibid., 334, related Du Bois' personal recollections of racist treatment, his "double consciousness" so heartbreakingly expressed in *The Souls of Black Folk*, 44 (published in 1903), which most certainly empowered him in his 1935 book, *Black Reconstruction*, 9 (quoted by Coates, ibid.) to demolish the false equivalency of oppression and exploitation in slavery and in wage labor: "there was in 1863 a real meaning to slavery different from that we may apply to the laborer today. It was in part psychological, the enforced personal feeling of inferiority, the calling of another Master; the standing with

hat in hand. It was the helplessness. It was the defenselessness of family life. It was the submergence below the arbitrary will of any sort of individual. It was without doubt worse in these vital respects than that which exists today in Europe or America", and more analogous, Du Bois went on to observe, to the sorts of practices he saw then occurring in China, India, Africa, and in Central and South America.

26 Sarah Frye, Probate file papers, will, June 1, 1776; inventory, May 1, 1781; accounting and distribution, September 7, 1790 ("To del^d [i.e., delivered to] Phillis + Rose two Negro's one Quarter part of the wearing apparel given them in the Will").

27 Anonymous, "Obituary" for Rosanna Coburn. The wording of the account about Phillis in the obituary was slightly changed from Anonymous, "Sketches of Octogenarians" (about Rose Coburn's family). Comparable evidence of oral histories about community lineage, preserved by African American women in memory, was examined by Fulton, *Speaking Power*; Sachs, "'Freedom By A Judgment'"; and by Schweninger, "Freedom Suits, African American Women, and the Genealogy of Slavery," revised and updated as the first chapter in his book *Appealing for Liberty*. See also Hancock, "'Tradition Informs Us,'" about African American traditions of oral history and social memory, and specifically about how those sources informed published histories of the American Revolutionary War.

28 The gravestone epitaph as quoted by Bailey, *Historical Sketches of Andover*, 44. "Memorial narratives" as "formal and respectful tributes" were "inherently performative texts" that continue to signify and function in a multivalent, polysemous manner, Brown, "Memorial Narratives of African Women in Antebellum New England," 40.

29 United States Census, *Population Schedules of the Second Census of the United States 1800, Roll 14*, Essex County, Andover, 200 ("Booss" is the rendering of Booso). Juba (Jack), Titus, and Tory, were the youngest children listed as slaves in Sarah Frye's estate inventory, Sarah Frye, Probate file papers, inventory, May 1, 1781. Their ages, ten years, (uncertain numeral, eight?) years, and six months, respectively, were provided in the inventory, although the numeral for Titus' age is indistinct. All the ages are indeterminate because they or the inventory takers may have misstated their ages. United States Census, *Population Schedules of the Second Census of the United States 1800, Roll 17*, Middlesex County, Wilmington, 1079 (Titus Coburn household with seven people of color).

30 United States Census, *Population Schedules of the Third Census of the United States 1810*, 248. Essex County Deeds, Book 184, pg. 280, Jonathan Griffin

to Titus Coburn, January 19, 1809, recorded January 26, 1809; Book 195, pg. 42, Titus Coburn to Sarah Stevens, November 8, 1811, recorded November 14, 1811, Southern Essex District Registry of Deeds, Salem, Mass.

31 I searched two volumes of microfilmed, manuscript Andover treasurer/overseers of the poor records primarily for the purpose of determining whether or not Phillis was the unnamed woman counted as a "slave" at the Andover almshouse in the 1830 federal census. Secondarily, I expected to find information that would fill out biographical details about Phillis' extended family. I began with a volume dating previous to the 1830 enumeration of the almshouse residents. (The questions asked by the census enumerator were about household residents on June 1, 1830.) Earlier entries might contain information about Phillis or another formerly enslaved woman at the almshouse —such as if Phillis had been moved to the almshouse prior to that date (which would be supporting information that she was indeed an almshouse resident on census day), or her death prior to that day (which would confirm that Phillis was not the "slave" counted there). By that effort, I determined conclusively that Phillis was not the woman designated as a "slave" at the almshouse. I discovered an entry that indicated that Phillis had died prior to January 5, 1829, when the town made payment for her coffin. I searched record entries after January 5, 1829 to February 7, 1831 to attempt to capture any later-submitted orders for payments regarding Phillis, or any notation about anyone else who might instead have been the woman counted as the "slave". I did find a few more entries that I included here for Rosanna and Colley dating after the entry for Phillis' coffin, but no other information to identify the "slave" woman at the almshouse. In other parts of the extensive treasurer/overseers of the poor records, there are indeed earlier entries for at least Booso and his family prior to his death, and for Rosanna and Colley following Phillis' death. I leave it to another researcher to locate and record all those entries in the manuscript town financial records and discover even more forgotten moments of their lives. The published annual town reports have entries for town support provided to Rosanna Coburn's household within the period of 1832–1856. For some years within that period she and/or Colley were not named, whether because no individuals were named those years, or whether they received no support those years, or whether payments for their support were inadvertently not included in the published report, Town of Andover, *Annual Town Reports*. For a summary of entries for Rosanna and Colley in the published annual town reports, see chap. 8, note 18.

These handwritten municipal treasurer/overseers records are in untitled and unpaginated bound volumes, microfilmed by GSU, that pose bibliographic challenges to identify specific entries for researchers. Each volume has entries that recorded the treasurer's payments for "orders" issued by the overseers of the poor over spans of years. The orders authorized payments to individuals who provided services or goods on behalf of the poor. The entries were arranged by year, then by date of payment. Each payment entry was sequentially numbered and noted who was paid, for what, and how much (e.g., among payments made May 5, 1823 is entry No. 10: "An order to Rose Coburn for boarding her mother to June 1ˢᵗ 1823", $6.50).

In the following summaries of information gathered separately under the bibliographic information for each of the two microfilmed volumes of manuscript records, I grouped the many entries of payments for Phillis and her extended family by broad subject (e.g., "Payments to Titus Coburn for supporting Phillis") as they are discussed in my text. In the summaries, I provided the date of the entry, the entry number, the payment amount, and for some entries relayed additional clarifying information, such as a variant name for Phillis: February 19, 1827 (No. 57, $2.17: "Phebe Boos"). An attentive researcher can rapidly relocate the manuscript entry with that information.

The payments were nearly all reimbursements for services or items *already* provided to the poor (e.g., the payment made to Titus Coburn on December 1, 1817, No. 100, "An order to Titus Coburn for supporting Phillice Wʷ [Widow] of Boos up to this date"). There was a time lag between when the service or item had been provided, and when payment was made. In a few instances, payments were made for near-term prospective support of poor individuals to be cared for by others (e.g., the payment made to Titus Coburn on February 23, 1818, No. 144, "An order to Titus Coburn for supporting Phillice Widᵒ of Boos up to the first of March next in part"; and, to Rose Coburn on February 19, 1827, No. 56, "for supporting her mother to March 1ˢᵗ 1827").

In these entries, names were rendered variously and spelling was not consistent and often phonetic, which is unsurprising for the time. Variations can be challenging to conclusively identify the person named, but are interesting because they can be specifically meaningful. Phillis' name was most frequently rendered by variations of "Phillice Widow of Boose", but also as Phillis, Phileus, and Phillies as a single name, and also combined with her late husband's single name used as her surname, as in Pillice Boose, Phillice Boos, Phillse Boose, and Phillis Boos. Phillis was surely the same person called Phebe Boos (so-named only once, which I conclude was a scrivener's error) as a patient of Dr. Abiel Pearson (1756–1827). Phillis had been seen by Dr. Pearson from about 1817 to 1827. After Dr. Pearson ended his practice months before his death on May 22, 1827 (he was 71 years old), Phillis became a new patient of Dr. Nathaniel Swift (1778–1840). Both doctors were reimbursed on the same day for having attended to Phillis' medical care on some previous, likely recent dates (February 19, 1827, No. 57 Dr. Pearson, "Phebe Boos" and No. 63 Dr. Swift, "Wid^w [Widow] of Boos"). Even though Phillis had been seen recently by Dr. Pearson, her new physician Dr. Swift would have wanted to evaluate his new patient himself. Booso's name varied also in those records (e.g., Boos, Boose, Booso); Rose Coburn and Rosanna Coburn both occur; and names of even well-known individuals were rendered differently (Dr. Abiel Pearson was named Abial Parsons, Abiel Person, Abel Pearson, Abell Pearson, etc.).

The following lists of payment entries are arranged under the references to the two manuscript volumes in which they appear, then the entries are grouped by types of payments. The date of payment, the payment number, and amount are indicated. The first volume I searched has entries dating from at least 1798 to 1823 (despite the narrower date span given on the microfilm target). The second volume has entries for payments dating from 1823 to April 4, 1843 (No. 13), then richly detailed, itemized lists dating 1843–1847 that are the "Account of Stock Provision and Sundry Articles Belonging to the Almshouse Establishment Andover" (title from 1843 list). After discovering the January 5, 1829 entry for Phillis' coffin, I only further researched that second volume for entries related to Phillis' extended family to the bottom of the page that has entries of payments dated February 7, 1831 (last order paid on that page was No. 85). Additional entries for Rosanna Coburn and Colley Hooper (a/k/a Elizabeth Coburn) appear in that second volume, and presumably in other volumes of town records that I did not investigate.

Town of Andover, "Town Records, Tax Records 1799–1822" (untitled volume, title from microfilm target but actually treasurer records of payments for orders drawn by the overseers of the poor), n.p., first volume on GSU Microfilm Reel 878782.

> **Payments to Titus Coburn for supporting Phillis:** March 14, 1816 (No. 2, $6.50). June 8, 1816 (No. 22, $6.50). September 2, 1816 (No. 54, $3.00; No. 55, $3.50). December 2, 1816 (No. 117, $6.50). April 11, 1817 (No. 13, $6.50). June 3, 1817 (No. 34, $6.50). September 1, 1817 (No. 67, $6.50). December 1, 1817 (No. 100, $6.50). February 23, 1818 (No. 144, $4.50). July 8, 1818 (No. 31, $9.00). October 5, 1818 (No. 59, $6.50). January 4, 1819 (No. 84, $6.50). August 2, 1819 (No. 37, $6.50). October 4, 1819 (No. 57, $6.50). January 3, 1820 (No. 88, $6.50). April 3, 1820 (No. 10, $6.50). July 3, 1820 (No. 40, $6.50). October 2, 1820 (No. 70, $6.50). January 19, 1821 (No.115, $6.50). April 23, 1821 (No. 18, $6.50).
>
> **Payments to Rose Coburn for supporting Phillis:** July 2, 1821 (No. 41, $6.50). December 4, 1821 (No. 75, $6.50). February 22,

1822 (No. 133, $6.50). May 13, 1822 (No. 14, $6.50). September 2, 1822 (No. 54, $6.50). December 16, 1822 (No. 81, $6.50). March 1, 1823 (No. 161, $8.67).

Payments to Dr. Abiel Pearson for "medicine and attendance" for Phillis: February 24, 1817 (No. 165, $1.01). February 26, 1818 (No. 158, $0.50). February 19, 1819 (No. 102, $0.67). February 28, 1821 (No. 153, $0.50). February 4, 1822 (No. 121, $0.99).

Payments for others in or generally for Titus Coburn's household: November 5, 1816 (No. 102, $0.50: "An order to William Johnson 3ᵈ [...] To cash paid black man at Titus Coburns"). February 3, 1817 (No. 146, $1.75: "An order to Jeremiah Abbot for Rye delivered [...] For [...] Titus Coburn").

Payments to Titus/Others for Jane or June Coburn: June 8, 1816 (No. 20, $5.00: "An order to Titus Coburn for supporting his daughter [Jane/June?] in part"; No. 21, $6.54: Dr. Nathaniel Swift for "June Coburn"). October 7, 1816 (No. 62, $2.08: Dr. Nathaniel Swift for "Jane Coburn").

Town of Andover, "Town Records, Tax Records 1823–1847" (untitled volume, title from microfilm target but actually treasurer records of payments for orders drawn by the overseers of the poor), n.p., ninth volume on GSU Microfilm Reel 878782.

Payments to Rose Coburn for supporting Phillis: May 5, 1823 (No. 10, $6.50). September 1, 1823 (No. 27, $6.50). February 23, 1824 (No. 93, $6.50). June 14, 1824 (No. 12, $6.50). September 19, 1824 (No. 22, $6.50). January 10, 1825 (No. 40, $6.50). August 23, 1825 (No. 11, $13.00). January 2, 1826 (No. 30, $13.00). July 3, 1826 (No. 16, $6.00). October 23, 1826 (No. 24, $13.00). February 19, 1827 (No. 56, $13.00). July 16, 1827 (No. 10, $8.50). February 25, 1828 (No. 58, $6.50).

Payments to Dr. Abiel Pearson for "medicine and attendance" for Phillis: October 20, 1823 (No. 37, $0.50). February 25, 1824 (No. 98, $1.09). February 19, 1827 (No. 57, $2.17: "Phebe Boos").

Payments to Dr. Nathaniel Swift for "medicine and attendance" for Phillis: February 19, 1827 (No. 63, $2.75). June 5, 1827 (No. 8, $2.26). August 20, 1827 (No. 12, $6.75). February 4, 1828 (No. 46, $3.57). March 10, 1828 (No. 3, $4.95: "Phillise Boose").

Payments for Rose Coburn's household: March 3, 1825 (No. 61, $4.00: Benjamin Jenkins [probably Benjamin, Jr., 1786–1835] "for wood deli[ver]ed sundry poor persons viz [...] Rose Coburn"). March 10, 1828 (No. 7, $13.81: William Jenkins [probably Benjamin, Jr.'s brother William, born 1795] "for wood deli[ver]ed Rose Coburn"). September 1, 1828 (No. 22, $15.28: Amos Abbot "for goodsi [goods] Deli[vere]d Phillis Boos"). February 2, 1829 (No. 40, $2.50: John L. Abbot: "for wood Deli[ver]ed [...] Phillis"). February 16, 1829 (No. 49, $2.00: Benjamin Jenkins "for wood Deli[ver]ed [...] Rose Coburn"). June 1, 1829 (No. 24, $2.00: David Holt "for wood delivered [...] Rosanna Coburn"). February 26, 1830 (No. 81, $4.12: Noah Abbot "for Supplies Granted the poor out of the [alms] house [...] Rose Coburn").

Payment for Coffin for Phillis: January 5, 1829 (No. 36, $3.00: "An order to Stephice [Stephen] Holt for a coffin for Phillis Wid[ow] of Boos").

[32] United States Census, *Population Schedules of the Fourth Census of the United States 1820*, 649 (Andover, aggregated data for 61 unnamed free persons of color). See ibid., iii, vi, about limited or no data for people of color in that census, with some names gathered separately for a few Essex County towns, but not for Andover.

[33] Titus Coburn, July 13, 1820 in Coburn and Coburn, RWPA. In the federal version of the 1820 application, "Phillis" was misread by the clerk who wrote "Chillin" in the federal copy, as was "Colley" in the original that was written as "Colby" in the federal copy. The 1820 document was copied by Ichabod Tucker, clerk of the Essex County Circuit Court of Common Pleas, Middle Circuit, who certified on July 17, 1820 that it was a true copy made from the original county court records. The original county court version of the 1820 application is Titus Coburn, RWPA, July 13, 1820, Essex County Circuit Court of Common Pleas for the Middle Circuit, Collection No. EC 43, Box 2, File 5 pension applications, "Collection of Essex County (Mass.) Court Records, 1628–1914," Phillips Library, Peabody Essex Museum, Rowley, Mass. The federal and county court versions were each written by different hands, and the federal version was a later copy. There are other inconsequential differences between the federal and county court versions of the July 13, 1820 application. *VRA*, Vol. 2, 573 ("Negroes," Titus Coburn death, May 5, 1821, age 81).

[34] For the specific citations, see chap. 4, note 31, Andover treasurer/overseers of the poor records, under Payments to Rose Coburn for supporting Phillis; under Payments to Dr. Nathaniel Swift for "medicine and attendance" for Phillis; and, under Payments for Rose Coburn's household.

[35] Town of Andover, *Annual Town Reports*, 1832, 1843, 1845–1847, 1851. (Rosanna and Colley as state paupers). For the specific entries for Phillis, see chap. 4, note 31, Andover treasurer/overseers of the poor records, under Payments to Dr. Abiel Pearson, and under Payments to Dr. Nathaniel Swift for "medicine and attendance" for Phillis. The financial records kept by Dr. Pearson, and those by David Gray while administrator of Pearson's estate, do not list Phillis or other members of her extended family, as the doctor's billings for his services to the poor were paid by the town, Taft Collection, Ms S 134, Sub-group I, Series A, David Gray, 1762–1844, folder 6, Accounts as administrator of estate of Abiel Pearson, M.D., 1827–1828; Sub-group III, Abiel Pearson, M.D., 1756–1827, ACHC.

[36] Colley died from "consumption" which could have been pulmonary tuberculosis or any other wasting disease; the symptoms may have appeared decades before her death in 1857. Colley lived with her mother her whole life. Conceivably, Colley may have had somatic or psychological developmental issues. However, her statement for her mother's pension application (albeit made in writing by another hand) was lucid and indicated she had access to her early childhood memories. Yet, in her will, Rose appointed her executor John Parnell to be Colley's trustee to manage Colley's financial affairs. Colley Hooper, August 8, 1854, in Coburn and Coburn, RWPA. Rose Coburn, Probate file papers, will, December 23, 1854. Colley Hooper, Death record, Town of Andover and State Vital Records.

[37] Town of Andover, "Town Records, Tax Records 1823–1847" (untitled volume, title from microfilm target but actually treasurer records of payments for orders drawn by the overseers of the poor), n.p., ninth volume on GSU Microfilm Reel 878782, January 5, 1829 (No. 36, $3.00: "coffin for Phillis Wid[ow] of Boos"). The treasurer intended the name to be "Stephen Holt". The coffin-maker must be the same man as "Stephen Holt 2^d" who on December 24, 1828, signed a house construction contract between the Tewksbury carpenter David Sherman and the prospective homeowner Benjamin R. Downes, Andover Preservation Commission, et al., *Andover Historic Preservation* webpage for 49 Red Spring Road, http://preservation.mhl .org/49-red-spring-rd, accessed August 22, 2017, quoting the document at the Southern Essex District Registry of Deeds, Book 252, pg. 234, recorded August 18, 1829.

[38] Anonymous, "Sketches of Octogenarians" (about Rose Coburn's family). The 1853 article said that Phillis "died about seventeen years ago" (about 1836), but that date was in error. Phillis probably died late 1828, and before January 5, 1829.

[39] Meltsner, *The Poorhouses of Massachusetts*, 124, indicated that an "inmates' cemetery" was on the ten-acre almshouse property sold as two parcels by the town to the American Woolen Company in 1921. Franklin, "Plan of Andover Town Farm" (1907), showed the location of the cemetery. Nancy Parker who died at the almshouse in 1825 was probably interred there. After the property was sold by the town, remains at the almshouse cemetery were exhumed and reinterred at Spring Grove Cemetery, Andover. Bessie Goldsmith, in her local news and history column called "Siftings" published on April 20, 1923, reported that 48 graves were disinterred up to that point. By May 11, 1923, the Andover newspaper reported that "The work of removing the bodies from the old town farm grave yard to the Spring Grove cemetery has been completed. One hundred and twenty-five bodies have been taken out of the old burying ground." Anonymous, "Local News Notes." I thank Heli Meltsner, Larry Murphy (Andover town clerk), Stephanie Aude (Memorial Hall Library, Andover), Alistair McBrien and Angela McBrien (ACHC) for assisting to locate Franklin's manuscript map of the almshouse property, which map is ACHC Accession No. 1990.015.144. Rather than her interment at the almshouse cemetery and reinterment at Spring Grove, it is possible that Phillis (and others of her extended family, except Rosanna and Colley buried at South Parish Cemetery) could be buried at another Andover or North Andover cemetery. Joan Patrakis reminded me that there is a section for African Americans at the Second or 1817 Burying Ground on Academy Road, Stevens, "The Old Burying Ground on Academy Road, North Andover," 15. Jane Cairns, "Andover Stories: Town Owes much more than Amusement to one-of-a-kind Bessie Goldsmith" and Patrakis, "Bessie [Goldsmith] Became a Town Legend," indicated that Goldsmith was the author of the "Siftings" column. Patrakis provided me Goldsmith's 1923 column, and shared her research note referring to Andover town clerk records of "Burial Removals 1921–1922" that cannot be located by the town clerk (Patrakis, emails, March 17 and 29, 2019; Andover town clerk Austin Simko, email, April 26, 2019).

Chapter 5 *Booso*

[1] Anonymous, "Sketches of Octogenarians" (about Rose Coburn's family); Anonymous, "Obituary" for Rosanna Coburn, n.p. [2] conveyed that "Booz was brought from the West Indies by Deacon Osgood". Abbott, "Historical Andover. No. 106. Africa to Andover," 3, referred to Booso as "Jubah brought from the West Indies, where he left a wife and four children and called Booz Chickering from his owner Sam Chickering. His wife was Phillis Frye". Abbott, "Historical Andover. No. 107. Africa to Andover.—(Concluded)," 3, again referred to him as "Jubah the West Indian". Note the additional vari-

ant rendering of Booso's earlier name as Jubah (phonetically the same as the ten-year-old child Juba). Abbott's sources for the precise information are unknown: "I have drawn from a great mass of gleaning [....] I have many details she [Bailey, *Historical Sketches of Andover*] had no time to gather up", "Historical Andover. No. 106. Africa to Andover," 3. For considerations of the trade of slaves to and from the West Indies to Massachusetts, and economic entanglements generally, see Bailey, "The Slave(ry) Trade and the Development of Capitalism in the United States: The Textile Industry in New England"; Desrochers, "Slave-for-Sale Advertisements and Slavery in Massachusetts"; Hardesty, *Unfreedom*; Kimball, "'What have we to do with slavery?': New Englanders and the Slave Economies of the West Indies"; Lewis, "Captives on the Move," and their cited sources.

² Hall, "Negro's Receiv'd from Barbados in the Year 1729," Hugh Hall account book, 1728–1733, 28, Hugh Hall Papers, 1709–1774, Ms. N-1352, Massachusetts Historical Society, Boston. I thank Lise Breen for noticing this entry. It indicates that the person named Juba was sold to J. Kellog. The Osgood family name is not listed among those that Hall did business with, but among Hall's many contacts could be an Andover connection to Osgood. Many of Hall's "Negro's" were transferred outside the Massachusetts Bay Colony to avoid duties, but others on Hall's list included slaves "he did not buy or sell", Hardesty, *Unfreedom*, 21, and others were apparently sold within the colony. Again, the Juba in Hall's account book may not be Booso. Booso was in Andover by 1755 (*VRA*, Vol. 2, 356, 358), but other slaves could have come to town from when Andover men traveled to the West Indies 1760–1761. According to Bailey, *Historical Sketches of Andover*, 273, "Capt. Peter Parker, of Andover, was in an expedition to Cape Breton [Nova Scotia], 1760, in Colonel Bagley's regiment, [...when] the vessel in which the company set sail for home was blown by storms to the West Indies, and did not reach home till 1761." The obviously dubious story may instead have been cover for a trading adventure.

³ Hanks, *Dictionary of American Family Names*, Vol. 1, 194, s.v. "Boos", "Boose", and "Booz". The latter is suggested as a Dutch variant of Boos, a nickname derived from Middle High German *boese*, "low-standing servant." But "Boso" is "from a Germanic personal name derived from a pejorative nickname meaning 'leader', 'nobleman', or 'arrogant person'", ibid., 194, 201.

⁴ Anonymous, "Obituary" for Rosanna Coburn; Anonymous, "Sketches of Octogenarians" (about Rose Coburn's family); Putnam, *A Genealogy of the Descendants of John, Christopher and William Osgood*, 19–20 (Deacon John Osgood, Hannah Osgood, and Samuel Chickering, Sr. and Jr.); *VRA*, Vol. 2, 356, 358 (Marriages, "Negroes," Boassee/Bussen and Moriah), 573 (Deaths,

"Negroes," Hepzabeth Boose at the almshouse, age 40). Charlotte Helen Abbott, "Historical Andover. No. 106. Africa to Andover," 3, referred to a bridge that crossed the Shawsheen River "called Boise's Bridge from a negro Boise about whom I could glean no more." (Quintal, *Patriots of Color*, 108 n4 quoted that same phrase and attributed the source of the information to "recollections of T.C. Frye", citing to Charlotte Helen Abbott's "Andover [MA] Families Notes. Manuscript at Andover [MA] Historical Society," 106–124, 422 [Quintal, ibid., 10, brackets in original; he abbreviated the source as "ABB2"].) In that first article, Abbott credited the family historian Theophilus C. Frye (1819–1907) for telling her that the location of the bridge was near where Caesar Frye lived "down in the Moose country," as that area in the West Parish was called, Bailey, *Historical Sketches of Andover*, 602. In her next article, Abbott, "Historical Andover. No. 107. Africa to Andover.—(Concluded)," 3, she supplemented with, "I will add to my item about Boise alias Bowser, that he was found to be, with wife Maria, of the household of Samuel Chickering, Jr." Boise/Bowser ("with wife *Maria*") could be another man, or the same as Booso, the Boassee/Bussen who married *Moriah*, emphasis added. For the information in her 1901 articles about Boise and the location of the bridge, Abbott may or may not have also relied on Robert H. Tewksbury's 1878 essay, "Lawrence," 237, but Tewksbury also indicated that Caesar Frye lived "in the same locality" of the bridge. Tewksbury—who may have heard independently the same historical information as Abbott did from Lawrence resident T.C. Frye—further provided that "Old Boise was a full-blooded African, who spent his years of final freedom in South Lawrence [formerly Andover]. The bridge over the old ferry-road crossing the Shawsheen was known as 'Boise's Bridge.'" Abbott was fond of relating colorful anecdotes, and I expect that if she had used Tewksbury's chapter as a source, she would have alluded to the story that Tewksbury conveyed about Boise's rage remembering "his capture by slavers; and, drawing a huge knife, would make furious attacks upon the trees, thus taking revenge upon an imaginary foe." The Andover treasurer and/or town meeting records may have notations about construction and maintenance of Boise's Bridge. For African-derived naming practices, see Handler and Jacoby, "Slave Names and Naming in Barbados"; Sachs, "'Freedom By A Judgment,'" 179 n13, 195 n71; Whiting, "'Endearing Ties,'" 117–120, and their sources cited. The attribution to Booso of the names "Benjamin" and "Booz Chickering" may be examples of attempts to retrospectively regularize his name. For that practice, see O'Toole, *If Jane Should Want to be Sold*, 96–99, 131.

[5] Booso's freedom suit (Booso v. Samuel Chickering, Essex County Court of Common Pleas Records, July 1778, 476, JA) ended in Booso's favor because, as in several freedom suits, the defendant failed to appear (defaulted). Other

Andover freedom suits were referred for arbitration, all of which resulted in freedom for the plaintiffs. Booso's case against Chickering was heard in the same July 1778 term of court as Prince v. Thomas Osgood (Essex County Court of Common Pleas Records, July 1778, 476, JA), with the same result for both Andover men recorded on the same page of the court records. The record for *Booso* appeared immediately after *Prince*, and together were the next-to-last identified Andover freedom suits. The last identified Andover freedom suit was Rose v. Joseph Osgood (Essex County Court of Common Pleas Records, May 1779, 507, JA). The defendant defaulted and the court ordered that "Rose recover against the said Joseph her Liberty & that the said Rose be no longer held in servitude by the said Joseph."

In all, nine suits for liberty dating 1769–1779 that involved people living in Andover have been identified. Assuredly there were more freedom lawsuits not yet found in Massachusetts judicial archives, so absolute numbers and meaningful statistics for Andover cannot be derived at present.

The first two freedom suit cases known to be brought by enslaved people in Andover directly involved eight people from that town: any one of the direct participants in the paired cases of *Peter* and *Kate* (1769) could have been the original source of legal information learned by other enslaved people and their allies in Andover of that legal avenue to emancipation. The case of Peter v. Moody Bridges (Essex County Court of Common Pleas Records, September 1769, 448, with the docket entries and the case file papers, JA) and the case of Kate v. Moody Bridges (Essex County Court of Common Pleas Records, September 1769, 449, with the docket entries and the case file papers, JA) appeared sequentially in the court docket and in the records of decisions, and the file papers also indicate that the cases were resolved concurrently.

Peter and Kate were brother and sister. Their mother was "Dido Indian Woman Servant to Mr S. Martin". She was admitted a member of the North Parish church between July 30, 1749 and February 4, 1750, Andover North Parish Church, "The Names of those, that were Communicants in the church at Andover, in the year 1686 and as such as have been since Admitted to full Communion," in "Andover North Parish Church Records 1686–1810 Communicants 1686–1810 Baptisms 1719–1810 Church Meetings 1692–1810 Marriages 1687–1807" (title from microfilm target, bound volume of printed photoreproductions of microfilmed manuscript records, n.p. but with microfilm frame numbers), NAHS Microfilm Frame 7245, NAHS. Dido had been characterized as "a mulatto" in the "Negroes" section of the *VRA*, Vol. 2, 356, 357, marriage with Abraham, October 31, 1744; both were servants of James Bridges. Dido's different characterizations as "mulatto" then "Indian" discloses how racialization suited purposes of commerce, in this regard the difference of enslaveability of Native people and people of African descent. See Greene, *The Negro in Colonial New England*, 126, 294, 322, who conveyed that the maternally rendered legal status was based in "custom and tradition" (126) not statutory law, and that children of "Indian women [...] were legally free" (294). Newell, *Brethren by Nature*, esp. 54, 167–168, emphasized the "legal vagueness" (306) of the "heritability of slave status for children of all enslaved persons" (54) in Massachusetts and in other New England colonies. Newell, "The Changing Nature of Indian Slavery," 126, 135 n41, 129 (quotation), concluded that legal reforms enacted in Massachusetts to protect Indians from enslavement (because of debt, for example) "failed to prevent the continuing enslavement of Native Americans." Dido's and her children's presence demonstrably challenges notions of Indian disappearance in historical Andover, as do records of several other "Indians" in historical Andover.

The cases of *Peter* and *Kate* were referred to arbitrators who granted Peter and Kate their liberty on the basis that they were freeborn. After winning her lawsuit against Moody Bridges in 1769, Kate stayed on as his servant. *VRA*, Vol. 2 (Marriages, "Negroes"), 358: "Kate [servant of Mr. Moody Bridges. int.], and Pompey [late servant of Mr. Henry Phelps. int.], free negroes, Jan. 15, 1772. [Jan. 16. CR1]" (brackets in original; "int." and "CR1" indicated the sources of the information in, respectively, the town clerk's records of marriage intentions, and in the North Parish Congregational Church records of marriages). The absence of the modifier "late" to the word "servant" for Kate but its use for Pompey in their marriage intention record suggests that Kate remained a servant of Bridges after she won her freedom. The term "late" appeared in other marriage records to indicate "former"; the notation that both were "free" persons when they married indicated Pompey was a former slave to Phelps. Whether Kate was paid for her labor or had some other remunerative arrangement with Bridges is undetermined. Similarly, after prevailing in his freedom suit in 1777, the formerly enslaved Andover man Timon entered into a two-year indenture with his former Andover owner Peter Osgood, Jr. (1744 or 1745–1801), Timon v. Peter Osgood, Jr., Essex County Court of Common Pleas Records, September 1777, 447, with the file papers, indenture dated October 3, 1777, JA.

To conceive why a former slave would remain with a former master, consider VanderVelde, *Redemption Songs*, 5: some chose "accommodation, perhaps with some slight improvement of their situation." And consider Berry, *The Price for Their Pound of Flesh*, 6: in adapting to enslavement or in setting their laboring rates as free persons, people "negotiated certain levels of commodification to survive". Elderly and feeble slaves with no family or savings had practical reasons to refuse emancipation: shelter, heat, food, and medical care. Relative socioeconomic, political, and legal power and powerlessness, facets of accommodated dispossession and self possession (Berry's "spirit or soul value" as "self worth"), and the conditional nature of freedom for people of color in historical Massachusetts are retrospectively obvious. Hardesty, *Unfreedom*, 2 and passim, encouraged the consideration of "the continuum of unfreedom" and dependence in social structure and legal parameters, particularly in labor relationships, with chattel slavery one of a number of possible situations. In Kate's consideration, however, there was a personal reason for remaining at Moody Bridges' household. Her mother Dido had come to live there as well. On June 28, 1771, an Andover doctor made an entry in his day book charging Moody Bridges for visiting Dido who had "extream pain in the abdomen" for which he bled her and prescribed medicine, Osgood and Osgood, Day Books, n.p., Vol. 1, October 8, 1770, https://iiif.lib.harvard.edu/manifests/view/drs:424481266$50i, digital image seq. 50, accessed October 16, 2019.

Timon v. Osgood was the 1777 case that legal historian William E. Nelson highlighted as an example of "a case in which the Essex County Court of Common Pleas held, as a matter of law, that a man could not be restrained of his liberty on the ground of his being a Negro slave", Nelson, *Americanization of the Common Law*, 101 (quotation), 228 n163 (the fancy stylized initial letter *T* of the plaintiff's name written in the manuscript court records was misread as an *S*, and Nelson referred to the case as "Simon v. Osgood"). The slaveholder's rote answer to being sued by his purported property—that the plaintiff was "his own proper Negro slave"—was not sufficient as a technical matter of law: the only correct formal response was to say, simply, "not guilty" (Nelson, ibid., 72–73). In *Timon*, however, the defendant's intentionally wrong response by Osgood's attorney William Pynchon—accompanied by a long and elaborate answer—was "sham pleading" (a knowingly wrong answer, Nelson, ibid., 16, 73) only made as part of a prenegotiated settlement to allow the plaintiff to prevail so that the court action would end. Nelson, ibid., 228 n163, noted that Timon's attorney, Theophilus Parsons, made the expected objection (demurrer) to Pynchon's deliberately wrong answer. Timon prevailed in his action by court order, not jury, because the technical issue of (deliberate and knowing) bad pleading was only a matter of law for the judges to decide. The damages and court costs that the court awarded Timon were *remitted* to Osgood.

What the court record, docket, and file papers together disclose is a crafty legal strategy by Theophilus Parsons to secure Timon's freedom from Osgood that limited costs and time for everyone. (Parsons successfully applied that strategy in other freedom suit cases, as well.) Timon essentially purchased his liberty from Osgood at the lesser price of his own attorney's fee and paying his own and Osgood's court costs. With Parsons' participation as a negotiator, Timon transformed his laboring arrangement with Osgood from slavery to a paid indenture for a set term. The final document in the file papers (October 3, 1777) is an indenture agreement for a term of two years between Osgood and Timon "a free negro who hath no Master", which provided that Timon would receive £6 and a suit of clothes.

Investigating the biographies of the people involved in these freedom suits, before and after the cases, assists to understand motivations and strategic timing. VanderVelde, ibid., 4–6, 199, recognized that the decision to finally bring a freedom suit was not impulsive, but involved balancing alternative outcomes including financial exposure and "risks of retaliation" (ibid., 4). Each filing of a freedom suit was ultimately impelled by a "triggering action" (ibid., 4). Some lawsuits were abandoned by plaintiffs because some chose "accommodation, perhaps with some slight improvement of their situation" (ibid., 5), or because some choose survival over freedom, or because of attorney or client issues. In the Chesapeake area, Banks, "Dangerous Woman," 821 and n122 with sources cited, recognized that "many servants understandably were reluctant to sue for their freedom," fearing retaliation if they lost their case.

The case file papers for *Timon* include an earlier document that fills in Timon's biography and discloses motivating circumstances that prompted his lawsuit. The bill of sale for Timon, who was purchased by Osgood from Thomas Chadwick (1751–1831) of Boxford, called a "Traider" (i.e., trader, merchant), was dated June 4, 1776. The bill of sale indicated that Timon had fled from Chadwick: "which s^d servant [Timon] is now absent & the s^d. Osgood is to take him wherever he can find him". The 1776 bill of sale underestimated (perhaps deliberately) Timon's age by about 8 years. Timon had left Chadwick, possibly to Newbury. At the time of his lawsuit, Timon was married, probably: when he was still a servant to Chadwick in Boxford, he and Phillis, a servant of Capt. Joseph Hale of Newbury, published a marriage intention on April 6 or 7, 1769, cf. *Vital Records of Newbury*, Vol. 2, 531 (Marriages, "Negroes," "Tymon", April 6) and *Vital Records of Boxford*, 219 (Marriages, "Negroes," "Simon", April 7). Timon and Phillis had a son named after his father, who was baptized on May 31, 1778 at the Byfield Parish Church in Newbury, *Vital Records of Newbury*, Vol. 1, 568 (Births, "Negroes").

Timon used the surname Freeman and sometimes used the surname Chadwick. Joan Patrakis (emails, March 7–9, 2019) asked me if there might be a sibling relationship between Timon Chadwick and Dinah Chadwick, but I have found no documentary support for such relationship, only supposing that Timon used the surname Chadwick because at one time he was enslaved by Thomas Chadwick (the dissipated son of Deacon Thomas Chadwick who had enslaved Dinah), [Deacon] Thomas Chadwick, Probate file papers (will 1786, "my Negro Woman, Named Dina" manumitted 1788); Thomas Chadwick, Probate file papers (Bradstreet Tyler, April 18, 1820, guardian of Thomas Chadwick, "a person given to excessive drinking and idleness"). The Andover "Negroe woman" named Catherine Timan may have been the daughter of Timon Chadwick/Freeman, Timan v. Fields (Case No. 19, December 4, 1797), and, Simpson v. Timan (Case No. 26, April 9, 1798), in Nathaniel Lovejoy, "Processes of Confessions," 1797–1800 (Justice of the Peace Records, Andover, Mass.), n.p., Collection No. EC 43, Box 6, File 4, "Collection of Essex County (Mass.) Court Records, 1628–1914," Phillips Library, Peabody Essex Museum, Rowley, Mass.

The published *Vital Records of Boxford*, 108 (Births, "Negroes"), indicated that Timon was baptized May 13, 1744 and seems to have been enslaved by the Rev. John Cushing (1709–1772) who indicated that Timon was "My Negro Child". Perley, *The History of Boxford*, 158, was more certain: "The Rev. John Cushing had a small negro-boy named Timon." Timon married Flora Dole on November 15, 1779 in Andover, and with his new wife moved to Boxford by November 5, 1788, where he and Flora lived out their lives, Perley, "The Dwellings of Boxford," 71; *VRA*, Vol. 2, 357 (Marriages, "Negroes," "Timan Chadwick" and Flora Dole were "residents in Andover"). Timon Chadwick/Freeman appeared in several entries in the Andover Drs. Osgood's day books, charged for visits to Boxford and medicine, Osgood and Osgood, Day Books, n.p., Vol. 2, February 9, 1789, https://iiif.lib.harvard.edu/manifests/view/drs:424481342$50i, digital seq. 50; Vol. 2, February 16, 1789, https://iiif.lib.harvard.edu/manifests/view/drs:424481342$51i, seq. 51; Vol. 2, May 29, 1790 ("Timon Freeman of Boxford"), https://iiif.lib.harvard.edu/manifests/view/drs:424481342$120i, seq. 120; Vol. 2, August 2, 1791 ("Timan a Man of Colour near Boxford Meeting [^]House[^]"), https://iiif.lib.harvard.edu/manifests/view/drs:424481342$181i, seq. 181; Vol. 3, June 4, 1794, https://iiif.lib.harvard.edu/manifests/view/drs:424481566$37i, seq. 37, accessed October 19, 2019. Timon Freeman died May 2, 1804, 68 years old, *Vital Records of Boxford*, 274 (Deaths, "Negroes") contra Perley, ibid. (July 10, 1805 at age 84).

The 1769 cases of *Peter* and *Kate* were the earliest yet-identified Andover cases that potentially spread word among enslaved people and their allies of that legal route to emancipation. Any of the Andover people directly involved in the several suits for liberty could have been vectors of legal information. Overheard talk was another source of information that was repeated and passed around. Andover resident Salem Poor was the appellee-plaintiff's witness at the appeal of the freedom suit of Caesar (of Andover) against Samuel Taylor (heard first at Essex County Court of Common Pleas September 1771, and in appeal as Taylor v. Caesar at the Superior Court of Judicature, Essex County, November 1771, continued to June 1772; SFC, File #132190 [Deposition of Salem Poor, and bill of cost for seven days attendance], JA). At that appellate trial, Salem Poor testified to the truth of Moses Hart's account of a heated conversation between Caesar and Taylor, which Salem also heard, while they were "Standing by the Door of the Court House" at Newburyport in September 1771. The reason that Salem Poor was at the Newburyport courthouse that day was for his fiancée's freedom suit decided at the same term of court as Caesar's lower court case (Nancy v. James Parker, Jr. and Dinah Parker, Essex County Court of Common Pleas Records, September 1771, 147, JA).

Salem Poor was a likely transmitter of legal information about emancipation in Andover, having had several occasions to learn about legal process. Salem Poor had purchased his freedom in 1769, and a legal manumission paper was drawn up by his owner John Poor, Jr. (1718–1811), Manumission paper of Salem Poor, July 10, 1769, MSS 0.569, Salem Poor Collection, Phillips Library, Peabody Essex Museum, Rowley, Mass., and copy recorded February 12, 1772, Book 130, pg. 21, Southern Essex District Registry of Deeds, Salem, Mass. He was directly familiar with the courtroom setting and legal process through his fiancée's freedom suit with legal activities occurring from at least May through December 1771. The December term of court at Salem, Mass., where Nancy's second action against James Parker, Jr. was decided, was not adjourned until March 31, 1772. Salem Poor's 1769 manumission paper was finally recorded in the Registry of Deeds on February 12, 1772—three months after his marriage to Nancy, conceivably at his wife's insistence, and probably during one of the several trips to Salem, Mass. (and Newburyport) that they (possibly she alone at times) made for her two lawsuits against the Parkers. As Salem Poor helped Nancy to arrange financing for her two legal actions in 1771, she could have contributed earlier to Salem's manumission payment in 1769 and/or the fee for recording his proof of freedom in the county records in 1772. While waiting to testify for Caesar in Samuel Taylor's appeal, Salem Poor attended Superior Court for seven days, watching and listening to performative ritualized speech and actions of learned attorneys and justices. For the interaction of speech events, performance, and courthouse architecture and its proxemics, see McNamara, *From Tavern to Courthouse* and St. George, "Massacred Language." McNamara provided detailed information about the Essex County courthouses and other public venues where Andover-related legal activities occurred.

Proficiency in social skills of attentive listening and observation, memory, self-regulated speech, "linguistic dexterity, cultural plasticity, and social agility" were advantageous traits for navigating and surviving the brutality of enslavement, as those abilities were strategic to leaving it, to assisting others to gain their contingent freedom, and during intersectional moments of disparate power, position, and authority. Lewis, "Fires of Discontent"; Morgan, "African Americans," 150 (quotation, quoting Berlin, *Many Thousands Gone*, 24).

Obtaining legal freedom was an empowering act that influenced others: the tool of the freedom suit was passed hand to hand by word of mouth. Andover may have been a locus of "legal consciousness" about freedom suits particularly but also about other legal and official matters. Scott Hancock, "'The Law Will Make You Smart,'" 7–11 (quotation at 7), wrote that "Legal beliefs are perceptions of how the law does or should work, perceptions based on personal experience, on information passed through the neighborhood, or by watching what happens to others who encounter the law." Streams and eddies of legal information flowed around Andover from the 1760s and into the nineteenth century too with land transfers, probate process, court activities, poor relief, banks, and other legal and bureaucratic encounters involving interactions with attorneys, justices of the peace and local magistrates, judges, town, county, and state clerks and other officials, federal census takers, and federal pension administrators.

Two volumes of Andover Justice of the Peace Nathaniel Lovejoy's records of decisions are preserved, dated 1787–1790 and 1797–1800. The later volume has records of decisions for two cases involving Andover people of color who brought civil actions called *processes of confession* (for which process, see Massachusetts Chapter 43 of the Acts of 1786 and Massachusetts Chapter 67 of the Acts of 1788, both titled "An Act for rendering processes in law less expensive"). The two actions were brought in a process of confession in a plea of the case (i.e., the writ called *trespass on the case* commonly used for promises not kept such as to pay a debt, or for indirect but consequential damages caused by negligence or nonfeasance). The particular issues in the cases were not detailed in the records of the hearings, which referred to the writs and notes on file (which are not preserved with the hearing records) but most likely the issues were in regard to debts not paid for goods or services. Catherine Timan v. Prince Fields, Case No. 19, December 4, 1797; and, Cesar Simpson v. Catherine Timan, Case No. 26, April 9, 1798, in Nathaniel Lovejoy, "Processes of Confessions," 1797–1800 (Justice of the Peace Records, Andover, Mass.), n.p., Collection No. EC 43, Box 6, File 4, "Collection of Essex County (Mass.) Court Records, 1628–1914," Phillips Library, Peabody Essex Museum, Rowley, Mass. In Timan v. Fields, Catherine Timan was identified as a spinster (unmarried), a "Negroe Woman" of Andover, and Fields was a laborer, a "Negroe Man" of Gloucester. Fields defaulted (did not appear) and Timan was awarded $50.28 in damages and $4.27 costs of suit. In Simpson v. Timan, Caesar Simpson (Dinah Simpson's husband) was identified as an Andover laborer, a "Negroe Man" and Timan was an Andover "Negroe Woman". Timan defaulted and Simpson was awarded $36.58 in damages and $2.58 costs of suit. Catherine Timan was possibly the daughter of Timon Chadwick/Freeman. Timon's 1777 negotiated freedom suit against Peter Osgood, Jr., and the processes of confession brought by Catherine Timan and by Caesar Simpson, were among many legal actions by Andover people of color that made legal knowledge familiar to many others.

I thank Jeanne Pickering for mentioning to me that she noticed Salem Poor's name in the Caesar v. Taylor case file papers (SFC, File #132190, JA), and for discussing with me the implications in relation to information gathering and information exchange by and among enslaved people and their allies. I guided Pickering during her initial research about Essex County freedom suits for her thesis, "Suing Slavery," and provided her my preliminary data of the so-far identified Essex County freedom suits—a comprehensive search of the JA has not been accomplished to identify and document all the Massachusetts freedom suits. Pickering has developed a website that provides sorted data on the participants and chronology of the identified Essex County freedom suits, http://northshoreslavery.com/freedomcases/index .php. Pickering, "Suing Slavery," and in conference and public presentations, considered precedential effects of decided legal issues (common law) in unpublished court decisions (in the tradition of, e.g., Nelson, *Americanization of the Common Law*, 101) that relied on the memories of attorneys and jurists. In particular and technical legal matters, case-after-case evolved the common law to make legal defense of slavery untenable. More broadly, and in the mode of the many modern historians cited by Pickering, ibid., who have paradigmatically shifted causative focus and emphasis to determined individuals, their allies, and communities, Pickering was interested in finely tracing the sociological effects of freedom suits and other emancipative efforts that synergistically fostered individual and community knowledge ("consciousness") about antislavery, how that changed hearts and minds, and how that impelled further actions to permit slavery's slow demise in Massachusetts. Again, even among those opposed to enslavement, equality and economic justice was not necessarily embraced (Warren, *New England Bound*, 237: "antislavery sentiment did not imply an inclusionary worldview").

[6] Nelson, *Americanization of the Common Law*, 101–102, 264 (s.v. "jurisdiction", i.e., the types of matters courts were variously authorized to hear). For the evolution of the ordinary rules of jurisdiction of the courts, see Hindus,

"A Guide to the Court Records of Early Massachusetts." In fact, courts of General Sessions of the Peace decided civil matters when doing so "conserved the peace." Hendrik Hartog, "The Public Law of a County Court," 282, 283 (quotation), 285, 317, conveyed the statutory vagueness of the jurisdiction of the General Sessions courts and noted many examples of civil cases that they heard, although their purpose was hearing lesser criminal cases, referrals from local magistrates, and conducting county administrative matters. So too, there are freedom suit cases where that issue of improper jurisdiction was raised by defense counsel effectively. Another point here is that the appearance of several freedom suits in the General Sessions courts of Essex, Middlesex, Suffolk, and Bristol counties advises searching for more cases in the General Sessions records, dockets, and file papers.

Familiarity with the statutory and "common law rules of jurisdiction, pleading, and procedure" along with the special definitions and intentions of legal vocabulary—understanding that formalized phrasing may include boldly fictive assertions, purposely, as a mere formality, merely to fit the issue with the form and requirements of the legal action—is critical to understand the contents and purposes of preserved historical legal documents, Nelson, "Court Records as Sources for Historical Writing," 502. Close reading of legal records of the freedom suits indicate that rules were rules except when they weren't. If no one timely objected to technical errors—such as, e.g., improper jurisdiction or venue; not adhering to precise terms, forms, and processes inherent to ancient writs of action (pleadings); the defendant bringing appeal after defaulting, etc.—then the matter stood: but even that principle had exceptions, as issues that were not preserved or that had been adequately litigated previously were raised again on appeal. The trend was away from formality and toward the merits and substance of the injustice, "as long as the forum was a fair and convenient one," Nelson, *Americanization of the Common Law*, Chapter 5, 78 (quotation, specifically regarding venue, i.e., proper location where a matter ought to be heard, ordinarily the county where the tort or dispute occurred), 188 n34 (for fictional venues invoked).

Propaedeutic information conveyed here (in the main text and among these endnotes) was derived from my unpublished research summaries of, so-far, 69 Massachusetts freedom suits dating 1660–1784. The Essex County Common Pleas and General Sessions freedom suit cases presently identified date from 1722 to 1782. Two earlier cases, 1660 and circa 1672, were heard in the predecessor county quarterly courts or by a local magistrate. My unpublished compilation also includes other legal actions that were characterized by others as freedom suits, but upon further review they do not appear to me to be suits for liberty. The summaries I compiled and continue to revise are of cases cited by others, and while looking for those, records of more cases

I happened to notice. A comprehensive search of the JA to identify and record all the freedom suit documents would be a major contribution toward understanding judicial abolition in Massachusetts.

7 The first of the two earliest Essex County cases involved Mall, an Indian girl from Nantucket put in involuntary servitude in Newbury, John Bishop v. John Hathorne and Edward Richards (In re Mall Indian) (caption created for referencing purposes), Essex County Quarterly Court Records, Ipswich, September 25, 1660, 89 (No. 16) and file papers, JA. Mall had escaped to Lynn, where local men physically defended her and attempted to protect her when Bishop and another Newbury man arrived to repossess her. While the case did not involve a slave-for-life, her attorney-advocate John Hathorne (1641–1717, later a judge, but the nephew of the Lynn tavern-keeper of the "ordinary" where Mall took refuge) attempted to free her by arguing significant, general issues. In effect, Hathorne tried to turn her master's case against Mall and the Lynn men into a freedom suit.

Hathorne's arguments to the court on behalf of Mall provide insight to the evolving legal positions of Native and African people in colonial Massachusetts: "[T]he law is undeniable that the indian may have the same distribusion of Justice with our selves: ther[e] is as I humbly conseive not the same argument as amongst the negroes for the light of the gospell is a begineing to appear amongst them—that is the indians." Hathorne further argued to the court that Mall was a minor (about 16 years old, a "legal infant" under English law, who could not make an indenture contract on her own) and her mother did not grant consent for the arrangement either: "I should thinke it a hard measure to have the same don[e] to any child of mine : by our law here established". Hathorne challenged the hearsay nature of statements made in evidence, the unreliability of translation between Massachusett (Wampanoag) and English, and the legality of the indenture, which supposedly was for five years, then if she wished to continue, for another five years. Hathorne emphasized that even if the purported verbal agreement for her servitude was accepted, its terms let Mall decide if she "liked" the situation with Bishop, which she did not. Mall was "extremely discontent to live with John bishop now there is some reason for it : for she was so when she came first to my house" and both Harry—the Nantucket Indian middleman who arranged the indenture through Thomas Macy—and Bishop "much commooton her". Hathorne asked that the court "would not forse [force] her to live ther[e]" with Bishop. Hathorne argued, finally, that even if Mall had agreed to serve for five years, which she denied, she did not like it. It defied "comon sence" to make her serve five years and only then decide if she "liked" the situation enough to serve five more years (Bishop v. Hathorne and Richards, quotations from *Records and Files of the Quarterly Courts of Essex County*, Vol. 2,

240–242, reference to which published abstracts were placed in references cited under Bishop v. Hathorne and Richards; in text quoted from the published abstracts, I substituted *u* for *v*). Ultimately Hathorne failed to secure Mall's freedom from an unhappy situation of involuntary servitude, which the court allowed to continue without setting an endpoint. The case is exemplary of uncertain arrangements of servitude in which vulnerable children of Native and African ancestry were placed in English households without a written contract of indenture that specified expectations and duration. The lack of formal agreement resulted in the distinct prospect of free people of color becoming slaves in fact and law, as considered by Newell, "Indian Slavery in Colonial New England," 34–35. I am grateful to Margaret Ellen Newell, *Brethren by Nature*, 126–127, 281 n60, for bringing Mall's case to my attention. For the circumstances which most likely figured in Mall's indenture, of Indian indebtedness on Nantucket and elsewhere that led to debt peonage, involuntary servitude, and "judicial enslavement," and for legislative attempts to reform the indenture system for Indians and others, see also Newell, "The Changing Nature of Indian Slavery"; Silverman, "The Impact of Indentured Servitude on the Society and Culture of Southern New England Indians"; Vickers, "The First Whalemen of Nantucket"; and, Vickers, "Credit and Misunderstanding."

The second of the two early cases from what became Essex County was brought by James Indian, a man from Virginia enslaved in Salisbury, Mass. (at the time located within the old county of Norfolk). The case, captioned here for referencing convenience as James Indian v. George Carr, was noted in Newell, *Brethren by Nature*, 203–204, 293 n45. It was first heard prior to March 1672 in an old Norfolk County Quarterly Court of which no record was preserved, but James obtained his freedom at the lower court. His purported owner appealed to the Court of Assistants in Boston, and James responded, seemingly through an attorney who has not been identified.

The case is known only by a single, poignant document: "James Indian⁵ answere to his Mʳ: Carrs reasons of Appeale To bee Delivered to mʳ Rawson Sect:[Secretary] to be pʳ[e]sented to yᵉ Court of Assistants yᵉ 5 : March : 1671/2," Ayer MS 446, Edward E. Ayer Manuscript Collection, Newberry Library, Chicago, Ill. (Elizabeth Bouvier, Head of Archives of the JA, and I both searched extensively and we could find no other documentation for that case. The records and files of the old Norfolk/Essex County courts are incompletely preserved and fragmentary. Hindus, "A Guide to the Court Records of Early Massachusetts," 534; Historical Records Survey, *Inventory of the County Archives of Massachusetts*, 92.) The document was witnessed by two Salisbury men, William Bradbury (1649–1678) and Samuel Ffellows (circa 1619–1698).

In dispute was the 1649 bill of sale for James from William Hilton to George Carr that was not recorded until 1670. Carr's purchase of James was in exchange for Hilton receiving "y^c q^{r}ter vessell", interpreted to be a quarter share in a ship. It bears the mark of "James y^c Indian" and stated that he "doth manifest his consent" for his sale. In his 1672 answer to Carr's appeal, James said that he did not understand the terms of the bill of sale that he put his mark to, and expressed that Hilton and Carr coerced or deceived him to do so. James contested that he was legally enslaved under the terms of the 1641 Body of Liberties for captives taken in "just" wars and those who sold themselves, Newell, ibid., 204. How and when James came to be taken as a slave in Virginia, and if he ever returned to his homelands, is unknown. While Carr averred that James was a war captive, James asserted he was "brought away by allurem^{ts}" (allurements). Sachs, "'Freedom By A Judgment,'" 181 n20, 183 (quotation), 184, summarized that "Virginians' approach to Indian slavery changed many times during the seventeenth century." Virginia passed a law in 1670 that made Indian slavery illegal, only to legalize it in 1682.

The bill of sale for James from William Hilton to George Carr (dated December 29, 1649) was recorded December 24, 1670, Old Norfolk County Deeds, Book 2, pg. 197, Southern Essex District Registry of Deeds, Salem, Mass. Transcriptions or quotations of portions of the disputed 1649 bill of sale have appeared in numerous publications, e.g., Coffin, *A Sketch of the History of Newbury*, 337; Elliott, "Slavery in New England," 180–181; Hassam, "Hilton," 333; Merrill, *History of Amesbury*, 41–42; and, Perley, "Essex County in the Abolition of Slavery," Vol. 1, No. 1, 2. Historical biographies of George Carr (circa 1613–1682) and William Hilton (1617–1675) are many, and the 1649 bill of sale was quoted in those works. Marilynne K. Roach, *Six Women of Salem*, 42–61, 68, provided in her biographical summary that Carr (involved in shipbuilding and boat repair at Salisbury) also "owned a wharf in Boston" and with Simon Bradstreet and Richard Saltonstall, Esq. (1610–1694) owned a part of a ship, ibid., 43. Both Carr and Hilton had trade with the West Indies. Hilton plied the eastern seaboard, and it was during Hilton's adventures that James was taken captive, Crapo, *Certain Comeovers*, Vol. 2, 529–540 (at 538, for Carr "shipping oak staves to the West Indies"); Lowell, "The Ancient Ferry Ways of the Merrimack" (Carr's businesses); Pickett, *Captain William Hilton and the Founding of Hilton Head Island* (Carr's and Hilton's business activities; at 35, the bill of sale was quoted).

It was probably James who was referred to as "y^c Indian" by George Carr's 16-year-old servant James Ffreese (Ffreeze, Freese) in a September 1657 case heard by the Court of Assistants about the culpability of Robert (Robbin) Quimby (Quenby/Quinby) (circa 1623–1677) in the April 17th drowning of Henry (Harry) Horrell at Salisbury. Quimby, a ship carpenter, and

Horrell, a servant of John Lewis (Lewes), had been drinking on Lewis' ship anchored near Carr's Island in the Merrimack River. Quimby and Horrell took a skiff from the ship to the adjoining Ram Island where Horrell either slipped or was "thrust" into the river. To no avail that day, Lewis, Quimby, Carr, Ffreese, and "yᵉ Indian" searched around Ram Island and other places for Horrell, whose body was only found a month later. The grand jury did not find Quimby guilty of Horrell's death, but still expressed that "wee finde some suspition". Indeed, the circumstances were curious. On the day of the drowning, Quimby had not answered Lewis when asked "what business he had abord" Lewis' ship on that Sunday morning. But at court, Quimby testi-fied that Horrell "desiered mee uppon Satterday att night [...] to goe aboard wᵗʰ him to drinke a cup of strong waters, but he [Quimby] refused to go yᵗ night wheruppon he desiered mee to come aboard on yᵉ Sabboath day morn-ing to drinke a cupp & then they would goe to yᵉ [church] meeting togeth-er"; "they drunke about a pint of Strong Liqʳˢ" before leaving the ship in the skiff to go ashore together on Ram Island. Ffreese testified that Quimby told Carr that "Horrell went downe uppon his hands & knees into yᵉ water, & yᵉ said Quenby said, prithie Harry come ashoare good Harry come a shoare, & said yᵉ sd Harry told him [Quimby] he would come a shoare again." Ffreese added, mysteriously, that "he saw Quenby pull off his gloves, when hee cam ashoare uppon his masters Iland". When Quimby was asked about Ffreese's testimony, he "denied that hee had any gloves" and "denyed that ever he sd Horril went downe on his hands & knees into the water as also that he ever spake to Horrill Good Harry come out of yᵉ water and Horrils answer that he would come out againe, wᶜʰ are both testifyed by James Freese and affirmed to be true by George Car[r]".

If Horrell's drowning had been an accident merely, Quimby's reported behavior and statements were inconsistent (and there are further anomalous details in Lewis' and Ffreese's depositions that are not conveyed here). Qui-mby was concealing what else happened between himself and Horrell on Ram Island. There was a desire by Horrell for Quimby's companionship, but whether Horrell's desire was platonic only, what Quimby desired or expect-ed, and what else was said and occurred between them on Lewis' ship and then on Ram Island, can only be conjectured.

While the records of the Court of Assistants are not preserved for Qui-mby's case (editorially captioned as Presentment of Robert Quimby for the death of Henry Horrell, Court of Assistants, Boston, September 2, 1657), transcriptions of several of the case file papers are in Cronin, *Records of the Court of Assistants of the Colony of the Massachusetts Bay 1630–1692*, Vol. 3, 63–66 (*u* substituted for *v* in the quotations from the printed transcriptions). Two of the original file papers are in SFC, File #271, JA. A third original file paper (not included in Cronin, ibid.) is in SFC, File #26696, JA: it is the bill of costs from the Salisbury constable for transporting Quimby, as a prisoner, to Ipswich, which Quimby was ordered to pay. Additional original file papers (transcribed by Cronin, ibid., 64–66) are MS Ch.E.10.114 in the Chamberlain Collection at the Boston Public Library Rare Books and Manuscripts Department, Boston, Mass., which is presently under renovation and closed to researchers until well into 2021, Sean Casey and Jay Moschella, emails, November 15, 18, 2019. File papers indicated that it was John Lewis who brought this case as a complaint against Robert Quimby, first to a constable and a magistrate (commissioner) in Salisbury, who referred it to officials in Ipswich, who in April 1657 then referred the complaint to the grand jury at the Court of Assistants at Boston which decided the matter in September 1657. Names were spelled variously in documents: Car/Carr/Carre, Ffreese/Ffreeze/Freese, Harry/Henry, Horell/Horrell/Horril/Horrill, Lewes/Lewis, Quenby/Quimby/Quinby, and Robert/Robbin.

I thank Margaret Ellen Newell, Lisa Schoblasky and Lauren VanNest of Newberry Library who facilitated access to digital images of the 1672 "James Indian" document, and Jeffrey Glover for collegial correspondence and information sharing about that freedom suit case and the related archive of the Quimby case. Glover provided me the image of the recorded bill of sale and encouraged that James was probably the "Indian" mentioned in the 1657 Quimby case. Roach, ibid., 43–44, 68, also seemed to surmise that James and the Indian mentioned in the 1657 case was probably the same person. Sean Casey and Jay Moschella at the Boston Public Library researched and confirmed that file papers are preserved there, and provided images of the catalog cards.

[8] The documentary evidence in judicial and attorney archives for the Massachusetts freedom suits, and complementary documentary evidence about the individuals and their allies involved in those cases, show that slave owners and their attorneys eventually came to realize that slavery in Massachusetts had become legally indefensible, and that the time, travel, and costs of mounting defense or pursuing appeal were fiscally imprudent and unpragmatic. Edgar J. McManus, *Black Bondage in the North*, 163–164, noticed that "many [...] freedom suits went virtually undefended. [...M]asters frequently rid themselves of troublesome, litigious slaves by turning freedom suits into manumissions by legal default." Once free, the former owner had no obligation to support them. On that point, McManus, ibid., 163, quoted Massachusetts Supreme Judicial Court Chief Justice Theophilus Parsons in Winchendon v. Hatfield (4 Mass. Reports 123 [March 1808], at 128): "The defence of the master was faintly made for such was the temper of the times, that a restless,

discontented slave was worth little; and when his freedom was obtained, in a course of legal proceedings, the master was not holden for his future support, if he became poor." Parsons had significant experience as plaintiff's counsel in Essex County freedom suits. Case records in which Parsons appeared as counsel disclose technical finesse in his knowledge of pleading and practice, and effective negotiation skills to settle cases that limited costs and achieved legal freedom for his enslaved clients. Likewise, Parsons craftily resolved a matter for a slave owner that Parsons represented in an appeal. That latter case involved Parson's representation of Joshua Wyman in Silas Royal v. Joshua Wyman (captioned on appeal as "Wyman vs Royall"), Superior Court of Judicature Records, Middlesex County, October 1778, 42, JA; see pleadings for that case by Parsons in SFC, File #148316, JA. In that matter Parsons used a prenegotiated strategy to deliberately lose by sham pleading; Royal received a symbolic one penny for damages but no court costs from Wyman. Thus, Wyman needed to only cover his costs.

The General Sessions court case of 1722 was about Priscilla ("a Freeborn New England Native", born in Hartford, Conn.), married to Jupiter ("a Negro"), who complained that she and her two children had been sold as slaves, Priscilla and Jupiter v. Nathan Simmons and Jonathan Chadwick (caption created for referencing purposes), Essex County Court of General Sessions of the Peace Records, March 27, 1722, 65 (Ipswich); August 1, 1722, 77 (Salem); September 25, 1722, 83 (Newbury), JA. At the first court session, March 27, 1722, 65, the court issued an interim protective order not to remove Priscilla and her children from the court's venue: "in ye mean time ye s^d Woman + her s^d Children be not disposed off either by Indenture or Otherwise unless for some short time in Bradford or some place adjacent within ye County of Essex from Day to Day week to week Month to Month so as to have them forth coming at ye Court". While the March hearing stated three children were involved (and rendered Chadwick's name as "Chadduck"), the record of the September hearing indicated two children. At the last session, September 25, 1722, 83, the court decided that the "Deed of Conveyance" between Simmons and Chadwick was "illegal", and that Priscilla and her children "have y^r [their] Liberty & Freedom". While Simmons indicated his intention to appeal and made sureties, there is no record of an appeal of the case in the records of the Superior Court terms of October 1722 through October 1724, and no entries were found in the SFC indices. In the conventions used in the General Sessions court records, Priscilla's case was not formally captioned. As a married woman, Priscilla was subject to the rules of coverture, and a married woman ordinarily came into court by her husband, Nelson, *Americanization of the Common Law*, 103. The court records suggest, however, that Priscilla took the lead in this matter and so I listed her first in the created case caption; the case file papers might disclose what role Jupiter had in this case. I thank John Hannigan for locating two entries for this case in the General Sessions court records, and for determining that file papers for those terms of the General Sessions court are preserved but require conservation treatment before they can be viewed. This case was noted by Blanck, *Tyrannicide*, 178 n70; Cross, "Slavery in Essex County," 73 (who adapted and modernized quotations from the court records); Greene, *The Negro in Colonial New England*, 165 ("1772" was a typographic error for 1722, and 165 n111 misstated that it was Chadwick rather than Simmons who intended to appeal); Hill, "Slavery and Its Aftermath in Beverly, Massachusetts," 120 n35 (the year of the case "(1865)" was a typographic error); Moore, *Notes on the History of Slavery in Massachusetts*, 21 n1; and, Towner, *A Good Master Well Served*, 186–187 n66.

9 Carter Jackson, *Force and Freedom*; Egerton, "Slave Resistance," 455–456 (quotations); Frey, *Water from the Rock*, 48 (quotation, "a major form of resistance), 51 (quotations, "the shape and degree"; "prerevolutionary"; "ideology, strategy, and meaning"); Hardesty, *Unfreedom*, Chapters 2 and 3; Hardesty, "Social Networks and Social Worlds," 234 (quotation, "hierarchy, deference, and dependence"); Konig, "The Long Road to *Dred Scott*," 55 (quotation). For the recognition of the upsurge of freedom suits during the revolutionary era in Massachusetts, see especially Blanck, "Seventeen Eighty-Three"; Blanck, "The Legal Emancipations of Leander and Caesar"; Blanck, *Tyrannicide*; and, Breen, "Making History."

10 McNamara, *From Tavern to Courthouse* and St. George, "Massacred Language" conveyed the settings, scenes, and actions of court proceedings.

11 Legal documents prepared during this time ordinarily included "legal fictions." Nelson, "Court Records as Sources for Historical Writing," 505–506. These formalistic assertions that only appear to be specific biographical facts were understood by the involved legal professionals as merely necessary technicalities, and no one objected to the fictive statements. Law professor Nancy Knauer's phrase, "the legal detritus of formalism" captured the conventional phrasing and assertions in historical legal documents that only posed as legal facts, as part of formal legal claims, Knauer, "Legal Fictions and Juristic Truth," 82. Historian and law professor David Thomas Konig considered the treatment of legal fictions by legal historians, and addressed the history of "[t]he artful use, and willing acceptance, of sham pleadings," including "[L]egal fictions [...that] made no innate sense outside the artificial reason of the law." "[T]he common law allowed facts to be contrived to fit the rule; known to all concerned as 'fictions,' they were legal and thereby accepted by the court." Konig, "Legal Fictions and the Rule(s) of Law," 99 (quotation), 102, 105 (quotation), 105 n21, 107 (quotation).

Legal fictions were required in order for the court to accept jurisdiction over a private, non-criminal dispute, and for the legal action to be maintained, so that a citizen might obtain justice in a public, regulated venue for a private and personal wrong. One recurring example in civil suits for liberty was the merely formulaic assertion that the purportedly wrongly enslaved person had been taken with "force and arms," that they were detained from a particular date to the present time, and that it disturbed the king's (later the public's) peace. That wording was required as a technical matter in slavery cases sued on a writ of trespass vi et armis (personal trespass with force and arms, alleging assault, battery, kidnapping, illegal detention). Abstractly, the legal reasoning was this: because one of the monarch's free subjects claimed to have been forcefully trespassed upon and held against their will, and that condition of wrongful detainment persisted, and the realm's peace was thereby disturbed, the king's court would then surely be keen to hear that matter. In actuality, slaves were purchased and they may not have known or remembered the date decades later when they finally brought suit against their purported owner; the enslaved person was brought to their new owner's place perhaps initially shackled but at some time unfettered and not constantly under threat of club, sword, or gun for the duration of their enslavement; few were particularly disturbed by yet another slave being purchased and put to labor; certainly the king was not aware of that particular enslaved person's predicament; and, by the date of the lawsuit, some formerly enslaved people not yet legally free had already walked away and were no longer being detained, but desired a judicial declaration of their liberty.

There has been mistaken assumption that freedom suits were about seeking back wages for past labor. Cotter, "The Somerset Case and the Abolition of Slavery in England," 40–41, provided corrective information to Wiecek, "Somerset," 115, as had Moore, *Notes on the History of Slavery in Massachusetts*, 112 n1. Massachusetts freedom suits were suits for liberty. They were not suits of quantum meruit ("as much as deserved" for back wages or services when the amount due was not specified by contract). There were two exceptional cases so-far identified, described immediately below in this endnote, one that achieved freedom for a person who was awarded court costs but not the back wages she sued for, and the other that supposedly established freedom for another person who was the subject of the action but not a party to the case. As in all civil actions, court costs were awarded to the winning party. Additionally, money damages to compensate for the claimed torts were awarded to winning plaintiffs in some civil actions. Depending on the technical writ used to bring a lawsuit, money damages may or may not have been allowed by established rules, but such rules were not rigidly and consistently applied either. There were many civil actions when the money owned for court costs and/or damages were seemingly never paid. Several freedom suits were brought on variations of ancient writs de homine replegiando (personal replevin) and de libertate probanda (to prove freedom). Both actions usually required the plaintiff to post a bond. The former ordered the sheriff to take custody of the plaintiff until judgment and the latter usually came with a protective order against removal of the plaintiff from the court's venue while the case was pending. Both forms of action provided a winning plaintiff their court costs but usually not also money damages. Most of the Massachusetts freedom suits were brought to court on a plea of trespass vi et armis, which provided both money damages and court costs and was a less-convoluted process. When money was sought it was not for back wages, but for damages for the tort of having been assaulted and wrongfully enslaved, and for court costs to bring and prosecute the legal actions. Cotter, ibid., quoted Lord Mansfield specifically on that point, and as also framed by Nelson, *Americanization of the Common Law*, 54–55, quantum meruit was inapplicable to slaves because they were laborers for no pay. There was no reasonable expectation that wages were promised slaves, so none were due. On that point and also about the supposed effect of Somerset to prompt Massachusetts freedom suits, Wiecek, ibid., 115, relied on Belknap, "Queries Respecting the Slavery and Emancipation of Negroes in Massachusetts," 202. Belknap was mistaken that freedom suits sought "recompense for their service" in slavery, and mistaken that the first freedom suit was brought "in 1770". The misunderstanding that appeared in Belknap's 1795 writing that suits for liberty were suits for back wages has persisted. Nevertheless, the unlikely idea that legally free former slaves could use courts to get paid wages for their unpaid slave labor (no such suits that achieved payment for back wages are yet known) was on the minds of the Massachusetts populace. One petition for emancipation, published in *The Massachusetts Spy* on July 29, 1773 and reprinted in Twombly, "Black Resistance to Slavery in Massachusetts," 45–47 (quotation at 46), sought to allay that issue: "We are not insensible, that if we should be liberated, and allowed by law to demand pay for our past services, our masters and their families would by that means be greatly damnified, if not ruined: But we claim no rigid justice".

There were at least two exceptional cases in venues other than Essex County, one in Plymouth County that fictively or not involved wages promised to a once-enslaved person that only won her freedom, and the other in Nantucket County about wages claimed by the supposed owner of a once-enslaved person that purportedly established freedom for that former slave. In the Plymouth County case, attorney David Johnson creatively used a form of action predicated on wages due an ostensibly free laborer that legally established the plaintiff's freedom. Hagar Hill v. Elijah Hayward (Plymouth

County Court of Common Pleas Records, July 1773, 53, JA; Nelson, *Americanization of the Common Law*, 199 n48) was sued on trespass on the case about wages promised. Hayward countered that Hill was his slave for life. The jury decision arrived at the substantive issue only to find that Hill was a free woman and awarded her court costs. The back wages she ostensibly sued for were not mentioned in the decision. The amount of Hill's court costs was not tabulated, and that part of the decision was left unwritten in the court record. While Hayward posted bond to appeal, he never prosecuted that action at the Superior Court of Judicature. There was no indication that an execution of judgment was issued against Hayward for Hill's court costs, which Hayward may or may not have ever paid, and no case was found of any subsequent action by attorney Johnson to get Hill or Hayward to recompense him for his legal work. Thus, it seems only that Hill v. Hayward resulted in freedom for the plaintiff. She did not get her back wages and she and her attorney may never have been recompensed for the costs of bringing her legal action. In the Nantucket County case, money earned by and paid to a whaleman was claimed by that man's supposed owner that only according to local tradition resulted in emancipation for the once-enslaved laboring man who was not a party to the lawsuit. John Swain v. Elisha Folger (Nantucket County Court of Common Pleas Records, October 1773, 297; Superior Court of Judicature Records, Suffolk County, August 1774, 238; SFC, File #102427, all at JA) was also sued on trespass on the case on promises for the value of shares from a whaling voyage that had been earned and paid directly to Prince Boston (1750–?) who Swain claimed to be his "Negro Servant man". The jury found for the defendant, narrowly that Folger never promised to pay Boston's earnings to Swain. While Swain appealed the decision to the Superior Court of Judicature sitting at Boston where Nantucket County cases were heard, Swain did not prosecute his action, judgment was made against him, and the court issued an execution to recover Folger's court costs. While not evident in the judicial documentation, local tradition insists that the case established Prince Boston's freedom. Locally focused historical writers, some of whom apparently did not review the original case records and file papers, misstated dates and involved parties and discerned far more about that case than the archival records and general historical facts indicate.

[12]   Recent and developing scholarship deemphasizes agency and intentionality involved in suing for liberty, accentuates the small number of known freedom suits in comparison to other modes of emancipation that by numbers alone were more effective, and focuses on the particular and limited effect of these private legal actions that only freed the plaintiffs. This countervailing perspective may arise from perceptions that in the modern historiography of

emancipation, the import of freedom suits has been overemphasized. Historian Manisha Sinha, in her book *The Slave's Cause*, 2, which highlighted resistance as "central to abolition", also noticed this historiographic reversion. In a counterpoise, Sinha, ibid., 2, 67, provocatively asserted that while "[r]ecent historians have declared black resistance to enslavement passé," "[i]n New England, where slaves possessed certain judicial and civil rights, including the right to sue their masters for freedom, African Americans initiated and enforced emancipation. [...] [B]lack activism was necessary to make freedom a reality." Perhaps more broadly, this counterswing in interpretive emphasis on degrees of agency is in response to perceptions that too much verve had been ascribed to enslaved individuals and that their "small triumphs of agency" may not have been so momentous.

Peter A. Coclanis' candid assessment of decades of "slavery/agency studies" found most to be "imbalanced, partial (in more than one sense of the word), lacking in formal rigor, and lacking even more in historical empathy and imagination," the latter particularly but not only involving empathy toward slave masters and mistresses who "creat[ed...] a stable and economically vital regime (however morally repugnant from our standpoint) that was sufficiently flexible, portable, and recapitulative to have lasted in the South for at least a century and a half." Coclanis, "The Captivity of a Generation," 551, 554. Coclanis, 544, 551, used the "(not very) peculiar," transgressive situation of southern plantation slavery (Ira Berlin's "slave society") as an exemplary, theoretical foil to contrast the "small triumphs of agency" achieved by enslaved persons.

While the economic significance of slavery in New England (Berlin's "society with slaves") and its destabilization following the Revolutionary War has been established (for which, see, e.g., Bailyn, "Slavery and Population Growth in Colonial New England," 254–255; Melish, *Disowning Slavery*, 7–8, 15–18; Newell, "The Birth of New England in the Atlantic Economy," 60; Richardson, "Slavery, Trade, and Economic Growth in Eighteenth-Century New England"; Rockman, "The Unfree Origins of American Capitalism"; Whiting, "'Endearing Ties'"), I am uncertain about whether and for whom the South's economy was "stable" and "vital". Mindful of severe class inequities in both regions that disproportionately affected health and well being, which should provoke empathy, I suggest that what is being contrasted are matters of import at different scales of view. What people of different times consider to be significant, sustaining, or affirming is obviously reflected and embodied in the forms of *created* and *applied* history, e.g., Berlin, "American Slavery in History and Memory and the Search for Social Justice"; Hancock, "'Tradition Informs Us'"; and, Hancock, "From 'No Country' to 'Our Country!'"

Enthusiastic historians of slavery and emancipation in their particular studies necessarily highlight different modes of resistance and agency, be they violence, riots, rebellions, military service, lawsuits, petitions, bills, fiery oration, persuasive literature, etc. Emily Blanck, "The Legal Emancipations of Leander and Caesar," 244, for example, contrasted the locus of power involved in manumissions effected by a willing slave owner through "wills, indentures and self-purchase," with the freedom obtained by lawsuits whereby "slaves ended their own enslavement" relying on the rule of law. Wroth and Zobel, *Legal Papers of John Adams*, Vol. 2, 49, emphasized that freedom suits were "an exceptionally sophisticated way of testing an issue which could have been determined either by force or by flight." David Thomas Konig, in "The Long Road to *Dred Scott*," 55, considered that while freedom suits "might arguably be seen, to be sure, as allowing the law to provide legitimacy for slavery by making a relatively insignificant concession to a statistically small number of successful petitioners," Konig emphasized that the transformative effects on thousands of individuals involved in any way in myriad freedom suits over hundreds of years are not to be dismissed so casually. At the microhistorical and individual scale that I am focused, it is evident to me that litigants, such as Nancy Parker, evinced financial and logistical planning, courage, exertion, and tenacity in bringing and prosecuting legal actions. Nancy returned to court a second time to sue James Parker, Jr. again when he failed to pay what he owed her for her initial freedom suit (Nancy v. James Parker, Jr. and Dinah Parker, Essex County Court of Common Pleas Records, September 1771, 147; December 1771, 197, JA). As in Nancy Parker's case (not in her case, but in several other cases where the court awarded a symbolic one penny in "damages"), few winning plaintiffs got much money—at the end Nancy may have only lost hard-earned money in court and attorney fees and her travel costs. What they got, most importantly, was their *freedom* and that was no small achievement for them.

Historian Kendra Taira Field, in the review essay "The Violence of Family Formation," 256, intriguingly proposed that microhistory "may offer a viable" dialectic to navigate through argumentation about the power of agency and resistance on the one hand, and the power of states, institutions, or a cabal on the other: "enslaved (and freed) people's small stories and collective insights about their experiences can matter in big ways. Indeed, their voices can illuminate the political and economic structures that constrained their own lives, and, in turn, how they interpreted the meaning of freedom." Biography as microhistory, with its pursuits down narrow and winding pathways, with its simultaneous broad perspective of pertinent chorography and epoch, can be leveraged to discern how captive and constrained people obtained their degrees of liberties (their freedom *from*), what they did with it (their freedom *to*), and how they instituted change for themselves, for their allies, and for their adversaries too.

13 Field, "The Violence of Family Formation," 256. See also Ashcraft-Eason, "Freedom among African Women Servants and Slaves," 68; Whiting, "'Endearing Ties,'" 126–133; Whiting, "Power, Patriarchy, and Provision," and especially 585 n2, for alternative configurations of families, considering James H. Sweet, "Defying Social Death: The Multiple Configurations of African Slave Family in the Atlantic World." While her focus was in the post-bellum South, Tera W. Hunter, *Bound in Wedlock*, documented a continuum of relationship practices, arrangements, and commitments. Hunter, ibid., 7, adopted a heuristic of "marriage [...] to encompass committed conjugal relationships, whether legal or not, monogamous, bigamous, polygamous, or serial. Black heterosexual intimacy comprised a wide range of domestic arrangements out of necessity [and choice], not all of which were described as marriage."

14 Sarah Frye, Probate file papers, accounting and distribution, September 7, 1790 ("taken their Freedom").

15 United States Bureau of the Census, *Heads of Families at the First Census [...] 1790*, (Essex County, Andover), 64.

16 Juba (Jack), Titus, and Tory, were the youngest children listed as slaves in Sarah Frye's estate inventory, Sarah Frye, Probate file papers, inventory, May 1, 1781. In 1800, Rosanna and her daughter Colley Hooper were probably living in Wilmington, with Rosanna's husband Titus Coburn: he lived with six other people of color that year. United States Census, *Population Schedules of the Second Census of the United States 1800, Roll 14*, Essex County, Andover, 200; *Population Schedules of the Second Census of the United States 1800, Roll 17*, Middlesex County, Wilmington, 1079.

17 Anonymous, "Sketches of Octogenarians" (about Rose Coburn's family), n.p. [2] ("Booz" and Phillis' house); Anonymous, "Obituary" for Rosanna Coburn, n.p. [2] (same). Dorman's 1830 map, "A Plan of Andover," shows "D. Peters" on the southwest side of Salem Turnpike (now Turnpike Street, between Haverhill Street and Elm Street, in North Andover) in the vicinity of several properties of "J. Peters". The Andover Preservation Commission, et al., *Andover Historic Preservation* website identified a four-acre parcel owned by William Peters in the vicinity of what is presently 79–93 Haverhill Street with parts extending to 5–8 Liberty Street, but that location is at some distance from the present location of Salem Turnpike (Route 114). No entry in the grantee or grantor indexes for Essex Deeds was found for Booso, searching alternative spellings including the surname Bowes and Chickering.

Nancy Parker occupied land she did not own in Andover. In Concord, Mass., former slaves occupied agriculturally marginal land, Lemire, *Black Walden*, 10.

[18] Town of Andover, "Town Records, Treasurer's Records 1767–1874" (untitled volumes, title from microfilm target), n.p., GSU Microfilm Reel 878787.

[19] Ibid. Payments to reimburse Booso for Member while she stayed with his family were made on February 4, 1793 (Nos. 184 and 185), March 1, 1793 (No. 277), and on March 18, 1793 (No. 6). Interesting among other payment records was "An order to pay Martin Farnum for Schooling Members Child" (February 17, 1800, No. 177). In another volume, on a different microfilm reel, was a similar entry made a year earlier: "Paid one Dollar for Schooling Members Child", February 22, 1799 (unnumbered entry), Town of Andover, "Town Records, Tax Records 1799–1822" (untitled volume, title from microfilm target but actually treasurer records of payments for orders drawn by the overseers of the poor), n.p., first volume on GSU Microfilm Reel 878782. That volume contains many entries for Member's child. Rev. Bentley of Salem, *The Diary of William Bentley*, Vol. 3, 382, visited the "African school" in Andover on September 5, 1808. He described its location as "the bank of the S. [Shawsheen] river". Bentley found 36 students in attendance on the day of his visit, was told that full attendance of that school was 60 students, and commented, "We were pleased to find anything done for this race." For the numbers and percentages of children of color attending school 1850–1900, drawn from federal census data, see Martin, "On the Landscape for a Very, Very Long Time," 168–169.

"Member's Child" appeared on three manuscript lists of expenses for the poor, 1801–1803, seemingly prepared by Joshua Chandler (1758–1817) as an Andover overseer of the poor. Town of Andover, Overseers of the Poor, "An Account of the Expence of Supporting poor of Andover from the first of March 1801 to the first of March 1802" ("Members Child" $27.00, "Clothing & [^]Nursing[^] Doct[or] Bills"); "An account of the Expence of Persons Supported by the Town; also of Persons in part Supported Viz. from the first of March 1802 to the first of March 1803" ("Members Child" $27.24); and, "A List of Persons to be Let out for the present year Viz Expences for 1803 1802 1801" ("Members Child" 1803, $21.19), all in Joshua Chandler (1758–1817) Papers, Ms S 52, Sub-group I, Joshua (7) Chandler, Series C, Official Town Documents, Sub-series 2a–2c, Overseers of the Poor, ACHC.

Member was Remember Sawyer, the "illegitimate" child of Mariah Lamson of Haverhill. Member's daughter was Phillis Russell, who gave birth to Elizabeth West Russel, January 13, 1814, *VRA*, Vol. 1, 391 ("Negroes"). Abbott, "Historical Andover. No. 107. Africa to Andover.—(Concluded),"

3, appeared to link Phillis Russell to Bristow/Brister's family line, but the connection was uncertain. Abbott noted that Phillis Russell married Porter Richardson "called negro" and then wrote, mysteriously, that Phillis was "a dusky belle whose career I judge, from records, was an exception to the rule among these young maidens of servitude." Russell and Richardson's marriage intention is noted in *VRA*, Vol. 2, 286, 293 (January 3, 1820). An entry for the death of Phillice Sawyer, age 98 on April 29, 1828, who might have been a relative, is in *VRA*, Vol. 2, 540. Joan Patrakis (email, April 20, 2019) found the information about Remember Sawyer and Phillis Russell in a manuscript volume that she identified as the Andover Overseers Records 1815–1839 at the Andover town clerk's office, and found the entries for Elizabeth West Russel and Phillice Sawyer in the *VRA*.

For Member and the Dr. Kittredges, see *VRA*, Vol. 2, 574 (Deaths, "Negroes," "Remember, woman of colour at Dr. Kittredge's, June 8, 1825"); and, Bailey, *Historical Sketches of Andover*, 157–159, and index entries at 621 (s.v. "Kittredge") for the Dr. Kittredges and for a few of their very many "colored servants or slaves" (ibid., 159). See also the 1806 letter from Peter Kittredge to the Town of Medfield Selectmen, GLC #GLC01450.702, Gilder Lehrman Institute of American History, New York, N.Y. Peter Kittredge (circa 1750–?), of African ancestry, was enslaved by Dr. Thomas Kittredge in Andover. Carol Majahad and Inga Larson of the NAHS (email, July 7, 2017) conveyed that when Remember died "in 1825 there was only one doctor from the Kittredge family here in town and that was Joseph (1783–1847), son of [Dr.] Thomas [Kittredge] (1746–1818). [...] Thomas had an older son, John [1775–1822], who also became a doctor, he took up residence in Newburyport, while younger son Joseph took over the North Parish of Andover practice." Majahad and Larson suggested that Remember could have been enslaved by Dr. Thomas Kittredge, then became a servant of his son Joseph. Majahad and Larson directed me to Kittredge, *The Kittredge Family in America*, for more details about the family. Many in the family practiced medicine, including "Elezebith Kittredge 'the bone-setter'" born 1751 in what is now North Andover and who moved to Londonderry, N.H.; her father was Dr. John Kittredge (1709–1776), ibid., 15–16, 35 (quotation).

The "Cato Freeman" who boarded Member's child was most likely Cato Freeman of Andover (1768–1853). Bristow/Brister ("Bristol") was charged 7s. 1p. for a doctor's visit and medicine while he was at Cato's (presumably with his son-in-law and daughter, Cato and Lydia [Bristow] Freeman), Osgood and Osgood, Day Books, n.p., Vol. 3, April 18, 1795 (page headed April 15, 1795), https://iiif.lib.harvard.edu/manifests/view/drs:424481566$99i, digital image seq. 99, accessed October 19, 2019. (There was another same-

named man in town at least briefly in 1793: a marriage intention was recorded in Andover for Cato Freeman "of Newburyport" and Rose Parker on November 21, 1793, *VRA*, Vol. 2, "Negroes," 357, 359. They did not marry. The
Newburyport Cato Freeman married Sally Smith in that town on February
10, 1796, *Vital Records of Newburyport*, Vol. 2, "Negroes," 531, 533. "Rose
Parker" married Prince Walker in Andover in 1812, *VRA*, Vol. 2, "Negroes,"
358, 359.)

Entries in the Drs. Osgood's day books for Primus indicated he was being
cared for in Caesar's household, but which of the Andover Caesars was not
indicated. Primus had been enslaved by Maj. John Osgood, *VRA*, Vol. 2, 358
(in Marriages, listed under "Negroes" as "Primas"), and so was well-known to
the doctors. Doctor visits and medicine were charged to the Town of Andover,
Osgood and Osgood, Day Books, n.p., Vol. 2, April 29, 1789, "dld [delivered
to] Cesar for Primus [/] by order Mr James Barnard", https://iiif.lib.harvard
.edu/manifests/view/drs:424481342$60i, digital image seq. 60; Vol. 2, July
6, 1789, https://iiif.lib.harvard.edu/manifests/view/drs:424481342$69i,
seq. 69, and while Caesar was not named in that entry, Primus may have been
with Caesar's family. Subsequent entries in the day books indicate that Primus
boarded at Caesar's, Vol. 2, May 18, 1790 (medicine "for Primus [/] dld Cesars
Wife", https://iiif.lib.harvard.edu/manifests/view/drs:424481342$117i,
seq. 117; Vol. 2, May 26, 1790 for Primus "To Visit to him at Cesars", https://
iiif.lib.harvard.edu/manifests/view/drs:424481342$119i, seq. 119, accessed
October 19, 2019. Kunal M. Parker, "Making Blacks Foreigners," 110–111
(internal editing modified), quoted Andover selectmen who in January 1792
sought state reimbursement for "Primus Freeman a native of Ginne [Guin-
ea] who is not abel to Labour". The state legislative Committee on Accounts
disallowed that claim. Primus Freeman may have been the same or another
man, as so too with the Primus indicated to be "a servant of Mr. Benj[amin]
Stevens, jr.", *VRA*, Vol. 2, Deaths, "Negroes," 574 , July 25, 1792, age 72 years,
5 months, 16 days.

Dudley Dole (1776–1835, a man of color) was reimbursed by the town
for "taking care of Prince Walker Jr in his last sickness", Town of Andover,
"Town Records, Tax Records 1799–1822" (untitled volume, title from microfilm target but actually treasurer records of payments for orders drawn by
the overseers of the poor), n.p., first volume on GSU Microfilm Reel 878782,
April 23, 1816 (No. 12, $2.00).

The widow Nichols boarded in Bristow/Brister's household either intermittently or for the duration of a three-year term, 1788–1791. The fees for
doctor visits and medicine for her were charged to the Town of Andover when
she lived with his family, Osgood and Osgood, Day Books, n.p., Vol. 2, June 22,

1788, https://iiif.lib.harvard.edu/manifests/view/drs:424481342$22i, digital image seq. 22; Vol. 2, July 5, 1790, https://iiif.lib.harvard.edu/manifests/view/drs:424481342$128i, seq. 128; Vol. 2, September 2, 1791 ("Nickols"), https://iiif.lib.harvard.edu/manifests/view/drs:424481342$185i, seq. 185, accessed October 19, 2019. The *VRA*, Vol. 2, 250–251, 510, included entries for several women with that surname, spelled variously, who lived into the early nineteenth century. None of the entries in *VRA* for those women's marriages or deaths were placed under "Negroes," so Mrs. Nichols may not have been a person of color but she boarded with a family of color.

Laurel Daen, "'To Board & Nurse a Stranger,'" 3, 13, 16, observed that selecting poorer households to board the needy poor provided income to those households as it partly mitigated the overall town expenses for poor relief (16); that decisions to board people of color with people of color were based in ideologies about "gender, race, class, and capacity," (13 [quotation], 14, 18); and, that the chiefly "unrecognized and uncompensated work of women [...] allowed towns to absorb and attend to the poor ailing strangers in their midst" (3). Daen, ibid., 14, especially considered caretaking by people of color who boarded the poor or needy, and who were also hired laborers that "assisted paupers [boarded] in the homes of white townspeople". If the Widow Nichols was not a person of color, it is interesting that the town placed her with Bristow/Brister's household. Daen, ibid., 10, 13, 24 n23, 25 n29, included data drawn from Andover's 1791 request for state reimbursements for state paupers. Daen's more general conclusions are highly significant historical findings: that prior to the establishment of almshouses, and afterwards while the boarding out system for some paupers continued, the intimate degree of homecare provided chiefly by women to incapacitated people from different backgrounds and circumstances brought measures of familiarity with "strangers" (the broad term used then) that would diminish as institutionalization was adopted (12, 18). "[T]he deeply personal and physical nature of caregiving and receiving—which often occurred between people from different racial, ethnic, and social backgrounds and continued for periods of multiple years and even decades—suggest that the bounds of eighteenth-century Massachusetts communities were flexible and capacious" (3).

The only entry I noticed in the Drs. Osgood's day books for Booso ("Bosse Man of Colour") was under the page heading for January 21, 1793. A note in the margin for the entry ("March 30") was either the date of the visit or the date that Booso paid the bill that totaled 3s. 8p., Osgood and Osgood, Day Books, n.p., Vol. 2, January 21, 1793, https://iiif.lib.harvard.edu/manifests/view/drs:424481342$208i, digital image seq. 208, accessed October 16, 2019.

[20] Town of Andover, Overseers of the Poor, "An Account of the Expence of Supporting poor of Andover from the first of March 1801 to the first of March 1802"; "An account of the Expence of Persons Supported by the Town; also of Persons in part Supported Viz. from the first of March 1802 to the first of March 1803" ("Cesar Sibson"); and, "A List of Persons to be Let out for the present year Viz Expences for 1803 1802 1801" (Caesar Sibson absent), all in Joshua Chandler (1758–1817) Papers, Ms S 52, Sub-group I, Joshua (7) Chandler, Series C, Official Town Documents, Sub-series 2a–2c, Overseers of the Poor, ACHC.

When I previously researched the microfilmed volumes of manuscript town records, it was for a different related research project, searching and recording all entries for Nancy Parker and Salem Poor. During that time-consuming, focused effort, I noticed many fascinating and thus distracting entries for numerous other people of color, and I discerned the interesting practice of the town reimbursing men of color for boarding and providing other necessities and services for other people of color. The entries for other people of color in all the town's vast historical record series—vital, tax, selectmen, treasurer, overseers of the poor, town meeting, etc.—were so numerous that I only noted a few examples passim, only so that I could share them encouragingly with a colleague doing parallel research. For this monograph, I researched parts of two volumes of the microfilmed manuscript records of the Andover treasurer/overseers of the poor. That research foray was to determine whether or not Phillis was the unnamed "slave" at the almshouse in 1830 (she was not), and to gather more biographical information about her and the extended family. I was not able to undertake a complete search of the town records for Phillis and her extended family, but encourage another researcher to do so. A comprehensive search of the town records for all the entries regarding Phillis, Booso, other members of that extended family, and the many other people of color in historical Andover, should be undertaken to better understand their presence, movements, relationships, contributions, difficulties, and fates. Another researcher would be informationally rewarded to undertake a comprehensive research effort.

The Andover town clerk holds the historical town's original municipal records, only some of which were imaged during microfilming projects. The "Andover Infirmary Records" cited by Brown, "Black Lucy's Garden" (which may be the same as the "Andover Overseers Records 1815–1839" found by Joan Patrakis in the town clerk vaults) and the records of the Andover almshouse cemetery "Burial Removals 1921–1922" seen by Patrakis in the vaults, have eluded rediscovery (Patrakis, emails, March 17 and 29, and April 20, 2019; Andover town clerk Austin Simko, email, April 26, 2019). Obviously the historical town records embed rich documentary potential, with astonishingly detailed information about many people and many subjects. Pressing municipal concerns of public welfare for those in need in Andover are especially well-represented in Andover town records, in the records of other Massachusetts towns, in state records when Andover sought payment from them for supporting nonresident paupers who lived or died while in Andover, and in other public and private historical records.

There would appear to be rich information about Andover poor, including people of color, and there may be additional information about Phillis' extended family, in two related state archival series, Massachusetts General Court Committee on Accounts, Account Rolls, 1786–1862 (CO6/2268x) and Account Roll Submissions, 1786–1860 (CO6/9x), M-Ar. Finding aids to the related archival series include descriptions of the archival series; a box of photocopies of the itemized account rolls from the printed Massachusetts *Acts and Resolves* series that include the pauper accounts; as well as the analyzed tables and container lists included with the CO6 archival series finding aids that indicate what if any related and supplemental records are preserved for the printed accounts for state expenditures. Daen, "'To Board & Nurse a Stranger,'" 10, 13, 24 n23, 25 n29, related that there is detailed information about care of the poor in the 1791 Andover account roll submission, so a comprehensive search of that archival series is advisable. Occasionally, Andover also wrote to towns in Massachusetts and other states seeking reimbursement for caring for their people, and notations about or copies of that correspondence are in the town records, and are likely also preserved in historical records of other towns. Meltsner, *The Poorhouses of Massachusetts*, provided a guide to the development and evolution of the Andover institution with bibliographic references for her sources.

At the ACHC there is a research file, "Almshouse, Town Farm, Town Infirmary," and other research files on related subjects, on families, and for photographs. ACHC manuscript collections include official town records of the Andover overseers of the poor, treasurer, the "auditors" who prepared the earlier annual town reports, and other town offices. A list of ACHC manuscript collections titled "Town Records" was made for the ACHC manuscript collections guides and finding aids (prepared in the 1980s by Mary F. Morgan), which supplemented entries in the now-superseded card catalog for their printed and manuscript collections. Most of the overseers and treasurer records are in the Joshua Chandler (1758–1817) Papers (Ms S 52, Sub-group I, Series C, Sub-series 1–2) and in the Taft Collection (Ms S 134, Sub-group I, David Gray, 1762–1844, Series A, with accounts and information both as town official and for his personal business; Sub-group X, Series A and B). Other ACHC manuscript collections that include overseers and treasurer records are Ms S 2, Ms S 60, Ms S 63, Ms S 96, Ms 202, Ms 203, Ms S 467, and Ms S 512. The collection of earlier *Annual Town Reports* at ACHC span 1820–1851, and have been assigned Ms S 643, S 647, S 671 and Accession No. 1980.101.4, .17–.18; 1994.063.1–.6; 2019.105.1–.14, .16; and 2019.106.1 (multiple copies of the same issue were separately accessioned; within the same accession, the Accession No. for multiple copies of the same issue is suffixed with letters a, b, etc.). As she accomplished for the ACHC objects collections, Angela McBrien, ACHC collections manager, is undertaking a renewed effort to process and systematically catalog the ACHC manuscript collections. Andover historian Joan Patrakis has been assembling information in files about people of color in historical Andover, and those files are anticipated to be provided to the ACHC.

At Baker Library, Harvard Business School, Boston, Mass., there is the collection of the Samuel Abbot Business Papers, dating 1754–1819, with personal and business financial, legal, and correspondence records made and received by Samuel Abbot (1732–1812) when he lived in Boston and environs, and then when he returned to Andover where he was town treasurer. Abbot sold goods and supplies to the town almshouse and seemingly also lent money to the town. Abbot lent money and sold items to many people in exchange for promissory notes, labor, and their products (such as yarn or thread they made from wool and flax). His records detail interactions with an enormous number of people in and beyond Andover. That vast and well-organized manuscript collection has been digitally imaged. Carole Foster, who prepared the Samuel Abbot Business Papers finding aid with "enhanced description", helpfully and particularly noted information about enslaved and free people of color among the records that can be readily found by searching Foster's finding aid for "African", "black", "enslaved", "free", and "negro". Abbot purchased and sold several slaves, and hired enslaved and free people of color for day labor, outwork, and service, variously, when he was in Boston and in Andover. In his notations regarding people of color, Abbot regularly used common racialized terms and abbreviations including "Negro", "N", "Blackman", "Blkman", etc. Abbot's records note dealings with and information about several familiar and some previously unidentified people of color in Andover and elsewhere (in Abbot's records from his time in the Boston area) including Lucy Chandler/Foster, Pompey Lovejoy, Caesar and Dinah Simpson/Sibson, Peter Lovejoy, Primus Jacobs, Fortune Porter, Pomp Blackman, Meria Bigers, Joel Saunders, True Butler whose clothes were mended by a Mrs. Parker who may have been Nancy Parker, Corner Cobourn (i.e., Coburn) of Dracut, many unnamed people of color, and many with single names, Bartholomew, Black Peag, Bristol, Caesar/Cesar, Flora, Hambleton, January/Prince, Pertheney, and Scipio. Related entries, and separate papers that supplement entries, are among separate items and files in the collection. Embedded in the collection are social, economic, material, and technological data (such as notations about textile production, agriculture, culinary arts, etc.), with information that tracks locations and mobility: these records have significant analytic and interpretive potential.

Three volumes of day books kept from 1770 to 1796 by the Andover physicians Joseph Osgood (1719–1797) and his son George Osgood (1758–1823), curated at Boston Medical Library, Francis A. Countway Library of Medicine, Boston, Mass., have been digitally imaged, Osgood and Osgood, Day Books. The doctors resided in the North Parish and were deacons of the church there, Abbot, *History of Andover*, 83, 137–138, 150, 151; Bailey, *Historical Sketches of Andover*, 22, 331, 469. Manuscript entries in the day books encode information on geographic locations of patients, laborers, and other people with whom the Osgoods had accounts in Essex, Middlesex, and Suffolk counties. Entries for their patients included travel for visits, medical procedures, and abbreviated notations for dispensed medicines. (Clinical diagnoses were not indicated for patients. It is impossible to discern the maladies treated from the medicines that were dispensed. Pharmacological substances were employed in humoral medicine for a variety of purposes, and the Osgoods practiced "polypharmacy," prescribing multiple drugs at initial and follow-up visits, Estes, "Therapeutic Practice in Colonial New England," 292, 314.) There were entries that record labor in exchange for credit (farm work and textile production and processing) for and by the Osgoods. Labor was sometimes performed to pay medical bills, and some entries for the cost of medical treatments were intriguingly marked "void", seemingly indicating that those bills had been paid by labor, goods, or cash, but perhaps at other times indicating pro bono treatment. There were entries for supplies purchased or received (frequently medicines that were purchased, but also foodstuffs and other items) that were characteristically gathered under "stock" but also under individual names. In addition to the many entries about named and unnamed people of color—only some of which notations are cited among these endnotes, and I encourage others to search for more—there were entries under "Town of Andover" for treatment of named poor who were boarded in named households, and for visits to patients with other named doctors for consultation. The dated entries have genealogical information that may not be recorded elsewhere, such births, approximate dates of deaths ("late"), and family relationships of individuals (entries refer to mothers, wives, daughters, sons, uncle, cousin, etc.). As with Samuel Abbot's business papers, the Drs. Osgood's day books have important research potential for studying a range of subjects.

Chapter 6 Colley Hooper

[1] While Hooper was also used as a forename, there were many men with the surname Hooper in Essex and Middlesex counties. Pomp Hooper, if born about 1771, would have been about 14 to 15 in 1785–1786, when Rosanna became pregnant at about 17 to 23 years old, *VRA*, Vol. 2, Deaths, "Negroes," 574 (age 39 in 1810). Sarah Holt, August 31, 1854, in Coburn and Coburn, RWPA, said that her cousin, Abigail Downing, told her repeatedly that Rosanna was 21 years old when Colley was born.

[2] Colley Hooper, Death record, Town of Andover and State Vital Records, "Colley Hooper (colored)"; Andover North Parish Church, "Andover North Parish Church Records Minister's Book 1810–1850 [i.e., 1848–1937] Baptisms Admissions to Membership Marriages Deaths," 79 ("Collie Coburn Colored Woman age 70"). The Andover doctor who made the entry for visiting and treating the "Negro Garl Colle" at Sarah Frye's was probably Joseph Osgood. His son George Osgood worked with his father and continued making entries in the day books, Abbot, *History of Andover*, 137–138, 150, 151; Osgood and Osgood, Day Books, n.p., Vol. 1, October 8, 1770, https://iiif.lib.harvard.edu/manifests/view/drs:424481266$23i, digital image seq. 23, accessed October 16, 2019.

[3] Colley Hooper, August 8, 1854, in Coburn and Coburn, RWPA. Rose Coburn, Probate file papers, will, December 23, 1854. Colley Hooper, Death record, Town of Andover and State Vital Records.

[4] Colley Hooper, August 8, 1854, in Coburn and Coburn, RWPA.

[5] Town of Andover, "Town Records, Tax Records 1823–1847" (untitled volume, title from microfilm target but actually treasurer records of payments for orders drawn by the overseers of the poor), n.p., ninth volume on GSU Microfilm Reel 878782, January 5, 1829 (No. 36, $3.00: "coffin for Phillis Wid[ow] of Boos"). United States Census, *Population Schedules of the Fifth Census of the United States 1830, Roll 61*, Essex County, 181.

[6] Their signatures by mark appear on several original and copied documents: *Titus Coburn*, February 5, 1787 ("Titus Cober", payment request copied by Massachusetts Secretary of Commonwealth, September 14, 1854), April 8, 1818 (two documents), July 13, 1820 (twice), May 5, 1821 (will copied by Essex County register of probate, August 8, 1854); *Rosanna Coburn*, August 8, 1854 (three documents), April 17, 1855 (two documents); *Colley Hooper*, August 8, 1854, all in Coburn and Coburn, RWPA; *Titus Coburn*, July 18, 1818 (promissory note to Moses Wood) in Gurney and Packard v. Coburn, Essex County Circuit Court of Common Pleas for the Middle Circuit, March 1819, file papers, JA; *Titus Coburn*, July 13, 1820 (thrice) in Ti-

tus Coburn, RWPA, Essex County Circuit Court of Common Pleas for the Middle Circuit, Collection No. EC 43, Box 2, File 5, pension applications, "Collection of Essex County (Mass.) Court Records, 1628–1914," Phillips Library, Peabody Essex Museum, Rowley, Mass.; *Titus Coburn*, May 5, 1821 (copy of will), and *Rosanna Coburn*, August 8, 1854 (petition), both in Titus Coburn, Probate file papers; and, *Rose Coburn* will, December 23, 1854, in Rose Coburn, Probate file papers.

[7] Carpenter, et al., *Digital Archive of Massachusetts Anti-Slavery and Anti-Segregation Petitions*, "House Unpassed Legislation 1842, Docket 1153, SC1/series 230, Petition of Mary S. Jenkins" and 100 other women of Andover for repeal of marital antimiscegenation laws and all laws making distinction on color (specifying Commonwealth of Massachusetts, *The Revised Statutes*, Chapter 75, Sec. 5 [475] and Chapter 76, Sec. 1 [479]), https://doi:10.7910 /DVN/DHXWG, digital image seq. 16 ("Rosanna Coban" and "Colly Coban"), accessed August 15, 2017. The antimiscegenation marriage laws were repealed by Massachusetts Chapter 5 of the Acts of 1843. Kantrowitz, "Fighting Jim Crow in the Cradle of Liberty," 64, ascertained that after years of legislative opposition, passage of the repeal act had become less politically difficult. Governor Marcus Morton rhetorically separated the issues of marriage rights from radical abolitionism, Earle, "Marcus Morton and the Dilemma of Jacksonian Antislavery in Massachusetts," 79–80. Richard Archer, *Jim Crow North*, Chapter 9, summarized the legislative history. Moulton, *The Fight for Interracial Marriage Rights in Antebellum Massachusetts*, 187 n6, 226 n17, 228 n39, cited the 1842 Jenkins petition. Zaeske, *Signatures of Citizenship*, addressed Andover women's petitions to Congress.

Mary Saltmarsh Farnham Jenkins (1796–1891) was the wife of William Jenkins (1796–1878). The couple was deeply committed to abolition: their home was a meeting place for the town antislavery society and a stop on the Underground Railroad. She was the lead signatory on an 1872 petition for women's suffrage, Massachusetts House of Representatives, *Journal of the House of Representatives*, 234. For more on the Jenkins and their house as a stop on the Underground Railroad, and as hosts to Frederick Douglass, William Lloyd Garrison, George W. Latimer, and other famous activists, see Goldsmith, *The Townswoman's Andover*, 20–22; Greater Lawrence Underground Railroad Committee, *The Anti-Slavery Movement and the Underground Railroad in Andover & Greater Lawrence*; Mofford, "The Underground Railroad Ran Through Andover"; and, Patrakis, *Andover in the Civil War*, 19–20. Alice M. Hinton (1870–1951) avuncularly remembered the couple as "Uncle Bill and Aunt Mary" and related their actions as part of the Underground Railroad, Hinton, "Memory Pictures," 1. Daniel Carpenter and Colin D. Moore, "When Canvassers Became Activists"—in an exceptional analytic and interpretive study, contextualized in references to historiography about women's political activism in the nineteenth-century nation—located the effective "mechanisms" of petitioning that leveraged women's skills in education and moral suasion grounded in gendered norms and evangelical Christianity; in developed and expansive local social networks that fostered consciousness-raising about political issues; and, in skills of organizing and practical logistics. The experience and talents developed in antislavery and antidiscrimination petitioning were formative for activists about women's suffrage and other reform movements long after.

[8] Carpenter, et al., ibid., "Senate Unpassed Legislation 1842, Docket 11057, SC1/series 231, Petition of Fanny Downs" and 113 other women of Andover, to define rights that no distinction be made on Massachusetts railroad cars on account of color, https://doi:10.7910/DVN/PKDGY, digital image seq. 157 ("Colly Coban"), accessed August 15, 2017. Pryor, *Colored Travelers*, 175 n86, cited that petition. For background on the campaign against this issue in tandem with the effort to repeal the discriminatory marriage laws, see Ruchames, "Jim Crow Railroads in Massachusetts."

[9] Carpenter and Moore, "When Canvassers Became Activists," 482, 487, and their further discussion regarding writing names for others in their separately paginated appendix of supplementary material, 5–7. Richard Archer, *Jim Crow North*, 142–143, indicated that in 1839 the state legislature investigated the genuineness of signatures written by others on petitions from other towns to repeal the marital antimiscegenation laws.

[10] Titus Coburn, July 13, 1820 (Colley aged 27, thus born 1793); Rosanna Coburn, August 8, 1854 (Colley age 68, thus born 1786); Colley Hooper, August 8, 1854 (Colley age 68, thus born 1786); Joseph V. Allen, August 28, 1854 (Colley over 64 or 65 years old, thus born 1789 or 1790); Elizabeth Blanchard, September 1, 1854 (Colley age 5–6 in 1792, thus born 1786–1787); Sarah Holt, August 28 and 31, 1854 (Colley "as much as four" when Rosanna went to live with Titus; Colley 65–67 years old, thus born 1787–1789); all in Coburn and Coburn, RWPA. Massachusetts House of Representatives, RCEC, 16 (Colley aged 40, thus born 1805); Massachusetts Census, 1855 (Colley aged 69, thus born 1786); Colley Hooper, Death record (December 26, 1857, age 70 thus born 1787), Town of Andover and State Vital Records.

A possible birth record for Colley Hooper was noticed by Joan Patrakis (email, February 19, 2019); that information is problematic and poses further questions. Because the original text of that record is not preserved, and surmised transcriptions of the writing are contradictory, it is not possible to

conclude what the birth record actually indicated. In a book of original Andover birth records, a line of text was written at the bottom of a page, but that
area of the page is now lost (Andover town clerk Austin Simko, email, April
26, 2019). The line of text of interest here once appeared immediately below
an entry for Lydia Clark. The text was written over the descending parts of
letters of Clark's entry, further complicating its reading. Town of Andover,
"Town Records, Births, Marriages, Intentions, Deaths, 1701–1800" (title
from microfilm target; spine title is "Births, Marriages, Deaths and Intentions 1701–1800 Town of Andover"), 370, second volume on GSU Microfilm Reel 878780, digital image 195 of 266, https://www.familysearch.org
/ark:/61903/3:1:3QS7-L97M-YRSB?i=269&cc=2061550&cat=143281,
accessed February 19, 2019. That now-lost line was transcribed in *VRA*, Vol.
1, 388 ("Surnames Missing," brackets in original) as "–––, Colby Cooper, d.
[torn] and Polly, –––, [1791?]". The question mark in *VRA* conveyed that
the original entries on that and other nearby pages had been later fit and
interlineated into whatever small blank areas had been available, some entries written vertically, creating a palimpsest effect. The practice of the clerks
around that time was that information was added as it was brought to their
attention, and the clerks attempted to fit in the written information close to
its chronologically appropriate place on the page.

Prior to the loss of the bottom of the page with the original birth record,
a surmised transcription of that line of text had been copied into another
book of Andover birth records (but the information of that copied entry was
not included in *VRA*): "Colby Cooper daughter of Rosanna Sawyer", born on
July 20, 1791, Town of Andover, "Town Records, Births, 1649–1801" (title
from microfilm target; spine title is "Records Births [torn] –1801; title page
reads "Copy of an Ancient Record of Births in Andover Mass. commencing
at 1651. 1649."), n.p., third volume on GSU Microfilm Reel 878780, digital image 497 of 515, https://www.familysearch.org/ark:/61903/3:1:3QS7
-L97M-YR2G?i=496&cc=2061550&cat=143281, accessed February 19,
2019.

Despite the parallels in the names of Colby Cooper/Colley Hooper and
the mother's name of Rosanna, is that 1791 record actually about Colley
Hooper, who by most accounts was born about 1786? By her own testimony and that of Elizabeth Blanchard and Sarah Holt in Coburn and Coburn,
RWPA, Colley Hooper was between four and six years old in September
1792 when she was in Wilmington at her mother's wedding with Titus Coburn. Questions that cannot be resolved include: Was the 1791 year of birth
indicated in the original record another falsification of Colley's age? Did the
word "Cooper" appear in the original, and if so, was that an original error for
"Hooper"? Or, rather, did the original entry read "Hooper"? Is "Polly" a mis-

reading of the remaining upper parts of the letters of "Rosanna"? What about the name "Sawyer" never known to be used by Rosanna Coburn? Was that a misreading of the mother's surname? There is an entry in *VRA*, Vol. 2, 540 for the death of Phillice Sawyer on April 29, 1828, age 98. If Rosanna ever truly used "Sawyer", does that 1828 record relate to her mother Phillis? Or, was Phillice Sawyer a relative to Remember Sawyer (died 1825, *VRA*, Vol. 2, "Negroes") and Remember's daughter Phillis Russell (*VRA*, Vol. 1, 391, Births, "Negroes," Elizabeth West Russel, daughter of Phillis; Joan Patrakis, email, April 20, 2019, citing to Andover Overseers Records, 1815–1839, Andover town clerk's office)? Did the compilers of the *VRA* neglect to review the volume of copied records, and if so, are there additional vital records in that volume of copied records that were not included in *VRA*? Or, had the *VRA* editors discounted the surmised transcription in the copied records, and produced their own?

[11] Berry, *The Price for Their Pound of Flesh*, 6.

[12] Darlene Clark Hine, *Hine Sight*, xxviii (quotations), employed the concept of "dissemblance" to particularly confront "rape [...], domestic violence, [... and] economic oppression born of racism and sexism," 38. See also ibid., 41–43 on "secrecy." I am aware of sociological critiques of Hine's theoretical proposition, as was Hine who addressed them, ibid., xxix, 49–58. I suggest that "dissemblance" was employed in other situations to confront disparate power and authority, and that it implicated a gendered ideology of feminine modesty and mystery. For one influential consideration of the gendered problematic, see Sontag, "The Double Standard of Aging."

[13] Brown, "Death-Defying Testimony," for privacy, 131, that reflected "preservation in the face of [...] sociopolitical duress" in "home, intimacy, and knowledge of self and quality of life", 135.

[14] Consider Berry, *The Price for Their Pound of Flesh*, 6, for her poetic phrase "spirit or soul value" as "self worth".

Chapter 7 Titus Coburn

[1] Coburn, *History of Dracut*, 338–339, in the section about "Colored People" named Coburn, adopting the family name from their former owners who were numerous in Dracut, and Coburn, *Genealogy of the Descendants of Edward Colburn/Coburn*. I thank Harvey Whitcomb for the book reference. The Lew family, which famously included the Revolutionary War soldier Barzillai Lew [Sr.] (1743–1822) from Groton, Mass., settled in the Pawtucketville section of Dracut (now within the City of Lowell), Coburn, *History of Dracut*, 322, 332–336; Dorman, *Twenty Families of Color in Massachusetts*,

271–329; Mayo, "The Lew Family"; Morrison, "Negroes Who Fought at Bunker Hill." The soldier's son Barzillai Lew [Jr.] (1777–1861), who moved to Andover, was "well acquainted" with Titus and Rosanna Coburn, and was instrumental assisting Rosanna to navigate legal processes for her late husband's probate filing and for her federal application for the Revolutionary War widow's pension, Barzillai Lew [Jr.], August 8, 1854 in Titus Coburn, Probate file papers; Coburn and Coburn, RWPA.

Titus Coburn's birth year may be estimated from his pension application statements of April 8, 1818 that he was 62, and July 13, 1820 that he was 64 (born 1756), and from the *VRA* his probably erroneous age at death of 81 in 1821 (born 1740). An enlistment record stated he was 22 years old on July 25, 1779 (ignoring months by convention, born 1757). Coburn and Coburn, RWPA; Massachusetts Secretary of the Commonwealth, *Massachusetts Soldiers and Sailors of the Revolutionary War*, Vol. 3, 686 ("Cobin, Titus" enlisted July 25, 1779); *VRA*, Vol. 2, 573 (Deaths, "Negroes," Titus Coburn, May 5, 1821, age 81). Titus Coburn's original town death record reads, "Titus Coburn Negro aged Eighty one years", Town of Andover, "Births & Deaths from 1800 to May 1844 Andover, Mass." (spine title), n.p., third volume on GSU Microfilm Reel 767599, May 5, 1821. In that original record, the words "Eighty one" were added later and written in a different hand. In making entries around that time, the town clerk often wrote "aged" and "years" and left space for where the age might be added later. From who came the seemingly erroneous information about Coburn's age at death, or when it was added to Coburn's original town death record entry, cannot be known.

Titus Coburn was baptized (with Edward Hircom's other slave as "Peggy & Titus} Negro Ser[van]ts of Capt Hircom") at the Second Church of Christ in Reading on August 23, 1767, Reading, Mass., Second Church of Christ Records, 1720–1806, RG5021, n.p., The Congregational Library & Archives, Boston, Mass., http://nehh-viewer.s3 -website-us-east-1.amazonaws.com/#/content/ReadingSecond/viewer /Church20Records2C2017201806/64, digital image 64. The same source, ibid., digital image 14, 90, recorded that "Edward Hurcom" was admitted as a member of the church on June 12, 1726, and was in full communion. The Wilmington town clerk retrospectively recorded Titus Coburn's arrival in Wilmington: "Capt Edward Hurcum & Wife and Family Came to Town in in [sic] ye Spring of ye year AD 1774 Names of their family is as follows (viz) Nathaniel Russel Sarah Russel and Titus Cober and Peggy Hurcum", Town of Wilmington, "Town Records Town Meetings Intentions 1762–1834" (title from microfilm target; spine title "Town Meetings Etc. 1807–1834 Intentions Town of Wilmington"), 345, first volume

on GSU Microfilm Reel 887763, digital image 190 of 430, https://www
.familysearch.org/ark:/61903/3:1:3QSQ-G979-M9D8-R?i=189&cc
=2061550&cat=146917, accessed February 16, 2019. A different man
named Titus was noted in the Reading First Church records, enslaved by
Thomas Green of Malden, Mass., baptized on November 22, 1741 and received to full communion on July 4, 1742. The possibly free woman of color
named Margaret, received to full communion on July 12, 1762 but not indicated to be anyone's servant, was not Hircom's Peggy. Cooper and Minkema,
The Colonial Church Records of the First Church of Reading, 145, 146, 151.

Edward Hircom may be the unnamed male child of Henry and Joane
Hurcome, christened on November 10, 1698 in Uley, Gloucestershire, England, FamilySearch, *England Births and Christenings*, https://familysearch
.org/ark:/61903/1:1:JWDC-KPY : 11 February 2018, data from GSU Microfilm Reel 427797 and 855625, accessed July 7, 2019. During Hircom's
probate proceedings, the court appointed Samuel Thompson to make inquiries about any heirs and was informed that Hircom was a "Foreigner" with
no relatives in the country, Edward Hurcum, Probate file papers, return of
citation, September 11, 1781. The characterization of the long-time Massachusetts resident as a "Foreigner" is curious. Perhaps the term was merely
intended legally, but if so that had no bearing on the administration of Hircom's Massachusetts estate, White, *A View of the Jurisdiction and Proceedings
of the Courts of Probate in Massachusetts*, 55.

Hircom was in the North Precinct of Reading by 1720, appearing on a
list of taxpayers as "Edward Hurcom", Eaton, *Genealogical History of the Town
of Reading*, 138. "Edward Hirkcum" married Priscilla Russell in Andover on
March 6, 1730/31, *VRA*, Vol. 2, 173, 293. Hircom's first and third marriages occurred in Reading: "Edward Hurcum" married Hannah Eaton on July
21, 1720, and "Edward Hircom" married Prudence Walcott on December 6,
1732/33, *Vital Records of Reading*, 326, 373 (Eaton), 368, 469 (Walcott). In
1737, Hircom purchased a 148-acre farm located in Reading and Andover
from "Joseph Frie" (i.e., Joseph Frye, 1712–1794) for £580, and sold it four
months later to Ebenezer Walcott for £600, Essex County Deeds, Book 81,
pp. 59, 60. Capt. Hircom may have been an officer during the earlier colonial
wars: in 1746 he was appointed administrator of the estate of an Andover
man who died at the Cape Breton expedition, John Bolton, Probate file papers. Hircom signed his name to the administrator's bond. Hircom was on a
1747 committee for laying out roads in the North Precinct of Reading, and
his property was traversed by a road from Robert Russell's property to the
Andover town line, Anonymous, "The Old Town of Reading Massachusetts.
Early Land Grants and Town Bounds from 1638 to 1802," 121, 122. In May
1762, Hircom purchased a 32-acre Andover tract of woodland and swamp

for £100, then in December sold it for £11 3s. 1p., Essex County Deeds, Book 110, pp. 156, 215. The Andover tract was purchased from John Holt 3rd of Andover, and then Hircom sold it to John Holt of Hollis, N.H. While the rendering of Holt's name and place of residence differed, the concluding section of the later deed would appear to indicate that the land was purchased from and sold back to the same man: "The Design of this Deed is to Convey to the said John Holt all ye Land that I the said Edward Hircom bought of said John Holt Essex of Andover". Alternatively, the property could have been purchased from the father, then sold to the son, Abbott, "Early Records of the Holt Family of Andover," 7.

Hircom had purchased and sold at least one other slave before March 1768 when Hircom was in Reading, before he moved to Wilmington with Titus Coburn and Peggy in the spring of 1774. In 1771, Capt. Edward Hircom, then residing in Reading, was summonsed as a witness in the appeal of the freedom suit of Caesar v. Taylor (Superior Court of Judicature, Essex County, November 1771, continued to June 1772; appellate case file papers in SFC, File #132190, JA). Caesar was once owned by Hircom who sold him to Samuel Taylor on March 24, 1768. A copy of Hircom's 1768 bill of sale was made for that case file. The bill of sale for Caesar from Hircom to Samuel Taylor was witnessed by Timothy Russell. I have not determined a genealogical relationship of Timothy and Nathaniel Russell, but I suspect there was connection to Hircom through his second wife, Priscilla Russell. A baptism record for "Cesar, Negro Ser^t of Capt Hircom" (November 27, 1763) was made in Reading, Mass., Second Church of Christ Records, 1720–1806, n.p., RG5021, The Congregational Library and Archives, Boston, Mass., http://nehh-viewer.s3-website-us-east-1.amazonaws.com/#/content/ReadingSecond/viewer/Church20Records2C2017201806/61, digital image 61. That same source, ibid., digital image 87, indicated that "Cesar (Capt Hircom's S[ervan]^t)" owned the covenant the day he was baptized, but was not "received" or "admitted" to "full Communion". After he was sold in July 1768, Caesar "threatened Capt Edward Hurcom [...] that he would hurt him in his Person or Estate" (deposition of Ezra Damon, November 12, 1771, SFC, File #132190, JA). There are several similarly worded depositions in the *Caesar* file papers that indicate Caesar was brought before a local magistrate and fined for threatening Hircom. The copy of Hircom's 1768 bill of sale in the court file papers indicated that Hircom had signed it with his name (not signed by a mark), suggesting that Hircom had become incapacitated for writing by the time he signed by mark in 1781. The copy of the bill of sale spelled the surname "Hircom" but it was spelled variously in other court file papers (such as Hirchum or Hirkum, Hircom, Hurcom, etc.). Capt. Hircom did not appear as a witness at the appellate trial of Caesar v. Taylor, but

Timothy Russell, who witnessed the 1768 bill of sale, attended court and was deposed on November 12, 1771. Hircom was on a list of voters in the Second Parish of Reading in 1771, Eaton, ibid., 170.

2 During his lifetime, Capt. Edward Hircom's surname was rendered variously such as Hirchum or Hirkum, Hircom, Hurcom, Hurcum, etc. He signed his name as "Edward Hircom" in 1746 and 1768, and I generally used that spelling, except in quotation and, of course, except in references, many of which cited works are arranged by a particular spelling (e.g., alphabetized and indexed names in *Massachusetts Soldiers and Sailors of the Revolutionary War*, the published *Vital Records* series, deeds, probate, etc.).

3 Intriguing summaries of 1776 service records for a man named Titus (no surname) are in Massachusetts Secretary of the Commonwealth, *Massachusetts Soldiers and Sailors of the Revolutionary War*, Vol. 15, 792. That Titus appeared on a July 1776 list "of men hired to perform turns of service on [the] Crown Point [N.Y.] expedition; said Titus sent by Capt. Ed'd Hurcum; credited with 1 turn; reported a Negro". Capt. Edward Hircom of Wilmington was Titus Coburn's owner. An entry for "Hurcum" is in ibid., Vol. 8, 561: "Hurcum" is named on a July 1776 list "of drafted men who hired men to perform turns of service on the Crown Point expedition; said Hurcum, Captain, sent his Negro man Titus and is credited with 1 turn." The entry for Titus (no surname), ibid., Vol. 15, 792, continued with a Titus in Capt. Wheeler's Co. who signed a receipt for wages for September 1776 that was given to the 4th regimental paymaster; he was a Private in Capt. Adam Wheeler's (2nd) Co., Lt. Col. Thomas Nixon's (4th) Reg.; he was listed on a regimental return at North Castle, N.Y., dated November 9, 1776; discharged on November 20, 1776. A note at that entry referred to an entry for Titus Tuttle which is in ibid., Vol. 16, 209: that cross-referenced entry has information about the same 4th regimental paymaster, receipt signed by Titus Tuttle for wages for October and November 1776; just above that entry in ibid., Vol. 16, 209, is another for a Titus Tuttle from Acton, and some of the summary of the Acton man's records of service may be intermixed with the summary of records for Titus (no surname) in ibid., Vol. 15, 792. Bishop, ed., *Wilmington Minute Men*, n.d. (1997?), n.p., (s.v., "Titus Cober", "Edward Hurcum") has summaries of Coburn's service, and some information about another Titus Coburn; at the end of the volume appear reproductions of unidentified handwritten notes or records that include the information about Hircom and Coburn in the Crown Point matter.

Titus Coburn's 1778–1780 service on behalf of the town of Wilmington was summarized in Coburn and Coburn, RWPA: Titus Coburn, April 8, 1818 (military service, enlisted July 1, 1778 in Capt. Pierce's Co., Col.

Michael Jackson's Reg., discharged on May 1, 1779 by Col. Jackson at West Point, N.Y.); Titus Coburn, July 13, 1820 (military service, June 20, 1778 to March 20, 1779 in Capt. Pierce's Co., Col. Michael Jackson's Reg.); Benjamin Berry, August 5, 1818 (military service, July 1, 1778 in Capt. Pierce's Co., Col. Michael Jackson's Reg., discharged beginning of May 1779); Massachusetts Secretary of the Commonwealth, September 14, 1854 (military service for Wilmington, nine months 1779 and 1780, from records dated January 27 and February 5, 1787). Massachusetts Secretary of the Commonwealth, *Massachusetts Soldiers and Sailors of the Revolutionary War*, Vol. 3, 686 ("Cobin, Titus", 22 years old, 5' 6" tall, "complexion, negro", enlisted on July 25, 1779, discharged on April 25, 1780), 744 (the second man named "Colburn, Titus", enlisted on November 24, 1779).

Rosanna's husband, the Titus Coburn from Wilmington (and later Andover), has been confused with another man named Titus Coburn who was from Shirley, Harvard, and Littleton, Mass., and who at one point lived in "Cambdon" (Campton?), N.H. according to a Harvard marriage intention record, and possibly the same man born 1742 in Hudson, N.H. That other person was a Minuteman on April 19, 1775, fought at Bunker Hill, and died at Valley Forge in 1778. Record summaries for that other Titus Coburn are in ibid., Vol. 3, 687 ("Coborn, Titus", service with main guard under Lt. Col. Loammi Baldwin, June 22, 1775; cf. "Baldwin, Loammi", in ibid., Vol. 1, 521, the main guard in Cambridge and vicinity before and after that date), ibid., Vol. 3, 695 ("Coburn, Titus", from Shirley, Harvard, and Littleton, Mass.), ibid., Vol. 3, 736 ("Colbourne, Titus" from Shirley, Mass. and "Colbrn, Titus"), ibid., Vol. 3, 744 (the first man named "Colburn, Titus" from Shirley, Mass.). Nell, *The Colored Patriots*, 21; Parker, Letter to George Bancroft; the anonymous pamphlet *The Loyalty and Devotion of Colored Americans in the Revolution and War of 1812*, 14 (sometimes attributed to William Lloyd Garrison but having identical wording regarding Coburn as Nell's *The Colored Patriots*, 21); and, Quintal, *Patriots of Color*, 87, are among innumerable secondary historical sources that confused the two Titus Coburns. Wilmington historian Larz Neilson attempted to detangle the records of the two men in his articles, "Who was Titus Colburn?"; "Wilmington voted to free slaves in 1777"; "Wilmington black man served in Revolution"; "The day the slaves were freed"; "Wilmington's first town meeting"; and, "Freedom for the slaves of Massachusetts." Neilson noticed Titus Toney (Tonia) who married Phillis (a slave of Ebenezer Jones of Wilmington), in Billerica, Mass., in 1768, Kelley, *Wilmington Records*, 77; Spraker, "The Lost History of Slaves and Slave Owners in Billerica," 123; *Vital Records of Billerica*, 336 (Marriages, "Negroes"). But Neilson also noticed the record for the birth of Jennie, Titus Coburn and his wife Violet's daughter, born on May 27, 1789, on which date

Titus and Violet were indicated to be "Servants of Ebenezer Jones" according only to Kelley, ibid., 26, which may be an editorial error.

[4] Massachusetts Secretary of the Commonwealth, September 14, 1854, in Coburn and Coburn, RWPA. This document is a copy made in 1854 from the state treasurer records of Titus Coburn's February 5, 1787 payment request for nine months service 1779–1780, £7 13s. 4p. The 1854 document indicated that affixed to Coburn's original 1787 payment request was a certificate dated January 27, 1787 from the Wilmington selectmen attesting to Coburn's war service for the town. Coburn requested that the amount owed to him be paid to Samuel Thompson, Esq. (1731–1820) of Woburn, at some time a Justice of the Peace and a state representative. (In 1781, Samuel Thompson witnessed Edward Hircom's will; acted on behalf of the Middlesex County Probate Court to serve notice of probate of Hircom's estate; and, was one of the three appraisers of that estate, Edward Hurcum, Probate file papers, will, July 14, 1781; Probate Judge Oliver Prescott citation, September 5, 1781; Samuel Thompson return of citation, September 11, 1781; Judge Prescott appointment of inventory takers, September 12, 1781.) Samuel Thompson also witnessed or affirmed deeds involving Titus Coburn, Middlesex County Deeds, Book 88, pg. 460 (Foster to Cober, witnessed September 6, 1782); Book 106, pg. 398 (Cober to Eames, witnessed January 16, 1792). The 1787 payment request was witnessed by Benjamin Wyman of Woburn and Ebenezer Thompson of Wilmington. Woburn is adjacent to Wilmington. Titus Coburn's relation to these men is otherwise undetermined.

[5] Edward Hurcum, Probate file papers, will, July 14, 1781, devising half the land to Titus and Peggy and half to Nathaniel Russell; Probate Judge Oliver Prescott citation, September 5, 1781; Samuel Thompson return of citation, September 11, 1781 ("Foreigner"); inventory, October 5, 1781 ("Capt. Edward Hurcum"); that inventory has further docketing verso "lodged 4 April 1782 [/] Sept. 16, 1785" and twice more "16 Sept. 1785". The inventory estimated the land area as "Two hundred Acres of Land in one piece be it more or less" plus one other parcel "one quarter of and [*sic*] Acre be it more or less". On the same day he signed his will (which devised half his land to be shared by Titus and Peggy), Hircom deeded all his land estimated as "two hundred acres be it more or less" to Titus and Peggy, Middlesex County Deeds, Book 83, pg. 243, Edward Hircum to Titus Cober and Peggy Hircum, July 14, 1781, witnessed July 23, 1781, recorded June 5, 1782 ("1781" was error). Because he had transferred by deed the 200¼ acres to Titus and Peggy prior to his death, it is confusing that the land was included in the inventory of Hircom's estate. So too, when Nathaniel Russell sold to Samuel Eames the parts of the buildings that he inherited from Hircom, it is puzzling that the

area of the land he also transferred to Eames was described as "ninety Acres
be the same more or less", Middlesex County Deeds, Book 97, pg. 503, Nathaniel Russell to Samuel Eames, July 9, 1788, witnessed same day, recorded August 6, 1788. No entry appears in the Grantor or Grantee indexes for
Russell either selling to or purchasing from Titus or Peggy half of Hircom's
land, which of course was about 100 acres, not the 90 acres Russell sold to
Eames. Hircom's Probate file papers do not include an account of administration showing the distribution of Hircom's assets. Considering that the matter regarding Hircom's land might have been the subject of a court action, I
searched each volume index to the Middlesex County Court of Common
Pleas records 1770–1790, but there was no index entry for a court action
involving Titus Cober/Coburn/Colburn, Peggy Hircom (etc.), or Nathaniel
Russell. I also searched the card indexes to the Middlesex Folio Collection
of county court file papers with no results, but Melinde Lutz Sanborn (now
Byrne) has cautioned that the indexes to the Middlesex Folio Collection
were hastily prepared, faulty, and incomplete, Sanborn, *Middlesex County,
Massachusetts Deponents*. (The Middlesex County Court of Common Pleas
records, and the indexes and folios of the Middlesex Folio Collection are at
JA, and digital images from microfilm are available on FamilySearch.org, but
are not included in the references cited.)

6 Edward Hurcum, Probate file papers, will, July 14, 1781. Nathaniel was
devised "the one half of a Bond that I have against Eleazer Flynt of Reading"
and the other half was devised to Peggy. The amount of the bond with Flynt
(£93 6s. 8p.) was specified in the inventory, October 5, 1781 with further
docketing verso "lodged 4 April 1782 [/] Sept. 16, 1785" and twice more "16
Sept. 1785". Nathaniel Russell was a Private in Capt. Timothy Walker's Co.,
Col. Green's Reg. "which marched on the alarm of April 19, 1775; service 4½
days." Massachusetts Secretary of the Commonwealth, *Massachusetts Soldiers
and Sailors of the Revolutionary War*, Vol. 13, 697. Nathaniel Russell arrived in
Wilmington with Edward Hircum in the spring of 1774, Town of Wilmington, "Town Records Town Meetings Intentions 1762–1834" (title from microfilm target; spine title "Town Meetings Etc. 1807–1834 Intentions Town
of Wilmington"), 345, first volume on GSU Microfilm Reel 887763, digital
image 190 of 430, https://www.familysearch.org/ark:/61903/3:1:3QSQ
-G979-M9D8-R?i=189&cc=2061550&cat=146917, accessed February 16,
2019. That retrospective record made by the town clerk indicated that Sarah (Stewart) Russell was, at the time the record was made, part of Hircom's
"family" but she may have moved to Hircom's Wilmington farm after her
marriage to Nathaniel on December 6, 1775, which marriage record indicated that both parties were from Wilmington, Kelley, *Wilmington Records*,
179, 185. Nathaniel and Sarah Russell had four children—Hannah, Nathan-

iel, Edward, and Pattey—born between 1778 and 1785, ibid., 70. Their second son was possibly named after Edward Hircom. When Nathaniel sold his part of his inheritance of the Hircom farm in 1788, the deed was made "with Sarah my now married wife consenting", Middlesex County Deeds, Book 97, pg. 503, Nathaniel Russell to Samuel Eames, July 9, 1788, witnessed same day, recorded August 6, 1788.

[7] Middlesex County Deeds, Book 83, pg. 243, Edward Hircum to Titus Cober and Peggy Hircum, July 14, 1781, witnessed July 23, 1781, recorded June 5, 1782 ("1781" was error). That deed stated that Edward Hircom received £1,000 from Titus and Peggy for the property transfer—"lawful silver money paid me in hand before signing and sealing this Instrument"—which I assume was fictive formalism. The deed (which Hircom signed by mark, as was the will that he completed the same day) did not mention the status of Titus and Peggy as Hircom's slaves, or their manumissions that would become effective only upon Hircom's death, which occurred prior to October 5, 1781.

[8] Edward Hurcum, Probate file papers, inventory, October 5, 1781 with further docketing verso "lodged 4 April 1782 [/] Sept. 16, 1785" and twice more "16 Sept. 1785". The inventory estimated the land area as "Two hundred Acres of Land in one piece be it more or less" plus one other parcel "one quarter of and [*sic*] Acre be it more or less". The land area was estimated as "two hundred acres be it more or less" in Middlesex County Deeds, Book 83, pg. 243, Edward Hircum to Titus Cober and Peggy Hircum, July 14, 1781, witnessed July 23, 1781, recorded June 5, 1782 ("1781" was error). The 200¼ acres listed in the inventory of Hircom's estate is unexpected because prior to his death he had transferred all of it by deed to Titus and Peggy. Hircom's Probate file papers do not include an account of administration showing the distribution of Hircom's assets.

Edward Hircom did not advantage the 30-day window of opportunity to free Titus and Peggy when the town of Wilmington voted on March 3, 1777 that any emancipated slaves who had been freed within a month of the town vote would be supported by the town if they required poor relief, Town of Wilmington, "Town Meetings, etc. 1730–1807," 164. The vote meant that during the 30-day period, the owner was not required to post a bond with the town for any poor relief expense the emancipated person might require, pursuant to Massachusetts Chapter 1 of the Acts of 1703.

Abbott, "Historical Andover. No. 107. Africa to Andover.—(Concluded)," 3, found Hircom's probate records, but in her summary muddled details and left out significant facts, particularly Titus Coburn's manumission and his major inheritance of shared interest in buildings, land, livestock, and tools of a working farm: "Titus or Tite, perhaps was Titus Coburn husband of Rose Frye (daughter of Jubah the West Indian, of whom Miss Bailey speaks [in *Historical Sketches of Andover*, 43, but only as "Benjamin"].) Titus got a bequest in 1781 of the clothes of a wealthy old widower, resident of Reading, Edward Hurcom. He gave his homestead to slave Nathaniel Russell, and Peggy a mulatto servant and all the house goods, $6000 in Continental money, $600 in bad notes but plenty of Spanish coins of Silver." Hircom (it was spelled "Hurcum" in the probate file, but he signed by mark) was a Wilmington resident at the time of his death, but had indeed once resided in the adjacent town of Reading; "Rose Frye" was a unique rendering of Rosanna Coburn's name; Russell was not a slave; and, there was no indication that the notes and bonds were all unredeemable.

Abbott, ibid., also found the probate records for Timothy Russell (1733–1818), of Reading then Boxford, Mass., but her report of the details was similarly confused. Abbott perceptively compared Edward Hircom's conveyance of his estate to his slaves, to Timothy Russell's plan to do similarly. Timothy Russell's 1796 will intended to convey half his estate to his wife Margaret, and the other half to Anthony Ballard (Abbott, ibid., Russell's "servant") who died 1818. Russell had real estate in Reading and Andover that he proposed to give to Anthony along with Russell's livestock and his husbandry, agricultural, and carpentry tools. In contrast to his prospective largess to Anthony, Russell perfunctorily bequeathed to one brother and five sisters only $1 to $2 to be paid to each of them between two and three years after his death; to his "kinsman" Timothy Russell Buxton, the amount was $10 to be paid four years after. Notably, Timothy Russell also left a legacy for two Andover women of color, Flora Chandler and Dinah Chadwick, who were Anthony Ballard's sisters. Flora was to receive $5 in two years after Russell's death (1820) and Dinah was to receive $3 in five years (1823). Anthony, Flora, and Dinah probably were Timothy Russell's laborers. There was no inventory or administration account in Timothy Russell's probate file papers that might have indicated that the legacies were paid. Timothy Russell's will made a special bequest to his wife of "a set of hand organs which was formerly Princs". Prince Russell (a "member of Mr. Timothy Russels family", *Vital Records of Reading*, 563) had died on July 6, 1795, 25 years old. "Prince, Timothy Russels Negrow Child" was baptized October 25, 1772, Reading, Mass., Second Church of Christ Records, 1720–1806, RG5021, n.p., The Congregational Library & Archives, Boston, Mass., http://nehh-viewer.s3-website-us-east-1.amazonaws.com /#/content/ReadingSecond/viewer/Church20Records2C2017201806/67, digital image 67; Timothy Russell, Probate file papers, will, June 11, 1796 and codicil, March 25, 1818; *Vital Records of Reading*, 492 ("Antony" Ballard), 563 (Prince Russell ["Russel"], error in year of death "1725" that cited his gravestone at Park Street Cemetery in North Reading, but the photograph of the gravestone on the Find A Grave website indicated 1795 as the year of Prince Russell's death, https://www.findagrave.com /memorial/11003343/prince-russell, accessed March 10, 2019). Flora and Dinah were identified as Anthony Ballard's sisters in his Probate file papers (Edmon [his spelling, but also rendered by the court as Edmund] Damon, April 7, 1818, Anthony Ballard, Probate file papers). Regrettably, Timothy Russell outlived both his wife Margaret and Anthony Ballard, so he prepared a codicil in 1818 to leave everything to another "brother" who had not been named as a beneficiary in the 1796 will.

9 I used the Middlesex South Registry of Deeds grantor and grantee indexes to find entries under Cober (entries separated from Coburn and its other variants), under Hircum/Hircom (all variants gathered under those headings), and under Russell. Middlesex County Deeds, Book 97, pg. 503, Nathaniel Russell to Samuel Eames, July 9, 1788, witnessed same day, recorded August 6, 1788. A rare page reference error ("505") was made in the Grantee and Grantor indexes for that deed. The Russell deed referred to the real estate "being the Property of Peggy Hurcum (reserved and excepted)" meaning that her portion of the property was not transferred by Russell's deed to Eames.

10 Middlesex County Deeds, Book 88, pg. 460, Ebenezer Foster to Titus Cober, September 6, 1782, witnessed same day, recorded May 4, 1785; Book 88, pg. 460, Titus Cober to Samuel Eames, November 30, 1782, witnessed May 2, 1785, recorded May 4, 1785.

11 Kelley, *Wilmington Records*, 114, 167 (marriage, "Titus Cober" and "Vilot Noble", August 28, 1785). The original entry for Titus and Violet's marriage in the town's vital records was made from a copy of a record of marriages performed by the Rev. Isaac Morrill, August 28, 1785, "Titus Cober & Vilot Noble", both of Wilmington. Town of Wilmington, "Vital Records Cattle Records 1716–1851" (spine title), n.p., first volume on GSU Microfilm Reel 761324, digital image 121 of 288, https://familysearch .org/ark:/61903/3:1:3QSQ-G97M-59T2-G?i=120&cc=2061550&cat =146741, accessed August 12, 2017. Rev. Morrill (1718–1793) was at the First Church of Christ in Wilmington; he owned two slaves named Dinah and Phillis, Smith, *Morrill Kindred in America*, 50–67 (60 for the slaves). The Wilmington town clerk recorded Violet's manumission on March 29, 1777 from Benjamin Thompson of Wilmington. As with Isaac Morrill freeing his slave Dinah on March 10, 1777, recorded on the previous page, Thompson's action would also appear to have been prompted by the March 3, 1777 town meeting vote that suspended for 30 days the requirement that slave owners post a bond with the town prior to manumitting a

slave. Before the town clerk, Thompson (spelled "Tompson") "Declared that he had given his Negro Girl Named Vilot her Freedom – & Desired that I would Enter it upon Record", Town of Wilmington, "Town Records Town Meetings Intentions 1762–1834" (title from microfilm target; spine title "Town Meetings Etc. 1807–1834 Intentions Town of Wilmington"), 345, first volume on GSU Microfilm Reel 887763, digital image 190 of 430, https://www.familysearch.org/ark:/61903/3:1:3QSQ-G979-M9D8-R?i =189&cc=2061550&cat=146917, accessed February 16, 2019. The manumission was recorded at the top of the same page that retrospectively recorded the arrival of Edward Hircom and his family from Reading, Mass.

[12] Middlesex County Deeds, Book 92, pg. 318, Titus Cober to Peggy Hircom, November 22, 1785, witnessed December 16, 1785, recorded April 5, 1786.

[13] Middlesex County Deeds, Book 97, pg. 503, Nathaniel Russell to Samuel Eames, July 9, 1788, witnessed same day, recorded August 6, 1788. Samuel Eames and Nathaniel Russell had both been in Capt. Timothy Walker's Co. (Wilmington), Col. Green's Reg. "which marched on the alarm of April 19, 1775", Loring, "Robert Eames of Woburn, Mass., and Some of his Descendants," 151; Massachusetts Secretary of the Commonwealth, *Massachusetts Soldiers and Sailors of the Revolutionary War*, Vol. 13, 697. Samuel Eames, Esq. was referred to as "Squire Eames" in Passmore, *250th Anniversary, Wilmington*, 31, 36, 37, 44, 67. (Passmore, ibid., 37, 44, included four photographic images of the "Squire Eames House" and related buildings and their setting; there are additional historical photographs of that property that I found searching online, including one in the Harriette Merrifield Forbes collection at the American Antiquarian Society, Worcester, Mass.) Passmore, "Solved: The riddle of the Pearson Tavern," summarized property transfers involving Squire Eames and his son Samuel Eames, Jr. that may pertain to the former Hircom farm. Additional research and analysis is needed to determine if what was once the Hircom farm was the same as the "Squire Eames House" property, which I suspect it was. The descriptions of the metes and bounds with the names of abutters of parcels purchased, sold, and subdivided have parallels. Passmore, *250th Anniversary, Wilmington*, 44, indicated that the property—also called the "1730 House" and later known as "The Shamrock"—was purchased by Squire Eames "sometime about 1780 and [he] lived there until his death in January 1834." That tradition may in fact elide what appear to be Hircom's purchases 1733–1734 of what became his farm, and Squire Eames' purchases 1788–1793 of the former Hircom farm. Edward Hircom and Squire Eames were involved in many Wilmington land transactions. Samuel Eames' probate file papers described his "Homestead" containing 140 acres, part of which was sold to settle the estate. I only sur-

veyed the numerous entries for Edward Hircom and Samuel Eames in the grantee and grantor indexes for Middlesex County Deeds, and perused Samuel Eames' probate file papers. As I have not determined which of those documents are pertinent to the former Hircom farm, none are included in the references cited.

[14] Middlesex County Deeds, Book 106, pg. 397, Peggy Hircom to Titus Cober, April 11, 1789, witnessed January 9, 1792, recorded January 18, 1792. At the time of that transaction, Titus was styled as "Yeoman" and Peggy as "Spinster". The former term of legal status meant a free, property-owning adult male. The latter term probably intended in that document only to convey her legal status as an unmarried adult woman, able to transact on her own, unfettered by coverture. The word "spinster" could otherwise or doubly convey occupation in textile production as a spinner. "Pegge Hurcum of Wilmington" was visited by an Andover doctor who traveled 11 miles to dispense medicine to her, costing 10s. 4p., Osgood and Osgood, Day Books, n.p., Vol. 2, June 24, 1789, https://iiif.lib.harvard.edu/manifests/view /drs:424481342$67i, digital image seq. 67, accessed October 19, 2019.

[15] Kelley, *Wilmington Records*, 26 (birth of Jennie, May 27, 1789, parents are "Servants of Ebenezer Jones"). I have not been able to locate the original entry for Jennie's birth in the town's manuscript book of original vital records—which is chronologically disordered, worn, and faded in parts—to determine if the information Kelley indicated about Titus and Violet being servants appeared in the original. Perhaps Kelley, ibid., 26, 77, conflated Titus Coburn ("Cober") with Titus Tonia/Toney, the latter man and his family also indicated by Kelley to be servants of Jones. I suspect that the identical, editorially added notes for both Tituses ("Servants of Ebenezer Jones") were well-meant attempts by Kelley to signal his thought that the two similarly named men were one and the same. The original birth records are in Town of Wilmington, "Vital Records Cattle Records 1716–1851" (spine title), n.p., first volume on GSU Microfilm Reel 761324, https://www.familysearch .org/search/film/007009576?cc=2061550&cat=146741, accessed August 24, 2017.

Seemingly it was Jennie whose name was rendered as Jane and June in 1816, Town of Andover, "Town Records, Tax Records 1799–1822" (untitled volume, title from microfilm target but actually treasurer records of payments for orders drawn by the overseers of the poor), n.p., first volume on GSU Microfilm Reel 878782, June 8, 1816 (No. 20, $5.00: "An order to Titus Coburn for supporting his daughter in part"; No. 21, $6.54: Dr. Nathaniel Swift for "June Coburn"); October 7, 1816 (No. 62, $2.08: Dr. Nathaniel Swift for "Jane Coburn").

¹⁶ United States Bureau of the Census, *Heads of Families at the First Census [...] 1790*, 159. The separate "Ceaser Russell" household in Wilmington had three people of color in 1790; he may have arrived in Wilmington from Andover, possibly once enslaved by the Andover Russell family. Among Andover Revolutionary War soldiers, "Cesar Russell" was noted by Bailey, *Historical Sketches of Andover*, 359, and Abbott, "Historical Andover. No. 107. Africa to Andover.—(Concluded)," 3, named "Caesar Russell of John Russell, Jr." Caesar Russell and Sally Richardson, both of Wilmington, married May 25, 1790, Kelley, *Wilmington Records*, 179.

¹⁷ Middlesex County Deeds, Book 106, pg. 398, Titus Cober to Samuel Eames, December 25, 1791, witnessed January 16, 1792, recorded January 18, 1792. In that deed, Titus was styled a "Laborer" and Eames a "Gentleman". See Loring, "Robert Eames of Woburn, Mass., and Some of his Descendants," 151, for Samuel Eames, Esq.

¹⁸ Middlesex County Deeds, Book 112, pg. 226, Peggy Hircom ("Spinster") to Samuel Eames ("Gentleman"), March 11, 1793, witnessed same day, recorded March 12, 1793; *VRA*, Vol. 2, 148, 173 (Peggy Hircom and Samuel George, "residents in Andover").

¹⁹ Rosanna Coburn, August 8, 1854; Elizabeth Blanchard, August 10, 1854; Sarah Holt, August 28 and 31, 1854 (marriage to Titus Coburn solemnized by Samuel Eames, Esq. in Wilmington); William H. Carter, Wilmington town clerk, August 10, 1854 (no town record of Titus and Rosanna Coburn marriage), all in Coburn and Coburn, RWPA. Eames apparently was not a minister, so the marriage was probably a civil ceremony, Loring, "Robert Eames of Woburn, Mass., and Some of his Descendants," 151.

²⁰ United States Census, *Population Schedules of the Second Census of the United States 1800, Roll 17*, Middlesex County, Wilmington, 1079.

²¹ For the "diverse array of nonnuclear families," see Ashcraft-Eason, "Freedom among African Women Servants and Slaves," 68; Whiting, "'Endearing Ties,'" 126–133; and Whiting, "Power, Patriarchy, and Provision," 584 (quotation), and 585 n2. Gloria McCahon Whiting, ibid., considered James H. Sweet, "Defying Social Death: The Multiple Configurations of African Slave Family in the Atlantic World," 271. Sweet stressed that "African Atlantic families operated at several overlapping registers not always apparent to Europeans" (271), with meaningful and not literally fictive (253, 256) "idioms of kinship" (264, 271) that along with "natal kin were often one [among several possible] expression[s] of broader communities" (271). Tera W. Hunter, *Bound in Wedlock*, recognized a continuum of relationship practices, arrangements, and commitments among enslaved and free people of color.

Hunter, ibid., 7, adopted a heuristic of "marriage [...] to encompass commit-ted conjugal relationships, whether legal or not, monogamous, bigamous, polygamous, or serial. Black heterosexual intimacy comprised a wide range of domestic arrangements out of necessity [and choice], not all of which were described as marriage."

[22] Essex County Deeds, Book 184, pg. 280, Jonathan Griffin to Titus Co-burn, January 19, 1809, recorded January 26, 1809; Book 195, pg. 42, Titus Coburn to Sarah Stevens, November 8, 1811, recorded November 14, 1811. Southern Essex District Registry of Deeds, Salem, Mass. The location was de-scribed as on the southerly side of the road that leads from Daniel Wardwell's to Simon Wardwell, Jr.'s house, adjoining land belonging to Jonathan Griffin, and land belonging to the late Rev. Jonathan French (minister of the South Parish church). On Dorman's 1830 map, "A Plan of Andover," numerous Wardwells and Stevens appear in the northeast part of Andover and farther into present-day North Andover. The Andover Preservation Commission, et al., *Andover Historic Preservation* webpage that summarized property trans-fers for what is now 8–10 Central Street noted the 1811 sale from Coburn to Stevens as part of her buying and selling many parcels, not necessarily at that location, http://preservation.mhl.org/8-10-central-street, accessed August 4, 2017. Less likely to be the location of the property, Dorman's 1830 map labeled the house of "Wid. Stevens" in the southwestern part of Andover, east of Haggett's Pond, on the northwest side of present-day Bellvue Road between I-93 and Greenwood Road. Poore, "A Genealogical-Historical Vis-itation of Andover, Mass., in the Year 1863," *Essex Institute Historical Collec-tions* 51 (4) (1915): 306, wrote that Titus and Rose "lived near the seminary" (the Andover Theological Seminary, the area now encompassed by Phillips Academy), which is closer to the Wardwells and Stevens mentioned above in the northeastern part of Andover and North Andover. Carpenter, "Glimpses of Life in Andover Eighty Years Ago, from an Old Family Expense-book," conveyed that "the Historical Society ladies" remembered that Rose and Col-ley lived on Missionary Lane, now called Woodland Road, which is east of Phillips Academy, Goldsmith, *The Townswoman's Andover*, 72; Ralston, "Last-ing Tribute to Andover's Early Missionaries." Dorman's 1830 map shows the house of "C. Wardwell" on the east side of what was Missionary Lane. Two unnamed residences were immediately north of Wardwell, and perhaps (or not) one of those was intended to represent the location of Rose and Colley's house. However, in 1852 and 1856, Rosanna Coburn's house was located far-ther north on Missionary Lane, at the northeast corner of the intersection of what is now Highland Road and Woodland Road (the modern street address is 4 Woodland Road). The house of "R. Coburn" was plotted at that location on Walling, "Map of the Town of Andover" (1852) and Walling, "A Topographi-

cal Map of Essex County" (1856). To determine modern street locations, I used the Harvard Library, *Harvard Geospatial Library*, which is a computer program that georeferences digital images of historical maps to modern maps, available via https://library.harvard.edu/services-tools/harvard-geospatial-library.

I identified Coburn's house location on the 1852 and 1856 maps only because the Andover South Church, *South Parish Burial Grounds Cemetery Database* created for grave markers included a note that conveyed (incorrectly, as it turned out) Rosanna Coburn "lived in Isaac Blunt House, 167 Highland". The source of the error was the historical building survey inventory form for the Isaac Blunt House prepared in 1975–1977. That form indicated (incorrectly) that the 1856 Walling map "shows R. Coburn, S.P. Blunt, and H. Jaquith located here." In fact, the 1852 and 1856 maps showed them in three separate houses. Andover South Church, *South Parish Burial Grounds Cemetery Database*, http://www.southchurch.com/cemetery/recordDetail .php?IDnum=2727; Massachusetts Historical Commission, Inventory of Historic Assets of the Commonwealth, Historical Building Inventory Form, Isaac Blunt House (ANV.269, 167 Highland Road, Andover), http:// mhc-macris.net/Details.aspx?MhcId=ANV.269; information from the 1975–1977 form was used for the Andover Preservation Commission, et al., *Andover Historic Preservation* webpage for the property, http://preservation .mhl.org/167-highland-road, all accessed August 4, 2017. I shared my findings with the website administrators of the *South Parish Burial Grounds Cemetery Database* and *Andover Historic Preservation*, and prepared a supplemental information sheet for the state inventory form. The cemetery database information was revised before October 4, 2017 to indicate that Rosanna Coburn's last known residence was on Woodland Road.

[23] Anonymous, "Sketches of Octogenarians" (about Rose Coburn's family). Dorman's 1830 map, "A Plan of Andover," shows "D. Peters" on the southwest side of Salem Turnpike (now Turnpike Street, between Haverhill Street and Elm Street, in North Andover) in the vicinity of several properties of "J. Peters". The Andover Preservation Commission, et al., *Andover Historic Preservation* website identified a four-acre parcel owned by William Peters in the vicinity of what is presently 79–93 Haverhill Street with parts extending to 5–8 Liberty Street, but that location is at some distance from Salem Turnpike (Route 114).

[24] United States Census, *Population Schedules of the Third Census of the United States 1810*, 248.

[25] Town of Andover, "Town Records, Tax Records 1799–1822" (untitled volume, title from microfilm target but actually treasurer records of payments for orders drawn by the overseers of the poor), n.p., first volume on GSU

Microfilm Reel 878782, June 8, 1816 (No. 20, $5.00: "An order to Titus Co-burn for supporting his daughter in part"; No. 21, $6.54: Dr. Nathaniel Swift for "June Coburn"); October 7, 1816 (No. 62, $2.08: Dr. Nathaniel Swift for "Jane Coburn"); November 5, 1816 (No. 102, $0.50: "An order to William Johnson 3ᵈ [...] To cash paid black man at Titus Coburns").

²⁶ Abbot, *History of Andover*, 189; Atkins, *History of the Town of Hawley*, 86 (the Franklin County writer); Coburn, *History of Dracut*, 341 ("Poverty Year" and the quoted lines "frosts every month [...] suffering for the fami-lies"); Sheldon, *Life of Asa G. Sheldon: Wilmington Farmer*, 146–147 (pigs). I thank George Walters for directing me to the Wikipedia page "Year With-out a Summer", https://en.wikipedia.org/wiki/Year_Without_a_Summer, accessed August 25, 2017, which included the lines quoted from Atkins.

²⁷ Document at front of file headed "(2,859) Massachusetts Roll" bearing dates September 24, 1818 and October 20, 1820; undated document head-ed "Titus Coburn 56" with payment schedule and bank branch location, in Coburn and Coburn, RWPA. A summary of Titus Coburn's pension infor-mation was published in 1835. It indicated that he had received $279.20, that payments commenced (retroactively to) April 8, 1818, and that he was placed on the pension roll on September 24, 1818. His death was not noted in the published summary, although others who died after him were so in-dicated. United States Secretary of War, *Report from the Secretary of War [...] in Relation to the Pension Establishment of the United States*, Vol. 1, Massachu-setts Pension Roll, 70. The manuscript ledger of pension payments indicated biannual payments of $48 (paid March and September) that commenced April 8, 1818, paid March 1818 through March 1821, United States Rev-olutionary War Pension Payment Ledgers, Roll 2, Volume B, Revolutionary War Pensioners under Act of 1818, 1818–32, 12 ("Titus Cobarn"). That re-cord provided that Titus had been paid biannually; it did not indicate the larger, lump-sum retroactive payment. Additional detailed information, in-cluding when and to whom payments were made, is likely to be found in the Pension Agency Payment Books, 1805–1909, RG 15, NM-21, Series 2 (the index cards to the books are RG 15, NM-21, Series 1), National Archives, Washington, D.C., not included in the references cited, but noted in Prech-tel-Kluskens, "Follow the Money."

²⁸ Alpheus Gurney and Silvanus Packard v. Titus Coburn, Essex County Circuit Court of Common Pleas for the Middle Circuit Records, March 1819, 72, and file papers. For Moses Wood, see Abbott, "The Wood Fam-ily," 1 ("was for a time an assistant in the old Shipman store"); Carpenter, *Biographical Catalogue of the Trustees, Teachers and Students of Phillips Acade-my*, 52 ("Clerk, trader, etc."). For Shipman's store, see Robbins, *Old Andover*

Days, 20–21, who remembered it as a "little country store". Gurney and Packard were listed in the Boston street directories of 1818 and 1820 as "grocers", meaning that they purchased and sold goods in gross, Boston Athenaeum, *The Boston Directory 1789 to 1900*.

[29] The references to the court records of decisions for the 15 Gurney and Packard cases against Andover men are listed in the references cited under Essex County Circuit Court of Common Pleas for the Middle Circuit Records. The decisions were: September 1818, 240 (Jacob Abbot), 241 (Andrew W. Dunklee and Andrew W. Dunklee, Jr.), 243 (Abiel Upton, Jr.); December 1818, 428 (Samuel Lummus), 429 (William Hawley and Samuel Lummus), 531 (Zachariah Gurney, Jr. v. Jacob Abbot), 532 (Jacob Abbot), 533 (Peter Holt); March 1819, 72 (Titus Coburn), 146 (Levi Trull), 147 (Benjamin Berry); June 1819, 259 (Moses Wood), 316 (Richard Sherwin), 375 (Levi Davis); March 1820, 156 (Richard Sherwin), JA. The involvement of so many plaintiffs from the same town, none of whom appeared in court, poses questions that could be addressed by further research, including searching for the file papers and records of executions for the 15 cases and checking Essex and Suffolk County court records for any collateral legal actions. In the Southern Essex District Registry of Deeds grantee index for 1820–1834, there are several entries for Gurney and Packard, including an assignment of property from Moses Wood. The possibility of coordinated protest by the Andover men should be investigated, e.g., in letters, diaries, newspaper articles, etc. Extralegal actions in response to the debt cases might have occurred in Andover, Boston, or at the Salem courthouse.

[30] Dupre, "The Panic of 1819 and the Political Economy of Sectionalism," 272. Nelson, *Americanization of the Common Law*, 153–154, saw that the Panic of 1819 prompted changes to Massachusetts statutory law for debtors and creditors.

[31] Gurney and Packard v. Coburn, Essex County Circuit Court of Common Pleas for the Middle Circuit, March 1819, file papers (docketed as No. 127), JA. The file papers for Coburn's case include three items. The promissory note of $35.72 to Moses Wood was dated July 18, 1818, which Titus Coburn (rendered as "Corburn") signed by mark. The back of the promissory note indicated that on that same day Wood had endorsed it to pay Gurney and Packard. Interest was charged ($0.35 and $0.17), bringing the debt to $36.24. On October 11, 1818, payment of $10 was made, reducing the debt to $26.24. Interest of $0.52 and $0.13 was added to that, bringing the total remaining debt to $26.89. The court clerk's docketing on the back of the note spelled the defendant's last name as "Caburn". The second file paper was the writ issued by the court on December 1, 1818 for "Titus Caburn". The writ

was served on Titus Coburn (so-spelled) by Deputy Sheriff Moody Bridges on December 5, 1818. The clerk's docketing on the writ spelled Titus' surname as "Caburn". The third file paper was the bill of the plaintiff's costs, issued by the court clerk that misrendered the caption as "Gurney & al [i.e., et al.] v Packard". The bill indicated that the case was first brought to court in the December 1818 term. Had Titus Coburn obtained an attorney and appeared at court, it is conceivable he could have motioned for the writ to be quashed because of the misspelled name on the promissory note and on the writ. Elizabeth Bouvier (email, September 26, 2017) found the file papers, but could not locate the execution records for the case in the JA. There may be additional documentation of the Gurney and Packard cases, including execution records for Coburn's case, in the Essex County, Mass., "Collection of Essex County (Mass.) Court Records, 1628–1914," Collection No. EC 43, Phillips Library, Peabody Essex Museum, Rowley, Mass. In the library's finding aid for that collection, what must be execution records were termed "Notices to Seize Property." Because the inclusive dates of those records in the library's finding aid did not comport with the Gurney and Packard cases, I did not search them. For Titus Coburn's real estate in Andover, I searched the Southern Essex District Registry of Deeds grantor and grantee indexes 1800–1819 and 1820–1834; there were no entries for Titus Coburn other than his 1809 purchase and 1811 sale of his acre and building in Andover. Nelson, *Americanization of the Common Law*, 41–45, 147–154, and passim (262, s.v. "debt," "debtor and creditor," "debts") provided exquisite details of transformations of the statutory and common law of debtor and creditor. For the detailed process and rules for executing judgments, and the sheriff's options and limits, see Coleman, "Massachusetts," in *Debtors and Creditors in America*; Goodwin, *New England Sheriff*. Goodwin, ibid., 100, explained the rule that required creditors to explicitly request that the sheriff attach real estate, otherwise the sheriff was under no obligation to do so. See Goodwin, ibid., 95–103 for attachment of real estate, and 35, 86, 91, 99 for seizing rent of leased land and produce. Agricultural produce required to sustain a debtor's family was later exempted by state statutes of 1826 and 1828, Goodwin, ibid., 218.

[32] The value of Titus Coburn's possessions totaled $6.15, but $5.32 was indicated as a result of an error by the inventory taker, as explained below. Titus Coburn was "very badly ruptured in the groin and often sick in consequence thereof and unable to perform any kind of labor – he is a laborer –", Titus Coburn, July 13, 1820 (quotations); document at front of file headed "(2,859) Massachusetts Roll" bearing dates September 24, 1818 and October 20, 1820; undated document signed by W.[?.] Taylor, acting third auditor indicating pension payments made to March 4, 1821 (written on verso of letter

of inquiry to auditor from Pension Office signed by S. [Dole?], September [?th,] 1854), all in Coburn and Coburn, RWPA. Compare the items listed in the 1820 pension application inventory of Titus Coburn's possessions, with the items listed in Edward Hurcum, Probate file papers, inventory, October 5, 1781 with further docketing verso "lodged 4 April 1782 [/] Sept. 16, 1785" and twice more "16 Sept. 1785".

The original county court version of Titus Coburn's 1820 pension application is Titus Coburn, RWPA, July 13, 1820, Essex County Circuit Court of Common Pleas for the Middle Circuit, Collection No. EC 43, Box 2, File 5 pension applications, "Collection of Essex County (Mass.) Court Records, 1628–1914," Phillips Library, Peabody Essex Museum, Rowley, Mass. The federal and county court versions were each written by different hands, and the federal version was a later copy. There are inconsequential differences between the federal and county court versions of the 1820 application. The federal copy indicated that payments under the previous pension act had commenced April 18, 1818, while the county court version indicated April 8, 1818. The name of Titus' mother-in-law Phillis was misread by the copyist who wrote it as "Chillin" in the federal version; his stepdaughter Colley's name was misread for the federal version as "Colby." Both names were interlineated in the county court version. The county court version of the file has a separate paper with the inventory of Titus Coburn's possessions dated June 22, 1820, and attested on July 7, 1820. In the body of the county court version of the application that listed his possessions (copied from the separate inventory), after "one pair of tongs", the clerk mistakenly added "+ no shovel", which does not appear in the federal version of the application or the separate inventory in the county court file. There was an error in the subtotal column of the original inventory: the sum of $0.83 ($0.58 for the axe plus $0.25 for the pair of tongs) was not carried over to the subtotals column. The value of Titus Coburn's possessions totaled $6.15, but "$5.32" was indicated as the total in the separate inventory. That total of $5.32 was mistakenly repeated in the bodies of the federal and county versions of the application, although all the possessions and their separate values were enumerated in the two versions of the application.

[33] United States Census, *Population Schedules of the Fourth Census of the United States 1820*, 649 (Andover, aggregated data for 61 unnamed free persons of color). See ibid., iii, vi, about limited or no data for people of color in that census, with some names gathered separately for a few Essex County towns, but not for Andover. Town of Andover, Overseers of the Poor, List of supplies delivered to the poor, 1820–1821, Taft Collection, Ms S 134, Sub-group X, Andover – Town Office, Series A, Overseers of the Poor, Sub-series 1, ACHC. For the town support provided to the household, see chap. 4, note 31.

[34] Titus Coburn will, May 5, 1821, in Coburn and Coburn, RWPA (copy by Essex County register of probate, August 8, 1854), and in Titus Coburn, Probate file papers (copy of will, August 8, 1854). The clerk did not retain the original will, but instead made a copy for the probate file, likely because the 33-year-old original document may have been fragile and worn. Two affiants (a son, and a son and nephew of the witnesses) attested that the signatures of the witnesses to the original 1821 document were genuine. Neither of the affiants mentioned the handwriting of the original will, only the signatures of the witnesses. Robert Callahan, Jr. and William Chickering, August 8, 1854 in Titus Coburn, Probate file papers (affiants about genuine signatures of Holt, Callahan, and Chickering on original will).

[35] Titus was baptized at the Second Church of Christ in Reading on August 23, 1767, Reading, Mass., Second Church of Christ Records, 1720–1806, RG5021, n.p., The Congregational Library & Archives, Boston, Mass., http://nehh -viewer.s3-website-us-east-1.amazonaws.com/#/content/ReadingSecond /viewer/Church20Records2C2017201806/64, digital image 64. A copy of a record of marriages performed by the Rev. Isaac Morrill, August 28, 1785, "Titus Cober & Vilot Noble", both of Wilmington, appeared in Town of Wilmington, "Vital Records Cattle Records 1716–1851" (spine title), n.p., first volume on GSU Microfilm Reel 761324, digital image 121 of 288, https://familysearch.org/ark:/61903/3:1:3QSQ-G97M-59T2-G?i=120&cc =2061550&cat=146741, accessed August 12, 2017. On Rev. Morrill, who owned two slaves named Dinah and Phillis, see Smith, *Morrill Kindred in America*, 50–67 (60 for the slaves).

[36] Rosanna Coburn, August 8, 1854; Elizabeth Blanchard, August 10, 1854; Sarah Holt, August 28 and 31, 1854 (marriage to Titus Coburn solemnized by Samuel Eames, Esq. in Wilmington); William H. Carter, Wilmington town clerk, August 10, 1854 (no town record of Titus and Rosanna Coburn marriage), all in Coburn and Coburn, RWPA. Loring, "Robert Eames of Woburn, Mass., and Some of his Descendants," 151.

[37] *VRA*, Vol. 2, 573 (Deaths, "Negroes," Titus Coburn, May 5, 1821, age 81, probably erroneous, more likely 64 years old if birthday was after July 25, 1765; Massachusetts Secretary of the Commonwealth, *Massachusetts Soldiers and Sailors of the Revolutionary War*, Vol. 3, 686 ["Cobin, Titus" enlisted July 25, 1779, 22 years old]). Titus Coburn's birth year of 1756 estimated from his enlistment record is consistent with the information that he provided in his pension application statements of April 8, 1818 that he was 62, and July 13, 1820 that he was 64 (born 1756), Coburn and Coburn, RWPA. Titus Coburn's original town death record reads, "Titus Coburn Negro aged Eighty one years". The words "Eighty one" were added

later and written in a different hand. In making entries around that time, the town clerk often wrote "aged" and "years" and left space for where the age might be added later; the added information for Coburn's age is only unusual among the other entries around that time in that words for numbers rather than numerals were written. From who came the seemingly erroneous information about Coburn's age at death, or when it was added to Coburn's original town death record entry cannot be known. Town of Andover, "Births & Deaths from 1800 to May 1844 Andover, Mass." (spine title), n.p., third volume on GSU Microfilm Reel 767599, May 5, 1821. Coburn's town death record in a volume of copied records prepared in 1879 reads, "Titus Coburn, negro, Aged 81 years". Town of Andover, "A Record of Deaths in the Town of Andover (Including North Andover), Essex County, Massachusetts, from 1650 to 1844 Covering a Period of 194 Years Chronologically Arranged and Transcribed from the Original Records Verbatim et Literatim by Samuel W. Blunt and Completed March 1, 1879," 133. In any regard, the apparently erroneous information for Titus Coburn's age at death in the original and copied town records was the source of the information that appeared in *VRA*, Vol. 2, 573.

Titus Coburn's place of death was not specified at the almshouse (unlike others around that time who were indicated to have "died at the almshouse"). I assume he died at home expectantly, after having completed his will that same day. Titus Coburn, Probate file papers, copy of will, May 5, 1821; his will devised all to Rose and named her executrix. In the probate file papers, the text of the will actually appears twice, once recited as part of Rosanna Coburn's petition, and a second time recited as part of the Probate Judge's order. Coburn and Coburn, RWPA (copy of Titus Coburn will by Essex County register of probate, August 8, 1854). Titus Coburn's will was witnessed by David Holt, Joel Jenkin, Robert Callahan, and Zachariah Chickering. When the original will was submitted to the probate court in 1854, three of the witnesses' signatures were affirmed as genuine by the son of Callahan, and by the son of Chickering who was also the nephew of Holt. Robert Callahan, Jr. and William Chickering, August 8, 1854 (affiants about genuine signatures of Holt, Callahan, and Chickering on original will); and, Barzillai Lew [Jr.], August 8, 1854 (affiant well-acquainted with Rose Coburn, remembered Titus and Rose as married, and affirmed facts of Rose's petition for probate), all in Titus Coburn, Probate file papers. The August 1854 probate court session was held at Andover, but exactly where is undetermined. The Town Hall at 20 Main Street was not constructed until 1858, but it included space for local court hearings in the lower meeting hall, Andover Preservation Commission, et al., *Andover Historic Preservation* webpage for 20 Main Street, http://preservation.mhl.org/20-main-st, accessed August 25, 2017. Minardi, "Freedom in the Archives: The Pension Case of Primus Hall," observed that when official records were lacking (as they often were), supplementary evidence was assembled for federal veteran pension applications. Jecmen, "Writing the Revolution," is also helpful for understanding the pension process. Barzillai Lew [Jr.]'s sisters, Lucy Dalton and Dinah Freeman, both signed their names to a petition in their mother's probate file papers, indicating their signature literacy, and they may have been literate in reading and writing as was their brother, Dinah Lew, Probate file papers.

Chapter 8 Rosanna Coburn

[1] Massachusetts House of Representatives, RCEC, 16 (quotation of 1846 overseer interview published in 1847). Anonymous, "Sketches of Octogenarians" (about Rose Coburn's family) (published 1853) and Anonymous, "Obituary" for Rosanna Coburn, n.p. [2] (published 1859) ascertained Rosanna Coburn's birthday as July 29, 1766, which is consistent with her gravestone epitaph stating age at death of 92 on March 19, 1859. The obituary said "Her age is not precisely known, but [her birth on July 29, 1766 was deduced] from the best information that the writer could obtain […]; although some persons believe her to have been one hundred at the time of her death." Her town and state death records give her age at death as 97 (thus born circa 1762), Rosanna Coburn, Death record, Town of Andover and State Vital Records. Rosanna's age, as stated in her husband's 1820 pension application, was 48 (born 1772, death at 87), Titus Coburn, July 13, 1820 in Coburn and Coburn, RWPA. Rosanna made a statement on August 8, 1854 in her application for the widow's pension that she was 87 years old (born 1767, death at 92). In 1846, Rosanna told the state commissioners (Massachusetts House of Representatives, RCEC, 16) that she "suppose[d]" she was 76 (born 1770, death at 89), but the town had told the state differently: the town reported her age as 78 (if reported in 1846, born 1768, death at 91; if reported in 1845, born 1767, death at 92). In 1850, she told the federal census enumerator that she was 90 (born about 1760, death at 99), United States Census, *Population Schedules of the Seventh Census of the United States 1850*, 748 (page misnumbered 750 and struck-through), Andover House No. 687. Rosanna (and Colley, too) provided widely varying ages in several instances. Sarah Frye, Probate file papers, will, June 1, 1776; inventory, May 1, 1781.

Belknap, "Queries Respecting the Slavery and Emancipation of Negroes in Massachusetts," 200, is oft quoted that "Negro children were reckoned an incumbrance in a family; and when weaned, were given away like puppies. They have been publickly advertised in the news-papers 'to be given away.'" See the long list of "Negro Children Offered as Gifts in Boston Newspapers," in Lawrence William Towner's 1955 dissertation, "A Good Master Well Served," 440 (Appendix L), and Benes, "Slavery in Boston Households," 28–29. Wendy Warren revisited and delved further into the Boston newspaper advertisements in "'Thrown upon the world': Valuing Infants in the Eighteenth-Century North American Slave Market." Warren's review of the long-known practice of giving away infants to be enslaved noticed further that some advertisements even offered to pay people money to take infants, that some advertisements for infants promised "vaguer enticements" ("necessaries to go with it"—the neuter pronoun referring to the infant—or "additional good terms"), and that there were related practices of giving away children for a term and of giving away elderly slaves, ibid., 624 (on the use of the pronoun), 628, 629 (quotations), 630, 636 n6. Andover men and women took advantage of the bargain and brought infants to Andover to be raised as slaves, a strategy that may also have considered that infants and children reared as slaves were more "coercibile" than adults, "more controllable and less likely to rebel", Hollander, Review of *Amistad's Orphans* by Benjamin N. Lawrance, 847. Town of Andover, "Town Records, Town Meetings, Persons Warned to Leave Town 1790–1793" (untitled volume, title from microfilm target), n.p., second volume on GSU Microfilm Reel 887742 (February 9, 1791 warning out for Prince brought into Andover "when an infant" by Jonathan Cummings, Jr.). Salem Poor was brought from Salem to Andover as an infant by John Poor's mother-in-law or his wife, but I am uncertain which John Poor (1690–? or 1718–1811) was meant, Lambert, "Salem Poor" and Tewksbury, "Lawrence," 237, with several other sources that provided parallel information for Salem Poor.

² Sarah Frye, Probate file papers, will, June 1, 1776; inventory, May 1, 1781; accounting and distribution, September 7, 1790 (quotation).

³ Booso v. Samuel Chickering, Essex County Court of Common Pleas Records, July 1778, 476, JA. I searched with no results the consolidated index to Essex County court records of decisions for other freedom suits involving Phillis' extended family. (The Essex County consolidated index is on microfilm at JA, but not included in the references cited.) I also searched with no results in the case accounting records dating 1781–1790 of Essex County attorney Theophilus Parsons, Docket book, 1774–1800, n.p., HLS MS 4022, Harvard Law School Library, Cambridge, Mass. There may be records of actions brought by or involving them unlocated in the judicial archives or in another Essex County attorney's records. Judicial and attorney records indicate that in some cases attorneys settled disputes among parties informally. Sometimes an attorney might obtain a writ and have it served on a defendant to commence a lawsuit but the matter was not docketed for trial, presumably because the case was settled out of court or abandoned. Sometimes a case

would be docketed, continued, then dropped, either nonsuit (the plaintiff did not proceed) or settled. In these different outcomes for resolved disputes, judicial and attorney records may have sparse information; case information may be unindexed and require searching for entries in dockets, file papers, and attorney's financial accounting records. Essex County Common Pleas court clerks sometimes discarded but other times preserved file papers that had been filed for cases that were not docketed, that were not adjudicated by trial, that were nonsuit by the plaintiff, or that the plaintiff won by default when the defendant failed to appear.

[4] Sarah Holt deposed that Rosanna was 21 years old when Colley was born. Sarah Holt, August 31, 1854, in Coburn and Coburn, RWPA. There were many Hoopers in the area, used as a forename or as a surname. Pomp Hooper, if born about 1771, would have been about 14 to 15 in 1785–1786, when Rosanna became pregnant, *VRA*, Vol. 2, Deaths, "Negroes," 574 (age 39 in 1810).

[5] Kelley, *Wilmington Records*, 114, 167 (marriage, "Titus Cober" and "Vilot Noble", August 28, 1785), and 26 (birth of Jennie, May 27, 1789, parents are "Servants of Ebenezer Jones"). A copy of a record of marriages performed by the Rev. Isaac Morrill (August 28, 1785, "Titus Cober & Vilot Noble", both of Wilmington) appeared in Town of Wilmington, "Vital Records Cattle Records 1716–1851" (spine title), n.p., first volume on GSU Microfilm Reel 761324, digital image 121 of 288, https://familysearch.org /ark:/61903/3:1:3QSQ-G97M-59T2-G?i=120&cc=2061550&-cat=146741, accessed August 12, 2017. Rosanna Coburn, August 8, 1854; Colley Hooper, August 8, 1854; Elizabeth Blanchard, August 10, 1854; Sarah Holt, August 28 and 31, 1854 (marriage to Titus Coburn solemnized by Samuel Eames, Esq. in Wilmington), all in Coburn and Coburn, RWPA. Eames apparently was not a minister, so the marriage was probably a civil ceremony, Loring, "Robert Eames of Woburn, Mass., and Some of his Descendants," 151. United States Census, *Population Schedules of the Second Census of the United States 1800, Roll 17*, Middlesex County, Wilmington, 1079. Town of Andover, "Town Records, Tax Records 1799–1822" (untitled volume, title from microfilm target but actually treasurer records of payments for orders drawn by the overseers of the poor), n.p., first volume on GSU Microfilm Reel 878782, June 8, 1816 (No. 20, $5.00: "An order to Titus Coburn for supporting his daughter in part"; No. 21, $6.54: Dr. Nathaniel Swift for "June Coburn"); October 7, 1816 (No. 62, $2.08: Dr. Nathaniel Swift for "Jane Coburn").

[6] Anonymous, "Sketches of Octogenarians" (about Rose Coburn's family), n.p. [2]. Dorman's 1830 map, "A Plan of Andover," shows "D. Peters" on the

southwest side of Salem Turnpike (now Turnpike Street, between Haverhill Street and Elm Street, in North Andover) in the vicinity of several properties of "J. Peters". The Andover Preservation Commission, et al., *Andover Historic Preservation* website identified a four-acre parcel owned by William Peters in the vicinity of what is presently 79–93 Haverhill Street with parts extending to 5–8 Liberty Street, but that location is at some distance from Salem Turnpike (Route 114).

[7] Carpenter, "Glimpses of Life in Andover Eighty Years Ago, from an Old Family Expense-book," credited "the Historical Society ladies" who remembered "the two colored women who lived in old time on Missionary Lane, known as 'Rose and Colley.'" Missionary Lane is now Woodland Road, Goldsmith, *The Townswoman's Andover*, 72; Ralston, "Lasting Tribute to Andover's Early Missionaries." Joan Patrakis (email, August 6, 2017) shared from her research notes an entry dated April 4, 1843, "No. 4: An order to Joseph S. Holt for rent of Garden and House for Rose and Colly Coburn.....$15.00". Patrakis found that entry in the "Treasurer's Record Book 1832–1874," which is the fifth volume in Town of Andover, "Town Records, Treasurer's Records 1767–1874," GSU Microfilm Reel 878787. Patrakis used the copy of that microfilm at Memorial Hall Library, Andover. The house and garden that Holt rented to Rosanna and Colley was probably their last known residence on Missionary Lane, located in the neighborhood where numerous members of the Holt family lived. In 1852 and 1856, Rosanna Coburn's house was shown to be located at the northeast corner of the intersection of what is now Highland Road and Woodland Road (the modern street address is 4 Woodland Road). The house of "R. Coburn" is plotted at that location on Walling, "Map of the Town of Andover" (1852) and Walling, "A Topographical Map of Essex County" (1856). To determine modern street locations, I used the Harvard Library, *Harvard Geospatial Library*, which is a computer program that georeferences digital images of historical maps to modern maps, available via https://library.harvard.edu/services-tools/harvard-geospatial-library. Massachusetts Census, 1855, Andover Dwelling No. 79, showed that the two women lived together.

[8] Town of Andover, "Town Records, Tax Records 1799–1822" (untitled volume, title from microfilm target but actually treasurer records of payments for orders drawn by the overseers of the poor), n.p., first volume on GSU Microfilm Reel 878782, June 8, 1816 (No. 20, $5.00: "An order to Titus Coburn for supporting his daughter in part"; No. 21, $6.54: Dr. Nathaniel Swift for "June Coburn"); October 7, 1816 (No. 62, $2.08: Dr. Nathaniel Swift for "Jane Coburn"); November 5, 1816 (No. 102, $0.50: "An order to William Johnson 3[d] [...] To cash paid black man at Titus Coburns").

⁹ For the specific citations, see chap. 4, note 31, Andover treasurer/overseers of the poor records, under Payments to Rose Coburn for supporting Phillis.

¹⁰ For Phillis' doctor bills, see chap. 4, note 31, Andover treasurer/overseers of the poor records, under Payments to Dr. Abiel Pearson, and under Payments to Dr. Nathaniel Swift. The largest payment to Dr. Swift for "medicine and attendance" for Phillis was $6.75, made on August 20, 1827 (No. 12).

¹¹ Colley Hooper, August 8, 1854, in Coburn and Coburn, RWPA. Rose Coburn, Probate file papers, will, December 23, 1854. Colley Hooper, Death record, Town of Andover and State Vital Records. Town of Andover, "Town Records, Tax Records 1823–1847" (untitled volume, title from microfilm target but actually treasurer records of payments for orders drawn by the overseers of the poor), n.p., ninth volume on GSU Microfilm Reel 878782, January 5, 1829 (No. 36, $3.00: "coffin for Phillis Wid[ow] of Boos").

¹² See Hine, *Hine Sight*, xxviii, for "dissemblance," and 41 for "enigmatic." See Brown, "Death-Defying Testimony," especially page 135 for privacy that reflected "resilient interiority."

¹³ The Rev. Charles Carroll Carpenter (1836–1918) moved to Andover in 1886. He was a local historian, antiquarian, genealogist, writer, and editor of *The Andover Townsman*. Adams, "A Man for All Seasons"; Anonymous, "Obituary Rev. C.C. Carpenter." Claude Fuess, *Andover: Symbol of New England*, 365, characteristically disparaged Carpenter's accumulation of local history sources, his methods, and his focus on details (as he did in his evaluation of local historians Abiel Abbot and Charlotte Helen Abbott, ibid., 357, 365–366). Rev. Carpenter donated six now rare publications from Andover's 250th anniversary celebration held in 1896, and a seventh publication from an 1896 Andover interdenominational missionary meeting, to the Massachusetts State Library, *Report of the Librarian*, 20. ACHC has a collection of his papers. Rosanna and Colley were mentioned in his 1913 article in that newspaper, "Glimpses of Life in Andover Eighty Years Ago, from an Old Family Expense-book" (May 2, 1913, 3), drawn from a talk he gave to the AHS in April. Carpenter extracted entries from the account book of Josiah B. Clough's household that showed Rose Coburn delivered eggs from Capt. Joseph Holt and traded "whortleberries" she collected for flour. Carpenter dated some of the exchanges with Rose to April 1834, but noted that the entries for Rose were "repeated often," so perhaps the entry for the blueberries was made in the late summer. "How interesting to think of that woman, with her remarkable history, bringing eggs from Capt. Joseph Holt's and 'huckleberries' which she had picked to Andover homes. Elder residents of Andover must remember her well." Drawing from Bailey, *Historical Sketches of Andover*, Carpenter summarized Rosanna's biography and mentioned that "Rose

Coburn [...] lived until she was 92 years old" and was "the last slave born in Andover".

John Plummer Foster, Account book, Vol. 1 (1842–1856), n.p., January 31, 1853, "Paid Mrs. Coburn for two weeks taking care of Ann" $2.50; John Foster Plummer, Diary, Vol. 6 (1851–1855, "John P. Foster Journal No. 2"), 49 (December 23, 1852, birth of daughter), John Plummer Foster Diaries, 1848–1888, DIA 63, Phillips Library, Peabody Essex Museum, Rowley, Mass. I was not able to read through the entire collection of Foster's incredibly interesting diaries and account books. After noticing the entry for Mrs. Coburn in the account book, other entries for his frequent visits to "South Andover", that he delivered loads of hay to Andover attorney Nathan W. Hazen who knew Rosanna and Colley, and that Foster described attending funerals, I selected periods to search in his journals for any related entries around the date of the entry for paying Mrs. Coburn and around the dates when Colley Hooper and Rosanna Coburn died, but there was no mention of either of them among the pages I reviewed. "Mrs. Coburn" may as well have been another woman from another town. Foster traveled beyond Andover to seek female laborers, such as for a wet nurse and for "a girl" to help with household labor. Foster also assisted with childcare and seemed to have taken on other tasks Ann could not perform while she recovered from childbirth. Foster's Diary, Vol. 7 (1855–1861, "John P. Foster Journal No. 3"), 152 (February 1–3, 1860) has several entries that said "I helped take care of the baby", and there are other entries that appear to indicate he took on some of Ann's work. Foster's journal entries broaden notions about gendered labor tasks involving childcare and other usually female-gendered household tasks that Foster managed to do "besides doing the chores" of farm work.

14 Anonymous, "Sketches of Octogenarians" (about Rose Coburn's family), n.p. [2].

15 Andover South Church, Records of the Samuel Phillips and Samuel Abbot Funds for the Relief of Indigent Persons in the South Parish (untitled, bound volume, n.p.), Andover South Parish Church I Records, Ms S 665, Subgroup IV, Series B, Subseries 1, ACHC. The absence of Rosanna Coburn from the annual lists of indigent persons from 1825–1835 is curious. Perhaps during that period she and Colley lived in another parish. Colley's name did not appear on the lists.

16 Town of Andover, Overseers of the Poor, "Return of the Poor in the Town of Andover during the year ending on the last Monday of December, 1833," Ms. S 203, ACHC, which was endorsed by a clerk January 18, 1834. The manuscript, a printed form with handwritten entries, indicated that Rosanna Coburn was 61 years old, "coloured" as indicated by ditto marks in the col-

umn for "Color", that she could neither read nor write, misstated that she had no children, was temperate, was supported outside the almshouse, and received annually $27.83 ("X" represented "8" in the entry, as it did in another part of the manuscript).

The wood delivery in 1839 to Rose Coburn was made by David Gray (1762–1844), who was an overseer of the poor, a selectman, and appraised property for tax purposes. His notebook includes notations of information made in his official role and for his personal business. Pertaining to the latter, Gray made the following entries: "to 12 feet of small pine wood to Rose Cobborn" (March 23, 1839, $3.00) and "to 14¼ feet white pine wood Delivered to Rose Colburn" (December 23, 1839, $5.00). Gray's arithmetic and calculations on that page, seemingly the amounts he recorded to be later claimed with the town treasurer, do not appear to be correct. David Gray, Account book, census and appraisal of townspeople's farm animals (and other property for tax purposes), May 1, 1838–October 11, 1839 (and later), n.p., Taft Collection, Ms S 134, Sub-group I, Series A, David Gray 1762–1844, Folder 9, ACHC. Whatever amount Gray was paid by the town for the two deliveries of fuel, presumably that was included in the total amount of support of $23.00 that the town reported it provided to Rosanna Coburn's household that year, Town of Andover, *Annual Town Reports*, 1839.

[17] Town of Andover, Overseers of the Poor, Notebook with accounts of activities and expenditures, 1843–1845, n.p., Ms. S 96, ACHC. The list of food provisions and other items provided to Rosanna Coburn appears on the tenth page of the notebook, after an entry dated August 22, 1843. With the layout and line breaks of the handwritten list retained for this quotation, the list reads:

> Rosanna Coburn –
> 1 Jug Mulasses
> 1 "   Oil – Butter
> Saltfish + Cheese –
> Flour – Dark Calico 2 dresses –
> ½ [lt?] Ginger, ground –
> 2 pr. Sheets – Tea
> Sugar – Cocoa –

[18] Town of Andover, *Annual Town Reports*, 1832, 1835–1839, 1843, 1845–1848, 1850–1856. I thank Angela McBrien for alerting me to the ACHC's collection of original printed town reports dating at least 1820–1851. The ACHC collection of annual reports is not serially complete, but the report may not have been published in some years. For years that the report was published, but which are not in the ACHC collection, the town clerk may

preserve those reports. The State Library and Memorial Hall Library presently host digital images of the reports in their collections for 1845–1846, and 1851–1856+, and images of earlier reports may be added. During my research, I passed over reports that did not list names of any individuals that received support. I noted that in 1829 the report listed names of the poor that were housed with named individuals. In 1829, Rosanna Coburn and Colley Hooper lived independently so were not named as boarding with others, but yet they received support that year. In the 1831 report, the Coburn-Hoopers were not listed among those who received financial support, and from 1840 to 1842 the published report specified no names of the poor, but again support for the Coburn-Hoopers was likely provided during those years. Items or services (wood, "goods", "supplies", "medical attendance", "board", etc.) provided to named individuals were not always specified in the annual report, but were itemized for those individuals in other town records, such as in the manuscript Andover treasurer and/or overseers of the poor financial records. Entries for support provided by the town to the Coburn-Hooper household for earlier and intervening years, but not indicated in the published town reports, were noticed in the manuscript town financial records, see chap. 4, note 31. During this research, I was not able to comprehensively search all the manuscript town financial records for entries for Phillis' extended family, but I expect additional entries could be found by another researcher. Rendering of names in the printed annual town reports varied (e.g., 1843: "Rose & Colly Coburn"; 1846: "Roxana Coburn and daughter"; 1847, 1850–1851: "Elizabeth Coburn"). Prior to 1852, the annual town report was printed as a broadside. From 1852 forward, the report was published as a paginated booklet, so in the summary below the page number where information appeared in the booklet was specified after the year. In the summary below, "id." indicates that the name was rendered identically as the previous quoted entry.

1832 ("Rose Coburn" state pauper $13.80); 1835 (id. $21.62); 1836 (id. $27.42); 1837 (id. $14.92); 1838 (id. $27.11); 1839 (id. $23.00); 1843 ("Rose & Colly Coburn" state paupers $35.20); 1845 ("R. Coburn and daughter" state paupers $31.39); 1846 ("Roxana Coburn and daughter" state paupers $65.23); 1847 ("Rose and Elizabeth Coburn" state paupers "goods" $59.75, wood $7.25, $67.00); 1848 ("Rose Coburn" wood $5.94, "Board and Support" $13.62); 1850 ("Rose and Elizabeth Coburn" wood $6.50, "Board and Support" $26.18, "Rose Coburn" "Medical Attendance" $4.00); 1851 ("Rosanna Coburn" wood $6.88, "Board and supplies" $34.57, "Medical Attendance" $3.00, "Elizabeth Coburn" state pauper wood $6.87, "Board and supplies" $34.57); 1852, 8 ("Rosanna Coburn" wood $20.25, "Board and supplies" $38.41); 1853, 10 ("Rose

Coburn" wood $28.31, "Board and supplies" $25.81); 1854, 10 (id.
wood $9.35, "Board and supplies" $42.94); 1855, 13 (id. $23.35);
1856, 14 ("Rose Coburn (1854)" $2.50).

All the costs of items and services listed in the printed town reports for
Rosanna and Colley (Elizabeth) were for support provided outside the almshouse. In this context, "board" could mean meals only, not also lodging when
staying with another family. Rosanna and Colley lived together in their own
home but their house was rented for them. Perhaps their rent was included in
the yearly amount for "board". The names on the lists of those who received
support outside the almshouse often seem to be heads of households. In some
cases the amounts listed for them included support for other unnamed people residing with them. The amounts of the expenditures vary considerably
for each listed person: in some years the amounts were noticeably greater
than for other named persons.

[19] Rose Coburn, Probate file papers, will, December 23, 1854. John Parnell
and his wife Sarah were neighbors of Rosanna and Colley: the Parnells also
lived on Missionary Lane. Massachusetts Census, 1855, Andover Dwelling
No. 77 (Parnell), Dwelling No. 79 (Coburn); Walling, "Map of the Town of
Andover" (1852); Walling, "A Topographical Map of Essex County" (1856).
Colley Hooper's estate was not probated, and Rose had no other heir. Executor John Parnell was the sole residuary legatee of Rose Coburn's estate. Regrettably for historians, no personal items were enumerated in Rose Coburn's
inventory. Rose's only listed property was $446.55 in cash savings and bank
interest. Clearly, Rose managed to save a large part of four to five years of her
widow's pension payments. After deducting debt and expenses—including
$20 Parnell paid for her gravestone—the remaining $309.32 in Rose's estate
went to Parnell. Rose Coburn, Probate file papers, account of administration, June 11, 1861, Schedule B for the gravestone. Rosanna Coburn's relationship to her neighbor John Parnell, a tailor, or to the other individuals
whose names appeared in her probate file papers, has not been fully ascertained. Parnell was a lay delegate representing Christ Church (Episcopal),
in Andover, at the 1844, 1845, and 1846 Boston conventions of the Diocese of Massachusetts, *Journal of the Proceedings of the [...] Annual Convention*,
1844, 4; 1845, 5; 1846, 5. John Parnell signed antislavery and abolitionist
petitions in 1838 and 1839. Carpenter, et al., *Digital Archive of Massachusetts
Anti-Slavery and Anti-Segregation Petitions*, "Senate Unpassed Legislation
1839, Docket 10525, SC1/series 231, Petition of Timothy Foster" and 276
other male inhabitants of Andover to abolish slavery in Washington, D.C.
and against the admission of Florida and slave states, https://doi:10.7910/
DVN/8Y0TY, digital image seq. 358, accessed August 15, 2017; Carpenter,
et al., ibid., "Passed Resolves; Resolves 1839, c. 36, SC1/series 228, Petition

of Mark Newman" and 200 other citizens of Andover protesting the foreign slave trade, https://doi:10.7910/DVN/DRLBB, digital image seq. 2, column 2, accessed August 15, 2017.

Rose Coburn's will was witnessed first by Nathan W. Hazen (her attorney and a Justice of the Peace). Hazen was an overseer of the poor in 1846 and 1847, Town of Andover, *Annual Town Reports*, 1846, 1847. Hazen had drafted the 1846 letter about Rosanna Coburn and Colley written to Massachusetts Rep. John Sargent (one of the two commissioners appointed to prepare the 1847 report, Massachusetts House of Representatives, RCEC, that had disclaimed Rosanna and Colley as state paupers), Town of Andover, Overseers of the Poor, Nathan W. Hazen, draft letter to State Commissioner John Sargent, November 18, 1846, in Town of Andover, "Town Records, Selectmen Records 1841–1861" (untitled volume, spine title "Letter Book", title from microfilm target but actually orders for payments drawn by the overseers of the poor, and letters written and received regarding poor in Andover), n.p., third volume on GSU Microfilm Reel 887743. The other two witnesses to Rose Coburn's will were David I.C. Hidden, and her neighbor Charles C. Blunt. Mr. Hidden and Mr. Blunt were involved in town and county agricultural societies. For Hidden, whose mother was Mary Chandler, and who was "a builder", see Chase, "To Promote True Piety" and "Liberal Advantages," 40–43, 65–66, 200 n4, 201 n5; Goldsmith, *The Townswoman's Andover*, 72, 91 ("builder"); Massachusetts Census, 1855, Andover Dwelling No. 80 (Blunt), No. 185 (Hidden). Nathan W. Hazen, Mr. Hidden, and Albert Abbott (also an Andover resident, ibid., Dwelling No. 147 [Abbott]) were appointed appraisers of Rose Coburn's estate. Hazen also acted as Parnell's attorney when Coburn's estate was probated. In his role as a Justice of the Peace, Hazen also took Parnell's sworn oath to the final accounting of the estate. Hazen's multiple roles in Rose Coburn's probate proceedings were conflicts of interests. In 1856, Hazen had published *A Letter to the Inhabitants of Andover and North Andover* that denied he was self-dealing in real estate while representing the Essex Company in Lawrence.

[20] Colley Hooper, Death record, Town of Andover and State Vital Records. Anonymous, "Obituary" for Rosanna Coburn. As transcribed by Alfred Poore, "Andover Graveyards Old South Andover Graveyards," n.p. [6], in "Cemetery Records of Andover, Mass.," n.d., MSS 0.424, Phillips Library, Peabody Essex Museum, Rowley, Mass., Rosanna's original gravestone epitaph also conveyed that she "was a person of great honesty vivacity and intelligence", as did the anonymous *Boston Globe* reporter, "Andover's 250th Birthday," *The Boston Sunday Globe*, May 17, 1896, 40, reading it as "honesty, vivacity and intelligence". Sarah Loring Bailey's, *Historical Sketches of Andover*, 44, "honesty, veracity and intelligence" must be an error in transcription

or typesetting. The epitaph on the present gravestone (placed in 2002) does not include either "vivacity" or "veracity" and there are other minor variations among all the transcriptions.

[21] Rosanna Coburn, August 8, 1854, in Coburn and Coburn, RWPA.

[22] Knoblock, *African American Historic Burial Grounds*, 209, noticed that Coburn was assisted in her pension application by Barzillai Lew [Jr.]. His and Rosanna's interactions with legal and bureaucratic county probate and federal pension systems, Titus Coburn's purchase and sale of property, Rosanna's father Booso's freedom suit, and Phillis and the other Frye slaves having "taken their Freedom" are examples of "legal consciousness," sophisticated legal knowledge shared among and utilized by people of color, as discerned by Hancock, "'The Law Will Make You Smart,'" 7–11. The local newspaper announcement about Rosanna's pension, Anonymous, "A Wind Fall," *Andover Advertiser*, September 30, 1854, n.p. [2], did not mention Barzillai Lew [Jr.], but rather reported that Rosanna obtained the pension "through the exertions of Mr. I.[Israel] Perkins, of Danvers." Coburn and Coburn, RWPA. Titus Coburn, Probate file papers. Barzillai and Dinah Lew, RWPA, application commenced by Barzillai Lew [Jr.], August 8, 1854; Dinah Lew, Probate file papers. For more on the Andover Barzillai Lew [Jr.] and his family history, see Coburn, *History of Dracut*, 322, 332–336; Dorman, *Twenty Families of Color in Massachusetts*, 277–278, which at 272 indicated that the genealogical information he summarized about Barzillai Lew [Sr.], his wife Dinah (Bowman) Lew, and their 13 children derived largely from the Barzillai and Dinah Lew, RWPA; Martin, "On the Landscape for a Very, Very Long Time," 135–136; Mayo, "The Lew Family"; Morrison, "Negroes Who Fought at Bunker Hill"; and see chap. 3, note 9. Barzillai Lew [Jr.] appears to have achieved prominence as a leader-type figure within the Andover community of people of color. He assisted as a liaison when they interacted with other people in positions of power and authority, on occasions when Andover people of color were required to articulate with official bureaucratic systems. The manuscript ledger of pension payments indicated biannual payments of $48 (paid March and September) that commenced March 4, 1848, paid September 1848 through March 1859, United States Revolutionary War Pension Payment Ledgers, Roll 19, Volume R, Widow Pensions under Acts of February 2 and July 29, 1848, 1848–62, 174 ("Rosannah Coburn"). That record indicated that Rosanna had been paid the amounts due her biannually; it does not indicate that she initially received a larger, lump-sum retroactive payment. The amount of the retroactive lump-sum was not specified in Coburn and Coburn RWPA, but as 13 payments of $48 were due her for September 1848 through September 1854, she probably received $624 as her first pension payment. Additional detailed information, including when and

to whom payments were made, is likely to be found in the Pension Agency Payment Books, 1805–1909, RG 15, NM-21, Series 2 (the index cards to the books are RG 15, NM-21, Series 1), National Archives, Washington, D.C., not included in the references cited, but noted in Prechtel-Kluskens, "Follow the Money."

[23] Minardi, "Freedom in the Archives: The Pension Case of Primus Hall," 129, who cited the Barzillai and Dinah Lew pension application at 130 n7 in discussion of gathered testimonial evidence when official records were lacking. See also Jecmen, "Writing the Revolution," for the pension process.

[24] Andover town clerk, August 11, 1854, copy of Titus Coburn death record of May 5, 1821, in Coburn and Coburn, RWPA.

[25] Anonymous, "A Wind Fall," *Andover Advertiser* (Andover, Mass.), September 30, 1854, n.p. [2]; Anonymous, "Rose Coburn," *The Liberator* (Boston, Mass.), October 13, 1854, 163 (quotation); Anonymous, "Gleanings of News," Rose Coburn note, *Frederick Douglass' Paper* (Rochester, N.Y.), October 20, 1854, n.p. [3]; Anonymous, Rose Coburn note, *The Anti-Slavery Bugle* (Salem, Ohio), November 4, 1854, n.p. [2].

[26] Theodore Parker, Letter to George Bancroft, March 16, 1858, 235. Parker conveyed information from William C. Nell, author of *The Colored Patriots*, 21, about African Americans at the Battle of Bunker Hill, mistaking Rosanna's husband for another man named Titus Coburn who was from Shirley, Harvard, and Littleton, Mass., and who died at Valley Forge 1778.

[27] Anonymous, "Sketches of Octogenarians" (about Rose Coburn's family), n.p. [2]. Conspicuous in the history of Phillis' extended family are the very few indications of religious affect or affiliation. Booso (Boassee/Bussen) married Moriah by the Rev. John Barnard at the North Church in Andover (now North Andover), *VRA*, Vol. 2, 356, 358 (Marriages, "Negroes," February 13 or 15, 1755); Bailey, *Historical Sketches of Andover*, 438 (Barnard ministry). Titus Coburn was baptized when he was likely 11 years old (with Edward Hircom's other slave, as "Peggy & Titus} Negro Ser[van]ᵗˢ of Capᵗ Hircom") at the Second Church of Christ in Reading on August 23, 1767, Reading, Mass., Second Church of Christ Records, 1720–1806, RG5021, n.p., The Congregational Library & Archives, Boston, Mass., http://nehh-viewer .s3-website-us-east-1.amazonaws.com/#/content/ReadingSecond/viewer /Church20Records2C2017201806/64, digital image 64. Titus Coburn and Violet Noble were married by Rev. Isaac Morrill at the First Church in Wilmington, Town of Wilmington, "Vital Records Cattle Records 1716– 1851" (spine title), n.p., first volume on GSU Microfilm Reel 761324, https://familysearch.org/ark:/61903/3:1:3QSQ-G97M-59T2-G?i

=120&cc=2061550&cat=146741, accessed August 12, 2017, digital image 121 of 288, "Titus Cober & Vilot Noble" (August 28, 1785); Smith, *Morrill Kindred in America*, 50–67 (Morrill church). Titus Coburn's will written the day he died began with "In the name of GOD amen" and also included "blessed be almighty GOD", Titus Coburn will, May 5, 1821, in Coburn and Coburn, RWPA (copy by Essex County register of probate, August 8, 1854), and in Titus Coburn, Probate file papers (copy of will, August 8, 1854). Rosanna Coburn received a small annual stipend (1824, 1836–1854) from a charitable fund administered by the South Church because she was a poor person residing in the South Parish. The fund was not reserved for South Church members. Andover South Church, Records of the Samuel Phillips and Samuel Abbot Funds for the Relief of Indigent Persons in the South Parish (untitled, bound volume, n.p.), Andover South Parish Church I Records, Ms S 665, Subgroup IV, Series B, Subseries 1, ACHC. Also in ecclesiastical records, Rosanna and Colley's deaths were noted by the Rev. Charles C. Vinal, whose records were copied into the North Parish Church "Minister's Book." Andover North Parish Church, "Andover North Parish Church Records Minister's Book 1810–1850 [i.e., 1848–1937] Baptisms Admissions to Membership Marriages Deaths," 77 (Vinal's records), 79 (deaths). The Rev. Vinal served the North Parish (Unitarian) church from 1857 to 1870, ibid., 77. His notations of their deaths in the "Minister's Book" could suggest their membership in his North Parish congregation, but Colley Hooper's name was rendered as "Collie Coburn" and Rosanna's death was recorded in the wrong year, suggesting he did not know them very well. He may have attended or officiated their graveside services, which occurred at the South Parish Cemetery maintained by the South Church. Further research of Andover church records might discover whether or not any of them had attended or were members of local churches.

[28] Anonymous, "Obituary" for Rosanna Coburn, n.p. [2]. I have not been able to identify the author. The November 12, 1853 issue of the *Andover Advertiser* with the "Sketches" article about Rosanna Coburn was published by John D. Flagg; the April 2, 1859 issue with her "Obituary" was published by Warren F. Draper. The masthead under Flagg's and Draper's editorships only credited that the business of the paper was "conducted by an Association of Gentlemen." Paradise, *A History of Printing in Andover*, n.p. [19, counting full title page as 1], conveyed that the writers under Flagg's editorship "were the Hon. George Foster, Mr. Eastman Sanborn, and Mr. Moses Foster [...]. However [...George Foster] did most of the work, and later conducted an Andover column in the *Lawrence American*." The Hon. George Foster (1810–1885) held local and state political offices. He "intended to enter the Methodist ministry [...] Contributed very much to the Andover *Advertiser* and was reg-

ular Andover news correspondent for the Lawrence *American*. [...] He was a prominent worker in the Free Church (Congregational), deacon [...and Sunday School] superintendent", Marland, "Loan Collection and Historic Sites,"149; Mooar, *Mooar (Moors) Genealogy*, 45–46 (quotation). Textual analysis of George Foster's writings might indicate whether or not he or another was the author of the Rosanna Coburn pieces, and of the anonymous "Pomp and Pomp's Pond" article that concluded with the initial "G." A clipping of the Coburn "Sketches" article was glued in the back of a unique copy of Abbot's *History of Andover* with "69 extra pages with newspaper clippings" at the ACHC (Accession No. 1991.140). That copy has many clippings of articles and letters to the town newspaper on local historical subjects, some published anonymously. William G. Brooks, one of the former owners of the book, wrote initials on some of the clippings (but not the Rosanna Coburn pieces) to indicate their authorship.

[29] The phrase was adapted from William Cowper, "The Time-piece" (as the poem title appeared in the first edition, then more usually rendered as "The Timepiece"), lines 12–13, in Book II of *The Task*, 46: "He finds his fellow guilty of a skin [/] Not colour'd like his own". I am grateful to Jessy Wheeler in the Research Services Department of the Boston Public Library for identifying the origin of the phrase in the lines of Cowper's epic poem. Cowper's antislavery and abolitionist poems were popular among adherents to the cause, and those particular lines resonated powerfully. The repeated quotation and adaptation of Cowper's lines appeared in numerous antislavery and abolitionist speeches and writings. The modification of Cowper's lines and general lack of attribution suggest that while the original source and its original form became obscure to some, its politically signifying essence was broadly recognized. See Davis, *The Problem of Slavery in the Age of Revolution*, 368–373, 384, 558, and Turner, "Cowper, Slave Narratives, and the Antebellum American Reading Public," n.p. (quotations), for the myriad ways that adaptations of Cowper's phrasing circulated in England and in New England, including in "collections of anti-slavery poems published in Britain and America, and the abolitionist newspapers such as William Lloyd Garrison's *The Liberator*, Frederick Douglass' *North Star*, and Lydia Maria Child's *National Anti-Slavery Standard*. [...] Accounts of [anti-slavery society] meetings in [...] New England [...] are peppered with quotations from Cowper." Davis, ibid., 369 n32, concluded that Cowper's "poems were immensely popular on both sides of the Atlantic, and were read by many who would never have opened an antislavery pamphlet."

[30] Brown, "Memorial Narratives of African Women in Antebellum New England," 40 ("pronounced religiosity"), 39 ("transform[ed from] cultural values" quoting "cultural values and memory" from Hume's *Obituaries in*

American Culture, 15), for alterity, and for interpretive inspiration in several respects. Lois Brown delved incisively into "the politics of appropriation" (39) of biography and genealogy for locative historical and demographically communal ("collective," 39) narratives "that reflect the competing tensions and politics of the worlds in which they were produced" (57). Brown elucidated the process of creating stories from remembered, discovered, and assumed biographic bits, sorting out factual and fictive elements. Those stories often contain nuggets of factual information not preserved elsewhere, such as *idioma* in speech (idiosyncratic and characteristic language patterns, "idioms" meant broadly, as in expressive "stylings"). An example for Rosanna Coburn appeared in the Anonymous, "Sketches of Octogenarians" (about Rose Coburn's family), n.p. [2]: "She has a daughter, which she calls her 'one chicken.'" Characteristically the stories have "unruly chronologies, unattributed facts, and incomplete profiles of the subjects" (57). Obviously, it cannot be presumed that the individual would have acceded to their portrayal, which is but one facet of the "tensions" (57) and "politics of appropriation" (39) of creating biography, even in the role of amanuensis. Regarding the genre of recounted and presented narratives authored by others, DoVeanna S. Fulton Minor and Reginald A. Pitts, "Introduction. Speaking Lives, Authoring Texts," 29, considered that "Narratives recorded by interviewers inherently raise questions about the narrator's voice and textual interests, particularly when we consider the racial and gender dynamics between interviewer and interviewee." By "locative" I mean that those stories attached to places. The stories circulated in a "community" (however conceived) and persisted as long as they were remembered and meaningful. Brown perceived that biographical "memorial narratives" are not merely stories about those individuals: they "reflect" (57) personal and group truths and broader social, political, and cultural issues. The stories were transformed in their retelling and when fixed in writing. Those set forms were again changed when the writing was quoted, paraphrased, referenced, or reformatted by photocopy, microfilm, digitization, etc. Seemingly in the examples of Rosanna's memorial narratives per se—the obituary and gravestone—and generally in stories told and written about her, there were explicit and implicit intentions to contrast the historicalness of local slavery with modernity, to advocate for social parity, and to promote national "meta-political issues" (40) such as abolition, equal treatment, enfranchisement, etc. See Melish, *Disowning Slavery*; Minardi, *Making Slavery History*; and, O'Brien, *Firsting and Lasting*, 136–137 for analysis and interpretation of historicalness and modernity in that regard. Again, by "historicalness" I mean perceptively "of history," the perceived quality of being an antiquity or a relic, in contrast to historical factuality denoted in "historicity."

[31] Rosanna Coburn, Death record, Town of Andover and State Vital Records.

[32] The town death record spelled Rosanna as "Rosana". An index to the state death records prepared by staff of the Massachusetts Secretary of the Commonwealth rendered the forename as "Roxanna", a misreading of the Andover clerk's distinctive minuscule *s*.

Andover town clerks Henry Osgood and Edward Taylor made similar nonconforming entries in the town and state marriage and death registers that denoted the former slave status of other people. Henry Osgood's record for Cato Freeman's death in 1853 (registered in 1854) added "Slaves" after the parents' names. Edward Taylor made an entry in the 1863 Andover marriage record for Robert Rollings and Julia C. Palmer, whose marriage was officiated in Andover on November 29, 1863. Their marriage record indicated, in the column for place of birth, that he was born "Maryland—in slavery" and that she was born "South—in slavery". In the column for "What Marriage—Whether First, Second, Third, &c. [etc.,]" Taylor wrote that they had previously "married south according to the slave laws." Julia's father was Henry Palmer, but her mother's name was not noted. Robert and Julia may have been escaped slaves. Rollings and Palmer, Marriage record. (I thank Charlotte Lyons for sharing her photographs of the Rollings' Andover marriage record at the Andover town clerk's office, which has the identical wording as the state record at M-Ar.) Like for Cato Freeman's and Rosanna Coburn's death records, *additional* information not required by the form was added to the Rollings-Palmer record in 1863, but seemingly differently intentioned than Freeman's and Coburn's death records made in 1854 and 1860, respectively. The 1863 entry for Rollings-Palmer explained why the already-married couple was having their marriage officiated in Andover: their marriage in the "south according to the slave laws" may not have been officially registered. It also explained the missing information for the bride's mother's name. For Cato Freeman's and Rosanna Coburn's death records, the clerks' nonconforming additions of "Slaves" for Freeman's parents, and "in slavery" for Coburn's birth with those words being underscored for the state record, explained nothing missing or unusual about their death records. (Although in Rosanna's death record the column for "Names of Parents" was left blank, death records for many others on that page were also left blank or only partially completed, such as with only a first name of a parent.)

Taylor or another person recorded "In slavery" for place of birth in the death record of Mrs. Martha Matilda (Palmer) Henderson, who died on December 3, 1864. Mrs. Henderson was the sister of Mrs. Julia C. (Palmer) Rollings, Robert Rollings' wife. The handwriting of "In slavery" is different than the rest of that entry, possibly added later by another hand. Her death record indicated that she was born about 1838, was married, and that her father was Henry Palmer. A space was left for her mother's name, but it was not indicated. Under occupation was written, in parentheses, "(african)". In the state vital records was an additional column for parents' birthplace. Her father Henry Palmer's birthplace was also indicated as "In slavery". Her mother was not known. I have not been able to locate any additional information about Mrs. Henderson, her mother, her birthplace, or husband. She might have been an escaped slave. Martha Matilda Henderson, Death record, Town of Andover and State Vital Records; Anonymous, "Necrology. Trustee. Edward Taylor." The 1864 entry for Henderson seems to me to be differently intentioned than the similar entries for Cato Freeman and for Rosanna Coburn. The 1864 entry for Henderson explained the *missing* maternal parent's name and parents' birthplaces, all of which was information that was required by the form; for Freeman and Coburn, the nonconforming entries supplied *additional* information not required and not intended to explain any missing or otherwise unusual aspects of Freeman's or Coburn's death records.

[33] Rose Coburn's estate administrator John Parnell may have composed the long epitaph that appeared on her gravestone, drawing some facts and ideas from Anonymous, "Obituary" for Rosanna Coburn. Rose Coburn, Probate file papers, account of administration, June 11, 1861, Schedule B for the gravestone. Paradise, *A History of Printing in Andover*, n.p. [19, counting full title page as 1], provided a clue that George Foster may have authored the anonymous "Sketches of Octogenarians" (about Rose Coburn's family), and Rosanna Coburn's obituary.

[34] See Minardi, *Making Slavery History*, and Minardi, "Making Slavery Visible (Again)," 95–97, for the abolitionist era linkage of citizenship efforts that recounted patriotic Revolutionary War service by people of color. Anonymous, "Obituary" for Rosanna Coburn, n.p. [2]. The word "vivacity" appeared in the earliest transcription of the epitaph, in notes made by Alfred Poore, "Andover Graveyards Old South Andover Graveyards," n.p. [6], in "Cemetery Records of Andover, Mass.," n.d., MSS 0.424, Phillips Library, Peabody Essex Museum, Rowley, Mass. Instead of Poore's more sensible and irredundant *honesty* vivacity *and intelligence* that was consonant with her buoyant character described in the anonymous "Obituary," Bailey (*Historical Sketches of Andover*, 44) provided that the epitaph read *honesty*, veracity *and intelligence*. Most certainly, "vivacity" was the word used on the original gravestone. Sixteen years after Bailey's book appeared, a reporter for the *Boston Globe* featured a transcription of the epitaph in an article about the town's 250th anniversary celebration of 1896: she or he also read it as "honesty, vivacity and intelligence", Anonymous, "Andover's 250th Birthday," *The*

Boston Sunday Globe, May 27, 1896, 40. The present gravestone placed in 2002 does not include either "vivacity" or "veracity". The phrase is "honesty and intelligence" in Batchelder's 1975 drawing (published in Campbell, *West of the Shawsheen*, 25), and that was the source of the wording selected for Rose Coburn's 2002 replacement gravestone. Poore, ibid., and Batchelder's drawing spelled "pention" (pension) identically, and that spelling may have appeared on the original gravestone. Poore and Bailey both rendered the important characterization of Rose as *the last survivor of all born* here in *that condition* (i.e., the last slave born in Andover). Batchelder drew it as *born* with in *that condition* while the 2002 stone combined it as within, each of which conveys a slightly different sense. Poore's and Bailey's quotations also indicated a co-burial and shared gravestone with her daughter. The last line—*neither of them leaving any descendants*—that bolstered the sense of finality of Rose as *the last survivor* was not included in either Rose or Colley's replacement stones. The separate gravestone for Colley Hooper placed in 2002 states she was the *daughter* of Titus Coburn (she was his stepdaughter). Other minor and unimportant variations among the four texts include Poore's lack of commas in the phrase "honesty vivacity and intelligence" and his spelling of "surviver".

At this juncture, matters of precision and accuracy by the transcribers of the original epitaph should be considered. Poore's transcription of another gravestone epitaph was neither precise nor complete for that of Almira Quacumbush (1800–1830) at what is now called Phillips Academy Cemetery. Poore misspelled the name as "Almena Quaembush" and did not include "she was" and "in full Christian hope" in his transcription (cf. Poore, "Theological Seminary Burial Ground" in "Cemetery Records of Andover, Mass.," n.p. [3]; *VRA*, Vol. 2, 532, that corrected the name but quoted from Poore's entry that excised words; and, the gravestone epitaph photographed by John Glassford for the Find A Grave record, https://www.findagrave .com/cgi-bin/fg.cgi?page=gr&GRid=92270552, accessed August 17, 2017. For a biographical note about Quacumbush, see Bailey, *Historical Sketches of Andover*, 515). Poore, "A Genealogical-Historical Visitation of Andover, Mass., in the Year 1863," *Essex Institute Historical Collections* 49 (1) (1913): 62, also mistook Rosanna Coburn for Pompey Lovejoy's wife Rose ("servant [...] to" John Foster, *VRA*, Vol. 2, 358, Marriages, "Negroes"). Bailey, ibid., 42–43, published a transcription of Cato Phillips' (Cato Freeman's) locally well-known letter of 1789 that varied considerably from the original manuscript. If Bailey's source was the transcription published in 1853 by Brooks ["B."], Letter to editor about Cato Freeman, which also was not consonant with the 1789 manuscript, her rendering differed considerably from Brooks' version too. It would be unrealistic to expect that history work, then as now, was consistently unerring, or that the products would be concordant with present-day scholarly transcribing principles. At the time when Poore and Bailey were practicing, it was conventional to silently adapt and to modernize idiosyncratic historical texts to improve readability. The epitaph on the original marble gravestone is eroded and unreadable, and a gravestone rubbing made by Jim Batchelder prior to his drawing has not been located. If historical photographs of the original stone are discovered, or if non-contact 3-D laser scanning of the original stone and image processing can reveal its text, then the certain form and content of the original epitaph could be determined.

[35] Anonymous, Note about resetting gravestones, *Lawrence American and Andover Advertiser*, May 15, 1896, 5. The effort occurred around the same time as Andover's 250th anniversary (held on May 20, 1896) and continued after. The newspaper indicated that "The stones that have laid flat for a long time in the South Parish grave yard are gradually being set up. [...] Rose Coburn[']s [stone] has also been set up. [...] There is a deep depression of the shape of the stone, where it has lain for a long time." Rose Coburn's 2002 replacement stone was featured in the news article about the South Parish Cemetery preservation project by Piro, "Historic Undertaking: Repairing Stones is a Grave Undertaking." The South Church's Rev. Dana Allen Walsh in 2017, "'Bear Witness,'" conveyed the meaningful historiographic representation of Rose Coburn's and Pompey Lovejoy's gravestones, and highlighted the summary of my research project that she read about in the AHS' newsletter article, Anonymous, "Remembered as 'the last slave born in Andover' Found!" The cemetery at the South Church has been referred to by several names, including South Parish Cemetery, South Parish Burial Grounds, Old South Burying Ground, South Church Cemetery, and South Church Burial Yard.

[36] Bailey, *Historical Sketches of Andover*, 43–44. In this block quotation, I preserved the original centered layout, indentation, line breaks, hyphenated word divisions, and other typographic elements. Those typographic choices, however, were made by her publisher's typesetter and editor, and appear to have no correlation to the arrangement of the carved epitaph on the original stone. "Veracity" was a mistranscription or typographic error for "vivacity". As noted above, transcriptions of the epitaph vary among five known texts: Alfred Poore's circa 1863 to 1864 notes, Bailey's 1880 book, an anonymous 1896 *Boston Globe* reporter's article, Jim Batchelder's 1975 drawing (published in Campbell, *West of the Shawsheen*, 25), and the 2002 replacement stone. The original gravestone is eroded and unreadable. Knoblock, *African American Historic Burial Grounds*, 209, noticed that Rose's gravestone was replaced in 2002. Concurrently, a separate marker was created for Colley Hooper that

also commemorates "Titus Coburn Buried Elsewhere", and placed adjacent to Rose's marker.

[37] Charlotte Helen Abbott, in her 1901 newspaper article, "Historical Andover. No. 106. Africa to Andover," 3, summarized the history of Phillis' extended family in relation to the Frye family. Abbott mentioned Rosanna Coburn in her discussion of Sarah Frye's probate file papers. Abbott drew from Anonymous, "Sketches of Octogenarians" (about Rose Coburn's family) (1853) and/or from Anonymous, "Obituary" for Rosanna Coburn (1859). Abbott also relied in part on Sarah Loring Bailey's *Historical Sketches of Andover* (1880). Referring to Phillis, Abbott wrote that "Miss Bailey tells much of her character." Andover *Catalogue of a Loan Collection at Punchard Hall* (1896), 18 (No. 468) referred to Rose Coburn's ring as "worn by the last slave in Andover." The 1897 Boston exhibition catalog, DRCM, *Catalogue of a Loan Collection of Ancient and Historic Articles*, 104 (Item 1800), related that Rose Coburn's ring was "supposed to have been presented to her at the time she was freed." Carpenter, "Glimpses of Life in Andover Eighty Years Ago, from an Old Family Expense-book" (1913), 3, relied on Bailey, ibid., and the memories of "the Historical Society ladies". Probably also drawing from Bailey, ibid., Susan E. Jackson in her 1914 book, *Reminiscences of Andover*, 24, wrote that "The last slave born in Andover was Rose Coburn, who died in 1859, aged ninety-two."

Rosanna Coburn has been remembered by modern Andover historical writers, such as Claude Fuess, *Andover: Symbol of New England* (1959), 60; Eleanor Campbell, *West of the Shawsheen* (1975), 24–25; Joan Patrakis, "Blacks Have Lived in Andover for Over Three Centuries" (1990); Barbara Thibault, "Anti-Slavery Movement in Andover: Notable Sites" (1993), a map that included "graves of freed slaves" including Rose Coburn's grave, National Park Service, *Underground Railroad*, 146 (quotation; I thank Angela McBrien for locating the map at the ACHC and providing me a copy); Charlotte Lyons, "South Church: Founding History and Abolitionism" (2011), 1: "Rose Coburn's gravestone (1859) tells us she was the last slave to die who was 'born into that condition' in Andover"; Elaine Clements, "Andover Stories: Slavery Did Exist in Early Andover" (2012) republished as "Slavery in New England" (2015); Bill Dalton, "Dalton Column: Slaves in Andover" (2013); Andover Cultural Council (2016) "Andover Cultural Caper," an educational game designed chiefly for children in which the grave of "Rose Coburn, the last slave to die in Andover" appeared as a point of interest in the South Parish Cemetery; Lyons, "How is it that Two Andover Slaves are Buried Next to One Another in the South Church Burial Yard?" (2017); Anonymous, "Remembered as 'the last slave born in Andover' Found!" (2017); and Dana Allen Walsh, "'Bear Witness'" (2017). Public historians in Andover, North Andover, and Lawrence continue to convey histories of Rosanna Coburn and other people of color in historical Andover and to connect their stories to places in the deeply historical area.

[38] "The last slave" trope in New England history writings conceptually established temporal distance and confirmed notions of modernity and social reform, O'Brien, *Firsting and Lasting*, 136–137. Rose Coburn's original gravestone epitaph was specifically qualified: the "last survivor of all born here", in Andover, in slavery. The assertion of finality was logically bolstered in the last line of the original gravestone epitaph that neither Colley nor Rose had descendants. Recall, however, that Rosanna's mother Phillis was said to have had 14 children, Anonymous, "Sketches of Octogenarians" (about Rose Coburn's family): it is possible, then, that there were collateral descendants. Like with Nancy Parker's factually incorrect epithet "the last Indian", there were other former slaves in Andover after Rose's death. One can imagine that in regards to the proposition that Rosanna alone was the town's "last slave", that any of the other formerly enslaved individuals, their relatives, or acquaintances living in Andover might have thought that notion to be overly circumscribed. Regardless, there were other competitors for that discomfiture. Martha Matilda (Palmer) Henderson (1838–1864) died in Andover; her town and state death records indicated that she also was born "In slavery" but her birthplace is not known. She may have been an escaped slave. Robert Rollings (1828–1879) was born in slavery in Maryland. Rollings moved to Andover around 1862. He was in the 54th Regiment Massachusetts Voluntary Infantry (Colored) and his grave is at the South Parish Cemetery. Mr. Rollings and Julia C. Palmer had their marriage officiated in Andover on November 29, 1863. Julia was Martha Matilda (Palmer) Henderson's sister; their father was Henry Palmer. The Rollings-Palmer marriage record indicated, in the column for place of birth, that he was born "Maryland—in slavery" and that she was born "South—in slavery". In the column for "What Marriage—Whether First, Second, Third, &c. [etc.,]" Taylor wrote that they had previously "married south according to the slave laws." Robert and Julia may have been escaped slaves. Rollings and Palmer, Marriage record. (I thank Charlotte Lyons for mentioning Rollings, showing me his gravesite, and sharing her photographs of the Rollings' Andover marriage record at the Andover town clerk's office, which has the identical wording as the state record at M-Ar.)

Allen Hinton (1835, 1837, 1844, or 1847–1912), a former and apparently escaped slave from North Carolina, moved to Andover in 1864. In 1867, he married Mary Jane (Patmore) Johnson, a widow said to be another sister of Robert Rollings' wife, but the Hinton-Johnson marriage record indicated that Mrs. Johnson was born in Connecticut, and he in South Carolina. In 1877 he established a family ice cream business in Andover, AHS, "Allen Hin-

ton," http://www.andoverlestweforget.com/faces-of-andover/gleason-holt
/allen-hinton/, accessed August 25, 2017; Balboni, "Andover Stories: Hinton's Ice Cream was Sweet Success of Former Slave"; Hinton and Johnson,
Marriage record; Patrakis, *Andover in the Civil War*, 65–68. Claude Fuess,
Andover: Symbol of New England, 399, remembered "the former Negro slave,
whose farm off South Main Street was a popular and harmless rendezvous
for stray [Phillips] Academy students". Fuess, *An Old New England School*,
391, attempted to render Hinton's distinctive dialect when he detailed that
Hinton's business "continued to be a favorite gathering-place for the boys
who, on hot spring nights, chose to risk the chance of a 'cut' in order to get
a plate of frozen pudding and to have a chat with Allen [Hinton] about the
days 'befo' the wa.'" A former Phillips Academy student remembered the local
establishment was a meeting-place for less innocent purposes than Headmas-
ter Fuess may have been aware, Graham, *It Happened at Andover*, 228.

Allen and Mary Hinton's daughter, Alice M. Hinton (1870–1951), attended the New England Conservatory of Music. In 1915 Alice Hinton
spoke to the National Negro Business League in Boston, to the evident admiration of Booker T. Washington and other attendees, Hinton, "How I
Have Carried On the Ice Cream Manufacturing Business Established by my
Mother and Father," 12, 103–110, 307 ("Haiden" Road is error for Hidden
Road, Andover Preservation Commission, et al., *Andover Historic Preservation* webpage for 104 Hidden Road, the Hinton family residence, https://
preservation.mhl.org/104-hidden-rd, accessed March 11, 2019). Alice and
her brother Edward continued the Hinton's ice cream business until the
1930s. In 1941 Alice produced a concert with the Free Christian Church
at Memorial Auditorium: "I always wanted to bring a colored group of artists to Andover to let Andover folks know what we could do [....] Will you
tell the people that I'm very grateful to all who came and helped make my
dream come true", Anonymous, "Dream Comes True for Alice Hinton," 6.
Alice Hinton died August 28, 1951 (age 81), and was buried near her mother
and father at Spring Grove Cemetery, Andover. Hinton family papers, with
recollections by Alice (circa 1938, called "Memory Pictures," copy of pages
provided to me by Joan Patrakis, and 1939, "Story of Allen and Mary Hinton and their Ice Cream Business in Andover, 1877–1912," cited by Patrakis,
Andover in the Civil War, 119 n128), and correspondence, are at the ACHC.
In the circa 1938 memoir, Alice Hinton intriguingly identified herself as "Of
Indian and English descent with a touch of African." Additionally, she stated
that she was born in "Dinah's house" on Missionary Lane (now Woodland
Road), which was occupied by Dinah and Caesar Simpson (died 1809 and
1805, respectively, *VRA*, Vol. 2, 574, "Negroes," "Sibson"). The persistent as-
sociative memory of that house with the long-gone couple is notable. (For

other persistent local memories of the couple, see the 1899 article, Anonymous, "Ten Miles Awheel," 5.) Astonishingly, Alice Hinton avuncularly remembered the ardent Andover abolitionists William Jenkins (1796–1878) and his wife Mary Saltmarsh Farnham Jenkins (1796–1891) as "Uncle Bill and Aunt Mary", Hinton, "Memory Pictures," 1 (all quotations). Information about Alice Hinton was included in a March 2019 mailing to ACHC members from Executive Director Elaine Clements. I am grateful to Joan Patrakis for sharing a copy of Alice Hinton's "Memory Pictures." Alice Hinton correspondence dating 1928–1947 is in the Head of School Records, Claude M. Fuess 1933–1948 Collection, Box 9, http://www.noblenet.org /paarchives/?page_id=601, and there is a vertical subject file about the Hinton family, http://www.noblenet.org/paarchives/?page_id=287, at Archives and Special Collections, Phillips Academy, Andover, both webpages accessed March 12, 2019.

[39] Images of Pompey Lovejoy's gravestone, https://www.findagrave.com /cgi-bin/fg.cgi?page=gr&GRid=57466682, accessed May 23, 2017. Several iterations of the epitaph were quoted in publications that slightly altered the punctuation, e.g., *VRA*, Vol. 2, 574 (Deaths, "Negroes").

[40] The earliest history book of the town, Abiel Abbot's (1829) *History of Andover*, 7, 186 (quotation), included Pomp's Pond in the geography section. In the part about "Births and Deaths—Longevity," Abbot avoided mentioning Pompey Lovejoy's enslavement: "Feb. 1826, Pompey Lovejoy, aged 102 years; was born in Boston, and brought to Andover when nine years old. Rose, his wife, died in Dec. following, aged 98."

Anonymous ("G."), "Pomp and Pomp's Pond," *Andover Advertiser*, October 30, 1858, n.p. [1]. If "baudy" was not a typesetting error, it was a malaprop for *bandy*, curvature of the legs (rickets), a consequence of Vitamin D deficiency. That condition or another degenerative disease may be why Pompey Lovejoy required crutches. The transcription of Pompey Lovejoy's gravestone inscription differs from the gravestone only in punctuation placement. I have not been able to identify the author of the 1858 newspaper article. Perhaps the initial "G." placed at the end of "Pomp and Pomp's Pond" indicated that George Foster authored the lush writing. George Foster also may have authored the two *Andover Advertiser* articles about Rosanna Coburn: Anonymous, "Sketches of Octogenarians" (about Rose Coburn's family) (November 12, 1853); and, Anonymous, "Obituary" for Rosanna Coburn (April 2, 1859). Scott Paradise, *A History of Printing in Andover*, n.p. [19, counting full title page as 1], conveyed that the *Andover Advertiser* writers under John D. Flagg's editorship "were the Hon. George Foster, Mr. Eastman Sanborn, and Mr. Moses Foster [...]. However [...George Foster] did most of the work, and later conducted an Andover column in the *Lawrence American.*" The November 12, 1853 issue of the *Andover Advertiser* with the "Sketches" article about Rosanna Coburn was published by John D. Flagg; the October 30, 1858 issue with "Pomp and Pomp's Pond" and the April 2, 1859 issue with Rosanna Coburn's "Obituary" were published by Warren F. Draper. Wilson Flagg in his essay "Rural Architecture" (first published 1876 in *The Atlantic Monthly*, 433–434, and republished 1881 in his book *Halcyon Days*, 16–18), provided an astonishingly detailed recollection of the architecture, layout, and appearance of Pompey and Rose Lovejoy's cabin, garden, and yard. So too did Wilson Flagg appreciate the sentimental affect of its archaeological features joined with the intellectual satisfaction of knowing the meaningful history of the place. Joan Patrakis (email, April 2, 2019) shared the 1858 Andover newspaper source with me. For a description of the cellar hole, well, and setting of the homeplace written in 1928, with an added note about a modern house constructed there, see Goldsmith, *The Townswoman's Andover*, 22.

[41] Melish, *Disowning Slavery*; Minardi, *Making Slavery History*; Minardi, "Making Slavery Visible (Again)." For historicizing slavery in Andover, see, e.g., Bailey, *Historical Sketches of Andover*, 39–44, where the main discussion of "Negro Slavery" (subject captioned in the table of contents, vi) is in her first chapter "Memorials of the Early Settlers," which follows the geology chapter and precedes chronological and subject chapters. Sarah Loring Bailey, ibid., 41, recognized that while her authorial choice to gather examples about the history of slavery in that section of her book was "not strictly within the scope of this chapter," it flowed narratively. In that chapter on the early settlers, Bailey had digressed to advocate for place names and street names grounded in local history; brought up Pomp's Pond as an important example of a toponym to preserve because it was "almost the only local reminder that negro slavery was one of our early institutions, and that for more than a hundred years men and women were bought and sold in Andover"; then gave several examples dating from the late seventeenth century to underscore that slavery was practiced in Andover in the first 25 years of English settlement. She then continued to give further examples of enslavement "down to the time when it ceased to be legal in Massachusetts [....] merely to present enough to show how prominent a feature of the town history slavery was." Bailey additionally provided information about free and enslaved Andover people of color in many other parts of her book. In contrast to historical writers before and after her, Bailey neither ignored nor countenanced the implications of the difficult subject, nor dismissed that slavery was integral to household and local economy, nor ignored the participation of enslaved and free men of color in military service. As with the many historical and genealogical writings by Charlotte Helen Abbott that mention slaves and "servants"

with the families of their owners and employers, Sarah Loring Bailey's historical considerations of Andover people of color, and of the subjects of enslavement, manumission, antislavery, and abolition were foundational to convey details of those people and subjects when recounting the history of the town.

For a conceptually contrasting example, consider the narrative treatment of slavery by Albert Poor, "The Oration," 82–83, delivered at Andover's 250th anniversary celebration in May 1896. Albert Poor did not directly mention local slavery. He alluded to it by contrasting slavery with the principle of equality in the Declaration of Independence that he noted was signed by slave owners, then deflected by relating slavery to the cause of the Civil War. The other mentions of slavery in the published volume, 117, 134, 150, 170, are about antislavery, abolition, and emancipation, also in consideration of the result of the Civil War. For Albert Poor (1853–1900), see Adams, "Albert Poor." Claude M. Fuess, *Andover: Symbol of New England*, 60–61, 312 (whose 1959 book was expected in 1946, but delayed due to personal reasons, ibid., v) wrote an astonishingly revisionist, presentist, and historically uninformed characterization of New England slavery and its protest. Fuess seemed to me to be either unconscious of or untroubled by his overtly racist statements, ibid., 12, 29, 57, 82, 173, 311, 313. He stereotypically rendered Allen Hinton's dialect and pronunciation in *An Old New England School*, 391. Frederick S. Allis, Jr., *Youth from Every Quarter*, 616, provided other painful examples from Fuess' Phillips Academy correspondence of racist and also anti-Semitic attitudes and his intentionally discriminatory practices in school admissions. Intriguingly, the complex Fuess maintained a correspondence with Allen Hinton's daughter Alice M. Hinton between 1928 and 1947, Head of School Records, Claude M. Fuess 1933–1948 Collection, Box 9, Archives and Special Collections, Phillips Academy, Andover, Mass., http://www.noblenet.org/paarchives/?page_id=601, accessed March 12, 2019. Jeanne Schinto, "Claude Moore Fuess," recognized in Fuess' *Andover: Symbol of New England*, 267, his difficulties appreciating the diversity of cultural traditions brought and maintained by Lawrence's then-recent immigrant populations, characterizing the city as "a hurly-burly, a melting pot, a crowded and complex city with all the problems that a society without traditions or cultural background must meet. A large percentage of its alien population could not understand the principles upon which Andover had been established." Yet, according to Schinto, Fuess was speaker to Lawrence High School's graduating class "for several years."

[42] Andover *Catalogue of a Loan Collection at Punchard Hall*, 18 (Item 468, gold ring lent by Mrs. Benjamin [Susan F. Burr] Brown). The other exhibited objects associated with former Andover slaves and its antislavery movement were "piece of wedding dress of Pomp Lovejoy's wife" (ibid., 19, Item 525,

lent by Miss Mary A. Ballard); "Rope used to tie slave to the whipping post—cut from the post in Petersburg jail, April 13, 1865" (27, Item 883, lent by Charles Carpenter); "Banner carried in an anti-slavery procession at Frye Village about 1843. The picnic was in Foster's Woods; Mr. John Smith was chief marshal" (32, Item 1032, lent by Joseph W. Smith). "Charles Carpenter" was the Rev. Charles C. Carpenter who served in the United States Christian Commission during the Civil War: "after the summer of 1864 [...he] spent the next winter in City Point [now Hopewell], Va." about ten miles northeast of Petersburg. Adams, "A Man for All Seasons"; Anonymous, "Obituary Rev. C.C. Carpenter" (quotation). Salome Jane Abbott Marland (Mrs. William Marland) was on the Andover loan collection exhibition committee (Andover *Catalogue of a Loan Collection at Punchard Hall*, 2); see also Marland, "Loan Collection and Historic Sites." I thank Clare Curren and Stephanie Aude at Memorial Hall Library for their research assistance with the 1896 catalog.

43   DRCM, *Catalogue of a Loan Collection of Ancient and Historic Articles*, 104 (Item 1800, quotation about Rose Coburn's ring). The "genealogical index" in the catalog, ibid., 144, gave the lifespan of Rose Coburn as 1767–1859. The other exhibited object associated with former Andover slaves was a "Piece of wedding dress of Dinah, wife of Pompey Lovejoy. 'They were born slaves but died free'", ibid., 101, 102 (credited loan of that and other objects to Miss Mary A. Ballard), 105 (quotation, perhaps paraphrasing from Pompey Lovejoy's gravestone epitaph, "Born in Boston, a slave: died in Andover a freeman", and mistaking Dinah for Pompey's wife Rose). Rose Coburn's ring and a swatch from Rose Lovejoy's wedding dress were exhibited in Boston, among the artifacts gathered by the Andover Phoebe Foxcroft Phillips Chapter of the DRCM; the "Chairman" of the Boston exhibition "Catalogue Committee," Mrs. William Marland (Salome Jane Abbott Marland) gave an Andover mailing address, ibid., 3, 4, 98. Anonymous, "Collecting Historic Relics," appeared in the *Boston Globe* on April 3, 1897, 4. The news article announced the upcoming Copley Square exhibition in Boston, and recognized Mrs. Marland for her leadership in producing the Andover and Boston exhibition catalogs: "This large collection of relics has been most carefully catalogued and may serve as a valuable book of reference. The work of preparing the catalog has been in the hands of Mrs Wm. Marland, who put such valuable work into the loan exhibition catalog of Andover at the time of the 250th anniversary."

One year previous to the 1897 DRCM exhibition in Boston, an exhibition of loaned historical objects in Andover had been arranged for the May 1896 celebration of Andover's 250th anniversary. Salome Marland was secretary of the town loan collection exhibition committee. The lender of Rose Coburn's ring for the Andover exhibition was Mrs. Benjamin [Susan F.] Brown. Brown's half sister, Eliza R. Doe Flanders was credited with its loan for the Boston exhibition. Mrs. Marland or another member of the Andover DRCM chapter learned about Rose Coburn's ring, and secured it first for the Andover display and then for the Boston exhibition. Marland, "Loan Collection and Historic Sites," 165 for Salome (Mrs. William) Marland and Sarah Northey (Mrs. William S.) Marland. For Salome Marland, see Hicks, "Mrs. Salome Jane (Abbott) Marland." Daughters of the Revolution, Phoebe Foxcroft Phillips Chapter Records, 1895–1932, Ms S 619, Sub-group I, Series B, Minutes, 1895–1912, 17 (April 9, 1896, appointed to the town committee); 30 ("Annual Reports 1895–1896"); 33–38 ("The Loan Exhibition," May 20, 1896, paper read by Frances Whipple Abbott to the chapter on November 2, 1896; I thank Kenna Therrien for identifying Mrs. Abbott); 39 (November 2, 1896 meeting); 51 (March 12, 1897, arrangements being made for the Boston exhibition); Sub-group IV, Series B, Speeches, 1930 (1896 loan collection exhibits and catalog highlighted as important chapter accomplishments), ACHC; Morgan, "Inventory, Daughters of the Revolution Records in Andover Historical Society." In addition to DRCM, Salome Marland was involved in several social and charitable organizations, including secretary of the Andover Society for Organized Charity (founded 1894) later known as the Andover Guild, and a founding member of the Indian Ridge Association (1898) that merged in 1917 with the Andover Village Improvement Society (founded 1894).

The ACHC does not have Rose Coburn's ring, but it preserves swatches of the beautifully colorful textile said to be from Rose Lovejoy's wedding dress (Accession No. 1924.014 [Mary Ballard Estate], 1936.009 [Alice Carey Jenkins], and 1945.037 [Dr. Edward D. Lovejoy]), and also has a chair said to have been made by Pompey Lovejoy (Accession No. 1977.001.1), Angela McBrien, pers. comm., March 31, 2017, April 11, 2019, and email, July 1, 2019; Killorin, "Pompey's Corner Chair." As meaningful heirlooms, the circa 1740 chair and the circa 1751 fabric pieces were preserved by Andover families into the early to late twentieth century. The wedding dress fragments were featured in the 2019 article by Elaine Clements, "The Story of Rose Lovejoy's Wedding Dress" and in the ACHC's Winter 2020 issue of its newsletter *Connections*, Anonymous, "Born into Slavery and Brought to Andover: Four Pieces of Cloth are all that Remain of her Story of Slavery and Freedom." Their preservation conveys the persistent devotion to remembering Rose and Pompey Lovejoy, and by association, Andover's former slaves and its antislavery movement, Minardi, "Making Slavery Visible (Again)."

Public historians in Andover created an exhibition of "artifacts from the slave period" at Memorial Hall Library in 1996, described in a handwritten cap-

tion on a photograph in the ACHC collections (Accession No. 1996.120.35),
published in *The Andover Townsman*. For the town's 350th anniversary in 1996,
the AHS published Eleanor Motley Richardson's book, *Andover: A Century
of Change*, that included historical and contemporary information about Andover people of color. The AHS also produced a traveling exhibition with
the eight-page pamphlet published in 2001, Greater Lawrence Underground
Railroad Committee, *The Anti-Slavery Movement and the Underground Railroad in Andover & Greater Lawrence*, and with a separate brochure about the
exhibition, Anonymous, "Antislavery in Andover Exhibit Will Travel." The
pamphlet and the brochure are in the collections of Lawrence History Center,
Lawrence, Mass. (Accession No. 2004.013.002), http://www.lawrencehistory
.org/node/4179 and http://www.lawrencehistory.org/node/799, accessed
June 29, 2019. The AHS and Peabody Museum of Archaeology at Phillips
Academy collaborated on a 2003 exhibition at AHS called "Lucy's Acre: A
Place in Time" that exhibited artifacts, original documents, and dioramas
created by Eugene Winter, and developed a traveling educational kit for
schools, Ciolfi, "*Lucy's Acre: A Place in Time* Exhibit Shows Life of Former
Slave."

[44] Abbott, "Historical Andover. No. 47. Some Old Residents." Eliza Davis
Burr Doe, born in Andover, was the mother of Susan F. Burr Brown (Mrs.
Benjamin Brown) and Eliza R. Doe Flanders (Mrs. Lucian B. Flanders).
The half sisters lived together in 1893 at the Brown's house with others on
Park Street in Andover. Mrs. Eliza Davis Burr Doe does not appear among
the deponents in Rose Coburn's widow's pension application, nor in Rose's
probate file papers. Susan F. Brown's husband, Benjamin Brown had a shoe
shop "on The Hill" meaning in the vicinity of the Andover Theological Sem-
inary and Phillips Academy, which is in the same part of town where Rose
Coburn and her executor John Parnell both lived on Missionary Lane (now
Woodland Road), Massachusetts Census, 1855, Andover Dwelling No. 77
(Parnell), Dwelling No. 79 (Coburn); Walling, "Map of the Town of Andover" (1852); Walling, "A Topographical Map of Essex County" (1856). I
have not been able to establish a direct connection of Parnell with Benjamin
Brown or with his mother-in-law Eliza Davis Burr Doe. (Parnell's estate was
not probated. His widow Sarah M. Parnell's estate was probated but none of
the Browns, etc. were involved with Mrs. Parnell's estate: an inventory of her
possessions included a gold watch and a silver watch but no ring.) At some
time both Brown and Parnell had their shops in the same area of Main Street,
and would have been familiar to each other as businessmen in the same related trade. Perhaps Rose gave her ring to Eliza Davis Burr Doe, or perhaps
Parnell did. The ring is not mentioned in Rose's will or inventory, and the latter only listed Rose's savings account. How, when, or to whom her remaining

possessions were distributed or disposed of when her rented Missionary Lane home was cleared out after her death is undocumented. Andover Preservation Commission, et al., *Andover Historic Preservation* webpages for 41–43 Main Street, http://preservation.mhl.org/41-43-main-street (Brown's shoe shop on The Hill in 1861, then at 43 Main Street in 1870); for 54 Woodland Road, http://preservation.mhl.org/54-woodland-rd (Parnell's tailor shop in Flagg and Gould Press building on Main Street); for 33–35–37 Main Street, http://preservation.mhl.org/35-main-st (Flagg and Gould building); all accessed September 16, 2017; Susan F. Brown, Death record (home on Park Street); Eliza R. Flanders, Death record; Sarah B. Parnell, Probate file papers (the watches were listed in Parnell's "Schedule of Personal Estate in detail" in "Executors Inventory" filed September 21, 1872); Patrakis, *Andover in the Civil War*, 18 (The Hill); Sparrow, *The Andover and North Andover Directory* (1893), 33, 34, 35, 47, 88, 94 (Brown home on Park Street, Eliza R. Flanders and others board with Brown; Brown's shoe shop at that time on Main Street); Walling, ibid. (1852) and Walling, ibid. (1856) for the locations of the Coburn and Parnell houses.

For Charlotte Helen Abbott, the "indefatigable" local historian and genealogist, see Anonymous, "Charlotte Helen Abbott" (obituary) and Patrakis, "Charlotte Helen Abbott." Fuess, *Andover: Symbol of New England*, 365 ("indefatigable" simultaneously used to also so-characterize Charles C. Carpenter), 366, 428 ("indefatigable"). Fuess characteristically disparaged Charlotte Helen Abbott's accumulations of local history data, her methods, and her focus on documenting details: "No problem was too abstruse, no quest too complicated, no item too insignificant for her inquisitorial zeal. Her files, if they could be called such, were bulging with information which only she could identify and interpret but which substantiated history with a vast amount of detail, valuable in spite of its lack of organization." Immediately before his catty assessment of Abbott, Fuess, ibid, 365, dispensed with Rev. Charles C. Carpenter's local history efforts using similarly patronizing faint praise. Fuess, ibid., 357, called Andover's premiere local history book author Abiel Abbot "a jejune chronicler" and opined that his *History of Andover* "contained a considerable amount of miscellaneous detail, it was badly arranged, and has no great importance for us today." Sarah Loring Bailey was also "indefatigable", ibid. 20, 53, 89, an adjective Fuess employed even several more times. A laudatory obituary for Bailey was published in *The Andover Townsman* on September 11, 1896, Anonymous, "Sarah Loring Bailey." Charlotte Helen Abbott, Sarah Loring Bailey, Charles C. Carpenter, Alfred Poore, and Robert H. Tewksbury sought local oral history sources, largely obtained by listening to stories told by local women. They preserved the uniquely insightful information in their research notes and related it in their publications. Fuess' decision not to employ a scholarly bibliographic apparatus in *Andover: Symbol of New England*, xiii (quotation, and his research sources and their repositories), makes it challenging to discern particular sources of information. Some was derived from oral sources that had been fixed in the print sources, and information about "more recent events [...] relied to some extent on the recollections of older residents". Abbott is justly renowned locally for her astonishing discoveries of obscure information buried in vast troves of primary manuscript sources. Her discoveries that she obtained by uncountable hours of difficult searching were indispensible to my supplemental research and documentation efforts. Abbott undoubtedly anticipated that future researchers would pursue her clues and her insights about her findings to discover and further document related information. Another aspect of Abbott's, Bailey's, and Carpenter's historiography was that they objectively sought information about local people of color and treated their biographies with compassionate human interest and far more evenhandedly than did many other writers of their generations.

[45] Anonymous, "Andover's 250th Birthday," 40. Other transcriptions of the original gravestone epitaph indicate that there were two sentences, one ending with "condition" and the next beginning with "A Pension" (perhaps spelled "Pention"), that in this 1896 variant transcription were joined as one sentence. Combining the two sentences and changing "was the last" to "as the last" conveyed a slightly different meaning: that the pension was granted because of her survivorship of slavery and because of her husband's war service. In that article, the *Boston Globe* reporter continued by indicating Pompey Lovejoy was buried adjacent to Rose Coburn and quoted his gravestone epitaph.

Chapter 9 Conclusions

[1] Rosanna Coburn, Death record, Town of Andover and State Vital Records. Bailey, *Historical Sketches of Andover*, 44.

[2] Blanche Linden-Ward, *Silent City on a Hill*, 108 ("historical or commemorative consciousness"); 106–107, 126, 128 (Figs. 4.1, 4.2, 4.14, 4.16, images of the monuments); 321 ("community action"); and, 342, where she related the "distinction [...] between the civic and the funerary monument." The title of Linden-Ward's epilogue "Putting the Past Under Grass" (321) in part referred to the sense of comfort that a pastoral, naturalistic (albeit contrived and idealized) verdant lawn brought to cemetery visitors (341). "Americans put the past under grass, explicitly equating history and death" in "landscapes of memory [...] as historical agents" (342–343).

Renée Ater (e.g., "Slavery and Its Memory in Public Monuments") interpreted meaningful transformations in representations of the history of slavery and its abolition in historical and contemporary public art. Ater, reviewing Ana Lucia Araujo's *Shadows of the Slave Past*, related how efforts to commemorate the history of slavery and its abolition in public spaces have drawn "various special interest groups [that] often understood the slave past in fundamentally different ways, opening up the memorialization process to conflict and contestation. Rather than historical accuracy or accountability, the memorial process often ends up focused on particular political agendas, ideas, and sentiments of individuals, elites, and national governments. In the end [...] most of these engagements in the public sphere are unsuccessful because they desire to tell a one-dimensional story about the Atlantic slave trade and slavery rather than understanding this historical moment as multifaceted and complex," Ater, "Book review," n.p. Araujo's forthcoming book (2020), *Slavery in the Age of Memory*, also promises an international scope that "explores how different modalities of memory (collective, public, cultural, official) shape the ways slavery is memorialized", Araujo, "Bio," www.analuciaaraujo.org, accessed January 14, 2020.

Marc Howard Ross, *Slavery in the North: Forgetting History and Recovering Memory*, in his book that appeared in 2018, viewed contemporary commemorative history-making projects as public educational opportunities that undergird cultural and political action. Every practicing educator, scholar, and public historian of the history of enslavement in this region has experienced the common lack of deep knowledge of this region's slavery and other unfree laboring arrangements, of the region's entanglements with slavery and the slave trade nationally and internationally, of inheritances of racist forms, and that these matters are "inherently brutal, violent, oppressive, and dehumanizing [in their] evil and immorality," e.g., Jay and Lyerly, *Understanding and Teaching American Slavery*; Harvard Law School Shield Committee, "Recommendation to the President and Fellows of Harvard College on the Shield Approved for the Law School," 2 (quotation). Sven Beckert and Seth Rockman, "Introduction. Slavery's Capitalism," 6–8 (quotation at 6), within their subsection about "The Rediscovery of Slavery," gave many examples from recent news reports that exposed long-term institutional and corporate involvement of national financial concerns with slavery, as turning points in "several distinctive conversations in the scholarship, as well as [...] a swell of public interest and social activism."

Yet, local and regional historiography of accomplished and ongoing history-making projects does not support that there has been a normative forgetting, or that there is only recent remembrance of enslavement and emancipation, or more generally that there is a dearth of knowledge about the historical and current presence and experiences of people of color in this area. The ubiquitous material evidence does not support tenebrous conspiracies of evidential concealment or nebulously, historical "erasure," "invisibility," or "systematic exclusion" in archives, despite those charges appearing so frequently in postcolonialist narratives. Even any casual research reveals that such shopworn postcolonialist rhetorical assertions are unconvincing. There is neither amnesia about local, regional, and national repositories of archives and artifacts, nor is there lack of local knowledge about historical people, places, and events among cadres of historically and genealogically learned residents who actively engage in public history projects as, by, for, and about people of color in this region. Those old conclusory saws that claim supposed paucity, suppression of evidence, or local ignorance of historical material and places were once powerful lies that motivated historical investigation of people of color.

Frequent invocation of variations of "little is known" became a trope in modern narratives, Ernest, "Life Beyond Biography." It signaled that little or no determined effort was made to seek and investigate the profoundly vast historical information and materials pertinent to historical biographies of people of color. Similarly, Julia Laite, "The Emmet's Inch: Small History in a Digital Age," 12, wrote that "Being able to find these details for many, many more people than we ever have before means that saying 'we cannot know' and 'we can only glimpse' loses methodological and rhetorical power." Along those same lines are narrative entrances that incongruously propose novelty in historical investigation, seemingly to claim scholarly primacy over a subject of investigation. Writings that mistakenly assert a subject was "previously unexamined by scholars," etc. fragment historical understandings when they do not acknowledge previous, relevant scholarship. A lack of effort to identify and explicitly reference previous, relevant scholarship is a practice of intellectual dilution, and a devaluing marginalization of complementary efforts.

Heroic-sounding historical missions (fashionably called interventions) can carry along the same problematic assumptions and unreflexive position of colonialist "salvage anthropology" that was disinclined to credit local knowledge of local history or to appreciate that ongoing cultural traditions were neither obscure nor in any particular need of being rescued. An understandable reticence to distract purposeful focus from historical subjects and objects of study, and formal disciplinary training to eschew presentism and anachronistic politicization as commentary about current affairs, may play a part in the lack of explicit reflexivity. Historical research projects are themselves cultural practices of their own times that arise within broader intellectual and historiographic traditions. Those projects, particularly when characterized as interventions, create ethnographic moments during the research, fieldwork, and production, what Annie Dillard, *For the Time Being*, ix, so vividly depicted as "quizzical encounters with strangers." The privileged positions and ethical postures of historical interveners require a sophisticated consciousness about their own roles, relationships, and responsibilities in crafting accounts of historical traditions in historical places that are the subject and location of study. After "[d]econstructing the canonical texts of ethnohistory [...] and illuminating their political genealogies" to proceed to an engaged anthropology, Amy E. Den Ouden, "Locating the Cannibals: Conquest, North American Ethnohistory, and the Threat of Objectivity," 122, elicited "the possibility for participation [...] or alliance-building" as an ethical mode of research programs. As that intellectual orientation applies to African diasporic studies, Nedra K. Lee and Jannie Nicole Scott, "Introduction: New Directions in African Diaspora Archaeology," leveraged the power of multidisciplinary thinking with an "activist-oriented scholarship" (87) in "the racial vindicationist tradition" (86) "as a political and intellectual project that is transnational and comparative in approach" (89). Advantaging mutually convenient opportunities for interested constituencies to collaboratively participate in developing and articulating research questions of interest to them, to provide meaningful feedback on initial findings, and to learn about study results that they may apply to their interests, are reciprocally gratifying aspects of community-based history-making projects as public service scholarship. Taking measures to preserve research records, and depositing copies of finished work in local archives, research institutions, and public libraries ensure that generations of constituencies will benefit.

Curiosity should prompt applied effort to learn ethical and productive research and documentation practices, and to go about and actually do that as opportunities allow. Massachusetts has long and ongoing historical traditions, deeply and expansively complex histories, connected within and beyond the Atlantic World, with documentary, oral, artifactual, visual, linguistic, culinary, and cultural geographic aspects. Those traditions were and continue to be deliberately and purposefully perceived, created, transmitted, and sustained through multivocal efforts that differently but also indifferently and unevenly remember, recount, transform, or convey local and regional histories of people of color in enslavement and contingent freedom. Those efforts or lack of effort, historical consciousness or unconsciousness, occur at historical moments, just as Ross' book appeared during this national moment replete with purposefully divisive, retrograde racist rhetoric, conflict, and violence. To borrow from Giulia Bonacci and Alexander Meckelburg, "Revisiting Slavery and the Slave Trade in Ethiopia," 16–17, active and ongoing reconfiguration of histories by commemoration and placemaking are "inevitably shaped by current contexts and ideologies". Marc Howard Ross located and theorized his approach within the research avenues and historiography of memory and placemaking as contemporaneities. Ross' narrative turns and returns to this present moment, this popular culture, sanguine of progressive social reform through public education and commemoration of empowered places. Ross highlights storytelling, reconstructions of lost elements of historic sites, reenactments, and narratives, especially oral traditions.

Historian Marisa J. Fuentes, "A Violent and Violating Archive: Black Life and the Slave Trade," n.p., "does not desire a swing to narratives of resistance and heroism" as the only interpretive frame of reference. She asked directly "how do we subvert the reproduction of the logic of this archive and the violence that seems to dominate it? And, how does this history shape the present precarity of black life?" Conceptualizations in the research area of postslavery studies in many places with their own long histories of enslavement and related analogs assist to understand that the United States has not emerged from its own postemancipation period. Recall that Bonacci and Meckelburg, ibid., 7, quoted Rossi, "African Post-Slavery," 303, to define "post-slavery" to mean "historical and social circumstances identifiable in 'contexts where slavery was a fundamental social institution and its legal abolition was followed by resilient legacies of past hierarchy and abuse.'" They stressed that to "inform the national discourse [...] would entail acknowledging the ways in which slavery frames today's social fabric, and in particular how it influences the interethnic relations between former slaves and their descendants on the one hand, and former masters and their descendants on the other." Remember that Mimi Sheller, both an historian and a professor of sociology, in her book review essay "Beyond Post-Emancipation Studies?" 123, remarked that "the struggles that emerged in freedom's wake remain on our own horizon." Robert L. Reece, "Whitewashing Slavery," 2, recently used newly available empirical data in his social science research "to draw direct quantitative connections between slavery and today". He summarized that his method and approach was intended to more precisely investigate "generally reasonable and encompassing" conclusions of centuries of "scholarly and public discourse" about "the myriad ways the lingering effects of slavery continued to manifest", both in "how slavery disadvantaged black Americans and how those disadvantages have endured [...] to influence present-day inequalities" and in "how slavery *advantaged* white people and how those accumulated advantages may be reflected in the geographic distribution of white social outcomes today." In this postslavery society too, "the idea of slavery continues to haunt people's minds and morals", Bellagamba, et al., "Introduction. Slaves and Masters," 11.

Notice especially that we need not limit our understandings and audiences by evoking racialized terms ("black" : "white") that are not simultaneously acknowledged to be themselves historically derived as artificial, incongruously mutually exclusive binaries. The racialized terms confound multiplicities of ancestries, heritages, and identities as do status terms ("slave" : "free") that gloss a continuum of unfreedom. Unconscious or unintentional language can exclude interested people who are themselves profoundly conscious of parallel experiences of intersectional oppressions and protests. Again, recall that Laurel Daen, "'To Board & Nurse a Stranger,'" 3, perceived that "the racial, ethnic, and social [...] bounds of eighteenth-century Massachusetts communities were flexible and capacious in ways" that only later came to be so partitive and exclusionary in social relations. The ideals of progressive liberalism, that of attaining liberty, equality, due process, equal protection, with legal, social, economic, and demographic justice for all people, as ideas per se, do not themselves have "autonomous power" (Davis, *The Problem of Slavery in the Age of Revolution*, 274 n31). Those humanistic goals are not an inevitability: they continually require intentional and insistent actions to challenge and resist discrimination, segregation, oppression, and violence, as degrees and positions of power and powerlessness are exchanged and renegotiated.

My anthropological interests further consider polysemous purposes and meanings of historically based projects, be they more or less cohesive or divisive, more or less conciliatory or provocative, within cultural contexts of their times and localities. Biographies of history-makers can assist to intuit research goals and practices that were not explicit. Tracing genealogies of scholarship makes apparent the sources of information relied upon and transformed to create subsequent history projects, and suggests research avenues, methods, and sources of data not previously or sufficiently advantaged and likely to be productive. The sociological, technological, and historical contexts of archival and other curated collections of original material instruct about the very nature of extant factual data upon which conclusion and interpretation are based. Historical practice that applies literary methods and theories, narratology (in its broader sense), searching for disjunctions and interruptions in conventional or formulaic texts, can recognize identities and assertions ("voices") even in "documents copied or composed by paternalistic colonial institutions", Glover, "Early American Archives and the Evidence of History," 177. Intellectual history that considers sociological and economic positions of history-makers and audiences in their times and places can explore cultural conventions (common assumptions) that operate as ideologies. Oppressive intersectional biases grounded in fear and unfamiliarity of others, reproduced in purposeful structures and modes of power and powerlessness, are often unconscious and unstated, but not unnoticed, unchallenged, and resisted then as now.

[3] Charlotte Lyons (pers. comm. and email, August 9, 16, 17, 2017 and September 1, 2017) observed that the epitaphs for Pompey Lovejoy and Rose Coburn are uncommonly long among grave markers at the South Parish

Cemetery. The extra cost of long epitaphs for Pompey Lovejoy then for Rose Coburn, Lyons surmised, was a measure of benevolence. Lyons also determined that Rose Coburn's and Pompey Lovejoy's gravestones are the only two known in Andover to use the word "slave". All others but one used the euphemistic term "servant". Almira Quacumbush's epitaph called her a "domestic". Lyons pointed out that the Lovejoy and Coburn gravestones face a prominent pathway in the cemetery. Rather than being segregated, the bodies of Pompey Lovejoy, Rose Lovejoy, Colley Hooper, then Rose Coburn were seemingly welcomed in a section of the cemetery that Lyons identified as also having graves of people with known antislavery or abolitionist sentiments. Pompey and Rose Lovejoy, and Rose Coburn and Colley Hooper, are in the same area as the Chamberlain family and next to the Smart family. Jenkins, Poor, Blunt, Stevens, Richardson, and Clark families are close-by. She interpreted the inclusion of their four bodies among South Parish people with abolitionist sentiments as a "testament to equality", Lyons, "South Church: Founding History and Abolitionism," 5; Lyons, "How is it that Two Andover Slaves are Buried Next to One Another in the South Church Burial Yard?"

On the 1854–1861 Andover activism about Kansas, see Cairns, "Andover Stories: The Thirty-four Star Flag"; Greater Lawrence Underground Railroad Committee, *The Anti-Slavery Movement and the Underground Railroad in Andover & Greater Lawrence*; Patrakis, "Andover Sent Anti-Slavery Emigrants to Kansas"; and Patrakis, *Andover in the Civil War*, 20. In addition to her article, Joan Patrakis (email, June 21, 2019) sent me the text of Cairns' article. Jane Cairns (email, July 15, 2019), a former President of the AHS and currently on the Board of Directors of the ACHC, provided me the bibliographic information for her published article. Digital images of historical documents from many repositories are hosted on the website of the Kansas State Historical Society and University of Kansas, *Territorial Kansas Online 1854–1861*, including documents relating to the New England Emigrant Aid Company and its predecessor, the Massachusetts Emigrant Aid Company (formerly Society). For recent treatments of the effects of the Kansas-Nebraska Act that spurred tactical violence in abolitionist strategies, see Carter Jackson, *Force and Freedom*, and Schermerhorn, *Unrequited Toil*, 181–182, 185–186.

[4]   Charlotte Lyons (email, August 25, 2017).

References Cited

Abbot, Abiel, *History of Andover from its Settlement to 1829*. Andover, Mass.: Flagg and Gould, 1829. The unique copy with "69 extra pages with newspaper clippings" once owned by Jonathan Clement and William G. Brooks, Accession No. 1991.140, Andover Center for History & Culture, Andover, Mass.

Abbot, Anne Wales, "A Massachusetts Slave," *The Child's Friend and Family Magazine Designed for Families and Sunday Schools* 8 (5) (August) (1847): 233–238.

Abbot, Elinor, *Our Company Increases Apace: History, Language, and Social Identity in Early Colonial Andover, Massachusetts*. Dallas, Tex.: SIL International, 2006.

Abbot, Samuel, Samuel Abbot Business Papers, 1754–1819, Mss: 761 1754–1819 A122, Baker Library, Harvard Business School, Boston, Mass., http://id.lib.harvard .edu/alma/990006027230203941/catalog, accessed many times.

Abbott, Charlotte Helen, "Early Records and Notes of the Chandler Family of Andover," typescript, n.d., Memorial Hall Library, Andover, Mass., https://www .mhl.org/sites/default/files/files/Abbott/Chandler%20family.pdf, accessed April 4, 2019.

Abbott, Charlotte Helen, "Early Records of the Frye Family of Andover," typescript, n.d., Memorial Hall Library, Andover, Mass., http://www.mhl.org/sites /default/files/files/Abbott/Frye%20Family.pdf, accessed August 6, 2017.

Abbott, Charlotte Helen, "Early Records of the Holt Family of Andover," annotated version, typescript, n.d., Memorial Hall Library, Andover, Mass., https://www .mhl.org/sites/default/files/files/Abbott/Holt%20Family%20Annotated.pdf, accessed January 26, 2019.

Abbott, Charlotte Helen, Manuscript about Nancy Parker, n.d. ("1881(?)" written later on manuscript), photocopy in research files, "Poor, Salem," Andover Center for History & Culture, Andover, Mass.

Abbott, Charlotte Helen, "The Wood Family," typescript, n.d., Memorial Hall Library, Andover, Mass., http://www.mhl.org/sites/default/files/files/Abbott /Wood%20Family.pdf, accessed September 27, 2017.

Abbott, Charlotte Helen, "Historical Andover. No. 47. Some Old Residents," *Andover Townsman* (Andover, Mass.) (November 27, 1896): 2.

Abbott, Charlotte Helen, "Historical Andover. No. 106. Africa to Andover," *The Andover Townsman* (Andover, Mass.) (March 15, 1901): 3.

Abbott, Charlotte Helen, "Historical Andover. No. 107. Africa to Andover.— (Concluded)," *The Andover Townsman* (Andover, Mass.) (April 12, 1901): 3. (See *The Andover Townsman* [July 6, 1906]: 2, indicating that this article was intended to be published as "2nd part of No. 106. (numbered by error 107) 106 concluded.").

Abolition Visualized, *Abolition Visualized* (website), http://abolitionvisualized .com/tableview/, accessed July 16, 2017.

Adams, Catherine, and Elizabeth H. Pleck, *Love of Freedom: Black Women in Colonial and Revolutionary New England*. New York, N.Y.: Oxford University Press, 2010.

Adams, George M., "Albert Poor," in "Memoirs of the New England Historic Genealogical Society," *The New England Historical and Genealogical Register* 55 (Supplement to April Number) (1901): lxxix.

Adams, John, "John Adams to Dr. Belknap. Quincy, March 21, 1795," in "Letters and Documents Relating to Slavery in Massachusetts," *Collections of the Massachusetts Historical Society* (5th series) 3 (1877): 401–402.

Adams, Leila Norwood, "Old Norwood Homestead: Interesting Sketch of an Historic Annisquam Abode. Now 'Seven Acres,' Residence of Madame Hyatt," *The Cape Ann Shore* (Gloucester, Mass.) (August 11, 1923): 4, 21–23.

Adams, Tom, "A Man for All Seasons" (about Charles C. Carpenter), *Andover Townsman* (Andover, Mass.) (June 20, 2019), https://www.andovertownsman .com/news/townspeople/a-man-for-all-seasons----part-i/article_ab18b1fc-e2c2 -5784-985f-41bd94a5949b.html, accessed June 29, 2019.

Albakry, Mohammed, and Rhoesmary Williams, "Whitewashing Slavery in New England: A Corpus-Based Analysis of the Representation of Africans in Historical Newspaper Discourse," *Journalism and Discourse Studies* 1 (2) (2016): 1–17, http:// www.jdsjournal.net/uploads/2/3/6/4/23642404/albakry_williams-jdsjournal -vol1-issue2.pdf, accessed January 23, 2020.

[Allen, John], *The Watchman's Alarm to Lord N---H; or, The British Parliamentary Boston Port-Bill Unwraped. Being an Oration on the Meridian of Liberty; Not to Inflame but to Cheer the Mind: Or as an Apple of Gold in the Pictures of Silver for the Mourning Captives in America. : With Some Observations on the Liberties of the Africans. By the British Bostonian*. Salem, Mass.: E. Russell, 1774. Evans, *Early American Imprints*, Series 1, No. 13757. Transcription from https://quod.lib.umich.edu/e /evans/N10865.0001.001/1:4?rgn=div1;view=fulltext, accessed September 1, 2017.

Allis, Frederick S., Jr., *Youth from Every Quarter: A Bicentennial History of Phillips Academy, Andover*. Andover, Mass.: Trustees of Phillips Academy, 1979.

American Museum of National History, Smithsonian Institution, "Within These Walls: One House, Five Families, 200 Years of History," n.d., http://americanhistory.si.edu/within-these-walls, accessed July 6, 2017.

Andover *Catalogue of a Loan Collection at Punchard Hall, The Two Hundred and Fiftieth Anniversary Celebration, Town of Andover, Massachusetts*, s.l.: s.n., n.d. [1896].

Andover Cultural Council, "Andover Cultural Caper." Andover, Mass.: Andover Cultural Council, 2016, http://www.mhl.org/sites/default/files/uploads/uncategorized/scavenger-hunt-mapwith-descriptions.pdf, accessed August 6, 2017.

Andover Free Christian Church, *The History of Free Christian Church, Andover, North Andover, Massachusetts*. [Andover, Mass.: Free Christian Church], 2012, http://freechristian.co/history/, accessed July 15, 2017.

Andover Historical Society, "Allen Hinton," *Lest We Forget: Andover and the Civil War* (website), http://www.andoverlestweforget.com/faces-of-andover/gleason-holt/allen-hinton/, accessed August 25, 2017.

Andover North Parish, "A Booke of Records for the North Precinct in the Towne of Andover There Being a division in the Towne By His Excelency the Governer and Generall Assemblys Order and Apointment Anno 1708," n.p., NAHS object 1977.004.002, North Andover Historical Society, North Andover, Mass. The original manuscript volume is also called "North Parish Records 1710–1827." Digital images from NAHS Microfilm Reel 11 (filmed circa 1960) provided courtesy of the North Andover Town Clerk. The microfilm target titled the volume "Andover North Parish Church Records Meetings 1710–1827," while the digital file is called "North Parish Meetings 1710–1827."

Andover North Parish Church, "Andover North Parish Church Records 1686–1810 Communicants 1686–1810 Baptisms 1719–1810 Church Meetings 1692–1810 Marriages 1687–1807" (title from microfilm target, bound volume of printed photoreproductions of microfilmed manuscript records, n.p. but with microfilm frame numbers). North Andover Historical Society, North Andover, Mass. Digital images from NAHS Microfilm Reel 11 (filmed circa 1960) provided courtesy of the North Andover Town Clerk. The original manuscript volume is also called "Journal kept by Thomas Barnard, John Barnard and Dr. Symmes from 1687 [i.e., 1686] to 1810 of Church Matters Baptisms + Weddings no deaths," NAHS object 1977.004.001, North Andover Historical Society, North Andover, Mass.

Andover North Parish Church, "Andover North Parish Church Records Minister's Book 1810–1850 [i.e., 1848–1937] Baptisms Admissions to Membership Marriages Deaths" (title from microfilm target). Digital images from NAHS Microfilm Reel 11 (filmed circa 1960) provided courtesy of the North Andover Town Clerk. The disbound manuscript volume was microfilmed in two consecutive parts. The first part of the volume (1810–1860, pp. 7–69) on Reel 10; the second part on Reel 11 (1848–1937, pp. 70–end—there was mispagination, but the last page was since microfilming renumbered 171). The digital files of the two imaged parts were named, respectively, "N. Parish Vitals 1810–1850" (i.e., 1810–1860), and "North Parish

Church 1810–1850" (i.e., 1848–1937). The original manuscript volume is NAHS object 1977.004.010, North Andover Historical Society, North Andover, Mass.

Andover Preservation Commission, Andover Historical Society/Andover Center for History & Culture, and Memorial Hall Library, *Andover Historic Preservation* (website), http://preservation.mhl.org/.

Andover South Church, "A Book bought by the Chh in the south part of Andover for their use 1711" (photocopy of bound manuscript volume), Andover South Parish Church I Records, Ms S 665, Subgroup I, Series A, Subseries 1, Andover Center for History & Culture, Andover, Mass.

Andover South Church, Records of the Samuel Phillips and Samuel Abbot Funds for the Relief of Indigent Persons in the South Parish (untitled, bound volume, n.p.), Andover South Parish Church I Records, Ms S 665, Subgroup IV, Series B, Subseries 1, Andover Center for History & Culture, Andover, Mass.

Andover South Church, *South Parish Burial Grounds Cemetery Database* (website), https://southchurch.com/south-parish-burial-grounds-2/, accessed June 30, 2019.

Andover, Town of, "Andover, Massachusetts, Town Meeting Records, 1709–May 21, 1776 [North Andover Historical Society Microfilm Frame No.] 5128–5263, Preliminary rough draft typed by Betty Senechal from records dictated by Forbes and Rosamond Rockwell." North Andover, Mass.: North Andover Historical Society, 1961, n.p. but with microfilm frame numbers indicated. Digitized from copy at Memorial Hall Library, Andover, Mass., https://archive.org/details/andovermassachus00unse_0, accessed February 21, 2019.

Andover, Town of, *Annual Town Reports*. Imprint varies, e.g., *Expenses of the Town of Andover* (1828–1839); *Annual Report of the Receipts and Expenditures of the Town of Andover* (1843); *Auditors' Report of the Receipts and Expenses of the Town of Andover* (1845–1849); *The Auditors' Annual Report of the Receipts and Expenditures of the Town of Andover* (1852–1854); *The Auditors' Report of the Receipts and Expenditures of the Town of Andover* (1855–1856). Printed broadsides (1820–1851), thereafter bound volumes (1852+), Ms S 643, S 647, S 671, Accession No. 1980.101.4, .17–.18; 1994.063.1–.6; 2019.105.1–.14, .16; 2019.106.1 (there are multiple copies of the same issue separately accessioned; within the same accession, the Accession No. for multiple copies of the same issue is suffixed with letters a, b, etc.), Andover Center for History & Culture, Andover, Mass. Digital images of the annual reports (1852–1856+), Memorial Hall Library, Andover, Mass., https://mhl.org/andover%E2%80%99s-digital-collections-links; and (1845–1846, 1851–1856+), Massachusetts State Library, Boston, https://archives.lib.state.ma.us/handle/2452/427013/browse?type=dateissued, accessed April 4 and 29, 2017.

Andover, Town of, "A Record of Deaths in the Town of Andover (Including North Andover), Essex County, Massachusetts, from 1650 to 1844 Covering a Period of 194 Years Chronologically Arranged and Transcribed from the Original Records Verbatim et Literatim by Samuel W. Blunt and Completed March 1, 1879" (title page, bound manuscript volume). Andover Town Hall, Andover, Mass. Second volume on Microfilm Reel 767599, "Town Records, Births, Marriages, Deaths 1647–1844, 1800–1850, Out of Town Marriages 1723–1858." (Despite the rendered Latin phrase, the original entries were not transcribed exactly.) Reproduction System for the Genealogical Society of Salt Lake City, Ut., 1971.

Andover, Town of, "Births & Deaths from 1800 to May 1844 Andover, Mass." (spine title), n.p. Andover Town Hall, Andover, Mass. Third volume on Microfilm Reel 767599, "Town Records, Births, Marriages, Deaths 1647–1844, 1800–1850, Out of Town Marriages 1723–1858." Reproduction System for the Genealogical Society of Salt Lake City, Ut., 1971.

Andover, Town of, "Records of Information of Persons Taken into Town – Since the last Act of Court in Regard of the Maintenance of poor persons +c" (i.e., etc.), in "Town Records, Treasurer Meetings 1767–1791" (untitled volume, title from microfilm target), n.p. Andover Town Hall, Andover, Mass. First volume on Microfilm Reel 878787, "Town Records, Treasurer's Records 1767–1874." (This document is located between selectmen's orders for payments made between April 30, 1792 and May 14, 1792; the date range is provided only to locate the list, which may have been started and been added to before or after that date range.) Reproduction System for the Genealogical Society of Salt Lake City, Ut., 1971.

Andover, Town of, "Town Records, Births 1649–1801" (title from microfilm target; spine title is "Records Births [torn] –1801; title page reads "Copy of an Ancient Record of Births in Andover Mass. commencing at 1651. 1649."), n.p. Andover Town Hall, Andover, Mass. Third volume on Microfilm Reel 878780, "Births, Marriages, Deaths, and Intentions 1651–1801" (title from catalog). Reproduction System for the Genealogical Society of Salt Lake City, Ut., 1971.

Andover, Town of "Town Records, Births Marriages Deaths 1651–1700" (title from microfilm target). Andover Town Hall, Andover, Mass. First volume on Microfilm Reel 878780, "Births, Marriages, Deaths, and Intentions 1651–1801" (title from catalog). Reproduction System for the Genealogical Society of Salt Lake City, Ut., 1971.

Andover, Town of, "Town Records, Births, Marriages, Intentions, Deaths, 1701–1800" (title from microfilm target; spine title is "Births, Marriages, Deaths and Intentions 1701–1800 Town of Andover"). Andover Town Hall, Andover, Mass. Second volume on Microfilm Reel 878780, "Births, Marriages, Deaths, and Intentions 1651–1801" (title from catalog). Reproduction System for the Genealogical Society of Salt Lake City, Ut., 1971.

Andover, Town of, "Town Records, Selectmen Records 1841–1861" (untitled volume, spine title "Letter Book", title from microfilm target but actually orders for payments drawn by the overseers of the poor, and letters written and received regarding poor in Andover), n.p. Andover Town Hall, Andover, Mass. Third volume on Microfilm Reel 887743, "Town Records, Selectmen Records 1836–1856, 1840–1873." Reproduction System for the Genealogical Society of Salt Lake City, Ut., 1971.

Andover, Town of, "Town Records, Tax Records 1799–1822" (untitled volume, title from microfilm target but actually treasurer records of payments for orders drawn by the overseers of the poor), n.p. Andover Town Hall, Andover, Mass. First volume on Microfilm Reel 878782, "Town Records, Tax Records 1799–1847." Reproduction System for the Genealogical Society of Salt Lake City, Ut., 1971.

Andover, Town of, "Town Records, Tax Records 1823–1847" (untitled volume, title from microfilm target but actually treasurer records of payments for orders drawn by the overseers of the poor), n.p. Andover Town Hall, Andover, Mass. Ninth volume on Microfilm Reel 878782, "Town Records, Tax Records 1799–1847." Reproduction System for the Genealogical Society of Salt Lake City, Ut., 1971.

Andover, Town of, "Town Records, Town Meetings, Persons Warned to Leave Town 1790–1793" (untitled volume, title from microfilm target), n.p. Andover Town Hall, Andover, Mass. Second volume on Microfilm Reel 887742, "Town Records, Boundaries 1715–1767, Meetings 1790–1793." Reproduction System for the Genealogical Society of Salt Lake City, Ut., 1971.

Andover, Town of, "Town Records, Treasurer's Records 1767–1874" (untitled volumes, title from microfilm target), n.p. Andover Town Hall, Andover, Mass. Microfilm Reel 878787, Reproduction System for the Genealogical Society of Salt Lake City, Ut., 1971.

Andover, Town of, Overseers of the Poor, "An Account of the Expence of Supporting poor of Andover from the first of March 1801 to the first of March 1802"; "An account of the Expence of Persons Supported by the Town; also of Persons in part Supported Viz. from the first of March 1802 to the first of March 1803"; "A List of Persons to be Let out for the present year Viz Expences for 1803 1802 1801," Joshua Chandler (1758–1817) Papers, Ms S 52, Sub-group I, Joshua (7) Chandler, Series C, Official Town Documents, Sub-series 2a–2c, Overseers of the Poor, Andover Center for History & Culture, Andover, Mass.

Andover, Town of, Overseers of the Poor, William Johnson, David Gray, and Stephen Abbot letter to Alden Bradford, Massachusetts Secretary of the Commonwealth, September 22, 1820, Ms. S 202, Andover Center for History & Culture, Andover, Mass.

Andover, Town of, Overseers of the Poor, List of supplies delivered to the poor, 1820–1821, Taft Collection, Ms S 134, Sub-group X, Andover – Town Office, Series A, Overseers of the Poor, Sub-series 1, Andover Center for History & Culture, Andover, Mass.

Andover, Town of, Overseers of the Poor, "Return of the Poor in the Town of Andover during the year ending on the last Monday of December, 1833," with clerk endorsement January 18, 1834, Ms. S 203, Object No. 3500.249.1, Andover Center for History & Culture, Andover, Mass.

Andover, Town of, Overseers of the Poor, Notebook with accounts of activities and expenditures, 1843–1845, n.p., Ms. S 96, Andover Center for History & Culture, Andover, Mass.

Andover, Town of, Overseers of the Poor, Nathan W. Hazen draft letter to State Commissioner John Sargent, November 18, 1846, in "Town Records, Selectmen Records 1841–1861" (untitled volume, spine title "Letter Book", title from microfilm target but actually orders for payments drawn by the overseers of the poor, and letters written and received regarding poor in Andover), n.p. Third volume on Microfilm Reel 887743, "Town Records, Selectmen Records 1836–1856, 1840–1873." Reproduction System for the Genealogical Society of Salt Lake City, Ut., 1971.

Andover v. Canton, Supreme Judicial Court, November 1816, 13 Mass. Reports 547.

Anonymous, "A Fitting Memorial" (dedication of Lucy Foster cenotaph), *Andover Townsman* (Andover, Mass.) (May 16, 2019), https://www.andovertownsman.com/news/lifestyles/a-fitting-memorial/article_651368f5-d03d-56e0-99c1-79da37109775.html, accessed May 26, 2019.

Anonymous, "A Fugitive," *Andover Advertiser* (Andover, Mass.) (July 7, 1860): n.p. [2].

Anonymous, "Andover's 250th Birthday," *The Boston Sunday Globe* (Boston, Mass.) 49 (138) (May 17, 1896): 40.

Anonymous, "Another Society in Andover," *The Liberator* (Boston, Mass.) 10 (11) (March 13, 1840): 43.

Anonymous, "Antislavery in Andover Exhibit Will Travel," *Andover Historical Society Newsletter* (Andover, Mass.) 27 (3) (2002): n.p. [4].

Anonymous, "A Relic of Slavery in Massachusetts," *The Elevator* (San Francisco, Calif.) 5 (7) (May 21, 1869): 1.

Anonymous, "Auld Lang-Syne. Anti-slavery Experiences in Andover" (reprinting Bristol, *The Pioneer Preacher*, 47–55), *The Andover Townsman* (Andover, Mass.) (February 3, 1888): 2.

Anonymous, "Auld Lang-Syne. Anti-slavery in Andover fifty years ago" (reprinting Bristol, *The Pioneer Preacher*, 40–47), *The Andover Townsman* (Andover, Mass.) (January 27, 1888): 2.

Anonymous, "Auld Lang-Syne. A Snow-Storm Incident of Fifty Years Ago" (about Dinah Chadwick and Harriet Dole), *The Andover Townsman* (Andover, Mass.) (April 13, 1888): 2.

Anonymous, "Auld Lang-Syne. More from the 'Old Red School-house'" (about the Osgood District school), *The Andover Townsman* (Andover, Mass.) (April 27, 1888): 2.

Anonymous, "Auld Lang-Syne. More Old Letters" (from Rev. Jonathan French and from his daughter Abigail French to son/brother Jonathan French, 1794 [or error], 1795, about Salem [Phillips], his wife Rama/Rema/Remy/Rhena, their son Cato Phillips/Freeman, and the Osgood District school), *The Andover Townsman* (Andover, Mass.) (April 6, 1888): 2.

Anonymous, "Auld Lang-Syne. Old Times in Osgood District" (about the district school), *The Andover Townsman* (Andover, Mass.) (April 20, 1888): 2.

Anonymous, "A Wind Fall" (Rosanna Coburn's pension), *Andover Advertiser* (Andover, Mass.) (September 30, 1854): n.p. [2].

Anonymous, "Born into Slavery and Brought to Andover: Four Pieces of Cloth are all that Remain of her Story of Slavery and Freedom," *Connections* (Andover Center for History & Culture, Andover, Mass.) (Winter 2020): 2.

Anonymous, "Census of the Colored Population of the U.S.," *The Abolitionist: Or, Record of the New England Anti-Slavery Society* (Boston, Mass.) 1 (1) (January 1833): 10.

Anonymous, "Charlotte Helen Abbott" (obituary), *The Andover Townsman* (Andover, Mass.) (October 28, 1921): 4.

Anonymous, "Collecting Historic Relics. Daughters of the Revolution Preparing to Hold a Loan Exhibit in Copley Hall, April 19, 20, and 21," *The Boston Daily Globe* (Boston, Mass.) 51 (93) (April 3, 1897): 4.

Anonymous, "Deaths. Death of an Octogenarian" (Cato Freeman), *Andover Advertiser* (Andover, Mass.) (August 20, 1853): n.p. [3].

Anonymous, "Deaths" (Pompey Lovejoy), *New-Hampshire Statesman and Concord Register* (Concord, N.H.) (March 11, 1826): n.p. [3].

Anonymous, "Deaths" (Rose Lovejoy), *New-Hampshire Statesman and Concord Register* (Concord, N.H.) (December 2, 1826): n.p. [3].

Anonymous, "Dedication at North Andover [of the Johnson High School and Stevens Hall]. Address by Dr. George B. Loring," undated and unidentified newspaper article published May 1867, pasted into the unique copy of Abbot, *History of Andover from its Settlement to 1829*, with "69 extra pages with newspaper clippings" once owned by Jonathan Clement and William G. Brooks, Accession No. 1991.140, Andover Center for History & Culture, Andover, Mass.

Anonymous, "Dedication of the Johnson High School House and Stevens Hall," *Lawrence American and Andover Advertiser* (Lawrence, Mass.) (May 24, 1867): n.p. [2].

Anonymous, Diary of a woman, Andover, Mass., 1852–1855, with sporadic entries concerning teaching school, religious struggles, attending churches and noting sermons, visits and social groups in Andover and Reading, Mass., and joining the Free Church, n.p. Octavo Item No. 15 in "Diaries (unidentified) Collection,

1760–1855," Octavo vols. "D" Almanacs Collection, American Antiquarian Society, Worcester, Mass.

Anonymous, "Dream Comes True for Alice Hinton," *The Andover Townsman* (Andover, Mass.) (May 22, 1941): 6.

Anonymous, "Errors in the Census relating to the Slaves in the Free States," *The Genius of Universal Emancipation* (Washington, D.C. and Baltimore, Md.) (March 1830): 167.

Anonymous, "Gleanings of News" (Rose Coburn note), *Frederick Douglass' Paper* (Rochester, N.Y.) 8 (44) (356) (October 20, 1854): n.p. [3].

Anonymous, *Lawrence Up to Date, 1845–1895*. Lawrence, Mass.: Rushforth and Donoghue, 1898.

Anonymous, Letter to Daniel O'Connor, "Miscellanies," *Journal of the American Institute* 3 (1838): 95–97.

Anonymous ("C." and "Mrs. P.F.C."), Letter to the editor about Cato Freeman, *Andover Advertiser* (Andover, Mass.) (September 3, 1853): n.p. [2]. A clipping of this published letter, with handwritten emendation of authorship as "Mrs. P.F.C." is pasted in the unique copy of Abbot, *History of Andover from its Settlement to 1829*, with "69 extra pages with newspaper clippings" once owned by Jonathan Clement and William G. Brooks, Accession No. 1991.140, Andover Center for History & Culture, Andover, Mass.

Anonymous, "Local News Notes" (about exhumation at the almshouse cemetery and reburial at Spring Grove Cemetery), *The Andover Townsman* (Andover, Mass.) (May 11, 1923): 5.

Anonymous, "Longevity" (of Pompey Lovejoy), *Salem Gazette* (Salem, Mass.) (November 1, 1825): 2.

Anonymous, "Longevity" (of Pompey Lovejoy), *Independent Chronicle and Boston Patriot* (Boston, Mass.) (November 2, 1825): 2.

Anonymous, "Longevity" (of Pompey Lovejoy), *Essex Register* (Salem, Mass.) (November 3, 1825): 3.

Anonymous, "Longevity" (of Pompey Lovejoy), *Boston Traveler* (Boston, Mass.) (November 4, 1825): 2.

Anonymous, "Longevity" (of Pompey Lovejoy), *Salem Observer* (Salem, Mass.) (November 5, 1825): 3.

Anonymous, "Longevity" (of Pompey Lovejoy), *Haverhill Gazette* (Haverhill, Mass.) (November 5, 1825): 2.

Anonymous, "Longevity" (of Pompey Lovejoy), *Niles' Weekly Register* (Baltimore, Md.) (November 12, 1825): 176.

Anonymous, "Longevity" (of Pompey Lovejoy), *Alexandria Gazette* (Alexandria, Va.) (November 15, 1825): 3.

Anonymous, "Longevity" (of Pompey Lovejoy), *Massachusetts Spy* (Worcester, Mass.) (November 16, 1825): 2.

Anonymous, "Longevity" (of Pompey Lovejoy), *Ladies Museum* (Providence, R.I.) (November 26, 1825): 72.

Anonymous, "Memorandum of the Names of the Families in each District in the South Parish in Andover 1805 Taken in January 1805," n.p., Ms S 56, Andover Center for History & Culture, Andover, Mass.

Anonymous, "Necrology. Trustee. Edward Taylor.," *Andover Theological Seminary. Necrology, 1892–93*, Second Printed Series No. 3, 73–74. Boston, Mass.: Beacon Press, 1893.

Anonymous, Note about death of Pompey Lovejoy, *Salem Gazette* (Salem, Mass.) (February 28, 1826): 2.

Anonymous, Note about death of Pompey Lovejoy, *Boston Patriot and Daily Chronicle* (Boston, Mass.) (March 2, 1826): 2.

Anonymous, Note about death of Pompey Lovejoy, *Salem Observer* (Salem, Mass.) (March 4, 1826): 3.

Anonymous, Note about death of Pompey Lovejoy, *Portsmouth Journal of Literature and Politics* (Portsmouth, N.H.) (March 4, 1826): 3.

Anonymous, Note about death of Pompey Lovejoy, *The Christian Watchman* (Boston, Mass.) (March 10, 1826): 3.

Anonymous, Note about death of Pompey Lovejoy, *Boston News-letter and City Record* (Boston, Mass.) 1 (12) (March 11, 1826): n.p. [4].

Anonymous, Note about death of Rose Lovejoy, *Haverhill Gazette* (Haverhill, Mass.) (November 25, 1826): 3.

Anonymous, Note about death of Rose Lovejoy, *Salem Observer* (Salem, Mass.) (November 25, 1826): 3.

Anonymous, Note about resetting gravestones at the Andover South Parish Cemetery, "About Andover," *Lawrence American and Andover Advertiser* (Lawrence, Mass.) (May 15, 1896): 5.

Anonymous, Note about the Andover Colonization Society, *The African Repository and Colonial Journal* 15 (14) (August 1839): 228.

Anonymous, "Notes," *The Nation* (New York, N.Y.) 9 (209) (July 1, 1869): 10–12.

Anonymous, "Number of Negro Slaves in the Province of the Massachusetts-Bay, Sixteen Years Old and Upward, Taken by Order of Government in the Last Month of the Year 1754, and the Beginning of the Year 1755," *Collections of the Massachusetts Historical Society* (2nd series) 3 (1815): 95–97.

Anonymous, "Obituary" (Rosanna Coburn), *Andover Advertiser* (Andover, Mass.) (April 2, 1859): n.p. [2].

Anonymous, "Obituary Rev. C.C. Carpenter," *The Andover Townsman* (Andover, Mass.) (August 23, 1918): 5.

Anonymous ("G."), "Pomp and Pomp's Pond," *Andover Advertiser* (Andover, Mass.) (October 30, 1858): n.p. [1].

Anonymous, "Remembered as 'the last slave born in Andover' Found!" *Connections* (Andover Historical Society, Andover, Mass.) (Fall 2017): 2.

Anonymous, "Rose Coburn," *The Liberator* (Boston, Mass.) 24 (41) (1056) (October 13, 1854): 163.

Anonymous, Rose Coburn note, *The Anti-Slavery Bugle* (Salem, Ohio) 10 (4) (474) (November 4, 1854): n.p. [2].

Anonymous, "Sarah Loring Bailey," *The Andover Townsman* (Andover, Mass.) (September 11, 1896): 8.

Anonymous, "Sketches of Octogenarians" (about Lydia Freeman), *Andover Advertiser* (Andover, Mass.) (September 3, 1853): n.p. [2].

Anonymous, "Sketches of Octogenarians" (about Rose Coburn's family), *Andover Advertiser* (Andover, Mass.) (November 12, 1853): n.p. [2].

Anonymous, "Ten Miles Awheel. Some Things That May Be Seen on an Andover Bicycle Trip. No. 5. A Jaunt Awheel to Mill's Hill, North Andover," *The Andover Townsman* (Andover, Mass.) (August 11, 1899): 5.

Anonymous, "The Black Patriot of Bunker Hill," *The Liberator* (Boston, Mass.) (June 19, 1857): 100.

Anonymous, *The Colonizationist and Journal of Freedom*. Boston, Mass.: George W. Light, 1834.

Anonymous, "The Green Table," *The Southern Magazine* 11 (November) (1872): 637.

Anonymous (attributed to William C. Nell or to William Lloyd Garrison), *The Loyalty and Devotion of Colored Americans in the Revolution and War of 1812*. Boston, Mass.: R.F. Wallcut, 1861.

Anonymous, "The Old Town of Reading Massachusetts. Early Land Grants and Town Bounds from 1638 to 1802." Typescript volume of transcribed public records, n.d., Reading Public Library, Reading, Mass. In library catalog, mistitled, misattributed to "J.W. [*sic*] Wightman" (i.e., William J. Wightman), and misdated "1853." This work was possibly prepared under direction of Edward E. Eaton, Wakefield, Mass., circa 1935 and copied from "Records of the Town of Reading, A True Transcript of the Towns Old Books made in 1853 by W J Wightman Town Clerk," 1.

Anonymous, *The Poor-Poore Family Gathering at South Church, Andover, Massachusetts. August 30, 1899*. Lawrence, Mass.: Star Publishing Co., 1900.

Anonymous, "The Taney Hunt Against Colored Americans," *The Liberator* (Boston, Mass.) (August 28, 1857): 139.

Anonymous, "Why Do They Call it That," *The Andover Townsman* (Andover, Mass.) (September 3, 1942): 15.

Araujo, Ana Lucia, *Shadows of the Slave Past: Memory, Heritage, and Slavery*. New York, N.Y.: Routledge, 2014.

Araujo, Ana Lucia, "Bio," *Ana Lucia Araujo* (website), www.analuciaaraujo.org, accessed January 14, 2020.

Araujo, Ana Lucia, *Slavery in the Age of Memory: Engaging the Past*. London: Bloomsbury, forthcoming 2020.

Archer, Richard, *Jim Crow North: The Struggle for Equal Rights in Antebellum New England*. New York, N.Y.: Oxford University Press, 2017.

Asbury, Samuel E., Correspondence file. Photocopies of Asbury letters (May 25, 1948, July 9, 1948, July 21, 1948) to the Andover Historical Society, and of letters to Asbury from the United States Bureau of the Census (April 29, 1948, June 25, 1948), American Antiquarian Society (June 9, 1948), Massachusetts Historical Society (June 1, 1948, June 30, 1948), Massachusetts Supreme Judicial Court Clerk (n.d.), Harvard College Library (May 21, 1948), and from the Andover Historical Society (June 2, 1948, July 16, 1948), in research files, "African Americans," Andover Center for History & Culture, Andover, Mass.

Ashcraft-Eason, Lillian, "Freedom among African Women Servants and Slaves in the Seventeenth-Century British Colonies," in *Women and Freedom in Early America*, ed. Larry D. Eldridge, 62–79. New York, N.Y.: New York University Press, 1997.

Ater, Renée, "Slavery and Its Memory in Public Monuments," *American Art* 24 (1) (2010): 20–23.

Ater, Renée, "Book review: *Shadows of the Slave Past: Memory, Heritage, and Slavery*" by Ana Lucia Araujo, *Historical Dialogues, Justice, and Memory Network* (website), April 6, 2017, https://historicaldialogues.org/2017/04/06/book-review -shadows-of-the-slave-past-memory-heritage-and-slavery/, accessed May 4, 2019.

Atkins, William Giles, *History of the Town of Hawley, Franklin County, Massachusetts, from its First Settlement in 1771 to 1887*. West Cummington, Mass.: The author, 1887.

Bailey, Ronald, "The Slave(ry) Trade and the Development of Capitalism in the United States: The Textile Industry in New England," *Social Science History* 14 (3) (1990): 373–414.

Bailey, Sarah Loring, *Historical Sketches of Andover (Comprising the Present Towns of North Andover and Andover), Massachusetts*. Boston, Mass.: Houghton Mifflin and Co., 1880.

Bailyn, Bernard, "Slavery and Population Growth in Colonial New England," in *Engines of Enterprise: An Economic History of New England*, ed. Peter Temin, 253–259. Cambridge, Mass.: Harvard University Press, 2000.

Baker, Mary, Probate file papers. Essex County, MA: Probate File Papers, 1638–1881, Case 1476, New England Historic Genealogical Society, 2014, from records supplied by the Supreme Judicial Court Archives, https://www.americanancestors .org/databases/essex-county-ma-probate-file-papers-1638-1881/image ?pageName=1476:1&volumeId=13744, accessed March 14, 2019.

Baker, Vernon G., *Historical Archaeology at Black Lucy's Garden, Andover, Massachusetts: Ceramics from the Site of a Nineteenth-Century Afro-American*. Andover, Mass.: Robert S. Peabody Foundation for Archaeology, 1978.

Baker, Vernon G., "Archaeological Visibility of Afro-American Culture: An Example from Black Lucy's Garden, Andover, Massachusetts," in *Archaeological Perspectives on Ethnicity in America*, ed. Robert L. Schuyler, 29–37. Farmingdale, N.Y.: Baywood, 1980.

Balboni, Francesca, "Andover Stories: Hinton's Ice Cream was Sweet Success of Former Slave," *Andover Townsman* (Andover, Mass.) (July 7, 2011), http://www .andovertownsman.com/news/local_news/andover-stories-hinton-s-ice-cream -was-sweet-success-of/article_ec77410f-0fb1-58ec-8ea1-2154b9e29de9.html, accessed August 26, 2017.

Ballard, Anthony, Probate file papers. Middlesex County, MA: Probate File Papers, 1648–1871, Case 931, New England Historic Genealogical Society, 2014, from records supplied by the Supreme Judicial Court Archives, https://www .americanancestors.org/databases/middlesex-county-ma-probate-file-papers -1648-1871/image?pageName=931:1&volumeId=14459, accessed March 9, 2019.

Ballard, William, Probate file papers. Essex County, MA: Probate File Papers, 1638–1881, Case 1606, New England Historic Genealogical Society, 2014, from records supplied by the Supreme Judicial Court Archives, https://www .americanancestors.org/databases/essex-county-ma-probate-file-papers-1638-1881 /image?pageName=1606:1&volumeId=13744, accessed April 2, 2019.

Bancroft, George, *History of the United States of America, from the Discovery of the American Continent*, Vol. 7 (11th edition, revised): The American Revolution, Vol. 1. Boston, Mass.: Little, Brown and Co., 1873.

Banks, Taunya Lovell, "Dangerous Woman: Elizabeth Key's Freedom Suit—Subjecthood and Racialized Identity in Seventeenth Century Colonial Virginia," *Akron Law Review* 41 (3) (2008): 799–837.

Barker, Ellen Frye, *Frye Genealogy*. New York, N.Y.: Tobias A. Wright, 1920.

Barnard, Frederick A.P., and Arnold Guyot (ed.), *Johnson's New Universal Cyclopaedia: A Scientific and Popular Treasury of Useful Knowledge*, Vol. 2, Part 1 (F–Herman). New York, N.Y.: A.J. Johnson and Co., 1881.

Battle-Baptiste, Whitney, *Black Feminist Archaeology*. Walnut Creek, Calif.: Left Coast Press, 2011.

Beckert, Sven, and Seth Rockman, "Introduction. Slavery's Capitalism," in *Slavery's Capitalism: A New History of American Economic Development*, ed. Sven Beckert and Seth Rockman, 1–27. Philadelphia: University of Pennsylvania Press, 2016.

Belknap, Jeremy, "Queries Respecting the Slavery and Emancipation of Negroes in Massachusetts, Proposed by the Hon. Judge Tucker of Virginia, and Answered by the Rev. Dr. Belknap," *Massachusetts Historical Society Collections for the Year 1795* (i.e., *Collections of the Massachusetts Historical Society* [1st series] 4 [1795]): 191–211.

Bell, Edward L., *Historical Archaeology at the Hudson Poor Farm Cemetery, Hudson, Massachusetts*. Boston: Massachusetts Historical Commission, 1993.

Bell, Edward L., *Vestiges of Mortality & Remembrance: A Bibliography on the Historical Archaeology of Cemeteries*. Metuchen, N.J.: Scarecrow Press, 1994.

Bell, Edward L., "Archaeology and Native History of the Den Rock Area," in *The Birds of Den Rock Park, Lawrence and Andover, Massachusetts: A Guide to the History and Natural History of Den Rock Park and its Birds*, by Susan Hegarty, 4–11. Andover, Mass.: Mass Nature, 2013.

Bell, Edward L., "Discerning Native Placemaking: Archaeologies and Histories of the Den Rock Area, Lawrence and Andover, Massachusetts," *Bulletin of the Archaeological Society of Connecticut* 75 (2013): 69–101.

Bell, Edward L., "Obtaining Her Liberty: The 1771 Freedom Suit of Nancy Parker of Andover, Massachusetts (with Notes and Suggested Readings for Educators and Researchers on Massachusetts Slavery and Emancipation)." Research summary prepared for "Invisible Injustice: A Symposium on Discovering & Disseminating the Story of Slavery in the North," Salem State University, Salem, Mass., April 2, 2016. Copy available at http://independent.academia.edu/EdwardLBell and at the Andover and North Andover historical societies.

Bell, Edward L., "Freeing Eral Lonnon: A Mashpee Indian Presumed a Fugitive Slave in Louisiana, and the Role of Native People in the History of Judicial Abolition in Massachusetts," *Atlantic Black Box* (website), April 29, 2019, https://atlanticblackbox.com/2019/05/08/freeing-eral-lonnon-a-mashpee-indian-presumed-a-fugitive-slave-in-louisiana-and-the-role-of-native-people-in-the-history-of-judicial-abolition-in-massachusetts/.

Bellagamba, Alice, "Freedom from Below: Some Introductory Thoughts," *Journal of Global Slavery* 2 (1–2) (2017): 1–9.

Bellagamba, Alice, Sandra E. Greene, and Martin A. Klein, "Introduction. Slaves and Masters: Politics, Memories, Social Life," in *African Slaves, African Masters: Politics, Memories, Social Life*, ed. Alice Bellagamba, Sandra E. Greene, and Martin A. Klein, 1–14. Trenton, N.J.: Africa World Press, 2017.

Bellefontaine, Edgar J., "Theophilus Parsons as a Legal Reformer," *Boston Bar Journal* 36 (2) (1992): 14–19.

Benes, Peter, "Slavery in Boston Households, 1647–1770," in *Slavery/Antislavery in New England*, ed. Peter Benes, 12–30. Boston, Mass.: Dublin Seminar for New England Folklife, Boston University, 2005.

Benes, Peter, *Meetinghouses of Early New England*. Amherst: University of Massachusetts Press, 2012.

Bentley, William, *The Diary of William Bentley, D.D., Pastor of the East Church, Salem, Massachusetts*, 4 vols. Salem, Mass.: Essex Institute, 1905, 1907, 1911, 1914.

Benton, Josiah H., Jr., *Early Census Making in Massachusetts 1643–1765 with a Reproduction of the Lost Census of 1765 (Recently Found) and Documents Relating Thereto Now First Collected and Published*. Boston, Mass.: Charles E. Goodspeed, 1905.

Ben-Ur, Aviva, "Bound Together? Reassessing the 'Slave Community' and 'Resistance' Paradigms," *Journal of Global Slavery* 3 (3) (2018): 195–210.

Berlin, Ira, *Many Thousands Gone: The First Two Centuries of Slavery in North America*. Cambridge, Mass.: Harvard University Press, 1998.

Berlin, Ira, "American Slavery in History and Memory and the Search for Social Justice," *The Journal of American History* 90 (4) (2004): 1251–1268.

Berry, Daina Ramey, *The Price for Their Pound of Flesh: The Value of the Enslaved, from Womb to Grave, in the Building of a Nation*. Boston, Mass.: Beacon Press, 2017.

Besteman, Catherine, "Public History and Private Knowledge: On Disputed History in Southern Somalia," *Ethnohistory* 40 (4) (1993): 563–586.

Betty's Case, Supreme Judicial Court, November 9, 1857, Shaw, C.J., in chambers, 20 [new series 10] Monthly Law Reporter 455 (1858).

Bishop, John v. John Hathorne and Edward Richards (In re Mall Indian), Essex County Quarterly Court Records, Ipswich, September 25, 1660, 89 (No. 16), "Court Records, 1646–1666," (title from microfilm target; spine title "County Court 1646–1666 Ipswich"), Microfilm Reel 877462, Genealogical Society of Salt Lake City, Ut., 1971, digitized by FamilySearch, https://www.familysearch .org/ark:/61903/3:1:3Q9M-CSQQ-JSZ7-M?i=135&cat=40003, digital image 136 of 488, accessed November 9, 2019. Abstracts of the court record and some file papers are in *Records and Files of the Quarterly Courts of Essex County*, Vol. 2 (1656–1662), 240–242, Salem, Mass.: Essex Institute, 1912. Transcriptions of file papers are in Archie N. Frost (comp.), "Verbatim Transcriptions of the Records of the Quarterly Courts of Essex County, Massachusetts," Vol. 6, 1660–1661, 23-1–23-4, 24-1–24-3, 25-1, Typescript, 1938 ("WPA Transcripts" on microfilm), Supreme Judicial Court Archives, Massachusetts Archives, Boston.

Bishop, R. Marshall, Jr. (ed.), from research by William Meyer, *Wilmington Minute Men 1775–1783, Being a list of men of the Seventh Wilmington Company, Second*

Middlesex Militia Regiemt [*sic*] *of Foot who had served during the Revolution*. [Wilmington, Mass.: Wilmington Company of Minute Men], n.d. (1997?).

Blanck, Emily, "Seventeen Eighty-Three: The Turning Point in the Law of Slavery and Freedom in Massachusetts," *The New England Quarterly* 75 (1) (2002): 24–51.

Blanck, Emily, "The Legal Emancipations of Leander and Caesar: Manumission and the Law in Revolutionary South Carolina and Massachusetts," *Slavery & Abolition* 28 (2) (2007): 235–254.

Blanck, Emily, *Tyrannicide: Forging an American Law of Slavery in Revolutionary South Carolina and Massachusetts*. Athens: University of Georgia Press, 2014.

Bluemel, Lee, "Stepping Up to Our Past: Black History at North Parish (1760–1860), Preached at The North Parish of North Andover, MA, February 21, 2010," typescript, n.p., in binder "North Andover African-American History," North Andover Historical Society, North Andover, Mass., also available at http://www.northparish.org/wp-content/uploads/2013/01/Black-History-at-NP-2010-02-21.pdf, accessed February 8, 2017.

Bluemel, Lee, "An Invisible History: A Sermon Preached by the Rev. Lee Bluemel at The North Parish, Unitarian Universalist, of North Andover, MA, Heritage Sunday, October 23, 2016," n.p., http://www.northparish.org/wp-content/uploads/2016/10/2016-10-23-Invisible-History.pdf, accessed February 8, 2017.

Bly, Antonio T., "Pretty, Sassy, Cool: Slave Resistance, Agency, and Culture in Eighteenth-Century New England," *The New England Quarterly* 89 (3) (2016): 457–492.

Bolton, John, Probate file papers. Middlesex County, MA: Probate File Papers, 1648–1871, Case 2127, New England Historic Genealogical Society, 2014, from records supplied by the Supreme Judicial Court Archives, https://www.americanancestors.org/databases/middlesex-county-ma-probate-file-papers-1648-1871/image/?pageName=2127:1&volumeId=14460&rId=38178857, accessed August 26, 2017.

Bonacci, Giulia, and Alexander Meckelburg, "Revisiting Slavery and the Slave Trade in Ethiopia," *Northeast African Studies* 17 (2) (2017): 5–30.

Booso v. Samuel Chickering, Essex County Court of Common Pleas Records, July 1778, 476, Supreme Judicial Court Archives, Massachusetts Archives, Boston.

Boston Athenaeum, *The Boston Directory 1789 to 1900* (website), http://cdm.bostonathenaeum.org/cdm/landingpage/collection/p16057coll32, accessed September 28, 2017.

Boston Public Library, *Anti-Slavery (Collection of Distinction)* (website), https://www.digitalcommonwealth.org/collections/commonwealth:ht24xg10q, accessed January 26, 2019.

Bowen, Charles, *The American Annual Register for the Year 1830–31, or the Fifty-Fifth Year of American Independence*. Boston, Mass.: Charles Bowen, 1832.

Bradford, James, "James Chandler," Appendix B.1 to "An Address, Delivered at Rowley, Mass., September 5, 1839, at the Celebration of the Second Centennial Anniversary of the Settlement of the Town, Embracing its Ecclesiastical History from the Beginning," in *The History of Rowley, Anciently Including Bradford, Boxford, and Georgetown, from the Year 1639 to the Present Time*, by Thomas Gage, 91–94. Boston, Mass.: Ferdinand Andrews, 1840.

Bradley, Patricia, *Slavery, Propaganda, and the American Revolution*. Jackson: University of Mississippi Press, 1998.

Breen, Lise, "Inculcated Forgetfulness at a New England Port," *Black Perspectives* (June 20, 2019), https://www.aaihs.org/inculcated-forgetfulness-at-a-new-england -port/, accessed June 25, 2019.

Breen, T.H., "Making History: The Force of Public Opinion and the Last Years of Slavery in Revolutionary Massachusetts," in *Through a Glass Darkly: Reflections on Personal Identity in Early America*, ed. Ronald Hoffman, Mechal Sobel, and Fredrika J. Teute, 67–95. Chapel Hill: University of North Carolina Press, 1997.

Brewer, Jonathan, et al., "Recommendation of Salem Poor a free Negro for his Bravery at ye Battle of Charlestown," December 5, 1775. Massachusetts Archives Collection, Vol. 180, 241–241a, SC1/series 45X, Massachusetts Archives, Boston.

Briggs, L. Vernon, "White, Indian and Negro Slaves of Our Ancestors and Other Early Settlers, 1632–1830," in *History and Genealogy of the Briggs Family, 1254– 1937*, Vol. 1, 86–137. Boston, Mass.: Charles E. Goodspeed and Co., 1938.

Bristol v. John Osgood, Essex County Court of Common Pleas Records, December 1773, 38, Supreme Judicial Court Archives, Massachusetts Archives, Boston.

Bristol, Sherlock, *The Pioneer Preacher: Incidents of Interest, and Experiences in the Author's Life*. Chicago, Ill.: Fleming H. Revell, 1887.

Brom and Bett v. John Ashley, Berkshire County Court of Common Pleas Records, August 1781, 55; Supreme Judicial Court Records, Berkshire County, October 1781, 96, captioned as "Ashley apl Brom et al."; Suffolk Files Collection, File #159966, Supreme Judicial Court Archives, Massachusetts Archives, Boston.

[Brooks, William G.] ("B."), Letter to editor about Cato Freeman, *Andover Advertiser* (Andover, Mass.) (August 27, 1853): n.p. [2]. A clipping of this published item with handwritten emendation of authorship as "W.G.B." is pasted in the unique copy of Abbot, *History of Andover from its Settlement to 1829*, with "69 extra pages with newspaper clippings" once owned by Jonathan Clement and William G. Brooks, Accession No. 1991.140, Andover Center for History & Culture, Andover, Mass.

Brown, Barbara, "Black Lucy's Garden," n.d. Typescript, research files, "Foster Family," Andover Center for History & Culture, Andover, Mass.

Brown, Lois, "Memorial Narratives of African Women in Antebellum New England," *Legacy: A Journal of American Women Writers* 20 (1–2) (2003): 38–61.

Brown, Lois, "Death-Defying Testimony: Women's Private Lives and the Politics of Public Documents," *Legacy: A Journal of American Women Writers* 27 (1) (2010): 130–139.

Brown, Susan F., Death record. State Vital Records, Deaths Register, Deaths 1901, Vol. 519 (Suffolk), 411, No. 56, July 14, 1901, Massachusetts Archives, Boston.

Buckingham, James S., *America: Historical, Statistic, and Descriptive*, Vol. 3. London: Fisher, Son and Co., 1841.

Bullen, Adelaide K., and Ripley P. Bullen, "Black Lucy's Garden," *Bulletin of the Massachusetts Archaeological Society* 6 (2) (1945): 17–28.

Bullen, Ripley P., *Excavations in Northeastern Massachusetts*. Andover, Mass.: Robert S. Peabody Foundation for Archaeology, 1949.

Bullen, Ripley P., and Arthur M. Hofman, "The Stickney Site, Ballardvale, Massachusetts," *Bulletin of the Massachusetts Archaeological Society* 5 (2) (1944): 20–25.

Butler, Jon, *Awash in a Sea of Faith: Christianizing the American People*. Cambridge, Mass.: Harvard University Press, 1990.

Caesar v. Samuel Taylor, Essex County Court of Common Pleas Records, September 1771, 158; Superior Court of Judicature Records, Essex County, June 1772, 91 (as Taylor v. Caesar); Suffolk Files Collection, File #132190, Supreme Judicial Court Archives, Massachusetts Archives, Boston.

Cairns, Jane, "Andover Stories: Town Owes much more than Amusement to one-of-a-kind Bessie Goldsmith," *Andover Advertiser* (Andover, Mass.) (May 19, 2011), https://www.andovertownsman.com/news/local_news/andover-stories-town-owes-much-more-than-amusement-to-one/article_49954bfc-0c35-50d2-bf46-b89ecc236351.html, accessed June 29, 2019.

Cairns, Jane, "Andover Stories: The Thirty-four Star Flag," *Andover Townsman* (Andover, Mass.) (May 29, 2014): 12.

Campbell, Eleanor, *West of the Shawsheen: A Story of the People of West Parish Church in Andover, Massachusetts*. Andover, Mass.: West Parish Church, 1975.

Carpenter, Charles C., *Biographical Catalogue of the Trustees, Teachers and Students of Phillips Academy, Andover, 1778–1830*. Andover, Mass.: The Andover Press, 1903.

Carpenter, Charles C., "Glimpses of Life in Andover Eighty Years Ago, from an Old Family Expense-book," *The Andover Townsman* (Andover, Mass.) (May 2, 1913): 3.

Carpenter, Daniel, and Colin D. Moore, "When Canvassers Became Activists: Antislavery Petitioning and the Political Mobilization of American Women," *American Political Science Review* 108 (3) (2014): 479–498.

Carpenter, Daniel, Nicole Topich, and Garth Griffin, *Digital Archive of Massachusetts Anti-Slavery and Anti-Segregation Petitions, Massachusetts Archives, Boston MA,*

2015 (website), https://dataverse.harvard.edu/dataverse/antislaverypetitionsma. Cambridge, Mass.: Widener Library, Harvard University, 2015.

Carter, Susan B., Scott Sigmund Gartner, Michael R. Haines, Alan L. Olmstead, Richard Sutch, and Gavin Wright (ed.), *Historical Statistics of the United States: Earliest Times to the Present, Millennial Edition*, Vol. 2, Part B, Work and Welfare. New York, N.Y.: Cambridge University Press, 2006.

Carter Jackson, Kelli, *Force and Freedom: Black Abolitionists and the Politics of Violence*. Philadelphia: University of Pennsylvania Press, 2019.

Carvalho, Joseph, III, "Uncovering the Stories of Black Families in Springfield and Hampden County, Massachusetts: 1650–1865," *Historical Journal of Massachusetts* 40 (1–2) (2012): 58–93.

Catterall, Helen Tunnicliff (ed.), with additions by James J. Hayden, *Judicial Cases concerning American Slavery and the Negro*, Vol. 4: Cases from the Courts of New England, the Middle States, and the District of Columbia. Washington, D.C.: Carnegie Institution of Washington, 1936.

Caulfield, Ernest, "A History of the Terrible Epidemic, Vulgarly called the Throat Distemper, as it occurred in His Majesty's New England Colonies between 1735 and 1740," *Yale Journal of Biology and Medicine* 11 (3) (1939): 219–272.

Caulfield, Ernest, "The 'Throat Distemper' of 1735–1740 Part II," *Yale Journal of Biology and Medicine* 11 (4) (1939): 277–335.

Chadwick, [Deacon] Thomas, Probate file papers. Essex County, MA: Probate File Papers, 1638–1881, Case 4887, New England Historic Genealogical Society, 2014, from records supplied by the Supreme Judicial Court Archives, https://www.americanancestors.org/databases/essex-county-ma-probate-file-papers-1638-1881/image?pageName=4887:1&volumeId=13763, accessed March 6, 2019.

Chadwick, Thomas, Probate file papers. Essex County, MA: Probate File Papers, 1638–1881, Case 4888, New England Historic Genealogical Society, 2014, from records supplied by the Supreme Judicial Court Archives, https://www.americanancestors.org/databases/essex-county-ma-probate-file-papers-1638-1881/image?pageName=4888:1&volumeId=13763, accessed March 9, 2019.

Chandler, George, *The Chandler Family. The Descendants of William and Annis Chandler who Settled in Roxbury, Mass. 1637*. Worcester, Mass.: Press of Charles Hamilton, 1883.

Chandler, Hannah, Probate file papers. Essex County, MA: Probate File Papers, 1638–1881, Case 4932, New England Historic Genealogical Society, 2014, from records supplied by the Supreme Judicial Court Archives, https://www.americanancestors.org/databases/essex-county-ma-probate-file-papers-1638-1881/RecordDisplay?volumeId=13763&pageName=4932:1&rId=245167883, accessed April 8, 2019.

Chandler, Isaac, Account book (bound volume), n.p., Chandler-Hidden Family Papers, 1678–1866, Ms. N-358, Massachusetts Historical Society, Boston.

Chandler, James, Probate file papers. Essex County, MA: Probate File Papers, 1638–1881, Case 4936, New England Historic Genealogical Society, 2014, from records supplied by the Supreme Judicial Court Archives, https://www .americanancestors.org/databases/essex-county-ma-probate-file-papers-1638-1881 /image?pageName=4936:1&volumeId=13763&rId=30104326, accessed March 4, 2019.

Chandler, Joshua, Joshua Chandler Papers, Ms S 52, Andover Center for History & Culture, Andover, Mass.

Chandler, Nathan, Probate file papers. Essex County, MA: Probate File Papers, 1638–1881, Case 4962, New England Historic Genealogical Society, 2014, from records supplied by the Supreme Judicial Court Archives, https://www .americanancestors.org/databases/essex-county-ma-probate-file-papers-1638-1881 /image?pageName=4962:1&volumeId=13763&rId=30104661, accessed April 1, 2019.

Chase, David, "To Promote True Piety and Virtue" and "Liberal Advantages: The Founding of Abbot Academy," in *Academy Hill: The Andover Campus, 1778 to Present*, 33–66. Andover, Mass.: Addison Gallery of American Art, Phillips Academy, and New York, N.Y.: Princeton Architectural Press, 2000.

Chase, Theodore, "Harvard Student Disorders in 1770," *The New England Quarterly* 61 (1) (1988): 25–54.

[Chever, George Francis], *The Old Parish Church of North Andover: A Poem*. s.l.: s.n., (1849?).

Child, Christopher Challender, "Chance Bradstreet (1762–1810), Servant of Abraham Dodge of Ipswich, Massachusetts," *American Ancestors* 11 (4) (2010): 41–43, and https://www.americanancestors.org/chance-bradstreet, accessed April 19, 2018.

Choate Family Papers, MSS 380, Phillips Library, Peabody Essex Museum, Rowley, Mass.

Choate Family Reminiscences, Handwritten notes about slaves in the Francis Choate household, Ipswich, Mass., Essex Shipbuilding Museum, Essex, Mass.

Choate, Francis, Probate file papers. Essex County, MA: Probate File Papers, 1638–1881, Case 5339, New England Historic Genealogical Society, 2014, from records supplied by the Supreme Judicial Court Archives, https://www.americanancestors .org/databases/essex-county-ma-probate-file-papers-1638-1881/image/?pageName =5339:1&volumeId=13763, accessed July 6, 2017.

Ciolfi, Sandra, "*Lucy's Acre: A Place in Time* Exhibit Shows Life of Former Slave," *Andover Historical Society Newsletter* (Andover, Mass.) 28 (3) (2003): n.p. [1, 4].

Clements, Elaine, "Andover Stories: Slavery Did Exist in Early Andover," *Andover Townsman* (Andover, Mass.) (July 26, 2012), http://www.andovertownsman.com/news/local_news/andover-stories-slavery-did-exist-in-early-andover/article_781f6965-4bfd-5bf9-b0f8-f676a8b03389.html, accessed January 3, 2015.

Clements, Elaine, "Abolitionism in Andover," *Andover Townsman* (Andover, Mass.) (August 2, 2012), https://www.andovertownsman.com/news/local_news/abolitionism-in-andover/article_982f22a4-df61-5e63-82cc-d4f4b7768379.html, accessed January 3, 2015.

Clements, Elaine, "Cato Freeman," *Andover Stories* (website), Andover Historical Society, October 24, 2015, http://andoverhistoryandculture.org/explore-andover-stories-blog/cato-freeman, accessed August 7, 2019.

Clements, Elaine, "Slavery in New England," *Andover Stories* (website), Andover Historical Society, October 24, 2015, http://andoverhistorical.org/explore-andover-stories-blog/slavery-in-new-england, accessed August 6, 2017.

Clements, Elaine, "The Story of Rose Lovejoy's Wedding Dress," *Andover Stories* (website), Andover Center for History & Culture, September 13, 2019, https://andoverhistorical.org/andover-stories/the-story-of-rose-lovejoy-s-wedding-dress, accessed January 21, 2020.

Coates, Ta-Nehisi, "The Black Family in the Age of Mass Incarceration," *The Atlantic* (October 2015), https://www.theatlantic.com/magazine/archive/2015/10/the-black-family-in-the-age-of-mass-incarceration/403246/, accessed September 21, 2019.

Coates, Ta-Nehisi, "Reporter's Notebook: 'A Species of Labor We Do Not Want.'" *The Atlantic* (June 27, 2016), https://www.theatlantic.com/notes/2016/06/a-species-of-labor-we-do-not-want/488744/, accessed August 16, 2019.

Coburn, Rosanna, Death record. State Vital Records, Deaths Register, Deaths 1859, Vol. 129, 109, No. 16, March 19, 1859, Massachusetts Archives, Boston.

Coburn, Rosanna, Death record. Town of Andover, Death Register 1855–1896, 9, No. 14, March 19, 1859, rendered "Rosana Coburn", Town Clerk's Office, Andover, Mass.

Coburn, Rose, Probate file papers. Essex County, MA: Probate File Papers, 1638–1881, Case 35590, New England Historic Genealogical Society, 2014, from records supplied by the Supreme Judicial Court Archives, https://www.americanancestors.org/databases/essex-county-ma-probate-file-papers-1638-1881/image/?pageName=35590:1&volumeId=14206, accessed March 24, 2017.

Coburn, Silas R. (ed.), *Genealogy of the Descendants of Edward Colburn/Coburn*. Lowell, Mass.: Walter Coburn and Courier-Citizen Co., 1913.

Coburn, Silas R., *History of Dracut, Massachusetts*. Lowell, Mass.: Courier-Citizen Co., 1922.

Coburn, Titus, Probate file papers. Essex County, MA: Probate File Papers, 1638–1881, Case 35592, New England Historic Genealogical Society, 2014, from records supplied by the Supreme Judicial Court Archives, https://www .americanancestors.org/databases/essex-county-ma-probate-file-papers-1638-1881 /image/?volumeId=14206&pageName=35592:1&rId=259609449, accessed April 14, 2017.

Coburn, Titus, Revolutionary War Pension Application File, July 13, 1820, Essex County Circuit Court of Common Pleas for the Middle Circuit, Salem, Mass., Collection No. EC 43, Box 2, File 5 pension applications, "Collection of Essex County (Mass.) Court Records, 1628–1914," Phillips Library, Peabody Essex Museum, Rowley, Mass.

Coburn, Titus, and Rosanna Coburn, Revolutionary War Pension Application File #W.6734, Revolutionary War Pension and Bounty-Land Application Files, Microfilm M804, Reel 589, National Archives and Records Administration. Digital copy from microfilm at https://catalog.archives.gov/id/54252879, accessed many times.

Coclanis, Peter A., "The Captivity of a Generation," *The William and Mary Quarterly* (3rd series) 61 (3) (2004): 544–555.

Coffin, Joshua, *A Sketch of the History of Newbury, Newburyport, and West Newbury, from 1635 to 1845*. Boston, Mass.: Samuel G. Drake, 1845.

Coleman, Peter J., "Massachusetts," in *Debtors and Creditors in America: Insolvency, Imprisonment for Debt, and Bankruptcy, 1607–1900* (reprint of 1974 edition), 39–52. Washington, D.C.: Beard Books, 1999.

Commonwealth v. Thomas Aves, Supreme Judicial Court, March 1836, 18 Pick. (35 Mass. Reports) 193.

Commonwealth v. Nathaniel Jennison, Supreme Judicial Court Records, Worcester County, April 1783, 85; Suffolk Files Collection, File #153693, Supreme Judicial Court Archives, Massachusetts Archives, Boston. (See also Jennison v. Caldwell and Caldwell, and Walker v. Jennison.)

Cooper, Frederick, Thomas C. Holt, and Rebecca J. Scott, *Beyond Slavery: Explorations of Race, Labor, and Citizenship in Postemancipation Societies*. Chapel Hill: University of North Carolina Press, 2000.

Cooper, James F., Jr., and Kenneth P. Minkema (ed.), *The Colonial Church Records of the First Church of Reading (Wakefield) and the First Church of Rumney Marsh (Revere)*. Boston: The Colonial Society of Massachusetts, 2006.

Cotter, William R., "The Somerset Case and the Abolition of Slavery in England," *History* (Journal of The Historical Association) 79 (255) (1994): 31–56.

Cover, Robert M., *Justice Accused: Antislavery and the Judicial Process*. New Haven, Conn.: Yale University Press, 1975.

Cowper, William, "The Time-piece," in *The Task, A Poem, in Six Books*, Book II, 46. London: Printed for J. Johnson, 1785.

Crane, Elaine Forman, *Ebb Tide in New England: Women, Seaports, and Social Change, 1630–1800*. Boston, Mass.: Northeastern University Press, 1998.

Crapo, Henry Howland, *Certain Comeoverers*, Vol. 2. New Bedford, Mass.: E. Anthony and Sons, 1912.

Crenshaw, Kimberlé, "Mapping the Margins: Intersectionality, Identity Politics, and Violence Against Women of Color," *Stanford Law Review* 43 (6) (1991): 1241–1299.

Crimaldi, Laura, "'She deserves her place'" (Dedication of Lucy Foster cenotaph), *Boston Sunday Globe* (Boston, Mass.) (May 12, 2019): B1, B7.

Cronin, John F., *Records of the Court of Assistants of the Colony of the Massachusetts Bay 1630–1692*, Vol. 3. Boston, Mass.: The County of Suffolk, 1928.

Cross, Henry J., "Slavery in Essex County," *Essex Institute Historical Collections* 7 (2) (1865): 73.

Cushing, John D., "The Cushing Court and the Abolition of Slavery in Massachusetts: More Notes on the 'Quock Walker Case,'" *American Journal of Legal History* 5 (2) (1961): 118–144.

Cushing, William, "Legal notes by William Cushing about the Quock Walker case." Digital images and transcription of the William Cushing judicial notebook, 1783 (Ms. P-406) pertaining to Commonwealth v. Jennison, Massachusetts Historical Society, Boston, http://www.masshist.org/database/viewer.php?item_id =630, accessed August 3, 2019.

Cushing, William, "Notes of cases decided in the Superior and Supreme Judicial Courts of Massachusetts from 1772 to 1789; taken by the Hon. William Cushing, one of the judges during that period and most of the time Chief Justice," "Worcester—April Term A.D. 1783" i.e., Commonwealth v. Jennison, 34–35, HLS MS 4083, Harvard Law School Library, Cambridge, Mass. Digital images, https://iiif.lib.harvard.edu/manifests/view/drs:51409100$76i, seq. 76–78, accessed August 3, 2019.

Cutter, William R., "Longevity in Woburn," in *Woburn Records of Births, Deaths, and Marriages, from 1640 to 1873. Part II. Deaths*, arr. Edward F. Johnson, 155–160. Woburn, Mass.: Andrews, Cutler and Co., 1890.

Daen, Laurel, "'To Board & Nurse a Stranger': Poverty, Disability, and Community in Eighteenth-Century Massachusetts," *Journal of Society History* (2020), advance version (February 11, 2019) prior to print publication, https://academic .oup.com/jsh/advance-article-abstract/doi/10.1093/jsh/shy117/5315915, accessed March 25, 2019.

Dalton, Bill, "Dalton Column: Slaves in Andover," *Andover Townsman* (Andover, Mass.) (February 14, 2013), http://www.andovertownsman.com/community/dalton

-column-slaves-in-andover/article_e23cfd7e-48e7-521e-b666-78b036d10025
.html, accessed January 3, 2015.

Dana, Francis, Francis Dana Papers, 1749–1810, in Dana Family Papers, 1654–1950, Ms. N-1088, Massachusetts Historical Society, Boston.

Daughters of the Revolution of the Commonwealth of Massachusetts, *Catalogue of a Loan Collection of Ancient and Historic Articles, Exhibited by Daughters of the Revolution of the Commonwealth of Massachusetts, Copley Hall, April 19–20–21, 1897, Boston.* s.l.: Daughters of the Revolution of the Commonwealth of Massachusetts, 1897.

Daughters of the Revolution, Phoebe Foxcroft Phillips Chapter Records, 1895–1932, Ms S 619, Andover Center for History & Culture, Andover, Mass.

Davis, Angela, "Reflections on the Black Woman's Role in the Community of Slaves," *The Massachusetts Review* 13 (1–2) (1972): 81–100, originally published in *The Black Scholar* 3 (4) (1971): 2–15.

Davis, Angela Y., "The Legacy of Slavery: Standards for a New Womanhood," in *Women, Race & Class*, 3–29. New York, N.Y.: Vintage Books, 1983.

Davis, David Brion, *The Problem of Slavery in the Age of Revolution, 1770–1823.* Ithaca, N.Y.: Cornell University Press, 1975.

Davis, David Brion, *Inhuman Bondage: The Rise and Fall of Slavery in the New World.* New York, N.Y.: Oxford University Press, 2006.

Davis, David Brion, "Re-Examining the Problem of Slavery in Western Culture," *Proceedings of the American Antiquarian Society* (new series) 118 (Part 2) (2009): 247–266.

Davis, Kathy, "Intersectionality as Buzzword: A Sociology of Science Perspective on What Makes a Feminist Theory Successful," *Feminist Theory* 9 (1) (2008): 67–85.

Dawson, Henry B., "Books," *The Historical Magazine, and Notes and Queries Concerning the Antiquities, History, and Biography of America* (new series) 5 (4) (1869): 280.

Dayton, Cornelia H., and Sharon V. Salinger, *Robert Love's Warnings: Searching for Strangers in Colonial Boston.* Philadelphia: University of Pennsylvania Press, 2014.

Den Ouden, Amy E., "Locating the Cannibals: Conquest, North American Ethnohistory, and the Threat of Objectivity," *History and Anthropology* 18 (2) (2007): 101–133.

Desrochers, Robert E., Jr., "Slave-for-Sale Advertisements and Slavery in Massachusetts, 1704–1781," *The William and Mary Quarterly* (3rd series) 59 (3) (2002): 623–664.

Dighton v. Freetown, Supreme Judicial Court, October 1808, 4 Mass. Reports 539.

Dillard, Annie, "Author's note," in *For the Time Being*, ix–x. New York, N.Y.: Alfred A. Knopf, 1999.

Dinkin, Robert J., "Seating the Meetinghouse in Early Massachusetts," *The New England Quarterly* 43 (3) (1970): 450–464.

Diocese of Massachusetts, *Journal of the Proceedings of the Fifty-Fourth [Fifty-Fifth and Fifty-Sixth] Annual Convention of the Diocese of Massachusetts: Holden in Trinity Church, Boston [1844, 1845, 1846]*. Published as three separate volumes of the annual proceedings. Boston, Mass.: James B. Dow, 1844, 1845, 1846.

Dix, Dorthea, *Memorial to the Legislature of Massachusetts*. Boston, Mass.: Munroe and Francis, 1843.

Dorgan, Maurice B., *Lawrence Yesterday and Today, 1845–1918*. Lawrence, Mass.: Press of Dick and Trumpold, 1918.

Dorman, Franklin A., *Twenty Families of Color in Massachusetts, 1742–1998*. Boston, Mass.: New England Historic Genealogical Society, 1998.

Dorman, Moses, Jr., "A Plan of Andover Taken for the Town by Moses Dorman, Jr. 1830." Boston, Mass.: Pendleton's Lithography. Harvard Map Collection digital maps, Harvard Library, Cambridge, Mass., http://vc.lib.harvard.edu/vc/deliver/~maps/009480389, accessed April 23, 2017.

Douyard, Christopher M., "Property, Capital, and Race: Rural Capitalism and Racialized Landscapes in Nineteenth-Century Massachusetts," *Journal of African Diaspora Archaeology & Heritage* 3 (2) (2014): 175–196.

Drew, Bernard A., *If They Close the Door on You, Go in the Window: Origins of the African American Community in Sheffield, Great Barrington, and Stockbridge*. Great Barrington, Mass.: Attic Revivals Press, 2004.

Du Bois, William Edward Burghardt, *The Souls of Black Folk: Essays and Sketches* (3rd edition). Chicago, Ill.: A.C. McClurg and Co., 1903.

Du Bois, William Edward Burghardt, *Black Reconstruction: An Essay Toward a History of the Part which Black Folk Played in the Attempt to Reconstruct Democracy in America, 1860–1880*. New York, N.Y.: Harcourt, Brace and Co., 1935.

Dupre, Daniel S., "The Panic of 1819 and the Political Economy of Sectionalism," in *The Economy of Early America: Historical Perspectives and New Directions*, ed. Cathy Matson, 263–293. University Park: The Pennsylvania State University Press, 2006.

Earle, Jonathan, "Marcus Morton and the Dilemma of Jacksonian Antislavery in Massachusetts, 1817–1849," *Massachusetts Historical Review* 4 (2002): 60–87.

Eaton, Lilley, *Genealogical History of the Town of Reading, Mass. including the present towns of Wakefield, Reading, and North Reading, with Chronological and Historical Sketches, from 1639 to 1874*. Boston, Mass.: Alfred Mudge and Son, 1874.

Egerton, Douglas R., "Slave Resistance," in *The Oxford Handbook of Slavery in the Americas*, ed. Robert L. Paquette and Mark M. Smith, 447–462. New York, N.Y.: Oxford University Press, 2018.

Einhorn, Robin L., *American Taxation, American Slavery*. Chicago, Ill.: University of Chicago Press, 2006.

Elder, Rosalyn Delores, *African American Heritage in Massachusetts: Exploring the Legacy*. Boston: African American Heritage Massachusetts, 2016.

Ellery, Benjamin, Benjamin Ellery account book (bound volume), n.p., Cape Ann Museum Archives, Gloucester, Mass.

Elliott, Charles W., "Slavery in New England," in *The New England History, from the Discovery of the Continent by the Northmen, A.D. 986, to the Period When the Colonies Declared their Independence, A.D. 1776*, 167–205. New York, N.Y.: Charles Scribner, 1857.

Emery, Elizabeth, and Mary P. Abbott, "Andover Female A.S. Society," *The Liberator* (Boston, Mass.) 6 (35) (August 27, 1836): 138.

Emery, Sarah Anna, *Reminiscences of a Nonagenarian*. Newburyport, Mass.: William H. Huse & Co., 1879.

Ernest, John, "Life Beyond Biography: Black Lives and Biographical Research," *Common-Place: The Journal of Early American Life* 17 (1) (2016), http://common -place.org/book/life-beyond-biography-black-lives-and-biographical-research/, accessed April 10, 2019.

Essex County Circuit Court of Common Pleas for the Middle Circuit Records, September 1818, 240 (Gurney and Packard v. Jacob Abbot), 241 (Gurney and Packard v. Andrew W. Dunklee and Andrew W. Dunklee, Jr.), 243 (Gurney and Packard v. Abiel Upton, Jr.); December 1818, 428 (Gurney and Packard v. Samuel Lummus), 429 (Gurney and Packard v. William Hawley and Samuel Lummus), 531 (Zachariah Gurney, Jr. v. Jacob Abbot), 532 (Gurney and Packard v. Jacob Abbot), 533 (Gurney and Packard v. Peter Holt); March 1819, 72 (Gurney and Packard v. Titus Coburn), 146 (Gurney and Packard v. Levi Trull), 147 (Gurney and Packard v. Benjamin Berry); June 1819, 259 (Gurney and Packard v. Moses Wood), 316 (Gurney and Packard v. Richard Sherwin), 375 (Gurney and Packard v. Levi Davis); March 1820, 156 (Gurney and Packard v. Richard Sherwin), Supreme Judicial Court Archives, Massachusetts Archives, Boston.

Essex County Deeds, Book 81, pg. 59, Joseph Frie to Edward Hirkcom (Hircom in caption), November 12, 1737, recorded November 7, 1740; Book 81, pg. 60, Edward Hirkcom to Ebenezer Walcott, March 23, 1738, recorded November 7, 1740; Book 110, pg. 156, John Holt 3rd (of Andover, Mass.) to Edward Hircom, May 6, 1762, recorded May 11, 1762; Book 110, pg. 215, Edward Hircom to John Holt (of Hollis, N.H.), December 6, 1762, recorded December 15, 1762; Book 130, pg. 21, John Poor, Jr. to Salem Poor, July 10, 1769, recorded February 12,

1772; Book 184, pg. 280, Jonathan Griffin to Titus Coburn, January 19, 1809, recorded January 26, 1809; Book 195, pg. 42, Titus Coburn to Sarah Stevens, November 8, 1811, recorded November 14, 1811; Book 252, pg. 234, Articles of Agreement (Contract) between David Sherman (with Stephen Holt signing also) and Benjamin R. Downes, December 24, 1828, recorded August 18, 1829, Southern Essex District Registry of Deeds, Salem, Mass.

Essex County, Mass., "Collection of Essex County (Mass.) Court Records, 1628–1914," Collection No. EC 43, Phillips Library, Peabody Essex Museum, Rowley, Mass.

Estes, J. Worth, "Therapeutic Practice in Colonial New England," in *Medicine in Colonial Massachusetts, 1620–1820: A Conference Held 25 & 26 May 1978 by the Colonial Society of Massachusetts*, ed. J. Worth Estes, Philip Cash, and Eric H. Christianson, 289–383. Boston: The Colonial Society of Massachusetts, 1980.

FamilySearch, *England Births and Christenings, 1538–1975* (website), https://familysearch.org/ark:/61903/1:1:JWDC-KPY : 11 February 2018 (male child of Henry and Joane Hurcome, November 10, 1698) based on data from Genealogical Society of Salt Lake City, Ut., Microfilm Reel 427797 and 855625, accessed July 7, 2019.

Farlow, Charles Frederic (comp.), *Ballard Genealogy: William Ballard (1603–1639) of Lynn, Massachusetts and William Ballard (1617–1689) of Andover, Massachusetts and their Descendants*, ed. Charles Henry Pope. Boston, Mass.: Charles H. Pope, 1911.

Farnham, John, and Moses Abbot (surveyors), "A plan of the Town of Andover Taken by the Subscribers a Committee appointed by the Inhabitants of said Town for that purpose agreeable to a resolve of the General Court of June 18ᵗʰ one Thousand Seven Hundred and Ninety four," June 1, 1795, Maps and Plans #1082, Town Maps 1794–1795, SC1 47x, Massachusetts Archives, Boston.

Faucquez, Anne-Claire, "L'esclavage en milieu urbain: le cas de New York au xviiᵉ siècle," *Transatlantica* 2 (2012), http://transatlantica.revues.org/6221, accessed October 26, 2014.

Fay, Joseph Dewey, *Pauperism. To the Citizens of Philadelphia, Paying Poor Taxes*, Part 3. Philadelphia, Pa.: s.n., 1827.

Field, Kendra, "The Violence of Family Formation: Enslaved Families and Reproductive Labor in the Marketplace," *Reviews in American History* 42 (2) (2014): 255–264.

Find A Grave, *Find A Grave* (website), https://www.findagrave.com/.

Finkelman, Paul, *An Imperfect Union: Slavery, Federalism, and Comity*. Chapel Hill: University of North Carolina Press, 1981.

Finkelman, Paul, *Slavery in the Courtroom: An Annotated Bibliography of American Cases*. Washington, D.C.: Library of Congress, 1985.

Fischer, David Hackett, *Albion's Seed: Four British Folkways in America*. New York, N.Y.: Oxford University Press, 1989.

Fisher, Linford D., "Native Americans, Conversions, and Christian Practice in Colonial New England, 1640–1730," *The Harvard Theological Review* (102) (1) (2009): 101–124.

Fisher, Linford D., *The Indian Great Awakening: Religion and the Shaping of Native Cultures in Early America*. New York, N.Y.: Oxford University Press, 2012.

Fisher, Linford D., "'Why shall wee have peace to bee made slaves': Indian Surrenderers during and after King Philip's War," *Ethnohistory* 64 (1) (2017): 91–114.

Fitts, Robert K., "The Landscapes of Northern Bondage," *Historical Archaeology* 30 (2) (1996): 54–73.

Fitzpatrick, Marilyn, "Joseph Parker of Andover—Part 1," *The Essex Genealogist* 18 (3) (1998): 154–163.

Fladeland, Betty, *Men and Brothers: Anglo-American Antislavery Cooperation*. Urbana: University of Illinois Press, 1972.

Flagg, Charles A. (comp.), *A Guide to Massachusetts Local History*. Salem, Mass.: The Salem Press Co., 1907.

Flagg, Wilson, "Rural Architecture," *The Atlantic Monthly: A Magazine of Literature, Science, Art, and Politics* 37 (222) (April 1876): 428–435.

Flagg, Wilson, *Halcyon Days*. Boston, Mass.: Estes and Lauriat, 1881.

Flanders, Eliza R., Death record. State Vital Records, Deaths Register, Deaths 1905, Vol. 2, 119, No. 42, April 18, 1905, Massachusetts Archives, Boston.

Forbes, Harriette Merrifield, Photographic image of Squire Eames House (Wilmington, Mass.), June 24, 1935, Scan number: 000420-0595. *Photographs of Seventeenth and Eighteenth Century Structures in Massachusetts taken 1887–1945 by Harriette Merrifield Forbes* (website), American Antiquarian Society, Worcester, Mass., https://www.americanantiquarian.org/forbes.htm, accessed February 10, 2019.

Forebears, *Forebears* (website), https://forebears.io, accessed September 15, 2019.

Forsyth-Vail, Gail, "African Americans and the North Parish and Church of North Andover, Massachusetts: 1760–1860," typescript, 2000, Special Collections, Lawrence Public Library, Lawrence, Mass.

Foster, Carole, *Mss:761 1754–1819 A122, Abbot, Samuel, 1732–1812. Samuel Abbot business papers, 1754–1819 (inclusive): A Finding Aid*. Boston, Mass.: Baker Library Special Collections, Harvard Business School, 1998, https://hollisarchives.lib.harvard.edu/repositories/11/resources/685, accessed many times.

Foster, John Plummer, John Plummer Foster Diaries, 1848–1888, DIA 63, Phillips Library, Peabody Essex Museum, Rowley, Mass.

Fowler, William C., *The Historical Status of the Negro in Connecticut: A Paper Read before the New Haven Colony Historical Society*. New Haven, Conn.: Tuttle, Morehouse and Taylor, 1875.

Francisco, In re, Supreme Judicial Court, December 4, 1832, Shaw, C.J., 9 American Jurist 490 (1833), headed as "A slave of a foreign country coming to Massachusetts is entitled to his liberty."

Franklin, John, "Plan of Andover Town Farm Andover Mass. Scale 100 Ft. = 1 in – Surveyed July 1907 John Franklin C.E. Lawrence Mass," Accession No. 1990.015.144, Andover Center for History & Culture, Andover, Mass.

[Freeman], Cato, Letter, May 24, 1789, North Andover Historical Society, North Andover, Mass.

Freeman, Cato, Death record. State Vital Records, Deaths Register, Deaths 1853, Vol. 75, 102, No. 70, August 9, 1853, Massachusetts Archives, Boston.

Freeman, Cato, Death record. Town of Andover, Register of Births, Marriages and Deaths in the Town of Andover, Commonwealth of Massachusetts, 1843–1855, 29, No. 70, August 9, 1853, Town Clerk's Office, Andover, Mass.

French, Jonathan, Manuscript about Nancy Parker, n.d. ("about 1881" written later on manuscript), in Rev. Charles C. Carpenter Collection, photocopy in research files, "Indians," Andover Center for History & Culture, Andover, Mass.

French, Jonathan, "Parson Phillips's Slaves – Also, Pomp and Rose," n.d. ("about 1881" written later on manuscript), in Rev. Charles C. Carpenter Collection, photocopy in research files, "African Americans," Andover Center for History & Culture, Andover, Mass.

Frey, Sylvia, *Water from the Rock: Black Resistance in a Revolutionary Era*. Princeton, N.J.: Princeton University Press, 1991.

Frye, Joshua, Probate file papers. Essex County, MA: Probate File Papers, 1638–1881, Case 10314, New England Historic Genealogical Society, 2014, from records supplied by the Supreme Judicial Court Archives, https://www.americanancestors.org/databases/essex-county-ma-probate-file-papers-1638-1881/image/?pageName=10314:1&volumeId=13766, accessed April 16, 2017.

Frye, Sarah, Sarah Frye draft estate inventory, "A true Inventory of the Estate of Mrs Sarah Frye Late of Andover decs^d taken by the Subscribers who being Sworn to the faithfull discharge of the Trust," n.d., in "Collection of Essex County (Mass.) Court Records, 1628–1914," Collection No. EC 43, Box 13, Folder 3 "Estate papers of various individuals," fourth item in file, Phillips Library, Peabody Essex Museum, Rowley, Mass.

Frye, Sarah, Probate file papers. Essex County, MA: Probate File Papers, 1638–1881, Case 10339, New England Historic Genealogical Society, 2014, from records supplied by the Supreme Judicial Court Archives, https://www.americanancestors

.org/databases/essex-county-ma-probate-file-papers-1638-1881/image/?pageName
=10339:1&volumeId=13766, accessed March 24, 2017.

Fuentes, Marisa J., "A Violent and Violating Archive: Black Life and the Slave Trade," *Black Perspectives* (March 7, 2017), https://www.aaihs.org/a-violent-and-violating-archive-black-life-and-the-slave-trade/, accessed January 14, 2020.

Fuess, Claude M., *An Old New England School: A History of Phillips Academy Andover*. Boston, Mass.: Houghton Mifflin Co., 1917.

Fuess, Claude M., *Andover: Symbol of New England, The Evolution of a Town*. s.l.: Andover Historical Society and North Andover Historical Society, 1959.

Fulton, DoVeanna S., *Speaking Power: Black Feminist Orality in Women's Narratives of Slavery*. Albany: State University of New York Press, 2006.

Fulton Minor, DoVeanna S., and Reginald A. Pitts, "Introduction. Speaking Lives, Authoring Texts: African American Women's Voices Raised for Freedom," in *Speaking Lives, Authoring Texts: African American Women's Oral Slave Narratives*, ed. DoVeanna S. Fulton Minor and Reginald A. Pitts, 1–38. Albany: State University of New York Press, 2010.

Furstenberg, François, "Beyond Freedom and Slavery: Autonomy, Virtue, and Resistance in Early American Political Discourse," *The Journal of American History* 89 (4) (2003): 1295–1330.

Gale (a Cengage Company), *Slavery and Anti-Slavery: A Transnational Archive* (website), http://www.gale.com/primary-sources/slavery-and-anti-slavery.

Glover, Jeffrey, "Early American Archives and the Evidence of History," *Early American Literature* 46 (1) (2011): 165–184.

Gohn, Katie, "Cato Freeman, slavery and prejudice in early Andover," *Andover Townsman* (Andover, Mass.) (February 24, 2011), https://www.andovertownsman.com/news/local_news/andover-stories-cato-freeman-slavery-and-prejudice-in-early-andover/article_0b683fcd-f2e0-52e7-8107-f0a013e70677.html, accessed August 6, 2019.

[Goldsmith, Bessie P.], "Siftings" (note about graves found at the former Andover poor farm), *The Andover Townsman* (Andover, Mass.) (April 20, 1923): 5.

Goldsmith, Bessie P., *The Townswoman's Andover*. Andover, Mass.: Andover Historical Society, 1964.

Goodwin, Isaac, *New England Sheriff: or, Digest of the Duties of Civil Officers; Being a Compendium of the Laws of Massachusetts, with Reference to Those of the Neighboring States, Upon Those Subjects*. Worcester, Mass.: Dorr and Howland, 1830.

Gordon, Ann D. (ed.), *The Selected Papers of Elizabeth Cady Stanton and Susan B. Anthony, Volume I: In the School of Anti-Slavery, 1840–1866* (3rd printing). New Brunswick, N.J.: Rutgers University Press, 2001.

Graham, James Chandler, *It Happened at Andover, Well, Most of it Did, Anyway.* Boston, Mass.: Houghton Mifflin Co., 1920.

Gray, David, Account book, census and appraisal of townspeople's farm animals (and other property for tax purposes), May 1, 1838–October 11, 1839 (and later), n.p., Taft Collection, Ms S 134, Sub-group I, Series A, David Gray 1762–1844, Folder 9, Andover Center for History & Culture, Andover, Mass.

Gray, Horace, Jr., *The Case of Nathaniel Jennison for Attempting to Hold a Negro as a Slave in Massachusetts in 1781 from the Minutes of Chief Justice Cushing with References to Contemporaneous Records Communicated to the Massachusetts Historical Society, April 16, 1874.* Boston, Mass.: Press of John Wilson and Son, 1874.

Gray, Horace, Jr. *The Abolition of Slavery in Massachusetts. A Communication to the Massachusetts Historical Society, April 16, 1874.* Boston, Mass.: Press of John Wilson and Son, 1874.

Gray, Horace, Jr., "Note by Chief Justice Gray," *Proceedings of the Massachusetts Historical Society* (1st series) 13 (1875): 294–299.

Greater Lawrence Underground Railroad Committee, *The Anti-Slavery Movement and the Underground Railroad in Andover & Greater Lawrence, Massachusetts.* s.l.: s.n., 2001. This eight-page pamphlet has no stated authorship or publisher. Patrakis, *Andover in the Civil War*, 116 n15, attributed sole authorship to Juliet Haines Mofford. Public library catalogs attribute responsibility of authorship to the committee as a corporate author, additionally crediting from the pamphlet acknowledgements Punchard Trustees Fund, Andover High School Fine Arts Department, Andover Historical Society, Immigrant City Archives, Lawrence Public Library, North Andover Historical Society, Memorial Hall Library, Methuen Historical Society, and Phillips Academy.

Greene, Lorenzo Johnston, *The Negro in Colonial New England, 1620–1776.* New York, N.Y.: Columbia University Press, 1942.

Greenwood, William v. Benjamin Curtis, Supreme Judicial Court, March 1810, 6 Mass. Reports 358.

Greven, Philip J., Jr., *Four Generations: Population, Land, and Family in Colonial Andover, Massachusetts.* Ithaca, N.Y.: Cornell University Press, 1970.

Greven, Philip J., Jr., "Youth, Maturity, and Religious Conversion: A Note on the Ages of Converts in Andover, Massachusetts, 1711–1749," *Essex Institute Historical Collections* 108 (1972): 119–134.

Grinnell, Frank W., "The Constitutional History of the Supreme Judicial Court of Massachusetts from the Revolution to 1813," *Massachusetts Law Quarterly* 2 (5) (1917): 359–552.

Grover, Kathryn, and Neil Larson, with Betsy Friedberg, Michael Steinitz, Paul Weinbaum, and Tara Morrison, "The Underground Railroad in Massachusetts 1783–1865." National Register of Historic Places Multiple Property Documentation Form, Massachusetts Historical Commission, Boston, 2005.

Grzanka, Patrick R., Rajani Bhatia, Mel Michelle Lewis, Sheri L. Parks, Joshua C. Woodfork, and Michael Casiano, "Intersectionality, Inc.: A Dialogue on Intersectionality's Travels and Tribulations," *Atlantis: Critical Studies in Gender, Culture & Social Justice* 38 (1) (2017): 16–27.

Gurney, Alpheus, and Silvanus Packard v. Titus Coburn, Essex County Circuit Court of Common Pleas for the Middle Circuit Records, March 1819, 72 (with the file papers), Supreme Judicial Court Archives, Massachusetts Archives, Boston.

Guyette, Elise A., *Discovering Black Vermont: African American Farmers in Hinesburgh, 1790–1890*. Burlington: University of Vermont Press, 2010.

Hales, John G., "The County of Essex from Actual Survey, Made by John G. Hales, Engraved by J.V.N. Throop, Boston, June 19th, 1825," https://id.lib.harvard.edu /curiosity/scanned-maps/44-990095083330203941, accessed August 10, 2019.

Hall, Hugh, "Negro's Receiv'd from Barbados in the Year 1729," Hugh Hall account book, 1728–1733, 28, Hugh Hall Papers, 1709–1774, Ms. N-1352, Massachusetts Historical Society, Boston, https://www.masshist.org/database /viewer.php?item_id=736, accessed November 17, 2019.

Hamburger, Philip, *Law and Judicial Duty*. Cambridge, Mass.: Harvard University Press, 2008.

Hammond, Dorothy M., "A List of Town Officers and Others Rendering Patriotic Services for the Town of Andover, for the Years 1775, 1776, 1777, 1778, 1779, 1780, 1781, 1782, 1783," typescript, Memorial Hall Library, Andover, Mass., https://archive.org/details/listoftownoffice00hamm, accessed August 25, 2017.

Han, Sora, "Slavery as Contract: Betty's Case and the Question of Freedom," *Law & Literature* 27 (3) (2015): 395–416.

Hancock, Scott, "'The Law Will Make You Smart:' Legal Consciousness, Rights Rhetoric, and African American Identity Formation in Massachusetts, 1641– 1855." Ph.D. dissertation, University of New Hampshire, 1999.

Hancock, Scott, "'Tradition Informs Us': African Americans' Construction of Memory in the Antebellum North," in *Slavery, Resistance, Freedom*, ed. Gabor Boritt and Scott Hancock, 40–69. New York, N.Y.: Oxford University Press, 2007.

Hancock, Scott, "From 'No Country' to 'Our Country!' Living Out Manumission and the Boundaries of Rights and Citizenship, 1773–1855," in *Paths to Freedom: Manumission in the Atlantic World*, ed. Rosemary Brana-Shute and Randy J. Sparks, 265–289. Columbia: University of South Carolina Press, 2009.

Handler, Jerome S., and JoAnn Jacoby, "Slave Names and Naming in Barbados, 1650–1830," *The William and Mary Quarterly* (3rd series) 53 (4) (1996): 685–728.

Hanks, Patrick (ed.), *Dictionary of American Family Names*, 3 vols. New York, N.Y.: Oxford University Press, 2003.

Hardesty, Jared Ross, "An Angry God in the Hands of Sinners: Enslaved Africans and the Uses of Protestant Christianity in Pre-Revolutionary Boston," *Slavery & Abolition* 35 (1) (2013): 66–83.

Hardesty, Jared Ross, *Unfreedom: Slavery and Dependence in Eighteenth-Century Boston*. New York, N.Y.: New York University Press, 2016.

Hardesty, Jared Ross, "Creating an Unfree Hinterland: Merchant Capital, Bound Labor, and Market Production in Eighteenth-Century Massachusetts," *Early American Studies* 15 (1) (2017): 37–63.

Hardesty, Jared Ross, "Social Networks and Social Worlds: Eighteenth-Century Boston, Slavery, and Community in the Early Modern Urban Atlantic," *Journal of Global Slavery* 3 (3) (2018): 234–260.

Hardesty, Jared Ross, *Black Lives, Native Lands, White Worlds: A History of Slavery in New England*. Amherst: University of Massachusetts Press, 2019.

Hartog, Hendrik, "The Public Law of a County Court: Judicial Government in Eighteenth Century Massachusetts," *American Journal of Legal History* 20 (4) (1976): 282–329.

Harvard Law School Shield Committee, "Recommendation to the President and Fellows of Harvard College on the Shield Approved for the Law School," March 3, 2016, https://hls.harvard.edu/content/uploads/2016/03/Shield-Committee-Report.pdf, accessed August 11, 2017.

Harvard Library, *Harvard Geospatial Library* (website and program), https://library.harvard.edu/services-tools/harvard-geospatial-library, accessed June 30, 2019.

Hassam, John T., "Hilton," *New-England Historical and Genealogical Register* 31 (1877): 333.

Hazen, Nathan W., *A Letter to the Inhabitants of Andover and North Andover*. Boston, Mass.: Fetridge and Co., 1856.

HeinOnline, *Slavery in America and the World: History, Culture and Law* (website), https://home.heinonline.org/content/slavery-in-america-and-the-world-history-culture-law/.

Henderson, Martha Matilda, Death record. State Vital Records, Deaths Register, Vol. 174, 160, No. 112, December 3, 1864, Massachusetts Archives, Boston.

Henderson, Martha Matilda, Death record. Town of Andover, Death Register, 1855–1896, 29, No. 20, December 3, 1864, Town Clerk's Office, Andover, Mass.

Hendrick, Caesar v. Richard Greenleaf, Essex County Court of Common Pleas Records, September 1773, 8, Supreme Judicial Court Archives, Massachusetts Archives, Boston.

Herndon, Ruth Wallis, *Unwelcome Americans: Living on the Margin in Early New England*. Philadelphia: University of Pennsylvania Press, 2001.

Herndon, Ruth Wallis, "'Proper' Magistrates and Masters: Binding Out Poor Children in Southern New England, 1720–1820," in *Children Bound to Labor: The Pauper Apprentice System in Early America*, ed. Ruth Wallis Herndon and John E. Murray, 39–51. Ithaca, N.Y.: Cornell University Press, 2009.

Herndon, Ruth Wallis, "Children of Misfortune: Growing Up Poor in Early New England," Paper presented to the Boston Area Early American History Seminar, Massachusetts Historical Society, Boston, December 6, 2011, https://www.bgsu.edu/content/dam/BGSU/college-of-arts-and-sciences/ics/documents/ChildrenofMisfortune-Herndon.pdf, accessed July 5, 2019.

Herndon, Ruth Wallis, and John E. Murray (ed.), *Children Bound to Labor: The Pauper Apprentice System in Early America*. Ithaca, N.Y.: Cornell University Press, 2009.

Heywood, Linda M., and John K. Thornton, "'Canniball Negroes,' Atlantic Creoles, and the Identity of New England's Charter Generation," *African Diaspora* 4 (1) (2011): 76–94.

Hicks, Lewis Wilder, "Mrs. Salome Jane (Abbott) Marland," in "Memoirs of the New England Historic Genealogical Society," *New England Historical and Genealogical Register* 75 (Supplement to April Number) (1921): lxxvi–lxxvii.

Higginbotham, A. Leon, Jr., *In the Matter of Color. Race & The American Legal Process: The Colonial Period*. New York, N.Y.: Oxford University Press, 1978.

Hill, Charles L., "Slavery and Its Aftermath in Beverly, Massachusetts: Juno Larcom and Her Family," *Essex Institute Historical Collections* 116 (2) (1980): 111–130.

Hill, Hagar v. Elijah Hayward, Plymouth County Court of Common Pleas Records, July 1773, 53, Supreme Judicial Court Archives, Massachusetts Archives, Boston.

Hilton, William, Bill of sale to George Carr for James, December 29, 1649, recorded December 24, 1670. Old Norfolk County Deeds, Book 2, pg. 197, Southern Essex District Registry of Deeds, Salem, Mass.

Hindus, Michael S., "A Guide to the Court Records of Early Massachusetts," in *Law in Colonial Massachusetts, 1630–1800: A Conference Held 6 and 7 November 1981 by the Colonial Society of Massachusetts*, ed. Daniel R. Coquillette, 519–540. Boston: The Colonial Society of Massachusetts, 1984.

Hine, Darlene Clark, *Hine Sight: Black Women and the Re-Construction of American History*. Bloomington: University of Indiana Press, 1997.

Hinton, Alice M., "How I Have Carried On the Ice Cream Manufacturing Business Established by my Mother and Father," in *National Negro Business League Annual Report of the Sixteenth Session of the Fifteenth Annual Convention Held at Boston, Massachusetts, August 18, 19, 20, 1915*, Report of the Annual Convention, Vol. 16, reported by William H. Davis, official stenographer, 103–110. Washington, D.C.: National Negro Business League, n.d.

Hinton, Alice M., Correspondence dating 1928–1947, Head of School Records, Claude M. Fuess 1933–1948 Collection, Box 9, http://www.noblenet.org /paarchives/?page_id=601, and vertical subject file about the Hinton family, http:// www.noblenet.org/paarchives/?page_id=287, both websites accessed March 12, 2019, Archives and Special Collections, Phillips Academy, Andover, Mass.

Hinton, Alice M., "Memory Pictures." Typed memoir, n.d., "1938–15" handwritten on first page, research files, "Hinton Family," Andover Center for History & Culture, Andover, Mass.

Hinton, Alice M., "Story of Allen and Mary Hinton and their Ice Cream Business in Andover, 1877–1912." Typed memoir, 1939, research files, "Hinton Family," Andover Center for History & Culture, Andover, Mass.

Hinton, Allen, and Mary J. Johnson, Marriage record. State Marriage Records, Town of Andover, Marriage Register 1855–1896, 34, No. 4, January 26, 1867 (registered January 31, 1867), Massachusetts Archives, Boston, https://www .familysearch.org/ark:/61903/3:1:3QS7-8979-69MF-M?i=76&cc=2061550&cat =1257681, accessed August 25, 2017.

Historical Records Survey, *Inventory of the County Archives of Massachusetts, Prepared by the Historical Records Survey, Division of Women's and Professional Projects, Works Progress Administration, No. 5. Essex County (Salem)*. Boston, Mass.: Historical Records Survey, 1937.

Hollander, Craig, Review of *Amistad's Orphans: An Atlantic Story of Children, Slavery, and Smuggling* by Benjamin N. Lawrance, *Journal of the Early Republic* 36 (4) (2016): 846–848.

hooks, bell, *Yearning: Race, Gender, and Cultural Politics*. Boston, Mass.: South End Press, 1990.

Hooper, Colley, Death record. State Vital Records, Deaths Register, Vol. 111, 164, No. 56, November 26, 1857, Massachusetts Archives, Boston.

Hooper, Colley, Death record. Town of Andover, Death Register, 1855–1896, 6, No. 56, December 26, 1857, Town Clerk's Office, Andover, Mass.

Hopkins, Peter, "Pomp Lovejoy and 'lection cake," *Crane's Bond* (website), February 16, 2012, https://cranesbond.com/2012/02/16/pomp-lovejoy-and-lection -cake/, accessed April 7, 2019.

Horton, Lois E., "From Class to Race in Early America: Northern Post-Emancipation Racial Reconstruction," *Journal of the Early Republic* 19 (4) (1999): 629–649.

Hume, Janice, *Obituaries in American Culture*. Jackson: University of Mississippi Press, 2000.

Hunter, Tera W., *Bound in Wedlock: Slave and Free Black Marriage in the Nineteenth Century*. Cambridge, Mass.: Harvard University Press, 2017.

Hunter, Thea K., "Publishing Freedom, Winning Arguments: *Somerset*, Natural Rights, and Massachusetts Freedom Cases, 1772–1836." Ph.D. dissertation, Columbia University, 2005.

Hunter, T[hea] K., "Geographies of Liberty: A Brief Look at Two Cases [*Somerset and Aves*]," in *Prophets of Protest: Reconsidering the History of American Abolitionism*, ed. Timothy Patrick McCarthy and John Stauffer, 41–58. New York, N.Y.: The New Press, 2006.

Hunter, T[hea] K., "Transatlantic Negotiations: Lord Mansfield, Liberty and *Somerset*," *Texas Wesleyan Law Review* 13 (2007): 711–727.

Hurcum, Edward, Probate file papers. Middlesex County, MA: Probate File Papers, 1648–1871, Case 12321, New England Historic Genealogical Society, 2014, from records supplied by the Supreme Judicial Court Archives, https://www.americanancestors.org/databases/middlesex-county-ma-probate-file-papers-1648-1871/image/?volumeId=14463&pageName=12321:1&rId=38297669, accessed August 6, 2017.

Jackson, Leon, "The Rights of Man and the Rites of Youth: Fraternity and Riot at Eighteenth Century Harvard," *History of Higher Education Annual* 15 (1995): 5–49.

Jackson, Susan E., *Reminiscences of Andover*. Andover, Mass.: The Andover Press, 1914.

James Indian v. George Carr, Document intended for an appeal to the Massachusetts Court of Assistants. "James Indian' answere to his Mr: Carrs reasons of Appeale To bee Delivered to mr Rawson Sect:[Secretary] to be pr[e]sented to yc Court of Assistants yc 5 : March : 1671/2," Ayer MS 446, Edward E. Ayer Manuscript Collection, Newberry Library, Chicago, Ill.

Jameson, E.O., *The Choates in America. 1643–1896. John Choate and His Descendants. Chebacco, Ipswich, Mass.* Boston, Mass.: Alfred Mudge and Sons, 1896.

Jay, Bethany, and Cynthia Lynn Lyerly (ed.), *Understanding and Teaching American Slavery*. Madison: University of Wisconsin Press, 2016.

Jecmen, Timothy, "Writing the Revolution: Radicalism and the U.S. Historical Romance, 1835–1860." Ph.D. dissertation, University of North Carolina, Chapel Hill, 2007.

Jennison, Nathaniel v. John Caldwell and Seth Caldwell, Worcester County Court of Common Pleas Records, June 1781, 203; Supreme Judicial Court Records, Worcester County, September 1781, 79 (rendered "Jenison"); Suffolk Files Collection, File #153693, Supreme Judicial Court Archives, Massachusetts Archives, Boston. (See also Commonwealth v. Jennison, and Walker v. Jennison.)

Jennison, Nathaniel, Petition of Nathaniel Jennison, n.d., before or in June 1782. House Unpassed Legislation 1782, Docket 956, SC1/230, Massachusetts Archives, Boston. Digital images in Daniel Carpenter, Nicole Topich, and Garth Griffin, *Digital Archive of Massachusetts Anti-Slavery and Anti-Segregation Petitions, Massachusetts Archives, Boston MA, 2015*, http://dx.doi.org/10.7910/DVN/3TZYJ, Harvard Dataverse V4, accessed August 15, 2017.

Johnson, Edward F., *Woburn Records of Births, Deaths, and Marriages, from 1640 to 1873. Part II. Deaths.* Woburn, Mass.: Andrews, Cutler and Co., 1890.

Johnson, Walter, "On Agency," *Journal of Social History* 37 (1) (2003): 113–124.

Johnson, Walter, "Time and Revolution in African America: Temporality and the History of Atlantic Slavery," in *A New Imperial History: Culture, Identity, and Modernity in Britain and the Empire, 1660–1840*, ed. Kathleen Wilson, 197–215. Cambridge: Cambridge University Press, 2004.

Jones, Douglas Lamar, "The Transformation of the Law of Poverty in Eighteenth-Century Massachusetts," in *Law in Colonial Massachusetts, 1630–1800: A Conference Held 6 and 7 November 1981 by the Colonial Society of Massachusetts*, ed. Daniel R. Coquillette, 153–190. Boston: The Colonial Society of Massachusetts, 1984.

Jones, Jacqueline, "Race, Sex, and Self-Evident Truths, The Status of Slave Women during the Era of the American Revolution," in *Women in the Age of the American Revolution*, ed. Ronald Hoffman and Peter J. Albert, 293–337. Charlottesville: University Press of Virginia, 1989.

Jones, Jacqueline, "'Domestick Enemies': Bound Laborers in New England and the Middle Colonies, 1620–1776," and "The Emergence of Free Labor, Fettered, in the North," in *American Work: Four Centuries of Black and White Labor*, 109–140, 141–168. New York, N.Y.: W.W. Norton and Co., 1998.

Jones, Rhett S., "'Trifling Patriots and a Freeborn Pepel': Revolutionary Ideology and Afro-Americans," in *Liberty's Impact: The World Views 1776*. Providence, R.I.: *Brown Alumni Monthly* and John Carter Brown Library of Brown University, 1976, http://www.brown.edu/Facilities/John_Carter_Brown_Library/electronicpub /liberty+.pdf, accessed November 2, 2014.

Jones, Rhett S., "In the Absence of Ideology: Blacks in Colonial America and the Modern Black Experience," *The Western Journal of Black Studies* 12 (1) (1998): 30–39.

Kansas State Historical Society and University of Kansas, *Territorial Kansas Online 1854–1861: A Virtual Repository for Territorial Kansas History* (website), http:// www.territorialkansasonline.org, accessed August 31, 2019.

Kantrowitz, Stephen, "Fighting Jim Crow in the Cradle of Liberty," in *More Than Freedom: Fighting for Black Citizenship in a White Republic, 1829–1889*, 41–64. New York, N.Y.: Penguin Books, 2012.

Kate v. Moody Bridges, Essex County Court of Common Pleas Records, September 1769, 449 (with the docket entries and file papers), Supreme Judicial Court Archives, Massachusetts Archives, Boston.

Kelley, James E., *Wilmington Records of Births, Marriages and Deaths, from 1730 to 1898*. Lowell, Mass.: Thompson and Hill, 1898.

Kent, James, *Commentaries on American Law*, Vol. 2. New York, N.Y.: O. Halsted, 1827.

Killorin, Jennie, "Pompey's Corner Chair," *Andover Historical Society Newsletter* (Andover, Mass.) 2 (2) (1977): n.p. [4].

Kimball, David Tenney, "Apology for Anti-Slavery," *The Liberator* (Boston, Mass.) 3 (39) (September 28, 1833): 153–154, reprinted from the *Genius of Temperance*, and published also as a pamphlet, "Apology for Anti-Slavery, Theological Seminary, Andover, August 22, 1833," in Samuel J. May Anti-Slavery Pamphlet Collection, No. 2 in "Abolitionist & A.S. tracts," Division of Rare and Manuscript Collections, Cornell University Library, Ithaca, N.Y., http://ebooks.library.cornell.edu/cgi/t/text/text-idx?c=mayantislavery;idno=10842602, accessed October 7, 2017.

Kimball, Eric, "'What have we to do with slavery?': New Englanders and the Slave Economies of the West Indies," in *Slavery's Capitalism: A New History of American Economic Development*, ed. Sven Beckert and Seth Rockman, 181–194. Philadelphia: University of Pennsylvania Press, 2016.

Kittredge, Mabel T., *The Kittredge Family in America*. Rutland, Vt.: Tuttle Publishing Co., 1936.

Kittredge, Peter, Letter to the Town of Medfield Selectmen, April 26, 1806, GLC #GLC01450.702, Gilder Lehrman Institute of American History, New York, N.Y. Transcription at https://www.gilderlehrman.org/collections/f4190a89-c5a8-4f4a-a438-071452154610, accessed July 22, 2017.

Knauer, Nancy J., "Legal Fictions and Juristic Truth," *St. Thomas Law Review* 23 (2010): 1–51.

Knight, Sarah Kemble, *The Journal of Madam Knight*. Boston, Mass.: Small, Maynard and Co., 1920.

Knoblock, Glenn A., *African American Historic Burial Grounds and Gravesites of New England*. Jefferson, N.C.: McFarland and Co., 2015.

Konig, David Thomas, "Legal Fictions and the Rule(s) of Law: The Jeffersonian Critique of Common-Law Adjudication," in *The Many Legalities of Early America*, ed. Christopher L. Tomlins and Bruce H. Mann, 97–117. Chapel Hill: University of North Carolina Press, 2001.

Konig, David Thomas, "The Long Road to *Dred Scott*: Personhood and the Rule of Law in the Trial Court Records of St. Louis Slave Freedom Suits," *UMKC Law Review* 75 (1) (2006): 53–79.

Kopelson, Heather Miyano, *Faithful Bodies: Performing Religion and Race in the Puritan Atlantic*. New York, N.Y.: New York University Press, 2014.

Laite, Julia, "The Emmet's Inch: Small History in a Digital Age," *Journal of Social History* (2020): 1–27, advance version (February 11, 2019) prior to print publication, https://doi.org/10.1093/jsh/shy118.

Lambert, David Allen, "Salem Poor (1743/44–1802), A Forgotten Hero of Bunker Hill Rediscovered," *New England Ancestors* 8 (4) (2007): 40–41.

Lanesborough v. Westfield, Supreme Judicial Court, September 1819, 16 Mass. Reports 74.

Lasser, Carol, and Marlene Deahl Merrill (ed.), *Friends and Sisters: Letters between Lucy Stone and Antoinette Brown Blackwell, 1846–93.* Urbana: University of Illinois Press, 1987.

Lawrance, Benjamin N., *Amistad's Orphans: An Atlantic Story of Children, Slavery, and Smuggling.* New Haven, Conn.: Yale University Press, 2014.

Lee, Nedra K., "Boarding: Black Women in Nantucket Generating Income and Building Community," *Transforming Anthropology* 27 (2) (2019): 91–104.

Lee, Nedra K., and Jannie Nicole Scott, "Introduction: New Directions in African Diaspora Archaeology," *Transforming Anthropology* 27 (2) (2019): 85–90.

Lemire, Elise, *Black Walden: Slavery and its Aftermath in Concord, Massachusetts.* Philadelphia: University of Pennsylvania Press, 2009.

Leonard, Angela M., "The Instability and Invention of Racial Categories in the *Haverhill Gazette* (MA), 1824–1827," in *Semiotics 1998*, ed. C.W. Spinks and John Deely, 271–282. New York, N.Y.: Peter Lang, 1999.

Leonard, Angela Michele, *Political Poetry as Discourse: Rereading John Greenleaf Whittier, Ebenezer Elliott, and Hip-hop-ology.* Lanham, Md.: Lexington Books, 2010.

Levi, Giovanni, "The Uses of Biography," in *Theoretical Discussions of Biography: Approaches from History, Microhistory, and Life Writing* (revised and augmented edition), ed. Hans Renders and Binne de Haan, 61–74. Leiden, The Netherlands: Brill, 2014.

Levinson, David, Rachel Fletcher, Frances Jones-Sneed, Elaine S. Gunn, and Bernard A. Drew (ed.), *African American Heritage in the Upper Housatonic Valley: A Project of the Upper Housatonic Valley National Heritage Area.* Great Barrington, Mass.: Berkshire Publishing Group, 2006.

Levy, Leonard W., *The Law of the Commonwealth and Chief Justice Shaw.* Cambridge, Mass.: Harvard University Press, 1957.

Lew, Barzillai, and Dinah Lew, Revolutionary War Pension Application File #W.20461, Revolutionary War Pension and Bounty-Land Application Files, Microfilm M804, Reel 1553, National Archives and Records Administration.

Lew, Dinah, Probate file papers. Essex County, MA: Probate File Papers, 1638–1881, Case 45264, New England Historic Genealogical Society, 2014, from records supplied by the Supreme Judicial Court Archives, https://www.americanancestors.org/databases/essex-county-ma-probate-file-papers-1638-1881/image/?pageName=45264:1&volumeId=14211, accessed September 24, 2017.

Lewis, Kerima Marie, "Fires of Discontent: Arson as a Weapon of Slave Resistance in Colonial New England, 1650–1775." Ph.D. dissertation, University of California, Berkeley, 2014.

Lewis, Kerima M., "Captives on the Move: Tracing the Transatlantic Movements of Africans from the Caribbean to Colonial New England," *Historical Journal of Massachusetts* 44 (2) (2016): 145–175.

[Liffmann, Dee], "From Our Archives" (about Cato [Freeman's] May 24, 1789 letter), *North Andover Historical Society Newsletter* (North Andover, Mass.) (Winter 1990): 3. Unattributed copy in Andover Center for History & Culture research files, "African Americans," accompanied by an unidentified, undated typed transcription of the 1789 letter.

Lima, Tim, "Bridging Town History: Eagle Scout Candidate [Jeffrey Page] Builds Critical Link to Early Cemetery," *Andover Townsman* (Andover, Mass.) (September 11, 2014), https://www.andovertownsman.com/news/local_news/bridging -town-history-eagle-scout-candidate-builds-critical-link-to/article_e00f07b3 -4e49-5499-8bbb-4d5f8db8d812.html, accessed July 6, 2019.

Lincoln, Levi, "Brief of Levi Lincoln in the Slave Case Tried 1781," *Collections of the Massachusetts Historical Society* (5th series) 3 (1877): 438–442.

Linden-Ward, Blanche, *Silent City on a Hill: Landscapes of Memory and Boston's Mount Auburn Cemetery*. Columbus: Ohio State University Press, 1989.

Littleton v. William Tuttle, Middlesex County Court of Common Pleas Records, September 1794, 486; Supreme Judicial Court Records, Middlesex County, October 1796, 302; Supreme Judicial Court Docket (Minute Books), n.p., October 1795 (#29), April 1796 (#16), October 1796 (#9); Suffolk Files Collection, File #150987, Supreme Judicial Court Archives, Massachusetts Archives, Boston. (Abstract in Winchendon v. Hatfield, 4 Mass. Reports 123, at 128 n.)

Litwack, Leon F., *North of Slavery: The Negro in the Free States, 1790–1860*. Chicago, Ill.: University of Chicago Press, 1961.

Livingston, Edward, "Erroneous Return of Slaves–Fifth Census–Massachusetts, Maine, Ohio, Letter from the Secretary of State, Transmitting the information required by a Resolution of the House of Representatives, of the 25th of January, instant, in relation to the return of slaves in the 5th Census, in Maine, Massachusetts, and Ohio," January 28, 1832. United States House of Representatives, 22nd Cong., 1st sess., Doc. 84, January 31, 1832.

Loring, Arthur G., "Robert Eames of Woburn, Mass., and Some of his Descendants," *The New England Historical and Genealogical Register* 62 (April) (1908): 150–157.

Lovejoy, Nathaniel, "Processes of Confessions," 1787–1790 and 1797–1800 (Justice of the Peace Records, Andover, Mass.), n.p., Collection No. EC 43, Box 6, Files 3 and 4, "Collection of Essex County (Mass.) Court Records, 1628–1914," Phillips Library, Peabody Essex Museum, Rowley, Mass.

Lovejoy, Paul E., "The African Diaspora: Revisionist Interpretations of Ethnicity, Culture and Religion under Slavery," *Studies in the World History of Slavery, Ab-*

olition and Emancipation 2 (1) (1997), n.p., https://www.academia.edu/3624702/The_African_Diaspora_Revisionist_Interpretations_of_Ethnicity_Culture_and_Religion_under_Slavery, accessed September 18, 2019.

Lovejoy, Paul E., *The "Middle Passage": The Enforced Migration of Africans across the Atlantic*. Ann Arbor, Mich.: ProQuest Information and Learning, 2005, https://www.academia.edu/3651406/_Middle_Passage_-_Enforced_Migration_across_Atlantic, accessed September 15, 2019.

Lovejoy, Capt. William, Probate file papers. Essex County, MA: Probate File Papers, 1638–1881, Case 17081, New England Historic Genealogical Society, 2014, from records supplied by the Supreme Judicial Court Archives, https://www.americanancestors.org/databases/essex-county-ma-probate-file-papers-1638-1881/image?pageName=17081:1&volumeId=13778, accessed April 7, 2019.

Lowell, William D., "The Ancient Ferry Ways of the Merrimack," *Putnam's Monthly Historical Magazine* (new series) 3 (1895): 35–42, 71–77.

Lyons, Charlotte, "South Church: Founding History and Abolitionism: An Essay Regarding New Facts," 2011, http://www.southchurch.com/images/2011-Abolition-2.pdf, accessed August 6, 2017.

Lyons, Charlotte, "How is it that Two Andover Slaves are Buried Next to One Another in the South Church Burial Yard?" 2017, typescript provided by Lyons (email, September 1, 2017).

MacEacheren, Elaine, "Emancipation of Slavery in Massachusetts: A Reexamination, 1770–1790," *Journal of Negro History* 55 (4) (1970): 289–306.

MacLean, John C., "Resources for Researching Massachusetts Slaves and Slaveholders," n.d., New England Historic Genealogical Society, Boston, Mass., https://web.archive.org/web/20090116000509/http://www.newenglandancestors.org/research/services/articles_resources_mass_slaves.asp, accessed March 4, 2019.

Malloy, Tom, and Brenda Malloy, "Slavery in Colonial Massachusetts as Seen Through Selected Gravestones," *Markers: Journal of the Association for Gravestone Studies* 11 (1994): 113–141.

Mandell, Daniel R., *Tribe, Race, History: Native Americans in Southern New England, 1780–1880*. Baltimore, Md.: The Johns Hopkins University Press, 2008.

Marland, Salome J., "Loan Collection and Historic Sites," in *Andover, Massachusetts: Proceedings at the Celebration of the Two Hundred and Fiftieth Anniversary of the Incorporation of the Town, May 20, 1896*, 144–167. Andover, Mass.: Andover Press, 1897.

Martin, Anthony F., "On the Landscape for a Very, Very Long Time: African American Resistance and Resilience in 19th and Early 20th Century Massachusetts." Ph.D. dissertation, University of Massachusetts, Amherst, 2017.

Martin, Anthony F., "Homeplace Is also Workplace: Another Look at Lucy Foster in Andover, Massachusetts," *Historical Archaeology* 52 (1) (2018): 100–112.

Martin, Anthony F., "Haven to the East, Haven to the North: Great Barrington and Pittsfield, Massachusetts," *Historical Archaeology* 53 (2) (2019): 307–322.

Massachusetts *Acts and Resolves* passed by the General Court of the Commonwealth of Massachusetts (i.e., the legislature). Imprint varies and series includes volumes that span multiple years. The series has been digitized, with a guide available at http://www.mass.gov/anf/research-and-tech/oversight-agencies/lib/massachusetts-acts-and-resolves-1692-to-1959.html.

Massachusetts Census, 1855, Andover, Dwelling No. 77, John and Sarah Parnell; Dwelling No. 79, "Wid[ow] Rosanna Coburn" and "Miss Colly Coburn"; Dwelling No. 80, Charles C. Blunt; Dwelling No. 147, Albert Abbott; Dwelling No. 185, David I.C. Hidden, n.p., Massachusetts Archives, Boston. FamilySearch database with images, https://familysearch.org/search/collection/1459985, accessed April 5 and June 16, 2017.

Massachusetts Chapter 1 of the Acts of 1703 ("An Act Relating to Molato and Negro Slaves," passed July 28, 1703), printed in *The Acts and Resolves, Public and Private, of the Province of the Massachusetts Bay*, Vol. 1, 519. Boston, Mass.: Wright and Potter, 1869.

Massachusetts Chapter 43 of the Acts of 1786 ("An Act for rendering processes in law less expensive," passed February 15, 1786), printed in *Acts and Resolves of Massachusetts. 1786–87*, 105–111. Boston, Mass.: Wright and Potter, 1893.

Massachusetts Chapter 48 of the Acts of 1787 ("An Act to Prevent the Slave Trade, and for Granting Relief to the Families of such Unhappy Persons as may be Kidnapped or Decoyed Away from this Commonwealth," passed March 26, 1788), printed in *Acts and Resolves of Massachusetts. 1786–87*, 615–617. Boston, Mass.: Wright and Potter, 1893.

Massachusetts Chapter 67 of the Acts of 1788 ("An Act for rendering processes in law less expensive," approved by the Governor, February 16, 1789), printed in *Acts and Resolves of Massachusetts. 1788–89*, 116–131. Boston, Mass.: Wright and Potter, 1894.

Massachusetts Chapter 5 of the Acts of 1843 ("An Act relating to Marriages between individuals of certain races," approved by the Governor, February 25, 1843), printed in *Acts and Resolves Passed by the General Court of Massachusetts, in the Years 1843, 1844, 1845; Together with the Rolls and Messages*, 4. Boston, Mass.: Dutton and Wentworth, 1845.

Massachusetts Chapter 119 of the Resolves of 1844 ("Resolve concerning the manner of making claims for the support of State Paupers," approved by the Governor, March 16, 1844), printed in *Acts and Resolves Passed by the General Court of Massachusetts, in the Years 1843, 1844, 1845; Together with the Rolls and Messages*, 333. Boston, Mass.: Dutton and Wentworth, 1845.

Massachusetts Chapter 54 of the Resolves of 1847 ("Resolve concerning State Pauper Charges," approved by the Governor, April 20, 1847), printed in *Acts and Re-*

solves of the General Court of Massachusetts, 1846, 1847, 1848; Together with the Rolls and Messages, 523. Boston, Mass.: Dutton and Wentworth, 1848.

Massachusetts Chapter 100 of the Resolves of 1847 ("Resolve for the Payment of sundry Pauper Accounts," approved by the Governor, April 26, 1847), printed in *Acts and Resolves of the General Court of Massachusetts, 1846, 1847, 1848; Together with the Rolls and Messages*, 540. Boston, Mass.: Dutton and Wentworth, 1848.

Massachusetts, Commonwealth of, *The Perpetual Laws of the Commonwealth of Massachusetts, From the Establishment of its Constitution in the Year 1780 To the End of the Year 1800*, Vol. 3. Boston, Mass.: I. Thomas and E.T. Andrews, 1801.

Massachusetts, Commonwealth of, *The Revised Statutes of the Commonwealth of Massachusetts, Passed November 4, 1835, to which are subjoined, an Act in Amendment thereof, and an Act to Expressly Repeal the Acts which are Consolidated therein, both passed in February 1836; and to which are prefixed the Constitutions of the United States and the Commonwealth of Massachusetts*. Boston, Mass.: Dutton and Wentworth, 1836.

Massachusetts General Court, Committee on Accounts, Account Rolls, 1786–1862, CO6/2268x, and Account Roll Submissions, 1786–1860, CO6/9x, Massachusetts Archives, Boston, and archival collections descriptions, https://www.worldcat.org/title/account-rolls-1786-1862/oclc/83623060 and https://www.worldcat.org/title/account-roll-submissions-1786-1860/oclc/79918172, both webpages accessed May 12, 2019.

Massachusetts General Court, *Special Joint Committee Report on the Deliverance of Citizens, Liable to be Sold as Slaves*, House No. 38, March 1839.

Massachusetts Historical Commission, Inventory of Historic Assets of the Commonwealth, Historical Building Inventory Form, Isaac Blunt House (ANV.269, 167 Highland Road, Andover), prepared by Nancy J. Stack and Juliet Haines Mofford, 1975–1977, http://mhc-macris.net/Details.aspx?MhcId=ANV.269, accessed August 4, 2017.

Massachusetts House of Representatives, *Journal of the House of Representatives of the Commonwealth of Massachusetts, 1872*. Boston, Mass.: Wright and Potter, 1872.

Massachusetts House of Representatives, *Report of the Commissioners appointed by an Order of the House of Representatives, Feb. 29, 1832, on the Subject of the Pauper System of the Commonwealth of Massachusetts*. House Document No. 6. Boston, Mass.: Dutton and Wentworth, 1833.

Massachusetts House of Representatives, "Report of the Commissioners appointed under the Resolve of April 16th, 1846, to Examine the Claims presented to the Legislature of that Year for the Support of State Paupers," Document No. 21, February 1, 1847, in *Documents Printed by Order of the House of Representatives of the Commonwealth of Massachusetts, During the Session of the General Court, A.D. 1847* (each document independently paginated). Boston, Mass.: Dutton and Wentworth, 1847.

Massachusetts Register for the Year 1854, Embracing State and County Officers, and an Abstract of the Laws and Resolves, with a Variety of Useful Information. Boston, Mass.: George Adams, 1854.

Massachusetts Secretary of the Commonwealth, *Abstract of Returns of the Keepers of Jails and Overseers of the Houses of Correction, for the Year Ending November 1, 1849.* Boston, Mass.: Dutton and Wentworth, 1849.

Massachusetts Secretary of the Commonwealth, *Massachusetts Soldiers and Sailors of the Revolutionary War,* 17 vols. Boston: Massachusetts Secretary of the Commonwealth, 1896–1908.

Massachusetts Senate, Document No. 66, Report on the Report of Commissioners on Claims for Support of State Paupers, March 22, 1847, in *Documents Printed by Order of the Senate of the Commonwealth of Massachusetts, During the Session of the General Court A.D. 1847* (document title from volume index, vii; each document independently paginated). Boston, Mass.: Dutton and Wentworth, 1847.

Massachusetts Senate, Document No. 109, Report and Bill concerning Alien Passengers and Paupers, April 21, 1847, in *Documents Printed by Order of the Senate of the Commonwealth of Massachusetts, During the Session of the General Court A.D. 1847* (document title from volume index, iii; each document independently paginated). Boston, Mass.: Dutton and Wentworth, 1847.

Massachusetts State Library, *Report of the Librarian of the State Library, for the Year Ending September 30, 1897, and Eighteenth Annual Supplement to the General Catalogue.* Boston, Mass.: Wright and Potter, 1898.

Massachusetts Valuation of Towns, Andover 1767, Massachusetts Archives Collection, Vol. 130, 34–49 (Andover counts of "Negros" as property in households), 40 (Joshua Frye), 70, 74 (taxation committee minutes regarding rates for slaves called servants for life), 106 (Andover aggregate total of servants for life), Massachusetts Archives, Boston.

Matthews, Albert, "Hired Man and Help," *Publications of the Colonial Society of Massachusetts* 5, Transactions 1897, 1898 (1902): 225–256.

Mayo, Martha, "The Quork-Lewis Family (1754–1954)" and "The Lew Family," *African Americans in Lowell* (website), UMass Lowell Library Guides, n.d. (webpages last updated July 25, 2018), created from "Profiles in Courage: African-Americans in Lowell. An Exhibit by Martha Mayo, University of Massachusetts Lowell, The Center for Lowell History, Patrick J. Mogan Cultural Center, April 19 through June 30, 1993," https://libguides.uml.edu/c.php?g=520711&p=3560974, accessed February 22, 2019.

McCarthy, B. Eugene, and Thomas L. Doughton (ed.), *From Bondage to Belonging: The Worcester Slave Narratives.* Amherst: University of Massachusetts Press, 2007.

McCaskill, Barbara, *Love, Liberation, and Escaping Slavery: William and Ellen Craft in Cultural Memory.* Athens: University of Georgia Press, 2015.

McManus, Edgar J., *Black Bondage in the North*. Syracuse, N.Y.: Syracuse University Press, 1973.

McNamara, Martha J., *From Tavern to Courthouse: Architecture & Ritual in American Law, 1658–1860*. Baltimore, Md.: The Johns Hopkins University Press, 2004.

McWilliams, James E., "Butter, Milk, and a 'Spare Ribb': Women's Work and the Transatlantic Economic Transition in Seventeenth-Century Massachusetts," *The New England Quarterly* 82 (1) (2009): 5–24.

Melish, Joanne Pope, *Disowning Slavery: Gradual Emancipation and "Race" in New England, 1780–1860*. Ithaca, N.Y.: Cornell University Press, 1998.

Melish, Joanne Pope, "The 'Condition' Debate and Racial Discourse in the Antebellum North," *Journal of the Early Republic* 19 (4) (1999): 651–672.

Melish, Joanne Pope, "Northern Slavery and Its Legacies: Still a New (and Unwelcome?) Story," in *Understanding and Teaching American Slavery*, ed. Bethany Jay and Cynthia Lynn Lyerly, 115–132. Madison: The University of Wisconsin Press, 2016.

Meltsner, Heli, *The Poorhouses of Massachusetts: A Cultural and Architectural History*. Jefferson, N.C.: McFarland and Co., 2012.

Menschel, David, "Abolition Without Deliverance: The Law of Connecticut Slavery 1784–1848," *Yale Law Journal* 111 (1) (2001): 183–222.

Merrill, Joseph, *History of Amesbury, including the First Seventeen Years of Salisbury, to the Separation in 1654; and Merrimac from its Incorporation in 1876*. Haverhill: Press of Franklin P. Stiles, 1880.

Messinger, Thomas, Deposition, April 5, 1720, Suffolk Files Collection, File #13991 (file papers for Mary Auter Note v. Sarah Tomlin, Superior Court of Judicature Records, Suffolk County, November 1720, 328), Supreme Judicial Court Archives, Massachusetts Archives, Boston.

Middlesex County Deeds, Book 83, pg. 243, Edward Hircum to Titus Cober and Peggy Hircum, July 14, 1781, witnessed July 23, 1781, recorded June 5, 1782 ("1781" was error); Book 88, pg. 460, Ebenezer Foster to Titus Cober, September 6, 1782, witnessed same day, recorded May 4, 1785; Book 88, pg. 460, Titus Cober to Samuel Eames, November 30, 1782, witnessed May 2, 1785, recorded May 4, 1785; Book 92, pg. 318, Titus Cober to Peggy Hircom, November 22, 1785, witnessed December 16, 1785, recorded April 5, 1786; Book 97, pg. 503, Nathaniel Russell to Samuel Eames, July 9, 1788, witnessed same day, recorded August 6, 1788; Book 106, pg. 397, Peggy Hircom to Titus Cober, April 11, 1789, witnessed January 9, 1792, recorded January 18, 1792; Book 106, pg. 398, Titus Cober to Samuel Eames, December 25, 1791, witnessed January 16, 1792, recorded January 18, 1792; Book 112, pg. 226, Peggy Hircom to Samuel Eames, March 11, 1793, witnessed same day, recorded March 12, 1793, Middlesex South Registry of Deeds, Cambridge, Mass.

Miller, George L., "Common Staffordshire Cup and Bowl Shapes [...] for the Diagnostic Artifacts in Maryland Website, linked from Jefferson Patterson Park & Museum's Webpage (www.jefpat.org)," updated July 12, 2011, https://apps .jefpat.maryland.gov/diagnostic/Post-Colonial%20Ceramics/Cup%20Shapes /Essay%20on%20Cup%20&%20Bowl%20Shapes.pdf, accessed August 20, 2019.

Millward, Jessica, "On Agency, Freedom, and the Boundaries of Slavery Studies," *Labour/Le Travail* 71 (2013): 193–201.

Minardi, Margot, "Freedom in the Archives: The Pension Case of Primus Hall," in *Slavery/Antislavery in New England*, ed. Peter Benes, 128–140. Boston, Mass.: Dublin Seminar for New England Folklife, Boston University, 2005.

Minardi, Margot, *Making Slavery History: Abolitionism and the Politics of Memory in Massachusetts*. New York, N.Y.: Oxford University Press, 2010.

Minardi, Margot, "Making Slavery Visible (Again): The Nineteenth-Century Roots of a Revisionist Recovery in New England," in *Politics of Memory: Making Slavery Visible in the Public Space*, ed. Ana Lucia Araujo, 92–105. New York: Routledge, 2012.

Mofford, Juliet Haines, *The History of North Parish Church of North Andover, 1645– 1974: And Firm Thine Ancient Vow*. North Andover, Mass.: s.n., 1975.

Mofford, Juliet Haines, "The Underground Railroad Ran Through Andover," *Andover Historical Society Newsletter* (Andover, Mass.) 25 (2) (2000): n.p. [1–2].

Mooar, George, *Historical Manual of the South Church in Andover, Mass., August, 1859*. Andover, Mass.: Warren F. Draper, 1859.

Mooar, George, *Mooar (Moors) Genealogy. Abraham Mooar of Andover and His Descendants*. Boston, Mass.: Charles H. Pope, 1901.

Mooar, George, *The Cummings Memorial: A Genealogical History of the Descendants of Isaac Cummings, an Early Settler of Topsfield, Massachusetts*. New York, N.Y.: B.F. Cummings, 1903.

Moore, George H., *Notes on the History of Slavery in Massachusetts*. New York, N.Y.: D. Appleton and Co., 1866.

Moore, George H., "Slavery in Massachusetts. Mr. Moore's Reply to His Boston Critics," *The Historical Magazine and Notes and Queries, Concerning the Antiquities, History and Biography of America* (1st series) 10 (Supplement No. VI, article III, supplements appear after issue No. 12 [December] and are independently paginated from issues) (1866): 186–198.

Moore, George H., "Slave Marriages in Massachusetts," *The Historical Magazine and Notes and Queries, Concerning the Antiquities, History and Biography of America* (2nd series) 5 (2) (1869): 135–137.

Morgan, Mary F., "Inventory, Daughters of the Revolution Records [Ms S 619] in Andover Historical Society," Andover Historical Society, Andover, Mass., 1983.

Morgan, Philip D., "African Americans," in *A Companion to Colonial America*, ed. Daniel Vickers, 138–171. Malden, Mass.: Blackwell, 2006.

Morrison, Allan, "Negroes Who Fought at Bunker Hill: Black Patriots were Heroes at First Major Battle of Revolution," *Ebony* 19 (4) (February 1964): 44–46, 48, 49–50, 52–53.

Moulton, Amber D., *The Fight for Interracial Marriage Rights in Antebellum Massachusetts*. Cambridge, Mass.: Harvard University Press, 2015.

Mullen, Zach v. John Ashley, Berkshire County Court of Common Pleas Records, April 1781, 24; August 1781, 53; February 1782, 237, Supreme Judicial Court Archives, Massachusetts Archives, Boston.

Murrell, Nathaniel Samuel, *Afro-Caribbean Religions: An Introduction to their Historical, Cultural, and Sacred Traditions*. Philadelphia, Pa.: Temple University Press, 2010.

Nancy v. James Parker, Jr. and Dinah Parker, Essex County Court of Common Pleas Records, September 1771, 147; December 1771, 197, Supreme Judicial Court Archives, Massachusetts Archives, Boston.

Nash, Gary B., "African Americans in the Early Republic," *OAH Magazine of History* 14 (2) (2000): 12–16.

National Park Service, Boston African American National Historic Site, *Slave Advertisements* (webpage), https://www.nps.gov/articles/slave-advertisements.htm, accessed March 14, 2019.

National Park Service, *Poets, Shoemakers, and Freedom Seekers: Abolitionists and the Underground Railroad in Essex County*. Salem, Mass.: Salem Maritime National Historic Site, n.d., https://www.nps.gov/sama/learn/historyculture/upload/ugrrsm.pdf, accessed April 27, 2017.

National Park Service, *Underground Railroad: Special Resource Study, Management Concepts / Environmental Assessment*. Denver, Colo.: National Park Service, Denver Service Center, 1995.

Neilson, Larz, "The Wilmington Resolves on Civil Rights," *Town Crier* (Wilmington, Mass.) (September 26, 1974): 4.

Neilson, Larz, "Who was Titus Colburn?" *Town Crier* (Wilmington, Mass.) (August 1, 1979): 4. Abridged version, with author indicated, "Who was Titus Colburn? A Revolutionary War hero, possibly from Wilmington," *Town Crier* (October 14, 2015): 2W.

Neilson, Larz, "Wilmington voted to free slaves in 1777," *Town Crier* (Wilmington, Mass.) (December 26, 1990): 5.

Neilson, Larz, "Wilmington black man served in Revolution," *Town Crier* (Wilmington, Mass.) (July 9, 1992): 8.

Neilson, Larz, "The day the slaves were freed," *Town Crier* (Wilmington, Mass.) (October 13, 1993): 7.

Neilson, Larz, "Wilmington's first town meeting," *Town Crier* (Wilmington, Mass.) (October 20, 1993): 5.

Neilson, Larz, "Freedom for the slaves of Massachusetts," *Town Crier* (Wilmington, Mass.) (November 3, 1993): 7.

Nell, William C., *Services of Colored Americans in the Wars of 1776 and 1812* (2nd edition). Boston, Mass.: Robert F. Wallcut, 1852.

Nell, William C., *The Colored Patriots of the American Revolution, with Sketches of Several Distinguished Colored Persons: to which is added a Brief Survey of the Condition and Prospects of Colored Americans*. Boston, Mass.: Robert F. Wallcut, 1855.

Nelson, Henry M., "Georgetown," in *History of Essex County, Massachusetts, with Biographical Sketches of Many of its Pioneers and Prominent Men*, Vol. 1, comp. D. Hamilton Hurd, 330–362. Philadelphia, Pa.: J.W. Lewis and Co., 1889.

Nelson, William E., *Americanization of the Common Law: The Impact of Legal Change on Massachusetts Society, 1760–1830* (reprint of 1975 edition). Athens: University of Georgia Press, 1994.

Nelson, William E., "Court Records as Sources for Historical Writing," in *Law in Colonial Massachusetts, 1630–1800: A Conference Held 6 and 7 November 1981 by the Colonial Society of Massachusetts*, ed. Daniel R. Coquillette, 499–518. Boston: The Colonial Society of Massachusetts, 1984.

Newell, Margaret Ellen, "The Birth of New England in the Atlantic Economy: From Its Beginning to 1770," in *Engines of Enterprise: An Economic History of New England*, ed. Peter Temin, 11–68. Cambridge, Mass.: Harvard University Press, 2000.

Newell, Margaret Ellen, "The Changing Nature of Indian Slavery in New England, 1670–1720," in *Reinterpreting New England Indians and the Colonial Experience*, ed. Colin G. Calloway and Neal Salisbury, 106–136. Boston: The Colonial Society of Massachusetts, 2003.

Newell, Margaret Ellen, "Indian Slavery in Colonial New England," in *Indian Slavery in Colonial America*, ed. Alan Gallay, 33–66. Lincoln: University of Nebraska Press, 2009.

Newell, Margaret Ellen, *Brethren by Nature: New England Indians, Colonists, and the Origins of American Slavery*. Ithaca, N.Y.: Cornell University Press, 2015.

Newman, Richard, "The Grammar of Emancipation: Putting Final Freedom in Context," in *Beyond Freedom: Disrupting the History of Emancipation*, ed. David W. Blight and Jim Downs, 11–25. Athens: University of Georgia Press, 2017.

Nickles, Shelley, "Finding New Stories in an Old House: Chance Bradstreet and 'Within These Walls,'" *Oh Say Can You See: Stories from the National Museum of*

American History (website), December 18, 2017, Smithsonian Institution, Washington, D.C., http://americanhistory.si.edu/blog/new-stories-old-house, accessed April 18, 2018.

Noyes, Daniel P., *1730–1880. Wilmington. Historical Addresses: Delivered in the Meeting-House of the Church of Christ in Wilmington, Mass., Sept. 25, 1880, Upon the One Hundred and Fiftieth Anniversary of the Incorporation of the Town.* Boston, Mass.: Press of Cochrane and Sampson, 1881.

O'Brien, Jean M., *Firsting and Lasting: Writing Indians Out of Existence in New England.* Minneapolis: University of Minnesota Press, 2010.

O'Brien, William, "Did the Jennison Case Outlaw Slavery in Massachusetts?" *The William and Mary Quarterly* (3rd series) 17 (2) (1960): 219–241.

O'Donovan, Connell, "The Descendants of Mingo and Dinah: From West Africa to Colonial Massachusetts," n.d. (prior to September 6, 2008), http://web.archive.org/web/20151109091301/http://people.ucsc.edu/~odonovan/walker_family.html, accessed March 21, 2017.

O'Donovan, Connell, "The Mormon Priesthood Ban and Elder Q. Walker Lewis: 'An example for his more whiter brethren to follow,'" *The John Whitmer Historical Association Journal* 26 (2006): 48–100.

Odu, Asiri, *Ah Juba! A PleaPrayerPromise.* s.l.: Oya's Tornado, 2015.

Old Sturbridge Village, "Celebrations in the 1830s," OSV Documents, Sturbridge, Mass., 2002, http://resources.osv.org/explore_learn/document_viewer.php?DocID=1104, accessed August 28, 2017.

Osgood, John, Probate file papers. Essex County, MA: Probate File Papers, 1638–1881, Case 20218, New England Historic Genealogical Society, 2014, from records supplied by the Supreme Judicial Court Archives, https://www.americanancestors.org/databases/essex-county-ma-probate-file-papers-1638-1881/image?pageName=20218:49&volumeId=13789&rId=30381330, accessed November 16, 2017.

Osgood, Joseph, and George Osgood, Day Books of Joseph Osgood and son George, 1770–1796, 3 volumes, n.p., Boston Medical Library, Francis A. Countway Library of Medicine, Boston, Mass., http://id.lib.harvard.edu/alma/990065550010203941/catalog, accessed October 16, 2019.

O'Toole, Marjory Gomez, *If Jane Should Want to be Sold: Stories of Enslavement, Indenture and Freedom in Little Compton, Rhode Island.* Little Compton, R.I.: Little Compton Historical Society, 2016.

Oxford English Dictionary, *Oxford English Dictionary* (website), www.oed.com, accessed many times.

Paradise, Scott H., *A History of Printing in Andover, Massachusetts 1798–1931.* [Andover, Mass.]: The Andover Press, 1931.

Parker, Kunal M., "Making Blacks Foreigners: The Legal Construction of Former Slaves in Post-Revolutionary Massachusetts," *Utah Law Review* 2001 (1) (2001): 75–124.

Parker, Kunal M., "State, Citizenship, and Territory: The Legal Construction of Immigrants in Antebellum Massachusetts," *Law and History Review* 19 (3) (2001): 583–643.

Parker, Kunal M., *Making Foreigners: Immigration and Citizenship Law in America, 1600–2000.* New York, N.Y.: Cambridge University Press, 2015.

Parker, Theodore, Letter to George Bancroft, March 16, 1858, in *Life and Correspondence of Theodore Parker, Minister of the Twenty-Eighth Congregational Society, Boston,* by John Weiss, Vol. 2, 234–235. London: Longman, Green, Longman, Roberts, and Green, 1863.

Parks, Roger N., "Early New England and the Negro," OSV Documents, Sturbridge, Mass., 1969, http://resources.osv.org/explore_learn/document_viewer .php?Action=View&DocID=869, accessed June 2, 2016.

Parnell, Sarah B., Probate file papers. Essex County, MA: Probate File Papers, 1638–1881, Case 49210, New England Historic Genealogical Society, 2014, from records supplied by the Supreme Judicial Court Archives, https://www .americanancestors.org/databases/essex-county-ma-probate-file-papers -1638-1881/image/?pageName=49210:1&volumeId=14213, accessed September 16, 2017.

Parsons, Theophilus, Docket book, 1774–1800, HLS MS 4022, Harvard Law School Library, Cambridge, Mass.

Parsons, Theophilus [Jr.], *Memoir of Theophilus Parsons [Sr.], Chief Justice of the Supreme Judicial Court of Massachusetts; With Notices of Some of His Contemporaries.* Boston, Mass.: Ticknor and Fields, 1859.

Passmore, Adele C. (ed.), *250th Anniversary, Wilmington, Massachusetts, 1730– 1980.* Wilmington, Mass.: Hampshire Press, 1981.

Passmore, Adele C., "Solved: The riddle of the Pearson Tavern," *Town Crier* (Wilmington, Mass.) (July 22, 1981): 4.

Patrakis, Joan, "Charlotte Helen Abbott: Genealogist, Dressmaker, Naturalist," *Andover Historical Society Newsletter* (Andover, Mass.) 14 (1) (1989): n.p. [3].

Patrakis, Joan, "Blacks Have Lived in Andover for Over Three Centuries," *Andover Historical Society Newsletter* (Andover, Mass.) 15 (1) (1990): n.p. [3].

Patrakis, Joan, "Andover Sent Anti-Slavery Emigrants to Kansas," *Andover Historical Society Newsletter* (Andover, Mass.) 16 (4) (1992): n.p. [3].

Patrakis, Joan, "Nancy Parker: Old Records Reveal Her Probable Identity," *Andover Historical Society Newsletter* (Andover, Mass.) 18 (4) (1994): n.p. [3].

Patrakis, Joan, "Bessie [Goldsmith] Became a Town Legend," *Andover Historical Society Newsletter* (Andover, Mass.) 19 (4) (1995): n.p. [3].

Patrakis, Joan, "Recent Research Clarifies Black Lucy's Life Story," *Andover Historical Society Newsletter* (Andover, Mass.) 22 (2) (1997): n.p. [1–3].

Patrakis, Joan, "Who Killed Mehitable?" *Andover Historical Society Newsletter* (Andover, Mass.) 31 (3) (2006): n.p. [2].

Patrakis, Joan Silva, *Andover in the Civil War: The Spirit and Sacrifice of a New England Town*. Charleston, S.C.: The History Press, 2008.

Paynter, Robert, and Whitney Battle-Baptiste, "Contexts of Resistance in African American Western Massachusetts: A View from the W.E.B. Du Bois Homesite in Great Barrington, Massachusetts," *Historical Archaeology* 53 (2) (2019): 323–340.

Paynter, Robert, Linda Ziegenbein, and Quentin Lewis, "Excavating the 'Garden of the North': Five Centuries of Material and Social Change in Western Massachusetts: An Introduction," *Historical Archaeology* 53 (2) (2019): 236–250.

Pemberton, Thomas, "Thomas Pemberton to Dr. Belknap. Boston, March 12, 1795," in "Letters and Documents Relating to Slavery in Massachusetts," *Collections of the Massachusetts Historical Society* (5th series) 3 (1877): 391–394.

Perley, Sidney, *The History of Boxford, Essex County, Massachusetts, from the Earliest Settlement Known to the Present Time: A Period of about Two Hundred and Thirty Years*. Boxford, Mass.: The author, 1880.

Perley, Sidney, "The Dwellings of Boxford," *Essex Institute Historical Collections* 29 (1–3) (1892): 1–128.

Perley, Sidney, "Essex County in the Abolition of Slavery," *Essex-County Historical and Genealogical Register* 1 (1) (1894): 1–4; 1 (2) (1894): 25–27; 1 (3) (1894): 37–39; 1 (4) (1894): 52–54; 1 (10) (1894): 146–148; 2 (2) (1895): 23–25; 2 (6) (1895): 82–84.

Perley, Sidney, "Alfred Poore," *The New England Historical and Genealogical Register* 62 (January) (1908): 51–56.

Peter v. Moody Bridges, Essex County Court of Common Pleas Records, September 1769, 448 (with the docket entries and file papers), Supreme Judicial Court Archives, Massachusetts Archives, Boston.

Phillips Academy, *Notable Alumni: Long List* (website), https://web.archive.org/web/20170808005328/https://www.andover.edu/About/NotableAlumni/LongList/Pages/default.aspx, accessed November 17, 2019.

Phillips, [Rev.] Samuel, Probate file papers. Essex County, MA: Probate File Papers, 1638–1881, Case 21715, New England Historic Genealogical Society, 2014, from records supplied by the Supreme Judicial Court Archives, https://www.americanancestors.org/databases/essex-county-ma-probate-file-papers-1638-1881/image?pageName=21715:1&volumeId=13789&rId=30403104, accessed August 18, 2019.

Pickering, Jeanne M., "Suing Slavery: The Essex County Freedom Suits, 1765–1783." M.A. thesis, Salem State University, 2018.

Pickett, Dwayne W., *Captain William Hilton and the Founding of Hilton Head Island*. Charleston, S.C.: The History Press, 2019.

Pike, Julie, *The History of South Church in Andover, Massachusetts Founded on October 17, 1711*. North Reading, Mass.: The Cheshire Press, 2011.

Piper, Emilie, and David Levinson, *One Minute a Free Woman: Elizabeth Freeman and the Struggle for Freedom*. Salisbury, Conn.: Upper Housatonic Valley National Heritage Area, 2010.

Piro, Rebecca, "Historic Undertaking: Repairing Stones is a Grave Undertaking," *Andover Townsman* (Andover, Mass.) (February 21, 2002): 1, 4–5.

Pleck, Elizabeth, "Slavery in Puritan New England" (book review of *New England Bound* by Wendy Warren), *Journal of Interdisciplinary History* 49 (2) (2018): 305–313.

Poor, Albert, "The Oration," in *Andover, Massachusetts: Proceedings at the Celebration of the Two Hundred and Fiftieth Anniversary of the Incorporation of the Town, May 20, 1896*, 43–95. Andover, Mass.: Andover Press, 1897.

Poor, John, Jr., Manumission paper of Salem Poor, July 10, 1769, MSS 0.569, Salem Poor Collection, Phillips Library, Peabody Essex Museum, Rowley, Mass. Copy recorded February 12, 1772, Book 130, pg. 21, Southern Essex District Registry of Deeds, Salem, Mass.

[Poor(e), Alfred], "History of Andover. Woburn street continued.," *Andover Advertiser* (Andover, Mass.) (August 29, 1863): n.p. [2].

[Poor(e), Alfred], "Andover Graveyards Old South Andover Graveyards," n.p. [6], and "Theological Seminary Burial Ground," n.p. [3], in "Cemetery Records of Andover, Mass.," n.d. [circa 1863–1864], MSS 0.424, Phillips Library, Peabody Essex Museum, Rowley, Mass.

Poore, Alfred, "A Genealogical-Historical Visitation of Andover, Mass., in the Year 1863," *Essex Institute Historical Collections* 48 (3) (1912): 276–292; 49 (1) (1913): 50–64; 49 (2) (1913): 161–171; 49 (3) (1913): 239–252; 49 (4) (1913): 305–320; 50 (1) (1914): 41–56; 50 (3) (1914): 253–264; 51 (4) (1915): 306–312; 52 (1) (1916): 84–96; 52 (3) (1916): 281–288; 53 (1) (1917): 54–64; 53 (2) (1917): 187–192; 54 (2) (1918): 138–144; 54 (3) (1918): 246–250; 55 (1) (1919): 75–77.

Prechtel-Kluskens, Claire, "Follow the Money: Tracking Revolutionary War Army Pension Payments," *Prologue: Quarterly of the National Archives and Records Administration* 40 (4) (2008), https://www.archives.gov/publications/prologue/2008/winter/follow-money.html, accessed February 15, 2019.

Price, Thomas, *Slavery in America: With Notices of the Present State of Slavery and the Slave Trade Throughout the World*. London: G. Wightman, 1837.

Prince v. Thomas Osgood, Essex County Court of Common Pleas Records, July 1778, 476, Supreme Judicial Court Archives, Massachusetts Archives, Boston.

Priscilla and Jupiter v. Nathan Simmons and Jonathan Chadwick, Essex County Court of General Sessions of the Peace Records, March 27, 1722, 65 (Ipswich); August 1, 1722, 77 (Salem); September 25, 1722, 83 (Newbury), Supreme Judicial Court Archives, Massachusetts Archives, Boston.

Prude, Jonathan, "To Look Upon the 'Lower Sort': Runaway Ads and the Appearance of Unfree Laborers in America, 1750–1800," *The Journal of American History* 78 (1) (1991): 124–159.

Pryor, Elizabeth Stordeur, *Colored Travelers: Mobility and the Fight for Citizenship before the Civil War*. Chapel Hill: University of North Carolina Press, 2015.

Pryor, Elizabeth Stordeur, "The Etymology of Nigger," *Journal of the Early Republic* 36 (2) (2016): 203–245.

Putnam, Eben (ed.), *A Genealogy of the Descendants of John, Christopher and William Osgood, Who Came from England and Settled in New England Early in the Seventeenth Century. Compiled by the Late Ira Osgood*. Salem, Mass.: Salem Press, 1894.

Pynchon, William, "William Pynchon Papers, 1746–1789," I. Legal Records, Box 1, Folder 2, Court Fees, 1761–1773/Miscellaneous Legal Fees 1764–1771 (bound manuscript volume), Mss. 236, Phillips Library, Peabody Essex Museum, Rowley, Mass.

Quimby, Robert, Presentment of, for the death of Henry Horrell, Court of Assistants, Boston, September 2, 1657, Suffolk Files Collection, File #271 and #26696, Supreme Judicial Court Archives, Massachusetts Archives, Boston; Chamberlain Collection, MS Ch.E.10.114, Boston Public Library Rare Books and Manuscripts Department, Boston, Mass. Transcriptions of file papers (except File #26696) are in Cronin, *Records of the Court of Assistants*, Vol. 3, 63–66.

Quintal, George, Jr., *Patriots of Color "A Peculiar Beauty and Merit": African Americans and Native Americans at Battle Road & Bunker Hill*. Boston, Mass.: Division of Cultural Resources, Boston National Historical Park, National Park Service, 2004.

Rabushka, Alvin, *Taxation in Colonial America*. Princeton, N.J.: Princeton University Press, 2008.

Rael, Patrick, *Black Identity and Black Protest in the Antebellum North*. Chapel Hill: University of North Carolina Press, 2002.

Ralston, Gail L., "Lasting Tribute to Andover's Early Missionaries," *Andover Townsman* (Andover, Mass.) (April 17, 2014), http://www.andovertownsman.com/news/local_news/lasting-tribute-to-andover-s-early-missionaries/article_b8617d1b-a572-5077-b85a-5a59533f9960.html, accessed April 30, 2017.

Raphael, Ray, and Marie Raphael, *The Spirit of 74: How the American Revolution Began*. New York, N.Y.: The New Press, 2015.

Rawley, James A., with Stephen D. Behrendt, "The American Dimensions and the Massachusetts Contribution," in *The Transatlantic Slave Trade: A History* (revised edition), 277–304. Lincoln: University of Nebraska Press, 2005.

Reading, Mass., Second Church of Christ Records, 1720–1806, RG5021, n.p., The Congregational Library & Archives, Boston, Mass. Digital images of manuscript volume, http://nehh-viewer.s3-website-us-east-1.amazonaws.com/#/content/ReadingSecond/viewer/Church20Records2C2017201806.

Reece, Robert L., "Whitewashing Slavery: Legacy of Slavery and White Social Outcomes," *Social Problems* (2019), advance version (June 25, 2019) prior to print publication, https://doi.org/10.1093/socpro/spz016, accessed August 22, 2019.

Reef, Catherine, *Poverty in America*. New York, N.Y.: Facts on File, 2007.

Reisner, Alex, *Speed of Animals* (website), http://www.speedofanimals.com/animals/horse, accessed May 28, 2017.

Richardson, David, "Slavery, Trade, and Economic Growth in Eighteenth-Century New England," in *Slavery and the Rise of the Atlantic System*, ed. Barbara L. Solow, 237–264. Cambridge: Cambridge University Press, 1991.

Richardson, Eleanor Motley, *Andover: A Century of Change, 1896–1996*. Andover, Mass.: Andover Historical Society, 1995.

Riley, Padraig, *Slavery and the Democratic Conscience: Political Life in Jeffersonian America*. Philadelphia: University of Pennsylvania Press, 2016.

Rinehart, Nicholas T., "The Man that was a Thing: Reconsidering Human Commodification in Slavery," *Journal of Social History* 50 (1) (2016): 28–50.

Roach, Marilynne K., *Six Women of Salem: The Untold Story of the Accused and their Accusers in the Salem Witch Trials*. Boston, Mass.: Da Capo Press, 2013.

Robbins, Sarah Stuart, *Old Andover Days: Memories of a Puritan Childhood*. Boston, Mass.: Pilgrim Press, 1908.

Rockman, Seth, "The Unfree Origins of American Capitalism," in *The Economy of Early America: Historical Perspectives and New Directions*, ed. Cathy Matson, 335–361. University Park: The Pennsylvania State University Press, 2006.

Rollings, Robert, and Julia C. Palmer, Marriage record. State Marriage Records, Town of Andover, Marriage Register 1855–1896, 21, No. 28, November 29, 1863 (registered November 30, 1863), Massachusetts Archives, Boston, https://www.familysearch.org/ark:/61903/3:1:3QSQ-G979-6999-F?i=63&cc=2061550&cat=1257681, accessed August 25, 2017.

Romer, Robert H., *Slavery in the Connecticut Valley of Massachusetts*. Florence, Mass.: Levellers Press, 2009.

Rose v. Joseph Osgood, Essex County Court of Common Pleas Records, May 1779, 507, Supreme Judicial Court Archives, Massachusetts Archives, Boston.

Ross, Marc Howard, *Slavery in the North: Forgetting History and Recovering Memory*. Philadelphia: University of Pennsylvania Press, 2018.

Rossi, Benedetta, "African Post-Slavery: A History of the Future," *International Journal of African Historical Studies* 48 (2) (2015): 303–324.

Rossi, Benedetta, "Preface to the Second Edition," in *Reconfiguring Slavery: West African Trajectories* (2nd edition), ed. Benedetta Rossi, xiii–xvii. Liverpool: Liverpool University Press, 2016.

Rossi, Benedetta, "Dependence, Unfreedom, and Slavery in Africa: Towards an Integrated Analysis," *Africa* (Journal of the International African Institute) 86 (3) (2016): 571–590.

Rossi, Benedetta, "Freedom Under Scrutiny: Epilogue," *Journal of Global Slavery* 2 (1–2) (2017): 185–194.

Rothman, David J., *The Discovery of the Asylum: Social Order and Disorder in the New Republic*. Boston, Mass.: Little, Brown, 1971.

Royal, Silas v. Joshua Wyman (captioned as "Wyman vs Royall"), Superior Court of Judicature Records, Middlesex County, October 1778, 42; Suffolk Files Collection, File #148316, Supreme Judicial Court Archives, Massachusetts Archives, Boston.

Ruchames, Louis, "Jim Crow Railroads in Massachusetts," *American Quarterly* 8 (1) (1956): 61–75.

Ruchames, Louis (ed.), *The Letters of William Lloyd Garrison, Volume II: A House Dividing Against Itself, 1836–1840*. Cambridge, Mass.: Harvard University Press, 1971.

Russell, Timothy, Probate file papers. Essex County, MA: Probate File Papers, 1638–1881, Case 24433, New England Historic Genealogical Society, 2014, from records supplied by the Supreme Judicial Court Archives, https://www.americanancestors.org/databases/essex-county-ma-probate-file-papers-1638-1881/image?pageName=24433:1&volumeId=13855, accessed March 9, 2019.

Sachs, Honor, "'Freedom By A Judgment': The Legal History of an Afro-Indian Family," *Law and History Review* 30 (1) (2012): 173–203.

Sampson v. Caleb Dodge and Josiah Batchelder, Essex County Court of Common Pleas Docket, July 1774 (Case #2), September 1774 (Case #1/33, as "Samson"), December 1774 (Case #2/25), May 1775 (Case #3/20), July 1775 (Case #4/19 & #5/19, listed twice), Supreme Judicial Court Archives, Massachusetts Archives, Boston.

Sanborn, Melinde Lutz, "Angola and Elizabeth: An African Family in the Massachusetts Bay Colony," *The New England Quarterly* 72 (1) (1999): 119–129.

Sanborn, Melinde Lutz (comp.), *Middlesex County, Massachusetts Deponents, 1649–1700* (website), Ancestry.com Operations Inc., 2000, https://www.ancestry.com/search/collections/midlsexma1649/, accessed August 1, 2019.

Sanderson, George W., Herbert J. Harwood, and Edward Frost, *Records of Littleton, Massachusetts*. Littleton, Mass.: Printed by order of the town at Concord, Mass.: Patriot Press, 1900.

Saville, Julie, "Rites and Power: Reflections on Slavery, Freedom and Political Ritual," in *From Slavery to Emancipation in the Atlantic World*, ed. Sylvia R. Frey and Betty Wood, 81–102. London: Frank Cass, 1999.

Schermerhorn, Calvin, *Unrequited Toil: A History of United States Slavery*. New York, N.Y.: Cambridge University Press, 2018.

Schinto, Jeanne, "A Load of Hay," *Jeanne Schinto* (website), October 17, 2018, http://www.jeanneschinto.com/commentaries/a-load-of-hay, accessed July 7, 2019.

Schinto, Jeanne, "Claude Moore Fuess," *Jeanne Schinto* (website), November 9, 2018, http://www.jeanneschinto.com/commentaries/claude-moore-fuess, accessed August 28, 2019.

Schutz, John A., *Legislators of the Massachusetts General Court 1691–1780: A Biographical Dictionary*. Boston, Mass.: Northeastern University Press, 1997.

Schweninger, Loren, "Freedom Suits, African American Women, and the Genealogy of Slavery," *The William and Mary Quarterly* (3rd series) 71 (1) (2014): 35–62.

Schweninger, Loren, *Appealing for Liberty: Freedom Suits in the South*. New York, N.Y.: Oxford University Press, 2018.

Scobey, D.C., G.S. Towle, A. Grover, H. Eaton, and J.W. Pillsbury, "A Statement of the Circumstances which Induced Fifty Students of Phillips' Academy, Andover, To ask a Dimission from that Institution," *The Liberator* (Boston, Mass.) 5 (33) (August 15, 1835): 130.

Scott, Julius S., *The Common Wind: Afro-American Currents in the Age of the Haitian Revolution*. London: Verso, 2018.

[Sedgwick, Theodore, or Henry Dwight Sedgwick], *The Practicability of the Abolition of Slavery: A Lecture, Delivered at the Lyceum in Stockbridge, Massachusetts, February, 1831*. New York, N.Y.: J. Seymour, 1831.

Seeman, Erik R., "'Justise Must Take Plase': Three African Americans Speak of Religion in Eighteenth-Century New England," *The William and Mary Quarterly* (3rd series) 56 (2) (1999): 393–414.

Sesma, Elena, "Creating Mindful Heritage Narratives: Black Women in Slavery and Freedom," *Journal of African Diaspora Archaeology & Heritage* 5 (1) (2016): 38–61.

Shelburne v. Greenfield, Supreme Judicial Court Records, Hampshire County, September 1796, 252, Supreme Judicial Court Archives, Massachusetts Archives, Boston.

Sheldon, Asa Goodell, *Life of Asa G. Sheldon: Wilmington Farmer*. Woburn, Mass.: E.T. Moody, Printer, Journal Press, 1862.

Sheller, Mimi, "Beyond Post-Emancipation Studies?" *Slavery & Abolition* (22) (2) (2001): 119–125.

Sherburne, Michelle Arnosky, *Slavery & the Underground Railroad in New Hampshire*. Charleston, S.C.: The History Press, 2016.

Shiels, Richard D., "The Scope of the Second Great Awakening: Andover, Massachusetts, as a Case Study," *Journal of the Early Republic* 5 (2) (1985): 223–246.

Shipton, Clifford K., "James Chandler," in *Biographical Sketches of Those who Attended Harvard College in the Classes 1726–1730 with Bibliographical and Other Notes. Sibley's Harvard Graduates*, Vol. 8, 1726–1730, 375–381. Boston: Massachusetts Historical Society, 1951.

Shipton, Clifford K., "John Frye," in *Biographical Sketches of Those who Attended Harvard College in the Classes 1768–1771. Sibley's Harvard Graduates*, Vol. 17, 1768–1771, 158–159. Boston: Massachusetts Historical Society, 1975.

Siebert, Wilbur H., "The Underground Railroad in Massachusetts," *Proceedings of the American Antiquarian Society* (new series) 45 (Part 1) (1935): 25–100.

Silverman, David J., "The Impact of Indentured Servitude on the Society and Culture of Southern New England Indians, 1680–1810," *The New England Quarterly* 74 (4) (2001): 622–666.

Simpson, Cesar v. Catherine Timan, Case No. 26, April 9, 1798, in Nathaniel Lovejoy, "Processes of Confessions," 1797–1800 (Justice of the Peace Records, Andover, Mass.), n.p., Collection No. EC 43, Box 6, File 4, "Collection of Essex County (Mass.) Court Records, 1628–1914," Phillips Library, Peabody Essex Museum, Rowley, Mass.

Sinha, Manisha, "To 'Cast Just Obliquy' on Oppressors: Black Radicalism in the Age of Revolution," *The William and Mary Quarterly* (3rd series) 64 (1) (2007): 149–160.

Sinha, Manisha, *The Slave's Cause: A History of Abolition*. New Haven, Conn.: Yale University Press, 2016.

Sinha, Manisha, "The Mobile Resistance: Rumor and Revolution in Julius Scott's Black Atlantic," *The Nation* (May 20, 2019), https://www.thenation.com/article/julius-scott-the-common-wind-book-review/, accessed June 20, 2019.

Smith, Annie Morrill, *Morrill Kindred in America*. New York, N.Y.: Lyons Genealogical Co., 1914.

Smith, John David, "George H. Moore, 'Tormentor of Massachusetts,'" in *Slavery, Race, and American History: Historical Conflict, Trends, and Method, 1866–1953*, 3–15. Armonk, N.Y.: M.E. Sharpe, 1999.

Smith, Pam, "Andover Stories: Pompey Lovejoy – 'lection cake and ginger root beer," *Andover Townsman* (Andover, Mass.) (August 25, 2011), https://www .andovertownsman.com/news/local_news/andover-stories-pompey-lovejoy--- lection-cake-and-ginger/article_5aacf294-af14-5a3a-a8ee-99be38255ff2.html, accessed June 30, 2019.

Soifer, Aviam, "Status, Contract, and Promises Unkept," *Yale Law Journal* 96 (8) (1987): 1916–1959.

Somerset, James v. Charles Stewart, King's Bench, 12 Geo. 3, Easter Term 1772, 98 Eng. Rep. 499 and 20 Howell's State Trials 1 (rendered "Sommersett" and "Steuart").

Sontag, Susan, "The Double Standard of Aging," *The Saturday Review* (New York, N.Y.) 55 (39) (September 23, 1972): 29–38.

Sparrow, A.D. (comp.), *The Andover and North Andover Directory, 1893–4*. Shirley Village, Mass.: Sparrow and Farnsworth, 1893.

Spaulding, S[amuel] J[ones], "James Chandler," "Sketches of the Members of the Essex North Association," in *Contributions to the Ecclesiastical History of Essex County, Mass.*, Essex North Association, 59–61. Boston, Mass.: Congregational Board of Publication, 1865.

Spector, Robert M., "The Quock Walker Cases (1781–83)—Slavery, Its Abolition, and Negro Citizenship in Early Massachusetts," *Journal of Negro History* 53 (1) (1968): 12–32.

Spencer-Wood, Suzanne M., "A Feminist Approach to European Ideologies of Poverty and the Institutionalization of the Poor in Falmouth, Massachusetts," in *The Archaeology of Institutional Life*, ed. April M. Beisaw and James G. Gibb, 117–136. Tuscaloosa: University of Alabama Press, 2009.

Spencer-Wood, Suzanne M., "Feminist Theoretical Perspectives on the Archaeology of Poverty: Gendering Institutional Lifeways in the Northeastern United States from the Eighteenth Century through the Nineteenth Century," *Historical Archaeology* 44 (4) (2010): 110–135.

Spencer-Wood, Suzanne M., and Christopher N. Matthews, "Impoverishment, Criminalization, and the Culture of Poverty," *Historical Archaeology* 45 (3) (2011): 1–10.

Spraker, Christopher M., "The Lost History of Slaves and Slave Owners in Billerica, Massachusetts, 1655–1790," *Historical Journal of Massachusetts* 42 (1) (2014): 109–141.

Stevens, Charles Emery, *Anthony Burns, A History*. Boston, Mass.: John P. Jewett and Co., 1856.

Stevens, James, "The Revolutionary Journal of James Stevens of Andover, Mass.," *Essex Institute Historical Collections* 48 (1) (1912): 41–71.

Stevens, Kate Hasting, "The Old Burying Ground on Academy Road, North Andover," *Old-Time New England* 41 (141) (1950): 13–15.

Stewart, James Brewer, "Modernizing 'Difference': The Political Meanings of Color in the Free States, 1776–1840," *Journal of the Early Republic* 19 (4) (1999): 691–712.

St. George, Robert Blair, "Massacred Language: Courtroom Performance in Eighteenth-Century Boston," in *Possible Pasts: Becoming Colonial in Early America*, ed. Robert Blair St. George, 327–356. Ithaca, N.Y.: Cornell University Press, 2000.

Stowe, Harriet Beecher, "Oldtown Fireside Talks of the Revolution," in *Sam Lawson's Oldtown Fireside Stories*, 248–266. Boston, Mass.: Houghton, Mifflin and Co., 1891.

[Sullivan, James], "Law Cases," *Collections of the Massachusetts Historical Society for the Year M, DCC, XCVIII*. Boston: Samuel Hall, 1798, reprinted by John H. Eastburn, 1835, (i.e., *Collections of the Massachusetts Historical Society* [1st series] 5 [1798]): 45–52.

Sullivan, James, "James Sullivan to Dr. Belknap. Boston, April 9, 1795," in "Letters and Documents Relating to Slavery in Massachusetts," *Collections of the Massachusetts Historical Society* (5th series) 3 (1877): 402–404.

Swain, John v. Elisha Folger, Nantucket County Court of Common Pleas Records, October 1773, 297; Superior Court of Judicature Records, Suffolk County, August 1774, 238 (captioned as Folger v. Swain); Suffolk Files Collection, File #102427, Supreme Judicial Court Archives, Massachusetts Archives, Boston.

Sweet, James H., "Defying Social Death: The Multiple Configurations of African Slave Family in the Atlantic World," *The William and Mary Quarterly* (3rd series) 70 (2) (2013): 251–272.

Sweet, John Wood, "'More than Tears': The Ordeal of Abolition in Revolutionary New England," *Explorations in Early American Culture* 5 (2001): 118–172.

Sweet, John Wood, *Bodies Politic: Negotiating Race in the American North, 1730–1830*. Philadelphia: University of Pennsylvania Press, 2006.

Sword, Kirsten Denise, "Wayward Wives, Runaway Slaves and the Limits of Patriarchal Authority in Early America." Ph.D. dissertation, Harvard University, 2002.

Taft Collection, Ms S 134, Andover Center for History & Culture, Andover, Mass.

Taft, Henry W., "Judicial History of Berkshire," in *Four Papers of the Berkshire Historical and Scientific Society*, 89–115. Pittsfield, Mass.: Berkshire Historical and Scientific Society, 1886.

Tarbox, Jennifer, and Joan Patrakis, "Andover Stories: Digging into a life, a garden," *Andover Townsman* (Andover, Mass.) (July 14, 2011), https://www.andovertownsman .com/news/local_news/andover-stories-digging-into-a-life-a-garden/article _84b8325f-4ae3-51b9-89cb-17894f04c57a.html, accessed May 29, 2019.

Taylor, John L., *A Memoir of His Honor Samuel Phillips, LL.D.* Boston, Mass.: Congregational Board of Publication, 1856.

Taylor, Marla, "Peabody at the Smithsonian," *The Robert S. Peabody Institute of Archaeology Newsletter* (February 14, 2019), https://peabody.andover .edu/2019/02/14/peabody-at-the-smithsonian/, accessed May 29, 2019.

Teed, Paul, "'A Brave Man's Child': Theodore Parker and the Memory of the American Revolution," *Historical Journal of Massachusetts* 29 (1) (2001): 170–191.

Tewksbury, Robert H., "Lawrence," in *Standard History of Essex County, Massachusetts, Embracing a History of the County from its First Settlement to the Present Time, with a History and Description of its Towns and Cities. The Most Historic County in America*, 210–238. Boston, Mass.: C.F. Jewett and Co., 1878.

The Trustees of Reservations, *Elizabeth Freeman: Fighting for Freedom* (website), February 2012, https://web.archive.org/web/20181215115229/http://www .thetrustees.org/what-we-care-about/history-culture/elizabeth-freeman-fighting -for-freedom.html, accessed August 3, 2019.

Thibault, Barbara, "Anti-Slavery Movement in Andover: Notable Sites" (map in the pamphlet boxes, arranged by historical topics, under "Slavery," Andover Center for History & Culture). Andover, Mass.: Andover Historical Society, 1993.

Thomas, Felicia Y., "Entangled With the Yolk of Bondage: Black Women in Massachusetts, 1700–1783." Ph.D. dissertation, Rutgers University, 2014.

Thompson, J. Earl, Jr., "Abolitionism and Theological Education at Andover," *The New England Quarterly* 47 (2) (1974): 238–261.

Thompson, Lucy Susan, *The Story of Mattie J. Jackson; Her Parentage—Experience of Eighteen Years of Slavery—Incidents During the War—Her Escape from Slavery. A True Story. Written and Arranged by Dr. L.S. Thompson (Formerly Mrs. Schuyler) As Given by Mattie*. Lawrence, Mass.: Printed at Sentinel Office, 1866.

Timan, Catherine v. Prince Fields, Case No. 19, December 4, 1797, in Nathaniel Lovejoy, "Processes of Confessions," 1797–1800 (Justice of the Peace Records, Andover, Mass.), n.p., Collection No. EC 43, Box 6, File 4, "Collection of Essex County (Mass.) Court Records, 1628–1914," Phillips Library, Peabody Essex Museum, Rowley, Mass.

Timon v. Peter Osgood, Jr., Essex County Court of Common Pleas Records, September 1777, 447 (with the docket entries and file papers), Supreme Judicial Court Archives, Massachusetts Archives, Boston.

Towner, Lawrence William, "A Good Master Well Served: A Social History of Servitude in Massachusetts, 1620–1750." Ph.D. dissertation, Northwestern University, 1955.

Towner, Lawrence William, *A Good Master Well Served: Masters and Servants in Colonial Massachusetts, 1620–1750*. New York, N.Y.: Garland, 1998.

Trans-Atlantic Slave Trade Database, *Trans-Atlantic Slave Trade Database* (website), https://www.slavevoyages.org/.

Trow, William A., Collection, Ms S 556, Sub-group IV, Phillips Family, Series A, Rev. Samuel Phillips, 1689/90–1771, Bills to estate of Rev. Samuel Phillips for his slave Cato (Phillips/Freeman), 1772, 1773, Andover Center for History & Culture, Andover, Mass.

Trowbridge, Francis Bacon, *The Ashley Genealogy: A History of the Descendants of Robert Ashley of Springfield, Massachusetts*. New Haven, Conn.: The author, 1896.

Turner, Katherine, "Cowper, Slave Narratives, and the Antebellum American Reading Public," *The Cowper and Newton Journal* 6 (2016), http://www.cowperandnewtonmuseum.org.uk/j6-article-turner/, accessed May 3, 2017.

Twombly, Robert C., "Black Resistance to Slavery in Massachusetts," in *Insights and Parallels: Problems and Issues of American Social History*, ed. William L. O'Neill, 11–56. Minneapolis, Minn.: Burgess Publishing Co., 1973.

Ulrich, Laurel Thatcher, "'Daughters of Liberty,' Religious Women in Revolutionary New England," in *Women in the Age of the American Revolution*, ed. Ronald Hoffman and Peter J. Albert, 211–243. Charlottesville: University Press of Virginia, 1989.

United States Bureau of the Census, *Heads of Families at the First Census of the United States Taken in the Year 1790 Massachusetts*. Washington, D.C.: Government Printing Office, 1908.

United States Bureau of the Census, "Statistics of Slaves," in *A Century of Population Growth from the First Census of the United States to the Twelfth 1790–1900*, 132–141. Washington, D.C.: Government Printing Office, 1909.

United States Bureau of the Census, *Negro Population 1790–1915*. Washington, D.C.: Government Printing Office, 1918.

United States Bureau of the Census, *Bureau of the Census Catalog of Publications, 1790–1972*. Washington, D.C.: Bureau of the Census, United States Department of Commerce, 1974.

United States Census, *Population Schedules of the First Census of the United States 1790, Roll 4, Massachusetts*, Vol. 1, Essex County. National Archives and Records Service, Microcopy No. 637, Roll 4.

United States Census, *Population Schedules of the Second Census of the United States 1800, Roll 14, Massachusetts*, Vol. 2, Essex County. National Archives and Records Service, Microcopy No. 32, Roll 14.

United States Census, *Population Schedules of the Second Census of the United States 1800, Roll 17, Massachusetts*, Vol. 5, Middlesex County. National Archives and Records Service, Microcopy No. 32, Roll 17.

United States Census, *Population Schedules of the Third Census of the United States 1810, Roll 18, Massachusetts*, Vol. 2, Essex County. National Archives and Records Service, Microcopy No. 252, Roll 18.

United States Census, *Population Schedules of the Fourth Census of the United States 1820, Roll 49, Massachusetts*, Vol. 3, Essex County. National Archives and Records Service, Microcopy No. 33, Roll 49.

United States Census, *Population Schedules of the Fifth Census of the United States 1830, Roll 61, Massachusetts*, Vol. 3, Essex County. National Archives and Records Service, Microcopy No. 19, Roll 61.

United States Census, *Population Schedules of the Fifth Census of the United States 1830, Roll 68, Massachusetts*, Vol. 10, Worcester County. National Archives and Records Service, Microcopy No. 19, Roll 68.

United States Census, *Population Schedules of the Seventh Census of the United States 1850, Roll 314, Massachusetts Essex County (pt.)*. National Archives and Records Service, Microcopy No. 432, Roll 314.

United States Congress, *Journal of the House of Representatives*, 22nd Cong., 1st sess., January 25, 1832, 240; January 26, 1832, 242–243.

United States Congress, *Statutes at Large*, 22nd Cong., 1st sess., Res. 5, July 3, 1832, 606.

United States Department of State, *Abstract of the Fifth Census of the United States, 1830*. Washington, D.C.: F.P. Blair, 1832, 5.

United States Department of State, *Fifth Census; or, Enumeration of the Inhabitants of the United States, as Returned by the Several Marshals of the States and Territories. 1830*. Washington, D.C.: Printed by Duff Green, 1832, bound as the second and independently paginated part of *Fifth Census; or, Enumeration of the Inhabitants of the United States. 1830. To which is Prefixed a Schedule of the Whole Number of Persons within the Several Districts of the United States, Taken According to the Acts of 1790, 1800, 1810, 1820*. Washington, D.C.: Printed by Duff Green, 1832.

United States Department of State, *Fifth Census; or, Enumeration of the Inhabitants of the United States, as Corrected at the Department of State. 1830*. Washington, D.C.: Printed by Duff Green, 1832, bound as the third and independently paginated part of *Fifth Census; or, Enumeration of the Inhabitants of the United States. 1830. To which is Prefixed a Schedule of the Whole Number of Persons within the Several Districts of the United States, Taken According to the Acts of 1790, 1800, 1810, 1820*. Washington, D.C.: Printed by Duff Green, 1832.

United States House of Representatives, *Abstract of the Returns of the Fifth Census*, 22d Cong., 1st sess., Doc. 263, 1832, State of Massachusetts, 5, 51, http://www2

.census.gov/prod2/decennial/documents/1830a-01.pdf, accessed December 3, 2014.

United States House of Representatives, Joint Select Committee on Disposition of Useless Papers in the Executive Departments, "Disposition of Useless Papers in the Department of Commerce and Labor," House of Representatives, 60th Cong., 1st sess., Rpt. 1734, May 12, 1908.

United States Revolutionary War Pension Payment Ledgers, 1818–1872, Microcopy No. T-718, Ledgers of Payments, 1818–72, to U.S. Pensioners under Acts of 1818 through 1858 from the Records of the Office of the Third Auditor of the Treasury, Roll 2, Volume B, Revolutionary War Pensioners under Act of 1818, 1818–32, 12 ("Titus Cobarn"); Roll 19, Volume R, Widow Pensions under Acts of February 2 and July 29, 1848, 1848–62, 174 ("Rosannah Coburn"). Washington, D.C.: National Archives and Records Service, 1962.

United States Secretary of Commerce and Labor, "Useless Papers in Commerce and Labor Department," House of Representatives, 60th Cong., 1st sess., Doc. 793, March 17, 1908.

United States Secretary of War, *Report from the Secretary of War, in Obedience to Resolutions of the Senate of the 5th and 30th of June, 1834, and the 3d of March, 1835, in Relation to the Pension Establishment of the United States*, Vol. 1: Massachusetts Pension Roll. Washington, D.C.: Duff Green, 1835. Also incorporated in *United States Congressional Serial Set*, No. 249, 23rd Cong., 1st sess., Senate Doc. 514, 1835.

Uscilka, Jane M., *The Newburyport Black Heritage Trail: Searching for African-American History in Newburyport*. s.l. [Newburyport, Mass.]: s.n. ["Produced by Rosemarie Greene"], 2002.

VanderVelde, Lea, *Redemption Songs: Suing for Freedom before Dred Scott*. New York, N.Y.: Oxford University Press, 2014.

Vickers, Daniel, "The First Whalemen of Nantucket," *The William and Mary Quarterly* (3rd series) 40 (4) (1983): 560–583.

Vickers, Daniel, *Farmers & Fishermen: Two Centuries of Work in Essex County, Massachusetts, 1630–1850*. Chapel Hill: University of North Carolina Press, 1994.

Vickers, Daniel, "Credit and Misunderstanding on Nantucket Island, Massachusetts (1683–1763)," *Quaderni storici* (new series) 46 (137) (2) (2011): 415–440.

Vital Records of Andover Massachusetts to the End of the Year 1849, Vol. 1: Births; Vol. 2: Marriages and Deaths. Topsfield, Mass.: Topsfield Historical Society, 1912.

Vital Records of Billerica Massachusetts to the Year 1850. Boston, Mass.: New England Historic Genealogical Society, 1908.

Vital Records of Boxford Massachusetts to the End of the Year 1849. Topsfield, Mass.: Topsfield Historical Society, 1905.

Vital Records of Dracut, Massachusetts, to the Year 1850. Boston, Mass.: New England Historic Genealogical Society, 1907.

Vital Records of Gloucester Massachusetts to the End of the Year 1849, Vol. 1: Births. Topsfield, Mass.: Topsfield Historical Society, 1917. Vol. 2: Marriages. Salem, Mass.: Essex Institute, 1923. Vol. 3: Deaths. Salem, Mass.: Essex Institute, 1924.

Vital Records of Ipswich Massachusetts to the End of the Year 1849, Vol. 1, Births; Vol. 2: Marriages and Deaths. Salem, Mass.: Essex Institute, 1910.

Vital Records of Manchester Massachusetts to the End of the Year 1849. Salem, Mass.: Essex Institute, 1903.

Vital Records of Marblehead Massachusetts to the End of the Year 1849, Vol. 2: Marriages and Deaths. Salem, Mass.: Essex Institute, 1904.

Vital Records of Newbury Massachusetts to the End of the Year 1849, Vol. 1: Births; Vol. 2: Marriages and Deaths. Salem, Mass.: Essex Institute, 1911.

Vital Records of Newburyport Massachusetts to the End of the Year 1849, Vol. 1: Births; Vol. 2: Marriages and Deaths. Salem, Mass.: Essex Institute, 1911.

Vital Records of Reading Massachusetts, to the Year 1850. Boston, Mass.: Wright and Potter, 1912.

Vital Records of Rowley Massachusetts to the End of the Year 1849. Salem, Mass.: Essex Institute, 1928.

Vose, Lewis and Crane, Ledger of Liberty Paper Mill, Milton, Mass., 1770–1793, Crane Museum and Center for the Paper Arts, Dalton, Mass.

Walker, Matthew, "Barre," in *History of Worcester County, Massachusetts, with Biographical Sketches of Many of its Pioneers and Prominent Men*, Vol. 1, comp. D. Hamilton Hurd, 330–362. Philadelphia, Pa.: J.W. Lewis and Co., 1889.

Walker, Quock v. Nathaniel Jennison (rendered "Quork" and "Jenison"), Worcester County Court of Common Pleas Records, June 1781, 215; Supreme Judicial Court Records, Worcester County, September 1781, 79, 84; Suffolk Files Collection, File #153101, Supreme Judicial Court Archives, Massachusetts Archives, Boston. (See also Commonwealth v. Jennison, and Jennison v. Caldwell and Caldwell.)

Walling, Henry F., "Map of the Town of Andover Essex County Massachusetts Surveyed by Authority of the Town by Henry F. Walling, Civil Engineer, 81 Washington St., Boston. 1852." Lithography of A. Kollner, Philadelphia, Pa. [Boston, Mass.: Henry F. Walling, 1852?], Harvard Map Collection digital maps, Harvard Library, Cambridge, Mass., http://nrs.harvard.edu/urn-3:FHCL:562277?buttons=y, accessed August 3, 2017.

Walling, Henry F., "A Topographical Map of Essex County Massachusetts Based upon the Trigonometrical Survey of the State The details from actual Surveys under the direction of H.F. Walling Superintendent of State Map. 1856." Engraved by George Worley and William Bracher, and manufactured at R.P. Smith's map establishment, 17 and 19 Minor Street, Philadelphia, Pa. Boston, Mass.: Smith and Morley, 1856, Harvard Map Collection digital maps, Harvard Library, Cambridge, Mass., http://nrs.harvard.edu/urn-3:FHCL:2809339?buttons=y, accessed August 3, 2017.

Walsh, Dana Allen, "'Bear Witness,' Seekers & Skeptics: Faith in a Changing World." Sermon delivered at Andover South Church, Andover, Mass., October 1, 2017.

Warren, Wendy, *New England Bound: Slavery and Colonization in Early America.* New York, N.Y.: Liveright, 2016.

Warren, Wendy, "'Thrown upon the world': Valuing Infants in the Eighteenth-Century North American Slave Market," *Slavery & Abolition* 39 (4) (2018): 623–641.

Washburn, Emory, *Sketches of the Judicial History of Massachusetts from 1630 to the Revolution in 1775.* Boston: Charles C. Little and James Brown, 1840.

Weeden, William B., "The Early African Slave-Trade in New England," *Proceedings of the American Antiquarian Society* (new series) 5 (1888): 107–128.

Weierman, Karen Woods, *The Case of the Slave-Child, Med: Free Soil in Antislavery Boston.* Amherst: University of Massachusetts Press, 2019.

Welch, Richard E., Jr., "Mumbet and Judge Sedgwick: A Footnote to the Early History of Massachusetts Justice," *Boston Bar Journal* 8 (1) (1964): 12–19.

Wells, Frank L., Garrard B. Winston, and Henry P. Beers, "Historical Development of the Records Disposal Policy of the Federal Government Prior to 1934," *The American Archivist* 7 (3) (1944): 181–201.

White, Daniel Appleton, *A View of the Jurisdiction and Proceedings of the Courts of Probate in Massachusetts, with Particular Reference to the County of Essex.* Salem, Mass.: Cushing and Appleton, 1822.

White, Shane, and Graham White, "Slave Clothing and African-American Culture in the Eighteenth and Nineteenth Centuries," *Past and Present* 148 (1) (1995): 149–186.

Whitfield, Harvey Amani, *The Problem of Slavery in Early Vermont, 1777–1810.* Barre: Vermont Historical Society, 2014.

Whiting, Gloria McCahon, "'Endearing Ties': Black Family Life in Early New England." Ph.D. dissertation, Harvard University, 2016.

Whiting, Gloria McCahon, "Power, Patriarchy, and Provision: African Families Negotiate Gender and Slavery in New England," *The Journal of American History* 103 (3) (2016): 583–605.

Whiting, Gloria McCahon, "Emancipation Without the Courts or Constitution: The Case of Revolutionary Massachusetts," *Slavery & Abolition*, advance version (November 25, 2019) prior to print publication, https://doi.org/10.1080/0144039X.2019.1693484, accessed December 13, 2019.

Wiecek, William M., "*Somerset:* Lord Mansfield and the Legitimacy of Slavery in the Anglo-American World," *University of Chicago Law Review* 42 (1) (1974): 86–146.

Wiesner, Merry E., "Spinning Out Capital: Women's Work in Preindustrial Europe, 1350–1750," in *Women in European History* (3rd edition), ed. Renate Bridenthal, Susan Mosher Stuard, and Merry E. Wiesner, 203–231. New York, N.Y.: Houghton Mifflin, 1998.

Williams, George W., *History of the Negro Race in America from 1619 to 1880* (popular edition, two volumes in one). New York, N.Y.: G.P. Putnam's Sons, 1882.

Williams, Rhoesmary R., "Demonizing, Dehumanizing, and Whitewashing: Linguistic Examination of *The Connecticut Courant's* Coverage of Slavery." M.A. thesis, Middle Tennessee State University, 2012.

Wilmington, Town of, "Town Meetings, etc. 1730–1807" (title from microfilm target), Wilmington Town Hall, Wilmington, Mass. *Records of Middlesex Co., Mass. Towns through 1830: Wilmington*. First volume on Wilmington Microfilm Reel 1. Boston: Early Massachusetts Records, Inc., 1975.

Wilmington, Town of, "Town Records Town Meetings Intentions 1762–1834" (title from microfilm target; spine title "Town Meetings Etc. 1807–1834 Intentions Town of Wilmington"), Wilmington Town Hall, Wilmington, Mass. First volume on Microfilm Reel 887763, "Town Records Town Meetings Intentions 1766–1876" (title from catalog). Reproduction System for the Genealogical Society of Salt Lake City, Ut., 1971.

Wilmington, Town of, "Vital Records Cattle Records 1716–1851" (spine title), n.p., Wilmington Town Hall, Wilmington, Mass. First volume on Microfilm Reel 761324, "Town Records, Births Marriages Intentions, 1716–1851" (title from microfilm target). Reproduction System for the Genealogical Society of Salt Lake City, Ut., 1971.

Winchendon v. Hatfield, Supreme Judicial Court, March 1808, 4 Mass. Reports 123.

Winter, Eugene C., and Barbara Brown, "Black Lucy's Garden – Amendments," 2012, typescript, Robert S. Peabody Institute of Archaeology, Phillips Academy, Andover, Mass.

Wong, Edlie L., *Neither Fugitive Nor Free: Atlantic Slavery, Freedom Suits, and the Legal Culture of Travel*. New York, N.Y.: New York University Press, 2009.

Wood, Peter H., "'Liberty Is Sweet': African-American Freedom Struggles in the Years before White Independence," in *Beyond the American Revolution: Explorations in the History of American Radicalism*, ed. Alfred F. Young, 149–184. DeKalb: Northern Illinois University Press, 1993.

Worcester County Deeds, Book 274, pg. 11, Elizabeth Walker, et al., to William Robinson, September 19, 1812, recorded March 4, 1830, Worcester Registry of Deeds, Worcester, Mass.

Wright, Carroll D., *Report on the Custody and Condition of the Public Records of Parishes, Towns, and Counties*. Boston, Mass.: Wright and Potter, 1889.

Wright, Conrad Edick (ed.), *Pedagogues and Protesters: The Harvard College Student Diary of Stephen Peabody, 1767–1768*. Amherst: University of Massachusetts Press, 2017.

Wroth, L. Kinvin, and Hiller B. Zobel (ed.), *Legal Papers of John Adams*. 3 vols. Cambridge, Mass.: Harvard University Press, 1965.

Zaeske, Susan, *Signatures of Citizenship: Petitioning, Antislavery, and Women's Political Identity*. Chapel Hill: University of North Carolina Press, 2003.

Zilversmit, Arthur, "Quock Walker, Mumbet, and the Abolition of Slavery in Massachusetts," *The William and Mary Quarterly* (3rd series) 25 (4) (1968): 614–624.

Zimmerman, Rebecca, "Secretive Slavery in Essex County," Essex LINCs (i.e., Local History in a National Context), a classroom lesson plan prepared July 2009 and 2010 at the Summer Institute Workshop, held at the Royall House, Medford, Mass., funded by a Teaching American History grant from the United States Department of Education, http://www.essexlincs.org/resourcesjuly2009medfordwkg.shtml#, accessed June 2, 2016.

Acknowledgements

Susan Hegarty first prompted my attention to histories of people of color in historical Andover. I am grateful to Nicole Topich who encouraged me to study the 1830 census quandary. For their guidance, encouragement, and generosity to locate and discuss information, I thank Stephanie Aude, Jim Batchelder, Whitney Battle-Baptiste, John Ward Beekman, Keith S. Blake, Emily Blanck, Elizabeth Bouvier, Joyce Bradshaw, Lise Breen, Shirley Brown, Margo Burns, Melinde Lutz Sanborn Byrne, Jane Cairns, Matthew Cameron, Richard M. Candee, Chris Carter, Sean Casey, Ashley Cataldo, Suzanne Cherau, Christopher Challender Child, Elaine Clements, Joyce M. Clements, James M. Cosman, William R. Cotter, Clare Curren, Karen Davis, Amy E. Den Ouden, John Devine, Nancy Doherty, Barbara Donohue, James T. Downs, Stephanie Dyson, Rosalyn Delores Elder, Susan Elliott, James C. Fannin, Minxie Jensvold Fannin, Jennifer Fauxsmith, Patricia E. Feeley, Kendra Taira Field, Alex Flick, Ferron Foisy, Betsy Friedberg, Jonas Gardsby, Jeffrey Glover, Indigo Godinez, Lorinda B.R. Goodwin, Patrick R. Grzanka, Ben Haley, Philip Hamburger, Scott Hancock, Russell G. Handsman, John Hannigan, Jared Ross Hardesty, Mary Guillette Harper, Joseph G. Hayes, Kristen B. Heitert, Marilyn Helmers, Holly Herbster, Ruth Wallis Herndon, Meadow Dibble Hilley, Cheryll Toney Holley, Karen Hutchinson, Leon Jackson, Elizabeth James-Perry, Caitlin Jones, Sandra I. Kay, Lauren Kosky-Stamm, Kathy Kottaridis, Erica Lang, Inga Larson, Nedra K. Lee, Elise Lemire, Kerima M. Lewis, Kimberly S. Lynn, Charlotte Lyons, Maria Madison, Nancy Maida, Carol Majahad, Anthony F. Martin, Alistair McBrien, Angela McBrien, Kate E. McMahon, Heli Meltsner, Margot Minardi, Volga Morren, Jay Moschella, Larry Murphy, Stephan Nance, Margaret Ellen Newell, James O'Brien, Sade Olatunji, Marjory Gomez O'Toole, Joan Silva Patrakis, Jonathan K. Patton, Robert Paynter, Nosapocket Ramona Peters, Jeanne Pickering, Thomas Merton Pietropaoli, Gail L. Ralston, Catherine Reef, Catherine Robertson, Louise Sandberg, Geoff Sawers, Lisa Schoblasky, Austin Simko, Gracelaw Simmons, Brona Simon, Sue Simonich, Tony Sophia, Chris Spraker, Michael Steinitz, Robert A. Stoesen, Susan Taylor, Kenna Therrien, Lauren VanNest, George Walters, Nadia Waski, Jessy Wheeler, Harvey Whitcomb, Gloria McCahon Whiting, Joseph Wylie, and Daniel M. Zoto. I benefitted from keen editorial suggestions of Maryana Bhak, James T. Connolly, L. Alex Green, David Joseph Hill, Jesse M. Kahn, Ellen Kaplan-Maxfield, and Thomas P. Mailhot. I thank Dave Hassel for his IT expertise. At Phillips Library, Peabody Essex Museum, Tamara Gaydos granted permission for quotation and illustration of manuscript material, and Claire Blechman provided the digital images. Jim Batchelder granted permission to include his 1975 drawing. Photographs by John Glassford © 2011 from the Find A Grave website are used as authorized. Other images are reproduced from digital images of public domain material courtesy of FamilySearch, Google Books, Harvard Library, Internet Archive, Library of Congress, Memorial Hall Library, National Archives and Records Administration, New England Historic Genealogical Society, Supreme Judicial Court Archives, and United States Census Bureau.

Name Index

Note: In the page locators, endnotes are indicated as *n*, figures as *f*. Identical note numbers assigned to different book parts appear on some pages of the endnotes (e.g., page 106, *Editorial Conventions* nn2–3 and *Chapter 1* nn2–3) but are not differentiated in the indexes. See also personal names included in the Subject Index.

Martin, Mr. S., 255n5

Mary (in Claverack, N.Y., in Sheffield; enslaved woman purchased and indentured by Gen. John Ashley), 200n26

Matthews, Albert, 112n15, 164n10

Matthews, Christopher N., 174n19

Mayo, Martha, 136n6, 164n9, 290n1, 321n22

McBrien, Alistair, 252n39

McBrien, Angela, 112n15, 114n17, 156n5, 252n39, 283n20, 317n18, 330n37, 337n43

McCarthy, B. Eugene, 136n6

McCaskill, Barbara, 9, 115n19, 158n7

McConnell, Peter. *See* Sigourney, Peter (Peter McConnell)

McManus, Edgar J., 268n8

McNamara, Martha J., 260n5, 270n10

McWilliams, James E., 220n8

Meckelburg, Alexander, 40, 227n11, 241n23, 343–344n2

Med (Maria Sommersett), xi, 205n26. *See also* Aves, Thomas; Commonwealth v. Aves

Melish, Joanne Pope, 38, 117–118n3, 127n3, 164n10, 200n26, 220n8, 221n8, 233n19, 233n21, 236n21, 241n24, 244n25, 274n12, 325n30, 334n41

Meltsner, Heli, 138n8, 148n2, 252n39, 282n20

Member's child. *See* Russell, Phillis (Member's daughter); Sawyer, Remember (Member)

Menschel, David, 117n3

Merrill, Joseph, 266n7

Merrill, Marlene Deahl, 115n17

Messinger, Thomas, 186–187n23

Middlesex, Salem, 151n4

Mighill, Stephen, 130n3

Miller, George L., 183n21

Millward, Jessica, 158n7

Minardi, Margot, 6, 37, 72, 108n9, 112n17, 117n3, 130n3, 149–150nn3–4, 156n5, 187n26, 199n26, 201n26, 232n19, 310–311n37, 322n23, 325n30, 327n34, 334n41, 337n43

Mingo (in Barre; Quock Walker's father), 136n6

Minkema, Kenneth P., 291n1

Minot, Stephen, 95f8

Mofford, Juliet Haines, 113n17, 119–120n3, 157n6, 207–208n28, 228n13, 233n20, 287n7

Mooar, George, 122n3, 128n3, 137n8, 168n18, 171n18, 177n21, 180n21, 205n27, 211n28, 223n10, 324n28

Moore, Colin D., 286n7, 287n9

Moore, George H., 34, 108n5, 117n3, 121n3, 147n2, 193n26, 195n26, 204n26, 217n5, 223–224n10, 234n21, 270n8, 271n11

Morgan, Mary F., 156n5, 282n20, 337n43

Morgan, Philip D., 228n13, 261n5

Moriah (Maria; in Andover; Booso's wife), 47, 50–51, 209n28, 212n30, 253–254n4, 322n27

Morrill, Isaac, 18, 65, 148–149n2, 209n28, 299n11, 309n35, 313n5, 322–323n27

Morrison, Allan, 162n9, 164n9, 290n1, 321n22

Morton, Marcus, 286n7

Moschella, Jay, 268n7

Moulton, Amber D., 166n17, 286n7

Mullen, Zack, 197n26

Murphy, Larry, 252n39

Murray, John E., 130n3, 174n19

Murray, Judith Sargent, 126n3

Murray, William (Lord Mansfield). *See* Mansfield, Lord

Murrell, Nathaniel, 212n30

Nancy (Nan; in Andover; enslaved by John and Joseph Osgood), 160n9

Nancy. *See* Parker, Nancy; Weed, Nancy

Nash, Gary B., 19, 158n7

Ned (Ned Choate; in Ipswich; husband of Sabina [Binah]; enslaved by Francis Choate), 133n3

Subject Index

Note: In the page locators, endnotes are indicated as *n*, figures as *f.* Identical note numbers assigned to different book parts appear on some pages of the endnotes (e.g., page 106, *Editorial Conventions* nn2–3 and *Chapter 1* nn2–3) but are not differentiated in the indexes. All placenames are in Massachusetts, unless otherwise indicated. Within entries, Rosanna Coburn is abbreviated as *RC*, Titus Coburn as *TC*, and Colley Hooper as *CH*. For personal names as entries and cross-references, also see the Name Index.

Abbot, Abiel: *History of Andover from its Settlement to 1829*: Claude M. Fuess' criticisms of, 315n13, 339n44; on Pompey and Rose Lovejoy and Pomp's Pond, 333n40; on Joseph and George Osgood's medical practice, North Parish residency, and as North Parish Church deacons, 284n20, 285n2; on "Poverty Year" (1816, "Year Without a Summer"), 61–62, 305n26; unique copy of *History of Andover* with pasted-in newspaper clippings, some with handwritten initials of authors of anonymous articles, 114n17, 124n3, 324n28

Abbot, Samuel: Andover town treasurer, business dealings with Andover, with many people of color in Andover and Boston, and buying and selling enslaved people, 283–284n20; business dealings with Lucy Foster and Dinah Simpson, 19, 158n6, 180–181n21, 183n21, 225–226n11; charitable fund for South Parish residents, 70, 210n28, 316n15, 323n27; finding aid (by Carole Foster, 1998) for archive of business papers of, 283n20

Abbott, Charlotte Helen: biography and historiography of: Claude M. Fuess' criticisms of, 315n13, 339n44; obituary of, 339n44; Joan Patrakis' appreciation of, 339n44; use of oral traditions, 122n3, 224–225n11, 254n4, 339–340n44; use of printed sources, 253n1, 254n4, 330n37; and writing about people of color, 334–335n41, 340n44; as a local historian, genealogist, and her "Historical Andover" column for the *Andover Townsman*: on Anthony Ballard, 170n18, 298n8; on Booso and his name variants, 109n14, 211n29, 212n30, 252–253n1, 254n4; on Bristow/Brister ("Old Bristoe") and family, 162n9, 277–278n19; on Dinah Chadwick's death caused by Harriet Dole, 129n3, 167–168n18, 170n18; on Chandler family, 168n18, 170n18; on TC and RC and their name variants, 297–298n8, 330n37; on RC's gold ring, 76; on Lucy Foster, 179n21; on Cato Phillips/Freeman and family, 120n3, 122n3, 124n3; on Cato Frye, 217n6; on Frye family, 229n15, 330n37; on Edward

Andover (historical Andover) (*cont.*)
historical Native American places
and traditions, 150–151n4,
227n11; annual town report: *see*
Andover (historical Andover), town
and vital records; Andover Center
for History & Culture; Ballard's
Pond: *see* Pomp's Pond, *below*;
Boise's Bridge, 254n4; churches:
see Christ Church (Episcopal);
Free Christian Church; North
Parish Church; South Church,
West Parish Church, *and see also*
religion; Den Rock area, 151n4;
"Dinah's road" (Dinah Simpson's
residence, probably Missionary
Lane/Woodland Road), 225n11,
332n38, *and see also* Highland
Road *and* Missionary Lane, *below*;
distances and travel-time to Boston
and Salem, 31, 216n3; districts in:
circa 1795, 123–124n3; and circa
1805, 227n11; and 1852, 99f18;
epidemic (1738) in, 32, 216n4;
Highland Road, 99f18, 225n11,
303n22, 304n22, 314n7; "The Hill"
(vicinity of Andover Theological
Seminary and Phillips Academy),
338–339n44; Holt District, 99f18,
227n11; Indian Ridge, 113n17,
337n43; libraries: *see* Memorial Hall
Library; Stevens Memorial Library;
maps: "The County of Essex" (John
G. Hales, 1825), 155n5; and "A Plan
of Andover Taken for the Town"
(Moses Dorman, Jr., 1830), 92–
93ff5–6, 276n17, 303n22, 304n23,
313–314n6; and "Map of the Town
of Andover" (Henry F. Walling,
1852), 99f18, 303–304n22,
314n7, 319n19, 338–339n44; and
"A Topographical Map of Essex
County" (Henry F. Walling, 1856),
303–304n22, 314n7, 319n19,
338–339n44; and "Plan of Andover
Town Farm" showing almshouse
and cemetery (John Franklin,

1907), 252n39; and "Anti-Slavery
Movement in Andover" (Barbara
Thibault, 1993); Memorial Auditorium, 332n38; Missionary Lane
(Woodland Road) area, 68, 99f18,
225n11, 303–304n22, 314n7,
319n19, 332n38, 338–339n44;
"Moose country" (in West Parish),
254n4; Native Americans in, 1,
149–151n4, 166n17, 185–186n22,
220n7, 227n11, 255–256n5,
332n38; newspapers: *see Andover
Advertiser; Andover Townsman;
Lawrence American and Andover
Advertiser*; Osgood District, 99f18,
123–124n3; Panic of 1819, 62–63,
306n30; Pomp's Pond (formerly
Ballard's Pond), 75, 111n13, 151n5,
153–155n5, 333n40, 334n41, *and
see also* Lovejoy, Pompey: homestead; "Poverty Year" (1816, "Year
Without a Summer"), 61–62,
305n26; religious history: *see*
churches, *above, and see also* religion; slavery and slave trade in, ix,
xii, 3–4, 14, 18, 25, 26, 31–33, 35,
38, 47, 52, 67, 75, 80–81, 114n17,
120n3, 121n3, 151n5, 159n9,
160n9, 167n18, 169n18, 214n1,
216–217n5, 219–220n7, 278n19,
302n16, 312n1, 334–335n41, *and
see also* enslaved people; formerly
enslaved people; slave trade; slavery
and abolition, historical memories
of, 1–2, 9–12, 76, 80–83, 334n31,
337–338n43, 344n2; slavery, anti-
slavery, and people of color in local
history: exhibitions on (1896, 1897,
1996, 2001, 2003, 2018), 29, 76, 77,
79, 156n5, 182–183n21, 330n37,
335–338nn42–43, 337–338n43;
and modern historical explorations of, xvi–xvii, 1, 9–12, 80–83,
111–112n15, 112–114n17, 126n3,
151n4, 186n22, 208n28, 211n28,
227n11, 329n35, 330–331n37,
334–335n41, 337–338n43, 342n2,

Mofford's paper on Underground Railroad (1999) as source of speculative factoid about Poor family wagon with hidden compartments to assist formerly enslaved people to escape, debunked by Jeanne Shinto, 113n17; Nancy Parker information at, 149n4; Abiel Pearson records at, 251n35; photograph of Memorial Hall Library exhibition of "artifacts from the slave period" (1996) at, 337–338n43; published 350th town anniversary book (Eleanor Motley Richardson, *Andover: A Century of Change*, 1996), 338n4; research files: "African Americans," 106n5, "Almshouse, Town Farm, Town Infirmary," 282n20; South Church records at, 124n3, 168n18, 177n21, 178n21, 209n28, 210n28, 316n15, 323n27; town records at, 129n3, 138n8, 140n9, 141n9, 143n9, 168n18, 170n18, 226–227n11, 277n19, 281n20, 282–283n20, 308n33, 316–317n16, 317n17, *and see also* annual town reports at, *above*; town and church records reformatting (microfilm) and transcription projects (ca. 1960) with North Andover Historical Society, xxi–xxii, 210–211n28. *See also Andover Historic Preservation* (website); Batchelder, Jim; Cairns, Jane; Clements, Elaine; Greater Lawrence Underground Railroad Committee; McBrien, Alistair; McBrien, Angela; Mofford, Juliet Haines; Morgan, Mary F.; Patrakis, Joan

Andover Free Christian Church. *See* Free Christian Church, Andover

Andover Guild (formerly Andover Society for Organized Charity), 337n43

Andover Historic Preservation (website about historical properties by Andover Preservation Commission, Andover Historical Society/ Center for History & Culture, and Memorial Hall Library), 124n3, 167n18, 251n37, 276n17, 303–304nn22–23, 310n37, 314n6, 332n38, 339n44

Andover Historical Society. *See* Andover Center for History & Culture

Andover Society for Organized Charity (Andover Guild), 337n43

Andover Theological Seminary: antislavery activities, 40, 238n22, 239n23; cemetery, 328n34; history and setting (including "The Hill" and Missionary Road/Woodland Road), 68, 99f18, 206n28, 225n11, 303–304n22, 314n7, 319–320n19, 332n38, 338–339n44. *See also* Phillips Academy; Quacumbush, Almira

Andover Townsman: "Auld Lang-Syne" column: on Dinah Chadwick's death caused by Harriet Dole, 129n3, 167n18; and on antislavey and colonization movement at Phillips Academy, 112n17, 239n23; and on Salem and Rama at South Church parsonage, and decrepit Osgood District schoolhouse moved there (1794 to 1795) for their housing, 123–124n3, 223n10; Sarah Loring Bailey obituary, 339n44; Charles C. Carpenter editor, 315n13; "Historical Andover" column: *see* Abbott, Charlotte Helen; Memorial Hall Library exhibition (1996) of "artifacts from the slave period," 337–338n43; on Pomp's Pond, and mistaken that slavery ended in Andover in 1859 when RC, "Andover's last slave" died, 111n15; "Siftings" column by Bessie P. Goldsmith, 184n21, 252n39; "Why Do They Call it That" column, 111n15. *See also* Abbott, Charlotte Helen; *Andover Advertiser*; Goldsmith, Bessie P.; *Lawrence American and Andover Advertiser*

orative monuments; emancipation; formerly enslaved people: escaped (fugitives, "runaways"); freedom suits; manumission; petitions; self-emancipation; suffrage

The Anti-Slavery Bugle (Salem, Ohio): reprinted *The Liberator* article about RC's pension (1854), xii, 8, 12, 72, 108n11, 322n25

archaeological investigations: "Black Lucy's Garden" (Lucy Foster home-site, Andover), 25, 177–178n21, 181–183n21, 185n21, *and see also* Foster, Lucy; Boston-Higginbotham House (Nantucket), 157n6, 169n18, 183n21; Den Rock area (Andover and Lawrence), 151n4, 227n11; W.E.B. Du Bois Boyhood Homesite (Great Barrington), 201–202n26; Stickney Site (Andover) as part of regional study of ancient Native American sites, 185n21

archives and archival preservation. *See* historiography

Ashcraft-Eason, Lillian: on African women's cultural sense of colonial English ways, 215n2; on family configurations, 276n13, 302n21; historiography and scholarship, 223n8, 241n23; on levirate (brother-in-law and sister-in-law marriages), 163–164n9; on parallels of African and Christian rituals and hierarchies, 206n28

attorneys: performative formalities in court, 50, 260n5; records: information in to extend data in judicial archives, xxxiii, 160n9, 268n8, 312–313n3; and information in about travel of people of color, 159n9; and information in trial notes and memory about common law made in unpublished decisions and bench rulings, 6, 196n26, 197n26, 202n26, 262n5; recursive effects of historical writings about freedom suits on understanding previous case

outcomes and applying common law, 189n26, 202–205n26; as sources of legal knowledge for laypersons, 160n9, 260–261n5; strategies used in freedom suits, 48–49, 150n4, 196n26, 198n26, 257–258n5, 265–266n7, 268–269n8, 270–273n11, 275–276n12, 312–313n3. *See also* Hathorne, John (attorney); Hazen, Nathan W.; Johnson, David; Lincoln, Levi; Lowell, John; Parsons, Theophilus, Sr.; Perkins, Israel; Pynchon, William; Reeve, Tapping; Spaulding, Amos; Sullivan, James

Auter Note v. Tomlin (1720), 186–187n23

Aves. See Commonwealth v. Aves

Bailey, Sarah Loring: biography in obituary of, 339n44; *Historical Sketches of Andover* (1880): Charlotte Helen Abbott's use of, 253n1, 298n8, 330n37; anecdotes about people of color, 224n11; anecdote about wedding at North Parish Church probably of Cato Phillips/Freeman and Lydia Bristow, 119n3, 163n9; on Anthony Ballard's military service, 170n18; on Rev. John Barnard at North Parish Church, 209n28, 322n27; on Booso's name as "Benjamin," 47, 74, 111–112n15, 298n8; on RC's biographical information and gravestone epitaph transcribed in, 74, 101f21, 110–112n15, 247n28, 320–321n20, 327–329n34, 329n36; on RC as the "last slave" born in Andover, and as the main source for RC's biography, 74, 111n15, 330n37; on dedication ceremony (1867) at Johnson High School and Stevens Hall, North Andover, 114n7; on Cato Phillips/Freeman's self-emancipation letter (1789), 119n3, 328–329n34; Claude M. Fuess' assessment of, 339n44;

Coburn, Rosanna (RC) *(cont.)*
53, 71, 112n17, 165n16, 251n36,
319–320n19, 327n33, 338n44;
and will, 53–54, 71, 98f14,
165n16, 251n26, 285n3, 286n6,
315n11, 319–320n19; TC's will
probate by RC under direction
of attorney Israel Perkins (1854),
65–66, 71, 97f13, 290n1, 310n37;
TC's will probate facilitated by
Barzillai Lew, Jr., 66, 71, 164n9,
290n1, 310n37, 321n22; residence
in Andover, home locations, 43, 51,
54, 61, 64, 67–68, 99f18, 303–
304nn22–23, 313–314nn6–7,
316n15, 319n19, 338–339n44;
residence in Wilmington, 43, 54,
61, 68, 276n16, 288n10; Revolutionary War veteran widow's pension: xii, 8, 12, 19, 29, 53, 65–66,
69–70, 71–72, 74, 76, 77, 97ff11–
12, 98ff15–16, 101–103ff21–23,
108n11, 111n15, 144nn11–12,
285–286n6, 290n1, 311n1, 321–
322n22, 322n25, 328n34, 338n44;
and pension application facilitated
by Barzillai Lew, Jr., 66, 71–72,
164n9, 290n1, 310n37, 321n22;
and pension application prepared
by attorney Israel Perkins, 65–66,
71–72, 321n22; and pension
known to George Bancroft, William C. Nell, and Theodore Parker,
8, 72, 109n13, 322n26; ring owned
by, exhibited in Andover and Boston (1896, 1897), 29, 76, 77, 79,
80, 330n37, 335n42, 336–337n43,
338n44; signature by mark, 54,
97–98ff11–16, 285–286n6; signature written by another, 286n7;
"slave" notations in official town
and state death records (1860):
xii, 3, 4, 8, 73, 100ff19–20, 106n3,
326–327n32. *See also* Booso; Booz,
Jack; Coburn, Titus (TC); Hooper,
Colley (CH); "last slave"; Phillis
(Booso's wife)

Coburn, Titus (TC): baptism in
Reading (1767), 57, 209n28,
290n1, 309n35, 322n27; birth
year estimated, 57, 65, 287n1,
290n1, 309–310n37; "black man
at Titus Coburns" (1816), 61–62,
69, 249n31, 305n25, 314n8; census
enumerations of household: in
1790 federal census, 60; and in
1800 federal census, 43, 61, 68,
245n29, 276n16, 302n20, 313n5;
and in 1810 federal census, 43, 54,
61, 68; confused for Titus Coburn
of Harvard, Littleton, and Shirley,
109n12, 294n3, 322n26; daughter
(with Violet Noble Coburn), Jennie
(Jane/June), x, 54, 60, 61, 68–69,
294–295n3, 301n15, 313n5; and
CH as stepdaughter, 15, 110n15,
308n32, 328n34; death (1821), 43,
65, 69, 250n33, 290n1, 309–
310n37, 322n24; debt case during
Panic of 1819, Gurney and Packard's lawsuit (1819) against, 62–64,
69, 95f9, 285n6, 305n28, 306n29,
306–307n31; Dracut, TC's possible
origins in, 57, 289–290n1; enslavement by Edward Hircom in Reading
and Wilmington, x, 57, 67, 209n28,
290n1, 292n1, 293n3, 297nn7–8;
fame, 8, 9, 72, 109nn12–13,
293n3, 294–295n3, 297–298n8,
322n26; grave location unknown,
65, 252n39; inheritance from
Edward Hircom, 57–58, 59, 64,
295–296n5, 297nn7–8, 300n12,
301n14, 308n32; injury and inabil-
ity to labor, 43, 54, 64, 69, 307n32;
inventory of possessions (1820, part
of Revolutionary War veteran pension application), 64, 307–308n32;
laborer, 302n17, 307n32; lawsuit
against: *see* debt case, *above;* manumission by Edward Hircom's will
(1781), 57–59, 148n2, 297n7; marriage to RC (1792), 53–54, 60–61,
65, 68, 288n10, 302n19, 309n36,

Institution) exhibition of artifacts, 182n21; research prospects of archive of, 177n21; singing voice, 179n21; social gatherings at home of, 169n18, 182–184n21; son Peter Foster, 25, 177–178n21, 180n21, 182n21; South Church baptism and member at, 25, 177–178n21, 180n21, 182n21, 184n21; state pauper designation, xii, 23–25, 44, 165n12, 173n19, 175n20, 182n21; "warning out" of Andover, 25, 176–177n21, 179–180n21

Francisco, case of, (In re Francisco, 1832), 190–191n26; and Paul Finkelman and Leonard W. Levy on, 190n26

Frederick Douglass' Paper (Rochester, N.Y.), reprinted *The Liberator* article about RC's pension, xii, 8, 12, 72, 108n11, 322n25

Free Christian Church, Andover, 80, 113n17, 115n17, 207n28, 324n28, 332n38. *See also* antislavery activism

freedom suits: accelerated emancipation in Massachusetts by evolving the common law, 48, 50, 197n26, 230n16; John Allen on, 234–235n21; in Andover, 50, 255n11; appealed to Court of Assistants, 48, 265n7; appealed to or heard in original jurisdiction at Superior Court of Judicature/Supreme Judicial Court, xi, xxvi, 26–27, 116n21, 117–118n3, 135n5, 187–190n26, 190–191n26, 192n26, 195–198n26, 200n26, 202n26, 204–205n26, 260n5, 269n8, 273n11, 292n1; Jeremy Belknap: on judicial abolition by Commonwealth v. Jennison (1783) and by the Declaration of Rights in the Massachusetts Constitution (1780), 189n26; mistaken about freedom suits as actions for "back wages" (quantum meruit) and that earliest freedom suit was brought "in 1770," 271–272n11;

courts, brought in quarterly county courts, in Court of Common Pleas, and in Court of General Sessions of the Peace, 48; depositions (testimony) in, 42, 186–187n23, 231n30, 259–260n5, 292–293n1; earliest so-far identified in Essex County, 48, 264–266n7; in Essex County, 48, 234n21, 263–264n6; as form of resistance, 6, 50, 274–275n12; Horace Gray, Jr., on, 189n26; "legal consciousness" (Scott Hancock), 36, 37, 68, 158n7, 232n17, 261–262n5, 321n22; historiographical approaches, 6–7; legal case outcomes: typically judgment for plaintiff, 37, 38, 50, 230n16, 254–255n5, 268–269n8, 275n12; and default by appellant (error in not sending up lower court file), 202n26; and default by defendant, 49, 187n26, 254–255n5, 268–269n8; and nonsuit by plaintiff and nullities, 194n26, 235n21, 312–313n3; legal costs and damages (monetary compensation for legal expenses and for tort, but not for "back wages"), 48, 198n26, 202n26, 257–258n5, 268–269n8, 271–273n11, 275n12; legal fictions: in writs (statement of case in summons to defendant), xxiv, 150n4, 270–271n11; and in judicial decisions, x–xi, xxiv, 6, 7, 27, 195n26; legal forms of action and pleading, xxiv, 263n6, 270–273n11, and sham pleading (a knowingly wrong response used strategically), 257–258n5, 269n8, 270n11; legal knowledge among enslaved people and their allies, 36, 150n4, 226n11, 232nn17–18, 255–262n5, 275n12, 321n22; legislative petitions for abolition in relation to, 232–233n19, 272n11, 275n12; liberty (not "back wages") as goal of, 271–273n11, 275n12;

historiography: African diaspora
studies, xi, 1, 25, 157n6, 185n22,
212n30, 215n2, 240–241n23,
343n2, *and see also* postemancipation/postslavery studies,
below; agency and resistance, 34,
35, 37–38, 49, 55, 58–59, 82,
116n21, 158n7, 184n21, 197n26,
199–201n26, 207n28, 224–
225n11, 227n11, 228n13, 232n17,
243n24, 244–245n25, 261n5,
273–276n12, 321n22, 345n2;
archival preservation, reformatting,
deterioration, and destruction, ix,
xx–xxiii, xxvii–xxxi, 5, 15, 16, 10,
28, 145n15, 209n28, 210–211n28,
287–288n10, 296n5, 301n15,
317–318n18, 325n30, 343n2;
archives, sociological contexts,
12, 221n8, 344n2; biographies of
historians, 345n2; Black feminism
and intersectionality, 19, 157n6,
159n8, 184n21, 289nn12–13,
315n12, *and see also* intersectionality, *below*; disability studies, 21,
24, 194n26, 280n19, *and see also*
disabilities; "Early Black Historians," 186n22, *and see also* Nell,
William C.; Williams, George W.;
feminist approaches, 19, 29–30,
32–33, 54, 138n8, 157–158n6,
217–218n7, 286–287n7, 289n12,
307n32, 316n3, 333n40; folklore
approaches, 227n11; gender studies,
19–20, 50, 55, 138n8, 140n8,
167n18, 211n29, 218n7, 240n23,
244n25, 280n19, 286–287n7,
289n12, 316n13, 325n30; genealogies of scholarship, 10, 342n2,
343n2, 345n2; historical amnesia
and historical forgetting, "erasure,"
"invisibility," "systematic exclusion,"
and conspiratorial concealment
of historical records, 38, 126n3,
200n26, 223n8, 224n10, 312n1,
341–345n2; historical biography
and local studies as microhistory,

2, 9–12, 80, 115–116n21, 275n12,
325n29, 341–342n2, 345n2; historical memory in history-making, xii–
xiii, 1–2, 15, 19, 25, 28, 37, 38, 73–
75, 79–80, 82–83, 112n17, 126n3,
149–151n4, 156n5, 186n22,
187–188n26, 195n26, 200–
201n26, 213n30, 245n27, 274n12,
303n22, 314n7, 315–316n13,
324–325n30, 327n34, 329n35,
330–331n37, 331–333n38,
334–338nn41–43, 340–345n2;
historicalness vs. historicity, 150n4,
325n29, 325nn29–30; intersectionality, 19–20, 83, 159n8, 167n18,
174n19, 238n22, 240n23, 244n25,
261n5, 280n19, 345n2, *and see
also* Black feminism, *above*, *and see
also* judiciary; "interventions" as
"historical missions," 342–343n2;
linguistic analysis, including
discourse analysis, "marking" and
"markedness," xvi, 28, 34, 39, 75,
105–106n1, 164n10, 227n11,
228n13, 237–238n22, 240n23,
245n28, 324–325n30, 345n2;
"little is known" trope, 342n2; microhistory, xiii, 11, 116n21, 164n11,
221n8, 275n12, 342n2; mobility
(of body): *see* disabilities; mobility (travel): *see* livestock; travel;
narratives and narratology: heroic
narratives, 37, 50, 151n4, 188–
189n26, 197n26, 201n26, 240n23,
342n2, 344–345n2; and historical
narratives: Andover people of color,
120–121n3, 149–151n4, 212n30,
225n11, 227n11, 334–335n41; and
RC and Pompey Lovejoy considered
together in historical narratives, 75;
and as cultural heritage, 1, 81; and
national emancipation narratives,
40, 112n17, 187n26, 201n26;
and grand narratives, metaphoric
regionalism, normative essentialism, subjectivism, and objectivism,
11, 12, 34, 40, 116n21, 274n12,

mobility (of body). *See* disabilities

mobility (travel). *See* livestock; travel

Monson: formerly enslaved person (escaped, "runaway") or only his children in (1846), determined to be state paupers, 165n12

Mooar, George: on Flora Chandler's South Church membership and death, 128n3, 168n18, 171n18; on Joseph Cummings as Andover almshouse superintendent, 137n8; *The Cummings Memorial* (1903), 137n8; on George Foster, 323–324n28; on Lucy Foster's South Church membership, 177n21, 180n21; *Historical Manual of the South Church* (1859), 122n3, 128n3, 168n18, 171n18, 177n21, 180n21, 205n27, 211n28, 223n10; information from *Historical Manual* to estimate number of graves in South Parish Cemetery, 205–206n27; *Mooar (Moors) Genealogy* (1901), 323–324n28

"Moor." *See* Africa; racialized language

Moore, George H.: on John Allen's allusion to Sampson v. Dodge and Batchelder (1774–1775), and as source of factoid about that freedom suit, 234–235n21; on enslaved females counted in tax valuations, 217n5; on the federal census of 1790, absence of counted enslaved people in Massachusetts unreliable indication of statewide abolition, 117n3; on "A Form for a Negroe-Marriage" (Rev. Samuel Phillips, 1760), 34, 121n3, 223n10; on freedom suits for liberty, not "back wages," 271n11; on the judicial abolition of slavery, 108n5; on Littleton v. Tuttle (1796), discrepancies noticed in published note about, and in judicial characterizations about, 193n26, 195n26; miscited Massachusetts Chapter 1 of the Acts of 1703 (bonds required to

manumit enslaved people), 147n2; *Notes on the History of Slavery in Massachusetts* (1866), 34, 108n5, 117n3, 147n2, 193n26, 195n26, 204n26, 217n25, 223–224n10, 234–235n21, 270n8, 271n11; and *Notes on the History of Slavery* as historical exposé that challenged revisionist histories, 34, 223n10; on Priscilla and Jupiter v. Simmons and Chadwick (1722), 270n8; "Slave Marriages in Massachusetts" (1869), 121n3, 223n10; "Slavery in Massachusetts" (1866), 193n26, 195n26

Morgan, Philip D., on paternalism, not inconsistent with capitalist interests, and not requiring benevolence, 228n13; on social, linguistic, and cognitive capabilities as key skills to surviving and leaving enslavement, and to navigating intersectional disparities of power, position, and authority, 261n5

"mulatto" ("Mallatoe," "Melatto," "Molato"). *See* racialized language

Mullen v. Ashley (1781–1782), 197n26

"Mum Bett" case. *See* Brom and Bett v. Ashley

music, musical instruments, and musicality: Lucy Foster's "wonderful singing voice," 179n21; Cato Phillips/Freeman, bass viol or violin, 120–121n3; Salem Phillips, "fiddling," 120n3; Alice M. Hinton, New England Conservatory of Music, and 1941 concert production, 332n38; Lew family, 120n3; Prince Russell's "hand organs," 298n8

Nancy v. Parker and Parker (1771), 150n4, 260n5, 275n12. *See also* Parker, Nancy

Nantucket: Prince Boston, whaleman, formerly enslaved at, 272–273n11; Boston-Higginbotham House,

Pickering, Jeanne M. (*cont.*)
  on Salem Poor's deposition in
    Caesar v. Taylor (1771–1772),
    262n5; thesis (2018) and website
    about Essex County freedom suits,
    262n5
Pittsfield: formerly enslaved person
  (escaped, "runaway") and child
  in (1846), determined to be state
  paupers, 165n12
Plymouth County: freedom suit of
  Hill v. Hayward (1773), 272–
  273n11; Plymouth Rock, 80
Ponkapoag Indians, 166n17. *See also*
  Andover v. Canton
Poor, Alfred. *See* Poore, Alfred
Poor, Nancy. *See* Parker, Nancy
Poor, Salem: in Andover town records,
  281n20; at Battle of Bunker Hill,
  1, 151n4, 186n22; confused for similarly named men, 151n4; death at
  Boston (1802), 149n4; enslavement
  by Poor family, 312n1; fame, 1,
  151n4, 186n22; financial assistance
  for fiancée's freedom suit, Nancy v.
  Parker and Parker (1771), 260n5;
  knowledge of the legal system, 259–
  260n5; manumission by self-purchase (1769) from John Poor, Jr.,
  260n5; marriage to Nancy Parker,
  1–2, 149–151n4, 260n5; Revolutionary War service, 1, 151n4,
  186n22; speculations about, 151n4;
  travels by, to Newburyport and
  Salem, 260n5; as witness in Caesar
  v. Taylor (1771–1772), 259–260n5,
  262n5. *See also* Parker, Nancy
Poor family: wagons with hidden compartments used in Underground
  Railroad, a speculative factoid debunked by Jeanne Schinto, 113n17.
  See also Poor, Salem
poor relief: citizens petitions against
  poor relief for foreign immigrants
  and all state reimbursements to
  towns, 174n19; former enslavement
  considered by judiciary in deciding

poor relief legal cases, 3, 6, 18, 21,
  149n3, 189–190n26, 191n26,
  192–195n26; housing arrangements, 23–24, 51–52, 168n18,
  278–280n19, 281n20; for medical
  treatment, 44, 194n26, 251n35,
  278–279n19; periodic need for,
  because of economic disadvantages
  among formerly enslaved people and
  their descendants, x, 3–4, 19–21,
  38, 157n6, 240–241n23, 344n2;
  purpose of "slave" designation in
  the 1830 census, x, 3, 5, 14, 16,
  107–108n5; records and reports
  of, 246–250n31, 281–284n20,
  316–319nn16–18, *and see also* Andover (historical Andover), town
  and vital records; Andover Center
  for History & Culture: town annual reports at, *and* town records at;
  residency determinations: *see* settlement (residency) laws; Samuel
  Phillips and Samuel Abbot Funds
  for the Relief of Indigent Persons,
  70, 210n28, 316n15, 323n27;
  state reimbursement to towns for,
  x, 5, 17, 171n19, 175–176n20;
  statutory and customary rules
  related to, 171–174n19, *and see
  also* settlement (residency) laws;
  "warning out" non-residents, 25,
  137n6, 176–177n21, 179–180n21,
  312n1; Wilmington vote to provide poor relief to those manumitted within 30 days, 18, 148–
  149n2, 230n16, 299n11; women
  more likely than men to require
  assistance because of economic disadvantages, 29, 157n6, 240n23; the
  "worthy poor" and social constructions of poverty and alterity, 23,
  174n19. *See also* almshouse, Andover; Andover v. Canton; overseers
  of the poor; settlement (residency)
  laws; state paupers; "warning out"
  practices; *and see also specific names
  of individuals*

Reading: Anthony Ballard in, 169–
170n18, 298–299n8; baptism of
people of color in: at First Church,
291n1; and at Second Church of
Christ, 57, 209n28, 290n1, 292n1,
298n8, 309n35, 322n27; and baptism of Caesar enslaved by Edward
Hircom, 292n1; and baptism of TC
and Peggy Hircom, enslaved by Edward Hircom in, x, 57, 290–292n1,
300n11; contiguity with Andover,
57, 93f6, 227n11; contiguity with
Wilmington, 57, 93f6; Edmon/
Edmund Damon, administrator of
Anthony Ballard's estate and overseer of the poor in, 169–170n18,
299n8; Edward Hircom in, 57,
291–293n1, 300n11; Margaret
Russell, Prince Russell, and Timothy
Russell in, 169n18, 298–299n8;
Vital Records publication (1912),
291n1, 298–299n8

references cited: abbreviations in notes,
xix, 105; bibliographic conventions
applied: for anonymous works, xix;
and for archival documents and artifacts, purposes generally, 10, 12; and
for titles, xix, xx; and for corporate
authors and works by governments,
xix–xx; and for digital sources,
xx–xxiii, 10, 161n9, 296n5; and for
email, xxi; and for government files
on individuals alphabetized by surname, xx; and for judicial archives
and other legal documentation, xx,
xxiii, xxiv–xxxii; and for legal case
titles (captions), xxv–xxvi; and for
microforms and other reformatted
materials, xx–xxii, 246–247n31;
and for Revolutionary War veteran
and widow pension application files,
xxv, xxvii, 144–145nn11–12; and
for serials, xx; and for United States
congressional publications and statutes, xx; and for variant names, xvii,
xix; sources of information in notes
not included in, xxi, 10, 128n3,

132n3, 151n5, 172n19, 223n8,
225n11, 296n5, 301n13, 305n27,
312n3, 322n22. *See also* transcriptions and quotations

reflexivity. *See* historiography: privilege, position, and reflexivity

regional exceptionalism. *See* historiography: narratives and narratology

religion, religiosity, and religious
history: in African, Caribbean,
and African-American traditions,
206n28, 212n30; in Andover and
New England regionally, xxi–xxiii,
28–29, 34, 35, 82, 119–124n3,
152n5, 157n6, 184n21, 206–
211n28, 223n10, 228n13; as aspect
of identity and social position,
19–20; baptism, and record-making of, 28, 60, 177n21, 178n21,
206–207n28, 208n26, 209n26, *and
see also specific churches and names
of individuals*; Christianity and
Islam among indigenous African
religious traditions, and influence of
converts teaching faith traditions in
the Americas, 212n30; communion,
207n28, 255n5, 290n1, 291n1,
292n1; confession (testimony),
134n3; covenant (declaration),
207n28, 292n1; discriminatory
admission practices by Claude M.
Fuess at Phillips Academy against
Jewish people, 335n41; in "memorial narratives" (Lois Brown), 72–73;
Muslims in Africa and the Americas,
among people enslaved or in other
laboring arrangements, 212n30;
in Native American traditions
and hybridized Indian Christianity, 206n11; in Phillis' (Booso's
wife) extended family, 28–29, 65,
209–210n28, 322–323n27. *See also*
Andover Theological Seminary;
churches; Congregational Library &
Archives

remembrance. *See* historiography: historical memory in history-making

(1846), determined to be legal town resident, 165n12, 173n19

Town Officer guides to Massachusetts law and legal procedure, 172n19

Trans-Atlantic Slave Trade Database (website), 214–215n1

transcriptions and quotations: conventions applied to, xviii, 165n15, 267n7, 317n17, 329n36; errors and variations: of Andover death records copied by Samuel W. Blunt (1879), despite *verbatim et literatim* in title, 142n9, 180n21, 310n37; and of Andover town meeting records (1709–1776, preliminary rough draft typed 1961), 160n9; and of Andover vital records, official and published *Vital Records*, 142n9, 287–289n10, 309–310n37, *and see also* Andover (historical Andover), town and vital records; and of "Mum Bett" and "Quock Walker" judicial records of case decisions and file papers, xxvi, 136–137n6, 205n26; and of James Chandler's will (1787), 130–131n3; and of RC's original gravestone epitaph, 73–74, 101f21, 110–111n15, 320–321n20, 327–329n34, 329n36, 340n45; and of TC's pension application, xxxi, 144–145nn11–12; and of Lucy Foster information from town and church records, 177n21, 180n21; and of Cato Phillips/Freeman's letter (1789), 119n3, 328n34; and of Pompey Lovejoy's gravestone epitaph, 333nn39–40; and of Samuel Phillips' "A Form for a Negroe-Marriage" (1760), 223n10; and of Almira Quacumbush gravestone epitaph, 328–329n34; and of Prince Russell's gravestone epitaph, 298–299n8. *See also specific municipalities* for vagaries, lacunae, errors, and inconsistencies in records

travel: Andover men traveling to and from Andover, Cambridge, and Maine, 159–160n9; coastal and river ship travel, 264n7, 266–267n7; among courthouses, judges and staff riding circuit to hold sessions in all counties, xxvii, 205n26; distance and travel-time between Andover, Boston, Charlestown, and Salem, 31, 216n3; enslaved people from Africa and West Indies brought to Merrimack Valley, 31, 159n9, 214–215n1, 221–222n8, 252n1; enslaved people brought from or sold in other states, 118n3, 136n6, 137n6, 200n26, 265n7, 269n8; enslaved people accompanying slave-owners in post-abolition Massachusetts, xi, 13, 107n5, 116n21, 117nn1–3, 131–132n3, 135n4, 190n26; formerly enslaved people, escaped (fugitives, "runaways") from slave states in post-abolition Massachusetts: *see* formerly enslaved people: escaped (fugitives, "runaways"); enslaved and formerly enslaved people: to attorneys, courthouses, and registry of deeds, 159–161n9, 260n5, 275n12; and to Boston to United States Bank, 62, 69, 159n9, 305n27; and couriering letters to Andover from Harvard College students, 159n9; and discrimination and assaults traveling roads and railroads, 158n7, 287n8; and driving livestock from Andover to Brighton and Roxbury markets, 159n9; and for courtship, on errands, for labor, and for visits, 18, 20, 35, 159n9, 183n21; and hauling rags and returning with paper from Andover to Milton paper mill, 152n5, 159n9; and as mariners, 134n3, 159n9, 233n20; and range and frequency of travel captured in documentary sources, 159n9, 227n11; and throughout Northeast in military service, 57, 154–155n5, 169n18, 293–294n3, *and see also* Civil War;

James Indian from, enslaved in Salisbury, 265–266n7; newspaper articles about Pompey and Rose Lovejoy and nieces (probably Dinah Chadwick and Flora Chandler) published in Alexandria, 153n5; rope from Petersburg jail "used to tie slave to the whipping post," displayed in Andover at 250th anniversary exhibition (1896), 336n42

Vital Records published series. *See specific municipalities*

wage laborers: enslaved people earning cash by working for individuals other than their owners, 35, 260n5, 275n12; error that freedom suits sought "back wages" rather than freedom, 271–273n11; gendered household labor unpaid, 19, 51–52, 62, 157n6; reactions by wage laborers to slavery and emancipation, 41, 244–245n25; state paupers put to paid and unpaid labor, 138n8, 173n19; uncertainties if or when people in ambiguous, slavery-like laboring situations received wages, 7, 17, 60, 124n3, 126n3, 130–131n3, 133n3, 146–147n1, 158n7, 200n26, 221n8, 231n16, 244n25, 256n5, 273n11

Walker, Prince (in Barre, Worcester County): as "perhaps, the last survivor of the Massachusetts slaves" (1856), 136n6; "slave" counted in his household in 1830 census, then corrected, 14, 15, 87–89ff1–3, 136n6, 145–146n16; sold in East Windsor, Conn., and escaped back to Barre, 136n6

Walker, Quock: "Quock Walker" cases (1781–1783): about the three cases, xxvi, 118n3, 202–205n26; ambiguity of, 195n26, 197n26, 204n26; common law effect of,

187n26, 198–199n26, 203n26; John D. Cushing on, 136n6, 188n26, 202n26, 205n26; William Cushing's contemporaneous trial notes and jury instructions (1783), and revised and elaborated notes (after 1789), about Commonwealth v. Jennison (1783), 188–189n26, 196n26, 203–204n26; first instance of explicit citation in Supreme Judicial Court decision of record (1867), 197n26; and Philip Hamburger on, 188n26; and Thea K. Hunter on, 195n26, 196n26, 204n26; Nathaniel Jennison characterization of effects of, having freed "all Negro Servants" including his "Ten Negroes," 204–205n26; as legal fiction in subsequent judicial decisions, of having judicially abolished slavery, and referred to in a dissenting opinion and obiter dicta, 188–190n26, 195n26, 197n26, 204–205n26; Levi Lincoln as the Caldwells' attorney, 196n26, 206n26; and the Massachusetts Constitution (1780), 188–189n26, 203–204n26; as myth about abolishing slavery instantly and statewide, xi, 26, 27, 117–118n3, 135–136n5, 179n21, 187n26, 195n26, 198–199n26; research prospects to pursue, and vagaries and lacunae to address, xxvi, 136–137n6, 205n26; Somerset v. Stewart (1772) parallels, 195–196n26; symbolic importance, 50, 197n26, 198–199n26. *See also* Caldwell, John and Seth; Commonwealth v. Jennison; Cushing, William; freedom suits; Jennison, Nathaniel; Jennison v. Caldwell and Caldwell; Walker v. Jennison

Walker v. Jennison (1781), xxvi, 118n3, 135n5, 202n26. *See also* Walker, Quock: "Quock Walker" cases